PEOPLE, MARKETS, GOODS:
ECONOMIES AND SOCIETIES IN HISTORY

Volume 25

The Political Economy of Ghana in the Long Twentieth Century

People, Markets, Goods: Economies and Societies in History

ISSN: 2051-7467

The interactions of economy and society, people and goods, transactions and actions are at the root of most human behaviours. Economic and social historians are participants in the same conversation about how markets have developed historically and how they have been constituted by economic actors and agencies in various social, institutional and geographical contexts. New debates now underpin much research in economic and social, cultural, demographic, urban and political history. Their themes have enduring resonance – financial stability and instability, the costs of health and welfare, the implications of poverty and riches, flows of trade and the centrality of communications. This paperback series aims to attract historians interested in economics and economists with an interest in history by publishing high quality, cutting edge academic research in the broad field of economic and social history from the late medieval/early modern period to the present day. It encourages the interaction of qualitative and quantitative methods through both excellent monographs and collections offering path-breaking overviews of key research concerns. Taking as its benchmark international relevance and excellence it is open to scholars and subjects of any geographical areas from the case study to the multi-nation comparison.

PREVIOUSLY PUBLISHED TITLES IN THE SERIES
ARE LISTED AT THE BACK OF THIS VOLUME

The Political Economy of Ghana in the Long Twentieth Century
1891–2011

Edited by
Gareth Austin and Kofi Adjepong-Boateng

THE BOYDELL PRESS

First published 2026
The Boydell Press, Woodbridge

ISBN 978 1 83765 314 0

The Boydell Press is an imprint of Boydell & Brewer Ltd
and of Boydell & Brewer Inc.
website: www.boydellandbrewer.com

Our Authorised Representative for product safety in the EU is Easy Access System Europe – Mustamäe tee 50, 10621 Tallinn, Estonia, *gpsr.requests@easproject.com*

A catalogue record for this book is available
from the British Library

Contents

Illustrations

Tables

Figures

Full credit details are provided in the captions to the images in the text. The editors, contributors and publisher are grateful to all the institutions and persons for permission to reproduce the materials in which they hold copyright. Every effort has been made to trace the copyright holders; apologies are offered for any omission, and the publisher will be pleased to add any necessary acknowledgement in subsequent editions.

Notes on Contributors

Emmanuel Abbey is a Senior Lecturer in the Department of Economics at the University of Ghana. He contributes to teaching and research in Development Economics, supporting both undergraduate and postgraduate training and scholarly enquiry. His research focuses on structural transformation and economic development, with a strong emphasis on empirical analysis and policy-relevant enquiry. His work engages with development issues in Ghana and the wider African context.

Prince Young Aboagye is a researcher in Economic History at Lund University School of Economics and Management. His research focuses on long-run economic development, inequality, taxation and state formation in Africa, particularly in Ghana and West Africa. His work has appeared in journals including *Explorations in Economic History*, *African Affairs* and the *Journal of Agrarian Change*. His current research examines fiscal capacity and sustainability in Sub-Saharan Africa.

Kofi Adjepong-Boateng is Associate Director, Centre for Financial History at the University of Cambridge and a Research Affiliate, History Section, Massachusetts Institute of Technology. Prior to this, he served in several banking roles including as a Vice Chairman at Standard Chartered Bank. He currently serves on several asset management company and learned society boards, including the United Kingdom's Royal Economic Society. His work has been published in, among other places, *African Economic History*, the *Historical Journal* and *International Review of Applied Economics*.

Emmanuel Adu-Danso is a development economist and lecturer at the Department of Economics, University of Ghana. His research interests span labour economics, entrepreneurship and environmental economics.

Rod Alence is Associate Professor of International Relations at the University of the Witwatersrand in Johannesburg. He has also held teaching and research positions at the University of the Western Cape and the Human Sciences Research Council in South Africa, and in 1992 he was a Fulbright scholar based at the University of Ghana. His research has appeared in journals such as the *Journal of African History, African Economic History,* the *Journal of Modern African Studies* and the *Journal of Democracy.*

Cyrelene Amoah-Boampong is the Head of the Department of History at the University of Ghana. She was a Fulbright Scholar in Residence at Mount Saint Mary's University (2021–2022) and a Queen Elizabeth Scholar at Concordia University (2023–2024). She is a gender historian working on women's activism in the cocoa sector in Ghana. Her work has been published in, among other places, *Ghana Studies, MISR Review* and *Journal of West African History.*

Ernest Aryeetey is an Emeritus Professor of Development Economics at the Institute of Statistical, Social and Economic Research (ISSER), University of Ghana. Until July 2024, he was the Secretary-General of the African Research Universities Alliance (ARUA), a network of 20 of Africa's flagship universities. He is a former Vice-Chancellor of University of Ghana and was also previously Director of ISSER. Ernest Aryeetey was the first Director of the Africa Growth Initiative of Brookings Institution, Washington DC. He has published very extensively on development economics, including many works on the Ghanaian economy.

Gareth Austin is Emeritus Professor of Economic History at the University of Cambridge. He also taught at the University of Birmingham, the University of Ghana, the London School of Economics and the Graduate Institute in Geneva. His work has appeared in, among many other places, *Business History Review, Economic History Review* and the *Journal of African History.* His book *Labour, Land and Capital in Ghana: From Slavery to Free Labour in Asante, 1807–95* was published in 2005.

George M. Bob-Milliar is a Professor of African Politics and History at the Kwame Nkrumah University of Science and Technology, Kumasi. His primary research focuses on political parties, political behaviour and informal institutions, complemented by interests in social, economic and political histories, as well as the African Diaspora. He has published articles in *African Affairs, Journal of African History, African Economic History, Ghana Studies, History and Anthropology, Africa Today,* the *Journal of Modern African Studies, Africa* and *Democratization* among others. He currently co-edits *African Affairs* and *African Economic History.*

Gavin Hilson is Professor and Chair of Sustainability in Business at the University of Surrey Business School. Through a program of sustained research that has spanned more than two decades, Professor Hilson has explored a variety of issues in Ghana's artisanal and small-scale mining (ASM) sector. These include understanding why ASM is persistently informal in the country; what connections it has with farming, and the implications this relationship has for local food security; and how mercury can be managed more effectively at sites. Professor Hilson received Bachelors and Masters degrees from the University of Toronto, and his Ph.D. from Imperial College London.

Nikolay Kamenov holds a Ph.D. from ETH Zurich. He has taught at Swiss universities including Bern, Basel and Lucerne, and at the Centre for Modern Indian Studies at the University of Göttingen, and at the University of St Andrews. His research focuses on cooperatives and capitalism in the Global South. Currently, he is completing his second monograph, *Cooperatives and Capitalism in the Global South: India and Ghana, 1900–1970*.

Ravi Kanbur is T. H. Lee Professor of World Affairs and Professor of Economics at Cornell University. He has served on the senior staff of the World Bank including as Resident Representative in Ghana and Chief Economist for Africa. He has published extensively on Ghana, on Africa and on economic development. His past positions include Chair of the Board of United Nations University-World Institute for Development Economics Research, member of the OECD High Level Expert Group on the Measurement of Economic Performance and President of the Human Development and Capability Association.

Manuel J. Manu-Osafo is a Past and Present fellow at the Institute of Historical Research, University of London, and a MUWUG postdoctoral fellow at the Department of History, Political Science, and Public Administration, Kwame Nkrumah University of Science and Technology. He completed his doctoral studies in History at the University of Ghana, Legon (2019–24). His work appears in the *Journal of Social History*, the *Journal of African History*, *History in Africa* and the *International Journal of African Historical Studies*.

Katie Monaghan is a Pre-Doctoral Research Fellow in Economic History at the University of Birmingham. She completed her BA in History and English Literature at the University of Manchester in 2023, and her MPhil in World History at the University of Cambridge in 2024. She looks forward to beginning her doctoral research in 2027.

Paul Nugent is Professor of Comparative African History at the University of Edinburgh and previously taught Comparative Politics at Keele University. He has published one book on the politics of the Rawlings period in Ghana and two others on the Ghana-Togo border, the most recent being *Boundaries, Communities and State Making in West Africa: The Centrality of the Margins*

(2019). His work has been published in numerous journals including *Journal of African History*, *Journal of Modern African Studies*, *Comparative Studies in Society and History* and the *New Left Review*. He sits on the advisory board of the United Nations Development Programme Resilience Hub for Africa in Nairobi and is the founder/chair of the African Borderlands Research Network (ABORNE).

Nana Yaw Boampong Sapong is a Senior Lecturer in the Department of History, University of Ghana. He has taught at Southern Illinois University Carbondale (United States of America) and University of Hradec Kralove (Czech Republic) and is a visiting scholar at the Faculty of History, Cambridge University in 2026. His current research project focuses on the political economy of higher education in Ghana, especially academic labour. His work has been published by Oxford, Wiley Blackwell and Cambridge (forthcoming). He is the co-editor of *Ghana Studies* journal.

Gerardo Serra is Senior Lecturer in Economic Cultures at the University of Manchester. Located at the intersection between history of political economy, intellectual history and the sociology of quantification, his work has appeared in outlets such as *Comparative Studies in Society and History*, *Global Intellectual History* and the *Journal of African History*. His first monograph, *Marching with the Times: Economic Knowledge and Political Imagination in Nkrumah's Ghana*, is forthcoming with Cambridge University Press.

Abbreviations

ASM	Artisanal and small-scale mining
BBC	British Broadcasting Corporation
BCA	Balliol College Archives
BFA	Banque de France Archives
BGA	Barclays Group Archives
BGC	Bank of the Gold Coast
BoE	Bank of England
BOEA	Bank of England Archives
BoG	Bank of Ghana
BOGA	Bank of Ghana Archives
CADN	Centre of Diplomatic Archives in Nantes
CCA	Chief Commissioner of Ashanti
CDR	Committee for the Defence of the Revolution
CFA (franc)	Colonies Françaises d'Afrique (franc)
CMB	Cocoa Marketing Board
CPP	Convention People's Party
EPA	Environmental Protection Agency
ERP	Economic Recovery Programme
FAO	Food and Agriculture Organization
GCB	Ghana Commercial Bank

GDP	Gross Domestic Product
GGDC	Groningen Growth and Development Centre
GGMU	Ghana–Guinea--Mali Union
HIPC	Heavily Indebted Poor Countries Initiative
IMF	International Monetary Fund
ISI	Import-Substitution Industrialisation
KKFU	Kuapa Kookoo Farmers' Union
MDR	Multilateral Debt Relief
MMIP	Multi-Sectoral Mining Integrated Project
NATO	The North Atlantic Treaty Organization
NDC	National Democratic Congress
NERC	National Economic Review Council
NLC	National Liberation Council
NLM	National Liberation Movement
NPP	New Patriotic Party
NRC	National Redemption Council
NSC	National Service Corps
NSS	National Service Scheme
NTs	Northern Territories
PDC	People's Defence Committee
PNDC	Provisional National Defence Council
PNP	People's National Party
PP	Progress Party
PRAAD	Public Records and Archives Administration Department
SAP	Structural Adjustment Programme
SMC	Supreme Military Council

TNA	The British National Archives
UAC	United Africa Company
UGFC	The United Ghana Farmers' Council
WACB	West African Currency Board
WDC	Workers Defence Committee

Preface

This book is the outcome of a project to produce a tightly edited, coherent volume that integrated discussion of Ghana's colonial and post-colonial history in the cocoa era. The book is intended to express the analyses and arguments of a range of Ghanaian and foreign scholars expert on one or other aspect of the country's political economy. We held a writers' conference in late July 2023, at King's College, Cambridge. The first drafts of all but one of the chapters were presented there. We thank everyone who contributed to a very rich – and lively – two days of discussion, including Dr Priscilla Twumasi Baffour (Department of Economics at the University of Ghana), Professor Akua Britwum (University of Cape Coast), Professor Andreas Eckert (Humboldt University), and Professor John Dunn, long-time fellow of King's, who published on Ghana before anyone in this volume.[1]

We are very grateful for the financial support which made possible the conference and therefore, ultimately, the book. In Cambridge, grants were provided by the King's College Research Committee and by four University sources: the Ellen McArthur Fund, which supports economic history throughout Cambridge; the Smuts Memorial Fund, which supports research on Commonwealth subjects; the Trevelyan Fund, in the Faculty of History; and Gareth Austin's personal research budget from the University. Two of the speakers were in Cambridge anyway for a preceding workshop on labour and work in Ghana, their flights covered by a grant (AH/W010852/1) from the UK Arts and Humanities Research Council and the Deutsche Forschungsgemeinschaft.

We were particularly delighted to receive generous funding from GCB, formerly Ghana Commercial Bank, the oldest indigenous bank in the country. GCB were marking their seventieth anniversary, and they enriched the intellectual vitality of the conference, both by financing the participation of additional authors from the University of Ghana, and by the active presence at the conference of a whole delegation of GCB top executives and their expert guests, who contributed valuably to the discussions. In particular, we thank

1 John Dunn and A.F. Robertson, *Dependence and Opportunity: Political Change in Ahafo* (Cambridge, 1973).

Messrs Kofi Adomakoh, Kofi Osei-Asibey and Daniel Kwaku Tweneboah Asirifi, who at the time were, respectively, GCB's managing director, executive business manager, and chair.

We are grateful to Michael Middeke and Crispin Peet of Boydell for their encouragement, guidance and patience. We also thank the peer reviewers for their suggestions. Finally, we thank Felicity ('Pip') Austin for her work on the index.

Gareth Austin and Kofi Adjepong-Boateng
Cambridge, 19 March 2026

Introduction: The Political Economy of Ghana in the Cocoa Era

Gareth Austin and Kofi Adjepong-Boateng

Ghana has often been considered a test case of economic development in Africa. Much the same can be said of the country's modern political history, with which its economic problems and achievements have been closely intertwined. The purpose of this collaborative and interdisciplinary volume is to review and analyse the political economy – the interaction of economic forces and political choices – of the country over the era from the beginning of cocoa exports in 1891 to their peak, in crop year 2010/11, which coincided with the beginning of petroleum exports. In treating this 120-year time span as a single era, we connect, and analyse in longer-term perspective, periods that have usually been considered separately: colonial or post-colonial, or a sub-set of either of these.[1] The ambition of the project is exemplified by Alence's chapter which contrasts the economic policy regimes of the early colonial government until the great cocoa hold-up of 1937–8 and the outbreak of world war in 1939, and the early post-colonial government until the advent of economic liberalisation in 1983, in how they responded to external trade shocks. This is a very acute way of approaching the differences between the mid-colonial and early post-colonial states.

1 Leading examples include Walter Birmingham, I. Neustadt and E.N. Omaboe (eds), *A Study of Contemporary Ghana*, vol. 1, *The Economy of Ghana* (London, 1966); G.B. Kay (ed.), *The Political Economy of Colonialism in Ghana: A Collection of Documents and Statistics 1900–1960* (London, 1972); Emmanuel Hansen and Kwame A. Ninsin (eds), *The State, Development and Politics in Ghana* (London, 1989); Wisdom J. Tettey, Korbia P. Puplampu and Bruce J. Berman (eds), *Critical Perspectives on Politics and Socio-Economic Development in Ghana* (Leiden, 2003); Kwame Boafo-Arthur (ed.), *Ghana: One Decade of the Liberal State* (London, 2007); Ernest Aryeetey and Ravi Kanbur (eds), *The Economy of Ghana: Analytical Perspectives on Stability, Growth and Poverty* (Woodbridge, 2008); Ernest Aryeetey and Ravi Kanbur (eds), *The Economy of Ghana Sixty Years After Independence* (Oxford, 2017); Lindsay Whitfield, *Economics After Colonialism: Ghana and the Struggle for Power* (Cambridge, 2018).

It should be noted that while the 'long twentieth century' is defined by the structure of exports, our interest is the political economy of Ghana as a whole. Therefore we consider economic growth and structural change, government revenue and expenditure, and the institutional settings and political struggles which responded to economic pressures and opportunities and also shaped them. Had space and the availability of contributors permitted, we would have liked to include chapters on other topics, notably food crops and large-scale mining, and to have had regional and district perspectives.[2]

The authors use a wide range of primary sources. Most chapters cite archival records (from a total of four countries) and some also use oral history, as well as official publications and databases. We also draw on the academic literature in economic history, economics, history and political science. The contributors come from all these disciplines.

Before going further, let us recall that the Ghanaian state that achieved independence in 1957 was not a pre-colonial kingdom now restored to sovereignty, like Ethiopia following the expulsion of Mussolini's troops in 1941. The Asante kingdom had once achieved varying degrees of control over the majority of what later became Ghana,[3] but independent Ghana was no renascent Asante.[4] Rather, it was a new nationalist political project that developed within, and ultimately superimposed itself upon, a colonial compilation of territories and populations. The colonial construction began in 1874, when British control moved inland from the handful of forts previously under British or other European ownership. Specifically, in that year Britain declared a protectorate over what later became the Gold Coast Colony, essentially comprising the land between the River Pra and the sea. The area under colonial control was approximately quadrupled in 1896, when Britain occupied the Asante kingdom (which became the colony of Ashanti) and its savanna hinterland (which became the Northern Territories). In 1914 British and French troops occupied the German colony of Togo; in 1919, part of it became British Mandated Togoland (now the Volta Region, along with Anlo district, which had been part of the Gold Coast Colony rather than Togo). In reading the earlier chapters in this book it is important to consider that the 'Gold Coast Colony' comprised only a quarter (25.5 per cent) of the territory of what became Ghana, with just under half the population according to the 1931 and 1948 censuses. The additions of

2 A pioneering example is John Dunn and A.F. Robertson, *Dependence and Opportunity: Political Change in Ahafo* (Cambridge, 1973), which interprets political change very broadly.

3 See the maps in Ivor Wilks, *Asante in the Nineteenth Century: the Structure and Evolution of a Political Order* (Cambridge 1975; 2nd edition, 1989), 19, 45, 62.

4 And surely would not have been, even had the Ashanti-based federalist party, the National Liberation Movement, succeeded in its pre-independence struggle against the Convention People's Party. On the NLM see Jean Marie Allman, *The Quills of the Porcupine: Asante Nationalism in an Emergent Ghana* (Madison WI, 1993).

1896 and 1919 were administered from Accra, however, and by the 1930s the whole territory was described by the British government as 'the Gold Coast'. This formed the boundaries of the independent state of 1957 – after surviving a United Nations (UN)-supervised referendum on whether the former German territory should become part of independent Togo.

Before colonisation the polities that occupied the space that later became Ghana varied greatly in size and structure, from autonomous villages that formed coalitions for defence, through small states up to the Asante kingdom, whose tentacles of control extended to the extraction of tribute from neighbouring polities in the savanna north. Both the Asante kingdom and the coastal region had thriving extra-subsistence production over the several decades – and centuries – before 1891. This included both 'legitimate commerce' (after the British ban on slave trading in 1807) on the coast, where palm oil and palm kernel exports developed, and in the interior, notably Asante exports of gold dust to the south and kola nuts to Kano in the Sokoto Caliphate. In the 1880s there was a short-lived boom in wild rubber, supplied by African entrepreneurs in Asante and further south.[5]

The cocoa take-off in the early colonial period, largely through African entrepreneurship, reinvesting the proceeds of earlier commercial activity, moved the Gold Coast Colony and Ashanti from exporting no cocoa beans in 1890 to becoming the world's largest producer in 1910/11. This famous episode in the broader cash-crop revolution in tropical Africa has often been seen a mere 'vent for surplus', in which growth was the result of adding further inputs of land and labour without increasing productivity.[6] But, as Austin's chapter highlights, this is greatly to underestimate the degree of innovation. Not only was cocoa a new, exotic crop as far as the farmers were concerned, but as a tree crop it took several years to come into bearing. Thus, as Hill emphasised in a classic work, adopting cocoa cultivation was bold, risk-taking, and long-sighted, the more so where farmers migrated and purchased land on credit.[7] To be sure, the cocoa take-off did involve extending the area under cultivation,

5 Kwame Arhin, 'The economic and social significance of rubber production and exchange on the Gold and Ivory Coasts, 1880–1900', *Cahiers d'études africaines* 20:77–8 (1980), 49–62; Raymond E. Dumett, 'African merchants of the Gold Coast, 1860–1905: dynamics of indigenous entrepreneurship', *Comparative Studies in Society and History* 25:4 (1985), 661–93 (reprinted in Dumett, *Imperialism, Economic Development and Social Change in West Africa* [Durham NC, 2013]); Ivor Wilks, 'Wangara, Akan, and Portuguese in the fifteenth and sixteenth centuries', in Wilks, *Forests of Gold: Essays on the Akan and the Kingdom of Asante* (Athens OH, 1993), 1–39; Gareth Austin '"No elders were present": commoners and private ownership in Asante, 1807–96', *Journal of African History* 37:1 (1996), 1–30.

6 For references see chapter 1.

7 Polly Hill, *The Migrant Cocoa-Farmers of Southern Ghana: A Study in Rural Capitalism* (Cambridge, 1963; 2nd edition Hamburg 1997).

taking advantage of the historic abundance of cultivable land in relation to labour, and the specific availability of forest ochrosols. But it also required a new ratio of inputs of labour, land and capital and a major reallocation of labour from earlier forms of extra-subsistence production (oil palm, small-scale gold mining, and even from the relatively recent trade in wild rubber). It was a shift from annual to vintage crop-growing, and to a new and more remunerative production function.[8]

The Gold Coast emerged as probably the most prosperous colony in tropical Africa, based on specialising in the most profitable export crop of the time. According to Broadberry and Gardner's estimates of real Gross Domestic Product (GDP) per head for seven British colonies in tropical Africa, the Gold Coast/Ghana was significantly ahead of the rest of the sample in every year for which they give figures until the 1970s.[9] This is going back to 1885 though, as will be explained later, it is necessary to be very cautious about any guesstimates for the period before 1920.

Table I.1 Colonial and Early-Independent Ghana's GDP per head in comparative perspective

(1990 international dollars)

Year (sample size)	Ghana	2nd in sample	3rd in sample
1920 (of 4)	815	Nigeria 620	Zimbabwe 404
1930 (of 7)	1094	Kenya 704	Nigeria 569
1950 (of 7)	1122	Nigeria 753	Zimbabwe 701
1956 (of 7)	1236	Zimbabwe 892	Nigeria 821
1960 (of 7)	1378	Zambia 960	Zimbabwe 938
1970 (of 7)	1424	Zimbabwe 1282	Nigeria 1094

Source: Stephen Broadberry and Leigh Gardner, 'Economic growth in Sub-Saharan Africa, 1885–2008: evidence from eight countries', *Explorations in Economic History*, 83 (2022), table A1, https://doi.org/10.1016/j.eeh.2021.101424 (accessed 25 May 2026).

8 Gareth Austin, 'Vent for surplus or productivity breakthrough? The Ghanaian cocoa take-off, c.1890–1936', *Economic History Review* 67:4 (2014), 1035–64. See, further, Austin's chapter in this volume.

9 They have no Ghana data for 1912–19 and 1940–41 inclusive. Ghana lost the lead in 1972. The other countries in the sample (not mentioned in Table I.1) are Uganda and Malawi.

During the colonial era itself, the Gold Coast came to be considered a model of what could be achieved by African economies without European settlement or widespread forced labour.[10] This policy was championed in imperial arguments about British West Africa by Sir Hugh Clifford, governor of the Gold Coast from 1912 to 1919. His successor, Gordon Guggisberg, introduced a Ten-Year Development Plan that involved more ambitious infrastructural investment than in comparable British colonies, extending to health and elite education but very much in the framework of continued specialisation in export agriculture.

Notoriously, the average prosperity of colonial Ghana was not experienced equally by the regions. As Bob-Milliar and Manu-Osafo explore in their chapter, the northern savanna – the 'Northern Territories' – remained poorer than Ashanti and the south as a whole throughout the colonial period, and indeed throughout the 'long twentieth century'. It is no surprise that when a free labour market developed across Ghana, the main form it took was a flow of mostly seasonal, mostly male workers from savanna communities of the Northern Territories and neighbouring French colonies, migrating for work on the cocoa farms and mines of the forest zone.[11] This voluntary flow accelerated when it became safe to move, following the prohibition of slavery and pawning in Ashanti and the North in 1908 (they had already been banned in the Gold Coast Colony in 1874). It also probably accelerated after the colonial administration ended its early practice (especially before 1910 and during 1919–24) of putting pressure on northern chiefs to send young men south to work in mines or for the government.[12] Northern labour in Ashanti is the focus of Bob-Milliar and Manu-Osafo's chapter, which takes the story into the post-independence era, with a focus – unlike in earlier literature — on female migration.

Aboagye examines in detail the quantitative evidence on inequality in Ghana generally, across the long twentieth century. He asks whether fiscal policy – taxation and government expenditure – affected inequality, given that redistribution in favour of the poor is considered one of the functions of government in developed economies. His findings are pessimistic: whether inequality rose or fell seems to have had little to do with government policy. Rather, the state passively presided over increasing inequality during the original cocoa take-off and in the late twentieth and early twenty-first centuries, in the era of economic liberalisation. Inequality declined between 1961 and 1982, but that

10 Benoit Daviron, 'Mobilizing labour in African agriculture: the role of the International Colonial Institute in the elaboration of a standard of colonial administration, 1895–1930', *Journal of Global History* 5:1 (2010), 479–501.

11 The fullest account remains Nicholas van Hear, 'Northern Labour and the Development of Capitalist Agriculture in Ghana' (Ph.D. dissertation, University of Birmingham, 1982).

12 Roger G. Thomas, 'Forced labour in British West Africa: the case of the Northern Territories of the Gold Coast 1906–27', *Journal of African History* 14:1 (1973), 79–103.

was a function of general economic shrinkage. Amoah-Boampong's chapter reviews the history of gender inequality in cocoa growing, with women's labour inputs being unmatched by their access to resources or income, especially in the early decades.

The series of cocoa hold-ups, 1908–38, when Ghanaian farmers and brokers challenged the price-fixing of successive cartels of European cocoa-buying firms by withholding their crop from the market, were acts of organised, collective and increasingly sustained economic protest unparalleled across Africa. Alence's chapter includes an incisive analysis of the culminating hold-up, of 1937/38, which has been astonishingly neglected in recent decades.[13]

The Second World War saw the commodity terms of trade worsen further for Ghanaians. Meanwhile thousands of Ghanaian soldiers fought in Ethiopia and Burma,[14] before returning to high inflation and severe shortages of imported commodities. By 1948, the effects of high inflation and urban discontent led first to a boycott of consumer goods, aimed at forcing prices down, and then to protests from ex-servicemen and eventually to riots. This led a former member of the colonial civil service to write that it 'is difficult to over-emphasize the extent of the social and political revolution which has taken place in the Gold Coast.'[15]

The emergence of a political movement demanding a greater share of power for the indigenous population, and ultimately independence, propelled the Gold Coast to the front of the crowd of African colonies pushing for freedom from colonial rule. The movement was originally led by members of the coastal educated elite, above all J.B. Danquah. But the riots of February–March 1948, and the effective articulation of their political significance – leading to the formation of the Convention People's Party (the CPP) in 1949, under Kwame Nkrumah – rather quickly led the British government to adopt a timetable for early independence.[16] The latter progressed in stages ('joint rule' 1951, internal self-government 1954) before full independence on 6 March 1957, ahead of any other 'black' African country.

Kwame Nkrumah, leader to independence, achieved fame also for his championing of the cause of continental unity. Ghana received widespread

13 Indeed, since Alence's own 'The 1937–38 Gold Coast cocoa crisis: the political economy of commercial stalemate', *African Economic History* 19 (1990–91), 77–104.

14 David Killingray, 'Military and labour recruitment in the Gold Coast during the Second World War', *Journal of African History*, 23:1 (1982), 83–95. See further, David Killingray with Martin Plaut, *Fighting for Britain: African Soldiers in the Second World War* (Woodbridge, 2010).

15 Reginald Saloway, 'The New Gold Coast', *International Affairs* 31:4 (1955), 469, 476.

16 Adu Boahen, *Ghana: Evolution and Change in the Nineteenth and Twentieth Centuries* (London, 1975), 155–65. For the impact of events on the ground on the evolution of colonial thinking see, Richard Rathbone (ed.), *Ghana*, Part I, *1941–1952* in *British Documents on the End of Empire*, Series B Volume 1 (London, 1992).

international attention for its early independence and its leadership in continental and global debates (such as championing the creation of the UN Economic Commission for Africa). Serra and Monaghan's contribution to this volume is an intriguing examination of one of Nkrumah's major but less well remembered initiatives, the neglected but significant episode of the formation of the Ghana–Guinea–Mali Union. Rather than seeing it simply as a story of idealistic ambition running into the brick wall of reality, Serra and Monaghan combine wide-ranging archival research, theoretical reflection and Akan proverbs in developing their idea of the union as a 'spectre' that has haunted the imagination of Ghanaian and African nationalists and pan-Africanists ever since.

Cooperation at micro level has been an idealistic dream in international and national contexts. In Ghanaian cocoa production, however, formal cooperatives were introduced from above. If the dream was realised, it then receded, before coming true again in a different form. Kamenov's chapter provides an extended account of the cocoa cooperatives of the colonial era, which were originally instigated by the Department of Agriculture in the late 1920s, in the hope of raising the quality of cocoa beans. Kamenov examines the struggle of the cooperative 'movement' to expand its following among cocoa farmers, and its share of the crop, in the 1930s and 1940s. In the 1950s, the cooperatives broke through to become a major force in cocoa production and selling. Kamenov asks how far these cooperatives should be understood as instruments of state control in agriculture, or how far they became vehicles or frameworks through which farmers – including small capitalists – pursued their own interests. Ghana's first president perhaps gave his own answer, in the Dawn Broadcast of April 1961, which announced the CPP's exclusion of cooperatives from cocoa marketing, in favour of the state (or, more precisely, the ruling party). In describing and analysing the rise and fall of cocoa cooperatives in the years before and after independence, Kamenov fills an important gap in the literature.

Much of Amoah-Boampong's chapter is an examination of the Kuapa Kokoo Farmers' Union (KKFU), which was the pioneer (1993) of the new wave of cocoa cooperatives that emerged a decade after the beginning of the general liberalisation of economic policy in 1983, and specifically following the establishment of the Fourth Republic. In particular, Amoah-Boampong reveals a remarkable story of how women's empowerment, in terms of securing their rights to farms as well as in representation and leadership, was advanced within the KKFU.[17] Whether these independent cooperatives have been more effective as champions of farmers' interests than their state-promoted predecessors of

17 For another possibly counter-intuitive case of female advance see Jérôme Destombes, 'From long-term patterns of seasonal hunger to changing experiences of everyday poverty: north-eastern Ghana c.1930–2000', *Journal of African History* 47:2 (2006), 181–205. For Nangodi, Destombes shows statistically that average nutritional status improved between

the colonial period is perhaps unclear, because in the liberal era the authorities have had their own reasons for ensuring that cocoa farmers receive a high proportion of the world price.

The 1950s and 1960s, indeed 1939 onwards, can be seen as a period of experimentation in economic policy. The outbreak of war prompted the British government, especially in the light of the recent cocoa hold-ups, to create a state Produce Marketing Board with a monopsony of exports from British West Africa. The initial intention was to enable the government to avoid unrest behind the lines by giving support to the prices paid to export-producers in the event of a price collapse in the Atlantic market. By war's end, however, the board had proved to be a very effective means of doing the opposite: taxing the farmers, by paying them significantly less than the board received (after deduction of marketing costs) on the international market. The decision was taken to make the marketing board permanent, as the Gold Coast (later Ghana) Cocoa Marketing Board.

The creation of a state export monopsony over the major export commodity created the fiscal potential for more ambitious state intervention. Before independence, Nkrumah and his colleagues explored options for accelerating economic development. This included hiring as an advisor Professor W. Arthur Lewis, already a star of development economics and himself from the Caribbean. Kanbur's chapter gives a close reading of Lewis's *Report on Industrialisation and the Gold Coast* (1953), which, as Kanbur notes, greatly disappointed the new government in its insistence that Ghana was not yet ready to pursue an active policy of industrialisation. By 1961, Ghana had embarked on just such a policy, the Seven-Year Plan. As Kanbur demonstrates, it is very interesting to consider the outcome of the plan, and of industrial strategy in the 1960s and 1970s generally, in the perspective of Lewis's warnings against a 'premature' push for industrialisation.

It was also under the CPP that Ghana got a central bank, the Bank of Ghana, after much debate about how far it should actively lend to promote development. The Bank of England persistently argued that a Ghanaian central bank should follow its own, highly conservative, model. Counter-arguments were made, including by Danquah, that the central bank should lend long-term to producers to promote economic change. This debate and its outcome is examined in Adjepong-Boateng's chapter. By the end of Nkrumah's presidency, Ghana had effectively declared currency independence, leaving the West African Currency Board and the sterling area.

The Nkrumah period was also an important moment for population policy. Ghana's population, like that of tropical Africa as a whole, did not necessarily grow continuously until after the global influenza pandemic of 1918. Even after

1963/4 and 1999/2000, with the 'hungry season' before the harvest losing some of its severity – the biggest gains being for women.

that, the increases shown in official figures are at least largely attributable to the 'censuses' becoming more comprehensive. The first true census (really counting almost everyone) was not until after independence. But the incomplete evidence does suggest that there was a genuine upward trend of population from *c.* 1920 onwards (Table I.2), which accelerated in mid-century, as did rural–urban migration. In the 1950s and early 1960s, as Ashford has documented, there was a clash of perspectives between the World Health Organisation and UN systems, both of which had become alarmed at the growth of world – and especially African – population, and public opinion and government in Ghana, which wanted more people.[18] On this, Nkrumah and Lewis were perhaps aligned: the latter had pointed to a shortage of (especially male) labour as a constraint on economic development in the country.

Table I.2 Population Growth and Urbanisation

Census Year	Population enumerated [adjusted estimate]	Urban population as share of total population
1921	2,296,400 [2,543,000]	7.9% [7.2%]
1931	3,160,568 [3,164,000]	9.2% [9.2%]
1948	4,118,450 [4,876,000]	17.1% [14.5%]
1960	6,726,815	23.1%
1970	8,559,313	28.9%
1984	12,296,081	32.0%
2000	18,912,079	43.8%
2010	24,558,823	50.9%

Sources: the Gold Coast and Ghana censuses, with some modifications to the earlier figures. The figures in square brackets are upward revisions either by Austin or accepted by Austin from earlier authors. They are estimated to the nearest thousand.[19] Urban means towns of at least 5,000 people.

18 Holly Ashford, 'Reproducing the nation in Nkrumah's Ghana, 1951–1966', in Ashford, *Development and Women's Reproductive Health in Ghana, 1920–1982* (Abingdon, 2023), 123–56.

19 For explanation, see Gareth Austin, 'Labour and land in Ghana, 1874–1939: a shifting ratio and an institutional revolution', *Australian Economic History Review* 47:1 (2007), at 105–7.

As it turned out, as Table I.2 shows, Ghana's population nearly quadrupled in the half-century after the 1960 census, while the proportion of the population living in towns (communities of 5,000 or more) more than doubled. One result has been to put enormous pressure on the supply of cultivable land, leading to landholders becoming less willing even to lease (still less sell) land to strangers, and to a perceived decline in the security of stranger-farmers' property rights.[20] One could certainly argue that the aggregate labour shortage is now over, despite the growth of emigration over recent decades. Ghana's rate of population growth peaked in the 1980s, but the proportion of young females in the population ensured that the population continued – and continues – to rise well into the twenty-first century.[21]

Nkrumah's overthrow, in the military coup of February 1966, appeared to mark the hugely disappointing end of a major experiment in import-substitution industrialisation as a means of breaking with the colonial economic pattern of specialisation in the export of unprocessed primary products, especially cocoa, gold and timber.[22] In the 1970s, a period of slow and fluctuating economic growth gave way to an extraordinary fall: from 1975 to 1983 real GDP per head fell at least a third.[23] By the early 1980s, in the words of a Harvard economist, Ghana was considered 'a model of how *not* to develop'.[24] Political instability seemed to become endemic: J.J. Rawlings' second 'revolution', on 31 December 1981, was the fifth military takeover, and within just fifteen years.

Rawlings returned determined both to arrest hyper-inflation and economic shrinkage by strict enforcement of the regime of quantity and price controls over most aspects of economic life – an approach that had worked temporarily

20 Stefano Boni, *Clearing the Ghanaian Forest* (Legon, 2005); Markus Goldstein and Christopher Udry, 'The profits of power: land rights and agricultural investment in Ghana', *Journal of Political Economy* 116:6 (2008), 981–1022.

21 For concerns about rapid population growth, see Baffour K. Takyii and Isaac Addai, 'Demographic processes, economic growth and socio-economic development in Ghana, 1960–2000', in Wisdom J. Tettey, Korbia P. Puplampu and Bruce J. Berman (eds), *Critical Perspectives on Politics and Socio-Economic Development in Ghana* (Leiden, 2003), 223–37.

22 A feeling captured in the title of an instant history written by two American Marxists: Bob Fitch and Mary Oppenheimer, *Ghana: End of an Illusion* (New York, 1966).

23 The process of decline is examined in Jonathan H. Frimpong-Ansah, *The Vampire State in Africa: The Political Economy of Decline in Ghana* ((London, 1991); Douglas Rimmer, *Staying Poor: Ghana's Political Economy 1950–1990* (Oxford, 1992). For a recent analysis, in comparative perspective, see Gareth Austin, 'Ghana and Kenya facing the 1970s commodity price shocks: the national and the global', in Shigeru Akita (ed.), *Oil Crises of the 1970s and the Transformation of International Order: Economy, Development and Aid in Asia and Africa* (London, 2023), 223–56.

24 Michael Roemer, 'Ghana, 1950–1980: missed opportunities', in Arnold Harberger (ed.), *World Economic Growth (*San Francisco, 1984), 201–30, at 202 (his emphasis).

during the brief June 4 Revolution in 1979 – but also, now, to replace 'bourgeois' democracy with a form of direct democracy embodied in Workers' and Peoples' Defence Committees.[25] These experiments in mass organisation helped establish Rawlings' Provisional National Defence Council (PNDC) as the top of a movement that invested in mass activism and relied on grassroots support to appeal to the broader populace, particularly the youth. In his contribution to this volume, however, Nugent draws attention to the shortcomings of analyses that tie the CPP very closely to the 'marginalised' youth in the lead-up to Independence. He highlights the role played by traditional leaders in the 1950s and 1960s, explaining why chieftaincy as an institution came through these decades relatively intact.

Sapong's chapter examines the history of youth organisations from the *asafo* companies of the pre-colonial Gold Coast to the various structures created by successive governments of independent Ghana – his focus is on 1966–81 – to both mobilise and control young adults. His account raises the question of whether there has been a transition from organisations that, for all the efforts at control by chiefs and elders, were ultimately led by young people themselves, to fundamentally 'top-down' structures aimed at averting spontaneous expressions of the views of younger citizens.[26]

Rawlings performed a U-turn in economic policy in 1983. Alence's chapter uses interviews with key participants and crucial documents from the time to show how the internal debate evolved within his government. One of the striking aspects is the realism: only a few months into the new regime, while its public position emphasised the moral and political imperative of enforcing the price and quantity controls that hamstrung the economy, there was confidential discussion of the economic need for – and the political arguments against – devaluation. Ghana's early adoption of economic liberalisation – what became 'Structural Adjustment' — took practical effect in the disguised devaluation in the budget of April 1983.[27] There was a staged transition to the floating of the cedi, completed in 1986. The programme of liberalisation was rewarded with economic growth per capita in every year through to the end of the era covered in this volume and beyond. Not only was the economic collapse of 1975–83 reversed, but real GDP per head, which had fallen back to pre-independence levels by 1983, more than doubled by 2010. The proportion of the population in

25 The background to these forms of organisation by the PNDC is described in Zaya Yeebo, 'Ghana: Defence Committees and the class struggle', *Review of African Political Economy* 32 (1985), 64–72.

26 Though perhaps things have changed again across Africa with the recent 'Generation Z' protests, for example in Kenya in 2024 and 2025.

27 Jeffrey Herbst, *The Politics of Reform in Ghana, 1982–1991* (Berkeley, 1993), 38–58.

absolute poverty, as measured by UN standards, also fell.[28] Inequality, however, rose as expansion continued in what was now, more than even in the colonial period, very thoroughly a market economy.[29] The economically liberal regime created by 'structural adjustment' has become more or less institutionalised: to the time of writing, it has been accepted in practice by both the major parties of the Fourth Republic. The debates have been about how to make the market economy work more equitably, and how to build more economic and human development within and upon it, rather than about any idea of reverting to detailed state regulation of the economy. The floating of the exchange rate has reduced the salience of devaluation in politics. It should also be remarked that it is surely no coincidence that, whereas economic instability and decline were highly correlated with attempted and actual military coups during 1966–83, sustained economic growth from 1983 onwards was accompanied by peaceful transitions from one government to the next.

In their chapter, picking up the theme of Kanbur's chapter, Abbey and Adu-Danso review the still largely unfinished pursuit of industrialisation since independence, including both the policy experiments of the early decades and the renewed efforts to promote manufacturing under the Fourth Republic. Kanbur considers the implications for industrial strategy in Ghana of the advent of petroleum exports, and the intensified global tendency for industrial technology to be labour-saving. As he comments, the 'jobs leaving China because of high labour costs will be far fewer by the time they get to Africa and Ghana'. And that was true even before the systematic application of artificial intelligence.

In the final chapter, Aryeetey investigates the political economy of deficits and deficit financing in Ghana, used initially by Nkrumah to fund investments in infrastructure and to pursue an industrialisation policy geared towards import substitution. In time, Aryeetey argues, deficit funding came to be used to meet the costs of maintaining a large civil service and to meet the cost of servicing government debt, leading to a debt trap. Debt funding, Aryeetey points out, has been raised either by borrowing from abroad or from the domestic banking system, including from the central bank. The lack of central bank independence is one of the themes discussed by Adjepong-Boateng in his chapter. Aryeetey formulates a powerful and provocative thesis about the absence of policy differences between the respective republics despite public and academic perceptions to the contrary. To Aryeetey, the lack of debate on the role of the Ghanaian state has contributed to an environment in which there is no contest of ideas

28 Andy McKay and Eric Osei-Assibey, 'Poverty and inequality in Ghana', in Ernest Aryeetey and Ravi Kanbur (eds), *The Economy of Ghana Sixty Years After Independence* (Oxford, 2017), 279–98.

29 McKay and Osei-Assibey, 'Poverty and inequality'.

and a lack of accountability, all of which has led to poor policy choices by successive governments.

This theme is also highlighted by Nugent in his analysis of what he describes as Ghana's 'social contract'. Like Aryeetey, he draws attention to the failure of successive governments to raise enough revenue to meet the expenditure necessary to support this social contract and therefore to the propensity of Ghanaian political parties to accumulate debt to meet the cost of electoral promises. Nugent's chapter explores back to the origins of the social contract in the Ghanaian context, beginning with the Bond of 1844 between Britain and the Fante chiefs, and upheld by successive governments. This contract set limits to several aspects of the relationship between the state and Ghanaian society, including limits to state interference in wider social questions, particularly as these relate to land and taxes. The contract also made the state responsible for the delivery of certain public goods, including infrastructure and public utilities. Finally, Nugent reasons that the contract made the state the guarantor of wider physical security across the country, including secure access to markets. This social contract was adhered to by both colonial and post-Independence governments and, over its long history, resulted in a political system which is generally accepted by the Ghanaian populace as legitimate, despite the failure by governments to uphold this very social contract being the primary source of political instability in the past.

The dream of industrialisation, which the Watson Commission investigating the causes of the 1948 riots had found itself 'pressed with' at 'every turn',[30] had, if anything, receded by 2010: 'the share of manufacturing in GDP was 6.7 per cent, less than it had been in the 1970s.'[31] But the lack of industrialisation does not mean there was no structural transformation. The 2010 census reported that, for the first time, the urban population exceeded the rural population. Urbanisation presupposes an expansion in food supply. Despite some imports, this primarily suggests a remarkable growth in domestic agricultural output. Urbanisation also creates opportunities for diversification in the range of occupational and entrepreneurial opportunities. While the growth of manufacturing remained disappointing, there was encouraging if uneven growth between the 1960 and 2010 censuses in the share of the employed population in service-sector occupations that are crucial for market integration: transport, storage and communication, together up from 2.6 to 4.1 per cent. There was also the emergence or expansion of certain service occupations characteristic

30 Great Britain, *Report of the Commission of Enquiry into Disturbances in the Gold Coast 1948* (Colonial no. 238; London, 1948), 54.

31 Nkechi S. Owoo and John Page, 'Industrial policy in Ghana: from a dominant state to resource abundance', in Ernest Aryeetey and Ravi Kanbur (eds), *The Economy of Ghana Sixty Years After Independence* (Oxford, 2017), 176–91, at 176. On the politics of industrial policy in the Fourth Republic see Whitfield, *Economies after Colonialism*.

of relatively sophisticated market economies ([formal] finance, insurance and real-estate, up from 0.09 to 4.0 per cent) and of modern economies in general (professional and technical, up from 2.3 to 7.3 per cent).[32] Ghana's sustained growth after 1983 stood in contrast to the 'lost' fifteen years of economic growth which the majority of African countries experienced until a continental boom began in 1995. So Ghana was, again, a test-case: this time at the positive end of a spectrum of experiences with economic liberalisation, at least as far as economic growth was concerned.[33]

It was not inevitable that political liberalisation would follow economic liberalisation.[34] But civil society, which had opposed military rule in the 1970s, created momentum towards the restoration of a multi-party electoral system accompanied by individual and press freedom. An important moment in this intellectual and political mobilisation was the historian Professor Adu Boahen's J.B. Danquah Memorial Lectures in February 1988.[35] The end of the Cold War, 1989–91, led to donor pressure on African countries to democratise in the name of 'good governance'. Chairman Rawlings declared his readiness to swop his air force fatigues for civilian clothes and to stand for president at the head of a new political party, the National Democratic Congress (NDC).

After the series of military coups that disfigured the reputation of Ghanaian democracy, the Fourth Republic – inaugurated on 7 January 1993 – has so far delivered not only constitutional stability but also four changes of ruling party through the ballot box (2000/01, 2008/9, 2016/17, 2024/25): a propensity for such changes that, if not unique, is highly unusual in the continent. Also striking is the resilience and strength of the two-party system in Ghana. The NDC and the New Patriotic Party (both founded in 1992) have alternated in power, at eight-year intervals; the latter being considered slightly to the right of the former. In Ghana, it has seemed more important to be the 'flag-bearer' of one or other major party than it is in Nigeria, where individuals with very deep pockets have had more scope to establish themselves as realistic contenders for power without necessarily harnessing themselves to deep party traditions.[36]

32 Ghana, *1960 Population Census of Ghana*, vol. IV (Accra, 1964); Ghana Statistical Service, *2010 Population & Housing Census: Summary Report of Final Results*, 75–7.

33 For a critical assessment of economic liberalisation see Kwabena Donkor, *Structural Adjustment and Mass Poverty in Ghana* (Aldershot, 1997; reissued Abingdon, 2018).

34 An interesting analysis is Eboe Hutchful, *Ghana's Adjustment Experience: the Paradox of Reform* (Geneva, 2002), 196–213.

35 Albert Adu Boahen, *The Ghanaian Sphinx: Reflections on the Contemporary History of Ghana 1972–1987* (Accra, 1989). In a recent publication, Bob-Milliar briefly describes the opinions of opponents of Boahen's thesis: George Bob-Milliar, 'Learned societies, knowledge production, and public engagement in colonial and postcolonial Ghana, 1930–90', *Journal of African History* 65:3 (2024), 396.

36 Discussion on money and politics in Nigeria can be found in Laurent Fourchard and Azeez Kayode Sikiru, 'The 2023 cashless election in Nigeria: the politics of withdrawing

Some chapters in this volume go beyond the end date in our title. In doing so, these chapters include references to Ghana's export of oil. The period from which Ghana exported material quantities of oil is outside the formal scope of this volume but is relevant as it sees the working out – or not – of some of the institutional trends and policy dilemmas that are discussed in this book. The continuing transition from cocoa to oil as the country's major export has profound implications for the control and distribution of export and fiscal revenue, with potentially important consequences for the country's whole political economy. But the growth of oil revenue has been fairly slow; meanwhile, at the time of writing, some years of international political instability have boosted the price of gold, igniting even greater interest from Ghanaians interested in artisanal and small-scale gold mining (ASM).

The existence of offshore oil deposits had been known since the early twentieth century, but it was early in the twenty-first that technological, institutional and policy conditions combined to facilitate their commercial exploitation. Very small quantities were exported, off and on, from the Saltpond Oil Field, about 24 metres down, from 1978. In 2007, however, the deep-water Jubilee Field was discovered, about 1100 metres down. Exports from there began in January 2011. That year oil exports came to about 4 per cent of GDP.

But, as explained by Aryeetey in his chapter, the expectation that oil exports would transform the country's revenue has yet to materialise. The contribution of oil and gas to GDP averaged 4.5 per cent of GDP during 2013–21. The peak so far was at 27 per cent in 2024. But data from the Ghana Statistical Service and the Bank of Ghana show that for the first three quarters of 2025 crude oil exports made up about 13 per cent of GDP. Clearly, fluctuations in the international price of oil can make a major difference, as does the growth of non-oil exports, notably gold.[37]

Small-scale and artisanal gold mining was legalised by the PNDC in 1989, as part of economic liberalisation, with producers being required to obtain a licence. The law defined ASM as using methods that required neither large capital nor specialised technology. While Ghana thereby became the first African state to legalise ASM since independence, it was a re-legalisation: in his chapter, Hilson notes that private African mining had been effectively prohibited by

money', *African Affairs* 122:488 (2023), 429–45; Mahmoud Alfa and John Marangos, 'An empirical appraisal of the role of money in Nigerian politics', *International Journal of Economic Policy in Emerging Economies* 9:1 (2016), 65–88.

37 Ghana Statistical Service, '*Third Quarter (Q3) 2025 Gross Domestic Product Estimates*' (released 10 December 2025); Bank of Ghana, '*Summary of Economic and Financial Data – January 2026*' (released 27 January 2026); Bank of Ghana, '*Semi-Annual Report on Petroleum Holding Fund: July 1 – December 31, 2025*' (released 2 February 2026); PwC Ghana: '*2026 PwC Budget Digest: Resetting for Growth, Jobs, and Economic Transformation*' (released 13 November 2025).

the colonial government when it banned the sale of mercury to Africans in 1933. The industry goes back centuries in 'the Gold Coast', but small-scale production apparently declined during the late nineteenth and early twentieth century because producers were attracted to cocoa farming, and some of the known surface sites were reaching exhaustion. The post-1989 revival of the industry has made much use of mercury and other environmentally damaging inputs. Despite the legalisation, the majority of output in recent years is often said to be from unlicensed producers.

Hilson's chapter is a very important intervention in the controversy about ASM in Ghana (and elsewhere). He sets out the historical context and uses a wealth of documentation rigorously to examine in some detail what he shows are often exaggerated claims about the negative consequences of ASM. He emphasises the importance of small-scale mining as a source of economic opportunity for much of the population. This includes the youth; a solution for some of the young people, the precarity of whose economic existence is documented in Sapong's chapter. Further, Hilson attacks the 'militarisation' of government policy towards small-scale miners in the 2010s. Rather, he advocates more positive and sensitive engagement: regulating, monitoring, and formalising the small-scale sector, such that this major source of employment and wealth can be maintained without the environmental recklessness that goes along with illegal activity.

Meanwhile, the relatively slow and volatile growth of the revenue contribution from oil exports, compared to some earlier expectations, may alleviate some of the concerns highlighted in this volume by Abbey and Adu-Danso about the risks to Ghana's non-oil sector if fossil-fuel exports drive up the exchange rate, so rendering non-oil industries less competitive internationally; and also about the potential for greater corruption.[38] Those concerns, however, remain.[39] The oil age is as yet young.

More generally, a striking feature of the pattern of economic development in Ghana since the 1890s is increasing demands on the natural environment. With the adoption of cocoa putting land into permanent cultivation, farmers began a long process of using ever more of what, as of 1890, was still a large

38 On the question of the effectiveness of the legal and institutional framework of the Fourth Republic in controlling corruption, see Michael Ofori-Mensah, 'The Politics of Anticorruption in Ghana, 1993–2006: Action, Inaction and Accountability' (Ph.D. dissertation, University of Edinburgh, 2009); Ernest Harsch, *Corruption, Class, and Politics in Ghana* (Athens OH, 2024), 195–290, 320–33. The starting-point for analysis of corruption in the country remains Ayi Kyei Armah, *The Beautyful Ones Are Not Yet Born* (Boston, 1968).

39 Augustin Kwasi Fosu, 'Oil and Ghana's economy', in Ernest Aryeetey and Ravi Kanbur, *Economy of Ghana*, 153; Shafic Suleman and Godfred Ennin, 'A stakeholder's perspective of petroleum revenue management after a decade of upstream exploration and production activities in Ghana', *Social Sciences & Humanities Open* (2024) 9. Art. 100809, 10.

reserve of unused soil fertility in the forest zone. Ghana's nearly 70-year reign as the world's largest exporter of cocoa beans was based on the availability of what Ruf calls 'forest rent', defined as the difference between producing a unit of cocoa on land newly cleared from forest rather than by replanting.[40] That resource was progressively tapped during the first and second waves of expansion in Ghanaian cocoa production, into the 1960s. It was the third wave, beginning gradually during Structural Adjustment and accelerating rapidly from 2002 to 2010/11, that saw the transition to major reliance on replanting. As Austin emphasises in his chapter, the third expansion represented another shift to a higher production function in the history of Ghanaian cocoa farming. This is part of a broader process of intensification in agriculture, in the country and the continent, as the historic pattern of labour being scarce in relation to land is reversed. The increased demands of cultivation, to feed the rising population as well as for export production, comes up against the hunger of small-scale gold mining for land, with some evidence that open-cast mining is reducing the area left for cultivation. The continuing increase in pressure on cultivable land, combined with the rise of the petroleum industry, mean that it is increasingly relevant to see contemporary Ghanaian economic and political history in the context of the global 'Great Acceleration' of the human impact on the natural environment, in multiple forms.[41]

Finally, let us consider the primary sources available to students, professional scholars and the public on the political economy of Ghana, colonial and post-colonial. Several chapters in this volume are based on detailed archival research, especially in the national archives of Ghana, now usually known by the unromantic acronym PRAAD (Public Records and Archives Administration Department), supplemented in some cases by archives in other countries. Several chapters make detailed use of national income and population statistics, some of them published by government or international organisations, others compiled by academics. A few chapters also make explicit use of oral history techniques, such as interviews.

We believe this volume exemplifies the rigorous and genuinely informative use of all these kinds of sources. Readers are cautioned, however, about certain problems. The basic limitation of oral sources is that informants are mortal. It is vital that each generation's voices are recorded (metaphorically and if possible literally) and conserved; and also that individual voices are not silenced in the depositories by over-zealous (though well-intentioned) ethical protocols.

40 François Ruf, 'From forest rent to tree-capital: basic laws of cocoa supply', in Ruf and P.S. Siswoputranto (eds), *Cocoa Cycles: the Economics of Cocoa Supply* (Cambridge, 1995). See Austin's chapter.

41 Cf. Gareth Austin, 'Africa and the Anthropocene', in Austin (ed.), *Economic Development and Environmental History in the Anthropocene: Perspectives on Asia and Africa* (London, 2017), 95–118.

The general limitations of GDP per capita as a measure, and the data problems involved in constructing national income series, are well-known in the general context of independent Africa.[42] In Ghana, though, the problems with the basic statistics are greater for the colonial period. There were six colonial 'censuses', each better-resourced and more comprehensive than its predecessor. But it was not until the first post-independence exercise, in 1960, that the census was fully worthy of the name, because it actually counted almost everyone in the country at the same time.[43]

Precisely because each colonial 'census' was more comprehensive, the rapid rise in the totals they report are inflated by better coverage. The 1891 censuses naturally excluded the parts of 'Ghana' not yet under British control. Even after that, the denominator in GDP per capita can only be estimated before 1960. While confidence that such estimates are much better than mere guesses becomes increasingly justified over the colonial period, it has to be particularly weak before the 1921 census, which at least covered the whole country though without doing a true count in all areas.

For the early years of the long twentieth century the numerator, output, is itself a guesstimate. To take an obvious example, we do not have data for government expenditure for Ashanti and the north before they came under British control, and much of their exports went uncounted, certainly by the British state. This does not mean that GDP per capita figures for 1891 are worthless; they are roughly in line with what would be expected from the rest of the research on the period. But they are 'heroic': meaning that we need to remember the difficulties of constructing these figures when we read and use them.[44]

The archives most used by authors of this volume is naturally the national archives of Ghana, to whose staff we are very grateful. One of PRAAD's great virtues is that – unlike the national archives of most states – it is decentralised, in that all but the newest regional capitals contain an office of the archives, making available the local records of colonial and early post-independence government for the use of researchers, including locally based students. But three problems deserve wider public attention. The first is conservation: paper records deteriorate over time. Digitising them would be an enormous service to future generations as well as to current users. The British Library's Endangered Archives Programme has made a start in the Tamale office, but how about a national effort to do this more comprehensively (could UNICEF help?).

42 Morten Jerven, *Poor Numbers: How We Are Misled by African Development Statistics and What to Do About It* (Ithaca NY, 2013).

43 Gerardo Serra, '"Hail the census night": trust and political imagination in the 1960 population census of Ghana', *Comparative Studies in Society and History* 60:3 (2018), 659–87.

44 Morten Jerven, 'A West African experiment: constructing a GDP series for colonial Ghana, 1891–1950', *Economic History Review* (2014), 964–92; Broadberry and Gardner, 'Economic growth'.

The second problem is access. PRAAD holds at least most of the records of the early independence governments, but its coverage of the 1980s onwards is pretty sparse. A major hindrance to civil-society and scholarly access is the fact that the ministries do not transfer files directly to the national archives, but instead to holding pens known as 'record centres'. There, papers are locked away indefinitely from public gaze, with no apparent oversight to ensure that they are released, for example, after a fixed number of years since their creation.

The third problem is the most disturbing: the covert removal of the papers of the PNDC government from PRAAD. In 2019 researchers were delighted and relieved to find that PRAAD had created a whole new series of records, 'RG 14 Provisional National Defence Council Papers'. 543 papers were listed in RG 14/1 alone, with titles ranging over many key issues of that period. One scholar photographed the whole list. But by the time another scholar returned on 19 April 2024, ready to focus on these papers while researching Structural Adjustment, the RG 14/1 catalogue had been totally rewritten. It contained no files at all dating even in part from the PNDC period. RG 14 as a whole, still called 'Provisional National Defence Council Papers', now had some 500 documents listed, of which only three which even continued into PNDC period (all three were started many years before). As for RG 14/1, it now had only 165 files listed, none of them covering even part of the PNDC. The main content is now from the CPP era. The fact that the documentation on such a crucial period of Ghana's modern history could vanish from the national archives is astonishing. Not only that, but the catalogue was rewritten as if to disguise the fact that the PNDC papers had ever been there. If scholars and public want to read first-hand about Ghana government policies of forty years ago, they will find more in the World Bank and IMF records – much of which are digitised and on open access – than in Ghana's own national archives.

* * *

This volume is structured in a broadly chronological fashion. The first three chapters cover all or most of the period 1891–1911: sketching the growth and volatility of cocoa production which provides the defining context of the 'long twentieth century', and then addressing the evolution of inequality, relating it to government fiscal policies, and to the north–south divide, and the implications of the latter for internal labour migration. Chapters four and five offer major analyses of the political economy of the country, focusing respectively on the impact of terms-of-trade shocks on policymaking regimes, and on the idea that an implicit social contract has been a key continuity in state–society relations since *c.* 1920, and indeed, before that. Chapters six to nine examine in depth different aspects of Ghana in the mid-twentieth century: the debates about what kind of national bank Ghana needed, whether the newly independent state should embark on industrialisation, whether Ghanaian independence could be the stepping-stone to a wider African unity, and the origins and very temporary triumph of producer cooperatives in cocoa production and marketing. Chapters ten and eleven start early in the colonial period but focus on the post-colonial, respectively for the resurrection of cooperatives and their possibilities as a vehicle for reducing gender inequality, and for the politics of youth movements and how elders sought to control them. The final three chapters focus fully on the years since independence: the controversial issue of artisanal and small-scale gold mining; the frustrating quest for industrialisation, and an argument for an unexpected degree of continuity in economic policy across the many different governments of the period.

I

Dynamics of Cocoa Cultivation in Ghana, 1891–2011[1]

Gareth Austin

The 'long twentieth century' in Ghana's economic history and political economy began with the Gold Coast becoming an exporter of cocoa beans in 1891, continued through an era in which Ghana was the world's largest producer and exporter of cocoa, and concluded with cocoa output reaching one million metric tonnes for the first time, in crop year 2010/11. It remains to be seen whether that new national record will last for ever. This chapter is the first single work to examine this 120-year story as a whole. Analytically, the history of cocoa production in Ghana has often been understood in terms of continuity in production techniques and social organisation. The general argument here is that there has been much more change, and much less continuity, than often supposed. The specific argument is that Ghanaian cocoa has moved from extensive to intensive methods of production, in response to a wider shift from relative abundance to relative scarcity of suitable land. In this it constitutes an instructive case of a broad African story. The expansion of production in extensive form, and more recently the adoption of intensive methods, has been accompanied by fundamental shifts in labour contracts and land tenure, and in the centre of agency, from small capitalists to the state.

The growth of output was far from continuous. Rather, it occurred in three distinct expansions. The three annual (crop-year) peaks were in 1936/7 (at 304,800 tonnes) with a trough in 1946/7 (195,173 tonnes); 1964/5 (580,869 tonnes) with a trough in 1983/4 (158,886 tonnes), and 2010/11 (1,024,553) tonnes. In between the great expansions of cocoa output and exports were two periods in which the volume of output trended downwards; in the second, gradual decline accelerated into free-fall. Because each expansion and each decline was different, a

1 This essay is dedicated to William Gervase Clarence-Smith, the leading comparative historian of cocoa dynamics, especially recalling our work on this in the early 1990s, which contributed to Clarence-Smith (ed.), *Cocoa Pioneer Fronts: the Role of Smallholders, Planters and Merchants* (Basingstoke, 1996).

section will be devoted to each of the five periods, preceded by an introduction to long-term perspectives on this complicated history.

Change rather than Continuity: From the Land-Extensive to the Land-Intensive Path

The one existing study covering the production story as a whole is the highly informative and insightful series of works by the economist Teal. In his account, dynamism was minimal. The original cocoa take-off was a vent-for-surplus story, i.e., of export demand enabling Ghanaian farmers to put to profitable use previously unused or underused supplies of land and labour. The expansion of output took place within the same production function (the same combination of inputs yielding one unit of output). This remained the case for the rest of the twentieth century, with growth the result of bringing more land under cocoa trees.[2] For the 2000s, Teal's survey evidence led him to conclude that productivity doubled during that decade; but he saw this as a revolution in government (marketing board) pricing policy, 'not in the methods farmers use to produce the cocoa'.[3] Instead, it will be argued here that both the first and third cocoa expansions were based on moves to new production functions. Further, I will suggest that both are part of a long-term path in Ghanaian – and African — economic history, through successive phases of 'land-extensive' choices of technique and institution, to the beginnings of agricultural intensification, defined as a process of increasing the ratio of labour and capital per unit of land.

In Sub-Saharan Africa, during the last centuries before European colonisation, the supply-side constraint on short-term expansion of agricultural output was generally not land but labour. In non-settler colonies like Ghana, this remained so into the post-independence era. In the very early years of cocoa planting in Ashanti there was room for land to be left fallow for 10–20 years in order to allow full restoration of fertility.[4] Johnson modelled land use around Kumasi in 1907. She concluded that, even close to the Asante capital, much of the land was outside the cycle of land rotation altogether.[5]

2 Francis Teal, 'Export policy and trade policy in Ghana in the twentieth century', *The World Economy*, 25:9 (2002), 1319–37.

3 Francis Teal, 'An Agricultural Revolution in Ghana?', CSAE 2013–378 (2013), Working Paper, Centre for the Study of African Economies, University of Oxford, 8.

4 See P.H. Nye and D. Stevens, 'Soil fertility', 137, and A. Foggie, 'The role of forestry in the agricultural economy', 229, both in J. Brian Wills (ed.), *Agriculture and Land Use in Ghana* (London, 1962).

5 Marion Johnson, 'Elephants for Want of Towns', 317–18, 329–30, in Christopher Fyfe and David McMaster (eds), *African Historical Demography* (Edinburgh, 1981).

'Land abundance' requires qualification. The general observation about pre-colonial and even early colonial tropical Africa is that while land availability was not the constraint on short-term expansion of agricultural output, in most areas the quality and sustainability of land for farming purposes was sharply constrained.[6] In the context of cocoa, in 1995 Ruf coined the term 'forest rent', defined as the difference between the cost of producing one unit of cocoa beans on land newly cleared from forest and on land replanted after a first cycle of cocoa cultivation had been completed. Ruf argued that, at any given time in the world history of cocoa production, the leading producing countries were those in which forested land was available. Thus, the growth of global output had been based on the capture of forest rent. Ruf highlighted, in contrast, the high cost of reviving old cocoa areas where primary forest was exhausted.[7] In the late nineteenth century, and well into the twentieth, the forest ochrosols of what is now southern Ghana offered plenty of forest rent, i.e., untapped soil fertility, of the kind specifically suitable for cocoa.

The meaning of 'expansion' in cocoa farming should be clarified. First, trends in output (or in current production capacity) lag trends in planting. Output is largely a function of the area of bearing cocoa trees, of a given variety. As cocoa is a tree crop, the start and finish of an output boom (a period of increasing annual output) necessarily follows a few years behind the start and finish of a planting boom (a period of net increase in production capacity, with the new plantings more than offsetting declining output from old trees). The lag was much longer with the variety of cocoa planted in Ghana's original cocoa take-off, Amelonado, which took five to seven years to start bearing, than with the hybrid varieties of cocoa planted in recent decades, which typically start bearing in three years. There is also a gap while trees move from first-bearing to peak-bearing; a gap which has again become smaller with hybrid varieties. Thus, whereas the first export expansion ended in 1936 (Figure 1.1), we can assume that the planting boom ended about 1930.

A second point of clarification concerns output and exports. The latter has been almost identical to marketed output. Some children – and adults – may suck cocoa beans, but marketed output has been almost entirely exported, throughout Ghanaian cocoa history, with two exceptions. One was the very early years of experimentation with cocoa farming, before 1891, when harvested beans tended to be sold to other farmers. The other is that since independence various governments have encouraged chocolate manufacturing within the

6 Gareth Austin, 'Resources, techniques and strategies south of the Sahara: revising the factor endowments perspective on African economic development, 1500–2000', *Economic History Review* 61:3 (2008), 587–624.

7 François Ruf, *Booms et crises du cacao: les vertiges de l'or brun* (Montpellier, 1995); Ruf, 'From forest rent to tree-capital: basic laws of cocoa supply', in F. Ruf and P.S. Siswoputranto (eds), *Cocoa Cycles: the Economics of Cocoa Supply* (Cambridge, 1995).

Figure 1.1 Ghana's First Cocoa Expansion, 1891–1936.

Sources: Hill, *Migrant Cocoa-Farmers*, 177; Geoffrey Kay, *The Political Economy of Colonialism in Ghana: a Collection of Documents and Statistics 1900–1960* (London, 1972), 336–7.

country; but even by 2010 the domestic chocolate industry took only a very small share of output.[8]

The most-written view of the original Ghanaian cocoa take-off is that it was a case of 'vent for surplus', implying that that it was purely extensive, happening merely by mobilising more resources of land and labour within the existing production function and at zero opportunity cost.[9] This hypothesis, based on the premiss that there were pre-existing reserves of unused land and labour (a leisure reserve) was intended to explain how it was possible for such a rapid growth of output to have occurred without an accompanying fall in food-crop production.

In an earlier paper I re-estimated the land and labour requirements of the original cocoa take-off, in the context of the seasonal and gender distribution of both food-farming and cocoa-farming tasks. I also detailed, as far as possible, the range of productive activities in which the future cocoa-farming populations of the forest belt of Ghana were involved before the late 1880s. I argued that the expansion of output was too large and too fast to be accounted for by the mobilisation of a reserve of leisure; which was anyway a highly implausible notion in a very labour-scarce economy. This fits with the decline of alternative forms of extra-subsistence production. In the short run, cocoa growing was indeed compatible with food growing, actually complementary to it, as tall food crops such as plantain were planted to shade young cocoa trees. But there were opportunity costs: the adoption of cocoa farming displaced or marginalised other exports in the areas suitable for cocoa farming. There was also greater market specialisation: the growth of cocoa incomes led to certain areas just outside the cocoa belt choosing to specialise in growing food crops for sale in the cocoa-growing areas.[10]

Even if the assumptions about spare land and labour could be justified, the vent-for-surplus story cannot be sufficient to explain the original cocoa take-off, because this was remarkably bold and transformative. Bold, because cocoa was an exotic crop. Tetteh Quarshie's famous importation of cocoa pods from Fernando Po, in 1876, followed unsuccessful experiments by the Basel Mission in growing cocoa at Akropong. Quarshie's planting at Mampong-Akwapim seems to have been the first case of a farm's-worth of cocoa trees (as distinct from perhaps a few individual trees) growing to maturity in the Gold Coast; and he gave or sold pods to others. He is said to have had the advantage of having

8 For an upbeat account see P.K. Akua, *The Success Story of Cocoa Processing and Chocolate Manufacture in Ghana* (Saffron Walden, 2002).

9 Hla Myint, 'The "classical theory" of international trade and the underdeveloped countries', *Economic Journal* 68:2 (1958), 317–37; R. Szereszewski, *Structural Changes in the Economy of Ghana, 1891–1911* (London, 1965); Teal, 'Export policy', among others.

10 Gareth Austin, 'Vent for surplus or productivity breakthrough? The Ghanaian cocoa take-off, c.1890–1936', *Economic History Review* 67:4 (2014), 1035–64.

observed in Fernando Po that cocoa plants should be planted under shade.[11] But most of those who became the first to plant it in their own districts, for example in Ashanti after 1900, had probably not personally seen a cocoa tree, at least not one mature enough to bear pods. The colonial administration was late on the scene: the Governor, Brandford Griffith, distributed some pods from 1885.[12]

The cocoa take-off was transformative, because the adoption of cocoa growing entailed a very different production function: a tree crop that in West Africa needed to be deliberately planted (unlike oil palms or kola trees), and which, as it turned out, took at least five years to yield any pods and therefore any return on the investment. Adopting cocoa raised farmers' returns fundamentally compared to alternative ways of using their resources. It created a 'producer surplus', such that until *c.* 1930 – and on a smaller scale, until the next price boom – it appeared profitable to plant almost whenever one had the savings and other resources to do so, irrespective of current price.[13]

Hill's work highlighted the fact that the pioneering cocoa farmers were committed to 'the continued expansion' of their business, taking a long-term view of investment and risk-taking. Her classic account of African economic agency in the original cocoa take-off in what was then the Eastern Province of the Gold Coast Colony, *The Migrant Cocoa-Farmers of Southern Ghana: A Study in Rural Capitalism* (1963),[14] refuted the then-conventional assumption that Ghanaian cocoa production had been (and remained) overwhelmingly the work of small farmers, specifically sedentary peasants adding a plot of cocoa trees to their food-crop farms.[15] Hill highlighted the migrant character of the take-off in the Eastern Province, emphasising the decisive role of Akwapims and Krobos who purchased land from Akim sub-chiefs in the neighbouring, then sparely-populated, district of Akim Abuakwa. Although much of the

11 Pascale Meyer, 'Cocoa in Ghana: how it all began', Swiss National Museum, posted 21 November 2024 (blog.nationalmuseum.ch); Gustav Adolf Wanner, *The First Cocoa Trees in Ghana 1858–1868* (Basel, 1962); Polly Hill, *The Migrant Cocoa-Farmers of Southern Ghana* (Cambridge, 1963) 170–3.

12 Hill, *Migrant Cocoa-Farmers*, 173–6.

13 The neatest illustration of this principle is based on Nigerian data: Sara S. Berry, 'Supply response reconsidered: cocoa in Western Nigeria, 1909–44', *Journal of Development Studies*, 13:1 (1976), 4–17. See also Austin, *Labour, Land and Capital in Ghana: From Slavery to Free Labour in Asante, 1807–1956* (Rochester NY, 2005), 330–2, 530.

14 Cambridge University Press. A second edition was published by LIT and James Currey with International African Institute: Hamburg and Oxford, 1997. The quotation is from p. 3.

15 Fame is temporary in the face of scholarly and journalistic amnesia. By 2011 a book on Ghanaian cocoa farming could appear which reverted uncritically to the assumption that Hill had debunked, and with no reference to Hill (Ŏrla O'Ryan, *Chocolate Nations: Living and Dying for Cocoa in West Africa* [London]). That assumption might no longer be a myth (conceivably, larger-scale producers might have disappeared) – but this needs to be shown not assumed.

land-buying was on credit, and although she downplayed the role of hired labour in the early years, she also emphasised that cocoa pioneering required cash. Specifically, she found that the pioneers had previously accumulated capital through palm oil production and other forms of extra-subsistence activity.[16] More recent research similarly highlights the importance of prior accumulation of cash and dependent labour (slaves imported from the north, but also pawns and additional wives acquired from among the free members of Akan households) – from the proceeds of artisanal gold mining, rubber and kola nut exports – in the post-1900 extension of cocoa planting into Ashanti.[17] This original Ghanaian cocoa-planting boom was a story of entrepreneurship involving reinvestment in the adoption of a new technology, enabling the formation of fixed capital (farms of cocoa trees) on a wide scale, a process reinforced by reinvestment within cocoa farming as farmers 'leap-frogged' each other (in Hill's phrase)[18] to establish additional farms as the cocoa frontier moved outward (mainly north and west but also east, beyond the Volta river, to Ho-Kpandu district).

If land was relatively abundant, at least in the districts in which cocoa was being introduced on a wide scale, labour was not. It was their acute appreciation of this distinction that enabled Ghanaian cocoa farmers to defeat competition from European plantations, which used more labour- and capital-intensive methods than did large African plantations as well as small farms.[19]

Hill maintained that wage labour was unimportant in the cocoa take-off in Akim Abuakwa. That was even more true in the early years of cocoa farming in Ashanti, where the first cocoa farms tended to be made for the local state (loosely, chieftaincy), using the chief's right to call upon the labour of his subjects; or to be planted by people who had accumulated a dependent labour force variously comprising (usually a combination of) slaves and pawns. Thereafter, hired labour became extremely important in all cocoa-growing areas.[20]

Although it was the colonial government that prohibited slavery (in the Gold Coast Colony in 1874; only extended to Ashanti and the Northern Territories in 1908), in Ashanti it was the adoption of cocoa growing by many thousands

16 Hill, *Migrant Cocoa-Farmers*.

17 Kwame Arhin, 'The economic and social significance of rubber production and exchange on the Gold and Ivory Coasts, 1880–1900', *Cahiers d'études africaines* 20:77–8 (1980), 49–62; Gareth Austin, '"No elders were present": commoners and private ownership in Asante, 1807–96', *Journal of African History* 37:1 (1996), 1–30; Gareth Austin, *Labour, Land and Capital*.

18 Hill, *Migrant Cocoa-Farmers*.

19 Gareth Austin, 'Mode of production or mode of cultivation: explaining the failure of European cocoa planters in competition with African farmers in colonial Ghana', in W.G. Clarence-Smith (ed.), *Cocoa Pioneer Fronts Since 1800: the Role of Smallholders, Planters and Merchants* (Basingstoke, 1996), 154–75.

20 Austin, *Labour, Land and Capital*.

of farmers that enabled masters of slaves to transition into employers of hired labour. In the present century, in which critics have sometimes accused cocoa farmers of labour coercion, it is interesting to look back to a period where export crops, freely grown by Africans, were critical to the transition from slavery to freedom. The same applies to the transition from pawning people to pledging cocoa farms.[21]

For their part, following the abolition of slavery, migrant labourers from the savanna succeeded in using their relative scarcity to win successively better terms in the labour market.[22] In turn, this delivered higher physical living standards in the savanna as well as in the forest zone where the cocoa trees were grown.[23] The first step in this process was the spread of annual wage contracts where slave-buying and pawning had previously been the main forms of labour recruitment from outside the household. In Ashanti, for example, annual wage contracts spread rapidly after 1918. There is no doubt that cocoa income enriched the south much more than the north, but more reached the latter, and with much more important effects on physical welfare, than has been recognised hitherto. The key was the fact that seasonal migration enabled the emergence of a national labour market from the 1910s.[24]

During the colonial period – from the first expansion and on to the beginning of the second – there was some demand for the issue of individual titles of ownership of land, and some advocacy within the colonial administration for individual titling to be made compulsory. But whenever the matter was debated, in the end the governor decided in favour of the status quo, under which – in accordance with Akan land tenure – the farmer's ownership over trees that he or she had planted was relatively secure, whereas the ownership of the underlying soil might be litigated between rival chiefs all the way up to the Privy Council in London.[25] Given that the existing land tenure system had proved compatible with very high levels of investment in cocoa trees, the economic case for reform lacked persuasiveness for colonial officials also worried that any British intervention in land would arouse fears of appropriation, as had happened in the settler colonies.[26]

Political conditions were generally, but not entirely, favourable to the original expansion of cocoa cultivation in the Gold Coast Colony, Ashanti, and the

21 *Ibid.*, ch. 13.

22 *Ibid.*, chs 16, 19.

23 Alexander Moradi, Gareth Austin and Jörg Baten, 'Heights and Development in a Cash-Crop Economy: Living Standards in Ghana, 1870–1980', final version in preparation. A significantly earlier version appeared in 2013 in the *African Economic History* Working Paper Series, AEHN WP 7; published by the African Economic History Network, Lund, Sweden.

24 Austin, *Labour, Land and Capital*, 316–17, 403–8, 424–5, 528, 540–1.

25 A.A.Y. Kyrematen, *Inter-state Boundary Litigation in Ashanti* (Leiden, n.d. [1971?]).

26 On the colonial policy debate as a whole: Austin, *Labour, Land and Capital*, 339–48, 531–3.

southern part of what, after the conquest of German Togo, became Southern British Togoland. But the correlation with colonial rule is loose. The states and peoples of the forest zone of what eventually became Ghana had already adopted export agriculture and silviculture before the waves of colonial occupation (kola to northern Nigeria, palm oil and palm kernels to Europe, then rubber). Ghanaians' adoption of cocoa cultivation enabled them to deepen their existing comparative advantage in export agriculture, by adopting a tree crop that made the most of the then-abundant forest rent, and working out how best to grow it and to prepare its produce for market. We have noted that the colonial administration made a late, small contribution to the supply of cocoa-planting material, which quickly became unnecessary as the output of cocoa pods increased. Griffith went on to establish a botanical garden at Aburi for experimentation with coffee and other crops, including cocoa; but until the 1940s the technical advice given to farmers by what became the Department of Agriculture proved ill-adapted to their economic and even botanical circumstances.[27] The colonial prohibition of slavery and human pawning affected the forms of labour and credit, but were clearly unnecessary for the adoption of cocoa.

What was crucial was the British avoidance of the mistake (in terms of economic growth) that the French made next door, where French planters were encouraged and assisted with a supply of forced labour. The competition between that model of cocoa development and the Gold Coast one of African farmers being free to take advantage of the forest rent was won unreservedly by the latter. In 1900, both Côte d'Ivoire and the Gold Coast exported one thousand tonnes of cocoa; in 1939, Ivorian exports had reached 55,200 tonnes but the Gold Coast exported well over five times as much, 302,800 tonnes.[28] Along the way, the few dozen Europeans who had started cocoa plantations in the Gold Coast were driven out in fair competition with African rural capitalists.

Otherwise, the main contribution of the British administration was to mobilise capital and labour for the construction of railways. Though these were initially intended primarily to facilitate the development of European-owned mechanised mining, and the movement of troops in case of a repetition of the 1900 Yaa Asantewaa rising,[29] the railways were very important, especially for the extension of cocoa production to Ashanti.[30]

The first cocoa expansion underpinned economic growth in this 'rural capitalist' economy. Two studies of real Gross Domestic Product (GDP) per

27 R.H. Green and S.H. Hymer, 'Cocoa in the Gold Coast: a study in the relations between African farmers and agricultural experts', *Journal of Economic History* 26 (1966), 299–319; Austin, 'Mode of production or mode of cultivation'.

28 Christer Gunnarsson, *The Gold Coast Cocoa Industry, 1900–1939* (Lund, 1978), 176.

29 Christian E. Tsey, 'Gold Coast railways: the making of a colonial economy, 1879–1929', Ph.D. dissertation, University of Glasgow, 1986.

30 Austin, *Labour, Land and Capital*, 68, 475; Remi Jedwab and Alexander Moradi, 'The permanent effects of transportation revolutions in poor countries: evidence from Africa', *Review of Economics and Statistics* 98:2 (2016), 268–84.

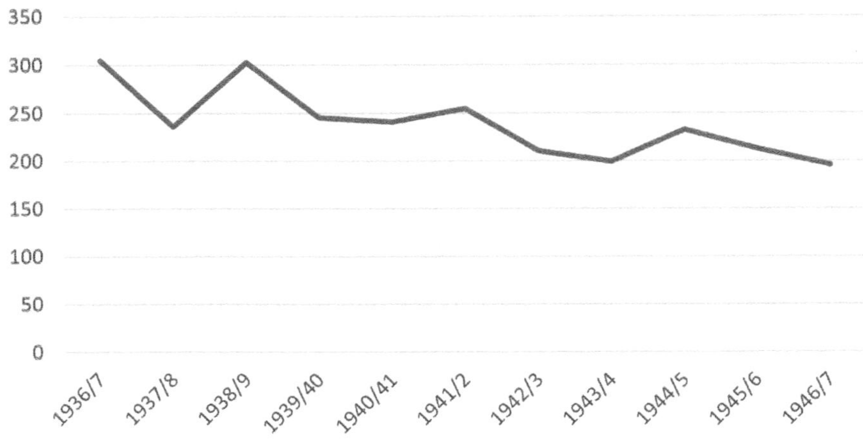

Figure 1.2 Ghana's First Coca Decline, 1937/38–1946/47.
Source: Merrill J. Bateman, 'An econometric analysis of Ghanaian cocoa supply', in R. A. Kotey, C. Okali and B. E. Rourke (eds), *Economics of Cocoa Production and Marketing* (Legon, 1974), 286–326. Volumes converted to metric.

capita indicate a near-doubling, or more than a doubling, for 1890–1936 as a whole.[31] Guesstimates for the period before even Ashanti and the Northern Territories, let alone part of Togo, were incorporated in the same jurisdiction, and long before real censuses, must be regarded with extreme caution. But more credible figures, though for the later and more precarious phase of the expansion, 1921–36, show a rise of 41.77 per cent, to 1,276 in 1990 international dollars.[32]

Peak-to-trough, the first decline of cocoa output and exports lasted ten crop-years and the trough was 64 per cent of the peak. The general cause was lower world cocoa prices, initiated by the international depression of the

31 Stephen Broadberry and Leigh Gardner, 'Economic growth in Sub-Saharan Africa, 1885–2008: evidence from eight countries', *Explorations in Economic History* 83 (2022), table A1, https://doi.org/10.1016/j.eeh.2021.101424 (accessed 25 May 2026); Morten Jerven, 'A West African experiment: constructing a GDP series for colonial Ghana, 1891–1950', *Economic History Review*, 67:4 (2014), 964–92.
32 Broadberry and Gardner, 'Economic growth', table A1.

early 1930s and reinforced by another event exogenous to colonial Ghana, the outbreak of the Second World War.[33]

Local parts of the story of decline included the decreased availability of land for first planting with cocoa in the older cocoa-producing areas of Akim Abuakwa and south Ashanti. In the latter, the cocoa-based diminution of local supplies of the most fertile land encouraged a shift in the 1940s towards adopting cassava, which would grow in less fertile soil, as part of the main local diet and crop repertoire. Cassava had once been grown only for livestock, or by slaves for their own consumption.[34] Indeed, it was because of concern that the spread of cocoa cultivation might deprive future generations of enough fertile land to grow food crops that, from 1938 to 1946, the Ashanti Confederacy Council of Chiefs, with the acquiescence of the colonial administration, banned the creation and extension of cocoa farms in Ashanti (including what is now Brong-Ahafo).[35] There was also the spread of swollen shoot disease, which was first observed in the 1920s precisely in the oldest cocoa-growing areas in the Eastern Region. For the first time, the government's agricultural experts lived up to their name, through A.F. Posnette's discovery (at the still-young Cocoa Research Institute at Tafo) in 1940 that the disease is caused by a virus.[36] Alas, the only remedy was the cutting out of potentially infected trees, even those not showing any symptoms.

The second expansion proved that, in aggregate, the end of the first was not because of constraints on land supply: there was plenty of 'forest rent' still to be tapped. Working back from the trend of output, it is evident that the net growth of productive capacity in colonial Ghana as a whole had stopped already *c.* 1930.[37] Producer prices were so low during the early 1940s that, along with fairly widespread evasion, the Ashanti chiefs' ban on new cocoa planting probably did not much delay the revival of cocoa planting.[38] If it seems paradoxical that the ban should have come in about eight years after the spread of cultivation had stopped, we should remember that, because of the use of tall food crops to shade young cocoa plants, periods when the area under cocoa is expanding tend to be better for food-crop output than years in which even the youngest cocoa trees are mature enough to have a shade canopy, which precludes weeds but also food crops from the cocoa farm.

33 For the impact of trade shocks on the Ghanaian political economy, see Alence's chapter.

34 Austin, *Labour, Land and Capital*, 66, 474.

35 *Ibid.*, 326–32, 529–30.

36 UK National Archives, CO96/768 1940 File 31265: A.F. Posnette, 'Transmission of Swollen Shoot disease of cacao', 16 February 1940, and subsequent correspondence in that and later files.

37 Austin, 'Vent for surplus or productivity breakthrough?', 1040–1.

38 Austin, *Labour, Land and Capital*, 328–32, 530.

The decline happened during an upward trend in the cost of hired labour. The 1930s saw a marked tendency in Ashanti, reinforcing a pattern already under way in the Eastern Region, for annual wage contracts to be replaced by a managerial form of sharecropping, within which the migrant worker got a third, later often a half, of the harvest. Economists might expect a switch to sharecropping to be an employers' strategy to delegate the risk of falls in cocoa prices. In this case, however, both written and oral evidence documents the change as a concession made to the labourers, who sought more control over their own work, and – as it turned out – gained more financially in an average year from their one-third (*abusa*) shares than they lost in the annual wage.[39] This labour transition was a striking departure from the conventional model of evolution towards wage labour – and it is one that also occurred, starting later, in the cocoa belts of Côte d'Ivoire and Nigeria.[40]

Long before the 1930s, briefer episodes of weaker world prices had precipitated collective action over the shares received by the European cocoa-buying companies on one side, and African intermediaries (brokers) and producers on the other. On the European side, a more concentrated ownership was complemented by the organisation of a series of cartels, known as 'pools', in which the European firms colluded to fix the price they paid at a rate lower than that on the competitive market. They also increasingly sought to reduce their marketing costs by agreeing to stop giving 'advances' to brokers, which in 'normal' years was a major weapon in their competition with each other for crop share. African producers and brokers responded with a series of equally organised 'hold-ups', in which participants refused to sell beans to the European firms until the price was raised and the pool dissolved. The series of cocoa hold-ups – some of them local – began in 1908 but the most widespread and prolonged were in the 1930s, after the initiation of what turned out to be a period of particularly low international cocoa prices. The largest hold-up so far happened in 1930/31, in the Gold Coast Colony and south Ashanti; which served as a prelude to the great hold-up of 1937/38, when the Gold Coast and Ashanti cocoa-farmers' unions succeeded in withholding most of the crop from sale to the European firms for most of the crop season. This was a crisis for the whole economy, including for the north, as tens of thousands of migrant labourers on southern cocoa farms went unpaid.[41] It was also a political crisis, with the colonial administration under pressure from both the hold-up movement which assumed it was (as in 1930) backing the European firms, and also from the latter, who were appalled by the 'weakness' of the governor in adopting a neutral stance, partly because the

39 *Ibid.*, chs 16, 19.

40 *Ibid.*, 423, 544.

41 Great Britain, *Report on the Commission of Enquiry into the Marketing of Cocoa in the Gold Coast* (London, 1938) (the Nowell Report). See, further, Bob-Milliar and Manu-Osafo in this volume.

governor was angry at the political irresponsibility of the firms in not consulting him before forming a pool, and partly because of the unprecedented strength of the hold-up movement. The Great Cocoa Hold-Up was only ended when the imperial government in London intervened and persuaded both sides to suspend their respective collective actions, the pool and the hold-up.[42] The hold-up movement, and especially the 1936/37 climax, were unparalleled in scale in colonial Africa as a form of collective protest by producers. Even in southwest Nigeria, where there was talk of a cocoa hold-up at the same time, nothing comparable happened – possibly the difference lay in the active (if quietly expressed) role of chiefs in the Ghanaian case.[43]

The system of statutory marketing boards, by which the state became the sole legal exporter of produce, was introduced to British West Africa in 1939, as a wartime measure initially designed to enable the colonial government to intervene to keep producer prices high enough to avoid serious discontent behind the military front line, if effective demand fell because of disruption and redirection of shipping. In practice, the marketing board was not really used for that purpose – to accumulate a surplus when the world price was relatively high, which would be used to subsidise farmers when prices were low. On the contrary, by the end of the war, policy-makers realised that the marketing board mechanism could be used for taxation: on a scale which might even solve the historic fiscal constraint on state-building in tropical Africa, namely the difficulty of extracting a high share of output in tax.[44] In 1946 the marketing board system was made permanent.[45]

Meanwhile, the cocoa decline contributed to a fall in real GDP per head: in 1945 it stood at an estimated 1,022 international dollars, 80 per cent of the 1936 level.[46]

The second cocoa expansion started at much the same time as systematic research at Tafo into improved cocoa varieties for West African conditions. Amazon, the first hybrid variety to be adopted in Ghana, began to be planted by 1950: quicker- and higher-yielding. Again, a specific insecticide, gammalin,

42 John Miles, 'Rural protest in the Gold Coast: the cocoa hold-ups, 1908–1938', in Clive Dewey and A.G. Hopkins, (eds), *The Imperial Impact: Studies in the Economic History of India and Africa* (London, 1978), 152–70, 353–7; Gareth Austin, 'Capitalists and chiefs in the cocoa hold-ups in South Asante, 1927–1938', *International Journal of African Historical Studies* 21:1 (1988), 63–95; Rod Alence, 'The 1937–38 Gold Coast cocoa crisis: the political economy of commercial stalemate', *African Economic History* 19 (1990–91), 77–104.

43 Austin, 'Capitalists and chiefs'.

44 On that constraint see, e.g., Jeffrey Herbst, *The Politics of Reform in Ghana, 1982–1991* (Berkeley, 1993).

45 Rod Alence, 'Colonial government, social conflict and state involvement in Africa's open economies: the origins of the Ghana Cocoa Marketing Board, 1939–46', *Journal of African History* 42:3 (2001), 397–416.

46 Broadberry and Gardner, 'Economic growth', table A1 (no figure for 1946).

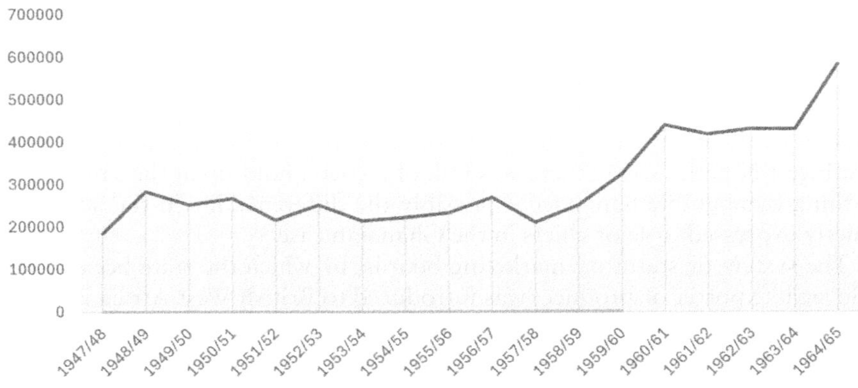

Figure 1.3 Ghana's Second Cocoa Expansion 1947/48–1964/65.
Source: Cocobod (with thanks to Rod Alence).

was found to be very effective against the most prevalent insect pest, capsid. But taking the expansion as a whole, neither technology was applied early enough and on a sufficiently large scale to account for most of the growth of output between 1947 and 1965.[47] For this episode, the evidence supports Teal's contention that expansion occurred mainly by extending the area under cultivation, within the same production function.[48] The supply of migrant labour from the savanna continued and even expanded.[49] The establishment of new cocoa farms in western Ghana (notably in Ahafo and Sefwi) more than made up for the erosion of output from the old cocoa-growing areas, especially in the Eastern Region which, as the main site of swollen shoot disease, was also therefore the focus of the government's programme of cutting-out diseased cocoa farms. Indeed, one reason why more was not done sooner to increase the supply of gammalin and Amazon was that the agricultural department's efforts focused on the seemingly existential struggle against swollen shoot. In its annual report for 1955/6, the Department said that it was now putting more

47 Dennis Leston, 1971. 'The diseconomy of insecticides in cocoa production in Ghana', in R.A. Kotey, C. Okali and B.E. Rourke (eds), *Economics of Cocoa Production and Marketing* (Legon, 1971), 96–104; Austin, *Labour, Land and Capital*, 84–7, 478.

48 Teal, 'Export policy'.

49 Nicholas van Hear, 'Northern Labour and the Development of Capitalist Agriculture in Ghana' (Ph.D. dissertation, University of Birmingham, 1982); see, further, the chapter by Bob-Milliar and Manu-Asafo in this volume.

emphasis on activities other than controlling swollen shoot, yet the latter 'still accounts for over over 80 per cent of the effort.'[50]

The marketing-board taxation has often been blamed for low producer prices, and by extension, for declines in output.[51] But the rate of extraction – the difference between the price it received for Ghanaian cocoa internationally, net of shipping and marketing costs, and the price paid to farmers – was not so high as to prevent the second cocoa expansion. The colonial government deposited marketing board surpluses in London, in UK government bonds, rather than investing them in the development of the Gold Coast. This they justified in the name of minimising inflation, in the context of continued shortages of imported consumer goods after the war.[52]

With African politicians taking over a share of political power, from 1951 (joint rule) and more so from 1954 (internal self-government), government expenditure rose rapidly. In October 1954 Kwame Nkrumah's Convention People's Party (CPP) government, confirmed in power by the recent elections, announced that the producer price of cocoa beans would be frozen, rather than rising in accordance with recent shifts on the world market. This decision precipitated the launch of a federalist opposition party, the Ashanti-based National Liberal Movement (NLM). Arguably, the defeat of the NLM in the pre-independence elections of 1956 defined the beginning of a period of state-led development policy unconstrained by any effective voice for the export-crop growers.[53] Yet, under Nkrumah the producer price was kept high enough for that government to preside over most of the country's second cocoa expansion. Overall, the marketing board's top-slicing of the money paid for Ghana's cocoa exports during the 1950s and early 1960s was not high to prevent farmers benefiting from, and responding to, the recovery of international cocoa prices after the Second World War.

In terms of agency, the boom involved farmers both large and small. Beckman had access to the subsequently lost records of the United Ghana Farmers Council, which from 1961 to 1966 enjoyed a monopsony of cocoa purchasing from the farmers. He reported that in the 1963/4 cocoa season,

50 UK National Archives, CO96/101, Gold Coast 'Annual Report of the Department of Agriculture, 1955–6', 23.

51 The major early critique was P.T. Bauer, *West African Trade* (Cambridge, 1954); among subsequent ones see especially Jonathon H. Frimpong-Ansah, *The Vampire State in Africa: the Political Economy of Decline in Ghana* (London, 1991); Douglas Rimmer, *Staying Poor: Ghana's Political Economy 1950–1990* (Oxford, 1992).

52 The inflation argument is examined sceptically in Rimmer, *Staying Poor*, 59–61.

53 Gareth Austin, 'National poverty and the "vampire state" in Ghana: a review article', *Journal of International Development* 8:4 (1996), 553–73, at 562–3.

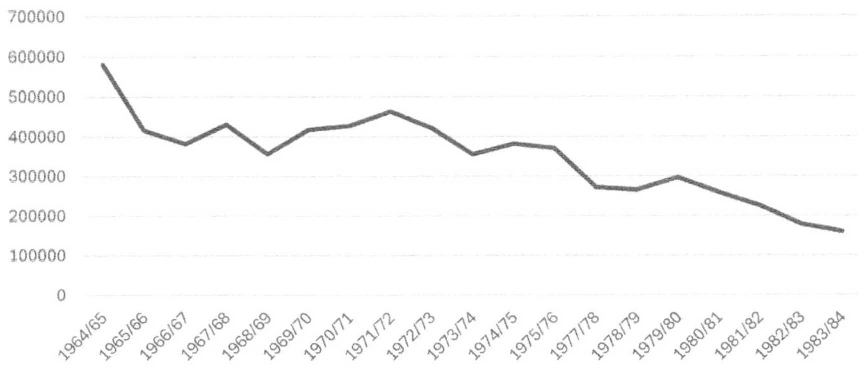

Figure 1.4 Ghana's Second Cocoa Decline 1965/66–1983/84.
Source: Cocobod (with thanks to Rod Alence).

15 per cent of farmers produced 100 or more 60lb loads of cocoa, and they accounted for 54 per cent of output.[54]

This second cocoa expansion was vital, helping real GDP per head to recover to around its 1936 peak shortly before independence in 1957; followed by a rise of 14.7 per cent to a new peak of 1,424 GK dollars in 1963. Over 1945 to 1965 as a whole, the growth of real GDP per head was 36 per cent.[55] The cocoa-planting boom also solved any food shortages by enlarging the food supply. Because of the practice of planting plantain and cocoyam to shade the young cocoa plants, the expansion of the area under cocoa brought with it a major increase in food supply. The 1950s–60s boom involved a renewal of the 1890s–1910s tendency to 'leap-frog': cocoa farmers jumping over each other (metaphorically) to establish new cocoa farms.[56]

The second decline in the volume of exports extended over nineteen crop years and the trough was only 27.3 per cent of the peak: so nearly twice as long as the first, with more than twice the fall in output. The downward trend accelerated between 1975 and 1983, to the point where the crisis in cocoa production seemed existential.

54 Björn Beckman, 1970. 'The Distribution of Cocoa Income, 1961–1985', Staff Seminar paper no. 13, Department of Economics, University of Ghana (Legon, 1970).
55 Broadberry and Gardner, 'Economic growth', table A1. It was only in 1954 that the figure (at $1,424) exceeded that of 1936 and it was slightly below it in 1956 and 1957.
56 Hill, *Migrant Cocoa-Farmers*.

The slippage in production began for a reason similar to the causes of the first decline: falling world prices (albeit passed on by the marketing board, which did not exist before 1939). What turned gradual slippage into precipitous descent was not the explicit taxation of cocoa exports through the gap between the world and producer prices, but rather the addition of implicit taxation of exporters via an increasingly over-valued, not freely convertible, currency. Nkrumah created the instrument, by moving from simply having a national currency (1957) to full monetary independence (in stages, 1964/5), with the option of adopting an official exchange rate that bore little or no relationship to its market value. But it was only under I.K. Acheampong's military regime from 1975 that monetary independence began to be used to create a currency that was over-valued compared to its market worth, not by some percentage points, but by several hundred per cent.

Ghana's commodity terms of trade actually rose in the 1970s (by 6.9 per cent, 1970–79), because the oil-price shock of 1973 was offset by the 1976–78 boom in beverage-crop prices. The world price of cocoa rose 7.5 per cent between 1970 and 1980.[57] Thus, the transition from gradual to near-terminal decline of cocoa planting and production was not the result of external shocks. Nor is it attributable to an excessive marketing board surplus. The producer's share of the border price of cocoa in 1977–80 averaged 47.5 per cent, compared to only 40 per cent in neighbouring Côte d'Ivoire which, during those years, overtook Ghana as a cocoa producer (initially helped by smuggling of cocoa from Ghana).[58]

Rather, the catastrophic fall between 1975 and 1983 was caused by the gross over-valuation of the currency, which served as a punitive tax on exporters. The marketing board sold the farmers' crop for US dollars, but paid the farmers' share in Ghanaian cedis, at the official exchange rate. By the early 1980s that was so overvalued that the purchasing power received by the farmers was only a few per cent of that received for their produce by the board.[59]

As with the first decline, pressure on land in the older cocoa-growing areas was increasing, with more land now under cocoa and the population rising even faster. In Ashanti the average fallow period was down to perhaps a third or a fifth of pre-cocoa levels, yet the Ministry of Agriculture could still report that 'Almost universally, reliance is based on the bush fallow for the maintenance of

57 World Bank, *Accelerated Development in Sub-Saharan Africa: an Agenda for Action* (Washington DC, 1981), 155, 157.

58 Gareth Austin, 'Ghana and Kenya facing the 1970s commodity price shocks: the national and the global', in Shigeru Akita (ed.), *Oil Crises of the 1970s and the Transformation of International Order: Economy, Development and Aid in Asia and Africa* (London, 2023), 223–56, at 238.

59 *Ibid.*

fertility'.[60] Some fertile land was still to be planted, especially in western Ghana and, as we have seen, scientific research – conducted in Ghana – had already begun to provide the technology needed to replant exhausted cocoa farms. Indeed, the third expansion was to demonstrate dramatically that Ghana had not come even close to realising its maximum productive potential in 1964/5.

Again like the earlier decline, the later one occurred – or least began – in a period of upward pressure on labour costs. The long-term trend of migrant labourers from the northern savannas achieving some success in negotiating better terms of employment on cocoa farms continued during the second cocoa expansion and even into the third. In between, during the early years of the second decline, state action made hired labour scarcer: in particular, the Busia government's Aliens Compliance Order of 1969 led to an exodus of foreign nationals who lacked the papers required to stay and work. The proportion of foreigners among 'permanent' cocoa labourers fell from 47 to 25 per cent.[61] The long-term upward trend in the bargaining position of the remaining labourers continued, manifested in a tendency for the one-third share of the harvest to be replaced by a half share. Part of this is attributable to the take-off of Ivorian cocoa farming which followed the abolition of forced labour in the French colonies in 1946. Thus, growing demand from Ivorian planters was pushing up the demand for labour, even while the supply was growing thanks to population growth. In the 1970s, the Cocoa Marketing Board also pointed to the growing average age of cocoa farmers (farm owners), which it put at 55 years in 1977 – three years higher than the average life expectancy at birth.[62] Important as these phenomena were in geographical and familial terms, they do not explain the reversals of expansion. That the cost and availability of labour was not the source of decline is shown by the fact that the second expansion happened precisely during the Ivorian take-off.

While the principle of a marketing board system was not to blame, having the state as the only legal exporter did create opportunities for corruption. However, the scale of that, and the extent to which such opportunities were taken, very much depended on the attitude of the government of the day. During the kleptocracy which emerged under Acheampong, there appears to have been major corruption in the marketing board's overseas sales: Douglas Rimmer

60 Ghana, Ministry of Agriculture (Crop Production Division), 'Production Programme 1972: Ashanti Region' (stencilled: n.d. but presumably Accra, 1971).

61 N.O. Addo, 'Some employment and labour conditions on Ghana's cocoa farms', in R.A. Kotey, C. Okali and B.E. Rourke (eds), *Economics of Cocoa Production and Marketing* (Legon, 1974), 204–21, at 210.

62 Ghana Cocoa Marketing Board, *Ghana Cocoa Marketing Board at Work* (6th edition, Accra 1977), 65. The life expectancy figure is from World Bank, *Africa Development Indictors* (Washington DC, 2013).

found evidence of massive under-invoicing in the period from 1973 to 1978.[63] Again, overmanning to the extent of continuing to pay employees who had actually died persisted until the marketing board was retrenched under the radical economic liberalisation that began in 1983.

In contrast to the first decline, when cocoa farmers and brokers united in the hold-up movement to struggle for higher shares of the world price, by the time the second decline started the cocoa farmers' capacity for collective action had been dissolved. The farmers' unions that represented, respectively, cocoa farmers in Ashanti and in the South (the former Gold Coast Colony) divided on party lines during the CPP–NLM conflict. Nkrumah followed up by establishing a party organisation that supposedly represented the cocoa farmers but in fact organised them to support the government, for example 'voluntarily' reducing their own share of the price.[64] It is also relevant that the government was actively cutting the political power and independence of chiefs, especially following the Asantehene's evident support for the NLM.[65] The free-rider obstacle to collective action, so strongly overcome in the 1930s by independent farmers' unions supported by the chiefs, now stymied any thought of a new hold-up. This political 'demobilisation' of the cocoa farmers, to use Beckman's term,[66] rendered them open to punitive taxation, as came to pass between 1975 and 1983.

Ghana's comparative advantage in cocoa growing remained overwhelming. Even in 1972, when output was on a downward trend which was soon to accelerate, and even at official exchange rates, the domestic resource cost per unit of foreign exchange from exporting cocoa was 0.30.[67]

A micro example of the paramountcy of price disincentive in the causes of the near-collapse of Ghanaian cocoa output is provided by twin World Bank 'Cocoa Rehabilitation' projects, in the Eastern Region (1970–80) and Ashanti (1975–83) respectively. They are particularly interesting because they anticipated the third cocoa expansion in the choice of site – replanting exhausted farms – and technology: hybrid cocoa. But both projects failed dismally. The farm owners were content to have the project replant their farms for them. But they declined to invest any of their own labour, except in planting and

63 Rimmer, *Staying Poor*, 133–4.

64 Björn Beckman, *Organising the Farmers: Cocoa Politics and National Development in Ghana* (Uppsala, 1976).

65 Richard Rathbone, *Nkrumah and the Chiefs: the Politics of Chieftaincy in Ghana 1951–60* (Accra and Athens OH, 2000).

66 Beckman, *Organising the Farmers*, 242–3.

67 World Bank, *Accelerated Development in Sub-Saharan Africa: an Agenda for Action* (Washington DC, 1981), 65.

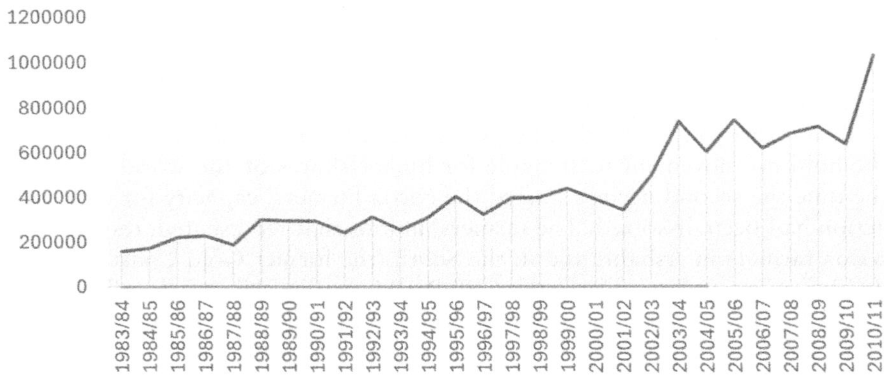

Figure 1.5 Ghana's Third Cocoa Expansion 1983/84–2010/11.
Source: Cocobod (with thanks to Rod Alence).

harvesting the food crop – plantain – that shaded the young cocoa plants.[68] The extreme repression of real producer prices for cocoa farmers, coupled with growing demand for foodstuffs, meant that the relative prices of food crops compared to cocoa had risen greatly since the mid-1960s.[69] These rehabilitation projects were the perfect illustration of the futility of the project approach to development aid, in the absence of a favourable price environment.

The second cocoa decline was at the heart of the fall in Ghana's real GDP per head, from 1,393 in 1990 international dollars in 1965 to 933 in 1983.[70] As Figure 1.5 shows, output/exports gradually climbed out of the pit of 1983/4. An extraordinary acceleration followed: in planting from the late 1990s, followed by a doubling of exports between 2001/2 and 2009/10, even before the record year of 2010/11. Exports averaged nearly 700,000 tonnes per calendar year between 2004 and 2010. In contrast to the second cocoa expansion, the third was achieved primarily by intensification.

The work of Kolavalli and Vigneri shows that the technology used was fundamentally different from that of the first and even the second cocoa booms.

68 World Bank Group Archives: Folder 30468727 Ghana – Eastern Region Cocoa – Credit 0205 – Project Performance Audit, 26.5.1981; Folder 1045467 Ghana – Eastern Region Cocoa – Credit 0205 – Correspondence (4.6.1980–29.6.1981); Folder 1066972 Ghana – Ashanti Region Cocoa – Loan 1181 – Project Completion Reports, Correspondence (7.3–18.7.1984).

69 V.K. Nyanteng, *The Declining Ghana Cocoa Industry: An Analysis of Some Fundamental Problems* (Legon, 1980), 15–19.

70 Broadberry and Gardner, 'Economic growth', table A1; Maddison Project Database (2013).

Whereas hybrid varieties were too little too late to contribute much to the growth of output in the late 1950s and early 1960s, these quicker-maturing, higher-yielding varieties were central to the cocoa rehabilitation efforts when they were relaunched in 1984 by the government with World Bank support. From 1995, it was virtually only hybrid varieties that were planted, yielding faster and more abundantly than 'Tetteh Quarshie' cocoa. If the modern varieties were the centrepiece of the new approach, other components included the provision of insecticide that was cheaper at the point of use (indeed, Cocobod had a free mass spraying programme in 2003) and – for the first time on a large scale in Ghanaian cocoa history – major use of fertiliser.[71]

The area harvested was 15.4 per cent lower in the peak calendar year of the third expansion (2010) than in the peak year of the second (1964).[72] Again, the panel survey of cocoa farmers reported by Teal shows a doubling of average land productivity, over eight years in which output itself only doubled, according to Cocobod.[73] Teal shows an intensification of farming practices, and attributes the higher productivity proximately to that. But, as noted earlier, he sees this as a function of higher producer prices, not of a change in the production function. Yet it seems clear that a new production function was adopted, in which higher ratios of capital and labour were applied per unit of land; and it was a higher production function, delivering higher yields and total factor productivity. In this it resembled the original cocoa expansion. But a significant difference should be noted: whereas the original cocoa expansion was a one-off shift to a new and higher production function in southern Ghanaian export agriculture, since the third expansion, the production technology has continued to advance, with the more recent introduction of hand-pollination.

It is often lamented that there has been no Green Revolution in Africa, in the sense of a transformation in yields based on quicker-maturing, more productive varieties of crop, to compare with those in parts of Asia. Yet the full adoption of hybrid cocoa in Ghana and elsewhere in West Africa perfectly fits the definition of a Green Revolution – for an export crop rather than a food grain. And the new varieties were bred locally, in this case (from Amazon onwards) at the national cocoa research station at Tafo.

This Green Revolution in cocoa marks a break with the era, identified by Ruf, where rapid expansions of cocoa cultivation were based on land newly cleared

71 Marcella Vigneri, 'Drivers of Change in Ghana's Cocoa Sector', Working Paper, Washington DC: International Food Policy Research Institute, 2008/9; Shashi Kolavalli and Marcella Vigneri, 'Cocoa in Ghana: shaping the success of an economy', in P. Chuhan-Pole and M. Angwafo (eds), *Yes Africa Can: Success Stories from a Dynamic Continent* (Washington DC, 2011); Kolavalli and Vigneri, *The Cocoa Coast: the Board-Managed Cocoa Sector in Ghana* (Washington DC, 2017). Also, Teal, 'An Agricultural Revolution in Ghana?'

72 Calculated from Food and Agriculture Organisation FAOSTAT_data_3.1.2020-Ghana cocoa.

73 Teal, 'An Agricultural Revolution in Ghana?'

from forest. While some of the land in western Ghana was probably newly cleared from forest, especially in the earlier years of the expansion, the acceleration of planting in the 1990s and early 2010s was primarily about replanting land already used for cocoa.

On land tenure, the further expansion of cocoa cultivation and the growth of population increased the demand for cultivable land in relation to a supply that is not even fixed but actually declining, given the hectarage taken out by other uses, including *galamsey* mining.[74] By the turn of the century, the argument that individual land tenure might be more efficient economically had grown stronger. Goldstein and Udry showed that 'stranger' farmers, however long-established, feared to fallow their land in case the local elders tried to seize it on the grounds of abandonment.[75] Goldstein and Udry were discussing food growing for the domestic market rather than cocoa growing, but there is other evidence to support the view that stranger-cocoa farmers' tenure became increasingly tenuous over the twentieth century.[76] On the face of it, the efficiency argument for individual land title is now stronger than before, even in the case of tree crops.[77]

In labour terms, one might have expected that a rapid increase in the volume of output, responding to higher world prices and a higher share of the world price, would have involved a major increase in the use of hired labour. So far, however, studies suggest that the intensification of production was mainly the work of family labour,[78] supplemented by the minimal form of hired labour, casual labour hired for a specific task and paid daily.[79] None of these studies devoted much space to labour, however: there is an urgent need for detailed research on the labour side of the story.[80] There is 'anecdotal' evidence from former participants in the 2000s expansion that much hired labour was involved, including in the novel form of 'spray guns': workers paid ultimately by the marketing board to spray farmers' farms.

In comparison with the literature on earlier production booms, something else is absent: anything on the agency and indeed entrepreneurship of farmers. The historiography of cocoa farming has moved from innovation and risk-taking

74 Illegal gold mining, discussed in Hilson's chapter.

75 Markus Goldstein and Christopher Udry, 'The profits of power: land rights and agricultural investment in Ghana', *Journal of Political Economy* 116:6 (2008), 981–1022.

76 Stefano Boni, *Clearing the Ghanaian Forest* (Legon, 2005).

77 Kojo Sebastian Amanor provided an elegant critique of the arguments that market-promoting land reform should be imposed by the state and, conversely, that individual land tenure is best left to emerge endogenously. Amanor, *Global Restructuring and Land Rights in Ghana* (Nordiska Afrikainstitutet, research report no. 108, Uppsala, 1999).

78 Vigneri, 'Drivers of Change'; Teal, 'An Agricultural Revolution in Ghana?'

79 Vigneri, 'Drivers of Change', 12.

80 A Ph.D. project on this, by Hedvig Lagercrantz, is in progress at Humboldt University, within the framework of the AHRC-DFG project 'Where Have all the Workers Gone? Labour and Work in Ghana, 1951–2010'.

to mere supply-response; from Hill's 'rural capitalism' to Kolavalli and Vigneri's 'board-managed' cocoa sector.[81]

The third cocoa expansion contributed importantly to Ghana's continuous economic growth, from a real GDP per head of 933 in 1990 international dollars in 1983, to 1,922 in 2010.[82]

Conclusions

This chapter examines the rise of Ghanaian cocoa production and exports, from zero to over one million tonnes a year, Ghana becoming the largest cocoa exporter on the planet for nearly seventy years, subsequently slipping into – but holding – second place. Three periods of expansion are identified, separated by two declines. This work is the first attempt to tell the story as a whole. In contrast to Teal's argument about continuity in the production function, I have emphasised that the adoption of cocoa in the first place, and the third cocoa boom of the 2000s, both entailed a shift to a new and more remunerative combination of factors of production: the first a one-off shift, the second embarking on a path of further technical innovation. Overall, it is a very positive story: while Ruf correctly associates expansions of cocoa production around the world with access to primary forest, in Ghana that was true of the first two great expansions, but the most recent was based upon replanting old cocoa farms with a higher-yielding variety of cocoa: a veritable 'Green Revolution', with higher output accommodated on a smaller area of land. It remains to be seen whether this intensification, which required higher inputs of fertiliser, insecticide and labour per hectare, is environmentally sustainable. The history from the 1890s to the 2000s as a whole marks one variant on the general path of economic development in Sub-Saharan Africa, from land-extensive to land-intensive choices in production technique and institutions: a path that, in food-crop farming around tropical Africa, has yielded examples of Boserupian advance to higher total factor productivity, worryingly mixed with cases of Geertzian agricultural involution, where higher output is achieved only by disproportionate rises in labour inputs.[83]

The two periods of decline in Ghanaian cocoa production have in common that they were responses to the weakening or disappearance of price incentives to plant and harvest cocoa. The overall duration and extent of both declines are

81 Kolavalli and Vigneri, *Cocoa Coast*.

82 Maddison Project Database (2013).

83 See special issue of *Food Policy* 48 (2014), especially T.S. Jayne, Jordan Chamberlin and Derek D. Headey, 'Land pressures, the evolution of farming systems, and development strategies in Africa: A synthesis' (pp. 1–17) and Derek D. Headey and T.S. Jayne, 'Adaptation to land constraints: is Africa different?' (pp. 18–33). Further, Gareth Austin, 'Africa and the Anthropocene', in G. Austin (ed.), *Economic Development and Environmental History in the Anthropocene: Perspectives on Asia and Africa* (London, 2017), 95–118.

entirely attributable to low producer prices, but the reasons those prices were low were different in that the slow decline after 1965 was turned into a potentially terminal collapse between 1975 and 1983 by policy: the state withholding all but a few per cent of the world price from the producers.

Ghana has had a strong comparative advantage in cocoa, such that, except when the state imposed punitive price disincentives, it was always in farmers' interests to expand production where rain and soil conditions were favourable for this tree crop. While cocoa has been central to the higher living standards achieved for a vastly larger population across the long twentieth century, other chapters in this volume explore the attempts to use cocoa surpluses to support structural diversification and transformation of the Ghanaian economy.[84]

Labour relations have changed radically in cocoa farming across the long twentieth century. While forms of coerced labour contributed to the initial expansion, especially in Ashanti, bearing cocoa trees played a huge role in creating effective demand (demand backed by purchasing power) for free labour. It is also important to underline the success of migrant labourers from the savanna in gradually winning better contracts from their employers, transitioning from regular annual wage contracts to a managerial form of sharecropping, within which the shares eventually increased. The result was that, while cocoa farming primarily benefited the areas where it was grown, some benefits were felt in the labour-supplying savanna: gains embodied in rises in the average heights of later generations. Hired labourers on cocoa farms had virtually disappeared by 1983 because farmers could not afford to pay them. More research is needed on labour in the third expansion, especially in the 2000s. So far, the work of economists suggests that the workforce overwhelmingly comprised the farmers themselves plus some family labour. If so, this suggests that cocoa farmers' holdings were on average smaller than ever before. If so, what has happened to Hill's 'rural capitalists' and the labour-hiring farmers who were the backbone of the hold-up movement in the 1920s and 1930s, and of the cooperative societies in the 1950s? But testimony from informed participants suggests that hired labour was again important in the 2000s, including in the new form of sprayers applying insecticide on farmers' farms but paid, ultimately, not by the farmers but by the marketing board.

The evolutionary theory of land tenure predicts that, as land becomes scarcer, property rights over it are likely to be made more strongly individual, facilitating buying and selling, whether of use rights or of the land itself. The original cocoa take-off in Akim Abuakwa involved purchase of land by groups of 'strangers', especially from Akwapim and Krobo. The colonial government saw to it that nothing on that scale was repeated as the cocoa frontier moved on, notably to Ashanti. The first and second expansions of Ghanaian cocoa

84 See chapters by Kanbur, Abbey and Adu-Danso, and Aryeetey.

production are actually significant in comparative terms as proving that wide-scale capital formation (cocoa tree-planting) for profit could happen without any general system of individual land titling. Secure ownership of the trees themselves was enough of a reward for investment, however much chiefs contested ownership of the underlying land. Again, further research is needed into how far land sales were part of the third cocoa expansion.

Finally, the politics of cocoa production have shifted dramatically across the long twentieth century. Backed by chiefs, the cocoa farmers' unions became a major force expressing the collective interests of producers (and of African brokers) in the 1920s and 1930s. That capacity for organised struggle for higher producer prices was lost when the unions split during the party conflict that preceded independence. The result was to facilitate the punitive taxation of export agriculture that actually threatened the survival of an activity in which the country had a strong comparative advantage. Economic liberalisation rescued cocoa growing from 1983 onwards, but not through any organised action by the farmers themselves: their role in the origins of Structural Adjustment was to stop planting cocoa, reduce their labour in harvesting it, and where possible sell it to smugglers. This spontaneous resistance to the price regime induced the fiscal and foreign-exchange crisis of the early 1980s that eventually persuaded the Provisional National Defence Council to abandon over-valuation and seek financial support from the IMF and World Bank. Since then, as Amoah-Boampong's chapter shows, independent cocoa cooperatives have emerged; but they do not appear to have acted as the farmers' champions in fighting for higher producer prices. In a remarkable historical irony, that role was taken in the 2000s by the marketing board itself. More generally, comparing the literature on the first and third great expansions of cocoa production, whereas the leading agents of change from Tetteh Quarshie himself to the early 1960s were entrepreneurial producers, in the first decade of the twentieth century the leading role was taken by the state, in the form of the marketing board.

2

Inequality in Ghana: Assessing the Impact of Government Tax and Expenditure Policies Over a Century

PRINCE YOUNG ABOAGYE

The role of taxation and government expenditures in alleviating economic inequality has long been recognised. Tax-funded government spending on welfare, education, health insurance, pensions, and infrastructural development has historically been instrumental in redistributing income in developed countries.[1] As a result, tax experts and policy makers have become more concerned with the role taxation and government spending might play in reducing the high levels of inequality in many developing countries.[2]

Historically, redistribution via taxation and social transfers has been least present in many underdeveloped countries where high levels of poverty and inequality persist.[3] In poor countries, personal income taxes have done little to reduce inequality because they are neither comprehensive nor progressive.[4] Further, the levels, coverage, and quality of government expenditure on social transfers in developing countries are significantly lower compared to developed countries. Although investments in public health, public schools and infrastructural development have increased since 1996 in sub-Saharan Africa, their impact

1 Peter H. Lindert and Jeffrey G. Williamson, 'Growth, equality, and history', *Explorations in Economic History* 22:4 (1985), 341–77; Peter H. Lindert, *Growing Public: Social Spending and Economic Growth Since the Eighteenth Century*, vol. 1 (Cambridge, 2004); Daron Acemoglu, Simon Johnson and James A. Robinson, 'The colonial origins of comparative development: an empirical investigation', *American Economic Review* 91:5 (2001), 1369–401; Thomas Piketty, *Capital in the Twenty-First Century* (Cambridge MA, 2014).

2 Richard M. Bird and Eric M. Zolt, 'Redistribution via taxation: the limited role of the personal income tax in developing countries', *UCLA Law Review* 52:6 (2005), 1627–96; Claire Kumar, *Africa Rising: Inequalities and the Essential Role of Fair Taxation* (Christian Aid, 2014).

3 Lindert, *Growing Public*, 15.

4 Bird and Zolt, 'Redistribution via taxation'.

on income distribution has been minimal. In some cases, the ability of fiscal policies to reduce inequality even declined between 1990 and 2014.[5]

Some scholars argue that the roots of African states' weak tax systems and inadequate expenditure on public goods to enhance citizens' welfare can be traced to the colonial era.[6] In some colonies, colonial governments established extractive institutions that prioritised the exploitation of labour and natural resources over broader economic and social welfare. In others, colonial governments described as 'gatekeeper states', focused on developing and taxing the export sector, rather than broadening the tax base. As a result, areas producing export crops were better off than their labour-supplying hinterlands, and fiscal systems remained underdeveloped, with limited resources allocated to social spending.[7] Other scholars argue that colonial fiscal policies contributed to broad-based social and economic development in certain contexts through investments in infrastructure, education, and public health.[8]

In light of the above discussion, this chapter explores two related questions: how have government tax and expenditure policies changed over the long term? How have they affected inequality over time? The essay focuses on colonial and post-colonial Ghana where successive governments from the colonial era onwards have been concerned with redistribution.[9] Governments have consistently prioritised distributive expenditures across a broad spectrum as well as targeted distribution to specific groups linked to ruling elites. While this is hardly exceptional, Ghana has also experienced several major political and economic changes in the long twentieth century. It therefore provides a suitable case for studying the impact of changing government policies on inequality trends over the long term. By cutting across the conventional dividing point

5 David E. Sahn and Stephen D. Younger, 'Expenditure incidence in Africa: microeconomic evidence', *Fiscal Studies* 21:3 (2000), 29–47. Ayodele Odusola, 'Fiscal space, poverty and inequality in Africa', *African Development Review* 29:S1 (2017), 1–14.

6 Acemoglu, Johnson and Robinson, 'Colonial origins'; Frederick Cooper, *Africa Since 1940: The Past of the Present* (Cambridge, 2000); Thandika Mkandawire, 'On tax efforts and colonial heritage in Africa', *Journal of Development Studies* 46:10 (2010), 1647–69.

7 Ewout Frankema, 'Colonial taxation and government spending in British Africa, 1880–1940: Maximizing revenue or minimizing effort?' *Explorations in Economic History* 48:1 (2011), 136–49.

8 John Sender and Sheila Smith, *The Development of Capitalism in Africa* (London, 2000), 61–6; Alexander Moradi, 'Confronting colonial legacies – lessons from human development in Ghana and Kenya, 1880–2000', *Journal of International Development* 20:6 (2008), 1107–21; Ewout Frankema and Marlous van Waijenburg, 'Metropolitan blueprints of colonial taxation? Lessons from fiscal capacity building in British and French Africa, c.1880–1940,' *Journal of African History* 55:3 (2014), 371–400.

9 Douglas Rimmer, *Staying Poor: Ghana's Political Economy, 1950–1990* (Oxford, 1992); Eboe Hutchful, *Ghana's Adjustment Experience: The Paradox of Reform* (Geneva, 2002); Lindsay Whitfield, *Economies After Colonialism: Ghana and the Struggle for Power* (Cambridge, 2018).

between colonial and post-colonial periods, this chapter identifies continuities and changes, and differences and similarities in governments' fiscal policies and priorities, and their implications for inequality. The chapter does not examine all aspects and purposes of government policies and does not suggest that tax and expenditure policies alone are responsible for inequality trends. In a trade-based economy such as Ghana's, commodity price booms and slumps on the world market influence income-distribution trends. Nonetheless, state interventions and policies, especially after the colonial era, have shaped general economic development more than external influences, highlighting the potential role of fiscal policies in the long-term evolution of inequality.[10]

The analysis of the relationship between fiscal policies and inequality covers four distinct periods, defined by shifts in fiscal policy regimes, rather than political events. Between 1891 and 1940, the colonial administration largely pursued minimalistic fiscal policies, prioritising revenue extractions from the cocoa export sector over broad-based taxation or social investments. As a result, regional inequality deepened and income inequality remained moderately high. Although progressive taxation and expansionary investments were introduced between 1941 and 1960, their narrow coverage limited their redistributive impact. Between 1961 and 1982 inequality declined, but this was the result of economic contraction rather than broad-based redistribution. Inequality has been on the rise since the implementation of structural adjustment reforms in 1983, with fiscal policies playing only a marginal role in redistribution.

Conservative Fiscal Policies and Inequality, 1891–1940

We begin our analysis from 1891, where we have the earliest inequality estimates, until 1940. During this period, the colonial administration mostly adopted conservative fiscal policies, maintaining minimal taxation and focusing on revenue extraction from the export sector rather than establishing a more inclusive tax system or investing significantly in social development. This period also saw the formal abolition of slavery in Ashanti and the Northern Territories in 1908, marking a significant shift in the structure of social and economic relations.[11] The gradual emergence of free wage labour, though uneven and highly gendered, created new opportunities for income generation and potentially altered the distribution of earnings – albeit within the constraints of a colonial economy still heavily shaped by extractive priorities. The extent

10 Jonathan H. Frimpong-Ansah, *The Vampire State in Africa: The Political Economy of Decline in Ghana* (London, 1991); Gareth Austin, 'National poverty and the "vampire state" in Ghana: a review article', *Journal of International Development* 8:4 (1996), 553–73.

11 Gareth Austin, *Labour, Land, and Capital in Ghana: From Slavery to Free Labour in Asante, 1807–1956* (Rochester NY, 2005).

to which colonial fiscal policies influenced economic and social welfare remains a subject of debate. Some scholars argue that government revenues and expenditures contributed to welfare improvements, especially through infrastructure investments.[12] Others have been critical of two aspects of fiscal policy during this era: first, the regressive nature of colonial tax systems, and second, the failure to spend on programmes that improved the welfare of the indigenous population.[13]

This section examines these contrasting views. We argue that, on one hand, the benign view of colonial taxation and spending is somewhat exaggerated. Although government spending on infrastructural developments led to an increase in cocoa production, welfare effects from the booming cocoa trade were confined to the south. On the other hand, criticisms against imperial beneficence need some revision. Colonisation is a generic term that subsumes a variety of historical situations, and a major aspect of this variety was time.[14] Between 1919 and 1927, the colonial government actively pursued policies that would be considered developmental today. Government expenditures increased rapidly and there were attempts to ensure widespread development. Admittedly, given the resources the colonial government had then, more could have been achieved. Following this, we first describe inequality trends in colonial Ghana between 1891 and 1940. Next, we analyse government tax policies and their distributional consequences. We end with a discussion of expenditure policies and priorities and their implications for income and regional inequality.

There is scarce quantitative information available about the income distribution effects of government tax and expenditure policies during the colonial era. In a recent attempt, Aboagye and Bolt construct social tables to estimate long-term changes in income distribution in colonial Ghana.[15] Social tables entail reconstructing income distributions based on occupational structures and income/wage data. Individuals or households are classified into broad

12 Gareth Austin, 'The "reversal of fortune" thesis and the compression of history: perspectives from African and comparative economic history', *Journal of International Development* 20:8 (2008), 996–1027; Sue Bowden, Blessing Chiripanhura and Paul Mosley, 'Measuring and explaining poverty in six African countries: a long-period approach', *Journal of International Development* 20:8 (2008), 1049–79; Remi Jedwab and Alexander Moradi, 'The permanent effects of transportation revolutions in poor countries: evidence from Africa', *Review of Economics and Statistics* 98:2 (2016), 268–84.

13 Rhoda Howard, *Colonialism and Underdevelopment in Ghana* (London, 1978); Nii-K. Plange, 'Underdevelopment in northern Ghana: natural causes or colonial capitalism?', *Review of African Political Economy* 15/16 (1979), 4–14; Frimpong-Ansah, *Vampire State*, 66–9; Austin, '"Reversal of fortune" thesis and the compression of history'.

14 Austin, '"Reversal of fortune" thesis and the compression of history', 1007.

15 Prince Young Aboagye and Jutta Bolt, 'Long-term trends in income inequality: winners and losers of economic change in Ghana, 1891–1960', *Explorations in Economic History* 82 (2021), no. 101405.

income groups and assigned estimated earnings. Population and income shares are then calculated to determine income distribution, often summarised by the Gini coefficient. Social tables are based on information on population, occupations, and incomes. African colonial population censuses are generally considered to be of relatively poor quality. For Ghana, for example, the 1911 census might have excluded up to 700,000 people in a population of about 1.5 million.[16] Aboagye and Bolt, therefore, use Frankema and Jerven's modified population counts for Ghana for all colonial census years, based on official census estimates, additional secondary literature, and census reviews.[17] The original regional population shares from the censuses are used to distribute the updated population estimates across different regions and to classify individuals into various social classes. Income and wage data are derived from colonial Blue Books, government reports, and economic and agricultural surveys.

Aboagye and Bolt find that inequality was high in the last decade of the nineteenth century and remained at relatively high but constant levels between 1901 and 1921 and declined in the early 1930s, primarily as a result of the global depression in prices in the 1930s. As Figure 2.1 shows, income inequality measured by the Gini coefficient stood at 0.37 in 1901, increased to 0.40 in 1911 and marginally declined between 1921 and 1931. Changing prices for the colony's major export crop, cocoa, and changing incomes for government employees, skilled and commercial workers account for the levels of inequality observed. The paper confirms earlier claims that there were some welfare effects from economic changes. Nonetheless, some people, especially in the southern cocoa-growing areas, benefited more than residents of northern colonial Ghana.

Although the authors do not explicitly relate their findings to changes in fiscal policies, and they measure pre-tax and pre-transfers inequality, government tax and expenditure policies directly and indirectly affected prices and income developments during this era. To begin with, the colonial government committed itself to a low level of taxation and hence taxes did not check the growth of incomes and did not have redistributive effects. Unlike many sub-Saharan African colonies at the time, the colonial administration did not impose direct taxation in the Gold Coast until the 1940s. Highly paid government officials and high-earning private sector employees paid no taxes. The colonial administration raised most of its revenues from trade taxes – import and export duties, which were not only relatively easy and cheap to collect, but also carried lower political risks compared to direct taxation.[18] Given that exports were less

16 Austin, *Labour, Land, and Capital.*

17 Ewout Frankema and Morten Jerven, 'Writing history backwards or sideways: towards a consensus on African population, 1850–2010,' *Economic History Review* 67:4 (2014), 907–31.

18 G.B. Kay and Stephen Hymer, *The Political Economy of Colonialism in Ghana: A Collection of Documents and Statistics 1900–1960* (Cambridge, 1972), 26; Frankema, 'Colonial taxation.'

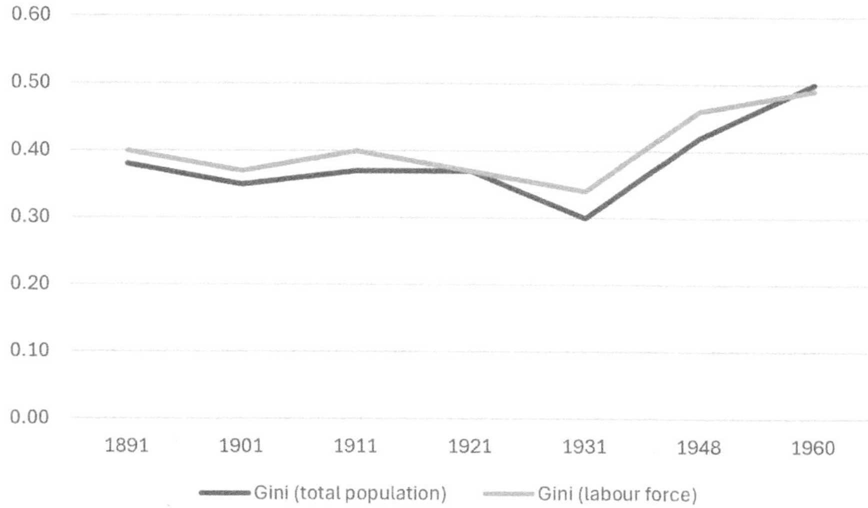

Figure 2.1 Income Gini Coefficients 1891–1960.
Source: Aboagye and Bolt, 'Long-term trends'.

heavily taxed than imports, the burden of taxation fell mostly on European manufacturers exporting to Africa and African consumers of imported European goods.[19] Even so, since the colonial government was careful not to reduce incentives for cocoa production and for private enterprise, trade taxes were kept low such that the tax burden was not punitive.

In fact, in times of economic prosperity, the government reduced trade taxes ostensibly guided 'by the great consideration that the reductions or proposed reductions will benefit the largest number of individuals, especially the poorer members of the country.'[20] However, the welfare effects created by the reduction in trade taxes were not diffusive. Tariff reductions only benefited producers of primary exports and consumers of European commodities who could bear greater tax burdens.[21] Given that high-earning public officials, private sector employees and producers of exports were not subjected to high levels of taxation, their income levels remained high relative to low-earning Ghanaians and many others who lived on subsistence. Therefore, there was little, if any, fiscal redistribution from taxation between 1891 and 1940.

19 N.A. Cox-George, *Studies in Finance and Development: The Gold Coast (Ghana) Experience, 1914–1950*, (London, 1973); Frankema and van Waijenburg, 'Metropolitan blueprints.'

20 Cox-George, *Studies in Finance*, 25.

21 *Ibid.*

Not much redistribution was achieved on the expenditure side either. Government expenditure was biased towards the cocoa export sector from which it raised much of its revenue. Aside from two periods of intense government activities, 1897–1907 and 1919–27, characterised by export expansion and improvements in transport and other social services, there were few attempts at broader economic development. Between 1900 and 1930, non-recurrent government expenditure on administrative, social, and economic infrastructure made up 55 per cent of total government expenditure. Government spending on economic infrastructure, which almost entirely covered expenditure on railways and harbours, accounted for 20 per cent of total government expenditure throughout 1900 and 1930.[22] Certainly, investment in transport infrastructure can result in a decline in transport costs and can lead to improvements in rural incomes by integrating labour and goods markets and therefore provide new economic opportunities to rural inhabitants.[23] The provision of transport infrastructure may have an unbalanced effect on the income and welfare of the poor and lead to a decline in income inequality. Transport infrastructure increases the value of the assets (such as land or human capital) of the poor and lowers the transaction costs poor people incur in accessing markets.[24]

Yet, in colonial Ghana, although government investment in transport infrastructure was fairly high, the expansion of rail and road transport was greatest in and around mining areas and the cocoa belt.[25] Better transport infrastructure diminished transport costs in cocoa-growing areas and led to increased incomes for cocoa growers and migrant labourers.[26] This might have further worsened income differences between Africans in cocoa-growing areas and those in non-cocoa growing ones.[27]

With greater emphasis on infrastructural development, the provision of other social services was limited. Admittedly, previous studies on the effects of social transfers on inequality elsewhere have shown that investment in social services such as education and health care may affect the distribution of income only after a relatively long time lag but they can also have immediate benefits. Government spending that reduces or takes away the costs (monetary and non-monetary) of educating children and providing health care for families

22 Kay and Hymer, *Political Economy*, 26–7.

23 Hanan G. Jacoby and Bart J. Minten, *On Measuring the Benefits of Lower Transport Costs* (Washington DC, 2008).

24 César Calderón and Luis Servén, 'Infrastructure and economic development in Sub-Saharan Africa', *Journal of African Economies* 19:S1 (2010), i13-i87.

25 Rita Hinden, *Plan for Africa: A Report Prepared for the Colonial Bureau of the Fabian Society* (London, 1941), 148; Kay and Hymer, *Political Economy* 20–5, 137.

26 Jedwab and Moradi, 'Permanent effects'.

27 Aboagye and Bolt, 'Long-term trends'. Detailed surveys of remittances indicate that the amount of income sent or taken home by migrant labourers was small, amounting to a pound per year per migrant, on average, in 1948.

reduces the income gap between rich and poor households as the cash benefit for low-income earning families is proportionately greater.[28] In colonial Ghana, government expenditure on basic education and health care was limited and accounted for between 2 and 8 per cent and 6 and 10 per cent respectively of total government expenditure, between 1905 and 1935.[29] Schools were mainly mission-run and were mostly located in the south and in large towns.[30] Health-care delivery was southern- and urban-biassed and other public services were only rudimentary in the towns, and unavailable in the villages.[31] Planned provision of public services and infrastructural developments in the north were sometimes abandoned and government resources were used to fund similar projects in the south.[32] To be sure, between 1919 and 1927 colonial government expenditure aimed at broader welfare development than before. During this time, spending was more than quadrupled and improvements in economic and social infrastructure had positive effects on incomes.[33]

However, the colonial government responded to economic challenges in the 1930s by cutting spending instead of raising taxes.[34] Investment in infrastructure averaged about 27 per cent of total expenditure in the 1930s as compared to an average of 57 per cent for the 1920s.[35] Government spending remained stagnant until 1941. Such cuts were unwarranted because despite the difficult economic conditions, the 1930s were, at least from 1932, a period of budget surpluses. 1931 was the only deficit year and by 1934 when the colony got out of the

28 Ke-Young Chu, Hamid Davoodi and Sanjeev Gupta, *Income Distribution and Tax and Government Spending Policies in Developing Countries* (Washington DC, 2000); Edward Anderson, Maria Ana Jalles D'Orey, Maren Duvendack and Lucio Esposito, 'Does government spending affect income inequality? A meta-regression analysis', *Journal of Economic Surveys* 31:4 (2017), 961–87; Oxfam, *The Power of Education to Fight Inequality*, Oxfam Briefing Paper (Oxford, 2019).

29 Prince Young Aboagye and Ellen Hillbom, 'Tax bargaining, fiscal contracts, and fiscal capacity in Ghana: a long-term perspective', *African Affairs* 119:475 (2020), 177–202.

30 Prince Young Aboagye, 'Inequality of education in colonial Ghana: European influences and African responses', *Economic History of Developing Regions* 36:3 (2021), 367–91.

31 K. David Patterson, *Health in Colonial Ghana: Disease, Medicine, and Socio-Economic Change, 1900–1955*, (Waltham MA, 1981), 17; Arlinde C.E. Vrooman, 'The development of colonial health care provision in Ghana and Côte d'Ivoire: c. 1900–55', *Economic History of Developing Regions* 38:3 (2023), 215–55.

32 Paul André Ladouceur, *Chiefs and Politicians: The Politics of Regionalism in Northern Ghana* (London, 1979).

33 Jedwab and Moradi, 'Permanent effects'.

34 Governor's Address, Opening of the 1930–31 Session of the Legislative Council, 17 February 1930, 4–11; Governor's Address, Opening of the 1931–32 Session of the Legislative Council, 23 February 1931, 11–16.

35 Kay and Hymer, *Political Economy*, 43.

depression its reserves and surpluses had increased.[36] Government surpluses could have been used to enhance the welfare of the indigenous population. However, accumulated reserves were invested mostly in the United Kingdom, in British Treasury Bills.[37] Large sums of potential public outlay therefore leaked out of the colonial economy. As a result, the levels of public expenditure and economic activity were kept lower than they should have otherwise been. In sum, the government's tax and expenditure policies had limited redistributive effects and inequality stayed at high, albeit constant, levels until the 1940s.

Decolonisation, Self-Government, and Rising Inequality, 1941–1960

During the decolonisation era and through the early years of Ghana's independence the government took a more active role in directing development, although its investments were still geared towards propping up the export sector. The dual societal structure from earlier decades rather than being eliminated was reinforced and inequality rose sharply. We begin by describing inequality trends during this period and subsequently, we first analyse government tax policies, and then expenditure priorities and their implications for distribution.

Like the previous era, not much information is available on the effects of government tax and expenditure policies on living standards and income distribution between 1941 and 1960. Nominal and real wages which reflect living standards appear to have increased substantially for many urban wage-earning Ghanaians during this period.[38] Nonetheless, there were large wage differences between skilled and unskilled workers and the relative position of workers at the low end of the remuneration spectrum did not improve.[39] Further, a majority of Ghanaians who earned a living from the non-cocoa sector fell behind. Inequality increased substantially after the 1930s world slump in prices with the Gini coefficient rising from 0.34 in 1931 to 0.49 in 1960 (see Figure 2.1). Incomes for commercial and skilled workers and government employees increased rapidly in the 1940s leading to increasing income inequality. Increasing cocoa prices in the 1950s also meant that Gold Coast cocoa farmers earned higher incomes. In 1960, nominal incomes per capita for large-scale cocoa farmers stood at £211, £63 for food farmers, £80 for petty traders and £87 for unskilled labourers.[40] At the end of the colonial

36 Cox-George, *Studies in Finance*, 110.

37 Frimpong-Ansah, *Vampire State*, 67.

38 Ewout Frankema and Marlous van Waijenburg, 'Structural impediments to African growth? New evidence from real wages in British Africa, 1880–1965', *Journal of Economic History* 72:4 (2012), 895–926.

39 Rimmer, *Staying Poor*, 68; Aboagye and Bolt, 'Long-term trends'.

40 Aboagye and Bolt, 'Long-term trends'.

era, large-scale cocoa farmers were better off and, in the north, where cocoa was not cultivated, many were poor.[41]

Although Aboagye and Bolt's estimates are for pre-tax inequality, it does not appear that much redistribution was achieved through taxation, notwithstanding the successful introduction of direct taxation by the colonial government in 1943. It was expected that the income tax would reach many of the richer Africans and become a much-needed remedy to the existing inequitable system of taxation. But only a small minority of Africans paid the income tax. It fell almost entirely on non-African sources of income and the tax rate was among the lowest in the British Empire.[42] In 1948, 5,000 non-Africans and only 693 Africans paid the income tax. The number of Ghanaian income taxpayers increased over time and, as Table 2.1 shows, by 1958/59 they accounted for 42 per cent of income taxpayers, but their contribution to total income tax returns (32 per cent) was still less than that of British and other Commonwealth nationals (41 per cent). As Table 2.1 indicates only 10,000 people (Africans and non-Africans) in a population of nearly six million paid income taxes by 1958. With inadequate staff and logistics, and limited coverage, the Income Tax Department was unable to reach many self-employed persons and other potential taxpayers, and as the 1954/55 report of the Income Tax Department indicates 'the field for expansion [remains] very large.'

Cocoa was the government's major tax handle. We must therefore briefly examine the nature of government's taxation of the cocoa sector to ascertain if much redistribution was achieved. State-controlled marketing was introduced during World War II which allowed the colonial government and immediate self-governing state to extract cocoa farmers' surpluses.[43] This war-time measure for supposedly stabilising prices paid to cocoa farmers became a permanent feature of Ghanaian cocoa trade from 1947 when the Cocoa Marketing Board (CMB) was established. The CMB fixed producer prices below the average market prices, and became the main instrument for state accumulation in the 1950s and thereafter. Between 1949/50 and 1957/58, cocoa farmers received 51 per cent of the total proceeds, 32 per cent of the proceeds was paid in export duty, 7 per cent was absorbed by other CMB costs, and 10 per cent accrued to the CMB as surpluses.[44]

41 Rimmer, *Staying Poor*, 30.

42 Lord Hailey, *An African Survey: A Study of Problems Arising in Africa South of the Sahara* (London, 1956), 666.

43 B. Björn Beckman, *Organising the Farmers: Cocoa Politics and National Development in Ghana* (Uppsala, 1976), 41–2; Rod Alence, 'Colonial government, social conflict and state involvement in Africa's open economies: the origins of the Ghana Cocoa Marketing Board, 1939–46', *Journal of African History* 42:3 (2001), 397–416.

44 Rimmer, *Staying Poor*, 55; Cocoa Marketing Boards, Annual Reports.

Table 2.1 Personal Income Taxpayers by Nationality 1954/55 – 1958/59

	1954–55		1955–56		1957–58		1958–59	
	Number	Income	Number	Income	Number	Income	Number	Income
Nationality	(%)	(%)	(%)	(%)	(%)	(%)	(%)	(%)
Gold Coast	24	20	23	21	29	24	42	32
Other African Territories	1	1	1	1	1	1	1	1
India	2	2	2	2	2	2	2	2
UK & Commonwealth	51	50	53	50	46	44	37	41
Other European & American	10	11	12	12	13	13	10	12
Middle East*	11	16	10	14	10	16	8	12
Total	8,641	10,963,702	8,678	11,862,076	10,061	14,562,681	12,879	16,827,128

Source: Income Tax Department Reports, 195 4–55 to 195 8–59.

*These were probably Levantines (Syrians and Lebanese) involved in commerce, often serving as intermediaries between European firms and African businesses.

In spite of the government's increased taxation of the cocoa sector, not much redistribution was achieved. Cocoa farmers were still better off in both relative and absolute terms especially between 1950 and 1958. They harvested on an annual average the same tonnage as in the immediate post-war year. Prices followed an upward trend during this period and farmers received a real price – the money-price deflated by the Accra cost-of-living index – nearly three times greater than in the immediate pre-war year.[45]

Tax policy is only one half of the fiscal equation, and the colonial government could have redistributed income through expenditures aimed at improving the incomes of the rest of the African population. However, not much redistribution was achieved on the expenditure side of the budget either. Indeed, the 1940s was the era of 'development-minded colonialism' where colonial governments began consciously to make investments for the general improvement of the welfare of their colonised people.[46] Between 1941 and 1948, the Gold Coast received a total of £858,778 under the Colonial Development and Welfare Act of 1940.[47] Grants from the Welfare Act were invested in agricultural research, the building of schools and urban water supply and electrification. Government spending rose significantly, with an annual average rate of 16 per cent to over £7 million from 1942 to 1950, and a large share of this expenditure was directed towards development and the expansion of social services. Development spending which had previously been neglected picked up rapidly from the mid-1940s as Table 2.2 shows.[48]

Table 2.2 Government Development Expenditure with Functional Breakdown 1940–60

Year	General Services	Community Services	Social Services	Economic Services
1940	0	0	0	0
1945	10.1	29.4	50.0	10.5
1950	1.4	41.4	30.9	26.3
1951	11.9	39.3	33.4	15.4

45 Rimmer, *Staying Poor*, 67; Tony Killick, 'The economics of cocoa', in Walter Birmingham, I. Neustadt and E.N. Omaboe (eds), *A Study of Contemporary Ghana: The Economy of Ghana*, Vol. 1 (London, 1966), 365–90.

46 Cooper, *Africa Since 1940*, 39. The Gold Coast had already initiated developmental investments earlier, particularly under Governor Guggisberg's 10-Year Development Plan (1919–29).

47 Frimpong-Ansah, *Vampire State*, 4.

48 *Ibid.*, 65, 78–9.

Table 2.2 continued

Year	General Services	Community Services	Social Services	Economic Services
1952	10	32	34	24
1953	4.7	28.3	27.5	39.5
1954	6.6	51.9	23.5	17.9
1955	10.9	44.7	16.5	27.9
1956	13.5	51.2	14.6	20.7
1957	14.1	39.4	15.5	31.0
1958	13.7	31.8	11.3	43.1
1959	29.0	30.8	16.0	24.1
1960	23.5	23.9	20.0	32.6

Note: General services refers to financial administration, tax administration, general economic regulations, defence and foreign affairs, justice and police, and other like expenditures. Community services include construction, fuel and power, roads, scientific services. Social services cover education and health services. Economic services include agriculture, mining, manufacturing and commerce, railways, harbours, transport and communications.

Source: Kay and Hymer, *Political Economy*, 375, Table 29; Frimpong-Ansah, *Vampire State*, 79, Table 5.1.

Still, developmental colonialism had defects. The south continued to benefit disproportionately from government expenditures relative to the north. Investments were made to develop the export economy of the south as a large share of government outlays went into economic and community services (see Table 2.2). There were more schools, hospitals, roads and other social services in the south than in the north, even allowing for the larger population of the south.[49] The nature of investments made by the colonial government was more likely to exacerbate inequality. As mentioned earlier, government spending on public transport directed towards the poor is more likely to reduce inequality, while public expenditure on developing infrastructure that favours the richer owners of capital tends to worsen the distribution of income.[50] Similar to the previous era (1891–1940), infrastructural development between 1941 and 1960 was concentrated in cocoa-growing and mining areas, leaving the majority of the poor under-served. Inequality was typified, on one hand, by the growth

49 Philip J. Foster, *Education and Social Change in Ghana* (London, 1965); Aboagye, 'Inequality of Education'.

50 Stephen J. Turnovsky, 'Economic growth and inequality: the role of public investment', *Journal of Economic Dynamics and Control*, 61:C (2015), 204–21.

of urban trading and administrative centres, concentrations of population in mining districts, and the emergence of wealthy indigenous farmers in the forest cocoa belts. On the other hand, outmoded agricultural systems still existed and many Africans barely scratched a living from the soil.[51]

Ghana became partly self-governing in 1951 and attained full independence in 1957. Compared to the British, the indigenous government from 1951 more actively used surpluses from the cocoa sector to fund development initiatives. As Table 2.2 shows, investments in community services increased rapidly. The ruling Convention People's Party (CPP), led by Kwame Nkrumah, in its 1951 election manifesto laid down such welfare aims as free technical and primary education up to the age of 16 years and a free national health service. This was to be rolled out under a five-year economic plan that would include infrastructural developments, electrification of the whole country, progressive mechanisation of agriculture, and a robust industrialisation programme. These would 'afford the people an increasingly higher standard of living which has long been denied to them under the Crown Colony system of government.'[52] From approximately £17 million per year between 1953 and 1958, development (or capital) expenditure rose to £26.1 million in 1958/59.[53] Some significant results were achieved as major improvements occurred in communications and public services. For example, road mileage maintained by the Public Works Department grew from 3,525 in 1950 to 4,277 in 1958.[54] The impact of these improvements on redistribution would be more discernible in the 1960s.

Overall, between 1941 and 1960 the tax net was still narrow, only a few people paid income taxes and although government expenditure increased, investments were still determined by the need to increase export earnings, and few resources were spent on improving the incomes of the majority of the African population. Inequality as measured by the Gini coefficient was 0.50 in 1960 (see Figure 2.1). After 1960, the independent state would extract more from cocoa farmers in a bid to change the structure of the export-based colonial economy. This would result in a more equitable distribution of income, but equity would be served only to the extent of making the former rich, less rich.

Big Push, Big Fall, and Income Redistribution, 1961–1982

From 1961, Nkrumah adopted fiscal policies different from those inherited from the British. Extraction of resources from the wealthier segments of society

51 Frimpong-Ansah, *Vampire State*, 67.

52 CPP, General Election Manifesto, 1951 'Towards a goal' in Metcalfe, *Great Britain and Ghana*, 705.

53 Rimmer, *Staying Poor*, 55.

54 Frimpong-Ansah, *Vampire State*, 82; Rimmer, *Staying Poor*, 66–7. See also, Kay and Hymer, *Political Economy*, 396. According to Rimmer, there were many other roads also and in 1958, the total road mileage was put at 18,866.

and the reallocation of government expenditures in favour of the poor resulted in a decline in inequality. Nkrumah's government was ousted from office in a military coup in 1966 and between 1966 and 1982 Ghana had eight different regimes. Nevertheless, generally there was much continuity rather than change in fiscal policies during this period.[55] Overall, inequality remained low due in part to increased redistributive expenditures, but also due to the general fall in incomes as a result of economic stagnation and decline. We begin with an analysis of Nkrumah's tax efforts and expenditure priorities and their effects on the distribution of income. We follow up with fiscal policies after Nkrumah and their distributional effects.

1961–66 marked a 'turning point' in the country's strategies. The government adopted 'big-push' development policies in order to build an industrialised and economically independent welfare state. As a result, expenditures increased, necessitating a larger tax effort. The independent state maintained control of marketing board surpluses and extracted an even larger share of cocoa farmers' income.[56] That the fiscal net was cast wider is illustrated by the increase in the share of taxes not directly related to external trade from 15.3 per cent in 1960/61 to 43.4 per cent in 1965, as a result of increased rates of personal and corporate income tax, higher excise duties, and the introduction of a purchase tax on imported consumer durables.[57] Relative to other African countries the tax burden on Ghanaians at this time was high, and perhaps for the first time, redistribution occurred through taxation.[58]

Other factors also pushed down inequality. For example, the decline in world cocoa prices in the first half of the 1960s, passed on by the marketing board, depressed cocoa farmers' incomes. Retail prices also increased and real wages declined both in absolute and relative terms to most other incomes.[59] The real incomes of urban wage earners, for example, declined by 46 per cent between 1960 and 1966.[60]

Redistributive consequences also followed from government expenditure policies. Major improvements occurred in public services, the most dramatic of which was in education, though this was a continuous trend from the previous decade.[61] Gross primary school enrolment rate increased from 33 per cent in 1960 to 60 per cent in 1965, a development related in part to the introduction of

55 Tony Killick, *Development Economics in Action: A Study of Economic Policies in Ghana* (2nd edition, London, 2010).

56 Aboagye and Hillbom, 'Tax bargaining'.

57 Rimmer, *Staying Poor*, 80.

58 Killick, *Development Economics in Action*, 159.

59 Keith Hart, 'Informal income opportunities and urban employment in Ghana', *Journal of Modern African Studies*, 11:1 (1973), 61–89; Rimmer, *Staying Poor*, 102–3.

60 Hart, 'Informal income opportunities', 64.

61 Killick, *Development Economics in Action*, 80–4.

the 1961 Education Act that made basic education free and compulsory.[62] There were steady improvements in the provision of health services, water supplies, electricity, and housing standards in both rural and urban communities.[63] Such investments can affect income distribution with a long-term lag but when they 'free' families from the costs of procuring such services, there can be immediate effects on the distribution of income. Under Nkrumah, free or highly subsidised social services became widely diffused and enjoyed by many.[64]

Government expenditures affected the distribution of income through other channels. The reallocation of cocoa income had important effects on the development of agriculture and agricultural incomes outside the cocoa sector. During the colonial era, public transport investments were concentrated in export-producing regions. Areas with high potential for food production received little development support, although the demand for foodstuffs in cocoa-buying centres had already stimulated market-oriented food production in neighbouring areas.[65] Under Nkrumah, investments in transport infrastructure further integrated local food production into the market economy, contributing to rising rural incomes. Food farmers' terms of trade rose from an index of 102 in 1962 to 132 in 1966, and on realistic assumptions about supply and demand elasticities, this might imply that their real incomes also increased.[66] Between 1960 and 1967, urban real incomes fell while rural incomes rose by 20 per cent and the growing urban–rural income differential of the 1950s contracted in the 1960s.[67] There were regional dimensions to redistribution under the CPP as well, as the north now benefited from investment in public services to a much greater extent than previously.[68]

Therefore, on both sides of the budget, redistribution occurred and although we do not have direct Gini estimates, the available evidence suggests that income disparities are likely to have declined between 1961 and 1966. However, redistribution was achieved by 'killing the goose that laid the golden egg.' As the cocoa sector continued to be squeezed for finance, there were reduced incentives for increasing production, the cocoa sector declined and led to adverse consequences on the Ghanaian economy. Nkrumah's government was overthrown in 1966 and a long period of economic stagnation followed.

62 M.M. Huq, *The Economy of Ghana*, (London, 1989), 71.

63 E.N. Omaboe, 'The process of planning', in Walter Birmingham, I. Neustadt and E.N. Omaboe (eds), *A Study of Contemporary Ghana: The Economy of Ghana*, Volume 1 (London, 1966), 439–63; G. Arku, 'Housing and development strategies in Ghana, 1945–2000', *International Development Planning Review* 28 (2006), 333–58.

64 Beckman, *Organising the Farmers*, 224–5.

65 Austin, *Labour, Land, and Capital*, 54–5.

66 Killick, *Development Economics in Action*, 80, 100–1.

67 J.B. Knight, 'Rural-urban income comparisons and migration in Ghana', *Bulletin of the Oxford University Institute of Economics & Statistics* 34:2 (1972), 199–228.

68 Beckman, *Organising the Farmers*, 225.

The National Liberation Council (NLC) government that took over from Nkrumah believed that taxes had become too high and there was 'the need to reduce the tax burden on the majority of our people.'[69] Several taxes were either reduced or abolished between 1966 and 1968.[70] At the same time, the government reduced public expenditure, but recurrent expenditures for education and social and general government expenditure increased.[71] By 1969, when the NLC government transferred control to the Progress Party government, public services had deteriorated. The effects of this government's reduced taxation and expenditure on income distribution between 1966 and 1969 are unclear given its short time in office. Gini estimates for this period are unavailable, except for a point estimate of 0.39 in 1970.[72] Income inequality therefore appears to have remained at a relatively low level. Nonetheless, rural–urban income disparities worsened as a result of the strong urban bias of government expenditure.[73]

The Progress Party, upon taking office, prioritised reducing the large disparities alleged to exist between rural and urban living standards. However, the government did not forcefully use the tax side of fiscal policies for redistribution. It only made slight adjustments to the tax structure to make it more equitable and to liberalise imports.[74] Other mechanisms have to be called into play. The government restrained wages, imposed a national development levy on wages and salaries, and reduced the fringe benefits of public servants. Higher rents for government housing and reduced allowances cut the effective incomes of senior civil servants.[75] Together, these factors might have contributed to keeping inequality in check. On the expenditure side, redistribution entailed greater public investment in agriculture and rural development programmes. Many rural areas certainly benefited from government investments in water supplies, electricity, health services and feeder roads.[76]

As public expenditure soared and a large import boom led to an economic crisis, the government devalued the currency in December 1971. Although it increased the wages of low-earning government employees and the

69 The National Liberation Council, Budget Statement for 1966–67, 12.

70 The National Liberation Council, Budget Statement for 1966–67, 12–14; The National Liberation Council, Budget Statement for 1969–70, 26; Rimmer, *Staying Poor*, 114; Killick, *Development Economics in Action*, 334.

71 Naomi Chazan, *An Anatomy of Ghanaian Politics: Managing Political Recession, 1969–1982* (Boulder CO, 1983), 158–9; Whitfield, *Economies After Colonialism*, 92.

72 Edward N. Muller, 'Economic determinants of democracy', *American Sociological Review* 60:6 (1995), 966–82.

73 Killick, *Development Economics in Action*, 90.

74 Budget Statement for 1970–71, 44, 49.

75 Piet Konings, *The State and Rural Class Formation in Ghana: A Comparative Analysis* (London, 1986), 33; Killick, *Development Economics in Action*, 64, 72.

76 K. Armah, *Ghana: Nkrumah's Legacy* (London, 1974), 167.

cocoa-producer price by 25 per cent, the devaluation was unpopular, especially in urban areas.[77] Devaluation led to an increase in prices of imported commodities and negatively affected the real incomes of urban workers. In January 1972, the government was ousted from office in a military coup. Overall, the reallocation of resources to rural areas, together with declining real incomes among urban workers, may have helped to keep both aggregate income inequality and urban-rural inequality relatively low.

The succeeding military government, the National Redemption Council, took much more forceful steps to reduce rural–urban and regional inequalities through redistributive expenditures to ensure that the fruits of development 'accrue, in an equitable fashion, to all sections of the population and to all regions of the nation.'[78] Budgetary allocations to the agricultural sector increased and the government subsidised the costs of fertiliser and cutlasses, and waived custom duties on agricultural machinery. It also placed tax exemptions on income from cocoa, abolished taxes on farming enterprises' incomes in their early years of operation and increased public loans to agriculturally related projects.[79] These measures were presumably intended to increase rural incomes. Resources were reallocated from higher education to primary, middle, and technical training and health services were expanded in poorer regions. Although recurrent expenditures were still more favorable towards richer regions, capital expenditures were more sensitive to corrective equity. Overall, Acheampong's record on distributive and redistributive equity was much better than that of the first two post-independence governments.[80]

Ghana's economy declined after 1975 as government revenues shrank much faster than expenditures and living standards fell. Although the economy benefited from a temporary boom in cocoa prices between 1975 and 1978, these windfalls were poorly managed and did not translate into sustained improvements.[81] Earlier, the 1973 oil price shock worsened Ghana's balance of payments by sharply increasing oil import costs. The 1979–80 oil price surge

77 Killick (*Development Economics in Action*, 64) reports that the currency was devalued by 90 per cent in local currency terms. Rimmer (p. 94), however, gives a figure of 44 per cent against the US dollar. He further notes that the actual increase in import prices was mitigated by the simultaneous removal of import surcharges and charges on invisibles, reducing the effective devaluation on the import side by about 12 percentage points. While Killick focuses on the nominal exchange rate adjustment, Rimmer considers policy changes that affected the real burden of imports.

78 Guidelines for the Five-Year Development Plan 1975–80, 45, quoted in Donald Rothchild, 'Military regime performance: an appraisal of the Ghana experience, 1972–78', *Comparative Politics* 12:4 (1980), 459–79.

79 Rothchild, 'Military regime performance', 471; Chazan, *An Anatomy*, 164.

80 Rothchild, 'Military regime performance', 475.

81 Gareth Austin, 'Ghana and Kenya facing the 1970s commodity price shocks: the national and the global', in Shigeru Akita (ed.), *Oil Crises of the 1970s and the*

and falling cocoa prices further aggravated the situation, ultimately 'put[ting] the boot to an already prostrate economy.'[82] Gross Domestic Product (GDP) per capita declined by 16 per cent between 1974 and 1978.[83] Hardship increased and people adopted a beat-the-system approach to survival.[84] People engaged in various malpractices – the smuggling of Ghanaian products, hoarding, black marketeering, and exploiting regulated blackmarket price gaps – in order to evade controls or maximise gains. Successive governments between 1978 and early 1983 were unable to halt the economic decline and the economy spiraled into the abyss.[85]

The indirect evidence presented in this section supports a reasonable generalisation that inequality declined between 1960 and 1982. However, scholars differ on the extent of inequality during this period. Bequele, for instance, drawing on the 1970 Agricultural Census, estimates a Gini coefficient of 0.64 for land distribution.[86] He also cites Beckman's data showing that, in 1963–64, 15 per cent of cocoa farmers produced 54 per cent of total output, while the poorest 18 per cent produced just 2 per cent. Further, Buxton's figures, cited by Bequele, indicate that the bottom 16 per cent of cocoa farmers produced only 1.3 per cent of the output while the top 18.2 per cent accounted for 60.5 per cent. Combined with rising food prices relative to agricultural wages, Bequele concludes that economic inequality in rural Ghana increased significantly after 1970.[87]

On rural–urban inequality, Jackson argues that urban–rural income gaps fell as a result of rapid inflation from 1974/75 and with food prices rising faster than other prices.[88] Similarly, Tabatabai shows that between the 1970s and at least until 1983, there was substantial redistribution within both rural and urban areas between two main groups; in rural areas, from cocoa producers (and agricultural labourers) to food producers, and in urban areas, from wage

Transformation of International Order: Economy, Development and Aid in Asia and Africa (London, 2023), 223–56.

82 Robert M. Price, 'Neo-Colonialism and Ghana's Economic Decline: A Critical Assessment', *Canadian Journal of African Studies/La Revue canadienne des études africaines* 18:1 (1984), 163–94, at 174.

83 Killick, *Development Economics in Action*, 402.

84 Chazan, *An Anatomy*, 194–7.

85 Rimmer, *Staying Poor*, 133.

86 Assefa Bequele (*Poverty, Inequality and Stagnation: The Ghanaian Experience* (Geneva, 1980), 16) derives the Gini coefficient from the 1970 Agricultural Census, using data on the number of holdings by size class. Since the Census did not report total acreage per class, his estimates rely on assumptions about the normal distribution of farm sizes within each class. Farms over 50 acres were treated as the residual. He refers to the resulting table as an 'interpretation' of land distribution and qualifies the estimate accordingly.

87 Bequele, *Poverty*, 17–19. Bequele (p. 18) gives the reference T.K. Buxton, The Distribution of Cocoa Income Among the Producers: Some Policy Implications (Centre for Development Studies, University of Cape Coast, 1976), mimeo.

88 Dudley Jackson, *Rural-Urban Gap and Income Distribution (A Comparative Sub-Regional Study): The Case of Ghana* (Addis Ababa, 1982).

earners to traders.[89] Real wages and salaries fell by an annual average of 16 per cent between 1970 and 1983. In that same period, the real cocoa-producer price – deflated using rural consumer price indices – declined by an annual average of 11 per cent. Given the increasing overvaluation of the currency during this period, the actual loss in purchasing power for cocoa farmers may have been even greater. Austin adds that in 1977–78, the real producer price had fallen to only 41 per cent of its 1974–75 level, despite world prices nearly doubling.[90] For food farmers, Tabatabai suggests that while they may have experienced some decline in returns, it was far less severe than the losses faced by wage earners and cocoa producers. Wholesale food prices deflated by rural consumer price indices rose by 29.6 per cent between 1970–77.[91] Finally, 'traders did even better,' as their real returns increased at an annual rate of 2.5 per cent between 1970 and 1983.

Taken together, the evidence suggests that inequality in Ghana probably declined between 1961 and the early 1980s, largely as a result of government fiscal policies. However, the extent and consistency of this trend – particularly after the mid-1970s – remain open to debate. As poverty and deprivation deepened and living standards fell, food farmers, traders, and those engaged in rent-seeking activities fared best, or least badly.

Distributional Effects of Structural Adjustment, 1983–2000

In April 1983, the Provisional National Defence Council, a quasi-military regime that seized power in December 1981, launched an IMF-World Bank supported Structural Adjustment Programme (SAP) to reverse decades of economic decline. Scholars differ on the effects of structural adjustment on inequality in Ghana, although there is some consensus that it resulted in a more uneven distribution of wage and income in its initial phase.[92] Roe and Schneider suggest that there were more gainers than losers from the SAP, and that the rich were more affected – both negatively, through reduced subsidies and increased taxation on formal-sector incomes, and positively, through expanded private-sector opportunities and market liberalisation. It is therefore not unreasonable, they argue, to suggest that overall equity may have somewhat increased as a result of adjustment.[93] Similarly, Bawumia concludes

89 Hamid Tabatabai, 'Agricultural Decline and access to food in Ghana', *International Labour Review*, 127:6 (1988), 703–26, at 726.

90 Austin, 'Ghana and Kenya', 239–42; Austin, 'National Poverty', 567.

91 Tabatabai, 'Agricultural Decline', 712–13, 722, 725. Calculated from Tabatabai's table on p. 722. Figures are based on official Ghanaian statistics and World Bank data, with real incomes calculated by deflating nominal values using the consumer price index.

92 Hutchful, *Ghana's Adjustment Experience*, 89.

93 Alan Roe and Hartmud Schneider, *Adjustment and Equity in Ghana* (Paris, 1992), 118.

that between 1983 and 1992, rural households are more likely to have benefited most from the SAP because of the high prices they received from their products and improved infrastructure.[94]

Konadu-Agyemang offers a contrasting view, arguing that rural–urban and regional inequalities in income and access to social services widened.[95] We argue that tax reforms during structural adjustment affected income distribution through price changes, but also more directly through tax cuts and exemptions that disproportionately benefited higher-income earners – primarily senior public servants, military officers, urban professionals and business elites. Although the number of individuals in this category was relatively small, they nonetheless stood to gain the most from reductions in top marginal tax rates and from import liberalisation measures that allowed access to goods and capital.

Structural reforms sought to restructure the tax system and expenditures to strengthen economic incentives for increased production and investment. After 1985, tax reforms were broadened to enhance the efficiency of tax administration and the equity of the tax system. On direct taxes, the government reduced corporate tax rates and by 1994 all rates had been reduced from 50–55 per cent to 35 per cent.[96] Government also reformed exemptions and tax brackets to reduce the progressivity of personal income taxes, which had been considered a major incentive for non-compliance.[97] However, improvements in tax administration after 1983 may have expanded the number of income tax payers. If compliance increased and more individuals entered the tax net, the overall effect of income tax on progressivity may have been more balanced than the rate cuts alone suggest. In the case of indirect taxes, the government integrated ad-hoc excise duties on many mass-consumption manufactured goods into a broadened sales tax.[98] The general sales tax rate was increased from 10 per cent to 20 per cent in 1987, and subsequently raised to 25 per cent, before being reduced to 22.5 per cent in 1989 and 17.5 per cent in 1991.[99] The government also reduced the 'tax' on cocoa farmers and other commodity producers, and

94 Mahamudu Bawumia, 'Understanding the rural-urban voting patterns in the 1992 Ghanaian presidential election: A closer look at the distributional impact of Ghana's Structural Adjustment Programme', *Journal of Modern African Studies* 36:1 (1998), 47–70.

95 Kwadwo Konadu-Agyemang, 'The best of times and the worst of times: Structural Adjustment programs and uneven development in Africa: the case of Ghana', *The Professional Geographer* 52:3 (2000), 469–83.

96 Newman Kwadwo Kusi, *Tax Reform and Revenue Productivity in Ghana* (Nairobi, 1998), 18.

97 Roe and Schneider, *Adjustment and Equity*, 75.

98 *Ibid.*

99 Kusi, *Tax Reform*, 20.

real producer prices for cocoa farmers almost quadrupled between the agricultural years of 1982/83 and 1987/88.[100]

The extent to which the tax side of governments affected the distribution of income can be assessed by examining the expenditure patterns of various socio-economic groups and the relative retail prices of food and non-food consumer goods. Roe and Schneider suggest that fiscal policies may have had progressive effects because food and other taxed items – some of which were considered luxury goods – constituted a larger share of the expenditure budgets of richer households than of poorer ones.[101] However, this interpretation is complicated by the composition of non-food expenditures. While food expenditures dominated the budgets of all households,[102] non-food goods and services, many of which were also subject to tax increases, made up a significant portion of the spending of poor households. Between 1983 and 1987, non-food prices rose by nearly 300 per cent, compared to a 64 per cent increase in food prices. These relative price changes arguably favoured richer households and urban food consumers, who were better positioned to absorb the price shocks or benefit from shifting market conditions.[103] In rural areas, rising cocoa prices benefited some farmers, but only a minority of the rural poor, around 19 per cent, were engaged in cocoa production.[104] Moreover, the removal of subsidies on farm inputs in 1990 further disadvantaged poorer farmers. Low-income farming households spent nearly 6 per cent of their agricultural income on inputs, while wealthier households spent less than 2 per cent. As such, the subsidy removal had a regressive effect, disproportionately burdening the rural poor.[105]

On the expenditure side, some positive welfare effects were achieved but were unevenly distributed between rural and urban areas and between regions. Unlike other African countries, Ghana's adjustment programme did not require major cuts in overall expenditures.[106] Government spending on education, health and social welfare as a share of GDP increased from 2.3 per cent in 1983 to 5.8 per cent in 1989, and from 29.1 per cent of total government expenditure in 1983 to 41.7 per cent in 1989.[107] However, much spending on education and health does not necessarily benefit the poor unless much of the outlays are directed towards basic education and preventive health care. Admittedly, government expenditures in basic education and health care increased and the primary school enrolment rate for example, increased from 65 per cent in 1987 to 72 per cent

100 Roe and Schneider, *Adjustment and Equity*, 75.
101 *Ibid.*, 111, 123.
102 Hutchful, *Ghana's Adjustment Experience*, 120.
103 Roe and Schneider, *Adjustment and Equity*, 114; Bawumia, 'Understanding', 61.
104 Konadu-Agyemang, 'The best of times', 480.
105 Roe and Schneider, *Adjustment and Equity*, 112.
106 Hutchful, *Ghana's Adjustment Experience*.
107 Bawumia, 'Understanding', 61.

in 1991 and expenditures on health, housing, electricity and water, and other social services provided large benefits to the poor.[108] Many roads, railways and highways were rehabilitated, facilitating the transport of exportable products from the hinterlands to the ports and enhancing market integration within Ghana. Certainly, these improvements in transport facilities positively affected rural incomes.

Nevertheless, other aspects of expenditure reforms had adverse effects on the poor. User fees and other charges were introduced in health, education and water. In the health sector, steeper increases in the costs of health services followed an initial round of increases in 1985 and a cash and carry system with increased charges for drugs and curative services was implemented in all regions by 1992. Increases in funding for hospitals improved health care delivery but this did not always mean the poor had greater access to health services.[109] The introduction of user fees led to a decline in hospital and clinic visits in both urban and rural areas.[110] In Ghana's capital, Accra, there was an instant drop of 25–50 per cent in hospital and clinic visits and in some rural areas, it was 45–80 per cent in the first eight months of the implementation of the 'pay as you use' system.[111] Declines in the use of out-patient services in government hospitals continued throughout the 1990s.[112] On education, the government restructured educational spending to direct more funding from tertiary to primary education. Gross primary enrolment increased from 68 per cent in 1988–89 to 72 per cent in 1989–90.[113] However, significant barriers remained, including teacher shortages, inadequate infrastructure, and the burden of indirect costs such as uniforms, supplies, and fees, all of which disproportionately affected rural and low-income households.

Further, capital expenditures on health, education and other social services were biased against rural areas and the northern regions of the country. Rural–urban and regional inequalities in the provision of health services were reinforced under SAP. For example, urban areas with one third of the population received 42 per cent of health spending in 1989; this increased to 48.7 per cent in 1992.[114] Access to education continued to be unequal between urban and rural areas and between regions.[115]

Another major government spending policy that affected income distribution was the increase in real wages of public-sector employees. The salaries of senior

108 *Ibid.*

109 Hutchful, *Ghana's Adjustment Experience*, 129.

110 Bawumia ('Understanding', 66) argues that rural households relied more on traditional sources of medicine so they might not have been affected by the increases in hospital user fees but provides no evidence to back this claim.

111 Konadu-Agyemang, 'The best of times', 478.

112 Hutchful, *Ghana's Adjustment Experience*, 130.

113 *Ibid.*, 132.

114 *Ibid.*, 119, 130.

115 Konadu-Agyemang, 'The best of times', 478–80.

civil servants were more than tripled between 1983 and 1988 while those of unskilled labour increased only by 50 per cent. The ratio of the highest to the lowest salary in the civil service increased from 2.5:1 in 1984 to 9.5:1 in 1990.[116] While the real minimum wage increased from an index of 54 in 1983 to 117 by 1992, real public-sector earnings increased from an index of 48 in 1983 to 270 by 1992.[117] The rise in incomes for civil servants might have improved the well-being of many households but the increase in wages and salaries came on the back of retrenchments in the public sector. More than 300,000 public sector employees lost their jobs during the implementation of SAPs.[118]

There are no income Ginis for this period and consumption-inequality trends from earlier surveys and recent inequality estimates suggest that inequality might have indeed started increasing from the SAP era, although overall welfare might have improved and poverty levels declined. Consumption-inequality Ginis rose from 35.3 in 1987 to 40.1 in 1998 and 42.8 in 2005.[119] Since consumption Ginis generally show lower inequality than income Ginis, the extent of inequality could be higher. Already in the late 1980s, rural residents were on average found to be worse off than urban residents.[120] In 1988, recognising that the economic recovery programme would increase the economic challenges of certain vulnerable groups, the World Bank and the government drew up the Programme of Actions to Mitigate the Social Costs of Adjustment. As a result of poor administration and poor targeting the programme was largely unable to alleviate the plight of retrenched workers and low-income urban and rural households.[121] Between 1992 and 1998 regional disparities in public spending in health and education were still noticeable and overall initial high public expenditures in social sectors were not sustained.[122]

Conclusion

This chapter has examined the distributional consequences of government fiscal policy in Ghana from the late nineteenth century to the end of the twentieth, contributing to the growing but still limited body of work on the intersection

116 Roe and Schneider, *Adjustment and Equity*, 113.
117 Bawumia, 'Understanding', 65.
118 Konadu-Agyemang, 'The best of times', 474–80.
119 World Bank, 'Gini index-Ghana', 2025.
120 Paul Glewwe and Kwaku A. Twum-Baah, *The Distribution of Welfare in Ghana, 1987–88*. World Bank Living Standards Measurement Study Working Paper (Washington DC, 1991), 75.
121 Lynne Brydon and Karen Legge, *Adjusting Society: The World Bank and Ghana* (London, 1996).
122 Sudharshan Canagarajah and Xiao Ye, '*Public Health and Education Spending in Ghana in 1992–98: Issues of Equity and Efficiency*', Policy Research Working Paper 2579 (Washington DC, 2001).

between taxation, public spending, and inequality in sub-Saharan Africa. Ghana's fiscal history provides a compelling lens through which to understand the constraints and contradictions of redistribution in a post-colonial export-oriented economy.

In the early colonial period (1891–1940), fiscal policy was largely minimalist and extractive, with little concern for equity. Inequality remained at relatively high but constant levels as state expenditure – limited as it was – flowed disproportionately to colonial officials, urban elites, and producers of export commodities. Between 1941 and 1960, although expenditures increased and took on a more developmental character, they remained concentrated in sectors and regions tied to export production. Redistribution was minimal, and inequality persisted. The post-independence period (1961–1982) saw an intensification of state intervention. Redistribution occurred not through the expansion of progressive taxation or targeted welfare spending, but largely through the extraction of cocoa surpluses and the erosion of real wages. This paradoxical form of redistribution – achieved by compressing incomes across the board – resulted in a decline in measured inequality, but not necessarily in an improvement in welfare. After 1983, with the onset of structural adjustment, fiscal policies shifted again – tax reforms and public spending patterns disproportionately benefited urban and higher-income groups. Inequality began to rise once more.

Ghana's experience reflects broader patterns across the continent. As in many African countries, efforts at redistribution have been hampered by narrow tax bases, weak administrative capacity, and over-dependence on a few primary exports. Social spending is often pro-cyclical and regressive in effect. Even when governments have aimed at equity, the instruments at their disposal have been politically constrained. What redistribution occurs often comes through implicit rather than explicit mechanisms – through controlled prices, marketing boards, and public-sector wages – rather than through sustained, progressive tax-and-transfer systems.

In sum, Ghana's fiscal history highlights the structural limitations of redistribution in African economies shaped by colonial legacies and post-independence policy choices that often prioritised short-term political gains over long-term strategies for inclusive growth. Without sustained economic transformation and stronger institutional frameworks, fiscal policy has served more as a mechanism of resource extraction and patronage rather than as a tool for sustained equity. Redistribution, when it occurred, was often temporary and rarely pro-poor.

3

From Mine Workers to *Kayayei*: National Inequality Regimes and Transformation in Northern Migrant Labour in Asante, *c*. 1896–*c*. 2011

George M. Bob-Milliar and Manuel J. Manu-Osafo

Migrations have always been part of life in Africa, and Ghana is no exception.[1] The movement of people and goods from northern to southern Ghana existed long before the heights of cocoa and gold mining in the colonial period. For instance, Wangara merchants migrated to trade in shea butter, leather goods, local cloth, and livestock.[2] However, this changed in the seventeenth century. The beginning of large-scale state formation in the forest zone of the South coincided with exponential increases in slave trading. New states such as Denkyera, Asante, and Akwamu actively participated in the slave trade to finance further expansion, especially through warfare.[3] The slave trade and ensuing wars created chaos which suppressed peaceful economic activity in the north. The British occupation of the area in 1896 led to the disruption of slavery activities. Subsequently, in 1908 when the Northern Territories (NTs) were designated as a protectorate, slavery was officially prohibited.[4]

The colonial government was focused on the provision of transport infrastructure to support the productive and more profitable sectors of the economy

1 For instance see chapters 2, 3, 8, 11, 13, and 14 of Michiel de Haas and Ewout Frankema (eds), *Migration in Africa: Shifting Patterns of Mobility from the 19th to the 21st Centuries* (London, 2022); Samantha R. Lattof, Philomena Nyarko, Ernestina Coast and Tiziana Leone, 'Contemporary female migration in Ghana: analyses of the 2000 and 2010 censuses', *Demographic Research* 39:44 (2018), 1181–226.

2 Ivor Wilks, 'Wangara, Akan and Portuguese in the fifteenth and sixteenth Centuries. I. The matter of Bitu', *Journal of African History* 23:3 (1982), 333–49; Wilks, 'Wangara, Akan and Portuguese in the fifteenth and sixteenth centuries. II. The struggle for trade', *Journal of African History* 23:4 (1982): 463–72.

3 For an overview, see Kwame Arhin, 'The financing of the Ashanti expansion (1700–1820)', *Africa: Journal of the International African Institute* 37:3 (1967), 283–91.

4 See Benjamin W. Kankpeyeng, 'The slave trade in northern Ghana: landmarks, legacies and connections', *Slavery & Abolition* 30:2 (2009), 209–21. On the history of the slave trade see Benedict G. Der, *The Slave Trade in Northern Ghana* (Accra, 1998).

in the Colony and Ashanti.[5] With no known exploitable commodities, the NTs could not justfy investment in transport infrastructure. However, its labour was required to support economic production in southern parts of the country. The general direction of state labour policies suggest that the government reserved the NTs as the source of labour for industries in the south. Thus, between the 1910s and 1930s recruiters were encouraged to mobilise young men from the north to work in mining, especially in Asante. The state's socio-economic underinvestment in the NTs compelled many young men to migrate south in search of gainful employment.[6] This situation was also influenced by northerners' desire for European goods like cloth and the introduction of a colonial monetary regime based on coinage to purchase such goods. Since there were few economic activities to earn cash, people migrated south for work.[7]

The historiography on Asante's colonial economy emphasises the push-pull factors that attracted young men from the NTs to trek south for work on cocoa farms, gold and manganese mines, railways, and other manual labour.[8] Despite the diversity of studies on this north–south migration, very few works examine the local Asante conditions within which northern migrant labour occurred.[9] What welfare conditions did the migrants meet on arrival in Asante?

5 See Kwamina B. Dickson, *A Historical Geography of Ghana* (Cambridge, 1969); Adu Boahen, *Ghana: Evolution and Change in the Nineteenth and Twentieth Centuries* (London, 1975).

6 Nii K. Plange, 'Underdevelopment in northern Ghana: natural causes and colonial capitalism?', *Review of African Political Economy*, 6:15–16 (1979), 4–14.

7 While most of the literature emphasises the state's role in pushing northerners south, Nicholas Van Hear offers compelling discussion of voluntary factors which influenced the decision to migrate south: 'Child labour and the development of capitalist agriculture in Ghana', *Development and Change* 13:4 (1982), 503. For the context of colonial Northern Ghana's monetary regime, see Domenico Cristofaro, '"Here there is no Gold Standard. Cows are the Standard": multiple currencies, colonial taxation and the monetary transition in Upper Ghana (1896–1936)', in Karin Pallaver (ed.) *Monetary Transitions: Currencies, Colonialism and African Societies* (Cham, 2021), 31–53.

8 For the historical context of colonial policy decisions which provoked north–south migrations, see A. Nyaaba and George Bob-Milliar, 'The economic potentials of northern Ghana: the ambivalence of the colonial and post-colonial states to develop the North', *African Economic History* 47:2 (2019), 45–67; see also Mariama Marciana Kuusaana, 'Migration and the production of informal economies in the Gold Coast', *African Economic History* 47:2 (2019), 68–83. While the literature on north–south migration emphasises exploitation, there is also evidence that at least by the second decade of colonial rule in Asante northern workers had begun to bargain their way to better contracts which allowed them to improve their income, living conditions, conjugal relations, and standards of health, see Gareth Austin, *Labour, Land and Capital in Ghana: From Slavery to Free Labour in Asante, 1807–1957* (Rochester NY, 2005), 412–30.

9 Notable exceptions include Nicholas Van Hear, 'Northern Labour and the Development of Capitalist Agriculture in Ghana' (Ph.D. dissertation, University of Birmingham, 1982); Van Hear, 'Child Labour'; Austin, *Labour*, 205–52, 504–15.

How did they seek redress for unfair labour conditions? Did British officials and the Asante see them as expendable labour or citizens with equal rights? In that regard, how did state officials and mining companies react to strikes by migrant labourers?[10] What policy positions did Asante chiefs assume, given their much older relationship with northerners, and how did these positions reinforce colonial state policies on northern migrant labour?

This essay uses archival records from the Kumase branch of Ghana's Public Records and Archives Administration Department, various government inquiry reports, population census data, and extant literature to make its contentions.[11] It posits that there was a racial and ethnic hierarchy of persons in colonial Asante, which government labour policies reinforced to the detriment of northern migrant labourers. This uneven hierarchy was inherited from the slavery-based social structure of pre-colonial Asante. It manifested itself in the labourers' work and living conditions, and generally constitutes a case of what Frankema, de Haas, and van Waijenburg have recently described as 'inequality regimes' at national and regional levels, where long-term distributions of wealth and economic value are held in people [and their labour], and not just in objects and financial capital.[12]

The chapter further contends that post-colonial Ghanaian governments have been unable to dismantle this socio-political hierarchy and the inequality regime it birthed owing to local and global socio-economic conditions. This has led to a recent phenomenon known as *kayayei*, where young northern girls migrate to serve as head-porters in Asante's markets. The essay therefore seeks to offer local evidence-based analysis of 'inequality regimes' in the Ghanaian context. It does this by tracing the fate of northern migrant labourers in Asante from the pre-colonial through the colonial to the post-colonial era.

The essay sets out its arguments in three sections. The next section offers the historical context of Ghana's labour migrations and the inequality regime

10 For the wider Gold Coast context of the experiences of northern labourers in mining, see Jeff Crisp, *The Story of an African Working Class: Ghanaian Miners' Struggles, 1870–1980* (London, 1984), 35–55. For commentary on labourers' relationship with mining companies in the late colonial period, see Ayowa Afrifa Taylor, 'An Economic History of the Ashanti Goldfields Corporation, 1895–2004: Land, Labour, Capital and Enterprise' (Ph.D. dissertation, London School of Economics, 2006), 189–221.

11 For insights into the contents of the Kumase branch of the Public Records and Archives Administration Department (henceforth PRAAD-Kumase), see Manuel Manu-Osafo, George Bob-Milliar and Ben Jones, 'Urban history in Kumase, Ghana: a note on archives,' *History in Africa* 51 (2025), 189–202; G. Austin, 'The Kumase branch of the National Archives of Ghana: a situation report and introduction for prospective users,' *History in Africa* 13 (1986), 383–9; and Samuel Aniegye Ntewusu, 'Serendipity: Conducting Research on Social History in Ghana's Archives', *History in Africa*, 41 (2014), 417–23.

12 Ewout Frankema, Michiel de Haas and Marlous van Waijenburg, 'Inequality regimes in Africa from pre-colonial times to the present', *African Affairs* 122:486 (2023), 57–94.

which sustains these migrations. The section after that examines case studies from colonial Asante's three main industries: cocoa, mining, and the railways. Through these case studies the essay outlines how the colonial state perpetuated the inequality regimes it inherited from the pre-colonial Asante state. The final section examines how northern labour migration transformed in the 1990s from male migrants in cocoa and mining to female head porters in Asante's markets. The essay concludes with an overview of the implications of Ghana's inequality regime for northern migrant labourers.

Northern Migrant Labour and Ghana's Inequality Regime: the Historical Context

Studies conducted in the 1960s and 1970s on labour migration were highly development-oriented.[13] Like many developing countries, Ghana has the problem of uneven development and inequitable distribution of basic social amenities between rural and urban areas. Facilities for higher education, quality healthcare, major sports and entertainment facilities, telecommunication, and the modern economy are all concentrated in the big cities such as Accra, Kumase, and Takoradi.[14] Dualism and disparities in development were inherited from the colonial state.

Historically, the movement of people from northern Ghana to Asante and other southern areas had been ongoing since pre-colonial times.[15] Population movements were, at the time, in part dictated by the search for fertile land, flight from internecine warfare, slave raids, and for trade.[16] Northern Ghana's strategic middle geographic location enhanced its control of the prosperous

13 See, for example, T.E. Hilton, 'Depopulation and population movement in the Upper Region of Ghana', *Bulletin of the Ghana Geographical Association* 11:1 (1966), 27–47; J.M. Hunter, 'Population pressure in a part of the West Africa savanna: a study of Nangodi, North East Ghana,' *Annals of Association of American Geographers* 57:1 (1967), 101–14; N.K. Plange, '"Opportunity cost" and labour migration: a misinterpretation of proletarianisation in northern Ghana', *Journal of Modern African Studies* 17:4 (1979), 655–76; Roger Thomas, 'Forced labour in British West Africa: the case of the Northern Territories of the Gold Coast, 1900–1927', *Journal of African History* 14:1 (1973), 79–103.

14 John Anarfi and Stephen Kwankye, 'Migration from and to Ghana: A Background Paper', University of Sussex, Development Research Centre on Migration, Globalisation and Poverty (Falmer, UK, 2003).

15 See Jack Goody, 'A note on the penetration of Islam into the West of the Northern Territories of the Gold Coast', *Transactions of the Gold Coast and Togo Historical Society* 1:2 (1953), 45–6; Ivor Wilks, 'The northern factor in Ashanti history: Begho and the Mande', *Journal of African History* 2:1 (1961), 25–34.

16 See Kankpeyeng, 'The slave trade in northern Ghana'; Der, *The Slave Trade in Northern Ghana*.

Kumasi-Kong-Djenne trans-Saharan caravan trade route.[17] The control of the flourishing kola nut trade and the collection of caravan tolls on cattle being sent to the south boosted the relative commercial status of towns in northern Ghana.[18] The resultant booming economy attracted people and merchants from both the Western Sudan and southern Ghana to trade in kola nuts, shea butter, livestock, salt, and fish.[19]

The southward migration of people increased with the arrival of British colonialists. The entry of colonialists and missionaries, along with the subsequent interactions with the local populations, became a significant factor for the ongoing labour migration to southern Ghana. This movement was further supported by a rise in the mining sector, following a temorary decline in gold production in South Africa due to the Boer War. As a result, there was a substantial demand for labour in the mines and plantations of the south.[20]

K. B. Dickson, reflecting on the labour migration situation in northern Ghana, notes that 'young men in northern Ghana were more attracted to the gold mines and cacao farms in Ashanti and southern Ghana than to the cotton farms' of the north.[21] In view of these culminating events, the colonial government identified and developed the NTs as labour recruitment centres to feed the mining and export agriculture concentrated in the south. This was done by way of deliberately dislodging indigenous self-sufficient peasant communities and livelihoods as a way of precipitating migration from agrarian societies in the north.[22] Colonial capitalist predatory inducements ensured the constant provision of cheap and hardworking labour for their economic establishments in the south.[23]

This began in 1906 after a carefully selected group of young men from all over the NTs were taken on a conducted tour of the gold mines, where they were highly impressed by the decent and higher standards of living enjoyed by the mining employees. A consequence of this was the subsequent abandoning of farms and unprecedented migration of economically active people from rural communities to the south to work in the mines.[24] Besides the recruitment

17 K.B. Dickson, 'Background to the problem of economic development in northern Ghana', *Annals of the Association of American Geographers*, 58:4 (1968), 686–96.

18 Kwame Arhin, *West African Traders in Ghana in the Nineteenth and Twentieth Centuries* (London, 1979).

19 Dickson, 'Background to the problem'.

20 Raymond E. Dumett, *El Dorado In West Africa: The Gold Mining Frontier, African Labor, and Colonial Capitalism* (Athens OH, 1999).

21 Dickson, 'Background to the problem', 690.

22 Plange, '"Opportunity cost" and labour migration: a misinterpretation'.

23 Jacob Songsore, *Regional Development in Ghana: the Theory and the Reality* (Accra, 2011).

24 See Mariama Marciana Kuusaana, 'Colonial labour policy and north–south migration in Ghana', *Journal of West African History* 8:2 (2022), 1–16; Mariama Marciana Kuusaana,

of northern labourers into the south's mining and agricultural sites, there were other factors that accounted for the continuous north–south migration. The NTs were characterised by isolation, neglect, and indifference by British policy design.[25]

The British government nevertheless took practical steps to integrate the north into the economy of the Gold Coast. These included encouraging trade with the rest of the country, collecting taxes on the caravan routes, establishing markets for European products, and introducing token currencies. After integrating the economy of the region with the rest of the country, they anticipated that the economic potentials of the region would gradually be realised. However, these economic policies did not save the region from comparative economic stagnation. The colonial administration failed to tap into the economic potential of the region, hence the delay in educational advancement and provision of few social amenities for the area. The area thus became a natural reservoir of labour for the rest of the country.

The colonial administration implemented a number of development programmes including mechanised agriculture to turn the fortunes of the area, but many development schemes proved unsuccessful.[26] Nevertheless, some physical developments were undertaken. For example, construction of roads was left to individual district officers, who relied on free and customary labour via chiefs.[27] Inadequate social amenities and educational advancement constrained the north. These policy decisions reinforced inequality regimes in existence since pre-colonial days.

In much of pre-colonial Gold Coast wealth was stored in people as it was in physical objects and financial capital.[28] Southern states such as Asante prospered in the eighteenth and nineteenth centuries because they could extract from northern tributary states slaves to man their armies for further wars of expansion, to mine gold, to farm cash crop and food plantations, and to be sold on the trans-Atlantic slave market in exchange for international trade goods such as guns, liquor, and exotic cloth.[29]

'A Historical Perspective of Migration from Northern Ghana to Asante, 1900–1955 (Ph.D. dissertation, KNUST, Kumasi, 2009).

25 N.J.K. Brukum, 'The Northern Territories of the Gold Coast under British Colonial Rule, 1897–1956: A Study in Political Change' (Ph.D. dissertation, University of Toronto, 1996).

26 Jeff D. Grischow, *Shaping Tradition: Civil Society, Community and Development in Colonial Northern Ghana, 1899–1957* (Leiden, 2005).

27 See Alice Wiemers, '"When the Chief takes an interest": development and the reinvention of "communal" labour in Northern Ghana, 1935–60', *Journal of African History* 59:2 (2017), 239–57; Wiemers, '"It is all he can do to cope with the roads in his own District": labor, community, and development in Northern Ghana, 1919–1936', *International Labor and Working-Class History* 92 (2017), 89–113.

28 Frankema et al., 'Inequality Regimes', 38.

29 See Arhin, 'Financing of the Ashanti expansion'.

We theorise that centuries of such socio-political relations between the northern and southern Gold Coast entrenched north–south inequality patterns. This perpetuated and calcified stereotypical perceptions by inhabitants of the two regions of each other, especially in ways of being, levels of civilisation, and 'social usefulness'.[30] In other words, northerners were cast as inferior to their southern counterparts. These deeply held socio-cultural perceptions were embraced by the British.[31] This influenced the socio-economic conditions that northern migrant labourers encountered in the south. In the next section we focus on colonial Asante, where rich and detailed archival records give us an idea of the unequal socio-political regime northern migrant labourers toiled under.

Northern Migrant Labour in Colonial Asante

The British toppled the government of Asantehene Prempeh I in 1896 and exiled him to the Seychelles Islands.[32] One of their main justifications for this coup was the eradication of slavery in Asante.[33] The Asante state was a key factor in the capture and sale of slaves in the Gold Coast. The institution of slavery therefore persisted in Asante society despite the ending of the slave trade in 1807. Northern slaves in Asante were designated as *nnɔnkɔ* (plural; singular: *dɔnkɔ*. According to studies by Wilks, Klein, Perbi and Austin, *nnɔnkɔ* occupied the lowest rungs of the Asante social structure.[34] They served in various capacities such as domestic servants, farmhands, mine boys, and head porters. They were also used as ritual oblations upon the death

30 See T.C. McCaskie, *State and Society and Society in Pre-Colonial Asante* (Cambridge, 1995), 93–101, especially n.61. See also Ivor Wilks, 'Consul Dupuis and Wangara: a window on Islam in early nineteenth-century Asante', *Sudanic Africa* 6 (1995), 55–72.

31 Sarah Balakrishnan, 'Imperial policing and the antinomies of power in early colonial Ghana', *International Journal of African Historical Studies* 53:2 (2020), 173–93; David Killingray, 'Imagined martial communities: recruiting for the military and police in colonial Ghana, 1860–1960', in Carola Lentz and Paul Nugent (eds), *Ethnicity in Ghana: The Limits of Invention* (Basingstoke, 2000), 119–36.

32 On Prempe's exile, see Joseph K. Adjaye, 'Asantehene Agyeman Prempe I and British colonization of Asante: a reassessment', *International Journal of African Historical Studies* 22:2 (1989), 223–49; Emmanuel Akyeampong, 'Christianity, modernity and the weight of tradition in the life of "Asantehene" Agyeman Prempeh I, c. 1888–1931', *Africa: Journal of the International African Institute* 69: 2 (1999), 279–311.

33 See Ivor Wilks, 'Asante at the end of the nineteenth century: setting the record straight', *Ghana Studies* 3 (2000), 13–59.

34 Ivor Wilks, *Asante in the Nineteenth Century: the Structure and Evolution of a Political Order* (Cambridge, 1975); A. Norman Klein, 'The two Asantes: competing interpretations of "slavery" in Akan-Asante culture and society', in Paul E. Lovejoy (ed.), *The Ideology of Slavery in Africa* (Beverly Hills CA, 1981), 149–67; Akosua Perbi, *A History of Indigenous Slavery in Ghana: From the 15th to the 19th Century* (Accra, 2004); Austin, *Labour*, 114–34, 483–90.

of high-ranking officeholders.[35] Given the centrality of the slavery question in British justifications for their takeover of Asante, one would have expected emancipation to follow immediately the 1896 overthrow of the Asante state. However, that did not happen. Despite disapproving British rhetoric on slavery, the colonial government allowed it to continue till 1908.[36] Even when slavery was eventually abolished, northern migrant labour remained a core part of the early colonial Asante economy. Why did this situation persist for so long?

British men on the spot offered several justifications for why slavery could not be expeditiously outlawed in Asante. Some argued that ending slavery would be a catastrophic blow to the financial power of Asante elites through whom the British effected indirect rule.[37] Weakening such elites would therefore affect the colonial state's power. They surmised that the institution would gradually fade away on its own as legitimate enterprises strengthened the colonial order and slave masters obtained the means of paying the wages free workers demanded.[38] Some even contrasted Asante elites with their Western counterparts who received monetary compensation for their emancipated slaves.[39] Asante slave owners needed more time to come to terms with their losses since they were getting no compensation.

Other officials considered the security implications of emancipation for the colonial state.[40] They contended that it was likely that many of the thousands of freed slaves bore grudges against their former masters. In addition, the former slaves had no lands of their own to live off and would thus constitute an enormous threat to social cohesion and security. Ending slavery would therefore lead to revolts by resentful owners or rootless slaves. They pointed to the colonial state's grossly undermanned and weakened security apparatus, which had itself been seriously undermined by the shock of the Yaa Asantewaa revolt in 1900.[41] Full emancipation therefore had to wait until such a time when security could be guaranteed.

35 See Clifford Williams, 'Asante: human sacrifice or capital punishment? An assessment of the period 1807–1874', *International Journal of African Historical Studies* 21:3 (1988), 433–41; Ivor Wilks, 'Asante: human sacrifice or capital punishment? A rejoinder,' *International Journal of African Historical Studies* 21: 3 (1988), 443–52.

36 See Austin, *Labour*, 206–12, 505–6.

37 Austin, *Labour*, 207–11, 505–6.

38 That eventually happened, as Austin points out: *Labour*, 315–21, 527–9.

39 Austin, *Labour*, 208, 505.

40 *Ibid.*, 210, 506. To compare colonial officials' defence of slavery in Asante with a similar situation in India, see Ranajit Guha, *Dominance without Hegemony: History and Power in Colonial India* (London, 1997), 28–9.

41 On the Yaa Asantewaa War, see A. Adu Boahen, *Yaa Asantewaa and the Asante-British War of 1900–1* (Oxford, 2003); S. Ukpabi, 'The British Colonial Office approach to the Ashanti War of 1900,' *African Studies Review* 13:3 (1970), 363–80.

Despite these apparently 'social' reasons, British officials counted the true cost of emancipation in economic terms. The purpose of the colonial enterprise was to exploit Asante's landed and natural resources (the broad forest rent in Austin's terminology). Asante had an abundance of gold and, from the 1910s, cocoa.[42] Gold mining had been worked under the previous dispensation by northern slave labour and slave labour was used in the take-off stages of cocoa farming. Without such a workforce, none of the labour-intensive sectors would survive.[43] This was the conundrum British officials faced. How could they free northern slaves yet continue to exploit northerners' toil for state benefit? The solution was to design policies which emphasised the north as the Gold Coast's labour pool. The NTs were deliberately underdeveloped to coerce young men to migrate south in search of gainful employment.[44] Recruiters were licensed to raise gangs of labourers in the NTs for mining companies.[45] Gangs usually numbered one hundred or more individuals. Northern chiefs were also incentivised to send men south for work. As shown above, these processes are well documented in both the Asante archive and historiography. But what employment conditions did the men meet upon their arrival in Asante's gold and manganese mines, cocoa farms, and railway tracks?

Mining

Gold and manganese mines in early 1920s Asante were at serious risk of collapse. Apprehensive mine bosses exchanged anxious correspondence with government officials: labour for their mines had suddenly dried up! Northern labourers were dying at high rates and replacements could not be found fast enough.[46] Frantic requests for labour recruits were sent to the French

42 See Austin, *Labour*, 253–77, 515–21.

43 This statement needs qualifying as the sectors mentioned here eventually adapted to changing times, as Austin correctly argues. They successfully moved from northern slave labour to free labour. The point, therefore, is not to argue that the lot of northerners did not improve, but rather that the improvement of their material and fiscal accumulation via means such as better negotiated sharecropping contracts did not lead to a greater share in the ownership of the overall enterprise. A greater share in the enterprise would have led to true emancipation in every sense of the word. For more on this, see Austin, *Labour*, 412–30, 542–5.

44 Nyaaba and Bob-Milliar, 'Economic potentials'; Kuusaana, 'Migration'.

45 See for example PRAAD-Kumase, ARG 1/37/3: Minutes of interview between the Governor and Mr Cogill, Secretary for Mines, at Coomassie, 30 April 1920; District Commissioner, Wa, to Chief Commissioner of Ashanti (henceforth CCA), 27 November 1921; Secretary of Mines to Chief Commissioner of Asante, 22 February 1922.

46 Surprisingly, as is explained below, mining bosses were conjecturally aware of the high death rates but kept no statistics and were therefore unable to say with surety the number of labourers that had died.

administrations in Côte d'Ivoire and Burkina Faso without success.[47] Lacking options, the government quickly engaged Sir W. J. Simpson, colonial expert on tropical medicine, to investigate the causes of the high death rates of northern labourers in Asante's mines.[48] They hoped that solutions he might proffer would help restore the workforce for the mining companies. His report, dated 29 September 1924, highlighted the poor conditions in which northern migrant labourers worked.[49]

Simpson's research was frustrated by the lack of statistics on morbidity and mortality in the various mines. Although there was universal agreement by mine bosses and colonial officials on northern labourers' high mortality, the lack of statistics made the situation appear more anecdotal than scientific. Why had none of the officials bothered to keep any figures on the deaths of miners? Simpson speculated that it was because the labourers 'come and go as they please, and there is no means of knowing the reason for going whether it is due to sickness or other cause.'[50]

The British government was displeased by the lack of data, with the secretary of state for the colonies, J.H. Thomas, lamenting that:

> the Colonial Government has been very inadequately supplied in the past with information on the health of the labourers employed in the mines, and it is only after repeated inquires that I have succeeded in obtaining trustworthy information. [It has been difficult] to elicit the facts with regard to the mortality of the mine[r]s, and that there was apparently so little readiness to realize the gravity of the situation. Accurate figures are of vital importance in any attempt to control mortality, but this does not appear to have been realized.[51]

In such a situation, facts threatened to give way to speculation.

Simpson's investigations covered the gold mines at Obuasi, Abosso, and Tarkwa, and the manganese mine at Nsuta. His first observation was that none of the mines had sanitary regimes in place to protect the workers. Neither were there any special recruitment processes for checking the labourers'

47 PRAAD-Kumase, ARG 1/37/3: Governor-General, Dakar, to Governor, Gold Coast, 9 September 1920.

48 For further context, see Akwasi Kwarteng Amoako-Gyampah, 'Sanitation and public hygiene in rural and mining communities in southern Gold Coast (colonial Ghana), c.1878–c.1950', *Journal of West African History* 9:2 (2023), 65–86.

49 See PRAAD-Kumase, ARG 1/37/7: Preliminary Report on Investigations Regarding High Death Rates of Mine Workers (1924–25).

50 PRAAD-Kumase, ARG 1/37/7: Preliminary Report by Sir W.J. Simpson on Investigations Regarding the High Death Rates of Mines Labourers, 29 September 1924.

51 PRAAD-Kumase, ARG 1/37/7: Secretary of State for Colonies to Governor Guggisberg, 21 October 1924.

fitness, as they were recruited ad hoc without any health screening. Based on these observations, he offered likely causes of the high death rates amongst the labourers.

The first was the extreme prevalence of hookworm in the population. This, he argued, 'lowers the vital powers of resistance and increases the liability to disease.'[52] Hookworm infestation was further 'aggravated by constant reinfection from infected latrines in the mines and villages.'[53] Simpson also found that a considerable number of the labourers suffered from tuberculosis, which inhibited underground work, soon breaking them down. The situation was worsened by the cramped and unhygienic houses the mines provided for the labourers. He pointed to the polluted water supply and inadequate medical arrangements in both the mines and surrounding villages, which aided the spread of diseases. What solutions did he recommend?

First, Simpson suggested that a medical officer be stationed in the NTs to screen labour recruits for diseases that made them unsuitable for mine work, such as tuberculosis, hookworm, defective eyesight, and other respiratory and circulatory conditions.[54] Those who tested positive were to be rejected while the healthy were to be issued identity tickets for the trip south. He also recommended similar tests at the mines, especially for local recruits. Simpson also made suggestions on sanitation. As early as April 1922, the Chamber of Mines had made new regulations on latrine design for mines which had apparently not been followed, partly because Asante's mines were not members of this body and were therefore not bound by its stipulations.[55] He recommended a strict enforcement of these requirements. New latrines were to be constructed entirely of concrete to a height of at least five feet, and with removable buckets two inches above the floor. The latrines were to be inspected twice daily by a European supervisor for cleanliness and disinfection.[56]

As stated above, Simpson noticed that the housing situation for northern labourers was unsatisfactory, particularly at Tarkwa, Abosso, and Nsuta. He therefore recommended the construction of new houses reserved for northern migrant labourers at all the mines. He further argued for new mining villages to be constructed 'with suitable provision for, and position of, playing grounds, squares, or open spaces, markets, slaughterhouse, water-supply, drains and sanitary conveniences including bath houses and incinerators.'[57] He also

52 PRAAD-Kumase, ARG 1/37/7: Preliminary Report by Sir W.J. Simpson.

53 *Ibid.*

54 *Ibid.*

55 *Ibid.*; PRAAD-Kumase, ARG 1/37/8: F.W. Applegate to Colonial Secretary, 22 May 1934.

56 PRAAD-Kumase, ARG 1/37/7: Preliminary Report by Sir W.J. Simpson.

57 *Ibid.*

stressed the need to improve the quality and quantity of water supply, especially at Tarkwa and Abosso.

These recommendations seemed sensible, especially in a tropical health environment such as Asante. One wonders, therefore, why it took so long for such basic health measures to be instituted. The sanitation situation in the mines was shocking, especially when one considers the high death rates officials had long observed, even if casually, among northern migrant labourers. Correspondence between mine bosses and government officials suggest that there was little care for the health of northern migrant labourers. This was until the labour pools apparently dried up in the early 1920s, threatening the profits and sustainability of the mines.[58] For instance, the management of Abbontiakoon Mines, operating from Tarkwa, wrote on 17 March 1924 to the Chief Commissioner of Ashanti (CCA), John Maxwell, that while 'it is not our intention to recruit indentured labour, this company, in common with other mining companies, is finding great difficulty in making both ends meet, entirely owing to the shortage of labour in the district for this kind of work.'[59] Apparently, the health and safety of northern migrant labourers got the attention of officials only after enough of them had died to threaten profits.

Gradual reforms in the subsequent years greatly improved labour conditions for the miners.[60] The companies therefore had a healthy population of northern labourers in Asante to draw from. There were also many local Asante and Fante labourers. Some people migrated from as far away as Nigeria to seek employment in the mines. The troubling labour situation that existed at the start of the 1920s had been banished. Yet almost a decade later, northern migrant labourers still suffered conditions which hampered their safety and wellbeing in Asante's mines. The work was tedious, their pay was low, and there was no job security, all of which made for a precarious living. The labourers therefore resorted to strike actions to compel favourable solutions to these problems. However, due to the abundance of labour, mining companies could now afford to lay off whole gangs of striking labourers as replacements were easy to find. An illustration is a series of events which unfolded at the Ashanti Goldfields Corporation mine at Obuasi in 1934.

On 9 April 1934 rumour spread through the Obuasi mine of an intended strike by the underground boys. Alarmed officials quickly telephoned Kumase for police officers to be dispatched to Obuasi.[61] Thirty were immediately sent

58 Another factor to consider is that mining competed with cocoa farming for northern labour. In years of high demand for labour by cocoa, mining lost out for a variety of reasons including the harshness of mining work, poor remuneration as compared to cocoa, and overall risk variability. See Crisp, *Story of an African Working Class*, 46–53.

59 PRAAD-Kumase, ARG 1/37/3: Abbontiakoon Mines Limited to CCA, 17 March 1924.

60 Crisp, *Story of an African Working Class*, 35–53.

61 PRAAD-Kumase, ARG 1/37/8: District Commissioner, Obuase, to CCA on 'Rumoured Strike of Mines Boys at Obuasi' (not dated); 'Obuasi – Alleged Labour Troubles at Ashanti Goldfields Corporation LTD,' CCA to Colonial Secretary, 9 May 1934.

from Kumase and another sixteen joined from Accra. Despite these rumours nothing happened. Yet mine officials remained worried; their sources had been credible. Further investigations revealed the grievances behind the intended strike.[62] First, the workers were disappointed that local mine bosses had not raised their wages although the rise had been authorised in London. They were also unhappy with the 6/- rent the mine charged per month for their accommodation. Importantly, they revealed that the families of those killed in mining accidents were not compensated. Furthermore, sick and injured labourers were not paid even though their European counterparts in similar conditions were.[63]

Some of these claims were true while others had been exaggerated. For instance, although the approval for pay increases had been agreed in London, the information reached local administrators after rumours of the strike.[64] In any case, the rumour prompted the deputy manager of the mine, R. Allen, to discuss in June 1934 with CCA Francis Jackson improvements in the conditions of the labourers.[65] The CCA was in favour of the suggested improvements. Allen subsequently tabled these proposals before the mine's board of directors.[66] He specifically asked for dependents of mine workers killed through accidents at work to be paid compensation commensurate with the circumstances of their death, such as the cause of mortality and their years of service. By the end of November 1934, the board had still not contemplated this proposal, never mind approved it.[67] Nevertheless, the rent was reduced on 1 July of that year to 4/6 per month ostensibly to placate the labourers.[68]

What can be observed about how mine bosses and government officials reacted to this ultimately phantom strike? First, it demonstrated officials' inclination to resort to coercion when dealing with labour agitations. Strikes in Asante's mines were generally peaceful. Workers often laid down their tools and picketed at vantage points in protest. On a few occasions striking workers compelled 'loyal' colleagues to join them. On the other hand, officials almost always responded to strikes with highhanded force. Even mere rumours of strike, as seen in this Obuasi case, were met with frantic calls for police detachments to be deployed. Ring leaders and headmen were often arrested. Threats were regularly issued to coerce their followers to work. Sometimes, striking workers were instantly dismissed and new ones employed. The lucky ones were fined portions of their wages. Labour was abundant, and the mining companies

62 RAAD-Kumase, ARG 1/37/8: District Commissioner, Obuase, to CCA on 'Rumoured Strike of Mines Boys at Obuasi' (not dated).

63 *Ibid.*

64 *Ibid.*

65 PRAAD-Kumase, ARG 1/37/8: R. Allen to District Commissioner, Obuase, 14 July 1934.

66 PRAAD-Kumase, ARG 1/37/8: District Commissioner, Obuase, to CCA, 27 November 1934.

67 *Ibid.*

68 PRAAD-Kumase, ARG 1/37/8: District Commissioner, Obuase, to CCA, 19 September 1934.

could therefore do as they pleased. The Obuasi mine, for instance, had in 1938 over 7000 men on its roll with more waiting on the sides.[69] Contrast this figure with the mere 1000 in 1924.[70] Northern migrant labourers were therefore at their mercy. How did the labourers fare in other sectors of the economy, namely cocoa and the railways?

Cocoa

In this section we reiterate the observation that despite northern labourers' long association with, and critical manpower inputs into, the cocoa sector, they never received the financial returns and compensations commensurate with their efforts (knowing their 'own value in the labour world' as Governor Guggisberg put it in 1920).[71] Austin's study of cocoa farming in Asante highlights how northern migrant labourers gradually negotiated better conditions of work using various strategies such as switching between cocoa and mining whenever favourable, negotiating with cocoa farmers to be paid in produce, and even staying away altogether and withholding their labour to increase demand for labour and, therefore, wages.[72] While these strategies allowed for the negotiation of better conditions of work, it did not lead to transformative shifts in terms of the distribution of the cocoa sector's overall financial returns. Northern labourers therefore continued to be exposed to the effects of long- and short-term crisis events from which other actors such as Asante farmers were better shielded. The clearest example of such exposure occurred in the 1937–38 cocoa season.

The 1937–38 cocoa season is mostly remembered for the cocoa hold-up which rocked the Gold Coast's economy.[73] Asante's cocoa farmers protested against unfair purchasing prices by refusing to sell their cocoa to the European cocoa-buying cartel led by Cadbury and the United Africa Company. Much is known about the causes of the hold-up, how it unfolded, its effects on the economy, and how it was eventually resolved. We also know the fate

69 PRAAD-Kumase, ARG 1/37/8: R.A. Stewart (acting mines manager) to CCA, 22 March 1938.

70 PRAAD-Kumase, ARG 1/37/7: Preliminary Report by Sir W.J. Simpson.

71 Quoted in Austin, *Labour*, 420.

72 See Austin, *Labour*, 316–20, 528–9.

73 On the cocoa hold-ups, see Alence in this volume; also Gareth Austin, 'Capitalists and chiefs in the cocoa hold-ups in south Asante, 1927–1938', *International Journal of African Historical Studies* 21:1 (1988), 63–95; Rod Alence, 'The 1937–1938 Gold Coast cocoa crisis: the political economy of commercial stalemate', *African Economic History* 19 (1990–91), 77–104; Rod Alence, 'Colonial government, social conflict and state involvement in Africa's open economies: the origins of the Cocoa Marketing Board, 1939–45', *Journal of African History* 42:3 (2001), 397–416.

of the northern migrant labourers who farmed Asante's cocoa.This section emphasises the hardships endured by northern labourers during this period. The hold-up economically destabilised the Gold Coast. To identify the causes and nature of the hold-up and offer possible solutions to prevent future occurrences, the British government established an investigative commission headed by William Nowell.

Nowell's report offers insights into the suffering of northern migrant labourers in the cocoa industry.[74] This appeared in a three-page appendix, which stated that northern migrant labourers were 'the backbone of the Gold Coast cocoa industry, being employed both by the merchants and by the farmers.'[75] Nowell distinguished between two types of northern migrant labourers. There were those who stayed in the Gold Coast throughout the year and those who migrated only for the cocoa season. The former migrated south many years ago, lived in permanent dwellings in the Zongos, and therefore constituted 'a large floating population ready to work for wages.'[76] However, even this large workforce was insufficient for the labour demands of the cocoa industry. It therefore had to be supplemented yearly by thousands of temporary migrant labourers from the NTs, Burkina Faso, and even as far away as Nigeria. These temporary migrants started the trek south in September, worked for six months, and migrated back north at the end of the cocoa season in May.[77]

The migrant labourers usually subsisted on food provided by the cocoa farmers such as cassava, plantain, and occasional additions of meat. The workday typically lasted ten hours. It involved carrying cocoa and wood, weed clearing, and other manual farm work. The labourers were paid at the end of the cocoa season in either cash or cocoa. In a good year, labourers received at least £8 for six months' work.[78]

In 1936–37 the Gold Coast experienced a bountiful harvest. This attracted more NTs labourers in 1937–38. By the middle of October 1937 thousands had arrived and found employment.[79] Everything went smoothly until late in the season when farmers informed the labourers of their inability to pay them because of the hold-up. By April, when they usually returned home, the labourers had still not been paid. As one labourer bitterly complained:

74 Great Britain, *Report of the Commission on the Marketing of West African Cocoa* (London, 1938).

75 *Ibid.*, 193.

76 *Ibid.*, 193. A Zongo was an area of town lived in mainly by northerners.

77 *Ibid.*, 193.

78 *Ibid.*, 194.

79 *Ibid.*, 194.

> I have been [in the Gold Coast] for thirty years working in cocoa farm[s]. Every year after the cocoa I go home and return. The Zugus who come down for the cocoa country are about 10,000. This year we have not been paid for the work we have done. Our parents in the North write asking us for money. We used to be paid one third of every load of cocoa which we collect.... This year the farmers will not give us one third of the cocoa to sell as they did in the past. This year they give us nothing.[80]

As Manu-Osafo and Ofosu-Mensah Ababio argue elsewhere, the hold-ups coincided with the rise of armed robberies in Asante. The blame for these robberies conveniently fell on supposedly vengeful northern labourers, who were said to be protesting about not only their lost wages for that particular year, but all the years of slavery northerners had endured under Asante suzerainty in the eighteenth and nineteenth centuries.[81]

Asante anxieties about northern labourers were familiar and had led to serious clashes before. In 1919 a riot in Bekwai against northerners, although not caused by farm–labour relations but by a gambling dispute, left eleven men 'killed and thirteen badly wounded.'[82] This riot was apparently led by the Omanhene, which raises questions about the role of chiefs in labour issues vis-a-vis northerners. Asante chiefs played limited roles in the labour issues of the mining industry, but they were central to the cocoa hold-ups. However, in neither sector did they intervene in favour of northern migrant labourers. Thus, 'even by the end of the cololnial period,' as Austin rightly observes, 'the northern labourers in Asante, despite the gains they had made in the cocoa-labour market, still obtained substantially smaller shares of cocoa-farm earnings than the Asante farmers did.'[83]

The Railway

In 1935 the British restored the Asante Confederacy and declared Osei Agyeman Prempeh II *Asantehene*. The Ashanti Confederacy Council (the union of Asante's constituent states) was re-established as a deliberative assembly under Prempeh's authority.[84] This new body allowed chiefs to play a more active role in labour disputes and related affairs in Asante. However, their involvement in

80 Great Britain, *Report*, 195.

81 Manuel Manu-Osafo and Emmanuel Ofosu-Mensah Ababio, 'Armed robberies in colonial Asante: official denial, private speculation, and the perpetuation of stereotype, 1935–1945' (forthcoming).

82 Austin, *Labour*, 420.

83 Austin, *Labour*, 430.

84 On the Asante Confederacy Council and Prempeh II's position in it, see Alessandro Triulzi, 'The Asantehene-in-Council: Ashanti Politics under Colonial Rule, 1935–1950,' *Africa: Journal of the International African Institute* 42:2 (1972), 98–111.

these matters did not radically challenge the power of the colonial government and corporate interests in any meaningful way. Rather, their actions tended to reinforce colonial power over African labourers, sometimes even leading calls for the dissolution of labour unions.

A case in point was a dispute which ensued between railway workers and the colonial government in late 1941. Details of this dispute were revealed at a public palaver held before the *Asantehene* on 1 December 1941.[85] J.S.O. Amoah, spokesman for the railway workmen, explained that the workers had two months earlier, together with their colleagues at Sekondi, submitted a petition of grievances to their general manager. This petition was ignored, which compelled the Sekondi group to embark on a strike on 26 November. The Kumase members were still in the process of deliberating their next course of action when policemen arrested members in their homes around midnight on 27 November. These unprovoked arrests spurred the rest of the men into action. They went to the police station to bail their colleagues. The workmen reconvened the next morning to deliberate on matters arising. It was to this meeting that policemen were sent to arrest all of them, numbering 128 individuals.

The group was of mixed ethnicities, but their names revealed some origins: Moro Moshie, Bakari Kanjarga, Kofi Grushie, Gwama Moshie, Ali Grumah, Senpuah Dagarti, Abu Dagomba, and Seidu Wangara, to name but a few.[86] They were detained at the prison yard until 10 a.m. the next day, when they were granted bail. Officials quickly arraigned them on charges of unlawful strike (under the Defence Regulations of 1939 which prohibited strikes by workers of certain public services such as the railways) and fixed the trial date for 1 December. This was obviously meant to intimidate the workmen, and it worked. The men, anxious to save their jobs and freedom, speedily petitioned the *Asantehene* for his intervention in the matter.

Asantehene Prempeh II begun by offering the men his sympathies. He, however, reminded them of the wartime conditions of the day: 'you know that in time of war it is not proper for any workmen, particularly railway workmen, to go on strike. When you go on strike you do great injury to the national cause.'[87] The men vehemently denied they were on strike but had only gathered to discuss the events outlined above. Nevertheless, the Asantehene cautioned that 'the government has power to punish people who do anything that goes to impede the successful prosecution of the war.'[88] He could thus 'not

85 PRAAD-Kumase, ARG 1/37/4: Asantehene to CCA, 5 December 1941; 'Notes Taken at a Palaver Held at Ahenfie Manhyia on Monday, December 1, 1941, in Connection with the Gold Coast Government Railway Workmen's Strike'.

86 PRAAD-Kumase, ARG 1/37/4: 'Notes Taken at a Palaver'.

87 *Ibid.*

88 *Ibid.*

assure you that you will not be punished for what you have done.'[89] The men responded with assurances that they would resume work immediately should they be freed. The Asantehene then advised them to march to the magistrate's court to stand trial, and that he would 'be there to see if I shall be permitted to plead for leniency for you.'[90]

At the trial the men protested their innocence again. The magistrate, D. Harbord, unconvinced by their arguments, found them liable to three months in jail and a fine of £100 or a further three months in default, making a total of six months imprisonment.[91] At this juncture the Asantehene pleaded for mitigation, arguing that the 'men were misled by their leaders not passing their representations through the proper channels to the government, and in consequence mistakenly felt resentment against government for not answering those representations.'[92] Harbord, taking the Asantehene's plea into consideration, passed a suspended sentence of three years within which the men could not strike 'whether they like their work or not, whether they are satisfied with their pay and conditions of work or not.'[93] Failure to heed this, the magistrate emphasised, would attract an immediate sentence of two years with hard labour. He further advised the workers to seek the Asantehene's help in such matters and 'make representations to the government through the proper channels as to their pay' and related matters.[94]

It was by such intimidating yet lawful methods that the colonial state trapped northern migrant labourers in unjust working conditions.[95] In many ways, the plight of these railway men mirrored the situation that northern migrant labourers as a group has endured in the long, entwined, but distinct labour histories of Asante (nineteenth century), Gold Coast (colonial), and Ghana (post-independence). These three distinct political entities relied on the same inequality regime which designated northerners as cheap labour for the south.

89 *Ibid.*

90 *Ibid.*

91 PRAAD-Kumase, ARG 1/37/4: Magistrate's Court Held at Kumasi on Monday the 1st Day of December 1941.

92 *Ibid.*

93 *Ibid.*

94 *Ibid.*

95 Unlike migrant cocoa labourers, railwaymen could not respond to threats of coercion or unfair treatment by staying away as migrant cocoa labourers did the season following the horrible experience of the 1937–38 hold-up. Unlike migrant cocoa labourers, railway workers tended to possess skills which required long periods of training, which meant investments of time and effort in residence in Asante. In effect, they tended to live permanently in Asante and could not surreptitiously leave, hence their resorting to strikes, a recourse the courts effectively blocked, at least for the duration of World War II. For more on this, see Komla Tsey, *From Head-loading to the Iron Horse: Railway Building in Colonial Ghana and the Origins of Tropical Development* (Bamenda, 2013), 99–116.

Wealth generated by northern labour did not disappear but was transferred from one epoch to the next. Northern labourers were – and still are – thus trapped in a temporal pattern of unequal labour relations with deep roots and resonances in the Ghanaian past. It is to the latest iteration of this phenomenon we now turn.

Farming in the Transition Belt, 1970s–2000

In March 1984, Ghana undertook its third post-independence population census and the ninth since 1891. The characteristics of Ghana's population in the early 1980s are pretty revealing. On close inspection of the population data, regional inequalities were being consolidated.[96] Separating the Upper regions into two administrative areas gave the northern savanna three administrative regions compared to seven for the southern half of the country.

Between 1970 and 1984, several thousands of northerners migrated to the Brong Ahafo, Ashanti and Western regions to seek employment. The areas closer to the north – Brong Ahafo and Ashanti – were more developed, urbanised, and possessed fertile lands for agricultural purposes.[97] As indicated above, Asante capitalists used northern labourers to produce cocoa and other food crops throughout the colonial period.[98] As unfavourable climatic conditions intensified in the arid north, citizens were compelled to travel outside the zone to seek employment and alternative agricultural lands for farming.[99] Additionally, the collapse of the Ghanaian economy in the mid-1970s saw the reversal of the industrialisation programme. In practical terms, unskilled and low-skill labourers had to seek better employment opportunities in the urban south.

Consequently, the voluntary mass migration of young people was established during this period – there was constant labour movement between the north and south. While some labour was seasonal, others relocated to the towns and farming villages in the Ashanti and Brong Ahafo regions. The unrestricted

96 Republic of Ghana, *1984 Population Census of Ghana – the Gazetteer 1* (Accra, 1989).

97 Ben Scully and Akua Opokua Britwum, 'Labour reserves and surplus populations: Northern Ghana and the Eastern Cape of South Africa,' *Journal of Agrarian Change* 19 (2019), 407–26.

98 Mohammed Iddrisu Kambala, 'Colonial origins of comparative development in Ghana,' *The Journal of Development Studies* 59:2 (2023), 188–208.

99 Kees van der Geest, Anton Vrieling and Ton Dietz, 'Migration and environment in Ghana: a cross-district analysis of human mobility and vegetation dynamics,' *Enviornment and Urbanisation* 22:1 (2010), 107–24; Jemina Nomunume Baada, Bipasha Baruah and Isaac Luginaah, '"What we were running from is what we're facing again": examining the paradox of migration as a livelihood improvement strategy among migrant women farmers in the Brong-Ahafo region of Ghana,' *Migration and Development* 8:3 (2019), 448–71.

movement of people swelled the populations in the south of the country. For example, the population of the Brong Ahafo region in 1970 was 766,509 and increased to 1,206,608 in 1984. Regarding occupation, agriculture employed 426,158 people, a sizable number.[100]

Many towns and farming communities in Ashanti and Brong Ahafo – Techiman, Atebubu, Goaso, Asutifi, Dormaa Ahenkro, Kintampo, Bekwai, Konongo-Odumase, Sekyere, Ejura, New Edubiase, and Agogo among others, saw an increase in the non-native population.[101] Because the region shares a border with Côte d'Ivoire, there was cross-border labour movement on both sides. While cocoa production in Ghana had declined from 1965 to 1983, it began to reviveafter that. Meanwhile cocoa production had been increasing steadily in neighbouring Côte d'Ivoire.[102] As Austin notes, the different politics of inequality in migrants' access to cocoa land in the two countries was important: at that time, migrant labourers had greater expectations of eventually becoming farm owners on the Ivorian side of the border.[103] Labourers from Ghana crossed over to work on the cocoa plantations in Côte d'Ivoire.

Until the 1980s, most northern labour migrants travelling to southern Ghana said they were 'going to Kumasi'. The reference to Kumasi, the capital of the Ashanti region, was all encompassing. Migrants came to Kumasi to travel to other Asante, Bono and Ahafo towns and farming villages. The administrative separation of the Brong Ahafo region out of Ashanti happened in the late 1950s. The 1980s were characterised by a rapid recovery of the economy after an injection of IMF/World Bank programmes.

Nevertheless, the north witnessed a significant transformation in labour migration. Isidore Lobnibe reminds us that labour migrants from the Upper West region introduced a new jargon into the migration discourse by saying – *ti kyeri ni jong* – (literally 'we are going to jong').[104] The colonial-era gold and cocoa migrants are contrasted with post-independence era semi-literate youthful

100 Republic of Ghana, *1984 Population Census of Ghana – Demographic and Economic Characteristics – Brong-Ahafo Region* (Accra, 1987), 94.
101 *Ibid.*, 46.
102 See Gareth Austin, 'The political economy of the natural environment in West African history: Asante and its savanna neighbors in the nineteenth and twentieth centuries,' in Richard Kuba and Carola Lentz (eds), *Land and the Politics of Belonging in West Africa* (Leiden, 2006), 187–212.
103 *Ibid.*
104 Isidore Lobnibe, 'Of Jong Migrants and Jongsecans: understanding contemporary rural out-migration from northwest Ghana,' *Journal of Dagaare Studies* 7–10 (2010), 7–8. See also Gariba B. Abdul-Korah, '"Where is not home?": Dagaaba migrants in the Brong Ahafo region, 1980 to the present,' *African Affairs* 106:422 (2006), 71–94; Gariba B. Abdul-Korah, '"Now if you have only sons you are dead": Migration, gender, and family economy in twentieth century northwestern Ghana', *Journal of Asian and African Studies* 46:4 (2011), 390–403.

migrants. The term *jong* was used broadly by labour migrants from the Upper West region to refer to the food-crop farming villages in the Brong Ahafo and Ashanti regions. The Brong Ahafo region is known for its production of various food crops, including cassava, yam, plantain, and maize.[105] The kind of manual labour required for yam cultivation is particularly suitable for northern farm labourers, as yams are planted on raised mounds, and thousands of such mounds are needed for large-scale production. Although yam production declined between the 1960s and 1970s, it saw a significant increase from the 1980s through to the 2000s, with an annual growth rate of 13.2%.[106] This rise in production can be attributed to several factors, including improved pricing and marketing opportunities for farmers, better extension services and more financial support, and the expansion of both local and international markets. The yam boom attracted different waves of migration into villages in Wenchi, Techiman and Kintampo in the Brong Ahafo region.[107] The *jong* phenomenon was labour migration linked to specific yam-producing villages.

Throughout the 1980s and 1990s, northern seasonal migrants worked as farm labourers in Asante and Bono areas. Groups of young men armed with hoes and cutlasses would clear large tracts of land and then raise yam mounds – big mounds requiring the use of a hoe with a wide blade. In the Akan areas, clearing of farmlands was done using the cutlass. The northern migrants combined the cutlass and the hoe in the clearing of lands for farming. Working from dawn to dusk, the young labourers would raise hundreds of yam mounds daily.[108] The farm owner paid for the labour based on the number of mounds raised each day or at the end of the process. The services of these skilful and hardworking labourers' were constantly in demand. Once the farming season ended, the migrants would trek back to the north. From the mid-1990s, couples migrated to seek employment in the south. The hometown associations and social networks created in the towns and farming villages enabled newly arrived migrants to integrate into their host communities. The migrants sought lands from the Odekro (village headman) for farming purposes. But they were refused, so many worked on the lands of wealthy subjects and chiefs for a portion of the farm produce. The process is repetitive and structured by an 'inequality regime' with variations.

105 See P. Anaadumba, 'Analysis of Incentives and Disincentives for Yam in Ghana', Technical notes series, MAFAP, Food and Agriculture Organisation, Rome, 2013; Noah Larvoe, 'Integration Assessment of Regional Yam Markets in Ghana: A Spatial Price Analysis', Master's thesis, Swedish University of Agricultural Sciences (Uppsala, 2015).

106 See Samuel Nii Ardey Codjoe, 'Supply and utilization of food crops in Ghana, 1960–2000,' *African Journal of Food Agriculture Nutrition and Development* 7:2 (2007), 5.

107 Lobnibe, 'Of Jong Migrants and Jongsecans'.

108 Each worker raised a minimum of 100 mounds per day. Interview, Techiman, 12 June 2024.

The Kayayei Phenomenon

Kayayei is a combination of Hausa and Ga language meaning female head-porters. '*Kaya*' in Hausa means load, luggage, goods, or burden. '*Yei*' in Ga means women or female. *Kayayei* are predominantly girls and young women, mostly from the northern regions in Ghana and neighbouring Burkina Faso and Togo.[109] The *kayayei* work has been in existence for a very long time.[110] According to Ziblim Shamsu-Deen, *kayayei* is a source of income for both male and female migrants from the northern savanna.[111] The men used to push items to various destination while the women used basins to carry loads on their heads in the major markets of southern Ghana.[112]

Currently, *kayayei* continues to be a major source of income for women from the northern regions of Ghana. *Kayayei* mainly carry loads on their heads to or from markets to lorry stations for a fee. They also assist market traders in stocking their shelves, packing, tidying up vending sites and other duties as required. Many local restaurants, popularly known as 'chop bars', engage *kayayei* in tidying up, preparing meals, and serving customers.

Until the early 1990s, the large-scale movement of young women into the cities was associated principally with the educated. The migration of young women or teenage girls with little or no education, though noteworthy, was not as voluminous as that of the educated.[113] Some stayed a short time as head-porters, working only during the 'lean' agricultural seasons. Others spent years working as *kayayei* to save up to buy utensils and other items for marriage, support their families, and contribute to the welfare of their communities back home. They engage in the *kaya* business because they see it as the only self-employment with low or no capital that could enable them to acquire minimum assets for either better marriage or prospects for future investment in more lucrative ventures and sedentary work.

However, there are other factors that influence the young girls to migrate south to work as *kayayei* despite anticipated challenges they may encounter.[114] Like much informal sector work, *kayayei* is not accounted for and thus is

109 James Adu Opare, 'Kayayei: the women head porters of southern Ghana,' *Journal of Social Development in Africa* 18:2 (2003), 33–48, at 34.

110 Mariama Awumbila and Elizabeth Ardayfio-Schandorf, 'Gendered poverty, migration and livelihood strategies of female porters in Accra, Ghana'. *Norsk Geografisk Tidsskrift*, 62:3 (2008), 171–9.

111 Ziblim Shamsu-Deen, 'Migration and health nexus: a case of female porters (Kayayei) in Accra, Ghana', *Research on Humanities and Social Sciences* 3:3 (2013), 103–9.

112 *Ibid.*

113 Based on estimates, see Opare, 'The women head porters in southern Ghana', 36.

114 Teni Agana, 'Understanding the Motivation and Circumstances of Kayayei in the Ghanaian Economy: The Kayayei Experience', Ph.D. dissertation, Asheshi University College (2018).

invisible within the Ghanaian labour market. The *kayayei* themselves do not regard their economic activity as permanent. They often pursue the activity on a short-term basis to meet financial obligations.[115]

Motivations for Migration

In Ghana, the northern regions are the poorest, with high levels of food insecurity and malnutrition. For more than a decade the rainfall pattern in the north has been disappointing.[116] It is estimated that about 80 per cent of the population in the northern regions are now living in abject poverty due to crop failure resulting from environmental stressors such as climate change.[117]

While many migrate due to hardship and poverty, others try to escape from outmoded socio-cultural practices such as forced marriages. It is recorded that the northern part of Ghana has an extremely high rate of child marriages, with children below the age of 18 given out for marriage by their parents.[118] Such marriages are arranged by the two families involved without the child's consent. Another outdated practice, female genital mutilation, is also prevalent in the northern belts.

The causes of the rise in the migration of young women from the north to the south has been changing since the phenomenon appeared. Lately, young girls migrate to the south to earn money to assist their parents, and also to earn money to buy a trousseau (materials considered necessary for a bride to take into married life). They need items such as clothes, shoes, jewels, kitchenware, and other essentials expected of a newly wed bride in her matrimonial home.

Peer pressure is another push factor. The perceived glamour of urban life, which they have heard about from the *kayayei* returnees, also contributes to the influx of northern migrants to Accra and Kumase. The *kayayei* returnees mostly exaggerate how profitable the business is to other girls, which tends to motivate them also to migrate, live independently and gain social skills to

115 Opare, 'The women head porters of southern Ghana' .

116 From the rainfall data, the 1980s were particularly bad years. See Jemima Nomunume Baada, Bipasha Baruah and Isaac Luginaah, 'Looming crisis – changing climatic conditions in Ghana's breadbasket: the experiences of agrarian migrants,' *Development in Practice* 31:4 (2021), 432–45; Benjamin Schraven and Christina Rademacher-Schulz, 'Shifting rainfalls, shifting livelihoods: seasonal migration, food security and social inequality in Northern Ghana', in Robert McLeman, Jeanette Schade and Thomas Faist (eds), *Environmental Migration and Social Inequality* (Cham, 2016), 43–56; Hanson Nyantakyi-Frimpong and Dinko Hanaan Dinko, 'Climate and non-climatic stressors, internal migration, and belonging in Ghana', in Tamar Mayer and Trinh Tran (eds), *Displacement, Belonging, and Migrant Agency in the Face of Power* (London, 2022), 153–65.

117 Opare, 'The women head porters of southern Ghana'.

118 This conclusion is based on anecdotal evidence, as many of these instances are under-reported due to cultural norms in the region.

prepare them for adult life. A lot of *kayayei* returnees come with lots of money from their savings, which gives the impression to other young girls that one can be wealthy in the south within a short stay.[119]

Challenges Kayayei Face

The *kayayei* girls and women are a noticeable, unique, and a concerning migration trend because they are positioned at the intersection of multiple disadvantages. Many of the girls and women are minimally educated and migrate to the southern cities in hopes of obtaining employment and better standards of living.[120] Among the challenges they face is that of accommodation.

Narrating their experiences, interviewees related that the lack of accommodation and having to sleep in the street was a frightening experience. For those who had to sleep in the street, it was a nightmare. While it was like sleeping in the compound during the hot season, this was different as there was no protection from intruders. They were often worried about assault, sexual harassment, or being forced into sexual activity. A 25-year-old *kayayo*[121] said, 'When we first arrived we did not have the chance to sleep in the room. I was afraid to lie outside because of bad people and too many mosquitos, but I could not do anything about it.'[122]

Kayayei face increased risks of economic and sexual exploitation and ill-health, including contracting sexually transmitted diseases. Apart from the surrounding swamps being infested by large colonies of malaria-carrying mosquitoes, sanitary conditions are deplorable and the unhygienic environment breeds other contagious diseases. Even though they now have more proximity to formal health services than they did in their villages in rural northern Ghana,[123] health becomes a challenge. Even though many of them might have access to the National Health Insurance, they would not get enough money to seek for quality health care.

On a typical day, *kayayei* carry all manner of goods for shop-owners and their customers. They reported that finding jobs was filled with uncertainty and

119 Agana, 'The Kayayei Experience,' 36.

120 Ahmed Bawa Kuyini, 'The Kayayo Girls' phenomenon: a child rights approach should be considered,' available at: www.modernghana.com/news/359753/the-kayayo -girls-phenomenon-a-child-rights-appr.html.

121 Kayayo refers to one person and kayayei refers to a group of girls involved in head portage.

122 Ahmed Bawa Kuyini et al., 'Narratives of internal migration experiences, health/well-being issues among females working as head-porters (Kayayei) in Ghana', *International Journal of Migration, Health and Social Care* 16:4 (2020), 518.

123 Aaron R. Denham, *Spirit Children: Illness, Poverty and Infanticide in Northern Ghana* (Madison WI, 2017).

also tiring because they have to keep walking around looking for opportunities. Sometimes, they can walk for an entire day and find very few opportunities. On the subject of how much they earn, a 27-year old interviewee said: 'How much you earn depends on your luck and your ability to negotiate with people [...] everyone wants the job so sometimes I have to charge less money. Sometimes I get many jobs in a day, but on other days I don't get any jobs. Also some people force you to accept less money.' Such a situation could mean that they are likely to have no food and go hungry for long periods.[124]

Many of the girls get worried about meeting their goals and/or being labelled as a failure. Most of the girls care about what their family members (parents/guardians and significant others) might say about their efforts to earn money. One *kayayo* said: 'I am always worried about what my parents will say if I don't meet their expectations.' For others, the concern about not earning enough money was more about what their peers (former *kayayei*) who are 'successful' would say about their failure. One of the young girls, aged 16, said: 'it is shame if you go back home with nothing or very little. [...] people will laugh and talk about you.' Another *kayayo*, 25 years of age, extended this point saying that it is not shame alone but 'the person can feel bad (guilty) because they have left their children at home and they don't bring back anything [...] it is like you have lost twice.'[125]

Conclusion

We have emphasised in this essay the plight northern migrant labourers faced in colonial Asante's three main cash-earning industries: mining, cocoa, and the railways. In the early years of colonial rule, migrant labourers in the mines were seen as an expendable resource. Their high death rates therefore never attracted official attention until their sudden unavailability threatened the mines' very existence. The conditions of service were no better for northern migrant labourers in the cocoa industry. They suffered greatly in the 1937–38 cocoa hold-up without any government intervention in their favour. In an environment which consigned them to second-class citizen status, northern labourers often initiated strikes as last resorts to compel official decisions in their favour. However, officials typically responded to such strikes with high-handed force including arrests, dismissals, and fines.

124 Ahmed Bawa Kuyini, Abdulai Abukari, Abdulai Kuyini Mohammed and Hughlett Omris Powell, 'Narratives of internal migration experiences, health/ well-being issues among females working as head-porters (Kayayei) in Ghana', *International Journal of Migration, Health and Social Care* 16:4 (2020), 511–25, at 518.
125 *Ibid.*

How officials responded to northern migrant labourers' agitations was indicative of broader unresolved tensions in colonial Asante's socio-political structure. Colonial rule did not up-end the ethnic hierarchy of pre-colonial Asante's social structure. On the contrary, British officials appropriated its implications for economic benefit. Just as *nnɔnkɔ* were at the bottom of the pre-colonial Asante social structure, northern migrant labourers occupied the lowest levels of the racial and ethnic hierarchy of colonial Asante.

Ghana's post-colonial governments failed to dismantle this hierarchy owing to global and local socio-economic realities.[126] Despite independence, industries such as cocoa and mining still relied on the exploitation of northern labour. Drastic changes in the flow of northern migrant labour would have threatened the economy. Northern Ghana after independence saw a series of development projects to eradicate poverty in the region. Ghana under Kwame Nkrumah and the Convention People's Party (CPP) government sought to bridge the development gap between the north and south. Nkrumah viewed industrialisation as the main requirement for development and modernisation.[127]

In fact Nkrumah made deliberate attempts to modernise agriculture, expand infrastructure, and improve education. The government implemented a campaign to promote home manufacturing of food products and processed foods. A rice mail was thus established in Nasia, halfway between Tamale and Bolgatanga, a tomato factory was established in Pwalugu, 21 km south of Bolgatanga, and a meat factory were established in Zuarungu, 6 km east of Bolgatanga. These establishments collectively provided a small economic boost in the form of post-harvest income and job security for the local population.[128]

The regime of the National Redemption Council (NRC), under the leadership of General Kutu Acheampong, was rated very high in terms of development projects in the northern regions. Shepherd et al. note that the Acheampong regime was the last regime which had a positive vision for the development of the north.[129] Commercial agriculture in the north was promoted under the government flagship policy of 'Operation feed your industry.' The regime's agricultural policy also impacted cash crops like cotton. Cotton farmers under a smallholder's scheme were able to produce cotton to feed the local textile industries.[130]

126 Austin, *Labour*, 213.

127 Charles Ackah and Denis Medvedev, 'Internal migration in Ghana: determinants and welfare impacts', *International Journal of Social Economics*, 39:10 (2012), 764–84.

128 *Ibid.*

129 Andrew Shepherd, Charles Jebuni, Ramatu Al-Hassan, Andy McKay, Colin Poulton, Ann Whitehead, and Jonathan Kydd, *Economic Growth in Northern Ghana, Revised Report* (DFID/CEPA, 2005).

130 Nyaaba and Bob-Milliar, 'Economic potentials', 56.

Despite policies geared toward bridging the developmental gap between the north and south, north–south migration patterns have persisted into twenty-first-century Ghana. Industries created after independence were not enough to accommodate the north's working classes. Post-colonial governments have tried to establish industries in the north to curb north–south migration but to no avail. Public industrialisation efforts are always greater for the south than the north. This leaves people no choice but to migrate south in search of jobs. As a result, migrations have continued with feeble government attempts to bridge the development gap between northern and southern Ghana.

In recent times this migration has transformed from predominantly male to young female migrants who serve as *kayayei* (head porters) in southern Ghana's markets. We contend that this sustained north–south migration and its causes point to a national inequality regime in existence since pre-colonial times. This regime is not just economic but also social in its origin, reproduction, and implication. We therefore call for more scholarship which will shed light on this under-researched aspect of Ghana's long-term social and economic history.

4

Nothing Less Than Revolutions? Terms-of-Trade Volatility and Policymaking Regimes in Ghana, 1937–47 and 1982–90

Rod Alence

> The transition in the economy of British West Africa can be called nothing less than a Revolution, so great sudden and radical has been the change.
>
> Allan McPhee (1926)

> I ask for nothing less than a revolution. Something that would transform the social and economic order of this country.
>
> Jerry Rawlings (31 December 1981)

Governments in Ghana, colonial and post-colonial, have regularly been forced to confront the domestic impact of large external trade shocks. Shocks emanate from fluctuations in the country's terms of trade – the ratio of world prices for its exports and imports – that arbitrarily add or subtract domestic purchasing power equal to several per cent of Gross Domestic Product (GDP). For most of the long twentieth century, their principal source has been the volatile world price of cocoa, Ghana's main export. As early as the 1920s and 1930s, exposure to terms-of-trade volatility was similar to levels seen during the global economic turbulence of the 1970s and 1980s. Shocks, especially those caused by sharp declines in the terms of trade, pose politically charged dilemmas for governments. Governments must decide whether to try to prop up aggregate domestic expenditure or sensitive industries, temporarily at least, and whether to intervene to buffer the impact on politically pivotal or socially vulnerable groups.

In this chapter I analyse responses to shocks by two governments in Ghana, one colonial and one post-colonial, that resulted in major changes in 'policy-making regime'. I define the regime as the set of primary policy instruments that governments have at their disposal when confronting terms-of-trade volatility. It comprises currency (monetary and exchange-rate) arrangements and the system of domestic cocoa pricing. Three major regime changes occurred during the long twentieth century. The first was the introduction of state-controlled cocoa marketing during the Second World War, which allowed governments to set the domestic producer price. The second (not covered in this chapter) was the introduction of a national currency within the Bretton Woods international monetary system shortly after independence. The third was the transition from administratively fixed to market-determined 'floating' exchange rates in the 1980s.

The two responses I analyse were both taken by government leaders 'against type' and have proved durable. Sir Arnold Hodson, the colonial governor who introduced state-controlled cocoa marketing in late 1939 had, only months earlier, categorically rejected a controlled marketing scheme proposed by a high-profile commission of inquiry. The control scheme he did support was a temporary wartime measure, later transformed into a permanent cocoa-marketing board, which persists to this day. Flight-Lieutenant Jerry Rawlings, head of the Provisional National Defence Council (PNDC) government that seized power at the end of 1981, was seen to be staunchly opposed to exchange-rate devaluation. Yet in 1983 his government began a regular series of large, discrete devaluations. They created momentum toward a floating exchange rate, phased in between 1986 and 1990, which also persists to this day.

The role of the state in setting the cocoa producer price and fixing the exchange rate features prominently in the literature on the political economy of Ghana. Economists have emphasised how low producer prices and overvalued exchange rates have short-changed cocoa farmers, especially during the first twenty-five years of independence, to the detriment of economic growth.[1] The marketing board's control of cocoa buying allows it to set the domestic producer price below the world price, the difference serving as a disguised tax on farmers. The government's control over a fixed exchange rate, meanwhile, allowed it to maintain an overvalued rate. Overvaluation reduces the local-currency value of export earnings, depressing cocoa farmers' returns further. Conventional accounts of the economic plight of cocoa farmers attribute it to their political marginality, especially compared with urban beneficiaries of state expenditure financed by their chronic under-payment. Such explanations fit Bates' influential argument about the political bases of agricultural policies

1 Jonathan H. Frimpong-Ansah, *The Vampire State in Africa: The Political Economy of Decline in Ghana* (Trenton, 1992); Douglas Rimmer, *Staying Poor: Ghana's Political Economy, 1950–1990* (Oxford, 1992); J. Dirck Stryker, *Trade, Exchange Rate, and Agricultural Pricing Policies in Ghana* (Washington DC, 1990); Francis Teal, 'Export growth and trade policy in Ghana in the twentieth century', *World Economy* 25:9 (2002), 1319–37; Francis Teal, 'The foreign exchange regime and growth: a comparison of Ghana and the Ivory Coast', *African Affairs* 85:339 (1986), 267–82.

in Africa, as well as more specific analyses of the agrarian basis of the post-colonial state in Ghana.[2]

Although low producer prices and overvalued exchange rates have unquestionably disadvantaged cocoa farmers, historical variation in these policies is out of sync with Ghana's politics. That is, major changes in the instruments used to effect the policies do not coincide with the political conditions supposed to explain them. From conventional accounts, one would expect state-controlled cocoa marketing to have been imposed when farmers were politically weak. Yet farmers' position in 1939 was unusually strong.[3] To oppose collusion among European merchant firms, they had recently organised a 'hold-up' and boycott of imported goods that brought external trade to a standstill through most of the 1937/38 crop season. With the outbreak of the Second World War, the colonial government and the Colonial Office in London were anxious to placate farmers and introduced controlled marketing to avoid renewed confrontation. From conventional accounts, one might also expect the transition to floating exchange rates in the 1980s, replacing the fixed rates that had become the main instrument driving the under-payment of cocoa farmers, to have occurred when farmers were politically strong. Yet farmers' position in the 1980s was unusually weak. The government was preoccupied with tackling a deep fiscal and economic crisis, not catering to organised farmers' demands.

Identifying and explaining changes in policymaking regimes is an important step in understanding Ghana's episodic trajectory of economic growth – and the dynamics of cocoa farming (see Austin's chapter in this volume) – during the long twentieth century. Cross-national econometric studies have shown that the growth rates are surprisingly weakly correlated over successive decades, meaning that economies that perform strongly in one decade often perform weakly in the next.[4] For individual countries, plotting long-term trends in national income rarely reveals a steadily rising hill of growth or an endless plain of stagnation. Especially for primary-exporting countries like Ghana, a varied terrain of mountains, rolling hills, and cliffs emerges.[5] Because variation over time cannot be explained by stable country characteristics, 'decompressing'

2 Robert H. Bates, *Markets and States in Tropical Africa: The Political Basis of Agricultural Policies* (Berkeley, 1983); Björn Beckman, 'Ghana, 1951–78: the agrarian basis of the post-colonial state', in Judith Heyer, Pepe Roberts and Gavin Williams (eds), *Rural Development in Tropical Africa* (New York, 1981), 143–67; Piet Konings, *The State and Rural Class Formation in Ghana: A Comparative Analysis* (London, 1986).

3 Gareth Austin, 'National poverty and the "vampire state" in Ghana: a review article', *Journal of International Development* 8:4 (1996), 553–73, at 563.

4 William Easterly, Michael Kremer, Lant Pritchett and Lawrence H. Summers, 'Good policy or good luck? Country growth performance and temporary shocks', *Journal of Monetary Economics* 32:3 (1993), 459–83.

5 Lant Pritchett, 'Understanding patterns of economic growth: searching for hills among plateaus, mountains, and plains', *World Bank Economic Review* 14:2 (2000), 221–50; also

the economic history of long-term development requires greater attention to potential causes that vary over time.[6] Changes in policymaking regimes in Ghana – undertaken by governments in response to external shocks and influencing how future governments respond – are candidates for understanding changes in growth trends.

My explanation emphasises how trade volatility exacerbates tensions within the prevailing policymaking regime, occasionally leading the government to make major changes. Under the restrictive colonial regime prior to the Second World War, volatile world prices fuelled rising social tensions that the government struggled to contain. In W.K. Hancock's terminology, West Africa was on the 'traders' frontier' of imperial expansion. Tensions flared in the Gold Coast along the transactional frontier between European merchant firms and African farmers and commercial intermediaries.[7] The government's primary impetus for introducing state-controlled cocoa marketing was to gain the ability to regulate the key price on the frontier: the domestic producer price. Much later, under a post-colonial policymaking regime – in which the government controlled the money supply, the exchange rate, and the producer price for cocoa – global economic turbulence exacerbated politically debilitating tensions and imbalances in the Ghanaian economy. The government ultimately recognised a paradox, articulated by Rawlings's close advisor Tsatsu Tsikata: the ubiquity of official economic 'controls' belied a situation in which real control over the free-falling economy was 'precisely what was lacking'.[8] The impetus for adopting a market-determined exchange rate was to eliminate the destabilising consequences of a key controlled price: the domestic price of foreign currency. Although colonial and post-colonial settings differed, in making major to policymaking regimes, governments in both cases sought to reconfigure the set of instruments available to manage the domestic impact of trade volatility.

The rest of the chapter proceeds as follows. The next section clarifies the periodisation of policymaking regimes during the long twentieth century. The following two sections contain case studies, of the shift to state-controlled cocoa

---

see Morten Jerven, 'African growth recurring: an economic history perspective on African growth episodes, 1690–2010', *Economic History of Developing Regions* 25:2 (2010), 127–54.

6 Gareth Austin, 'The "reversal of fortune" thesis and the compression of history: perspectives from African and comparative economic history', *Journal of International Development* 20:8 (2008), 996–1027.

7 W.K. Hancock, *Survey of Commonwealth Affairs*, vol. 2, *Problems of Economic Policy, 1918–39* (2 pts, London, 1940 and 1942), pt 2, 154.

8 'Human Dimensions of Africa's Recovery and Development: Ghana's Country Experience', paper presented at an Economic Commission for Africa conference, document number ECA/ICHD/88/51 (Addis Ababa, 1988), 8. For a similar, prescient analysis of the social consequences of economic controls, see Richard Jeffries, 'Rawlings and the political economy of underdevelopment of Ghana', *African Affairs* 81:324 (1982), 307–17.

marketing and of the shift to a market-determined exchange rate. Each describes how terms-of-trade volatility contributed to tensions within the existing policy-making regime and how the government responded. A conclusion, which includes a brief discussion of comparative implications, follows.

Periodising Policymaking Regimes

Ghana's economy has been heavily exposed to external volatility since the early twentieth century. The availability (or not) of three policy instruments are crucial for governments facing external shocks: the ability to print money, the ability to fix the exchange rate, and the ability to set the producer price for cocoa (the most important single domestic price in the tradable sector). Being able to print money allows the government to buffer, at least temporarily, the impact of an adverse shock on domestic expenditure, without resorting to foreign reserves or external borrowing, albeit at the expense of inflation. Being able to set the official exchange rate allows the government to influence relative prices between the tradable and non-tradable sectors of the economy, with implications for the balance of payments. Being able to set the cocoa producer price allows the government to regulate the purchasing power of cocoa farmers, with implications for aggregate expenditure and the distribution of income between the cocoa sector and the rest of the economy.

Governments' menu of possible responses to a shock is structured by the policy instruments at their disposal. The three major changes of the long twentieth century define four policymaking regimes. They are listed in table 4.1 with approximate dates. Until 1939, governments were locked into a highly restrictive colonial regime. With a colonial currency, governments could neither print money nor set the exchange rate. They also lacked a means for setting the cocoa producer price. The first major change came at the beginning of the Second World War, when state-controlled marketing was introduced. It allowed governments to set the price paid to cocoa farmers, within the otherwise restrictive colonial regime. The second change came shortly after Ghana's independence in 1957, when the government adopted a national currency, in keeping with the global Bretton Woods system of fixed (but adjustable) exchange rates. The initial post-colonial regime provided the widest possible policy discretion, allowing the government to print money, to set the official exchange rate, and to set the cocoa producer price. The third change came in the 1980s, with a transition to floating exchange rates. Government relinquished control over the exchange rate but retained the ability to print money and to set the cocoa producer price.

Table 4.1 Periodisation of Policymaking Regimes in Ghana 1891–2010

Government can:	1891–1939	1939–1961	1961–1986	1986–2010
Print money	○	○	●	●
Set the exchange rate	○	○	●	○
Set the cocoa producer price	○	●	●	●

Exposure to external shocks magnifies the importance of policymaking regimes. The degree of exposure can be thought of as the international price risk attached to the external sector of the economy. A useful indicator multiplies the share of the external sector in the national economy by terms-of-trade volatility within the external sector.[9] The size of the external sector is captured by the trade openness ratio: the average of exports and imports divided by GDP. Volatility is captured by the standard deviation of year-on-year changes in the log-transformed terms of trade (loosely, the size of a 'typical' percentage fluctuation). Trade openness multiplied by volatility expresses a typical fluctuation as a percentage of GDP.

Since the rise of its cocoa industry, Ghana's exposure to volatility has been substantial. Best estimates put the country's trade openness between 1911 and 1939 at roughly 15 to 20 per cent of GDP, while terms-of-trade volatility was about 20 per cent.[10] With 15 to 20 per cent of the colonial economy subject to volatility of 20 per cent, multiplication yields a reasonable estimate of the Gold Coast's exposure of about 3 or 4 per cent of GDP. Exposure to volatility before the Second World War is similar to exposure from the early 1960s through to

9 Dani Rodrik, 'Where did all the growth go? External shocks, social conflict, and growth collapses', *Journal of Economic Growth* 4:4 (1999), 385–412, at 394–5.

10 On trade openness, Francis Teal's estimates for 1911, 1919, 1929, and 1939 imply the external sector accounted for roughly 15 to 20 per cent of gross domestic income at prices adjusted for the terms of trade: 'Growth, Comparative Advantage and the Economic Effects of Government: A Case Study of Ghana' (Ph.D. dissertation, University of London, 1984), 108. A more recent estimate by Stephen Broadberry and Leigh Gardner puts the external sector at 24.6 per cent of GDP in 1929: 'Economic Growth in Sub-Saharan Africa, 1885–2008', *Explorations in Economic History* 83, no. 101424 (2022); they use constant 1950 prices without a terms-of-trade adjustment, so their estimate is not directly comparable with Teal's. On the barter terms of trade, Teal's 1984 ('Growth, Comparative Advantage', 268–9) series implies volatility of 21 per cent, while a series calculated from Stephen Hymer's indexes of export and import prices, in G.B. Kay (ed.), *The Political Economy of Colonialism in Ghana* (Cambridge, 1972), 332–3 and 338–40), yields a similar volatility estimate of 23 per cent.

the early 1980s, when trade openness ratio and external volatility were both about 20 per cent, so that exposure was roughly 4 per cent of GDP.[11] Available data therefore suggests that Ghana was heavily exposed to external volatility before and after independence.

The rest of the chapter analyses how governments have responded to terms-of-trade volatility under two policymaking regimes that are mirror images: the restrictive colonial regime of the inter-war years, and the discretionary regime of the early post-colonial era.

Taking Control of the Cocoa Producer Price, 1937–47

The policymaking regime before the Second World War combined a colonial currency with a privately ordered system of cocoa purchasing and marketing. It provided the platform for Ghana's first major growth episode of the long twentieth century, during which the country emerged as the world's leading cocoa exporter – exemplary of the economic transformation McPhee called 'nothing less than a Revolution.'[12] Yet export-led growth exposed the Ghanaian economy to the volatile world market for cocoa, which was to become a recurring source of social tension. The government's eventual decision to introduce state-controlled cocoa marketing sought to manage these tensions by setting the cocoa producer price.

The colonial monetary system, which tied the Gold Coast[13] to British sterling, was a crucial part of the policymaking regime. The West African Currency Board (WACB), established in 1912, formalised the arrangement.[14] It issued West African pounds fully convertible to British pounds at par, with convertibility ensured by a 100 per cent reserve requirement. The WACB thus operated as a currency converter, not an autonomous monetary authority. Changes in the money supply of each colony were determined passively by the balance of payments. Governments' access to external borrowing was also limited, with loans restricted to projects with reliable prospects for generating revenue, such as ports and railways. The regime embodied and enforced the British Treasury's well-known principle that colonialism should be self-financing.

11 Postcolonial trade openness ratios are from World Bank, *World Development Indicators*, 26 Oct. 2023 release (World Bank, 2023), and terms of trade are from Bernard Gruss and Suhaib Kebhaj, 'Commodity Terms of Trade: A New Database', *IMF Working Paper* WP/19/21 (2019). Trade openness is average exports as a percentage of GDP for 1960–71, before the endogenous collapse of the 1970s.

12 Allan McPhee, *The Economic Revolution in British West Africa* (London, 1926), 2.

13 I use 'Gold Coast' when referring specifically to the British colony whose boundaries approximate those of modern Ghana and 'Ghana' in general references to the country.

14 A.G. Hopkins, 'The creation of a colonial monetary system: the origins of the West African Currency Board', *African Historical Studies* 3:1 (1970), 101–32.

The Gold Coast economy achieved several decades of sustained economic growth under this restrictive regime. African farmers cultivated cocoa in the country's forest belt, which possessed suitable soils and climate, seeking lucrative proceeds from its sale on overseas markets. Exports were recorded consistently from 1891, initially in small quantities, and by 1911 the country was the world's leading exporter. On the eve of the First World War, exports were roughly 50 thousand tonnes; by the eve of the Second, they had grown sixfold.[15] Cocoa sustained a thriving two-way transoceanic trade. African farmers and traders sold produce to large European merchant and manufacturing firms, and the firms in return supplied the local market with imported merchandise.

The Gold Coast government benefited financially from the trade. Customs duties, though levied at modest rates, yielded buoyant returns that accounted for nearly all public revenue, making the Gold Coast a 'customs-post state'.[16] The government's main economic contributions were ports, railways, and eventually motorable roads. The extension of railways and roads dramatically reduced the cost of transporting cocoa to the coast, though the government did not give cocoa priority in planning routes.[17] Across most areas that were agronomically suitable for cocoa, cultivation was uneconomic if produce had to be conveyed by traditional head-loading alone. Rail was cheaper per kilometre by a factor of about ten, lorry transport by a factor of two or three.[18] The spread of cocoa cultivation responded quickly to the spatial pattern of transport infrastructure, and chiefs mobilised local communities to build and maintain feeder roads linking to trunk roads and railways.[19]

A stable and convertible currency, which reduced commercial risk, also supported the rapid growth of trade. Risks for European merchant firms in West Africa were considerable, particularly in light of the volatility of world cocoa prices. Firms held produce over long intervals between purchase in the Gold Coast and sale on overseas markets. Unexpected price shocks routinely wiped out under-capitalised firms. Survivors merged and colluded to fortify themselves. The largest merger, between the Niger Company and the African and Eastern Trade Corporation, gave birth to the United Africa Company (UAC) in 1929. Based in London, it accounted for about two-fifths of the Gold

15 Kay, *Political Economy*, 336.

16 Richard C. Crook, 'Decolonization, the colonial state, and chieftaincy in the Gold Coast', *African Affairs*, 85:338 (1986), 75–105, at 86.

17 Kay, *Political Economy*, 20–25.

18 Official estimates from 1923, quoted in Simon Heap, 'The development of motor transport in the Gold Coast, 1900–39', *Journal of Transport History* 11:2 (1990), 19–37, at 21.

19 Joint effects of railway proximity and land suitability on cocoa cultivation as of 1927 are mapped in Remi Jedwab and Alexander Moradi, 'The permanent effects of transportation revolutions in poor countries: evidence from Africa', *Review of Economics and Statistics* 98:2 (2016), 268–84, at 272. By this time motor transport was also widespread.

Coast's external trade at the time and was dubbed the 'commercial colossus of West Africa.'[20] Yet just two years later, the colossus struggled privately with its British bankers to secure basic credit needed to continue trading, evidence of the financial precarity of the trade.[21] The colonial policymaking regime limited governments' policy options, but it also promoted trade by creating what has been called a 'paradise of sound money in a wilderness of colonial backwardness.'[22]

Cocoa Hold-Ups and the Nowell Report

Growth of the cocoa industry enhanced the country's prosperity but left it vulnerable to external shocks. World cocoa prices, determined on the European and American commodity exchanges, fluctuated widely. Adverse price shocks were regular sources of domestic social tension. They triggered a series of cocoa hold-ups, in which African farmers refused to sell their cocoa to the European firms and boycotted imported merchandise.[23] Hold-ups occurred when sharp drops in cocoa prices were accompanied by news of collusion among the firms. The firms could not themselves engineer sustained drops in world prices. But once world prices did drop, buying agreements that set a common purchasing price were, according to internal UAC records, 'very useful for preserving a margin of profit temporarily and locally.'[24] As shown in figure 4.1, the three sharpest terms-of-trade declines during the inter-war period triggered hold-ups.[25]

Each major hold-up covered a wider area and lasted longer than its predecessors. The most effective brought external trade to a near-standstill through the 1937/38 crop year.[26] As world cocoa prices plummeted in September 1937,

20 Hancock, *Survey*, vol. 2, pt. 2, 208; market shares reported in William Nowell (chair), *Report of the Commission of Enquiry into the Marketing of West African Cocoa*, Cmd. 5845 (London, 1938), 191.

21 D.K. Fieldhouse, *Merchant Capital and Economic Decolonization: The United Africa Company, 1929–1987* (Oxford, 1994), 88–92.

22 P.J. Cain and A.G. Hopkins, '"Playing the game" in Tropical Africa, 1914–40', in *British Imperialism: Crisis and Deconstruction* (London, 1994), 201–34, at 207.

23 For overviews, see John Miles, 'Rural protest in the Gold Coast: the cocoa hold-ups, 1908–1938', in Clive Dewey and A.G. Hopkins (eds), *The Imperial Impact: Studies in the Economic History of Africa and India* (London, 1978), 152–70; Roger J. Southall, 'Polarisation and dependence in the Gold Coast cocoa trade, 1890–1938', *Transactions of the Historical Society of Ghana* 16:1 (1975), 93–115.

24 Quoted in Fieldhouse, *Merchant Capital*, 114.

25 Barter terms of trade are from Teal, 'Growth, Comparative Advantage', 268–9, rescaled with the period average set to 100.

26 For a more detailed account, see Rod Alence, 'The 1937–1938 Gold Coast cocoa crisis: the political economy of commercial stalemate', *African Economic History* 19 (1990–91), 77–104.

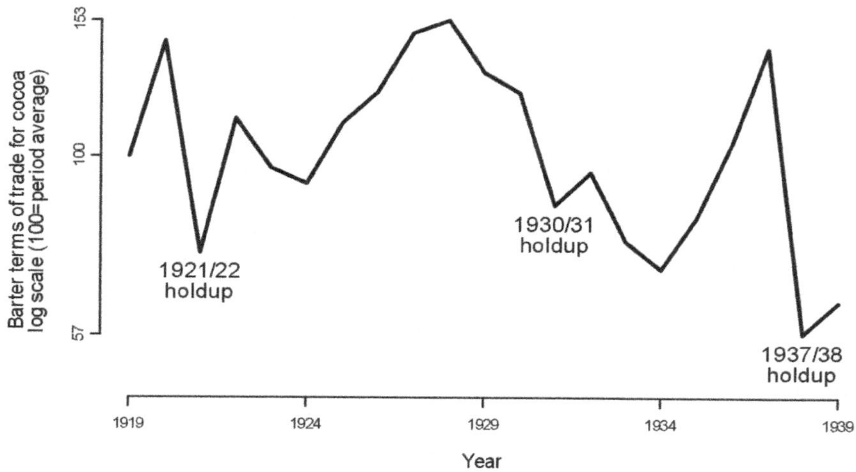

Figure 4.1 Terms of Trade for Cocoa and Hold-Ups in the Gold Coast 1919–39.

just before the start of the season, the European firms finalised a new buying agreement. UAC took the lead, and thirteen firms that purchased 94 per cent of the Gold Coast's cocoa the previous year participated. For the first time they included Cadbury and Fry, the chocolate manufacturer that was the second leading buyer, after the UAC.[27] As word of the agreement spread and local prices dropped, farmers' groups throughout the country mobilised the hold-up and boycott. It was the first hold-up endorsed by the Asantehene (king of the Asante people) and extended across all major cocoa-growing areas of the country.[28] By December, imported merchandise was accumulating in customs sheds. When officials threatened to invoke an obscure statute to auction goods left in storage for more than thirty days, Barclay's Bank quickly complained to the Colonial Office.[29] In January, when cocoa exports usually peak, they were at a trickle.

The hold-up posed serious challenges for the Gold Coast government. Beyond fiscal concerns, the governor, Sir Arnold Hodson, worried about the threat of social unrest. The firms, through the British secretary of state for the colonies, pressed him to endorse their agreement publicly. A sceptical Hodson

27 Nowell, *Report of a Commission*, p. 191.

28 Gareth Austin documents Asante local participation in prior cocoa hold-ups, mainly on the initiative of farmers, and shows that it was organised farmers who pressed their chiefs and the Asantehene to endorse the 1937–38 hold-up: 'Capitalists and chiefs in the cocoa hold-ups in South Asante, 1927–1938', *International Journal of African Historical Studies*, 21:1 (1988), 63–95.

29 Letter from Baxter (Barclay's Bank), 6 Dec. 1937, TNA, CO 852/133/1, The British National Archives (TNA) (CO 852: 'Colonial Office, official correspondence, economic').

would go no further than issuing a terse informational circular to his senior officials.[30] Asked his views directly by the secretary of state, he wrote that he believed 'the continuation of this agreement will embitter relations between Europeans and Africans and disorganise trade.'[31] In public the governor was careful to project impartiality, but he was blunt in private conversations with visiting representatives of the firms. He admonished them that their agreement risked provoking riots among the 'large number of people out of work' in the towns, who were 'ripe for mischief and the ready tool of agitators.'[32] John Cadbury, who led the firms' delegation, recorded his irritation at the governor's repeated 'reference to rioting, burning, loss of life and the necessity of using troops ... to impress us of the seriousness of the position into which we had put the country.'[33]

To break the stalemate, Hodson proposed an independent commission of inquiry. The governor of Nigeria, where a protest movement against the firms threatened to escalate into a hold-up, concurred.[34] The secretary of state gave his approval, provided the West African governments covered the costs themselves. The appointment of the commission was announced on 11 February, to be chaired by William Nowell, former director of the East African Agricultural Research Institute. The announcement came with a request for farmers 'to commence selling their cocoa forthwith in an orderly manner and to end the boycott.'[35] But farmers did not budge, meaning Nowell's first task when he arrived was to negotiate a 'truce.' Farmers and firms alike were anxious that if trade resumed abruptly, cocoa would flood the market and further depress the price, as happened after the 1930/31 hold-up collapsed. Nowell leveraged this anxiety, crafting an arrangement with temporary monthly export quotas, which was enough to convince the firms to suspend their agreement and farmers their hold-up.

The commission's report, published in September 1938, recommended 'radical changes in the conditions of cocoa marketing in the Gold Coast.'[36] It emphasised two systemic problems: weak commercial organisation of farmers

30 London to Agriculture Director and Provincial Commissioners, 17 November 1937, CSO 2815/30, sub-file 1/1, Public Records and Archives Administration Department (PRAAD), Accra, Ghana.

31 Hodson to Ormsby-Gore, 18 November 1937, TNA, CO 852/67/2.

32 Hodson to Ormsby-Gore, 9 December 1937, TNA, CO 852/67/2.

33 John Cadbury, 4 January 1938, Cadbury Papers, file 288/27, University of Birmingham.

34 On the Nigerian protest movement see Jan-Georg Deutsch, *Educating the Middlemen: A Political and Economic History of Statutory Cocoa Marketing in Nigeria, 1936–1947* (Berlin, 1995), 94–108.

35 The request was published in the official *Gold Coast News* and reproduced in Accra's two daily newspapers the next day.

36 Nowell, *Report of a Commission*, 161.

and speculative 'abuses' by African 'middlemen' that fed off short-term price movements. To improve the organisation of farmers, the commission proposed a single farmers' association with statutory control over all cocoa buying. Farmers would be required to sell to the association through designated local farmers' groups. The association would then sell to merchant firms within the colony or sell directly on overseas markets. Payments to the farmers' groups would be made retrospectively at the average price received over at least two or three weeks, minus the association's operating expenses. Period-pooling of proceeds was to remove incentives for middlemen to engage in short-term price speculation, holding back cocoa on a rising market and releasing it at the first sign of a price drop. Retrospective payment was crucial, as it would minimise the up-front trading capital required by the association.

After convening two local committees, Hodson flatly rejected the commission's recommendations. He wrote to the secretary of state in June 1939, arguing that the Nowell scheme was 'bound to fail' and its failure would 'be laid at the door of Government with disastrous results.'[37] In his view, the statutory association would neither raise producer prices nor eliminate the trading 'abuses' at the heart of the commission's case against competitive purchasing. Drawing upon the local committees' reports, he concluded that farmers would not accept fully retrospective payment. The association would need to make at least half payment on delivery, which would greatly inflate financial requirements. He put the initial capital outlay at not less than £1 million – more than three times the commission's estimate, and more than a quarter of the government's annual revenue. He also expected the association to require recurring operating subsidies. Hodson's sceptical views were well received in the Colonial Office, where the leading specialist on West African agriculture agreed that the 'radical reorganisation' proposed by the Nowell commission would have forced the government 'to bite off more than it could chew.'[38]

So despite the spectacular disruption of trade, the governor felt unable to introduce significant marketing reforms. Concerned about the financial and administrative commitments that would be required, he opted to retain an unsettled status quo. The episode highlights the tight constraints imposed by the colonial policymaking regime. Hodson's rejection of the commission's recommendations, bound to be controversial locally, was however never publicised. Less than four months later, he eagerly supported an alternative wartime scheme for state-controlled cocoa marketing.

37 Hodson to MacDonald, 1 June 1939, TNA, CO 852/192/1.
38 Minute by Stockdale, 3 July 1939, TNA, CO 852/192/1.

The Transition to State-Controlled Cocoa Marketing

The day after the United Kingdom declared war on Germany in September 1939, UAC executives approached the Colonial Office hoping to secure commercial protection.[39] During the First World War, the British government refused to guarantee the purchase of West African cocoa. Shipping disruptions and the closure of enemy markets led buying prices on the coast to fall by half, and even at these prices farmers failed to sell much of their produce.[40] The Gold Coast was more tense on the eve of the Second World War. As Eugene Melville, influential in the Colonial Office's economic department, put it, 'No one with a sense of responsibility could have contemplated ... a repetition of the cocoa hold-up of the previous year ... without foreseeing the quite serious possibility of political unrest.'[41] Hodson, in regular contact with the Colonial Office, supported any arrangement that would guarantee the purchase of the full crop at a price high enough to meet farmers' production costs.[42]

The firms and colonial officials hoped the British government would serve as buyer of last resort, paying a minimum price for unsellable 'surplus' cocoa. The stumbling block was that the Treasury, whose approval was required, had serious reservations about what could only be a loss-making proposition for the British taxpayer. After meeting with Treasury officials in late October, a Colonial Office representative lamented that there was 'not much prospect the proposals will be accepted.'[43] Then the Colonial Office conjured an ingenious proposal to address Treasury's concerns. A statutory board would buy the entire crop at a controlled price, rather than just buying surplus produce. 'Profits' earned on successful sales would offset losses on unsold stocks. The risk of cumulative net losses could be reduced by setting a conservative producer price. The Treasury accepted the proposal, conditional on cutting the Gold Coast government's recommended producer price for the current season by 10 per cent to reduce its own liability. The government and the Colonial Office readily agreed, as a concession 'to assist towards the acceptance of the scheme.'[44]

39 For a more detailed account, see Rod Alence, 'Colonial government, social conflict and state involvement in Africa's open economies: the origins of the Ghana Cocoa Marketing Board', *Journal of African History* 42:3 (2001), 397–416.

40 David Killingray, 'Repercussions of World War I in the Gold Coast', *Journal of African History* 19:1 (1978), 39–59, at 42–3.

41 Eugene Melville, 'The marketing of West African cocoa', in Cocoa, Chocolate and Confectionery Alliance (ed.), *Report of Cocoa Conference Held at Grosvenor House* (London, 1948), 70–84, at 71.

42 Hodson to MacDonald, 25 September 1939, TNA, CO 852/256/1.

43 Minute by Stockdale, 26 October 1939, TNA, CO 852/256/2.

44 Minute by Melville, 26 October 1939; Hale to Melville, 28 Oct. 1939, TNA, CO 852/256/2.

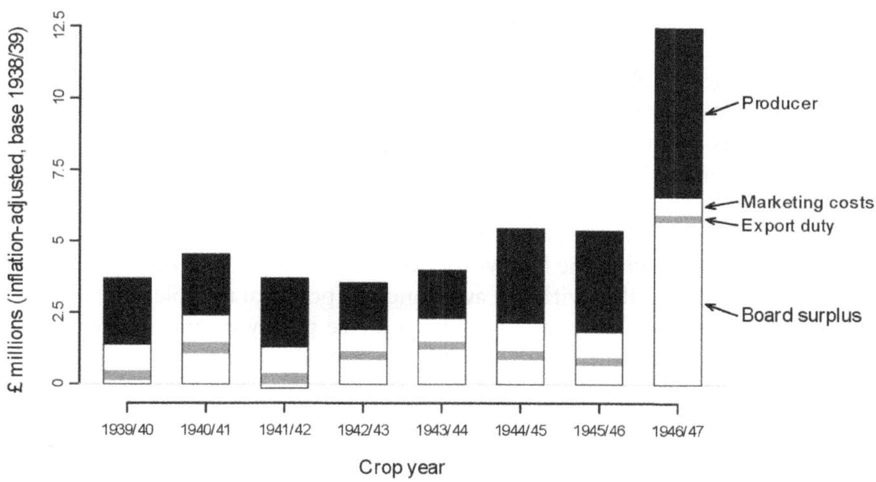

Figure 4.2 Allocation of the Gold Coast's Cocoa Proceeds 1939/40–1946/47.

The wartime scheme split cocoa proceeds four ways. Farmers received the producer price set by the control board. European firms, along with a few African ones, served as buying and shipping agents, paid according to an official cost schedule. West African governments levied modest export duties. The balance, surplus or deficit, accrued to the control board. The control scheme began as a temporary measure but continued without major changes from December 1939 through the end of the 1946/47 crop year. Figure 4.2 shows the annual allocation of inflation-adjusted proceeds.[45]

The board's conservative producer price policy reflected Treasury influence, but farmers were protected from a local market collapse in return. The protection was operative during the first four years of the war, when the board purchased one-fifth more cocoa in the Gold Coast than it could ship and sell,

45 Total proceeds and payments and payments to producers are based on data in Colonial Office, *Report on Cocoa Control in West Africa, 1939–43, and a Statement on Future Policy*, Cmd. 6554 (London, 1944), 14–16; Colonial Office, *Statement on the Future Marketing of West African Cocoa*, Cmd. 6950 (London, 1946), 10–12. Control board surpluses and deficits on Gold Coast cocoa are from P.T. Bauer, *West African Trade: A Study of Competition, Oligopoly and Monopoly in a Changing Economy* (Cambridge, 1954), 396. Marketing costs (including purchasing and shipping) are calculated as a residual. The inflation adjustment uses the UK price index for 'consumer goods and services' from Charles Feinstein, *National Income, Output and Expenditure of the United Kingdom, 1855–1965* (Cambridge, 1972), table 61. As each crop season spans two calendar years, I use the average price index for two years.

and it was forced to destroy surplus stocks.[46] Without a guaranteed buyer, excess supply would have depressed local prices, and many farmers would have failed to sell their produce. Worst was 1941/42, when the United States banned cocoa imports from West Africa, and nearly 40 per cent of the crop never left the coast. The marginally negative bar in figure 4.2 for that year represents the board's only annual deficit, but it was small enough to be financed by accumulated surpluses. Farmers complained about low producer prices, which they said failed to cover their costs, though they appreciated having a guaranteed buyer. With the Treasury having the last word, producer prices continued to be set 'at the minimum compatible with the avoidance of political trouble.'[47]

The official rationale for a conservative price policy evaporated after the 1942/43 season, when the Colonial Office acknowledged that the chance of being stuck with surplus cocoa was 'increasingly remote.'[48] Threats to the West African shipping route had receded, the American ban had been lifted, and international cocoa prices were rising sharply. Yet the control board continued to pay low producer prices, now justified as a domestic anti-inflationary measure. As part of British wartime policy, colonial imports of consumer goods were restricted, and these restrictions tightened as Britain's war debt mounted.[49] The board's cocoa producer price was the most effective means of curbing consumer demand, albeit one that placed the full burden on farmers by deliberately withholding income from them. Government concerns about unrest had meanwhile shifted from hold-ups by rural farmers to strikes by urban workers. For example, when Sir Alan Burns arrived in late 1941 to replace Hodson as governor, he faced a railway and harbour strike over the failure of wages to keep pace with inflation, which posed a 'serious hindrance to the movement of essential war supplies.'[50] Evidence emerged that low producer prices were leading cocoa farmers to neglect maintenance, and swollen-shoot disease was ravaging the older tree stock in the Eastern Province. Yet the government's stance on producer prices had flipped: early in the war it was the strongest advocate of paying farmers more; from 1944, concerned with

46 Data on destruction of surplus stocks is in Colonial Office, *Report on Cocoa Control*, 15.

47 David Meredith, 'State controlled marketing and economic "development": the case of West African produce during the Second World War', *Economic History Review*, 39:1 (1986), 77–91, at 82.

48 Colonial Office, *Report on Cocoa Control*, 6.

49 Michael Cowen and Nicholas Westcott, 'British imperial economic policy during the war', in David Killingray and Richard Rathbone (eds) *Africa and the Second World War* (Basingstoke, 1986), 20–67; Nicholas J. Westcott, 'Sterling and Empire: The British Imperial Economy, 1939–51', Institute of Commonwealth Studies seminar paper (1983).

50 Burns to Stanley, 27 Nov. 1941, CO 96/774, TNA (CO 96, 'Original correspondence, Gold Coast'); also see Alan Burns, *Colonial Civil Servant* (London, 1949), 186–7.

domestic inflation, the government had to be pressed hard by the Colonial Office to agree to raise producer prices.

Controlled marketing was never intended to outlive the war, but memories of the 1937/38 hold-up and the Nowell commission's analysis convinced the Colonial Office that 'a full return to pre-war arrangements could not be contemplated.'[51] As the board began racking up large surpluses 'on behalf of' African farmers, a palatable means was needed to return the funds when the war ended. As early as 1942 the Gold Coast government suggested retaining the structure of wartime controls, but shifting operational control and accumulated surpluses from London to a government-led board in Accra – an idea endorsed in a 1944 Colonial Office white paper.[52] The white paper provided political cover for continuing to withhold large surplus funds from farmers during the war. It attracted criticism from various quarters, not least the United States, which was concerned about effects on American consumers.[53] Two years later, the Colonial Office published a second white paper with the same proposals but a slicker rationale.[54] When the permanent Gold Coast Cocoa Marketing Board replaced the wartime control board from the 1947/48 season, it inherited the statutory monopsony powers and funds of its predecessor.

State-controlled cocoa marketing substantially modified the classic colonial policymaking regime. The impressive growth of the cocoa industry had brought prosperity to the Gold Coast but also exposed it to external shocks. The colonial regime provided a platform for export growth but limited the government's ability to manage conflict between African farmers and European firms. The war was a brief conjuncture when the British Treasury was willing to provide limited financial guarantees to back state-controlled marketing. The ability to set the producer price for cocoa turned out to be very useful to the government, not only in the ways originally envisaged, and no government in Ghana since has relinquished it.

Giving Up Control of the Price of Foreign Exchange, 1982–90

The post-colonial policymaking regime in Ghana, from just after independence until the mid-1980s, was a mirror image of the early colonial regime: incorporating a national currency with an administratively fixed exchange rate, while inheriting the state-controlled system of cocoa marketing established during

51 Melville, 'The Marketing of West African Cocoa', 72.

52 London to the Agriculture Director and provincial commissioners, 11 May 1942, TNA, CO 852/445/4; Colonial Office, *Report on Cocoa Control*.

53 David Meredith, 'The Colonial Office, British business interests and the reform of cocoa marketing in West Africa, 1937–1945', *Journal of African History* 29:2 (1988), 285–300, at 286.

54 Colonial Office, *Statement on Future Marketing*.

the Second World War. Politically, coups came to pose the greatest threat to the survival of governments, civilian and military alike. Confronted with external volatility, the actions of a series of insecure governments contributed to the country's most severe growth collapse. From 1971 through to 1981, real GDP per capita shrank by nearly a quarter. Against this bleak backdrop, Flight-Lieutenant Jerry Rawlings, in a post-coup radio broadcast on the last day of 1981, called for 'nothing less than a revolution. Something that would transform the social and economic order of this country.'[55]

For an insecure government facing a terms-of-trade shock, good economics often makes for bad politics, and vice versa. Responding to a large adverse shock, the economist's textbook advice is to adjust the domestic economy quickly to reflect changed external conditions. Prescribed policies include a calculated mix of 'expenditure reduction' (tight monetary and fiscal policies) to reduce aggregate demand and 'expenditure switching' to discourage imports and encourage exports (with exchange-rate devaluation preferred to ad hoc trade and exchange controls).[56] Yet a government with short political time horizons prefers to avoid or postpone the potentially destabilising side effects of adjustment. It resorts to financing fiscal shortfalls by printing money, imposes import and exchange controls to conserve foreign exchange, and devalues only when all else fails.[57] Short-term incentives are to avoid antagonising groups that threaten the government's survival. Yet failing to adjust compounds the domestic imbalances caused by the initial shock and results in deeper long-term economic damage. The collapse of the Ghanaian economy beginning in the 1970s was propelled by a protracted failure to adjust that fed a downward spiral.

Ghana's exposure to external volatility was on a similar scale in the 1970s to what it had been in the 1930s, but the social impact of adverse shocks differed. Under the colonial regime, the government's lack of policy instruments constrained it passively to transmit external shocks to the domestic economy. They inflamed tensions between African farmers and European firms, and the government was left to do its best to mediate. In contrast, the initial post-colonial regime gave governments an array of policy instruments. Large shocks could trigger downturns when the economy was otherwise performing well, and they could make a bad situation worse. Because government policies mediated the impact of external volatility, citizens held the government responsible for sharp declines in economic conditions, whatever the cause. When discontent rose, the most immediate political threat to the government was an opportunistic military coup.

55 Jerry John Rawlings, 'Resisting Injustice', radio broadcast to the nation, 31 December 1981, in *A Revolutionary Journey: Selected Speeches of Flt-Lt. Jerry John Rawlings, 31 Dec. 1981 to 31 Dec. 1982* (Accra, 1983), 1–3, at 1.

56 Paul Krugman, 'External shocks and domestic policy responses', in Rudiger Dornbusch, F. Leslie and C.H. Helmers (eds), *The Open Economy: Tools for Policymakers in Developing Countries* (New York, 1988), 54–79, at 64–73.

57 See Krugman, 'External shocks', 73.

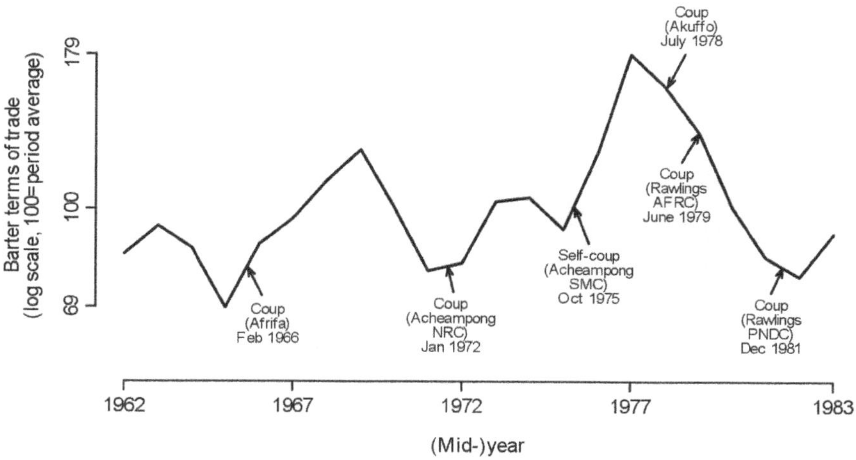

Figure 4.3 Terms of Trade and Military Coups in Ghana 1962–83.

The association of adverse shocks with coups from independence through the mid-1980s resembles the pattern of adverse shocks and cocoa hold-ups during the inter-war years. Figure 4.3 shows how the trend in terms of trade was punctuated by successful military coups.[58] External volatility increased in the 1970s, mainly due to rising and unstable world oil prices, which increased import price volatility alongside the usual volatility of the price of cocoa exports. Every notable trough in the terms of trade was accompanied by a successful coup, and every successful coup came on (or shortly after) a declining trend. The frequency of coups intensified from 1975, as economic growth collapsed.

Effects of an overvalued exchange rate are crucial to understanding Ghana's post-colonial growth collapse. Overvaluation occurs when a fixed exchange rate, set by government, dictates that local currency exchanges for more foreign currency than is justified by supply and demand. A political attraction of overvaluation is that it makes imported goods cheaper in local currency. Yet it also means that foreign exchange earned by exporters converts to fewer units of local currency and that (barring increased protectionism) domestic producers of importable goods must compete against cheaper imports. Overvaluation therefore benefits consumers of imports at the expense of producers in the tradable (export and import-competing) sector of the economy. By discouraging

58 Terms of trade are from an IMF database with 'rolling weights' based on lagged three-year averages; see Gruss and Kebhaj, 'Commodity terms of trade'. In the figure, terms of trade are annual averages and coup dates monthly. Year ticks for the terms of trade are placed 'mid-year'.

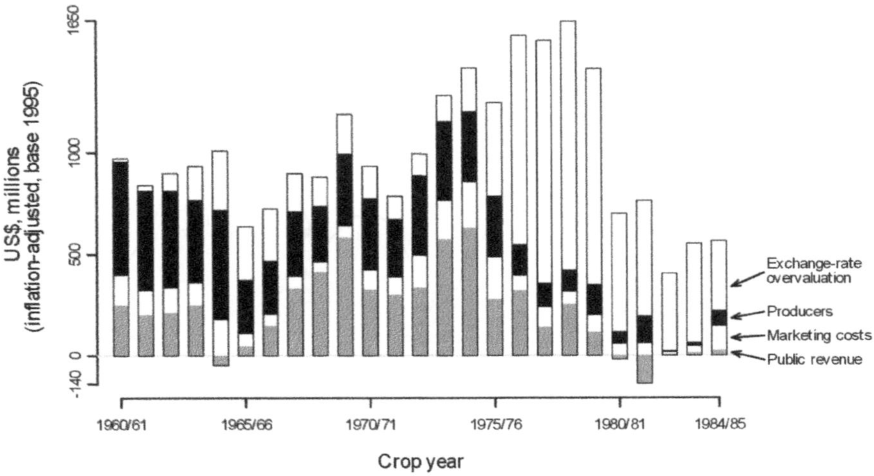

Figure 4.4 Allocation of Ghana's Cocoa Proceeds 1960/61–84/85.

exports and import substitutes, an overvalued exchange rate compounds balance-of-payments problems caused by an adverse terms-of-trade shock.

Overvaluation ravaged cocoa farmers' incomes. Figure 4.4 uses estimates of the degree of overvaluation to make its effects explicit. The height of each bar represents the real (inflation-adjusted) US dollar value of cocoa exports for the 1960/61 to 1984/85 seasons. The three domestic components – payments to producers, the marketing board's costs, and public revenue (export duties plus or minus the marketing board's surplus or deficit) – are based on the conversion of Ghanaian cedis to US dollars at the official exchange rate. As the exchange rate was always overvalued to some extent, the sum of the domestic components falls short of total export proceeds. The shortfall can be attributed to exchange-rate overvaluation.[59]

An unprecedented burden of overvaluation emerged in the mid-1970s. By the early 1980s, overvaluation accounted for the vast majority of proceeds from cocoa sold through official (legal) channels. Considering only the producer share in Figure 4.4, the trend might look like just a quantitative intensification of the 'underpayment' of farmers, but there was a qualitative difference. Deductions

59 Shares for producers, marketing costs, and public revenue are from Stryker, *Trade, Exchange Rate, and Agriculture*, 89–90 (table 8). Exchange-rate overvaluation is based on purchasing-power-parity real exchange rates in Stryker, 279–80 (table 2.1, fourth column), with the overvaluation factor equal to the real exchange rate divided by 0.71 (the rate assumed to be an 'equilibrium' 1957 through 1959). Shares of proceeds are then applied to real exports earnings in US dollars from Teal, 'Export growth'.

from farmers' income previously came mainly as public revenue and marketing costs – 'from below' in the geometry of the figure. Beginning in the mid-1970s, they intensified but came increasingly 'from above', soaked up by the overvalued exchange rate. Overvaluation was not only devastating farmers' income, it was doing the same to the marketing board and the state's fiscal base.

As the economy deteriorated, political instability ensued. The slide started when Lieutenant Colonel (later General) Ignatius Kutu Acheampong toppled the elected civilian government of Dr. K. A. Busia in January 1972. Busia's government had just implemented an adjustment programme with a large devaluation and public spending cuts. Acheampong reversed the programme, cancelling some spending cuts and partly revaluing the currency. He briefly abided by a 'self-reliance' pact with the Bank of Ghana, which included a build-up of external reserves and fiscal restraint.[60] But for the rest of his tenure, expenditure control was weak, and devaluation was off the table. The government printed money to finance fiscal deficits, the resulting inflation with a fixed exchange rate fuelled mounting overvaluation, overvaluation reduced the real value of public revenue from cocoa, revenue shortfalls necessitated further deficit spending, and the spiral continued. The spiral was the at the heart of Tsikata's paradox (noted earlier) of a highly 'controlled' economy that was in fact totally out of control. A boom in Ghana's terms of trade, which peaked in 1977, temporarily masked the extent of the decline (see figure 4.3). Then reality hit, when a sharp drop in world cocoa prices coincided with the decade's second major oil shock. On the downward slide, successful coups occurred in 1978 and 1979. Jerry Rawlings, who seized power in a June 1979 coup, handed over to an elected civilian government a few months later. Then, on the last day of 1981, he returned after toppling the same government.

The Devaluation Debate, 1982

Rawlings' second government was politically and institutionally eclectic. 'Revolutionary' organs operated alongside established structures of the post-colonial state. Defence committees formed in communities and workplaces, coordinated by a body eventually known as the National Democratic Congress (NDC). A Committee of Secretaries served as a more conventional cabinet, with each ministerial portfolio assigned to a secretary. The PNDC sat atop these parallel structures, the highest executive decision-making body. It initially consisted of six regular members, some civilian, some military, chaired by Rawlings as the head of state. Crucial decisions were taken by Rawlings and an inner circle of advisers, with the PNDC serving as a rubber stamp.

60 For the account of the then-governor of the Bank of Ghana, see Frimpong-Ansah, *Vampire State*, 108–10.

Within weeks of the coup, Rawlings announced a 'comprehensive review of the domestic economy'.[61] Behind the scenes, he and his inner circle solicited advice from intellectually diverse Ghanaian experts. Contrary to Rawlings's perceived radical tilt, his most trusted economic advisor was Joe Abbey. Abbey, economic commissioner in the military government that toppled Acheampong, had engineered 'disguised' devaluations (with IMF backing) in 1978 and 1979. Others consulted included, for example, Kwame Amoa, a socialist Ghanaian economist and deputy to Samir Amin at the United Nations Institute for Trade and Reconstruction (UNITAR) in Dakar. Amin and Amoa both flew in during January 1982 at Rawlings' invitation.[62]

With no finance secretary in place for several months, the National Economic Review Committee (NERC) managed the finance portfolio collectively. Its members' views spanned the spectrum of past Ghanaian economic policy. It came to be chaired by Kwesi Botchwey, a law lecturer known for his critiques of neo-colonialism, who was named finance secretary in May.[63] Botchwey mediated policy debates anchored at one end by the self-avowedly non-socialist Abbey and at the other by Kwesi Amoako-Atta, the 'scientific socialist' who had been Kwame Nkrumah's last finance minister. Rawlings deliberately engineered the heterogeneous committee. 'The nation had experienced all these characters and not made any headway', he explained. 'So I thought, put them together. Listen to them as they're talking and making their arguments. You'll be able to pick the solution out of it, the cross-point.'[64]

The committee's deliberations, secret except to Rawlings and his inner circle, included discussions of devaluation, with or without IMF backing. The objection of even the committee's deepest sceptic, Amoako-Atta, was mainly political. 'If you want to cut your throats, go ahead and devalue', he was paraphrased as saying.[65] Amoa, who was not on the NERC but prepared a twenty-two page paper for Rawlings in February, made a reasoned economic

61 Jerry Rawlings, 'Sovereign Power Lies with the People', introductory statement at a press briefing, 18 January 1982, in *Revolutionary Journey*, 14–15, at 14.

62 Samir Amin, *The Long Revolution of the Global South: Toward a New Anti-Imperialist International* (New York, 2019), 112–13. Amin reported that the visit was in 1981, which is impossible because Rawlings only returned to power on 31 December 1981. Kwame Amoa ('Interview by Author', Accra, 25 August 1992), who double-checked his passport, confirmed the visit was in January and February 1982.

63 For a sample of his academic work at the time, see Kwesi Botchwey, 'Transforming the "Periphery": A Study of the Struggle of the Social Forces in Ghana for Democracy and National Sovereignty', paper for the United Nations University Sub-Project on the Transformation of the World, UNU/HSDRSCA-83/UNUP-309 (1981).

64 Jerry Rawlings, 'Interview by Author', Accra, 27 January 2006.

65 Amoa, 'Interview by Author.' An irony of Amoako-Atta's position was that, during his tenure as finance minister, the Nkrumah government refused to devalue despite severe balance-of-payments problems – and was removed in a military coup.

case for devaluation. After disparaging the IMF as a 'surrogate ideologue for the capitalist system', he noted 'signs of increasing flexibility' within the IMF that might allow meaningful negotiation on standard policy prescriptions.[66] Contrary to the public appearance that the government firmly opposed devaluation, Rawlings and his close advisers were debating it internally within a few months of seizing power.

The first open discussion of devaluation within the government came in a joint meeting of the PNDC, the NDC, and the Committee of Secretaries, convened by Rawlings in August 1982. Abbey was tasked with presenting the NERC's work to a largely critical audience. Scrupulously avoiding the word 'devaluation', he used practical examples to show that 'it was economically unprofitable to produce for export because if you earned a dollar on any line of activity, and you surrendered this dollar to the central bank at the official exchange rate, ...you got less ... than your cost of production. And this was true whether you were in gold, cocoa, everything.'[67] When he finally admitted the exchange-rate 'adjustment' he advocated was a devaluation, it triggered a long and acrimonious debate. To bridge the economic divide within the government, a new committee was formed for critics to propose structural reforms and 'mobilisational' activities to accompany the NERC's macroeconomic proposals. Amoa and Amin (along with the Nigerian economist Eskor Toyo) were brought back in, ostensibly as technical advisors. But, in Amin's words, Rawlings and his team assigned them 'more directly political objectives': to try 'to contribute to the calmer exchange of views between the different parts of the movement'.[68]

The committee's report framed a fragile compromise. It juxtaposed a major concession on devaluation with a proposed set of illiberal structural and mobilisational measures and a call to disband the NERC. The language on devaluation was remarkably unequivocal – for example, 'The Cedi will have to be devalued', and, 'If the restoration of financial and price rationality will induce the IMF to come to the aid of revolutionary Ghana, well and good.'[69] Within the committee, the position on devaluation meant different things to different members. Some embraced it as a necessary but insufficient condition for addressing the country's economic crisis; others saw it as part of a political *quid pro quo* in which, as put bluntly by Emmanuel Hansen, NDC secretary

66 Kwame Amoa, 'Formulating an Economic Policy for Ghana (Notes for Discussion)', paper attached to memorandum to Jerry Rawlings, 23 February 1982, 12–13.

67 Joe Abbey, 'Interview by Author', Accra, 6 August 1992.

68 Amin, *Long Revolution*, 113.

69 Committee of the NDC and PNDC Secretaries, 'Report of the Committee of the National Defence Committee and the Secretaries on the Economy', unpublished, 10 September 1982.

at the time, 'The Right got its devaluation, and the Left got its radical developmental framework.'[70]

Political tensions within the government soon exploded. Rawlings and his inner circle rejected the committee's call to disband the NERC and referred its other proposals to the PNDC secretaries to implement if and how they saw fit.[71] Some committee members continued to work on a structural and mobilisational programme to accompany the NERC's macroeconomic framework. Those seeking to shift the balance of power within the government, however, realised they had been outmanoeuvred. A few began plotting an overthrow from within. PNDC member Chris Atim was secretly called upon to mobilise civilian opposition. Others began to do what one insider euphemistically called 'mobilise soldiers to implement the decision to change the leadership.'[72] Tensions came to a head on 23 November, when PNDC member Alolga Akata-Pore was arrested for a coup attempt. Rawlings announced publicly that the government would be 'purged from top to bottom.'[73] The purge removed the final obstacles to the NERC's work, in Abbey's view. He believed if 'we could get something that was hard-fought' from negotiations with the IMF and other donors, 'we could be on our way.'[74]

From Devaluation to a Floating Exchange Rate

The government and the IMF signed a memorandum of understanding in February 1983, which included a substantial devaluation. The devaluation was central to the government's Economic Recovery Programme (ERP), which Botchwey announced in his April 1983 budget speech. The rate of devaluation, from 2.75 cedis to the dollar to a trade-weighted average of 25, corresponded with the IMF's initial prescriptions. It would, the IMF noted, 'restore the exchange rate in real terms to close to what it was in 1972, which is the last year with a reasonable equilibrium in the balance of payments.'[75] The IMF's main concession was to permit a dual-rate system, which Ghanaian negotiators hoped they could use to convince the public that the ERP was not a 'standard IMF package.' In his budget speech, Botchwey adopted Abbey's rhetorical tactic, not using the word 'devaluation' once. He explained the exchange-rate changes as a 'system of bonuses and surcharges' on external transactions, a

70 Emmanuel Hansen, *Ghana Under Rawlings: The Early Years* (London, 1990), 116.

71 Zaya Yeebo, *Ghana: The Struggle for Popular Power, Rawlings: Saviour or Demagogue* (London, 1991), 125.

72 Yeebo, *Ghana*, 149.

73 'PNDC, NDC to Be Purged', *People's Daily Graphic* (Accra), 26 November 1982, 1.

74 Abbey, 'Interview by Author.'

75 International Monetary Fund, 'Memorandum of Understanding [with the Government of Ghana]', 18 February 1983.

more equitable way of allocating scarce foreign exchange, 'conferring on foreign exchange earners bonuses which are to be financed by surcharges on all users of foreign exchange.'[76]

Widespread public opposition focused on the steep increases in official prices of consumer goods and tested the government's nerve. Many senior officials gave public speeches defending the ERP, anchored by a radio and television address by Rawlings. He declared that Ghana had reached a 'moment of truth' and could not 'run away from it.' Batting away criticism of the bonus-surcharge system as a devaluation in disguise, he argued that 'it is not in our national interest that our hard-earned and increasingly scarce foreign exchange should be sold cheaply to users while exporters are denied adequate cedi compensation for the foreign exchange they earn.'[77] The political environment was tense, with a constant threat of coups. In mid-June, for example, plotters seized the national broadcasting headquarters and announced the government had been overthrown, only for their putsch to collapse later in the day.

The devaluation announced in the 1983 budget was the first in what became a regular series. The government meanwhile pursued restrictive fiscal and monetary policies and sought to rehabilitate exports. Yet these supporting measures could not quickly bring inflation down to near the rates of Ghana's trading partners. After each devaluation, the currency invariably became overvalued again, though less so than before. The second devaluation was in October 1983, when the lower tier of the bonus-surcharge system was abolished, resulting in a unified exchange rate of 30 cedis to the dollar. The government and IMF reviewed the exchange rate every quarter and made discrete devaluations. The last was in January 1986 and resulted in a rate of 90 to the dollar.[78]

Repeated discrete devaluations had economic and political disadvantages, which prompted a shift toward a floating exchange rate. A key economic concept is the 'real exchange rate': the nominal exchange rate adjusted for differences in price levels within the countries of each currency. Periodic devaluations could never fully track the real exchange rate, which depreciated continuously due to Ghana's domestic inflation. Politically, unpopular devaluation announcements were focal points for the government's opponents in a coup-prone environment.[79] The government introduced a foreign-exchange auction in 1986. It

76 Ghana, Ministry of Finance and Economic Planning, *Summary of PNDC's Budget Statement and Economic Policy for 1983* (Accra-Tema, 1983), 2.

77 Jerry Rawlings, 'Ghana's Moment of Truth', radio and television broadcast, 2 May 1983, in *Forging Ahead: Selected Speeches of Flt-Lt. Jerry John Rawlings, 1 Jan. 1983 to 31 Dec. 1983* (Accra, 1984), 16–21, at 16–18.

78 Exchange-rate policy during this period is summarised in Ishan Kapur et al., 'Ghana: Adjustment and Growth, 1983–91', *IMF Occasional Paper* 86 (1991), 18.

79 See Jeffrey Herbst, *The Politics of Reform in Ghana, 1982–1991* (Berkeley, 1993), 48–9.

helped depoliticise exchange-rate adjustments while pushing the rate toward a market-clearing equilibrium. Foreign-exchange receipts were still routed through the central bank, but they were sold domestically at auction rates. Technical issues delayed moves to a fully floating exchange rate. The latter included legalising private foreign-exchange bureaus (in 1988), phasing out import licensing (completed in 1989), and creating a unified 'wholesale' market for foreign exchange (1990).[80] After the last discrete devaluation in 1986, it took roughly four years for the country to achieve a floating exchange rate with 'full convertibility'.

Like the colonial currency regime but by different means, a floating exchange rate acts a safety valve to prevent severe overvaluation. The real exchange rate becomes overvalued when domestic inflation exceeds external inflation without a compensating depreciation in the nominal exchange rate. Under the colonial currency regime, the guaranteed exchange parity between British and West African pounds, coupled with unrestricted (usually) trade and capital flows, prevented the emergence of sustained inflation differentials in the first place.[81] Under a floating exchange-rate regime, excess domestic inflation is possible but immediately triggers a proportional increase in the local currency price of foreign exchange. Exchange-rate depreciation compensates for the domestic inflation, typically leaving the real exchange rate essentially unchanged. For this reason, a shift from fixed to floating exchange rates has been likened to a shift from fixed *nominal* exchange rates to one of 'fixed' *real* exchange rates.[82] Not only does a floating exchange rate alleviate balance-of-payments pressures, it also self-corrects relative prices between the tradable and non-tradable sectors of the economy.

The transition to floating exchange rates in the 1980s transformed the policymaking regime within which Ghanaian governments respond to external volatility. Governments retain the fiscal and monetary policy discretion accorded by a national currency but have surrendered the exchange rate to market forces. They can still resort to inflationary deficit finance but must accept that this brings an exchange-rate depreciation. Shielded from perils of overvaluation, Ghana ended the long twentieth century with its second major growth episode: real GDP per capita rose by more than 50 per cent between the mid-1980s and 2010.

80 For details, see Kapur et al., 'Ghana', 18–25.

81 Wartime and early post-war trade restrictions were a notable exception.

82 W. Max Corden, *Inflation, Exchange Rates, and the World Economy: Lectures in International Monetary Economics*, 3rd edn (Chicago, 1986), 130. An overvalued real exchange rate is possible under a colonial currency regime or a floating exchange-rate regime, but only for as long as it is financed by net capital inflows.

Conclusion

This chapter has analysed two major changes in Ghana's 'policymaking regime' during the long twentieth century. The first was the introduction of state-controlled cocoa marketing during the Second World War, within an otherwise restrictive colonial regime. This change established state control over the domestic producer price, historically the most important price within Ghana's tradable sector. The second was the transition from a fixed to a floating exchange rate in the 1980s, within a post-colonial policymaking regime that otherwise allowed wide policy discretion. By leaving the exchange rate to market forces, this change ended state control over a key price that influences relative returns between the tradable and nontradable sectors. Both changes, initiated to address immediate challenges, have become enduring features of Ghana's political economy.

Ghana's experience offers comparative insights for other primary-exporting countries. During the international economic upheavals of the 1930s, colonial governments in Africa and beyond adopted new forms of state intervention to regulate sensitive prices in externally exposed sectors. On Hancock's traders' frontier, marketing boards for export agriculture became increasingly common. In settler economies, where mining and plantation agriculture dominated exports, the transactional frontier of imperial expansion ran through a variety of labour relationships between European employers and African workers. Not coincidentally, officials became preoccupied with labour stabilisation and colonial welfare after shocks of the mid-1930s triggered 'disturbances' such as strikes on the Copperbelt in present-day Zambia and a wave of social unrest in the West Indies. During the economic turbulence of the 1970s, the fate of primary-exporting countries varied widely. This partly reflected differences in the degree of exposure to terms-of-trade shocks, but institutions mattered as well. Ghana, like many newly independent countries with national currencies and weak monetary institutions, fared poorly. Relevant comparators include African countries in regional monetary unions, such as the CFA franc zone. The CFA countries benefited initially from their membership in a more restrictive currency regime, but the benefits dissipated later as the CFA franc itself became increasingly overvalued.

Policymaking regimes can have powerful effects on how governments respond to external shocks and in turn on economic performance. During the long twentieth century, Ghana has had four distinct policymaking regimes, each lasting more than two decades. Across these periods, growth has been episodic – starting with an impressive growth climb, proceeding over rolling hills of relative stagnation, plunging off an economic cliff, and recovering to end the long century on a second extended upward climb. By zooming in on why governments – colonial and post-colonial – initiated major changes of the policymaking regime, this chapter has proposed a dynamic and historically 'decompressed' approach to making sense of the episodic trajectory of the Ghanaian economy over the long twentieth century.

5

Why Social Contracts in Ghana Matter: The Remarkable Durability of Understandings About the Relationship Between State and Society *c.*1920–2011

Paul Nugent

In trying to make sense of the political economy of the Gold Coast/Ghana over the long twentieth century, the challenge is to capture the intricacies of the historical record, whilst not allowing oneself to be overwhelmed by the detail. In this contribution, I deploy the concept of the *social contract* in order to expose the sedimentation of certain very particular understandings about the relationship between state and society. Needless to say, the concept of the social contract has a very long history within European political thought. Applying it to a different time and place in West Africa might not seem to be the obvious manoeuvre to make at this academic juncture. But for all the talk about decolonising the academy, scholars have yet to come up with emic models for talking about such things – not least concepts and models that lend themselves to making statements of a comparative nature.[1] The fact that the act of working may be experienced very differently does not render the concept of labour, or for that matter exploitation, invalid. Equally, James C. Scott has treated anarchy, in the sense of a stubborn commitment to remaining stateless, as a conscious praxis that resonates across cultures.[2] In the Gold Coast/Ghana, there have been decidedly few anarchists, but a lot of consideration has been

1 The 'social contract' does not need to be anchored to the European context. However, it is often deployed in a loose way, especially as it has crept into governance discourse. The concept has long been used to characterise the relationship between Sufi brotherhoods, citizens and the state in Senegal. See Cheikh Anta Babou, 'The Senegalese "social contract" revisited', in Mamadou Diouf (ed.), *Tolerance, Democracy, and Sufis in Senegal* (New York, 2013). For another recent academic application, see Relli Shechter, *Egyptian Social Contract: A History of State-Middle Class Relations* (Edinburgh, 2023). Social contracts are often viewed through the prism of tax bargains. For African comparisons, see Wilson Prichard, *Taxation, Responsiveness and Accountability in Sub-Saharan Africa: The Dynamics of Tax Bargaining* (Cambridge, 2015). Here I treat social contracts in a more expansive manner.

2 James C. Scott, *The Art of Not Being Governed: An Anarchist History of Upland Southeast Asia* (New Haven, 2011).

given to the question of where the right to govern emanates from. That is an invitation to think comparatively about how states have come to engage with their citizens.[3]

The broad concept of the social contract addresses the terms on which those who govern claim the right to do so and how this is received by those who are ruled. Whereas classical European social contract theory tended to envisage societies composed of atomised individuals, in Ghana the point of departure has always been the claim of the individual to belong within a 'home community' – even where the individuals concerned may have been physically residing a long way away. This means that what is regarded as legitimate, or otherwise, is typically construed in ways that transcend considerations of individual self-interest. Furthermore, the social contract does not imply harmony, but rather a willingness to bargain. The relationship of societal actors to the institutions of state may be explicitly coercive, it may involve the promise of the delivery of societal benefits and it may involve a degree of collusion in bending the rules. These variations provide the basis for what I have elsewhere referred to as coercive, productive and permissive social contracts.[4] These are obviously ideal types, and every concrete political configuration may manifest a dominant element but also embody aspects of the others. For people living in Mobutu's Zaire, the logic of Thomas Hobbes' version of the social contract – which is that only the sovereign stands between the citizen and chaos – would have been instantly recognisable. The reality was, however, that Mobutu increasingly presided over chaos, as large swathes of the country slipped from meaningful control. His political discourse famously involved an invitation to citizens to do what was necessary to survive – which was a coded way of winking at forms of corruption. Ghana manifests a different configuration because, while there were episodes of violence and repression, those who ruled typically subscribed to a version of the productive social contract. Equally, while there were periods when corruption proliferated, it was never normalised in the manner that it was under Mobutu.

Finally, I have preferred the social contract as a framing device to a political settlements approach which has gained academic traction in recent years. My reason is that the latter is mostly concerned with elite compacts, whereas I

3 On the need for intellectually ambitious, but genuinely reciprocal comparisons between Africa and elsewhere, see Gareth Austin, 'Reciprocal comparison and African history: tackling conceptual Eurocentrism in the study of Africa's economic past', *African Studies Review* 50:3 (2013), 1–28.

4 Paul Nugent, *Boundaries, Communities and State-Making in West Africa: The Centrality of the Margins* (Cambridge, 2019). An earlier formulation was contained in Paul Nugent, 'States and social contracts in Africa', *New Left Review* 63 (2010), 35–68.

am more interested in how those who rule relate to society as a whole.[5] To be sure, business and professional elites have wielded influence in Ghana beyond their crude numbers, but governments have also had to listen to the concerns emanating from the wider society.

The Social Contract and What it Explains

When it comes to the genealogy of the social contract in Ghana, it is necessary to go back to the nineteenth century, before the colonial state had settled into its existing borders. What I am advancing here is a more elaborated version of what I have proposed elsewhere.[6] The contract, which emerged out of long battles between the British and spokesmen for 'indigenous' interests, came to rest on three elements that existed in a complex relationship with one other. The first was the notion *that the state had its clear limits*. Although the Gold Coast, from the late 1920s onwards, is sometimes thought of in terms of the application of Indirect Rule principles, this is actually deeply problematic. In the imagining of the colonial relationship in the Gold Coast Colony (that is, the southern provinces), power was not devolved downwards to traditional authorities. On the contrary, the premise was that the colonial regime originated in rights ceded by the 'native states' to the British administration. Although the British authorities frequently sought to deny the validity of this construction, and to insist that this was a colony like others, Gold Coasters were insistent that the colonial state was constituted through consent. On this reading, what was not ceded was also retained, which helps to explain a collective determination to resist British claims to 'unoccupied' land and the right to levy direct taxes. The notional founding charter was the Bond of 1844 which was signed between Fante chiefs and the British. Its iconic status is comparable to the Treaty of Waitangi, which was signed four years earlier between Maori chiefs and the British and which has shaped ideas about the state–society relations in New

5 Tim Kelsall, Nikolai Schulz, William D. Ferguson, Matthias vom Hau, Sam Hickey and Brian Levy, *Political Settlements and Development: Theory, Evidence, Implications* (Oxford, 2022) are explicit that the focus is about the most powerful groups in society (chapter 2). See also Mushtaq Khan, 'Political settlements and the analysis of institutions', *African Affairs* 117:469 (2018), 636–55. For applications to Ghana, see Lindsay Whitfield, Ole Therkildsen, Lars Buur and Anne Mette Kjær, *The Politics of African Industrial Policy: A Comparative Perspective* (Cambridge, 2015), and Abdul-Garafu Abdulai, 'Political settlement dynamics and the emergence and decline of bureaucratic pockets of effectiveness in Ghana' in Sam Hickey (ed.), *Pockets of Effectiveness and the Politics of State-Building and Development in Africa* (Oxford, 2023).

6 Nugent, *Boundaries*.

Zealand ever since.[7] Writing in 1868, Africanus Horton pointedly observed that 'the inhabitants submitted themselves to the British Government, not as subjects, but as independent nations' and that when misunderstandings had arisen, this had 'been occasioned by the executive exceeding the charter of settlement'.[8] When J.B. Danquah later reflected on the meaning of the Bond, he was already building on a rich body of Ghanaian thought on the inherent limits of British powers.[9] Although Asante was added partially through conquest, Gold Coast intellectuals, who were initially in favour of military action, came to apply the same model to Asante as well. In the north, the British eventually decided to import something that was supposed to look like Indirect Rule, but in reality this meant building on the centralised polities that existed and affixing stateless peoples as administrative appendages.[10] The main difference in the Northern Territories was that the British claimed the right to interfere with respect to land and to direct taxes. But this did not really challenge the southern model which became hegemonic well before independence. All of this had important consequences for the language of politics, notably in terms of the claim to the existence of residual rights. In a scalar sense, British authority largely stopped at the District level. Beyond that point, officials were dealing with chiefly authorities who claimed ownership of local political and economic space. One additional consequence was that Gold Coast came to be imagined as an assemblage of 'native states' of different shapes and sizes – which remain important on the map today as 'traditional areas'.

The second element is the presumed responsibility of the state to *deliver particular kinds of public goods*. Infrastructure has always featured prominently since the nineteenth century, notably the construction of roads and bridges. However, health and educational services have also featured strongly.

7 Claudia Orange, *The Treaty of Waitangi* (Wellington, 1987). The difference is that in the context of settler colonialism, that treaty has been much more contentious.

8 James Africanus Beale Horton, *West African Countries and Peoples, British and Native* (London, 1868), 243.

9 See, for example, J.B. Danquah on the Bond of 1844 in *Liberty of the Subject: A Monograph on the Cocoa Hold-Up and Boycott of Foreign Goods (1937–1938)* (Kilsie, 1938), 35–41. I am grateful to Rod Alence for sharing a copy. See also J.B. Danquah, 'The historical significance of the Bond of 1844', *Transactions of the Historical Society of Ghana* 3:1 (1957), 3–29, and Gerardo Serra, 'Economic equality and political imagination in Ghana: J.B. Danquah on poverty, land and community', *Global Intellectual History* 9:1–2 (2022), 1–20.

10 Carola Lentz, *Ethnicity and the Making of History in Northern Ghana* (London & Edinburgh, 2006), ch. 3; Benjamin Talton, *Politics of Social Change in Ghana: The Konkomba Struggle for Political Equality* (New York, 2010), chs 2–3. This tendency was accentuated by the pursuit of Indirect Rule in the Northern Territories from the late 1920s. Martin Staniland, *The Lions of Dagbon: Political Change in Northern Ghana* (Cambridge, 1975), chs 5–6.

Demands for these public goods were initially made most forcefully at the coast, but gained increasing traction in the rest of the colony, especially as the economic centre of gravity moved to the cocoa-growing regions of the central belt. The third element was the role of the *state as a guarantor* of societal benefits. The colonial state historically grew out of the extension of mediation, which meant that the law (and lawyers) always loomed large.[11] The fundamental importance of customary law meant that the colonial edifice was itself widely seen as issuing from society rather than being imposed from an imperial template. Linked to the law was the role of the state in guaranteeing basic security and social order through policing. And finally, what came to be an important part of the governance jigsaw was the role of the state in guaranteeing equitable access to markets, both in an abstract and in a very practical sense. Markets were important because they were central to urban and rural livelihoods, but they were also fundamental to the possibility of consumption.

It is my contention that a broad consensus on the role of the state in relation to society emerged in colonial times as a product of active contestation, and that it remains with us to the present day. Indeed, it has been internalised to the extent that it is not even completely obvious to the actors that there is something particular about the currency through which politics is transacted. The catch is that the capacity of governments, operating in real time, to deliver on all aspects of the contract has tended to be uneven. Very often, prioritising one particular element has come at the expense of letting the others slip. The complexity of the task of governance is rooted in some fundamental structural constraints. A deep-rooted societal aversion to direct taxation, and the limited capacity to engage in extractive practices through control over land, meant that colonial and post-independent regimes leaned heavily on various forms of indirect and 'covert' taxation as well as government borrowing to balance the books. Import duties typically accounted for around half of all revenues in the inter-war years, as the spinoffs from cocoa drove increased levels of consumption.[12] During times of economic boom, it was possible to square the circle, whereas during periods of recession, the public authorities struggled to reconcile competing demands. The deterioration of basic infrastructure, and the proliferation of

11 Björn Edsman, *Lawyers in Gold Coast Politics, c.1900–1945: From Mensah Sarbah to J.B. Danquah* (Uppsala, 1979).

12 Beyond the Gold Coast/Ghana, across Africa, the possibility of dispensing with direct taxation was only present in south-western Nigeria, where cocoa similarly sustained high levels of import duty. See Leigh A. Gardner, *Taxing Colonial Africa: The Political Economy of British Imperialism* (Oxford, 2013), and Ewout Frankema and Marlous van Waijenburg, 'Metropolitan blueprints of colonial taxation? Lessons from fiscal capacity building in British and French Africa c.1880–1940', *Journal of African History* 55:3 (2014), 371–400.

the black market, have typically been the bell-wethers for the failure of governments to address the gap between expectations and delivery.

Using this interpretative framework, I now seek to show how this illuminates key moments over the course of the long twentieth century. The periodisation that I have adopted is somewhat unconventional, but is intended to shed light on key moments in the shaping and reshaping of social contracts. This is inevitably conducted in terms of broad historical brushstrokes, but hopefully those that are rooted in the rich historiography of the Gold Coast/Ghana.

The Forging of the Social Contract, 1920–1960

The starting point for this paper is what unfolded in the decades after the First World War when the colonial project finally began to manifest itself, albeit unevenly, across the whole territory it claimed. This process began with the consolidation of the Gold Coast Colony, which had the most sustained contact with the British, and was gradually extended to Ashanti, the Northern Territories and British Togoland. The early stages of this process have been exhaustively covered in the classic account of David Kimble, which I draw on here.[13] The first element, which concerns the *definition of the limits of the state*, is worth dwelling on because some parts of the story are counterintuitive. At an early point, the British had decided to accept, at least tacitly, the claim that the state derived its legitimacy from the agreements they had struck with coastal rulers in the nineteenth century – in stark contrast to the deportation of the Asantehene in 1896. In the 1920s, the British desire was to bring traditional authorities into direct engagement with the structures of governance beyond their immediate domains. This culminated in the formation of Provincial Councils of Headchiefs under the 1925 Constitution. This innovation was regarded by the educated elites in the coastal towns as an attempt to blunt their demands for representative government. The British authorities were prepared to concede the electoral principle at the municipal level, partly in the hope that this might be hitched to the obligation to embrace taxation – something to which Kimble notes there had been an almost pathological opposition ever since the demise of the poll tax in the nineteenth century.[14] With effect from 1924, a universal but qualified franchise was extended to the populations of the three main urban centres of Accra, Sekondi and Cape Coast.[15] When it came to the Legislative Council (Legco), the British authorities were keen to extend

13 David Kimble, *A Political History of Ghana, 1850–1928* (Oxford, 1963).

14 Kimble, *Political History*, 425.

15 The vote was extended to everyone over 21 years of age 'in occupation of a house with a rateable value of at least £8 per annum.' Kimble, *Political History*, 441.

representation to the leading paramount chiefs,[16] whereas the Aborigines Rights Protection Society (ARPS) wished the assembly to be based on direct election. In 1926, Legco was reconstituted to include three directly elected municipal members from each of the metropolitan areas, and six chiefly members chosen by the newly consecrated Provincial Councils of the Gold Coast Colony.[17] This reform was clearly limited, and was regarded by the ARPS as the thin end of the wedge. It gave chiefs more influence and it still left out Ashanti and the Northern Territories. But it did have the effect of giving the chiefs in the rural districts of the Colony a greater say in how state resources were dispensed. In addition, it brought chiefs into a national political space without undermining their dominion over their respective traditional areas. Hence the conception of the Gold Coast as the sum of its constituent traditional parts was formally entrenched in the constitutional arrangements. The restoration of the Asante monarchy did not lead to entry to Legco in the short-term, but British policy in Ashanti was informed by the same basic principles. Hence, Ashanti became a large building block in its own right, with its constituent parts broadly conforming to those of units in the Colony.

When it comes to the *delivery of services*, the British authorities recognised that recognition of their moral right to govern would rest on their effective delivery of public goods. While the administration was under pressure to cater to the interests of the mining industry,[18] it also accepted legitimacy of demands for spending that served local interests. When Gordon Guggisberg launched the first national development plan, he was making the terms of the contract very clear. His answer to the implicit question of whether colonialism was necessary was the practical benefits it would bring to the lives of Gold Coasters. The Ten-Year Development Plan (1920–27) was heavily skewed towards infrastructure, especially railways, ports and harbours. But there was also significant expenditure on roads as well as urban services (water, sewerage etc.) that were in demand.[19] During the 1920s, recurrent expenditure on construction expanded significantly, but the increased expenditure on education and health also reflected a wider concern with social development.[20] The question of road construction was in some ways the most crucial one for the majority living in the rural areas. The infamous 'roads gap' policy (shelved in 1929) sought to force some of the traffic onto the railways that had been constructed in part to serve

16 The Paramount Chief of Manya Krobo was the first chief to be appointed to the Legislative Council in 1911. Kimble, *Political History*, 432.

17 Kimble, *Political History*, 441–2.

18 This a recurring theme in Rhoda Howard, *Colonialism and Underdevelopment in Ghana* (London, 1978), 60–9.

19 G.B. Kay, *The Political Economy of Colonialism in Ghana: A Collection of Documents and Statistics* (Cambridge, 1972), table 14, at 322.

20 Kay, *Political Economy*, Table 27c, at 370.

the gold mines.[21] A recurrent demand that District Commissioners faced was for connection to the road network, especially as the cocoa frontier advanced. And, as is well known, communities often constructed their own roads in the hope that these would be adopted by the administration. The likelihood that this would happen hinged on the possibility of developing trade, which meant that the northern half of the country could boast only a few trunk roads and very few feeder roads during the inter-war years.

In terms of the revenue that was collected, entrenched opposition to direct taxation, which was matched by the reluctance of mining companies to pay export duties, forced the authorities into narrow channels. Aside from government borrowing, the solution that lay to hand was to lean heavily on import duties. These generally accounted for more than half of revenues in the 1920s,[22] whereas export duties made a more marginal contribution. Import duties were essentially a form of taxation on everyday consumption. The duties on imported alcohol, especially spirits, were by far the most important to the exchequer, accounting for well over half of the revenues from this source.[23] If the colonial state was not exactly fuelled by alcohol, it became heavily dependent on it. As I have sought to demonstrate elsewhere, this had governance implications in the borderlands to the east of the Volta River, because the proximity of the port of Lomé made the importation of much cheaper spirits highly attractive for traders there.[24] Imported tobacco, textiles and clothing were the other major sources of import duties (and of contraband) which underlined the manner in which these items were rapidly becoming items of everyday household consumption. This was a period when the right to consume, at something other than a subsistence level, came to be regarded as integral to the fulfilment of the social contract. Moreover, because the capacity to consume was very much linked to rising rural incomes derived from cocoa, the colonial state needed to be mindful of what was needed to support – or at least not to retard – the relentless process of expansion.[25] Hence the extension of rural production, increased consumption and road/bridge construction were integrally linked to one another.

During the tenure of Guggisberg, the colonial regime seemed to have established something approximating to a virtuous circle. However, the fiscal deficit

21 Howard, *Colonialism*, 174–5; Komla Tsey, *From Head-Loading to the Iron Horse: Railway Building in Colonial Ghana and the Origins of Tropical Development* (Bamenda, 2012), chs 1–2.

22 Kay, *Political Economy*, table 24a, at 348–9. This data is distilled from the Gold Coast *Blue Books*, various years.

23 Kay, *Political Economy*, Table 24b, at 358.

24 Nugent, *Boundaries*, 170–6. Paul Nugent, *Smugglers, Secessionists and Loyal Citizens on the Ghana-Togo Frontier: The Lie of the Borderlands Since 1914* (Athens OH, 2002), ch. 3.

25 See Gareth Austin, *Labour, Land and Capital in Ghana: From Slavery to Free Labour in Asante*, 1807–1956 (Rochester NY, 2005).

was an issue and when Guggisberg was replaced in 1927, the Plan was shelved. The Great Depression followed shortly thereafter, at which point the more ambitious initiatives ground to an abrupt halt. Government revenues declined rapidly, in large part because of the drop in import duties, and only climbed back to where they had been after 1936. Government expenditure had not returned to the level of the 1920s until the end of that decade – when the war struck a further blow. The official response to the Depression was to resort to retrenchment. Government departments shed staff and the budgets were pared back to the most needed recurrent expenditure. This all came at a cost to the relationship between the government and the population at large. Most people in urban and rural areas alike would have felt appreciably poorer during the 1930s. In the cocoa districts, the efforts of the buying firms to combine and dictate the producer price led to well-documented hold-ups, most notably in 1930–31 and 1937–38.[26] The colonial government tried to abstract itself from the fray, but was widely regarded as favouring the European firms – especially in the latter instance. As the independent press waxed increasingly critical of government performance, and linked this to a trans-Atlantic discourse of anti-imperialism, a thin-skinned Gold Coast administration became intolerant of critical voices. This was reflected in the censorship of the Gold Coast press and the attempt to muzzle journalists in the 1930s.[27] In this way, the government forfeited whatever goodwill had been built up in the 1920s. Although there were renewed expressions of loyalty when the Second World War broke out, the manner in which access to scarce consumer goods was managed became a source of underlying friction. Significantly, the urban grievances that culminated in the 1948 riots began with a consumer boycott of the European trading firms in Accra who stood accused of hoarding and inflating the prices of consumer items. The actual trigger for the events that followed was the killing of the ex-servicemen at the Christiansborg crossroads, but the evidence strongly suggests that the administration had already forfeited the sympathy of much of the urban population by this point.[28] When the Convention People's

26 John Miles, 'Rural protest in the Gold Coast: the cocoa hold-ups, 1908–1938' in Clive Dewey and A.G. Hopkins (eds), *The Imperial Impact: Studies in the Economic History of Africa and India* (London, 1978); Rhoda Howard, 'Differential class participation in an African protest movement: the Ghana cocoa boycott of 1937–38', *Canadian Journal of African Studies* 10: 3 (1976), 469–80. Gareth Austin, 'Chiefs and capitalists in the cocoa hold-ups in South Asante, 1927–1938', *International Journal of African Historical Studies* 21: 1 (1988), 63–95; Rod Alence, 'The 1937–38 cocoa crisis: the political economy of commercial stalemate', *African Economic History* 19 (1990–91), 77–104.

27 Stanley Shaloff, 'Press controls and sedition proceedings in the Gold Coast, 1933–1939', *African Affairs* 71:284 (1972), 241–63; Jarvis L. Hargrove, *Ghana's Ashanti Pioneer Newspaper: Aim High, Strive Hard, Go Forward* (Cham, 2022), ch. 3.

28 Great Britain, Colonial Office, *Report of the Commission of Enquiry into Disturbances in the Gold Coast, 1948* [Watson Commission] (London, 1948). For a glimpse of the rich evidence that never made it into the final report, see Jennifer Hart, 'One British archive:

Party (CPP) was established to take advantage of these events and to pursue a campaign for self-government, it is significant that much of their power base lay with the market women.

The rest of the story is very well known. The British decision to concede a democratically elected assembly meant that the genie could not be put back in the bottle even once the underlying economic conditions had dramatically improved. After 1951, with Kwame Nkrumah now installed as the Leader of Government Business, it was a matter of when rather than if full independence would come. The entrenched mythology surrounding the politics of these years often makes it difficult to get to the bottom of what really happened – which is not helped by the forced 'migration' of the archival record from Ghana. But a few points can be extracted that are relevant to the issue of social contracts. The first is that the CPP did not ride to power on the crest of a wave of popular support.[29] It won a safe Parliamentary majority but on a low turnout. It triumphed because it managed to suture its regional power-base in the coastal strip, where much of the population was located, to pockets of support elsewhere – often playing off chieftaincy disputes or opposition to chiefly authority where social tensions were acute. Secondly, the CPP was able to firm up a commitment to the social contract, but stripped of its colonial associations. The first Nkrumah government inherited a colonial Ten-Year Plan, but this was replaced by a more ambitious Five-Year Plan in 1952,[30] which then rolled forward in the shape of the Consolidated Plan for a further two years from 1957–59. This placed heavy weight on infrastructure, but now it was roads that received a much greater emphasis, alongside the construction of the Tema Harbour. Social Services also received a substantial allocation, with education taking the lion's share. These items of expenditure were precisely those that were valorised by the voting public.

In addition, the economic boom of the greater part of the 1950s meant that rural producers earned more money that they could spend on an even greater range of consumer goods, while urban and rural traders operated under far more favourable conditions than before. The 1950s was the period when Ghana experienced a veritable consumer boom which was reflected both in the arrival of the urban department store in Accra, but also in a proliferation of rural shops.[31] The CPP was able to capitalise on this period of optimism, and promoted the images of modernity that went with it. At the same time, it

---

archives of dissent – complicating anti-colonial histories through the Watson Commission (Gold Coast/Ghana)', *Journal of British Studies* 63 (2024), 517–20.

29 This is developed in more detail in Paul Nugent, 'Nationalism and decolonization in the Gold Coast', in T. Spear (ed.), *Oxford Research Encyclopedia of African History* (2021).

30 Austin, *Politics in Ghana*, 157.

31 Bianca Murillo, *Market Encounters: Consumer Cultures in Twentieth-Century Ghana* (Athens OH, 2017).

portrayed the opposition as backward-looking traditionalists. The notion that the CPP somehow crystallised the aspirations of the marginalised 'youngmen' hardly seems tenable in the light of the evidence we have.[32] While the chiefly establishment in Ashanti backed the National Liberation Movement (NLM), across the rest of the country the picture was mixed. While some chiefs did take exception to what they regarded as the excesses of youth – often linking unfettered access to alcohol to the lack of respect for chiefly authority – many chiefs actively supported the independence movement. Indeed, a new generation of 'modern' chiefs represented the fruits of the expansion of educational provision in the 1920s. It should also be noted that the NLM and its allies were themselves in favour of independence, provided it came about under a federal constitution. This was even true of the Togoland Congress, although its rider that French Togoland would also need to be part of a future arrangement inevitably created problems around sequencing.[33]

The 1950s was a decade when the CPP took ownership of the British developmental agenda. The institutions of state became visible across a large swathe of the country, as was reflected in the proliferation of rural post offices, schools, adult education centres, health clinics and the like. The CPP found itself at loggerheads with the chiefly establishment in Ashanti and the Eastern Province, and engineered the overthrow of those of whom it did not approve.[34] But its pragmatic impulse meant that it generally wanted to have chiefs in place who were supportive of its programme rather than seeking to demolish the existing structures. By the early 1960s, newly-enstooled chiefs generally needed to make a show of loyalty to the ruling party. Chiefs lost some of their autonomy, but the institution retained a great deal of legitimacy. Crucially, there was never a serious suggestion that the institution should be abolished, like in Guinea, or that stool lands should become state lands. To that extent, the pragmatism of the chiefs matched that of the ruling party. After the 1966 coup, those stools and individuals that had been rewarded for their loyalty were generally downgraded, whilst the former casualties were reinstated. This was the source of a great deal of discord, but chieftaincy as an institution came through the late 1960s relatively unscathed.

32 The classic account, which has shaped all subsequent debates, is that of Dennis Austin, *Politics in Ghana, 1946–1960* (London, 1970). See also Jean Allman, *The Quills of the Porcupine: Asante Nationalism in an Emergent Ghana* (Madison WI, 1993).

33 On the Togoland question, D.E.K. Amenumey, *The Ewe Unification Movement: A Political History* (Accra, 1989), chs 4–6; Nugent, *Smugglers*, ch. 5; Kate Skinner, *The Fruits of Freedom in British Togoland: Literacy, Politics and Nationalism, 1914–2014* (Cambridge, 2015), ch. 4.

34 Richard Rathbone, *Nkrumah and the Chiefs: The Politics of Chieftaincy in Ghana 1951–60* (Accra, Athens OH & Oxford, 2000).

There is a sizeable body of literature on the Nkrumah regime's embrace of socialism and industrialisation after 1960.[35] A few points are worth teasing out for the purposes of this discussion. The first is that the government inclined to the position that infrastructural investments needed to be made with a view to not merely maximising exports – given the vagaries of the cocoa economy – but also to stimulating new forms of production. At this time, import substitution seemed like the quick route to industrialisation. And, given the limited size of the domestic capitalist class, the presumption was that it was the state that would necessarily take the initiative through the creation of parastatals. The Seven-Year Plan was highly ambitious in its efforts to channel greater investment into state industries.[36] The government's particular obsession with seeing the Volta River Project through to completion was rooted in the easily comprehensible notion that industrialisation would hinge on generating sufficient levels of cheap hydroelectric power.[37] The development of goods made in Ghana would also make it possible to create sufficient locally produced goods to satisfy local consumers. The utopian vision of an urbanising population working in the factories to produce the goods that they would also consume, clearly owed something to the imaginaries of the Eastern bloc. But it was entirely consistent with the conception of the productive social contract that had taken shape earlier in the century. Indeed, the Nkrumahist vision took it to the next logical step by linking investments in infrastructure and services with the aspiration to create a modern consumer society.

The government sought to channel state resources to where it was most needed, and this implied resisting pressures from below for greater access to social amenities. In a remarkable passage, the *Programme for Work and Happiness* stated that:

> We would add here a comment upon the pressures brought to bear upon members of parliament by their constituents to force the establishment of projects in their villages or towns, irrespective of the value to the general community or to the wider needs of the nation. This has just as detrimental effects as bribery, and is, in fact, a form of corruption which deflects the national loyalty of parliamentarians to sectional interests.[38]

35 Tony Killick, *Development Economics in Action: A Study of Economic Policies in Ghana* (London, 1978); Jeffrey S. Ahlman, *Living with Nkrumahism: Nation, State and Pan-Africanism in Ghana* (Athens OH, 2017), especially chs 4–6; Jeff Grischow and Holger Weiss, 'Pan-Africanism, socialism and the future: development planning in Ghana, 1951–1966', in Jenny Anderson and Egle Rindzeviciute (eds), *The Struggle for the Long-Term in Transnational Science and Politics* (New York, 2015).

36 Republic of Ghana, *Seven-Year Development Plan, 1963–64 to 1969–70* (Accra, 1964).

37 Stephan Miescher, *A Dam for Africa: Akosombo Stories from Ghana* (Bloomington, 2022).

38 See *Programme of the Convention People's Party for Work and Happiness* (Accra, undated), 19.

But it is nevertheless worth noting that the number of children in public primary and middle schools jumped from 696,270 in 1960 to 1,404,929 in 1966, while over the same period the number attending secondary schools more than doubled from 20,110 to 42,628 [see Table 5.1]. There was also a significant increase in the number of government hospitals and health centres. The Nkrumah regime won lasting sympathy in the north by taking practical steps to extend basic infrastructure and social services to the part of the country that had no cash crops to offer. Evidently, the Nkrumah government remained attentive to demands for access to services, even if it might have wanted to channel more resources into directly productive activity. Indeed, it is striking that the share of government expenditure allocated to social services increased to 27.43 per cent, whereas economic services consumed 30.13 per cent and had actually risen more slowly than the former since 1957/58.

Table 5.1 Indicators of Government Performance in Service Provision

Indicator	1950	1955	1960	1966
Primary and Middle School attendance (Public)	266,850	543,407	696,270	1,404,929
Secondary School Attendance (Public)	2,776	10,017	20,110	42,628
Doctors in Government Service	n/a	126	227	296
Nurses in Government Service	n/a	936	1,848	2,944
Government Hospitals	21	32	32	53
Health Centres and Field Units		9	31	53

Sources: Ghana, *Economic Survey 1958*, table 39, p. 55, table 40, p. 58; Ghana, *1961 Statistical Yearbook*, tables 161–2, p. 146; tables 26–7, pp. 28–9; Republic of Ghana, *Statistical Handbook 1967*, table 9, p. 7, table 14 & 15, pp. 12–13; Republic of Ghana, *Statistical Yearbook, 1969–70*, tables 21–2, pp. 28–30, table 143, p. 153.

The fundamental problem was that the Nkrumah regime was running out of fiscal options during the straitened years of the early 1960s when the terms of trade deteriorated. Import duties remained the main source of revenue whereas export duties deriving from cocoa gradually declined in the latter 1950s in line with the plummeting world price. The Cocoa Marketing Board (CMB) had afforded a mechanism for taxing the cocoa farmers by paying them at well below the world market price, but this came at the cost of greatly increased smuggling and an increasing disincentive to replant trees. The introduction of a compulsory savings scheme for workers was a major factor in the railway workers' strike of 1961.[39] While individual earnings declined, basic goods also began to disappear from the market as the state factories struggled to meet demand at reasonable prices and as the government sought to reduce imports. As access to scarce consumer items became the privilege of those with political connections, there was an erosion of confidence in the Nkrumah regime.

By the time it was overthrown in 1966, it had ceased to be regarded as the guarantor of the social contract it had helped to define. Many were willing to accept that the civilian opposition might perform a better job, and when the National Liberation Council (NLC) gave way to the newly elected Progress Party (PP) government of Kofi Busia there seemed a reasonable chance that things might be put back on track.[40] The claim of the PP to have rural interests at heart and to be supportive of chiefly institutions was part of its appeal. The problem was that the 1966 coup had also underlined certain tensions between the institutions of state: that is, between the elected politicians, the Police and Armed Forces and the government bureaucracy. These were not resolved by the Busia regime, which found itself at odds with parts of the military and the civil service over plans for retrenchment.[41] When the military took over for a second time in January 1972, partly as a consequence of corporate grievances, the country looked set for a more significant shift in the relations between state and society.

The Social Contract in Question, 1966–1982

Over eleven turbulent years from 1972 to 1983, the country underwent two distinct efforts to redesign the social contract, which signalled a shift in the relations between central institutions and societal actors in the Regions. The first explicit attempt to revisit the terms of the contract was made by Lt.-Col I. K. Acheampong at the head of the National Redemption Council (NRC) and subsequently the Supreme Military Council (SMC). The NRC made it clear that it would take years before it could hope to piece the country's economy

39 Richard Jeffries, *Class, Power and Ideology: The Railwaymen of Sekondi* (Cambridge, 1978), ch. 5.

40 The best collection of essays on the NLC period and the elections of 1969 remains Dennis Austin and Robin Luckham (eds), *Politicians and Soldiers in Ghana, 1966–1972* (London, 1975).

41 Naomi Chazan, *An Anatomy of Ghanaian Politics: Managing Political Recession, 1969–1982* (Boulder CO, 1983), 224–30.

back together again. In its initial search for allies, it turned to the civil service and traditional authorities who were prepared to give the junta the benefit of the doubt.

The NRC was the first fully-fledged military regime, but it drew on older political repertoires. At one level, the NRC sought to return to some of the basic understandings of the Nkrumah period. Whereas the NLC and PP had gingerly sought to reverse the tide of statism, the NRC returned to the idea that economic independence would best be delivered by the parastatals that still existed. The difference was that whereas the Nkrumah regime was fixated on industrialisation, the NRC focused most of its attention on agriculture. Given that the country had become dependent on food imports, the main priority was to be on developing commercial agriculture through subsidies on imported machinery and fertilisers. Operation Feed Yourself (OFY) placed renewed emphasis on the State Farms Corporation and the Food Production Corporation, but it also involved a voluntarist appeal to Ghanaians in all walks of life to embrace farming – either full-time or as an adjunct to their main occupation.[42] Today, the early 1970s is remembered as a time when civil servants, military officers and school children devoted part of their time to farming activities which were hailed as a token of patriotism. The NRC identified the river basins of the north as ideal for the production of mechanised rice. To some extent this returned to the Nkrumahist position that the neglect of the north had hobbled Ghana as a whole. Cocoa remained the main foreign exchange earner, but the main concern for government was to ensure that what was produced actually made it to market. The Acheampong regime set up a National Economic Planning Council, staffed by senior military officers, technocrats and representatives of key interest groups. It also introduced its own Five-Year Plan in 1975/76 that referenced earlier planning efforts since the time of Guggisberg, and identified both a lack of political commitment and an over-dependency on cocoa as reasons for their shortcomings.[43] The document also identified improved tax collection as critical to its ambition to significantly increase development spending.[44] Once again, the emphasis was placed on the development of basic infrastructure, and most particularly that which would meet the needs of the agricultural sector. In the sphere of distribution, the

42 Alice Wiemers, '"A time of Agric": rethinking the "failure" of agricultural programs in 1970s Ghana', *World Development* 66 (2014), 104–17. Evidence of implementation is contained in Ministry of Agriculture files for the Volta Region that I was permitted to consult. See Nugent, *Boundaries*, 443–8. The official documentation for OFY as a whole remains inaccessible, although much of the vision can be gleaned from the state-owned newspaper for the period, the *Daily Graphic*.

43 Republic of Ghana, *Five-Year Development Plan, 1975/76–1979/80, Part I* (Accra, 1977), 85–6.

44 *Five-Year Development Plan*, 74–75.

Acheampong regime sought to ensure that there were enough imports entering the distribution chain to meet the demands of consumers. There was much that was familiar about the NRC's economic agenda. In effect, the junta's basis for legitimacy rested on the claim that it would make a better fist of addressing the country's many economic problems.

But at another level, the Acheampong regime also went much further in proposing a new constitutional arrangement which, it claimed, would be more in keeping with the culture of Ghana. Whereas I have argued that the political system developed in a more or less incremental fashion – born out of more than century of political contestation – the NRC/SMC insisted that the Parliamentary system was a culturally alien imposition that was bound to fail because it was not rooted in Ghanaian traditions. The NRC/SMC clearly intended chiefs to be given a leading role in national life, arguably echoing British plans from the 1920s. But the government also maintained that it was artificial to keep the military separated from society and argued this on the basis of the *asafo* tradition in southern Ghana. The government engaged in a national consultation exercise, but it was clear that it was angling towards a form of corporatism which it called Union Government (or Unigov). Although the regime claimed that nothing had been pre-judged, it was hoping to create a form of no-party government in which the most important interest groups would be directly represented.[45] The constitutional proposals that were eventually put to a referendum were in line with some of the older conceptions of a social contract: in that chiefs, professionals, the military and other social groups would have notionally shared power and have been guided in their work by the government bureaucracy. By pulling together, it was claimed governments would be better placed to meet the demands of Ghanaians for public goods. If the NRC had tabled these proposals early in its tenure of office, it might have made some headway, but their introduction came on the back of the failure of OFY, in part because of serious drought, and the demands of students and professional bodies for a return to civilian rule. Unigov looked like an attempt by the military hierarchy to perpetuate its grip on power. The woeful economic mismanagement, which led to a thriving black market, created all kinds of opportunities for the few who enjoyed privileged access to scarce commodities.[46] Opponents of the junta claimed that *kalabule*[47] was an economic system all of itself which was designed to benefit those who could corner scarce import

45 On Union Government, see Maxwell Owusu, 'Politics without parties: reflections on the union Government proposals in Ghana', *African Studies Review* 22:1 (1979), 89–108; Chazan, *Anatomy*, 245–67.

46 On the economic slide, see Jonathan Frimpong-Ansah, *The Vampire State in Africa: The Political Economy of Decline* (Trenton NJ, 1992).

47 *Kalabule* is a popular expression, the precise origin of which is contested, which refers to the secretive and illicit acquisition of wealth through various forms of profiteering, typically revolving around the black market, and outright corruption.

licences and consumer goods. The perception that members of the junta were directly benefiting from the crisis eroded popular support, but it was also corrosive for relations within the Armed Forces. On June 4 1979, Unigov was formally terminated. The Armed Forces Revolutionary Council was only ever intended as a short inter-regnum in which those implicated in the former junta would be held accountable.

The intervention of 31 December 1981 provided the second moment when a wholesale re-design of the social contract was on the cards – however fleetingly. As in Ethiopia, much of the initial impetus behind the revolution came from the University campuses and the barracks.[48] The June 4 Movement (JFM) had taken its inspiration from the 1979 intervention, but two years later it had come to espouse a more radical position. Members of the JFM played an instrumental role in the establishment of the People's Defence Committee (PDC) and the Workers' Defence Committee (WDC). This enabled them to shape government positions, and to proselytise freely across the regions. The position of the JFM militants was one that owed something to the *dependentista* orthodoxies of the day. But its focus was much on the domestic class enemy as on international capital. The PDCs and WDCs were conceived of as the antidote to a system of inequality that hinged on *kalabule*: all that was covert and shady was to be flushed out by structures that were open and participatory. The local enemy were those businessmen who fed off the existence of the black market, along with their bureaucratic accomplices.[49] In the border regions, much of the energy of the PDCs was absorbed by anti-smuggling campaigns at a time when the borders were closed for extended periods.[50] Chiefs were the target when they were regarded as being authoritarian or were suspected of abusing stool resources. The WDCs had a difficult relationship both with management and with the Trade Union Congress whose leadership the cadres regarded as having sold out. The PDC and WDC militants lost out in two of the early struggles over the course of the revolution: respect for the hierarchy was re-asserted within the Armed Forces[51] and cadres were instructed that their role was to keep an eye on the chiefs rather than seeking to displace them. The most difficult problem the militants had to deal with was how exactly government, and by extension the constituent institutions, could be rendered accountable to the mass of the population. The somewhat vague formulation was that PDCs at the base

48 Bahru Zewde, *The Quest for Socialist Utopia: The Ethiopian Student Movement, c.1960–1974* (Rochester NY, 2014).

49 For a detailed analysis, see Paul Nugent, *Big Men, Small Boys and Politics in Ghana: Power, Ideology and the Burden of History* (London, 1992), ch.2; Jeffrey Haynes, 'Revolutionary populism and democracy in Ghana', *Journal of Modern African Studies* 60:4 (2022), 503–26.

50 Nugent, *Smugglers*, 253–70.

51 Humphrey Asamoah, '"Monkeys play by sizes": the reconstruction of military hierarchy in Ghana's Armed Forces', *Africa* 91:5 (2021), 874–92.

would select the leaders at the ward and District levels and upwards to the Provisional National Defence Council itself. In this vision, the existing administrative building blocks were taken for granted. After 1982, Qaddafi's model of direct democracy found some favour in the shape of a proliferation of Green Book Study Clubs. But the level of influence over government itself was never very profound. In sum, the revolutionary vision was one that might conceivably have broken the mould, but the pragmatists surrounding Flt.-Lt. Jerry Rawlings asserted their control. A series of purges of the radicals followed in late 1982 and early 1983. This brought things back to a more familiar pattern. The PDCs lived on in the shape of the Committee for the Defence of the Revolution (CDRs), but their allotted role was to support the existing structures rather than to supplant them. Hence, in the rural areas they were expected to support community development initiatives in cooperation with chiefly authority.

The Social Contract Renewed, 1983–2000

Between 1983 and 1992, the Provisional National Defence Council (PNDC) offered a kind of benign dictatorship which incorporated some of the principal interest groups as it promised a period of stability.[52] During this hiatus, a solution would be found to the worsening economic crisis and the need for a viable political dispensation. Although the PNDC governed with a firm hand, it avoided a slide into authoritarianism and was broadly responsive to public pressure. It was also a regime that was characterised by a high level of competence in key Ministries, with PNDC Secretaries being shown the door when evidence of malfeasance came to light. It was during this decade of relative stability that the productive social contract was restored.

Firstly, having made its peace with the bilateral donors in 1983,[53] the PNDC committed itself to renewed investments in essential infrastructure that was needed to kick-start economic recovery. This included major improvements to the road network, which had largely collapsed by 1983. This was essential both for the rehabilitation of the main export sectors, gold and cocoa, but also to ensure that agricultural goods returned to the market after the acute food shortages of the early 1980s. The transport sector responded positively as spare parts and fuel once more became available. Towards the end of the decade, the government also committed itself to a rural electrification campaign, focusing

52 On the Rawlings era, see Nugent, *Big Men*. For a recent revisitation of the period, see Jeffrey Haynes, *Revolution and Democracy in Ghana: The Politics of Jerry John Rawlings* (London, 2022).

53 Eboe Hutchful, *Ghana's Adjustment Experience: The Paradox of Reform* (Geneva, 2002). See also Frimpong-Ansah, *Vampire State*, and Ernest Aryeetey and Ravi Kanbur (eds), *The Economy of Ghana: Analytical Perspectives on Stability, Growth and Poverty* (Oxford, 2009).

initially on the District capitals. Bringing the more remote rural areas onto the national grid signalled a qualitative shift of a kind that had not been witnessed since the 1950s. It had particularly profound consequences for the Northern, Upper East and Upper West Regions where much of the early support for the revolution had manifested itself.[54]

Secondly, the PNDC addressed the particular issue of access to markets through a combination of strategies. It liberalised import restrictions and abandoned price controls. This, together with improved infrastructure, ensured that while the yam lorries trundled southwards by road or along the Volta Lake, imported commodities were once more to be found across the length and breadth of the country. Market towns, in particular, witnessed a recovery of fortunes, whether based on the weekly market cycle or due to the increase in the number of permanent stores. The decline in the urban black market and in the incentive to smuggle in the border regions also reduced many of the points of friction between those charged with enforcement of the law and the public at large. The flip side to these measures was the reduction of the role of the state enterprises that came with the adoption of Structural Adjustment. The remaining parastatals were privatised, an effort was made to reduce the size of the public sector payroll and most subsidies were abolished. Hence the kind of support for agriculture that had been touted during the Acheampong years became a practical impossibility.

The PNDC had more difficulty defining what a 'true' democracy would look like once it had abandoned the notion of a pyramidal form of direct democracy based on defence committees. The first part of its answer was to render elected local government bodies the building blocks for the new dispensation. Its innovation was to insist on the election of the District Assemblies on a non-partisan basis. This was supposed to ensure that a range of interests would be reflected in the composition of the Assemblies, including the chiefs. But even if this addressed the question of representation at the local level, it hardly resolved the issue of the articulation between local and national structures. Ultimately, the government was forced to concede that there was no viable model out there that would enable citizens to relate to government more effectively than through the workings of the ballot box. By conceding the formation of political parties and the principle of the formation of a national government through regular elections, the PNDC went back on one of the early mantras of the revolution – namely that electoral democracy was bound to lead

54 In his doctoral thesis, Ivan Cuesta Fernandez demonstrated that electricity was more evenly distributed across national space in Ghana than in Tanzania. This underlines that the regime felt the need to be responsive to popular demands for power. 'Kilowatts, Megawatts and Power: Electric Territorialities of the State in the Peripheries of Ghana and Tanzania', unpublished Ph.D. thesis, University of Edinburgh, 2018. See also Naaborle Sackeyfio, *Energy Politics and Rural Development in Sub-Saharan Africa: The Case of Ghana* (Cham, 2017).

to the domination of a small elite and a corresponding loss of mass interest in the structures of political representation.

The formation of a Consultative Assembly to design a Constitution for Ghana inevitably brought forth debates about what the relationship between state and society should look like. The final document explicitly recognised that the institutions of central government had their limits. The Constitution of the Fourth Republic removed the right of government to interfere with chieftaincy and made the Regional and National Houses of Chiefs the arbiters of how chieftaincy should function as well as of particular disputes.[55] The main deal to be cut was over the distribution of revenues from stool lands. These provisions freed the chiefs from political interference, but also formally prohibited them from engaging in party politics. In the 1990s, the traditional authorities became very adept at restoring the recognition of what they regarded as their historic rights. While the central government appointed the District Chief Executives, the latter exercised no control over the chiefs who considered themselves sovereign within their domain. The lack of any right of command on the part of government representatives was strikingly different from Togo next door where the chiefs were very much under the thumb of the *préfets* appointed from the centre. One means by which chiefs increased their bargaining power was through the (re)-creation of cultural festivals. The revival of Odwira in Ashanti was the most visible manifestation of the use of festivals for multiple ends: to create a sense of community, to compete with neighbouring traditional authorities, but also to establish a platform for bargaining with government.[56] The invited guests at the festivals were typically other senior chiefs, but also politicians looking for their imprimatur. The latter were made acutely aware of the fact that they were entering the terrain of the chiefs and had to listen politely as demands were made upon them.[57] Indeed, with a short electoral cycle of four years, the politicians needed to be regular attendees. The representatives of government made a point of targeting the main festivals, where they announced new initiatives such as the construction of a new trunk road, a hospital and so on. By working through the traditional authorities, they validated the claims of the latter to be the true spokesmen for their communities. The chiefs were

55 *Constitution of the Republic of Ghana, 1992* (Accra, 1992), 164–8.

56 Carola Lentz, 'Local culture in the national arena: the politics of cultural festivals in Ghana', *African Studies Review* 44:3 (2001), 47–72; Richard Rathbone, 'Memory as theatre: using a Ghanaian ritual to recall past greatness and to redress recent reverses' in Peter Lambert and Björnn Weiler (eds), *How the Past Was Used: Historical Cultures c.1750–2000* (Oxford, 2017).

57 This argued in detail in Paul Nugent and Isabella Soi, 'Border festivals, closures, and practical governance: a comparison of Agbamevoza (Agotime) and Godigbeza (Aflao) on the Ghana-Togo border', *Africa: Journal of the International Africa* Institute, 95:3 (2025), 304–25.

fond of pointing out that Members of Parliament came and went, whereas the traditional leaders were ever-present and intent on ensuring that their areas received their share of the national cake.[58]

This was closely related to another phenomenon, namely the pressure to multiply Districts and Parliamentary constituencies. Until 2018, Ghana retained the same number of Regions, but many new Districts were created. The unstated principle was that traditional areas (often thought of as paramouncies) nest within Districts and should not cut across them. At the same time, Parliamentary constituencies needed to be congruent with the borders of the Districts because the MPs are also members of the Assemblies. The demand for new Districts arose from those political interests hoping to create new constituencies in the future, but it also arose from within the traditional areas. Winning a District implied the construction of new offices and administrative facilities, the rehousing of administrative personnel, and the upgrading of the infrastructure of the town in question. Because the District capital was typically where the seat of the paramouncy was located, this enabled the chiefs to gain even greater prominence and leverage over the authorities. The underlying logic of proliferating Districts may be regarded as a reworking of the old idea that Ghana was the sum of its traditional parts. The problem is that Districts and constituencies are supposed to be of a broadly similar size. This has been honoured in the breach for the simple reason that the underlying traditional units are of very different proportions. The anomalies became most apparent when the Akufo-Addo government decided to break up the existing Regions, but left Ashanti untouched. There is nothing that accords a privileged status to Ashanti in the Constitution, but it would be politically unthinkable to break up a Region that is still considered to be one kingdom. Creating new Districts and constituencies is also potentially sensitive because of the chiefly hierarchies that exist within Ashanti.

Finally, all this has been linked to the practicalities of politics. Under the Fourth Republic, what is striking is the absence of cohesive interest groups that might impart a clear direction to governance. Organised labour lost most of its capacity to influence government during the era of Structural Adjustment when employment in the public sector shrank considerably. The business community has been fractured and incapable of shaping a long-term economic strategy in its own interests.[59] The state bureaucracy has been highly permeated by political influence and unable to establish its own operational autonomy – far less to drive a technocratic agenda of its own design.[60] And finally, traditional

58 The one domain where the moral authority of the chiefs was called in question was in their complicity in illegal gold mining, or *galamsey*, which polluted many of the main rivers flowing through the forest belt.

59 Whitfield et al., *Politics of African Industrial Policy*, especially ch. 9.

60 Abdulai, 'Political settlement'.

authorities have insisted on maintaining the terms of the historic social contract rather than seeking to steer the agenda. Politics itself has partly turned largely on a symbolic differentiation between the two dominant parties, the National Democratic Congress (NDC) and the New Patriotic Party (NPP). While the NDC has pitched itself as the party of the common people – the traders and the farmers – the NPP has positioned itself as supportive of business and chieftaincy. But in reality, their social bases have been broadly similar, albeit spread differentially across national space. This matters in a context where regional disparities in access to public goods such as physical infrastructure, electricity and education remain entrenched. Symptomatically, while national road density increased considerably since the 1990s, the northern regions lagged significantly behind their southern counterparts.[61] Again, the commercialisation of oil exports has brought some infrastructural improvements to the old Western Region – which had always fared less well than south-central Ghana – but has also nourished a sense of grievance about having to bear the less positive downstream effects. These tensions have played out within the logic of a fiercely competitive electoral system in which swathes of the country have switched their allegiances at election time.

The productive social contract has been internalised to the extent that the main political parties do not even question what the terms of engagement should be. They have all campaigned on a platform of increasing the range and coverage of public goods. The main nuance is that the NDC has made more of a pitch for the northern and eastern peripheries, whereas the NPP has had to be attentive to its power-base in the centre. But not too much should be made of this because the NPP has attempted to win over northern votes with the promise of improved access to infrastructure in the shape of three north–south transport corridors that are notionally aimed towards Burkina Faso, but which are more than anything an exercise in linking the peripheries to the infrastructure grid. The politicians have made large spending promises at election time in an attempt to woo the voters. In practice, many projects are never completed, and when there is a change of government, as there has been every eight years,[62] they are effectively abandoned. At the same time, governments have been spending far ahead of their ability to raise new taxes, leading to successive debt crises. VAT, which was introduced in 1995, is notionally borne by consumers, but in practice it is largely evaded. Government has also added new taxes, but these have not plugged the gap between revenue generation and expenditure. Because it is politically dangerous to cut back on the electoral

61 For an analysis, see Olivier J. Walther, Paul Nugent and Susanna Goewey, 'The impact of transport policies on road accessibility in Ghana (2010–2019)', *African Geographical Review* 44:1 (2025), 1–17.

62 The pattern was repeated in December 2024 when the National Democratic Congress (NDC) returned to power after eight years in opposition.

promises, the temptation has been to accumulate debts. The spread of these debts through bond issues looks very different from the time when Ghana was beholden predominantly to the International Financial Institutions. The indifferent economic performance since the 1990s, punctuated by moments of crisis, is something that ordinary citizens and the business community have been affected by in different ways. The central paradox – which is that Ghana has a functioning democracy, but one that struggles to cover its bills – is one that had been prefigured as early as the 1920s. Today, it continues to cause concern.

Conclusion

In this essay, I have sought to demonstrate how a broad consensus took shape in Ghana over a period of more a hundred years. If Ghana has a founding charter, it is the Bond of 1844: that is some decades before the Partition of Africa. Since then, the dominant view has been of a state that has clear limits that are defined by the residual rights that were never ceded to the coloniser – or indeed, to any regime since independence. Although the Nkrumah regime chipped away at chiefly prerogatives, no government has seriously entertained the possibility of abolishing the institution or converting chiefs into the mere ciphers of government. Moreover, most of what was lost to erosion was emphatically regained in 1992. At the same time, there is an expectation that any government will deliver public goods that are in the greatest demand: infrastructure and markets. In the 1970s and early 1980s, much of the basic infrastructure collapsed, while Ghanaians struggled to secure access to basic commodities. Moreover, the thriving black market fuelled a perception that those who governed were actually profiting from *kalabule*. The perceived failure of particular governments to honour their obligations culminated in a series of coups, both attempted and actualised. The years of crisis had a corrosive effect on state institutions, as was manifested in the virtual implosion of the Armed Forces. The sense of systemic failure led some to call for a social revolution in 1982 which might have rewritten the social contract. In the end, this did not come to pass and what the Rawlings regime did was to restore the fundamentals of what had existed before the crisis years.

A lot of what has transpired since 1992 is counter-intuitive. Strikingly, parliamentary democracy has coincided with the reinvigoration of traditional authority. Although many countries have experienced the revival of chieftaincy since the 1990s,[63] this has often been associated with a retreat from democracy. In Ghana, the opposite has been the case because it has gone together with a reinforcement of ideas about the limits of state power. Moreover, even though

63 Claude Hélène Perrot and François-Xavier Fauvelle-Aymar (eds), *Le Retour des Rois: Les Autorités Traditionelles et l'État en Afrique Contemporaine* (Paris, 2003).

the Constitution does not say so, there is a common understanding that Ghana remains the sum of its traditional parts that necessarily come in different shapes and sizes. Although the current system drives governments to accumulate debt, and incentivises both corruption and waste, it is a system that is generally construed as legitimate. This peculiar configuration manifests many layers of history that are not adequately captured by portraying Ghanaians as living 'under the sign of neo-liberalism'. There is so much more going on, and it has been the business of this contribution to identify 'it' and to account for the patterns in historical terms.

Finally, it is worth considering how distinctive Ghana really is. The sedimentation of Ghana's social contract over the better part of two centuries is a large part of what explains its durability. In this, it bears some comparison with Ethiopia, but with the all-important difference that within a conquest state the default was always likely to be some variant on domination – even within the framing of ethnic federalism that was supposed to strip away the dead weight of that country's imperial history. Although the trajectories of Ghana and Ethiopia briefly seemed to converge in their respective revolutionary moments, they quickly spun off in different directions. Ghana mostly avoided the violence and repression that became a hallmark of Ethiopia under the Dergue,[64] and drifted back to constitutional rule. In Ghana, there was a much greater possibility of forging a contract based on a conception of governance where the state has its limits, but also its responsibilities to deliver. This was the product of successive struggles against the British urge to treat Ghanaians as colonised subjects and the efforts of some post-independence governments to revisit the ground-rules. Senegal perhaps comes closest to the Ghanaian case, being based on a comparable societal struggle to define the limits of the state – albeit in relation to religious rather than chiefly spaces.[65] The fact that electoral democracy has fared better in Ghana and Senegal than in most African countries is surely not coincidental because in both cases, the terms of the social contract are well-understood in the society at large and are ultimately based on expressions of consent that are constantly renewed. This picture would have been very familiar to European social contract theorists writing at a very different time and located in quite different places. What this serves to illustrate is that political theory can be related to the real world of political praxis, but also that certain concepts have a capacity to stray well beyond their original

64 Andargachew Tiruneh, *The Ethiopian Revolution, 1974–1987: A Transformation from an Aristocratic to a Totalitarian Democracy* (Cambridge, 1993).

65 For a discussion of the application of the social contract to Senegal, see Cheikh Anta Babou, 'The Senegalese '"social contract" revisited' and 'Negotiating the boundaries of power: Abdoulaye Wade, the Muridiyya, and state politics in Senegal, 2000–2012', *Journal of West African History* 2:1 (2016), 165–88.

temporal and geographical moorings. While being alert to the possible existence of universals in politics, the task of the historian is to account for why some ideas about the political realm have stuck whereas others have been passed or actively rejected.

6

Shaping the Bank of Ghana, 1924–62: What Type of Bank?

Kofi Adjepong-Boateng[1]

This chapter analyses the attempt by Gold Coast and Ghanaian nationalists to convert the first indigenous commercial banking institution into a modern central bank. The analysis presents the discussions on the design of a central bank in the Gold Coast in the context of wider discussions on central bank design which took place within the British Empire. The model of central banking recommended by Bank of England (BoE) in the Gold Coast was promoted against the wishes of Gold Coast and Ghanaian nationalists of different political persuasions and against recommendations of a more actively developmental central banking model. The analysis runs from 1924, when a nationalist, Frederick Nanka-Bruce, first advocated changing the Gold Coast's credit and banking system, to 1962 when debate on the design of the Bank of Ghana ceased.

Early History of an Idea

Well before the worldwide spread of central banks, Montagu Norman, Governor of the Bank of England (1920–44), had seen central banking as being 'young and experimental and [having] no tradition', leading to uncertainty; although this type of institution 'may last and may develop, or its usefulness, to fill a short post-war need and no more, [it could] soon come to an end'.[2] Still, the number of institutions between 1919 and 1939 that performed central banking functions surged, rising to 28 new 'central banks'.[3] After the Second World War

1 I am grateful to Gareth Austin, Charles Goodhart and Sarah Stockwell for their comments on an earlier draft of this chapter.

2 Letter from Montagu Norman to J.P. Morgan, 19 November 1926, Bank of England Archives (hereafter BOEA) G1/307.

3 Barry Eichengreen and Andreas Kakridis (eds), *The Spread of the Modern Central Bank and Global Cooperation: 1919–1939* (Cambridge, 2023), 3.

institutions with central banking functions proliferated, as colonial empires disintegrated and nation states emerged.[4] However, before 1950, in countries like the Gold Coast, calls for 'state-owned banks', 'state-aided banks', and 'national banks' barely specified the type of bank design needed.[5] Increasingly, central banks were seen as necessary for development, even as critics warned that these institutions, being easily integrated into governments, would be 'far too good as machines for inflation'.[6] Calls for central banks meant that looking to countries with sophisticated financial markets for blueprints was irresistible.[7] BoE had begun as a commercial bank in a similar mode to the early European public banks.[8] It was, however, BoE's twentieth-century model that was exported to the colonies, with BoE exerting 'itself to give [an impetus] to shape the new central banks in its own image'.[9] The governing principles for institutions of this type were being set just when monetary reforms in the colonies were demanded and when British imperial policy dictated shoring up the Sterling Area.[10] The goal of colonial administrations towards the end of Empire was to put in place 'the institutional and intellectual apparatus for managing money at arm's length from representative governments'.[11]

4 Forrest Capie, Charles Goodhart, Stanley Fischer and Norbert Schnadt, *The Future of Central Banking: The Tercentenary Symposium of the Bank of England* (Cambridge, 1994), 91.

5 In 1926, for example, McPhee had called for an investigation into establishing 'state banks' in West Africa: Allan McPhee, *The Economic Revolution in British West Africa* (London, 1972; orig. 1926), 243–4.

6 J.L. Fisher, 'Some reflections on Currency Boards and Central Banks in the Colonial Context', BOEA OV 7/36/604/2. This concern dates back to the central banks established after the Napoleonic Wars (Capie, et al., *Central Banking*, 5).

7 Juha Tarkka, 'The North European model of early central banking', in David G. Mayes and Geoffrey E. Wood (eds), *Designing Central Banks* (London, 2009), 34.

8 Ulrich Bindseil, *Central Banking Before 1800: A Rehabilitation* (Oxford, 2019); Stephen Quinn and William Roberds, *How a Ledger Became a Central Bank, A Monetary History of the Bank of Amsterdam* (Cambridge, 2024).

9 Richard S. Sayers, *The Bank of England, 1891–1944*, Volume 1 (Cambridge, 1976), 201.

10 Gerold Krozewski, 'Finance and empire: the dilemma facing Great Britain in the 1950s', *International History Review* 17:1 (1996), 48–68; Catherine R. Schenk, 'Finance and empire: confusions and complexities: a note', *International History Review* 18:4 (1996), 870–1.

11 Gopalan Balachandran, 'Central banking and colonial control: India, 1914–1939' in Eichengreen and Kakridis, *Modern Central Bank*, 383. In India's case, this led to BoE preparing guidelines leading up to the country's independence: 'Memorandum on Financial Safeguards' by R.A. Mant, H. Strakosch, L.J. Kershaw, and C.H. Kisch, 17 June 1931, BOEA G1/311.

Global Adoption of the Classic Model

The first noted attempt at a universal exposition of the doctrines associated with BoE's model – referred to here as the 'classic' model – was by Kisch and Elkin in 1928.[12] A foreword by Norman enhanced its standing. The work explained why a central bank, not the state, should manage a country's note issue and monetary policy, warning that if note issuance is left to government it risks causing inflation when it funds government expenditure.[13] The study also recommended that modern central banks, unlike the original BoE, should not make commercial loans in case the banks diverted credit to industries where their commercial banking customers required support.[14] This became one of BoE's principles for modern central banking.

Subsequent works by de Kock and Plumptre analysed central banking in countries with less sophisticated capital markets.[15] Before publishing his major study in 1939, de Kock had argued that, whatever stage of economic development a country had reached, centralised cash reserves were an asset and countries should ensure that a bank supported and regulated by government controlled currency and credit.[16] Plumptre repeated Norman's assertion that governments must have limited influence over central banks because of the concern that 'needy Governments' would turn to 'the printing press or to debasement of coinage' to create credit.[17] Plumptre's work, however, did highlight the limitations of the classic model. For one thing, central banks could not sell securities to reduce the money in circulation nor repurchase securities to inject money into the banking system.[18] He raised questions about the model's effectiveness in the absence of securities and money markets. Regardless, BoE tried to persuade colonial authorities to establish central banks which could propagate BoE's functions, supervise orthodox policies, and assist in strengthening the Sterling

12 C.H. Kisch and W.A. Elkin, *Central Banks: A Study of the Constitutions of Banks of Issue, with an Analysis of Representative Charters* (London, 1928).

13 In this work, Kisch revised his earlier view that central banks should have private shareholders to protect them from governments (Balachandran, 'Central banking', 397).

14 Kisch and Elkin, *Central Banks*, 110–11. Under Norman, the Bank of England had intervened in industry as a commercial lender during the inter-war period (William R. Garside and Julian Greaves, 'The Bank of England and industrial intervention in interwar Britain', *Financial History Review* 3:1 (1996), 69–86.

15 M.H. de Kock, *Central Banking* (London, 1946); Arthur W.F. Plumptre, *Central Banking in the British Dominions* (Toronto, 1940).

16 M.H. de Kock, 'The significance of the recent legislative amendments concerning the South African Reserve Bank', *Economic Journal* 41:161 (1931), 67–73.

17 Plumptre, *Central Banking*, 25.

18 These actions are referred to as 'Open Market Operations'. Plumptre, *Central Banking*, 25, 424.

Area.[19] To help with this, BoE established an Overseas Department.[20] Applying the classic model universally was, however, challenged.

The Niemeyer Memorandum

The challenge came from Otto Niemeyer, the BoE official who worked across several countries in the inter-war period and provided advice on establishing numerous central banks. His work was integral to rebuilding the international financial system after the First World War.[21] In 1935, Niemeyer wrote an internal memorandum describing circumstances which justified departure from the classic model.[22] He recognised that while the 'ideal' central bank does not lend to industry, central banking institutions mostly originating as commercial banks, may be 'in various stages of evolution towards the ideal'. He explained that in countries where commercial facilities are not 'adequate' or where money markets are less sophisticated, the new central banking institutions need commercial banking mandates in order to 'have a direct effect on the market by fixing a price' for commercial lending. He reasoned that those new central banks modelled on BoE 'have often either found their powers too narrow or have had to get round their too-restrictive statutes by various subterfuges'. Hence, Niemeyer believed that a new central bank should reserve the right to compete with commercial banks, though these powers should be used sparingly and only when more traditional methods of controlling credit were ineffective. Niemeyer acknowledged that these institutions may be able to persuade other commercial banks to keep reserves with them only by eventually dropping their own commercial operations.

Niemeyer's memorandum probably benefited from his work on establishing central banks in several countries as in several cases there was need for a determination on how existing commercial lending activities should be treated by institutions seeking to become central banks. In 1927, before the Niemeyer memorandum was written, he served on the Financial Committee

19 Josiah Stamp, 'Central banking as an Imperial Factor', lecture given at University College Nottingham (1934), 2; Peter J. Cain, 'Gentlemanly imperialism at work: the Bank of England, Canada, and the Sterling Area, 1932–1936', *Economic History Review* 49:2 (1996), 342–3.

20 Sarah Stockwell, *The British End of the British Empire* (Cambridge, 2018), 143.

21 For a more recent and detailed analysis of Niemeyer's work, see Robert Yee, *The City's Defense: The Bank of England and the Remaking of Economic Governance, 1914–1939* (Cambridge, 2025), 211–54.

22 'Central Banks undertaking Commercial Business', Memorandum by O.E. Niemeyer, 8 October 1935, BOEA OV50/9/23–24. Otto Niemeyer was a director of the Bank for International Settlements (1931–65) and, shortly after the memorandum was prepared, became a Director of the Bank of England (1938–52).

of the League of Nations, and later became the Committee's chair. In 1926, the League and BoE were involved in converting Estonia's National Bank, a commercial bank, to a central bank.[23] Niemeyer's advice was also sought by the Bulgarian authorities during the period in which the League's loans to Bulgaria (1926–28) resulted in the transformation of the Bulgarian National Bank to a central bank.[24] Aside from advising New Zealand (1930) and Argentina (1935) on establishing new central banks, Niemeyer also advised Brazil (1931) and Egypt (1936) on converting commercial banks in these countries to central banks.[25] One of these, National Bank of Egypt (NBE), had before its statutory conversion performed the functions of a central bank since 1898.[26] It justified its dual role by arguing that frequently 'the central bank is obliged to intervene in the market in order to restore normal conditions, especially if the market cannot be left to its own devices'.[27] However, NBE promised to refrain from becoming involved in 'smaller commercial operations not required by the public interest' and agreed not to fund advances from sums deposited at NBE by other commercial banks.[28]

Similarly, the Commonwealth Bank of Australia (CBA), a commercial bank, acquired central banking functions between 1924 and 1929.[29] It could intervene in credit markets by calling in deposits from other commercial banks and later sterilise them if credit grew inordinately. Through its savings bank operations, it could, if necessary, outbid other banks for deposits,[30] and use these savings to put competitive pressure on these banks to adjust their lending rates. In 1926, Montagu Norman had acknowledged that the wide differences between British and Australian conditions might make a 'rigid application' of

23 Eichengreen and Kakridis, *Modern Central Bank*, 31.

24 Roumen Avramov, 'The Bulgarian National Bank, 1926–1935: revamping the institution, addressing the Depression' in Eichengreen and Kakridis *Modern Central Bank*, 277.

25 Catherine R. Schenk and Tobias Straumann, 'Central banks and the stability of the international monetary regime', in Michael D. Bordo, Øyvind Eitrheim, Marc Flandreau and Jan F. Qvigstad (eds), *Central Banks at a Crossroads: What Can We Learn from History?* (Cambridge, 2016), 334.

26 National Bank of Egypt 1898–1948, Report to Board of Directors, Cairo (1948), 83. Niemeyer joined the London Committee of the National Bank of Egypt in 1931 ('Sir Otto Niemeyer', Richard Sayers Papers, Records of Interviews, BOEA ADM33/24/AB287/2).

27 Mohammed Ali Rifat, *The Monetary System of Egypt: An Inquiry into its History and Present Working* (London, 1935), 88.

28 Letter to the Shareholders by Aly Shamsy, President, National Bank of Egypt, dated 29 May 1950, BOEA O.E.N. 61.03 OV9/53/282/1.

29 John Singleton, 'Central banks in the British dominions in the interwar period' in Eichengreen and Kakridis, *Modern Central Bank*, 359.

30 Lyndhurst F. Giblin, *The Growth of a Central Bank: The Development of the Commonwealth Bank of Australia 1924–1945* (Victoria, 1951), 3; and Sydney J. Butlin, *Foundations of the Australian Monetary System, 1788–1851* (Melbourne, 1953).

central bank design difficult.[31] However, Norman's deputy, Ernest Harvey, was less accommodating: he saw conversion resulting in a central bank which was 'fundamentally unsound in principle' and 'transgress[ed] generally accepted principles of Central Banking as embodied in most modern statutes'.[32] Niemeyer had circulated a memorandum in 1930 by Theodore Gregory[33] which cautioned Australia against a radically different approach to establishing a central bank. Gregory believed that Australia's financial problems then were such that the timing was 'particularly unsuitable' for departing from the orthodox central banking approach.[34]

When Niemeyer wrote his 1935 memorandum, he was corresponding with Claude Reading, CBA's then chair (1934–1945). Reading had enquired whether it would be 'advisable or at least permissible' for a modern central bank to engage in commercial activities;[35] Niemeyer replied:

1. That the older central banks could function commercially, while modern central banks were closer to BoE's ideal but have sometimes found their charters too restrictive.

2. That every country should have its own variant of a bank '<u>primarily</u> concerned with central banking and <u>primarily thinking</u> in that direction.[36]

3. That countries which lack money markets, extensive commercial banking systems, developed financial systems, or large bill and discount markets, would probably have central banking systems remote from BoE's ideal and their monetary system might suffer from having a rigid central banking structure imposed on them.

Niemeyer was concerned that insisting on an 'orthodox' central bank in Australia would needlessly 'involve a number of difficulties and dangers'. If Australia found it convenient to retain a central bank with commercial (savings)

31 Letter from Montagu Norman to James Kell, Governor, Commonwealth Bank, 26 August 1926, BOEA OV13/33/682/2.

32 Cablegram from Ernest Harvey, Bank of England, to Robert Gibson, Commonwealth Bank, 7 April 1930, BOEA OV13/34/171/682/3/56.

33 560 Theodore Gregory was Sir E. Cassel Professor of Economics, University of London (1927–37).

34 T.E. Gregory, 'Observations on the Commonwealth Bank Bill (1930)' attached to letter from Otto Niemeyer to William Glasgow, Commonwealth Bank of Australia, 27 October 1930, BOEA G1/291 458.

35 Letter from Claude Hill Reading to Otto Niemeyer, 22 August 1935, BOEA OV13/50/686/1/85.

36 The emphases are Niemeyer's.

capability, he saw no reason to 'push theoretical objections' to it.[37] It was only in 1960 that CBA spun off its central banking functions to establish the Reserve Bank of Australia. During the Gold Coast debates, CBA was seen as a precedent.

Sayers

Reservations about the universality of BoE's model were also voiced by Richard Sayers.[38] He recommended that relatively immature economies should avoid a 'slavish imitation' of BoE's practices.[39] Sayers' position echoed a memorandum written for India's banking commission (October 1913).[40] This had explicitly advised against modelling India's new central bank on BoE and reflected Keynes' published view that 'the framers of the new [Indian central] bank's constitution' should look for models to the state banks of Germany, Holland or Russia, not the Bank of England.[41] Russia's central bank could lend to industry, commerce, and agriculture, as Keynes wanted India's to do.[42] What emerged indirectly from Keynes' advice was the Imperial Bank of India, which was appointed sole banker to the government, acted as a bankers' bank, and also was required to open branches across the country to help in developing India's banking sector. Similar to BoE at its founding and like the early European public banks, the Imperial Bank played the role of a central bank with commercial banking responsibilities.[43] At the time, even Montagu Norman acknowledged 'the possible development of the Imperial Bank of India into a true Central Bank.'[44]

Sayers also commented that establishing a new central bank must emphasise 'the development of a banking system to control'.[45] While acknowledging that a country's commercial banks could create a 'banking habit', he thought they could not act 'fast enough to make adequate provision for the country's economic potentialities' without the central bank's involvement, because

37 This was consistent with Keynes's position on India (see below).

38 Like Theodore Gregory before him, Sayers became the Sir Ernest Cassel Professor of Economics, London School of Economics (1947–68). He was the Bank of England's official historian for the years 1891–1944.

39 Richard S. Sayers, *Modern Banking* (Oxford, 1938), 249–52.

40 Anand G. Chandavarkar, *Keynes and India: A Study in Economics and Biography* (London, 1989), 4.

41 J.M. Keynes, *Indian Currency and Finance* (London, 1971; orig. 1913), 168.

42 Anand G. Chandavarkar, *Central Banking in Developing Countries* (London, 1996), 99. Sayers refers to Keynes' argument in a biographical essay (Richard S. Sayers, 'The Young Keynes', *Economic Journal* 82:326 (1972), 592.

43 Seshadriiyengar L.N. Simha, *History of the Reserve Bank of India (1935–51)* (Bombay, 1970), 25.

44 Letter from Montagu Norman to Lord Birkenhead, 24 February 1927, BOEA G1/312/19. The reasons for Norman's opinion are set out in Balachandran, 'Central banking', 394–99.

45 Richard S. Sayers, *Central Banking after Bagehot* (Oxford, 1957), 115.

distributing currency over geographically dispersed areas was expensive and required backing from 'some public authority.' Currency shortages such as occurred in Ashanti during the 1930s depression highlight the difficulties associated with inadequate currency distribution in countries in which the banking habit was not widespread. They had too few banks for many farmers to exchange bank notes for coins. Consequently, high-denomination notes were unwanted because they could not be converted easily into small change to divide between family members and pay labourers.[46] This increased the demand for low-denomination currency to counter poor bank penetration.[47] Moreover, data from a 1956–57 study suggested that cocoa producers in Ashanti were inclined to save.[48] These data, covering the period when the design of the central bank was still under discussion, evidently justified building the necessary banking infrastructure to encourage a savings habit and recycling capital productively, as Sayers' work on central banking advocated.

Gold Coast: The Shephard Report

These debates took place between the 1920s and 1960s, before the universal acceptance of BoE's model. During these years, the Gold Coast's economy expanded and pressure increased to improve the country's credit system. Newspapers like the *Gold Coast Independent* and the *Ashanti Pioneer* called for change.[49] In editorials in 1924, a few years before Kisch and Elkin published their work, Frederick Nanka-Bruce argued for monetary reform in the Gold Coast. He highlighted discrimination by banks against African businesses, calling for the establishment of a government-supported agricultural bank.[50] Similarly,

46 District Commissioner, Obuasi, to Chief Commissioner of Ashanti, Kumasi, 9 July 1937, Public Records and Archives Administratin Department (PRAAD) (Kumasi): ARG1/1/141.

47 District Commissioner Obuasi to Chief Commissioner of Ashanti, Kumasi, 13 July 1937, PRAAD (Kumasi): ARG1/1/141/147. For an analysis of currency problems in Ashanti, see Kofi Adjepong-Boateng, 'War, finance, and monetary reform in Ashanti, 1807–1935', *African Economic History,* 53:1 (2025), 21–59.

48 Barbara Ingham, 'Ghana cocoa farmers – income, expenditure relationships', *Journal of Development Studies* 9:3 (1973), 365–72.

49 The *Ashanti Pioneer* was founded in 1939 by John S. Tsiboe, a merchant. The *Gold Coast Independent* was founded in 1918 by Frederick Nanka-Bruce, its editor, also a physician and an elected African member of the Gold Coast Legislative Council.

50 Frederick Nanka-Bruce, 'Banking Facilities', *Gold Coast Independent*, Saturday, 27 September 1924, 790; and Frederick Nanka-Bruce, 'Wanted, an Agricultural Bank for the Gold Coast', *Gold Coast Independent*, Saturday, 13 December 1924, 990–1. For an analysis of discriminatory practices by British banks, see: Chibuike U. Uche, 'Credit for Africans; The Demand for a "National Bank" in the Gold Coast Colony', *Financial History Review* 10 (2003), 75–9.

Winifred Tete-Ansa, writing in 1934, argued for a 'Farmers' Bank.[51] In response to this nationalist pressure for monetary reform, particularly of rural credit, the colonial administration commissioned a report from C. Y. Shephard.[52]

Published in 1936, Shephard's report analysed the country's agricultural credit systems.[53] He highlights the dominance of rural moneylenders who extended longer-term loans secured against farms. Because land was not owned by individuals and was seen as being impignorable under Gold Coast customary law, these security arrangements amount to derivative pledges.[54] Shephard also highlights the role cooperative societies could, if encouraged, play in extending credit and marketing crops.[55] He reasons that creditworthy farmers should be able to borrow from these societies at lower rates than those charged by moneylenders who had to take the default rates of less creditworthy farmers into account when computing interest rate levels on a diverse portfolio.[56]

Unlike Nanka-Bruce and Tete-Ansa, Shephard did not support forming an agricultural bank, advocating instead a system of cooperative banks established by the Gold Coast's new network of cooperative societies. Shephard also proposed that these cooperative banks should hold funds in reserve though a 'central cooperative bank', beyond the reach of individual banks and that, through a commercial arrangement with existing joint stock banks, the centralised institution could offer lines of credit to the cooperative banks to meet depositors' demands for repayments at short notice.

Politics and Monetary Reform

By 1947, scarce goods and inflation were provoking discontent amongst the Gold Coast's growing urban population, often unemployed or paid little.[57]

51 Winifred Tete-Ansa, 'Our national economic independence – a farmers' bank, co-operative marketing, national funds and industrialization are essentials', Parts 1 and 2, *Gold Coast Independent*, 22 and 29 September 1934, 897 and 934, respectively.

52 Shephard was Carnegie Professor of Economics, Imperial College of Tropical Agriculture, St. Augustine, Trinidad and Tobago.

53 C.Y. Shephard, *Report on the Economics of Peasant Agriculture in the Gold Coast*, (Accra, 1936).

54 Gareth Austin, *Labour, Land and Capital in Ghana: From Slavery to Free Labour in Asante, 1807–1956* (Rochester NY, 2005), 278–303. A ruling by William Brandford Griffith, the Gold Coast's Chief Justice (1895–1911), encouraged the use of derivative pledges. This led to other judgements upholding claims that commercial land could be treated as private property and be pledged (S.K.B. Asante, 'Interests in land in the customary law of Ghana: a new appraisal', *Yale Law Journal* 74:5 (1965), 865). While money-lenders dominated the secured long-term lending activities, shorter-term loans were secured against crops and extended by African brokers. This distinction is covered in Gareth Austin, *Labour, Land and Capital*, 281–7.

55 See Kamenov's chapter in this volume.

56 Shephard Report, 51–2.

57 Dennis Austin, *Politics in Ghana 1946–1960* (Oxford, 1964).

In August 1947, Robert Scott, then the country's Financial Secretary (1947–1950), established an informal committee to discuss monetary conditions. It recommended investigating a 'state-aided bank' to provide capital to Africans involved in commerce; and recruiting Africans to work in the finance sector.[58] Until it was repealed in 1950, Section 5 of the Gold Coast's 1906 Companies Ordinance denied Africans permission to establish banks there.[59] Scott favoured an investigation noting that the two existing banks, Barclays (DCO)[60] and Bank of British West Africa (BBWA), did not compete effectively.[61] However, before a formal investigation of the colony's banking conditions was begun, economic discontent in 1948 provoked riots. In response, the Watson Commission was convened to investigate the riots causes and how disenchantment could be tackled. Its findings (June 1948) highlighted, amongst other things, the problem of rural indebtedness, asserting that the colony's credit system was unsatisfactory.[62] The report recommended forming a 'Cocoa Farmers Bank' or 'Discount House' to take over existing debts and to extend credit to farmers and industrialists in the rural areas. Similar points were made by J.B. Danquah, a founding member of the United Gold Coast Convention (UGCC). Danquah acknowledged his debt to the arguments that Nanka-Bruce had made in favour of

58 Letter from Robert Scott, Governor's Deputy, to Arthur Creech Jones, Secretary of State for the Colonies, 26 May 1948, BOEA OV69/1/478/2765/3/153A.

59 There is evidence of confusion about this legislation's ancestry. The Colonial Office confirmed that, following a record search, Section 5 was not in the original Bill and that the insertion had been made by a special committee after a second reading, for reasons not stated in the records. In his correspondence, G.E. London challenged the interpretation of the Bill that debarred Africans from engaging directly in banking (Letter from G.E. London, Colonial Secretary, Accra, to Gerald Creasy, Gold Coast Department, Colonial Office, 7 January 1936, PRAAD (Cape Coast) CSO3/15/19 No.2/36).

60 Barclays Bank (Dominion, Colonial and Overseas), which was the name used by Barclays for its international and overseas banking operations from 1925. Between 1954 and 1971, Barclays Bank (Dominion, Colonial and Overseas) was renamed Barclays Bank D.C.O. In October 1971, the bank officially dropped the D.C.O. designation and was renamed Barclays Bank International Limited.

61 Letter from Robert Scott to Arthur Creech Jones, 26 May 1948. BOEA OV69/1/478/2765/3/153A. Evidence of this close cooperation was the 'Agreement on Minimum Rates' between BBWA and Barclays which covered all the West African territories in which they operated. The agreement was also signed by the British & French Bank. (Letter from G. Redmayne, Assistant General Manager BBWA to A.F. Mallory, Assistant General Manager, Barclays Bank DCO, 26 July 1958, Barclays Group Archives (hereafter BGA) 11/2105; and Memorandum to General Managers: West African Agreement, 14 July 1958, BGA11/2105). The lack of competition is covered by Gareth Austin and Chibuike U. Uche, 'Collusion and Competition in Colonial Economies: Banking in British West Africa, 1916–1960', *Business History Review* 81:1 (2007), 1–26.

62 Report of the Commission of Enquiry into the Disturbances in the Gold Coast 1948, 53.

a 'national bank'.[63] When he published articles in 1948 and 1949, Danquah included a draft bill, stipulating that a new bank be established to provide credit to agriculture (particularly cocoa producers) and other African businesses. He also proposed that the bank eventually take over the colony's note issue from the West African Currency Board (WACB).[64] Danquah had, therefore, envisaged a commercial bank with a note-issuing function.

Scott circulated a draft bill which was based 'very substantially' on the 1939 legislation governing the establishment of Ceylon's 'state aided' bank.[65] In reaction, the Foreign Office accepted that establishing 'a state-aided' bank with safeguards was better than starting several indigenous banks which might fail and undermine confidence.[66] The colonial administration may have felt cautious after the bank failures that beset Nigeria at the time.[67] The Foreign Office and BoE expressed concern about Scott taking Ceylon as a precedent because, as observed in other British colonies, demands for 'state-aided' institutions ended up as calls for central banks which did not conform to BoE's approved model.[68] The persistent calls for monetary reform and Scott's argument for an investigation of the banking question led the colonial authorities to appoint G. D. Paton to examine the country's monetary conditions.

Paton Report and Armitage Committee

Paton's 1949 report advised against forming an agricultural bank, arguing that it was difficult to secure loans against land because the country had no system

63 'National Bank', by J.B. Danquah. Speech to Legislative Council, 9 December 1949, reprinted in Henry K. Akyeampong, *Joseph Boakye Danquah, Historic Speeches and Writings on Ghana* (Accra, 1966), 95.

64 J.B. Danquah, 'A National Bank, Letter to the Editor', *Ashanti Pioneer*, 24 October 1949, reprinted in Henry K. Akyeampong, *Journey to Independence and After (Dr. J.B. Danquah's Letters) 1949–1951* (Accra, 1970), 69.

65 The nationalists in Ceylon took advice from the United States on establishing a central bank (Hitihamy A. De S. Gunasekera, *From Dependent Currency to Central Banking in Ceylon: An Analysis of Monetary Experience, 1825–1957* (London, 1962), 261). The resultant institution's design was not to BoE's liking (Eric Haslam, *Central Banks in the Making: The Role of the Bank of England 1948–74* (1979), [BOEA OV18/2], 11).

66 Anonymous, Foreign Office memorandum, 12 August 1948 and addressed to F.F. Powell, Bank of England, BOEA OV69/1/478/2765/3/163. Powell was at the time the Adviser to Governors (1946–51), (John Fforde, *The Bank of England and Public Policy 1941–1958* (Cambridge, 1992), 103).

67 Between 1930 and 1948, the date of the said Foreign Office memorandum, there had been five bank failures in Nigeria (Chibuike Uche, 'Indigenous Banks in Colonial Nigeria', *The International Journal of African Historical Studies* 43:3 (2010), 469).

68 Letter from F.F. Powell to W.G. Boss, Colonial Office, 20 August 1948, BOEA OV69/1/478/2765/3/166.

of land registration.[69] This reasoning is, however, incomplete: moneylenders were already taking derivative rights in land as security, as noted. Chiefs also pledged land to raise funds for local development.[70] Finally, Paton also repeated Shephard's advice that cooperative societies should anchor the reforms to Gold Coast's credit system. Unlike Shephard, Paton believed that indebtedness was not a problem because the high cocoa prices then prevailing enabled farmers to pay off outstanding loans if they wished.[71] Paton also could not recommend a state-aided commercial bank because he had no 'economic grounds' for one.

Neither the Colonial Office in London nor the colonial administration in the Gold Coast accepted Paton's advice to drop the agricultural bank concept. The Colonial Office and BoE did, however, concede Paton's objections to a 'national bank', but the colonial administration in the Gold Coast argued that, with government and Cocoa Marketing Board's (CMB) support, the bank would be viable.[72] Arthur Creech Jones, Secretary of State for the Colonies, disagreed, believing that foreign banks in the country already met current demand and future needs.[73] Meanwhile, *Ashanti Pioneer* continued to publish editorials and Danquah's articles. It also cited Nanka-Bruce's earlier work on banking and called for a committee to investigate monetary reform. Gold Coast's Legislative Council subsequently resolved to institute this and appointed a Select Committee chaired by Robert Armitage, the new Financial Secretary.[74]

At its first meeting (March 1950), the Armitage Committee discussed the type of institution the Gold Coast required.[75] It wanted to study different banking

69 Paton was not alone in being cautious about government-supported agricultural lending institutions (M.P. Cowen and R.W. Shenton, 'Bankers, peasants, and land in British West Africa 1905–37', *Journal of Peasant Studies* 19:1 (1998), 26–58).

70 For examples of borrowing arrangements involving chiefs, see: Agreement covering Mortgage of Properties situated at Dunkwa between Ohene Kojo Amuakwa, Chief of Dunkwa and African & Eastern Trade Corporation Ltd., Branch of United Africa Company Ltd. The document is not dated but other archival evidence suggests it was signed on 30 November 1930, PRAAD (Cape Coast) ADM 23/1/759/54/11; Letter from W.H. Grey to the Colonial Secretary, Victoriaborg, Accra, 17 September 1929, PRAAD (Cape Coast) ADM 23/1/759/54/11; Letter from Acting Commissioner Central Province to the Secretary for Native Affairs, Victoriaborg Accra, 12 July 1932, PRAAD (Cape Coast) ADM 23/1/759/54; Letter from Acting Commissioner Central Province to the Secretary for Native Affairs, Victoriaborg Accra, 13 June 1932, PRAAD (Cape Coast) ADM. 23/1/759/51.

71 Report on the Development and Control of Banking and Agricultural Credit Facilities in the Gold Coast (Accra, 1949) (Paton Report), 7.

72 Letter from Mr. Mangin, Government House, Accra to A.B. Cohen, Colonial Office, 6 April 1949, BOEA OV69/1/478/2765/3/153A.

73 Letter from Arthur Creech Jones to The Officer Administrating the Government of the Gold Coast, 17 June 1949, BOEA OV69/1/478/2765/3/153A.

74 *Ashanti Pioneer*, 19 December 1949, 2; and *Ashanti Pioneer*, 10 December 1949, 3.

75 Minutes of the First meeting of the Select Committee appointed to investigate the establishment of a national bank for the Gold Coast, 27 March 1950, BOEA OV69/1/478/2765/3.

models, including BoE's interventions in British industry between the wars when it was a commercial lender. At its second meeting (31 May 1950), it was proposed that the new institution should absorb the newly created Agricultural Development Bank and any other proposed domestic development finance organisations and accept deposits. There was, however, no agreement that the new institution should take over the note issue functions of WACB; some members believed this premature. The minutes of this second meeting named the proposed institution the 'Gold Coast National Development Corporation' and mandated it to take deposits and make loans.[76] The deposit-taking operation was named 'the National Bank of the Gold Coast' and it was proposed that the government, CMB, and private shareholders, should jointly capitalise the bank, giving the government the right to appoint most of the directors. On 29 July 1950, the Armitage Committee recommended appointing an expert to study the constitutions of other bodies, including Central Bank of Ceylon and National Bank of Egypt. Several constitutional documents were circulated on 4 January 1951.[77] Another study was proposed, with Cecil Trevor as author.

Trevor Report and Jackson Memorandum

Trevor was recommended by BoE's then Deputy Governor, Dallas Bernard. In 1950 Trevor had retired as Deputy Governor from Reserve Bank of India, which he had joined at its formation in 1935 after working at the Imperial Bank (which had a commercial business and acted as government banker, as described above).[78] Of the three other suggested advisers, two, like Trevor, had worked at commercial banks with central banking functions: Arthur Poole (Imperial Bank of India) and C.N. Nixon (National Bank of Egypt). Trevor's mandate required him to examine banking conditions in the Gold Coast and, in particular, to investigate setting up 'a national bank on commercial lines' to provide finance and act as a central bank.[79] Early in the investigation Stanley W. Payton, Trevor's assistant, confirmed to BoE that discussions in the Gold Coast had not centred on a 'central bank'; but rather on credit access.[80]

76 Minutes of the Second meeting of the Select Committee appointed to investigate the establishment of a national bank for the Gold Coast, 31 May 1950, BOEA OV69/1/478/2765/3.

77 The documents circulated included the Report on the Establishment of a Central Bank of Ceylon, the Monetary Law Act No.58 of Ceylon 1949, and the Commonwealth of Australia Banking Act 1947.

78 Letter from D.G.M. Bernard to Hilton Poynton, 10 April 1951, BOEA OV69/2/478. At the time, Poynton was head of the Colonial Office's Economic Division (1948–1959).

79 Banking Conditions in the Gold Coast and on the Question of Setting Up a National Bank (Accra, 1951) (Trevor Report), 117.

80 Letter to F.F. Powell from S.W. Payton, 1 June 1951, BOEA OV69/2/478; and Letter to Leslie O'Brien from S.W. Payton, 7 July 1951, BOEA OV69/2/478. At the time, S.W. Payton was a Senior Clerk at BoE's Overseas Department.

Trevor's report was submitted on 16 August 1951. It recommended that a commercial bank controlled by the government should be established in the Gold Coast. Trevor repeated Shephard's (and, later, Paton's) recommendation that a lending business should be based on cooperative societies, particularly now that these were better established.[81] The report advised against the formation of a bank of issue for three reasons: first, since WACB served the Gold Coast adequately, a Bank of Issue was redundant; second, that a central bank could be created only after 'a Government security market, a bill market, a stock exchange, banking and insurance systems' had been established; and third, a central bank would not extend commercial long-term loans. Instead, Trevor recommended establishing a commercial bank, which would extend short-term loans, 'encourage a banking habit among the population', and in time assume central banking functions.[82]

Trevor's report was not welcomed at BoE. A memorandum by Maurice Parsons articulates BoE's disquiet, emphasising the inflationary risk associated with domestic credit.[83] Parsons was able to persuade Trevor to draw attention in his report to this risk.[84] A second memorandum by William Jackson encapsulated what eventually became the official BoE position on this 'national bank' question.[85] Jackson reasoned that it was quite legitimate for the Gold Coast to establish a commercial bank with issuing powers if it wished and claimed that if Trevor had rejected the National Bank idea, the Gold Coast would either have set up a bank anyway or else appointed an American adviser who might perhaps have 'recommended something worse in the shape of a half-baked Central Bank'. In saying this, Jackson acknowledged that the changing political conditions in the Gold Coast restricted choice, particularly given the United States Federal Reserve's growing influence in international monetary politics and the 'winds of change [being] fanned by the influence of the new Washington financial institutions, heavily weighted as they were by American ways of thought'.[86] Accepting Jackson's counsel, the colonial authorities and

81 Trevor Report, paragraph 117.

82 *Ibid.*, paragraphs 100–4. The report faced criticism (David Rowan, 'Banking adaptation in the Gold Coast: A Critique of the Recent Report by Sir Cecil Trevor', *South African Journal of Economics* 20:4 (1952), 345–65).

83 Memorandum from Maurice H. Parsons to The Deputy Governor, 16 August 1951. At the time, Parsons was Deputy Chief Cashier at the Bank. (F. Capie, *The Bank of England: 1950s to 1979* (Cambridge, 2010), 49).

84 Memorandum from S.W. Payton to Leslie O'Brien, 21 August 1951. The section of the Trevor Report amended to reflect Parson's input is Paragraph 155.

85 Memorandum from W.J. Jackson to Leslie O'Brien and Anthony Grafftey-Smith, 24 August 1951, BOEA E20/155. At the time, Jackson was Assistant in the Bank of England's Overseas and Foreign Department.

86 Haslam, *Central Banks*, 9. Haslam's reference was to the growing influence in international monetary affairs of the World Bank and the International Monetary Fund, as was

BoE agreed to establish a new financial institution, the Bank of the Gold Coast (BGC), along Trevor's lines.

A 'National Bank' with Commercial Operations

In 1951, following the elections, a transitional government took administrative control in the Gold Coast under Kwame Nkrumah and the Convention People's Party (CPP). This government wanted the new institution to have both commercial banking and note issuance powers, as CPP had told Trevor during the preparation of his report.[87] To retain oversight of the new bank, the British authorities sought a 'European Managing Director' as head. In April 1952, Alfred Eggleston, recommended by Cecil Trevor, was selected.[88] In August 1952, Eggleston sent Jackson a draft bill to establish BGC. This had a clause enabling the new bank to:

> carry on and transact a wide range of business on behalf of the government, namely: the paying, receiving, collecting and remitting of money, bullion and securities ... and the undertaking and transacting of any other business which the Government may from time to time entrust to the Bank (Clause 15).[89]

Jackson was concerned that this clause would make the new bank 'a maid of all work for the Government'.[90] To BoE, this implied that BGC could end up with central banking functions.[91]

During this period, nationalist politicians continued to call for a new institution with the dual purpose of being both 'the sole currency-issuing authority'

---

evidenced in colonies like Nigeria (Chibuike Uche, 'Bank of England vs the IBRD: Did the Nigerian Colony deserve a Central Bank?' *Explorations in Economic History* 34:2 (1997), 220–41). This concern was heightened by the United States itself being involved in establishing central banks in Ceylon, Sudan, and elsewhere. American influence had also extended to South Africa (Bradley Bordiss and Vishnu Padayachee, '"A superior practical man:" Sir Henry Strakosch, the Gold Standard and monetary policy debates in South Africa, 1920–23', *Economic History of Developing Regions* 26:1 (2011), 116).

87 Memorandum from the Secretary's Office, The Convention People's Party, to Cecil Trevor, Ministry of Finance, Accra, 10 July 1951, BOEA OV69/2/478/2765/4. This goal was also stated in CPP's General Election Manifesto (George E. Metcalfe (ed.) *Great Britain and Ghana: Documents of Ghana History, 1807–1957* (London, 1965), Document 508).

88 Four years prior, Eggleston had retired from the Imperial Bank of India. When the Reserve Bank of India was formed, he became for three years a director of its Central Board.

89 Clause 15 (a) of the Bank of Gold Coast Ordinance 1952.

90 Memorandum from W.J. Jackson to Maurice Parsons and Leslie O'Brien, 2 September 1952, BOEA OV69/2/478/2765/4/40.

91 Memorandum from W.J. Jackson to Maurice Parsons, Leslie O'Brien and G.M. Watson, 22 September 1952, BOEA OV69/2/478/2765/4/47.

and 'a lender'.[92] In response, Eggleston accused Danquah of proposing 'a Frankenstein Monster' which would cause inflation by relying 'on the handle of a note-printing press for funds with which to finance development'.[93] It is interesting to find Eggleston inveighing against a single bank, since he would later argue in favour of one (see below). Eggleston's attitude may owe something to Danquah' opposition to Nkrumah and Eggleston's wish to gain the government's favour.

The BGC bill was debated on 8 October 1952. In presenting it, Armitage said the government intended to hold most of the new bank's shares and sell the rest to the public, once the new institution became profitable and could pay dividends. He proposed that government should appoint most directors, including the Managing Director, ensuring government control. Even though the institution would not be a central bank, Armitage nonetheless proposed the name 'The Bank of the Gold Coast' because this was a 'very good analogy of Bank of England'![94]

Armitage presented the new institution as a commercial bank which would extend secured loans and execute 'a wide range of financial transactions' on government's behalf, including acting as agent on treasury issues and government bonds. He spoke against any changes to the country's monetary system that would ensue from establishing a Bank of Issue. Changes, he asserted, would cast doubt on the management of note issues, capital repatriation, and any trade balance forecasts. These concerns would, he believed, reduce overseas investment in the Gold Coast, particularly if British investors did not see the new institution as mirroring BoE.[95] Armitage's point that the existing monetary arrangements provided the stability which gave colonies access to capital markets was seen by British colonial policymakers as one of Empire's advantages.[96]

The substantive objections to Armitage's speech were as follows. First, members questioned whether the proposed institution was what the country needed, particularly since no provision had been made in the bill for the new bank to eventually become a Bank of Issue. Second, there was doubt whether the plan to sell shares to the public was necessary since these would later need to be repurchased once the bank became a Bank of Issue, wholly owned by

92 'National Bank should make own currency' by J.B. Danquah, *The Daily Echo*, 23 September 1952.

93 Note from Eggleston to Ohene Djan, Ministerial Secretary, Ministry of Finance, BOEA. OV7/35/17.

94 Gold Coast Legislative Assembly Debates, Session 1952, Issue No.3, 215–16: Cambridge University Library Rare Books Department RCS.L.448.2.1952c.

95 Gold Coast Legislative Assembly Debates, Session 1952, Issue No.3, 218.

96 Peter V. Mini, 'Keynes on markets: a survey of heretical views', *American Journal of Economics and Sociology* 55:1 (1996), 99–111.

government. Third, it was observed that even though the transition to a central bank would need to be gradual, the complementary roles of the government and minority shareholders needed clarification: where government disagreed with other shareholders, decisions would favour the government. A fourth point criticised the vagueness of Clause 15, as BoE had done. Fifth, the proposed institution, it was argued, failed to address the colony's need for credit and a further study was sought on this problem. Coupled with this was a call for the institution to be a 'Bank's banker' which would act as a lender of last resort to meet short-term demands for liquidity that might arise wherever long-term loans were granted.

At the bill's Second Reading, Armitage rebutted these points. First, he said that the bill could not confirm that the new institution would eventually become a Bank of Issue because it would be unjustified to force the government's hand prematurely by requiring immediate confirmation of the change. Second, that if it became appropriate for BGC eventually to become an orthodox central bank, the new bank could then shed its commercial banking business. In saying this, Armitage, abandoning BoE's preferred approach, was extending the possibility that BGC could eventually become a central bank. Third, Armitage objected to the new institution lending to the agricultural sector; rather, this role should belong to the Colony's Agricultural Loans Board. Lastly, Armitage confirmed that BGC would work to create a money market that a new central bank in due course would supervise.

With minor amendments, the bill became law on 9 October 1952 and BGC began operations on 20 May 1953. Its first staff included 25 Africans recruited from Barclays and BBWA, together with others who joined as school-leavers.[97]

Once established, Eggleston voiced support for BGC adopting central banking functions. In an undated memorandum, he pointed out that BGC was 'brought into being to fill a reputed vacuum in commercial banking facilities which did not, in fact, exist'.[98] He therefore argued that BGC should become a Bank of Issue, 'without necessarily being a Central Bank' since, as he observes, the Gold Coast had no traditional instruments through which a central bank controls credit (money markets and bill markets). Scottish banks and the Bank of England in its original incarnation exemplified for him commercial banks which had both trading and note-issuance functions. Eggleston argued that

97 One of these first recruits was Yaw Adjepong-Boateng, the father of the present author. He joined as a clerk, having completed his secondary school studies at Mfantsipim and ahead of leaving for the Wharton School in Pennsylvania for his undergraduate studies. He was later to join Bank of Ghana (1969–91).

98 'Gold Coast Currency: Notes and Proposals by the Managing Director, Bank of the Gold Coast' (undated), Future of the West African Currency Board, The British National Archives (hereafter 'TNA') CO 1025/5A. Eggleston's observation dates the memorandum as being either very late 1953 or 1954.

a 'periodically-reviewed convention' would protect the Gold Coast's existing private banks from BGC using its position to 'undercut' their rates. This position contrasted to the role envisaged for CBA as described above.

Bank of Ghana Bill

After the 1954 elections, internal Colonial Office correspondence confirmed the Nkrumah government's intention that 'the Board of the Bank of the Gold Coast should be the Executive Currency Authority' controlled by the Minister of Finance.[99] An unsigned 1955 memorandum spelt out BoE's opposition to the idea of a hybrid institution.[100] This was probably written by J.B. Loynes; it is consistent with subsequent documents he wrote in 1956 and 1957.[101] The memorandum argued that a hybrid institution might face conflicts since 'its commercial instincts might frequently be running counter to its Central Bank instincts, especially in times of economic expansion or contraction', making it difficult to locate central banking and commercial banking operations 'under one hat' (a point made previously by Kisch and Elkin). To Loynes, 'even greater than the danger of a central bank competing actively for commercial business is, of course, the danger of wrong policies in the central banking field itself'.[102] Shortly thereafter, Loynes circulated a warning that the model of a central bank with a commercial banking function was a 'fait accompli'.[103] BoE believed that Eggleston was promoting this design for personal reasons.[104]

After the CPP's victory in the 1956 elections, Loynes sent an internal memorandum confirming that the Finance Minister, Komla Gbedemah, had

99 Memorandum from R.J. Vile, Africa Department B, Colonial Office, to A.N. Galsworthy, Head of Finance Department, Colonial Office, 21 December 1954, BOEA OV69/3/2766/1/40D.

100 'Central Bank and Commercial Bank' – Unsigned memorandum, 13 January 1955, BOEA OV69/3/2766/1/40.

101 John Barraclough de Loynes worked in the Bank of England's Overseas and Foreign Department. He was involved on assignments in Ceylon, Gold Coast, Nigeria, Sierra Leone, and Gambia (Chibuike Uche, 'J.B. Loynes and central banking development in British West Africa', *South African Journal of Economic History* 15:1–2 (2000), 112–33).

102 Memorandum from J.B. Loynes to J.L. Fisher, G.M. Watson, and the Chief Cashier, 30 August 1955, BOEA OV69/3/2766/1/55.

103 Memorandum from J.B. Loynes to J.L. Fischer, and the Chief Cashier, 6 September 1955, BOEA OV69/3/2766/1/55C; Memorandum from J.B. Loynes to J.L. Fischer, and the Chief Cashier, 8 September 1955, BOEA OV69/3/2766/1/55D.

104 Haslam, *Central Banks,* 228. This view is further supported by Eggleston telling Barclays that he would extend his stay in Ghana following the merger because it would create a 'real bank' (Memorandum: Ghana Commercial Bank Ltd and Bank of Ghana Ltd., 10 November 1958, B GA 11/2105). Eggleston was later described within the Bank of England as 'an unfortunate choice' (Haslam, *ibid.*, 1108).

agreed to hive off BGC's commercial operations into a separate institution, converting what was left into a Bank of Issue.[105] This led Loynes to refer to the proposed institution as a 'central bank' rather than a 'Bank of Issue' to reflect its not only issuing currency but also its wider obligations in banking and policy.[106] This approach was subsequently modified. When Gbedemah presented the Bank of Ghana bill to Parliament on 5 February 1957, he proposed that BGC would continue as a commercial bank instead of becoming a Bank of Issue. It was to be renamed 'Ghana Commercial Bank', with no central banking functions; these would be discharged by a separate, central institution. Gbedemah explained that this decision had been taken 'to avoid any possibility of suspicion that the profits of the Issue Department or the currency backing were being used to finance commercial banking activities'.[107] In the bill, the government announced that a new currency, together with local treasury bills and other government securities issued by the new central bank to replace WACB notes, would be backed by Sterling, to ensure confidence in the new currency. Gbedemah said that he expected the new central bank to also help 'develop a local securities market' and to act as a 'Lender of Last Resort', particularly when new 'indigenous commercial banks' were established. Furthermore, Gbedemah assured Parliament that the directors of the new bank would be selected on merit, disregarding 'political affiliations'.

In the subsequent debate, Cobina Kessie, another founding member of UGCC, reminded Parliament that membership of WACB gave the Gold Coast a stable exchange rate against Sterling, a system through which the country's sterling reserves were managed, and an effective exchange control system. Given these advantages, Kessie asked whether the additional cost of maintaining a central bank was justified. He also criticised the lack of a recognised feature of central banking in the bill, i.e., to provide for the control of credit by centralising the reserves of the existing expatriate commercial banks.

Victor Owusu, another Opposition member, reasoned that notes could be issued without establishing a central bank, because the government could appoint any commercial bank, including BGC, as its agent for this purpose. Likewise, a legal requirement could oblige commercial banks to maintain adequate reserves without the need for a centralised reserve system. Owusu also raised questions about the ownership of the central bank and described models where the central bank's capital was owned not by the government but by the public, or other commercial banks, or a hybrid of the two. He recommended to Parliament that if the country was to have a central bank, 9 per cent

105 Memorandum from J.B. Loynes to F.C. Hawker, 20 July 1956, BOEA OV69/3/2766/1/112. Gbedemah had become Finance Minister in 1954 when the Finance portfolio moved from being a colonial appointment to the government.

106 Memorandum from J.B. Loynes to the Minister of Finance, 19 December 1956, BOEA OV69/3/2766/1/58.

107 Bank of Ghana bill, Second Reading, 703.

of its shares should be held by the public and 41 per cent (sic) by the commercial banks.[108] The government would hold the balance and the majority interest (51 per cent). Owusu also wanted directors appointed who had been recommended by the commercial banks.

In his response to these arguments, Gbedemah said that the government wanted to set up a new central bank because it would help to develop the financial sector, including establishing money and securities markets. He expressed concern that if commercial losses occurred adding an Issue department to BGC would undermine 'public confidence in the safety of a currency issued' by the bank. Gbedemah also confirmed that Bank of Ghana would not provide 'long-term development capital'; instead, this would be provided by establishing a domestic long-term debt market. He also rejected suggestions that the new central bank should be owned under different configurations of state, commercial banks, and the public, commenting that modern central banks were wholly state-owned. Finally, he rejected the suggestion that the commercial banks should nominate directors to the board of the new institution.

The bill passed its Second Reading on 14 February 1957 and established Bank of Ghana (BoG) as a separate legal institution from BGC. BoG was modelled on BoE. Eggleston was appointed Governor and Douglas Stone, seconded from BoE, was appointed its First Deputy Governor.

On 6 March 1957, WACB handed its operations to BoG and the central bank became responsible for currency issues and the enactment and enforcement of monetary laws.[109] By November 1957, settlement procedures were arranged between WACB and BoG, necessitated because Ghana's new currency, due about 1 July 1958, would be backed by Sterling and WACB notes and coins.[110] By December 1957, changes to the country's reserves management had been discussed with BoE.[111]

Opposition to the Classic Model

Even as the transition above was proceeding, a proposal to merge BoG and Ghana Commercial Bank (GCB) was being considered,[112] because the country was not satisfied with keeping the two institutions separate. Yet another study

108 Owusu's figures add up to 101 per cent. It is, therefore, likely that he intended to say that 40 per cent of the new central bank should be owned by the commercial banks.

109 Harcourt Fuller, *Building the Ghanaian Nation-State: Kwame Nkrumah's Symbolic Nationalism* (New York, 2014), 58.

110 Bank of Ghana: 'Preliminary Notes on the Establishment of an Issue Department', 20 November 1957, BOEA OV69/8/2767/2/65.

111 Letters exchanged between J.L. Fisher and the Chief Cashier, Bank of England, dated between 22 November and 2 December 1957, BOEA OV69/8/2767/2/67.

112 Letter from R.W.B. Carter, United Kingdom Trade Commissioner, Accra to R.C. Wright, Board of Trade, Commercial Relations and Export Department, London, 25

of banking conditions was under discussion.[113] Notably, by early 1957 Sudan's government was working with the United States to establish a central bank. In this regard, the Federal Reserve advised Sudan to acquire NBE's commercial banking branches in Khartoum and combine these with the then Sudan currency board's note issue functions.[114] To support commercial lending, Sudan's new central bank's statutes were drafted to enable it to lend 'in emergency situations when the urgent credit needs of the country are not being satisfied.'[115] Later, one of the advisers to Sudan reiterated that not only absorbing the functions of the currency board, the new central bank was also responsible for credit control and the expansion of banking services.[116] The Federal Reserve's advice to Sudan was known to BoE.[117] This would have contributed to concerns about American influence in promoting central banking models which were not to BoE's liking, the point that William Jackson had raised earlier.

Criticism of BoG's design also came from two British advisers to the Nkrumah government, Geoffrey Bing and Thomas Balogh. Bing was formally appointed in October 1956 as the constitutional adviser to Nkrumah.[118] He was later appointed Attorney General after Ghana's independence, and subsequently a Presidential adviser (1961–1966). Balogh, in contrast, had no official position in

---

February 1957, BOEA OV69/4/2766/2; Letter from J.B. Loynes to H. Reed, Commonwealth Relations Office, Downing Street, 9 April 1957, BOEA OV69/8/2767/2.

113 Letter from G.M. Watson to J.B. Loynes, 21 June 1957, BOEA OV69/8/2767/2/28; Note from G.M. Watson to the Deputy Governor, Bank of England, 10 September 1957, BOEA OV69/8/2767/2/29. Graham Towers, the first governor of Canada's central bank, was under consideration as an adviser for this new study.

114 The Economic and Financial background of Central Banking in the Sudan, 20 August 1957, Andrew F. Brimmer Papers, 1944–2014, Baker Library Special Collections, Harvard Business School Archives Box 40.

115 Preliminary Report on the Organisation and Functions of a Central Bank for the Sudan by Oliver P. Wheeler (Vice President, Federal Reserve Bank of San Francisco), Alan R. Holmes (Economist, Federal Reserve Bank of New York), and Andrew F. Brimmer (Economist, Federal Reserve Bank of New York), Ministry of Finance & Economics, Khartoum, 28 February 1957, Andrew F. Brimmer Papers, 1944–2014, Baker Library Special Collections, Harvard Business School Archives Box 40.

116 Andrew F. Brimmer, 'Banking and Finance in the Sudan', *South African Journal of Economics* 28:1 (1960), 34.

117 Letter from Claude Loombe, Bank of England to Oliver Wheeler, Federal Reserve Bank of San Francisco, 11 April 1957, Andrew F. Brimmer Papers, 1944–2014, Baker Library Special Collections, Harvard Business School Archives Box 40. Loombe was a member of Sudan's currency board (1956–60) (Fforde, *Bank of England*, 116).

118 Geoffrey Bing was a British barrister and politician and former Labour Member of Parliament (1945–55). Bing's close relationship to Nkrumah led to his involvement in several aspects of Ghanaian society, including founding membership of the Ghana Academy of Learning. At one stage he had an ambition – ultimately unfulfilled – to become the first substantive Vice-Chancellor of the new University of Ghana (Alexander A. Kwapong, *A Life in Education: A Memoir* (Accra, 2006),138 and 517).

Ghana. Between 1927 and 1931, Balogh worked for Henry Strakosch,[119] Oliver Sprague, and Hjalmar Schacht at the Reichsbank.[120] He had also worked at the Federal Reserve and Banque de France.[121] Despite working with these advocates of the classic model, Balogh was non-conformist and suspicious of monetary policy management.[122] Bing had sought to hire Balogh to advise on establishing a National Bank in the Gold Coast, the exchange control framework, and other financial legislation.[123]

Writing in 1957 on Malaya, Balogh argued that '[colonial] banking systems grew up to serve the needs of the metropolitan areas for the reliable and cheap supply of food and raw materials'.[124] To him, this applied to Africa.[125] He maintained that the goal of colonial monetary policy was to ensure that currencies used in the colonies were stable and 100 per cent backed by sterling assets.[126] Balogh argued that this level of reserve backing meant that the colonies provided loans to the metropolis. Balogh was not the first to criticise this approach. Writing to the Colonial Office in 1943, Keynes had perceived that because this reserves policy did not recognise a fiduciary component, it led to 'a high degree of conservatism in development' and he acknowledged that possibly 'too much conservatism has prevailed hitherto in Colonial finance'.[127]

119 At the time, Henry Strakosch served on the Council of India. He had served on the Royal Commission on Indian Currency and Finance (1925–26). In 1920, he had chaired the South African monetary economic commission which drafted legislation which led to South Africa's reserve bank being established (A. Chatterjee, 'Sir Henry Strakosch: Obituary', *Journal of the Royal Society of Arts* 91:4652 (1943), 656; Bordiss, and Padayachee, 'Henry Strakosch', 114–22).

120 Letter from H.A. Siepmann (Adviser to the Governors, 1926–1932) to J.M. Keynes, 3 September 1930, BOEA OV45/81/520/2909/3/111B.

121 June Morris, *The Life and Times of Thomas Balogh: A Macaw Among Mandarins* (Brighton, 2007), 9–11.

122 Letter from Henry Clay (Economic Adviser, Bank of England (1930–44)) to A.W. Flux (President of the Royal Statistical Society (1928–1930)), 2 February 1931, BOEA OV45/81/520/2909/3/159; and Roger Opie, 'The future of monetary policy' in Paul Streeten (ed.) *Unfashionable Economics: Essays in Honour of Lord Balogh* (London, 1970), 263.

123 Geoffrey Bing, *Reap the Whirlwind: An Account of Kwame Nkrumah's Ghana from 1950 to 1966* (London, 1968), 146–7. Bing confirms that Balogh had started working on Gold Coast problems ahead of the prospective appointment (*Ibid.*, 151). Bing suggests that the appointment was blocked by the British government.

124 Thomas Balogh, 'A Note on the monetary controversy in Malaya', *Malayan Economic Review* 4:2 (1957), 21–6.

125 Thomas Balogh, 'The mechanism of neo-imperialism', reprinted in Thomas Balogh (ed.), *Revival: The Economics of Poverty* (New York, 1966), 82.

126 For an early discussion on the inefficiencies of using sterling reserves as backing for local currency circulation see: Keynes, *Indian Currency*, 104–37.

127 'Financial development through fiduciary issues and uses of Colonial Currency Funds', Letter from J.M. Keynes to Sidney Caine, Colonial Office, Dover House, Whitehall, dated 18 May 1943, TNA, T 236/4090.

J. Mars was to make a similar point in 1947.[128] By 1954, colonial administrators calling for flexibility would describe this reserves policy in the Gold Coast as 'flat-footed'.[129]

Balogh also argued that the foreign banks operating in the colonies and who kept their assets in sterling in London, diverted wealth created in these colonies to the metropolitan market to feed imperial trade, resulting in higher borrowing costs in the colonies and reducing funds available to them for domestic industrial development. He also criticised the practice of funding colonial development projects by raising capital in London (and Paris). He found this flawed, since it 'conferred on private financial interests, and especially overseas banks operating in the capital cities, an absolute veto power on policy decisions in dependent areas'.[130] The reluctance of the colonies to raise tax revenue reinforced this. In his counter-argument, Balogh said that the Sterling Area needed to be reorganised by the British Government and BoE, allowing strong central banks to rise in the new Commonwealth countries (and the remaining colonies) which could direct savings and investment and compete with private banks.[131]

In a letter sent in 1957 and addressed to 'Robert' (apparently Robert Jackson), Balogh, referring to Sayers and making the point that Keynes had made in India, expressed doubts over 'whether a central bank fashioned after the pattern of BoE or the Federal Reserve System ... is adequate for underdeveloped areas'.[132] Because commercial banking in the Gold Coast was not widespread in the 1950s, Balogh contended, it was advantageous if the central bank was a direct lender and opened branches across the country. He argued that savings in the Gold Coast had to be mobilised to offset the funding shortfalls that would

128 John Mars, 'Monetary and banking system and loan market of Nigeria', in Margery Perham (ed.) *Mining, Commerce, and Finance in Nigeria* (London, 1947). The point is debated extensively in the literature (Arthur Hazlewood, 'Sterling balances and the colonial currency system: A Reply', *Economic Journal* 64:255 (1954), 616–17; Ida C. Greaves, 'The sterling balances of Colonial Territories', *Economic Journal* 61:242 (1951), 433–9.

129 Future of West African Currency Board, Memorandum from E. Melville, Secretary of State for the Colonies, to K.C. Tours, Colonial Office, Sanctuary Buildings, London, dated 1 February 1954, TNA, CO 1025/5A.

130 The emphasis on 'private' is Balogh's (Thomas Balogh, Memorandum on Exchange Control, Finance & Economic Policy Sub-Committee, Labour Party, R.161/September 1952, The Papers of Nicholas Kaldor, King's College Archives, Cambridge NK/11/13/392).

131 Thomas Balogh, 'The Economic Impact of Monetary and Commercial Institutions of a European Origin in Africa' – Presentation at the National Bank of Egypt (Cairo, 1964), 12.

132 Undated letter held at Balliol College Archives (BCA hereafter) Q2/17/7–13. Robert Jackson worked on the Volta Dam project in Ghana. I am indebted to Andrew Graham for his help in identifying Jackson as the recipient of this letter. Mr. Graham worked as an economic assistant to Thomas Balogh at No. 10 Downing Street (1966–67).

result from falling cocoa prices and the consequent inability of the country to raise capital easily in the London markets.[133]

Balogh recommended CBA as a model for the former colonies to follow, seeing it as an institution that could finance development, reinvest savings in the domestic economy, and carry out central banking functions.[134] He repeated points made by Niemeyer in the 1935 memorandum discussed above. Balogh must have been a persuasive critic of BoG's design and would have encouraged the government to bring BoG and GCB closer. Through Bing and Robert Jackson, Balogh would have had Nkrumah's ear, hence BoE's reference to him as a 'troublemaker'.[135]

Progressing the amalgamation proposal

At a Cabinet meeting in October 1958, Gbedemah reminded those present of the earlier objections to BGC having central banking functions: ministers were concerned that trading losses might undermine the currency's value; and that BGC's commercial banking interests would hinder its ability to discharge central banking functions. Gbedemah said that he did not consider these objections to be 'decisive' because '[so] long as the Issue Department and its assets remain by law distinct and inviolable, there is no reason to suppose that minor happenings of the commercial side would affect them'.[136] Gbedemah explained further that the country's financial system was too undeveloped for BoG to exercise the functions performed by an orthodox central bank and that these functions could be performed equally well by a commercial bank. To advance the amalgamation, he proposed several legislative changes, including additional clauses to the Bank of Ghana Ordinance to enable BoG to take over all GCB's assets and liabilities. Cabinet granted approval for work to begin on draft legislation.[137]

133 The article entitled 'Eyeless in Ghana' is amongst Balogh's papers held by Balliol College, Oxford (BCA Q2/17/5). It is likely to have been published in 1957.

134 Balogh had had a consultancy role at Commonwealth Bank (1941–64) – (Morris, *Life and Times*, 22). This recalls Junius Jayewardene's recommendation that Commonwealth Bank be a model for Ceylon's central bank (Haslam, *Central Banks*, 132).

135 Letter from J.B. Loynes to G.M. Watson, 1 July 1957, BOEA OV69/8/2767/2/29.

136 Cabinet Memorandum by the Minister of Finance, PRAAD (Accra) ADM13/2/53, CM 964/18.

137 Internal British documents show persistent opposition to the idea (Note from D.W. Spiers, Overseas Department, to Chief Cashier, 18 November 1958, BOEA OV69/8/2767/2/125; and Letter from R.W.B. Carter, United Kingdom Trade Commissioner, Accra to R.B. Dorman, Commonwealth Relations Office, London, 9 December 1958, BOEA OV69/8/2767/2/132).

At BoG's November 1958 board meeting, a letter from the Ministry of Finance was circulated confirming the decision to merge and promising to introduce supporting legislation at the National Assembly meeting in February 1959.[138] Stone, absent from the November board meeting, opposed the amalgamation at a subsequent meeting.[139] Another person with concerns was Arthur Lewis. He had become Nkrumah's Economic Adviser in October 1957.[140] In December 1958, Lewis attended the first meeting of the Cabinet Economic Committee established by Nkrumah. This meeting, however, postponed discussion of the amalgamation.[141]

A subsequent meeting of the Economic Committee in January 1959 agreed that work on draft legislation should continue but that the amalgamation itself should be delayed.[142] The Committee's minutes note a presentation by Lewis on the merger but do not record its content.[143] However, Lewis's position can be deduced from a disagreement he had with Eggleston the previous year. Eggleston had written to the Cabinet in 1958 saying that Loynes's recommendations were mistaken on two points: in claiming that, if a hybrid institution suffered losses in its trading business, this might shake confidence in the currency; and in alleging that competing with private commercial banks would affect its discharge of its central banking functions. Eggleston's criticism of Loynes made reference to Sayers' published work.[144] This drew opposition from Lewis, who contended that Eggleston had misrepresented Sayers. Lewis discussed his views with Stone, who in turn wrote to Gbedemah.[145] In his correspondence, Stone, also drawing on Sayers' work, asserts that instead of the merger, GCB should be strengthened so it could compete effectively with the foreign-owned banks and meet the needs of expanding indigenous enterprises. Lewis's presentation to the Economic Committee is likely to have been consistent with Stone's arguments and with his published work, in which he argues that the development of a banking habit 'with all the changes in attitudes and institutions and in techniques which accompany this conversion'

138 Bank of Ghana Board Minutes, Friday, 7 November 1958, Bank of Ghana Archives (BOGA) (it is Bank of Ghana policy to withhold call numbers of material held at its archives).

139 Bank of Ghana Board Minutes, Friday, 12 December 1958, BOGA (Call number withheld).

140 For a description of Lewis's responsibilities as Economic Adviser, see: Letter from Myer Cohen (signed on behalf of the Director General, Technical Assistance Administration, United Nations) to Kwame Nkrumah, 12 August 1957, PRAAD (Accra) RG 17/1/53/KN 130.

141 Minutes of the First Meeting of the Cabinet Economic Committee held in the Prime Minister's Office (18 December 1958).

142 Minutes of the Second Meeting of the Cabinet Economic Committee held in the Prime Minister's Office, 23 January 1959.

143 Nor is there a record of this presentation in Lewis's private papers at Princeton.

144 Haslam, *Central Banks*, 278–9.

145 *Ibid.*, 280–1.

was central to economic growth.[146] By opposing the amalgamation, Lewis may not have considered that the development of this habit in the Gold Coast required the type of central bank with commercial branches that Sayers, and later Thomas Balogh, described. Extending the banking habit through a public institution would have reduced pressure on the foreign-owned banks to incur the cost of expanding into rural areas.[147] It is, of course, possible that Lewis believed that this role could be played by GCB since it was also state-owned and that his reason for opposing the merger was governance concerns associated with a powerful government-controlled commercial bank which also had note-issuing functions.[148]

Gbedemah reported to Cabinet in February 1959 that the merger was still 'temporarily' on hold. Eggleston attended his last board meeting at BoG on 3 April 1959, leaving the bank thereafter. The following month, Gbedemah circulated another memorandum to the Cabinet in which he advised that draft legislation was still being prepared, but that no decision on implementation had been taken.[149] Eggleston was replaced by Hubert Kessels, recruited from Deutsche Bundesbank.[150] The discussion on the amalgamation continued but the merger was still not implemented, probably because of opposition from Kessels (see below). Another memorandum supporting the proposed merger was circulated at BoG's October 1961 board meeting. One director, Robert Blay, opposed the amalgamation, maintaining that a central bank with a commercial business would be less influential in advising the Treasury on fiscal measures.[151] Though Blay was the only bank director to oppose the merger proposal, it was

146 W. Arthur Lewis, *The Theory of Economic Growth* (London, 1955), 226. One author criticised Lewis for giving the development of a banking habit the prominence that he did: Peter Bauer, 'Review: Lewis' Theory of Economic Growth', *American Economic Review* 46:4 (1956), 636.

147 Sarah Stockwell, 'Instilling the "Sterling tradition": decolonization and the creation of a Central Bank in Ghana', in *Journal of Imperial and Commonwealth History* 26:2 (1998), 111.

148 Evidence of earlier government abuse of lending facilities in the cocoa sector may have reinforced these concerns: Report of the Commission of Enquiry into the Affairs of the Cocoa Purchasing Company Ltd. (Gold Coast, 1956); and Austin, *Politics in Ghana*, 342.

149 Cabinet Information Paper by Minister of Finance, Amalgamation of the Bank of Ghana and the Ghana Commercial Bank, May 1959, PRAAD (Accra) ADM 13/2/60.

150 Appointment of a Governor, Cabinet Memorandum by the Minister of Finance, Bank of Ghana, July 1959, PRAAD (Accra) ADM 13/2/62.

151 Bank of Ghana Board Minutes, Friday, 13 October 1961, BOGA (Call number withheld).

not adopted.[152] However, it remained under consideration, as confirmed by correspondence.[153]

Gbedemah resigned as Finance Minister in September 1961. Earlier that year, evidence had emerged of the government's tight liquidity position. In February 1961, a BoE memorandum recorded that Pember and Boyle, responsible for managing Ghana's reserves, were 'very worried' because of the repeated requests from the government to shorten the reserves portfolio – a sign of liquidity pressure.[154] Kessels gave an undertaking to the World Bank that the Government would not seek funding through an over-issue of currency.[155] Despite this commitment, amendments made to the fiduciary provisions in the Bank of Ghana Act led BoE to question whether the government's need for funding was 'structural rather than temporary'.[156] In mid-September that year, Kessels wrote to F.K.D. Goka, Gbedemah's successor, acknowledging that 'a considerable part of Government expenditure had to be financed by the Central Bank'.[157] This recalled the warnings about the risks of state control of note issuance by 'needy governments'.[158] Kessels also advised that the Government's surplus overseas balances had fallen as securities valued at £12 million had been sold to fund grants to Guinea and Upper Volta.[159]

In May 1962, a BoE memorandum records that Kessels had told Nkrumah that he would resign if the amalgamation was implemented, implying this was still under consideration.[160] A month later, another memorandum reported

152 Blay was Vice Chairman of UGCC. Nkrumah probably approved Blay's appointment because of Gbedemah's commitment to appoint independent directors on merit. In discussing Blay and C.E. Osei's appointments to Bank of Ghana's board, Nana S.K.B. Asante told the author that he believed that Nkrumah displayed 'notable pragmatism' in his political career. Once he felt politically secure, Nkrumah made several appointments of competent public officers irrespective of earlier political affiliation. Examples were the appointment of Kobina Arku Korsah as Ghana's first Chief Justice and of Edward Akufo Addo to the Supreme Court. Blay and Osei's appointments were, therefore, not unusual.

153 Letter from A.K. Kwarteng, Principal Secretary, Ministry of Finance to The Secretary, Bank of Ghana, 14 March 1962, Ghana Commercial Bank Archives (not catalogued).

154 Memorandum from D.W. Spiers to R. Heasman and J. Hollom, 17 February 1961, BOEA OV69/3/2766/50.

155 Memorandum from D.W. Spiers to D.F. Stone and G.M. Watson, 20 March 1961, BOEA OV69/3/2766/51a.

156 Letter from D.W. Spiers to H. Kessels, Governor, Bank of Ghana, 24 March 1961, BOEA OV69/3/2766/51c; Memorandum from D.W. Spiers to John Stevens, Director, Bank of England, 23 May 1961, BOEA OV69/3/2766/53.

157 Letter from H. Kessels, Bank of Ghana, to F.K.D. Goka, Minister of Finance, 14 September 1961, BOGA (Call number withheld).

158 Aryeetey's chapter in this volume discusses this point further.

159 For a discussion on the background to these credits, see Gerardo Serra and Katie Monaghan's chapter in this volume.

160 Note to Record, copied to J.B. Loynes, M. Parsons, D.F. Stone, and G.M. Watson, 15 May 1962, BOEA OV/69/8/478/103.

that H.E. Assan, then head of BoG's Banking Department, told BoE that the amalgamation was ill-advised.[161] A revised central bank act was circulated in September 1962, which was when W.M.Q. Halm became BoG's first Ghanaian Governor. This Act was described by BoE as 'probably an intermediary stage' ahead of amalgamation.[162] By then, however, circumstances were dire: BoE reported Goka lamenting that '[nothing] will change until we can all go to him (Nkrumah) and say there simply isn't any more foreign exchange'.[163] Table 1 shows the extent of the fall in the country's reserves. As illustrated, these reserves fell by 58 per cent between 1957 and 1962. During this period, the central bank's reserves rose by 24 per cent and reserves at CMB fell by 84 per cent. This was because of the transfer of funds from CMB to BoG to help meet the government's funding requirements.[164]

Table 6.1 Ghana's Gross Foreign Exchange Reserves by Holders 1957–62

(£ million Current Prices)

End of Year	Total	Central Government	Central Bank	Other Banks	CMB	Other
1957	171	59	38	11	49	14
1958	173	61	31	14	52	15
1959	167	60	43	11	37	16
1960	149	43	54	6	30	16
1961	73	11	48	3	7	9
1962	72	10	47	2	8	9

Source: Digest of Statistics, Office of the Government Statistician, Accra, March 1963.

161 BoE Memorandum addressed to J.B. Loynes and G.M. Watson, 13 June 1962, BOEA OV/69/8/478/105A.

162 Memorandum from J.S. Tunstall, Overseas Office, Bank of England, to J.B. Loynes and H.R. Stobbs, 3 September 1962, BOEA OV/69/8/478/108c.

163 690 *Ibid.*; Nugent reinforces the point in his chapter in this volume saying that the Nkrumah regime run out of fiscal options in the early 1960s. Also, J. Frimpong-Ansah (BoG's Deputy Governor, 1965–68) who attended Cabinet meetings at the time, writes that Nkrumah's absolute authority meant that his ministers and advisers were unable to point out flaws in his thinking about economic issues or disagree with him [Jonathan H. Frimpong-Ansah, 'The State and the Economy in Ghana' (Unpublished Ph.D. thesis, University of Salford, 1989], 180). Frimpong-Ansah was later to become BoG's Governor (1968–73).

164 An analysis of the taxation of cocoa incomes and of cocoa production dynamics during the 1950s and 1960s is provided by Austin's chapter in this volume.

The 1962 Central Bank Act raised the fiduciary issue, assisting the government in purchasing the cocoa crop.[165] It also increased BoG's powers to lend to government and by 1963 the annual deficit was about a third of total government expenditure, partly financed by the central bank.[166] These developments led BoE to express regret that BoG's standing as a 'sound' central bank was being undermined by 'the virtually uncontrolled demands for cash made upon it by government'.[167]

Conclusion

There is no evidence that the amalgamation was still under discussion after 1962 despite board changes in February 1963 entrenching government control of BoG.[168] Ghana's need to turn to the international capital markets may have caused the Nkrumah government to pause and retain, albeit reluctantly, the type of relationship with BoE that facilitated the country's access to capital (resembling that of the Gold Coast during its membership of the Sterling Area). Before 1961, Ghana's economy was said to have experienced a period of 'innocence'.[169] This was when government expenditure was fully funded by either current export proceeds or reserves accumulated from prior export earnings. However, with growing pressure for roads, utilities, education and health facilities and other public goods, total government expenditure rose from £50 million per annum in the mid-1950s to about £200 million in 1965, leading to the country's first budget deficit in financial year 1959–60. By 1963, this deficit was estimated to have risen to 33 per cent of government expenditure, which for two years prior had been funded by BoG's purchase of Treasury Bills using fiduciary issues.

The trend above continued and in 1964, the Bank of Ghana Act began to require commercial banks also to hold a high proportion of their liquid assets in Treasury Bills. It is likely that this period of Ghana's financial distress and the

165 Douglas Rimmer, 'The crisis in the Ghana economy', *Journal of Modern African Studies* 4:1 (1966), 24.

166 *Ibid.*, 23. Aryeetey's paper in this volume analyses the political context in which Ghana's deficits were normalised.

167 Memorandum from J.W. Rose, Overseas Office, Bank of England, to J.B. Loynes, H.R. Stobbs, G.M. Watson, R. Heasman, 7 September 1962, BOEA OV/69/8/478/110. It was not unusual for new central banks to experience a shift of power to governments (Barry Eichengreen and Andreas Kakridis, 'Interwar central banks, a tour d'horizon' in Eichengreen and Kakridis, *Modern Central Bank*, 25).

168 Blay could no longer oppose the amalgamation because he left the Bank's board to join the Supreme Court in August 1962 (Bank of Ghana Board Minutes, 30 August 1962, PRAAD (Accra) RG 17/2/183).

169 Rimmer, 'Crisis', 17.

need to look externally for capital meant that it was prudent to maintain BoG's design since this was easily recognised by external capital.[170] This justification recalls Gregory's warning to Australia mentioned above. It also evokes Balogh's observation (*c.* 1957) when BoG's design was originally adopted that 'both Dr Nkrumah and his Finance Minister felt that they must not antagonise at this juncture the power of Bank of England to make or mar Ghana's immediate financial future'.[171] Balogh's comment was prescient as in 1965 the then newly appointed BoG Governor, Albert Adomakoh, asked BoE for assistance in implementing a debt-refinancing operation to help Ghana meet its need for foreign exchange.[172] It is, therefore, not surprising that the discussion on amalgamation ended, leaving BoG and GCB as separate institutions. They have remained separate ever since.

170 This is consistent with research on Latin America which found that central banks there were established in part to attract foreign capital (J.F. Zendejas and Gianandrea Nodari, 'Latin American experiments in central banking at the onset of the Great Depression' in Eichengreen and Kakridis, *Modern Central Bank*, 331.

171 Letter from Balogh to Robert Jackson (undated), 7: BCA Q2/17/13.

172 Internal Memorandum prepared by J.D. Hennings, Head of Development Policy and West and East African Economic Development, Commonwealth Relations Office, London, 25 October 1965.

7

Arthur Lewis's Mid-Century Report on Industrialisation and the Gold Coast: A Long-Century Perspective

Ravi Kanbur

On 5 June 1953, Arthur Lewis sent a letter to K.A. Gbedemah, Minister of Commerce and Industry, transmitting his report *Industrialisation and the Gold Coast* to the Government of the Gold Coast.[1] The Report had been commissioned by the Ministry in a letter dated 29 November 1952. Lewis was in the Gold Coast from 15 December 1952, to 4 January 1953, his first visit and the start of a long and sometimes turbulent association as the colony of the Gold Coast transitioned to the independent nation of Ghana.

Arthur Lewis was not yet 40 years old, but he was a star, even before he had written his classic 1954 Nobel prize winning paper 'Economic Development with Unlimited Supplies of Labour'.[2] He held the prestigious Stanley Jevons Professorship in Political Economy at the University of Manchester and had been, and was, prominent in analytical and policy debates on development. This is not the place to go into his trajectory to this position from humble beginnings in the colonial West Indies, the overt and covert racial discrimination he faced in England including at the London School of Economics, and his fights with orthodox views on economics at the Colonial Economic Advisory Committee. Nor is this the place to delve into his interactions as an economist with the realities of Ghanaian political economy, most notably his relationship with Kwame Nkrumah, whose famous dictum was 'Seek ye first the political

1 W. Arthur Lewis, *Report on Industrialisation and the Gold Coast* (Accra, 1953).

2 W. Arthur Lewis, 'Economic development with unlimited supplies of labour', *The Manchester School* 22:2 (1954), 139–91.

kingdom'. These have been well covered in the biographies of Lewis and in related papers.[3]

Rather, in this paper I focus on the Industrialisation report itself and provide a close reading in the context of Ghanaian, African and global debates on industrial policy beginning in colonial times right up to the present. It is no exaggeration to say that whether there should be an interventionist industrial policy at all, and if so what form it should take, has been and still is at the centre of the development discourse. We have seen cycles of thought, from the colonial masters' perspective on the colonies as providers of raw materials for their (the masters') industry, through the deep post-colonial desire in the newly independent countries to match their former masters in industrial development, followed by a disenchantment and disavowal of these policies by some in the era of trade liberalisation, while others pointed to state interventions in aiding the industrialisation of East Asian tiger economies, to now a rethink of industrialisation in the time of labour-saving technological change. These cycles are also seen in Ghanaian policy.[4]

What did the Lewis report say, and how if at all does its analysis stand the test of time? Section 1 of this paper presents the key elements of the argument and findings of the report. Section 2 then looks at the global and Ghanaian debates on industrial policy in the long century in light of the Lewis report and vice versa. Section 3 asks where we go from here in Ghanaian policy, given the current trajectories of trade and technology. Section 4 concludes.

The Report

The Report consists of six chapters, starting with Chapter I, 'The Genesis of Industrialisation' which provides the analytical framework, ending with Chapter VI, 'Conclusions and Recommendations'. Chapter I frames the analysis by setting out three routes to industrialisation:

> Industrialisation starts usually in one of three ways: (1) with the processing for export of primary products (agricultural or mineral) which were previously exported in a crude state; or (2) with manufacturing for an expanding home market; or (3) with the manufacture for exports of light manufactures, often based on imported raw materials. (p. 1)

3 See for example, Robert Tignor, *W. Arthur Lewis and the Birth of Development Economics* (Princeton, 2010); and Ravi Kanbur, 'W. Arthur Lewis and the roots of Ghanaian economic policy', in Ernest Aryeetey and Ravi Kanbur (eds) *The Economy of Ghana Sixty Years After Independence* (Oxford, 2017), 16–27.

4 See Nkechi Owoo and John Page, 'Industrial policy in Ghana: from a dominant state to resource abundance', in Ernest Aryeetey and Ravi Kanbur (eds), *The Economy of Ghana Sixty Years After Independence* (Oxford, 2017), 176–91.

This framing sets in train the analysis in the next four chapters, which ends in Chapter VI with very sharp conclusions and recommendations:

> Measures to increase the manufacture of commodities for the home market deserve support, but are not of number one priority... Number one priority is... a concentrated attack on the system of growing food in the Gold Coast, so as to set in motion an ever increasing productivity. This is the way to provide the market, the capital and the labour for industrialisation... Priority number two is to improve the public services. To do this will reduce the cost of manufacturing in the Gold Coast, and will thus automatically attract new industries, without the government having to offer special favours... Very many years will have passed before it becomes economical for the government to transfer any large part of its resources towards industrialisation and away from the more urgent priorities of agricultural productivity and the public services. (pp. 43–4)

Lewis did go on to present a list of interventions to aid industry, but these pale in comparison to the stark conclusion that the best way to support industrialisation was to – support agriculture! In his Foreword to the report Gbedemah, inclined as he was to push for industrialisation, struck a cautious note:

> Early publication, however, should not be regarded as a declaration of Government policy and does not mean the Government has already reached decisions on the conclusions and recommendations contained in the Report. (p. v)

Specific recommendations on industrialisation, such as the training of African personnel by foreign firms, were highlighted and publicly welcomed, and in the Legislative Assembly Nkrumah said that the government accepted the general findings as well, but we know that the future turned out very differently.

What was the analytical basis of Lewis's stark conclusions? Start with the first of his three routes to industrialisation – processing materials for export. He notes that:

> ... the undeveloped country relies usually on two advantages: (a) low labour cost, based on low wages, and (b) an advantage in transport cost, if the material loses weight in the course of processing. (p. 1)

The key point Lewis makes on (a) is that 'Low wages are not the same as low labour cost' (p. 1). The difference is of course labour productivity, and this theme carries throughout the report, particularly as he stresses the role of public services in determining the productivity of the private sector, from where flows his number two priority recommendation, to improve public services. Further,

Lewis develops the argument against heavy manufactures by noting that the low labour cost advantage is stronger when labour cost is a large component of total cost, which is not the case for capital-intensive industry. For all of these reasons, the loss of weight in processing would give a decisive advantage in export, and Lewis concluded that on this basis a case for processing for export could be made for timber.

The second route to industrialisation, the production of manufactures for an expanding home market, 'shares the problems of processing for export', for example 'fuel is costly, engineering service expensive, public utilities inadequate and so on' (p. 2). But, further, it also obviously requires a large and growing home market. And, of course,

> The size of the local market for manufactures depends, given the size of the population, upon how rich or poor the people are... The development of manufacturing for the home market therefore essentially depends upon improving the productivity of other economic activities... From this point of view, the most usual path to progress is increasing efficiency in the production of food. (p. 4)

Lewis goes on to say that 'the surest way to industrialise the Gold Coast would be to multiply by four or five' (p. 4) the funds for increasing agricultural research and extension. He further highlights the importance of mechanisation: 'A high standard of living cannot be built upon an economy in which half the people are scratching the ground for food with a hoe.' (p. 4)

The third avenue is the production of light manufactures for export. But Lewis dismisses this possibility for the Gold Coast:

> A country which lacks advantageous natural resources can compete effectively in foreign markets only on the basis of low labour costs... The Gold Coast is not over-populated, and wages are high in the Gold Coast relatively to other under-developed countries.[5] The industrialisation of the Gold Coast is not likely to be based on importing light raw materials in order to export manufactures, so there is no point analysing this case. (p. 5)

However, Lewis had earlier alluded to success stories which formed the basis for much of the discussion of industrialisation in the coming decades:

5 A statement supported by Ewout Frankema and Marlous Van Waijenburg's paper comparing real wages in cities in British West Africa (including Accra) with cities in Asia, to 1965. 'Structural impediments to African growth? New evidence from real wages in British Africa, 1880–1965', *Journal of Economic History* 72:4 (2012), 895–926.

> There are, however, countries which have built up industrialisation on the basis of exporting, without possessing these advantages. Japan, Hong Kong and Puerto Rico are outstanding examples. Lacking fuel and raw materials, these countries have concentrated on importing raw materials which are light in relation to their value (so that transport cost is small), and which use little fuel in the process of manufacture. Textile fibres, rubber, leather and paper are the most important materials in the categories. (p. 5)

Quite remarkably, Lewis is presaging the East Asian miracle to come in the 1960s and 1970s, which was then held up as a model for Ghana, and for Africa in general.

This is the analytical heart of the report, the basic framing which is then applied in detail to the ground realities of the Gold Coast in the next four chapters before drawing the sharp conclusions and recommendations in the final Chapter VI, but which are already clearly present in Chapter I.

Chapter II, 'Analysis of Industries' considers export industries based on processing of raw materials and producing for consumption in the home market. For export industries the key factor identified in the framing chapter is 'whether weight is lost in the process of manufacture' (p. 6), which Lewis says pins down four commodities – bauxite, timber, cocoa and oilseeds. For reasons which are not made clear specifically, bauxite 'was outside my terms of reference' so only the last three are considered. Focusing on cocoa here for purposes of illustration, Lewis is sceptical of the prospects for processing either the whole bean to compete with chocolate manufacturing abroad, as the Gold Coast 'lacks fuel and skill, and is at a disadvantage climatically' (p. 6), or of the separation into cocoa butter and cake with existing processes: 'Research is being done on new process, but these are not ready yet' (p. 6).

Lewis then turns to the home market noting that:

> It will be seen that, apart from bauxite, the processing of raw materials does not offer any immediate prospect of increased manufacturing on a significant scale. If there is to be significant industrialisation it must be for the home market (p. 7)

He goes to the list of imported commodities and makes an assessment of favourability or unfavourability. From the earlier framing and analysis:

> 'Unfavourability' applies to industries where (a) a weight-losing raw material would have to be imported; or (b) fuel requirements are heavy; or (c) the local market is too small; or (d) very special skills are required (as in the manufacture of watches); or the ratio of capital to labour is abnormally high. (p. 7)

A detailed analysis is carried out for each of a large number of industries, classifying them as favourable, marginal or unfavourable. The favourable industries are oil expressing, canned fruit and vegetables, salt, beer, bricks and tiles, cement, glass, lime, industrial alcohol, miscellaneous chemicals and wood products. The marginal industries are biscuits, soap, confectionery, cigarettes, boots and shoes, hats and caps, shirts, knitwear, weaving cotton and rayon, jute bags, foundry products, candles, paints and colours, travelling bags and rubber manufactures.

Chapter III, 'Ownership and Management' poses the question: 'Is the industrialisation of the Gold Coast to be done by the Government, by African business men, by foreigners, or by these three in combination?' (p. 14). Lewis says 'This issue has still to be settled' (p. 14), a state of affairs which is still true despite seven decades of debate – not just for Ghana but for Africa and the rest of the developing world.

On Government, Lewis is very clear that its role in operating and owning enterprises should be minimal, with two exceptions – public utilities, and what he terms 'pioneering'. On public utilities, he further makes clear, without taking a position on which is better, that an alternative to public ownership 'is to leave the industry in private hands, but to control its prices or profits, and its conditions of sale' (p. 21). On pioneering, he takes the successful example of Japan between 1870 and 1900 to argue that 'In countries where entrepreneurs lack experience or confidence, there is a case for government to lead the way by establishing industries with its own money, and to show that it can be operated successfully; in the expectation that it can withdraw from industry once the pioneering stage is over' (p. 24).

On foreign investment, Lewis is again very clear that industrialisation will not succeed without the finance and knowledge of outsiders, despite the fact that 'Foreign capital is unpopular in all countries which are or have been in colonial status' (p. 16). However, Lewis is equally clear that 'foreigners are often reluctant to train up people in the secrets of their craft' (p. 17), referring to both scientific and managerial knowledge, and that the government should put conditions on foreign investment that ensures this will happen. On actual financing from foreign sources, this is also needed since the government's own funds, according to Lewis, should go towards providing public services. The need will remain till the economy grows and savings are sufficient to fuel substantial investment. So, Lewis returns again to the major theme of the report, the number one priority, to increase agricultural productivity:

> Much is talked about the speed of Japanese industrialisation; but it is not generally realised that what really made this possible was the spectacular increase in agricultural productivity which was taking place at the same time... We return thus to a point which Chapter I has already made: the secret of industrialisation is a rapidly progressing agriculture, and, more particularly since food production is the major part of agriculture, the number one priority in a programme of economic development is measures which increase food production per head. (p. 15)

Thus, in the middle of a chapter devoted to industry, Lewis highlights agriculture! However, he does discuss in detail industry-related measures, including the need to train African employees and managers, especially in a section entitled 'African Enterprise'. This discussion goes through to Chapter IV, 'Initiative and Aid', where perhaps the most interesting element, form a historical perspective, is the articulation of the infant industry argument:

> it takes manufacturing industry some time to find its feet...These difficulties decrease with time. Meanwhile a subsidy or protection for a limited item is thoroughly justified, so long as there is good reason to think that the factory will soon be able to pay its way. (p. 39)

Lewis takes his analysis to a policy conclusion:

> We may sum this up by recommending that the government should be prepared where necessary to give some assistance to any of the industries listed in Chapter II as 'favourable' or 'marginal'. The assistance should be for a short period only, say not exceeding five years, and be limited in amount, say to the equivalent of a 20 per cent tariff on imports. Industries which are not likely to be able to stand on their own feet without longer or greater assistance should not be supported. (p. 40)

Here again is Lewis the pragmatist, not tied to a free market dogma, but calling for careful benefit-cost analysis to delineate and delimit support. Chapter V, 'Government Agencies', then goes on to discuss the institutional basis for implementation.

Arthur Lewis's Mid-Century Report on *Industrialisation and the Gold Coast*: a Long-Century Perspective

Arthur Lewis's *Report on Industrialisation and the Gold Coast* comes slap bang in the middle of the long twentieth century 1891–2010. It is part of the great debates that were underway in the mid-twentieth century on the route to development and modernisation for newly independent and soon-to-become-independent former colonies of Africa and Asia, as well as other poor countries including those in Latin America. In this section of the chapter, I provide an account of these debates, first at the global level and then specifically for Ghana in the context of actual industrialisation outcomes in Ghana. In doing so we shall see the prescience of Lewis, but also ask the extent to which his analytical framework remains relevant for today's trade and technology realities, globally and in Ghana.

Global Debates

In the colonial era, and especially in the intense phase of anti-colonial struggle leading up to independence, the 'civilising mission' of the colonisers was countered by the fighters for independence through an account of the economic burden of colonialism on the indigenous population. There were many dimensions of this counterargument, including empirical demonstrations of the extent of poverty in the colony. In his 1901 book *Poverty and Un-British Rule in India* Dadabhai Naoroji wrote: 'My object… is to show… that under the present system of British administration India is suffering seriously in several ways, and is sinking in poverty', which he did with a mass of official statistics.[6] The National Planning Committee of the Indian National Congress, headed by Nehru, produced a report in 1936, which was referred to by Nehru in his book *Discovery of India*: 'there was lack of food, of clothing, of housing and of every other essential requirement of human existence' and independence was needed 'to ensure an adequate standard of living for the masses, in other words, to get rid of the appalling poverty of the people.' Nehru wrote these words in prison, having been put there by the British authorities for his role in the Quit India movement of 1942.[7]

A key element of the struggle for independence was the argument that colonial policies had stifled industrialisation in the colonies, keeping them solely as hewers of wood and drawers of water, producers of raw materials for processing in the metropole. While India produced about 25 per cent of world industrial output in 1750, this figure had fallen to only 2 per cent by 1900.[8] Here is how Naoroji puts it when discussing cotton and textiles:

> I take this opportunity of saying a few words about the recent telegram that Lord Salisbury had instructed the Indian Government to abolish the duties on cottons… The real object, says to-day's *Times of India*, is to 'nip in the bud' the rising factories in India – the ostensible reason assigned is free trade… I like free trade, but after what I have said…you will easily see that free trade between England and India in a matter like this is something like a race between a starving exhausting invalid, and a strong man with a horse to ride on. (p. 62)

6 Dadabhai Naoroji, *Poverty and Un-British Rule in India* (1901), https://www.vifindia.org/sites/default/files/povertyunbritishoonaoruoft.pdf (accessed 25 May 2026).

7 Jawaharlal Nehru, *The Discovery of India* (London, 1947).

8 David Clingingsmith and Jeffrey Williamson. 'India's Deindustrialization Under British Rule: New Ideas, New Evidence', National Bureau of Economic Research *(NBER) Working Paper* 10586 (2004) http://www.nber.org/papers/w10586 (accessed25 May 2026).

Whether colonialism per se, as opposed to broader technological trends for example, was responsible for the change in production structure is under debate. But the lack of industry clearly shaped the argument for independence.

In Ghana, the writings of Kwame Nkrumah and the stalwarts of the independence movement echoed these sentiments, and they were also core to their thinking post-independence. In India, the first two five-year plans after independence were focused on industrialisation, 'machines to make machines to make machines' being the mantra taken from the Soviet experience. An integral part of this strategy was import substitution aided by tariffs and trade restrictions.

One might have expected from Lewis, on the basis of his interactions in the England of the 1930s with the likes of C.L.R. James, George Padmore, Eric Williams and Paul Robeson, and his battles in the Colonial Economic Advisory Committee against the ruling laissez-faire orthodoxy of Sir Sidney Caine, that he would have fallen in line with the global progressive tendency for aggressive import-substitution-led industrialisation. Indeed, this might have been the hope of Gbedemah and his Convention People's Party (CPP) stalwarts when he commissioned Lewis to write the report. However, as I have argued elsewhere,[9] Lewis had by this time begun his journey towards a more pragmatic centrist position in economic policy, recommending state intervention in moderation and of the right sort, based on careful economic analysis.

As is well known by now, the intellectual tide began to turn in the 1980s against import substituting industrialisation *à l'outrance*, culminating most significantly in the reforms instituted in India by then Finance Minister Manmohan Singh. Manmohan Singh was a Nehruvian socialist who became disenchanted with the trajectory of Indian policy and made a decisive move towards a more open economy. But it might be better to categorise Manmohan Singh as an economic policy maker in the Arthur Lewis mould; not eschewing state intervention completely, but using it carefully and guardedly with careful cost-benefit analysis; taking ground-level realities of comparative advantage as given, but taking small pragmatic steps to change them. For Lewis, the realities of the Gold Coast meant that agriculture had to come first, followed by public services and education and training of African personnel, while grandiose schemes for manufacturing that did not satisfy elementary cost-benefit criteria were to be ditched. For Manmohan Singh, given India's realities of a labour-surplus economy opening up to labour-intensive manufacturing exports was the appropriate strategy. Now, it did not quite turn out that way, with the real success coming in information technology-based service exports, but that was to do with how the realities changed, and rapidly.

9 Ravi Kanbur, 'W. Arthur Lewis and the Roots of Ghanaian Economic Policy', in Ernest Aryeetey and Ravi Kanbur (eds) *The Economy of Ghana Sixty Years After Independence* (Oxford, 2017), 16–27.

In the debates of the 1980s and 1990s on openness and industrialisation, the experience of the East Asian Tigers in the 1960s and 1970s were examined carefully and put to the service of one argument or its counter. They were lauded as the success of an industrial policy which favoured open trade based on the advantage of low labour cost. This was then recommended for other countries, including those in Africa even though, as Lewis had pointed out, countries like the Gold Coast did not in fact enjoy a labour-cost advantage or at least not as large as might have been imagined. On the other hand, the East Asian experience was also lauded as the success of targeted government policy to encourage industries of particular types. Throughout, however, it was recognised that the initial conditions of these economies, in particular high and growing levels of human capital, played a key role.

The 1980s saw the era of 'structural adjustment' and reversal of policies of state-led import substitution and industrialisation in Africa, including in Ghana. This is not the place to go into a detailed assessment of this period, which culminated globally in the fall of the Berlin Wall and the declaration of the 'end of history'.[10] Suffice it to say that 'the end of history lasted for such a short time'.[11] The Growth Commission of the mid-2000s, chaired by Nobel Laureate Michael Spence and including leading economists and economic policy makers from the North and South, in 2008 declared the death of the orthodoxy of the past quarter century and heralded a new era of balanced and pragmatic approaches to state intervention including industrial policy, in the spirit of Arthur Lewis:[12]

> In recent decades governments were advised to 'stabilize, privatize and liberalize'. There is merit in what lies behind this injunction – governments should not try to do too much, replacing markets or closing the economy off from the rest of the world. But we believe this prescription defines the role of government too narrowly. Just because governments are sometimes clumsy and sometimes errant, does not mean they should be written out of the script. On the contrary, as the economy grows and develops, active, pragmatic governments have crucial roles to play. (p 4)

In reaching this conclusion the Commission rode a wave of intellectual reconsideration which also led to a more pragmatic approach to industrial policy, balancing the realities of comparative advantage with the need to change them

10 Francis Fukuyama, 'The End of History?'(1989) http://www.wesjones.com/eoh.htm

11 Ravi Kanbur, 'Economic Policy, Distribution and Poverty: The Nature of Disagreements', *World Development* 29:6 (2001), 1083–94.

12 Commission on Growth and Development, *The Growth Report: Strategies for Sustained Growth and Inclusive Development* (Washington DC, 2008).

over time.[13]. It has even led to a paper with two former World Bank Chief Economists as co-authors calling for industrial policy in Africa.[14]

However, even as the Growth Commission produced its report, discussions around a trend that had been visible at least for the past decade began to crystallise and come to the fore. This was the phenomenon of 'jobless growth' where productivity increases outstrip increase in total output leading to job losses or increasing underemployment. The strong trends in labour-saving technical change began to influence thinking on industrialisation policy and on policy in general. What can we say about industrialisation in an era of deindustrialisation?[15] This question will be taken up in Section 3 as we look forward to the coming policy challenges for Ghana.

Industrial Policy and Industrialisation in Ghana

Perhaps not surprisingly, the debates and policies on industrialisation in Ghana tracked the global trajectory of such debates. In early colonial times, the name of Governor Guggisberg (1919–27) is prominent, both lauded and criticised for his interventions.[16] Although unlike India there was no industry in Ghana to compete with the metropole, Guggisberg's development plans, and those of his predecessor Hugh Clifford (1913–19) built infrastructure to further develop the exploitation of natural resources and agriculture. This was a far cry from the manufacturing and the factories which those fighting for independence saw as the way forward for the nation.

As noted in the previous section, there was some hope among CPP stalwarts including Gebdemah and Nkrumah, that the Lewis report would support their stance on industrialisation as the centre-piece of development strategy. The report did not do this but, despite a respectful welcoming of the report, the policies of the newly independent Ghana went far beyond the limited and modest

13 Dani Rodrik, *Had Globalization Gone Too Far?* (Washington DC, 1997); Dani Rodrik, 'Industrial Policy for the Twenty-First Century', CEPR Discussion Papers 4767 (2004).

14 Joseph Stiglitz, Justin Lin, Celestin Monga and Ebrahim Patel, 'Industrial Policy in the African Context', World Bank Policy Research Paper 6633 (September 2013), https://openknowledge.worldbank.org/server/api/core/bitstreams/a0e6518d-a996-5428-9e2b-25c9ce6e3edb/content (accessed 25 May 2026).

15 Dani Rodrik. 'Premature deindustrialization', *Journal of Economic Growth* 21:1 (2016), 1–33; Rodrik, 'Prospects for global economic convergence under new technologies' in David Autor et al., *An Inclusive Future? Technology, New Dynamics, and Policy Challenges*, Brookings Institution (Washington DC, 2022).

16 Francis Agbodeka, 'Sir Gordon Guggisberg's contribution to the development of the Gold Coast, 1919–1927', *Transactions of the Historical Society of Ghana* (1972), 13:1, 51–64.

interventions that Lewis had envisaged in support of industry. However, as we know, the push was not successful. The review by Owoo and Page[17] observes:

> Today, 60 years after independence, Nkrumah's vision of Ghana as an industrial economy remains unfulfilled. Following a brief boom in the 1960s, industrial output has followed a rollercoaster pattern of rises and falls, and the growth of industrial output has seldom exceeded the growth of gross domestic product (GDP). In 2010 the share of manufacturing in GDP was 6.7 per cent, less than it has been in the 1970s. (p. 176)

The broad trajectory of Ghana's industrial policy regimes is now well known and has been set out in a number of papers.[18] A key dividing date is 1983, which delineates the periods before and after the Economic Recovery Programme (ERP). The earlier period was overall marked by a strategy of import-substitution industrialisation (ISI), although there were years of greater market orientation in between:

> At the centre of the ISI strategy was the development of large-scale, capital intensive state-owned manufacturing industries. Government invested heavily in infrastructure and was involved in domestic production of previously imported consumer goods, processing of exports of primary products (agricultural and mining), and the expansion and development of building materials and electrical, electronic, and machinery industries... From the mid-1960s the ISI strategy was characterized by a strong reliance on import substitution through high levels of effective protection...[19]

However, after initial results when manufacturing grew from 2 per cent of Gross Domestic Product (GDP) in 1957 to 9 per cent by 1969, the strategy had to be pulled back because the state could no longer finance the costs. Between 1969 and 1972 a more market-oriented approach was tried but this was reversed in 1972, and these policies stayed in place in broad contour till the crisis of 1983:

17 Owoo and Page, 'Industrial policy in Ghana'.

18 Owoo and Page, 'Industrial policy in Ghana'; Charles Ackah, Charles Adjasi and Festus Turkson, 'Industrial policy in Ghana: its evolution and impact' in Carol Newman et al. (eds), *Manufacturing Transformation: Comparative Studies of Industrial development in Africa and Emerging Asia* (Oxford, 2016), 50–71; Said Boakye, 'Ghana's Attempts at Industrialization: How Can the County Achieve the Success it Yearns For?', Institute for Fiscal Studies, Accra (2018), Occasional paper No.19.

19 Ackah, Adjasi and Turcson, 'Industrial Policy', 51.

> The Economic Recovery Package, adopted in 1983, abolished the import licensing regime, introduced market exchange rates, removed price controls. and liberalized interest rates…[Q]uantitative import controls were eliminated and tariffs were rationalized and lowered…The new approach to industrialisation focused greater attention on small-scale manufacturing, the use of local inputs and value-addition to primary products.[20] (pp. 178–9).

In many ways this was a return to Lewis, backing away from aggressive large-scale manufacturing through state intervention but rather using state intervention to help develop what he called African Enterprise. Many of the schemes introduced after 1983 to develop small and medium enterprises are echoes of the Lewis recommendations. However, once again, after initial success these reforms did not deliver the goals of strengthening manufacturing in GDP. As a fraction of total industrial output, manufacturing declined from 65 per cent in 1984–90 to 35 per cent in 1996–2000.[21]

After 2000 or so, the government turned away from industrial policy in the sense of specific support for specific industries towards improving the 'investment climate' in general. This is again reminiscent of Lewis's priority number two, improving public services, which he conceived of in a broad sense and included items which regularly appear in the investment climate list such as policy predictability. However, other items, like developing skills and infrastructure, did not figure large in the new policy orientation:

> In practice, Ghana's investment climate reform programme has mainly centered on reforms of trade policy and regulations, drawn from the World Bank *Doing Business Surveys*. With the exception of the Export Processing Zones (EPZs) that have been developed at Tema and Sekondi, investments in infrastructure and skills to support industrial development have been largely neglected…[22]

This was in 2000 but, as noted in the discussion on global debates, 'industrial policy is back'. The cycle of interventionist policy being on or off has turned and interventionism is once again on, not least because it has come back with a vengeance in competition between developed countries. As Walter says, 'For African governments the question is not *whether* to pursue industrial policy: it is, and has for a while been, *how* to maximize its chances of driving inclusive and sustainable economic transformation' (p. 7).[23]

In keeping with global trends, Ghana Government documents demonstrate a newfound enthusiasm for industrial policy:

20 Owoo and Page, 'Industrial Policy in Ghana'.

21 *Ibid.*

22 *Ibid.*, 189.

23 Max Walter, 'Industrial Policy Makes a Comeback in Africa' (Brookings Institution 2021), https://www.brookings.edu/blog/africa-in-focus/2021/12/01/industrial-policy-makes-a-comeback-in-africa/ (accessed 25 May 2026).

> The Vision of the Ministry is to: Establish Ghana as a globally competitive manufacturing and trading hub in Africa. In order to meet its Vision, the Ministry is implementing a Ten (10) Point Industrial Transformation Agenda aimed at establishing Ghana as a major manufacturing hub in Africa. (p. 1).[24]

The ten points of the agenda are:[25]

- National Industrial Revitalisation Programme (Stimulus Package)
- One District One Factory (Decentralising industrial development)
- Development of Strategic Anchor Industries (towards diversifying the economy)
- Establishment of Industrial Parks in all regions
- Development of small- and medium-scale enterprises (SMEs)
- Export Development Programme
- Enhancing Domestic Retail Infrastructure
- Improving the Business Environment through regulatory reforms
- Industrial sub-contracting exchange
- Improving Public-Private sector Dialogue. (p. 1)

More generally and in the broader discourse in Ghana, we find specific and detailed cost-benefit analysis of various industrialisation projects and proposals. Thus, for example, Quartey et al. calculate Benefit-Cost Ratios (BCRs) for a number of specific interventions. Among them:

> The analysis indicates that providing management training to local (non-multinational) factories with large turnovers (large firms) generates a BCR of 5.9. The total cost of this intervention is estimated at GHS1.62M per year per factory, and it is expected to generate total profits of GHS 2.1M for the first year.... An increase in R&D spending by 0.4 per cent of GDP is expected to generate a BCR between 1.5 and 1.75... Finally, for the... intervention that sought to provide subsidies or reduce the electricity tariffs payable by manufacturing firms and industry, a BCR of 1.8 is estimated. (p. 1).[26]

24 Government of Ghana, *Medium Term Expenditure Framework (MTEF) For 2022–2025: Ministry of Trade and Industry*; *Programme Based Budget Estimates for 2022* (Accra, 2022).

25 Government of Ghana, *Medium Term Expenditure Framework (MTEF) For 2022–2025: Ministry of Trade and Industry*; *Programme Based Budget Estimates for 2022. (Accra,* 2022).

26 Peter Quartey, Festus Ebo Turkson, Emmanuel Abbey, Daniel Chachu Mawuenyega and Makafui Butu, 'Cost-Benefit Analysis of Interventions in The Industrial Sector of Ghana', Copenhagen Consensus Center (2020), https://copenhagenconsensus.com/sites/default/files/gp_a4_industrial_policy_final.pdf (accessed 25 May 2026).

The authors point to the relatively small BCR for electricity subsidies to manufacturing and to the relatively high return from management training. While one can always debate the specifics, the general point is one of approach: no intervention is necessarily ruled out on *a priori* grounds, but each intervention is subjected to careful technical analysis, which is very much in the spirit of the Lewis report.

Entering the Next Long Century

The twists and turns of industrialisation policy debates in Ghana tracked global debates, and at the end of the long century under consideration, 1891–2010, found themselves somewhere in the pragmatic middle. No leap back to the heady era of state-driven import-substituting industrialisation of the immediate post-independence period, nor the hands-off laissez-faire stance of the post-ERP years, but a cautious opening to state intervention in some areas after careful cost-benefit analysis. This reflects in many ways the pragmatism and caution of Lewis in method and perspective.

Have we, then, reached relative stability in the discourse on industrialisation in Ghana? Perhaps so on method and perspective, but the ground-level realities in Ghana today are different in significant respects from those that Lewis found in the Gold Coast in 1950s. There are two features of the Ghanaian economy as we enter the second quarter of this century which stand out as requiring specific attention in light of the experience of the long century: oil, and labour-saving technical change.

Oil is of course a big factor in current Ghanaian economics and policy. When Lewis was writing in the 1950s, his candidate for major development in industrialisation was the processing of bauxite into aluminium:

> ...since it takes four tons of bauxite to make one ton of aluminium, transport charges are saved if bauxite is turned into aluminium on the spot, instead of being transported as bauxite to the country where the aluminium will be used. (p. 2)[27]

Further, the presence of oil changes the equation in other ways:

> If fuel is available side by side with the material which is to be processed, the producing country has thus a double advantage over all consuming countries which do not have their own fuel. (p. 2)[28]

Applying the Lewis perspective set out in *Industrialisation and the Gold Coast*, then, these two features change the balance of argument considerably

27 Lewis, *Report on Industrialisation.*
28 *Ibid.*

and make a stronger case for supporting the development of oil processing and for fuel-intensive manufacturing. However, the other side of the Lewis method is careful benefit-cost analysis of each proposal and project for state support and intervention.

More generally, recall that Lewis's priority number two is the improvement to public services, broadly construed. Although in the report itself Lewis stays focused on public services as directed towards industry, for example efficient production and supply of electricity for manufacturing plants, it is now well documented that in his later interactions with the government, especially with Nkrumah, Lewis broadened his concern to economic governance in general. Here is how he refers on 1 August 1958 to the drafting of the Five-Year Plan:

> It is not easy to make a good development plan for £100 million if the Prime Minister insists on inserting £18 million of his own pet schemes of a sort which neither develop the country nor increase the comfort of the people.[29]

In his overview of oil and Ghana's economy, Fosu highlighted well known macroeconomic issues like the 'Dutch disease' but turned more generally to the 'resource curse' and the deterioration of institutional quality and controls at precisely the time they were most needed: 'The need to avoid the oil curse is particularly germane for Ghana, given her past performance with non-oil mineral resources. ... It is therefore imperative that governance continue[s] to improve'.[30] However, Fosu is pessimistic about this prospect:

> Unfortunately, even though Ghana's measures of institutional quality (...) are well above SSA's average, they seem to have generally trended downwards since 2011...Especially troubling also is the downward trend in the 'control of corruption'... (p. 153).[31]

Fosu's concerns from almost a decade ago did materialise, with ballooning deficits and borrowing on the strength of oil reserves leading to a debt crisis. Lewis's perspective thus still remains valid. The discovery of oil suggests a change in the cost-benefit of industrialisation, but in the absence of institutional governance mechanisms such calculations will fall by the wayside as macroeconomic instability returns to Ghana.

Let us turn now to the second aspect for ground-level reality which is very different form the situation in the 1950s. Looking to the successful experience of East Asia in particular, policy analysts debated whether the option of industrialisation through light manufactures was open to Ghana, and if so how it

29 Quoted in Tignor, *W. Arthur Lewis*, 167.

30 Augustin Fosu, 'Oil and Ghana's Economy', in Ernest Aryeetey and Ravi Kanbur (eds) *The Economy of Ghana Sixty Years After Independence* (Oxford, 2017), 137–54, at 152.

31 Fosu, 'Oil and Ghana's Economy'. SSA means Sub-Saharan Africa.

should best be encouraged and implemented. In 1953 Lewis's analysis was fairly clear-cut. The Gold Coast was a land-surplus, not a labour-surplus, economy. Labour costs, wages combined with labour productivity, were relatively high so export-based industrialisation, with manufacturing of labour-intensive goods demanded in the rich countries, was not an option given the competition from the labour-surplus economies. The only option for Lewis 'for very many years', was improving labour productivity in agriculture thereby both increasing incomes and demand for manufactured goods and releasing labour for this manufacture.

As Ghana's population increased over the next half century it began to take on the characteristics of a labour-surplus economy, but at the same time that countries like China, India, Bangladesh and Vietnam opened up their economies to export, thus providing significant competition to industrialisation efforts by Ghana through this route. As these countries themselves exhausted their supplies of surplus labour and their wages started rising, there was hope that Ghana and other African countries could benefit from the relocation of labour-intensive industries from these countries, using local materials as appropriate. The development of a leather industry in Ethiopia is an example of this type of transition.

However, even as these hopes were being expressed the ground-level reality for the world as a whole was changing rapidly in the form of labour-saving technical change. These trends have questioned the whole notion of industrialisation in the sense that Lewis, and indeed all of us, thought of it in the half century after independence. The jobs leaving China because of high labour costs will be far fewer by the time they get to Africa and Ghana. This is not the place for a detailed review of this vast technical and policy literature. An extract from Rodrik will suffice to animate the discussion for Ghana:

> [E]ven in the most favorable scenario, convergence is likely to occur at a slower pace than in the past, when rapid, labour-absorbing industrialisation was still possible...The traditional model of export-oriented industrialisation is based on nurturing productive manufacturing firms that act as growth leaders ...[T]he next generation of growth strategies will have to target small- and medium-sized firms with the potential to enhance both productivity and employment and which are necessarily mostly in services. Traditional 'industrial policies' will have to be modified and extended to parts of the informal economy ... [S]ustainable poverty reduction and enhanced economic security will remain possible only by creating more productive, better jobs for workers at the bottom of the skill distribution. (p79).[32]

32 Dani Rodrik, 'Prospects for Global Economic Convergence Under New Technologies', in David Autor et al., *An Inclusive Future? Technology, New Dynamics, and Policy Challenges* (Washington, DC, 2022).

Comparing Rodrik's assessment of prospects for industrialisation with Lewis's *Report* from seven decades earlier, several features stand out. First, there is agreement across the decades on the importance of the fundamentals of education, skills, institutions and governance. As noted earlier, the political economy dynamics of oil have underlined the importance of institutions and governance. Second, while agriculture is given a role by Rodrik, it is far less prominent than in Lewis's report, for whom it was the 'number one priority'. This is understandable given the now much smaller share of agriculture in output and in employment. Third, although in a very different context, there is a great deal of consistency between Rodrik's twenty-first century focus on small- and medium-size enterprises and Lewis's mid-twentieth-century focus on 'African enterprise'. It is encouraging to see this emphasis also in the ten-point industrial policy programme of the Government of Ghana. Characteristically, however, Lewis also focused on implementation details:

> No loan should be made until the industrial Development Corporation is satisfied as to the technical and managerial experience of the borrower, as to his character, and as to his past record. A Development Corporation is not a device for helping lame dogs over stiles. (p. 25).[33]

Institutions and governance once again appear as key elements in policy development and implementation.

Conclusion

Arthur Lewis's 1953 *report on Industrialisation and the Gold Coast* is a remarkable document. It deserves to be better known in the wider development discourse because of its analytical sharpness and for the method and perspective it sets out for policy analysis. It is of course of its time, but it is also timeless. It is of its time because it is framed by the economic structures and trends that Lewis found in Ghana and in the world in the middle of the long century 1891–2010. Population growth has moved Ghana from land surplus towards a labour-surplus economy, and migration has turned the country towards an urban reality. His focus on agricultural productivity, while still relevant, would not perhaps rate as number one priority. Oil was not part of the picture when Lewis wrote his report. Its emergence in the last two decades may change some of the production-side advantages as analysed by Lewis but, more important, recent developments emphasise Lewis's timeless strictures on governance and quality of public expenditure. The world has also changed because of the dramatic trends in the twenty-first century towards labour-saving technical

33 Lewis, *Report on Industrialisation*.

change. Shift of policy away from large-scale labour-intensive manufactures and towards small and medium enterprises is called for by this global shift, but this emphasis was in any case also present in the Lewis report. In this sense the report is timeless. But it is also timeless because of its emphasis on education and skill building and the quality of institutions and governance, and because of its emphasis on careful benefit-cost analysis in considering policy and in particular large-scale government interventions and investments. These are lessons to which the Ghanaian polity would do well to pay heed as we enter Ghana's next long century.

8

Spectral Political Economies: Reassessing the Ghana–Guinea–Mali Union, 1958–63

Gerardo Serra and Katie Monaghan

On 23 November 1958, Ghana and Guinea issued a joint communiqué announcing their Union. This was the first example of two newly independent countries in Sub-Saharan Africa, formerly colonised by different European powers (in this case Britain and France), choosing to come together. The political significance of this act exceeded the simple union of the two countries as Ghana was the first British colony in Sub-Saharan Africa to achieve independence, and Guinea was the only country to vote 'non' in the 1958 French Union referendum issued by Charles de Gaulle.[1] Indeed, their declaration gestured at a future that diverged from the institutional topographies envisaged by Western powers for post-colonial Africa. Following a series of talks and joint communiqués in 1960, Mali joined the union in April 1961.[2] The resulting Charter for the Union of African States formalised the Ghana–Guinea–Mali Union's (GGMU hereafter, also known as the Union of African States) commitment 'to work jointly to achieve the complete liquidation of imperialism, colonialism and neo-colonialism in Africa and the building up of African Unity'.[3] Besides defence and domestic and foreign policy, the Charter also identified 'the complete decolonisation of the [economic] set ups inherited from the colonial system' and 'the rehabilitation and development of African culture' as key areas of intervention.[4] Hailed by an iconic Ghanaian highlife tune by E.T. Mensah and the Tempos as

1 This research has been partly funded by Gerardo Serra's University of Manchester, Faculty of Humanities Large Collaborative Grant ('Inequality and Crisis in West African Economic Thought, 1870-2022'). Serra thanks Luca Fantacci and Jacob Norris for their encouraging comments. For a detailed reconstruction of the bottom-up nature of Guinean anti-colonialism, see Elizabeth Schmidt, 'Top down or bottom up? Nationalist mobilisation reconsidered, with special reference to Guinea (French West Africa)', *American Historical Review*, 110:4 (2005), 975–1014.

2 Ghana and Guinea were also engaged in other cooperation projects, for example, the Community of Independent African States (with Liberia), whose charter is discussed in Kwame Nkrumah, *I Speak of Freedom: A Statement of African Ideology* (London, 1961), 176–7.

3 *Charter for the Union of African States and A joint communiqué issued later after a summit conference between the leaders of the Union* (Accra, no date [1961]), 2.

4 *Ibid.*, 3.

'Africa's strongest foundation', the GGMU promised fundamentally to reshape Africa's political and economic design.[5] Through fostering new patterns of integration, challenging boundaries and economic structures inherited from colonialism, and propelling the possibility of a continental Union of African States, the GGMU embodied a dense web of hopes and aspirations. The three countries modified their constitutions, including a clause which declared their willingness to give up part or all their national sovereignty.[6]

In 1963, the Union was dissolved, without having achieved any of its proposed goals. As a result, the GGMU does not occupy a prominent place in histories of Pan-Africanism and African political imaginaries. In the 1960s, the key problem was empirical:

> Because of the quiet functioning of this organization [...] very little has been written about it. Thus, a student of Africa is reduced to dependence upon short newspaper accounts of the various meetings of the leaders of the states involved, to brief references in more general works of African unity, and to conjecture.[7]

However, the paucity of archival traces does not fully account for the Union's relative neglect in later historiography, which emphasised the gap between the GGMU's ambition and reality. According to Birmingham, the union was 'magnanimous, ambitious and unrealistic'.[8] Nugent noted that although Sekou Touré, Kwame Nkrumah, and Modibo Keïta (Figure 8.1) were 'ideological soulmates', their 'different official languages, currencies, administrative traditions, and sheer physical distance created practical impediments that would have taken decades to overcome'.[9]

The dichotomy contraposing the GGMU's 'unrealistic' ambition, and the 'reality' of its ineffectiveness is not historians' invention but was divulged in contemporary discourse. Before Mali joined the union, Nnamdi Azikiwe, President of Nigeria, declared that Ghana and Guinea did 'not have yet one parliament or currency [...] and the so-called union remains a scrap of paper'.[10] Kofi Busia, the head of the opposition in Ghana, declared Nkrumah's approach

5 E.T. Mensah's tune here: https://www.youtube.com/watch?v=SBXHpe3y1mA (accessed 25 May 2026).

6 Kwame Nkrumah, *Africa Must Unite* (London, 1974, orig. 1963), 149.

7 Marc W. DeLancey, 'The Ghana-Guinea-Mali Union: a bibliographical essay', *African Studies Bulletin*, 9:2 (1966), 35–51, 35.

8 David Birmingham, *Kwame Nkrumah: The Father of African Nationalism* (Athens OH, 1998), 103.

9 Paul Nugent, *Africa since Independence: A Comparative History* (London, 2004), 79.

10 Quoted in Toyin Falola, *Nationalism and African Intellectuals* (Rochester NY, 2001), 172; however, at the time of the 1958 Joint Communiqué, Azikiwe expressed support for the Union ('What Zik Says', *Daily Graphic*, 28 November 1958).

Figure 8.1 Nkrumah, Keïta and Touré 'hold an informal discussion in Conakry'.

Source: Information Services Department, Ghana Ministry of Information, F46/RR/864/70. Reproduced with permission.

'unrealistic'.[11] Conversely, for the key actors involved, defending the Union's political project meant articulating its 'reality'. When asked by a journalist of the Italian left-wing daily *l'Unità*, Touré said it was a 'political union that aims to accelerate the unification of a free and independent Africa'.[12] Similarly, on the first anniversary of Mali's independence, Keïta reiterated that the Union

11 'Ghana Opposition Hits Approach to West African Union', *Christian Science Monitor*, 26 November 1958. However, not all opposition emphasised the unrealistic nature of the Union. Joe Appiah, instead, made the argument that, if Ghana and Guinea (with a combined population of only 7 million people or so) ended up proposing a constitutional model that could be embraced by other countries, this would 'wound' the national pride of other nations, Inward Telegram to Commonwealth Relations Office, p. 2, 13 December 1958, The British National Archives, London (TNA hereafter), PREM11/2894.

12 République de Guinée, *Textes des Interviews Accordeés aux Représentants de la Presse par le Président Sékou Touré* (Conakry, 1959), 20.

'was a West African reality'.[13] For Nkrumah, it represented the closest institutional embodiment of his dream of West African unity, which was articulated at the height of the anti-colonial struggle at the 1945 Pan-African Congress in Manchester, and expressed in *Towards Colonial Freedom*.[14] This chapter draws on the insight that, despite its pervasiveness, the juxtaposition of 'ambition' and 'reality' results in a flattening and erasure of the historical dynamics and imaginaries activated by the Union.

Recently, a few historians have mobilised the GGMU to challenge teleological narratives that treat the nation-state as 'the modal end-point of the evolution of colonial empires'.[15] Olubomehin provided a balanced reconstruction of the Union's overall trajectory, while Getachew used the GGMU as a case study of federalist political thought.[16] Grilli perceptively noted that, within Ghana, the Union illuminates the contested nature of the Pan-African project: while for Nkrumah the Union was a catalyst for continental union, for George Padmore (who was serving as Nkrumah's adviser on African Affairs) it acted as model of a regional-based federalism.[17] Building on these concerns, the chapter shifts the focus on the fears caused by the Union to colonial powers, and in so doing reconstructs the Union's wider political economy. Making it visible, however, requires recasting the Union as a 'spectre'.

In the Shadow of the *Nunum*: Re-thinking Spectrality

Jacques Derrida's *Specters of Marx* paved the way for a 'spectral turn' in cultural and social theory.[18] Derrida's use of 'spectre' aimed to capture a distinctive ontology which 'is neither substance, nor essence, nor existence, *is never present as such*'.[19] While the 'spectral turn', primarily associated with post-structuralism, raised important questions on issues as diverse as the

13 Modibo Keïta, *Discours et Interventions* (Moscow, 1965), 59.

14 Kwame Nkrumah, *Towards Colonial Freedom: Africa in the Struggle against World Imperialism* (London, 1962).

15 Frederick Cooper, 'Reconstructing empire in postwar French and British Africa', *Past & Present*, 210: supplement 6 (2011), 196–210, at 197.

16 O.O. Olubomehin, 'The Ghana-Guinea-Mali Union (1958–1964): an experiment in cooperation', *International Review of Politics and Development* 2:1 (2004), 100–112; Adom Getachew, *Worldmaking after Empire: The Rise and Fall of Self-Determination* (Princeton, 2019), 109–10.

17 Matteo Grilli, *Nkrumaism and African Nationalism: Ghana's Pan-African Foreign Policy in the Age of Decolonisation* (Cham, 2018), 90.

18 Jacques Derrida, *Specters of Marx: The State of the Debt, the Work of Mourning, and the New International*, trans. Peggy Kamuf (New York, 1994).

19 *Ibid.*, xviii.

politics of nostalgia and literary theory, this contribution shows that it can also illuminate past political economies.[20] But how? Unlike Derrida and some of his commentators, we are not concerned with spectres' capacity to 'reveal the complete functioning of the law of value'.[21] More modestly, while still retaining its function as a 'conceptual metaphor', we use the figure of the ghost to challenge 'the classical ontological oppositions of reality and illusion'.[22] Applied to the GGMU, this insight allows us to go beyond seeing the Union as a 'failed experiment' that remained, in Azikiwe's words, 'a scrap of paper', but rather as something more elusive: not conforming to its own design, and yet capable of producing political economy effects.

Proverbs represent another important element of our framework. Far from being entirely 'exogenous', proverbs were part of the discursive order through which the Union was discussed, as shown by the following excerpt from the archives of the Banque de France, in which M. Duwuona-Hammond (Guinea's Minister of Education), in response to a question related to the difficulties of the application of the agreement between Ghana and Guinea, stated 'when someone misses their meeting, do not blame them too much; they may be having domestic troubles'.[23] On the other hand, readers familiar with Akan proverbs will notice our unorthodox approach. Over time, a proverb's meaning emerges and coalesces through its deployment in specific contexts and social practices.[24] Yet, experimenting with new realms of application can stretch a proverb's heuristic potential, and illuminate phenomena that differ significantly from those of its inception and 'original' applicability. Specifically, we use the rich repertoire of Akan proverbs focusing on ghosts (*ɔsaman* pl. *asamanfo*) to corroborate our framework. Akan proverbs confirm both ghosts' elusiveness and distinctiveness: *ɔsaman ahoɔhwam ne nunum,* 'The smell of ghosts is like the

20 For an overview, see María Del Pilar Blanco and Esther Pereen, 'Introduction: conceptualising Spectralities', in *The Spectralities Reader* (London, 2013), 1–28.

21 Antonio Negri, 'The specter's smile' in Michael Sprinker (ed.), *Ghostly Demarcations: A Symposium on Jacques Derrida's Specters of Marx* (London, 1999), 6. For a recent insightful analysis of the potential of hauntology and spectrality in Marxist theory, see Christopher Loughlin, 'Hauntological Marxism: The Marxism of the crypt', in Vesna Stanković Pejnović and Ivan Matić (eds), *New Understandings of Capital in the Twenty-First Century* (Belgrade, 2020), 83–103.

22 Slavoj Žižek, 'The spectre of ideology', in Slavoj Žižek (ed.), *Mapping Ideology* (London, 2012), 1–33, at 20.

23 'Ouverture aujourd'hui de la conférence nationale du parti democratique de Guinée', 2/11/1960, Banque de France Archives (BFA hereafter), 1466200601 AR 430 (all translations from French archives by Monaghan).

24 For an exhaustive analysis of this aspect, see Kwesi Yankah, *The Proverb in the Context of Akan Rhetoric*, 2nd edn (New York, 2012).

nunum plant'.[25] The *nunum* plant's smell is very distinctive, but the emphasis on the olfactory sense is also a reminder of the spectre's elusive 'presence'.[26] Johann Gottlieb Christaller's Twi dictionary reported the meaning of *ɔsaman* as a 'departed spirit, ghost, spectre, apparition' and claimed that the Akan distinguished between three distinct types of ghosts: 'a) those who fell in battle (or by an accident, or by a falling tree); b) common spirits; c) lingering spirits'.[27]

It is helpful to think of the GGMU as a 'lingering spirit' that seldom appears. Since its dissolution, only rarely has the Union been attributed a *genealogical* role in African history. A key exception comes from Ghanaian diplomat K. B. Asante, who declared that 'the idea of ECOWAS started with Nkrumah, with the Ghana–Guinea–Mali Union'.[28] By linking the GGMU to ECOWAS (Economic Community of West African States) – the most studied West African integration project – this statement highlights the GGMU's capacity to inspire successive generations of policy-makers and Pan-Africanists.[29] On the other hand, in recent Africanist historiography, ghosts and shadows are mainly invoked to capture the fragmented, ephemeral, and dislocated nature of the 'post-colonial archive'.[30]

In contrast, our take on spectrality does not pertain primarily to the ways in which the Union still 'lingered' in African political imagination after its dissolution, nor to the nature of the archival evidence it left behind. Instead, this chapter excavates the hauntological nature of the Union as it was unfolding between 1958 and 1963. In the words of (Tom) Lewis: 'The specter thus may be said to represent more than the instability of the real; it also represents the ghostly embodiment of a fear and panic provoked by intimations of an impossible state of being'.[31] By following archival trails in Ghana, France,

25 Peggy Appiah, Kwame Anthony Appiah, Ivor Agyeman-Duah, *Bu Me Bɛ: Proverbs of the Akans* (Banbury, 2007), proverb no. 5223.

26 *Ibid.*

27 J.G. Christaller, *A Dictionary of the Asante and Fante Language Called Tshi (Chwee, Twi) with a Grammatical Introduction and Appendices on the Geography of the Gold Coast and Other Subjects* (Basel, 1881), 407.

28 Matteo Grilli, 'Kwame Nkrumah and Pan-Africanism in West Africa', in Reiland Rabaka (ed.) *Routledge Handbook of Pan-Africanism* (London, 2020), 289–301, at 298.

29 See, for example: Uka Ezenwe, *ECOWAS and Economic Integration in West Africa*, (London, 1983) and Thomas Jaye, Dauda Garuba and Stella Amadi (eds), *ECOWAS and the Dynamics of Conflict and Peace-Building* (Dakar, 2011).

30 Jean Allman, 'Phantoms of the archive: Kwame Nkrumah, a Nazi pilot named Hanna, and the contingencies of postcolonial history-writing', *American Historical Review* 118:1 (2013), 104–29; Kate Skinner, 'West Africa's first coup: neo-colonial and Pan-African projects in Togo's "shadow archives"', *African Studies Review* 63:2 (2020), 375–98.

31 Tom Lewis, 'The politics of "hauntology" in Derrida's *Specters of Marx*', in Michael Sprinker (ed.), *Ghostly Demarcations: A Symposium on Jacques Derrida's Specters of Marx* (London and New York, 1999), 134–167, at 140; Derrida, *Specters of Marx*, at 161.

and the United Kingdom, we document the multiple ways in which the Union elicited fears, projects, and assumptions. Rather than reifying the gap between 'rhetoric' and 'reality', the Union embodied 'a hybrid constellation of affect and political effect'.[32] We argue that the Union is a powerful entry point for capturing the complexity and open-endedness of debates about economic and political sovereignty in early independent Africa. While failing to achieve its expected impact, the GGMU manifested the capacity to haunt – and thus influence – the discursive articulations and political forms through which both African policymakers and former colonisers imagined alternatives to the nation-state and the national economy and interrogated their consequences.

The Spectres of Communism and Pan-Africanism

> 'A spectre is haunting Europe: the spectre of communism.'[33]

The Communist Manifesto's incipit remains the most iconic reference ever made to a ghost in Western social theory. Despite referring to its Soviet version rather than Marx's, the GGMU also summoned the 'spectre of communism'. The Union overlapped with Ghana, Guinea, and Mali's proclaimed allegiance to socialism, and their expanding strategic role within the Soviet orbit.[34] In successive years the leaders of the three countries were all awarded Lenin Peace Prizes: Touré in 1961, Nkrumah in 1962, and Keïta in 1963.[35] This does not imply that the relation between the USSR and the three countries was unproblematic, either in theory or in practice. The Soviets debated the possible existence of a 'non-capitalist path of development', but the management of aid and technical assistance was far from straightforward.[36] By the Union's dissolution in 1963, the Soviets' interest in West Africa was already declining.[37]

32 Homi K. Bhabha, 'Spectral sovereignty, vernacular cosmopolitans, and cosmopolitan memories', in Bruce Robbins and Paulo Lemos Horta (eds), *Cosmopolitanisms* (New York, 2017), 141–52, at 143.

33 Karl Marx and Friedrich Engels, *The Manifesto of the Communist Party* (1848) https://www.marxists.org/archive/marx/works/1848/communist-manifesto/index.htm (accessed 1 June 2023).

34 On the relationship between the Soviet Union and these countries, see Alessandro Iandolo, *Arrested Development: The Soviet Union in Ghana, Guinea and Mali, 1955–1968* (London, 2022).

35 Arthur Jay Klinghoffer, *Soviet Perspectives on African Socialism* (Rutherford NJ, 1969), 53.

36 Alessandro Iandolo, 'The rise and fall of the "Soviet model of development" in West Africa, 1957–64', *Cold War History* 12:4 (2012), 683–704.

37 Iandolo, *Arrested Development*, 147.

Until 1963 the situation was more open-ended, as Guinea became the first West African country to attract significant investment from the Eastern bloc. As noted by foreign companies, this was not limited to the Soviets. The Overseas Director of the Foundation of Netherland Industries and the Chairman of the Dutch African Institute visited Guinea in 1960 as part of a broader fact-finding mission about opportunities and constraints of investing in Africa. They described a country where 'the vacuum left by the French provided a convenient entrée' for communist presence, cemented by a Soviet 'Rouble 100 million loan convertible into any currency', but with 'the main nationalities in evidence being Czechs, East Germans and Chinese'.[38] By the summer of 1959, an unnamed French government official writing a report about Guinean independence claimed that 'the main concern born of the Guinean problem is to see the country imperceptibly or roughly tumble into the Eastern camp'.[39]

Besides altering patterns of aid, investment, and technical assistance, the Eastern bloc's involvement in Guinea provided the Union members with powerful discursive and strategic resources. Indeed, Nkrumah was capitalising on British fears of communist influence in Africa to reinforce ties between Ghana and Guinea, and thus consolidate the Union's legitimacy in the international sphere. A British memorandum reports that Nkrumah was allegedly concerned with Guinea because he thought 'that penetration by the Iron Curtain countries is going too far', and it would have been 'advantageous for the West if Ghana gave financial assistance to Guinea, and perhaps other newly independent territories, and if Ghana were then to be reimbursed by the U.K'.[40] To reassure Britain, Nkrumah also promised to terminate his special relationship with Guinea if the country 'went communist'.[41] While the Foreign Office was invited to consider that Nkrumah was 'exaggerating a little in saying that Guinea is in great financial difficulty and in suggesting that chaos threatens', the GGMU was pivotal in shaping how Pan-Africanism and socialism 'haunted' the former colonisers, and how Britain and France reconceptualised the relation between the two.[42]

38 D.F. Stone, Guinea, 29 April 1960, p. 1, Public Records and Archives Administration Department, Accra (PRAAD hereafter), RG6/3/31/79. French sources speak, instead, of a 140 million roubles loan from the USSR to Guinea. Cf. 'Après neuf mois de l'indépendance guinéenne', 27 June 1959, BFA, 1466200601 AR 430.

39 'Après neuf mois de l'indépendance guinéenne'.

40 Ghana-Guinea, memo from H.L. Jenkyns to Sir Denis Rickett, 9 May 1960, TNA, DO35/9383.

41 Secret Inward Telegram from Accra to Commonwealth Relations Office, 28 April 1960, TNA, PREM11/2894.

42 Hugh Jones, Telegram from Conakry to Foreign Office, 21 March 1960, TNA, DO 35/9383.

A French report declared that:

> if the wind from the East, which blows towards Guinea, is strong [...], the winds from the West are not lacking, or are at the very least comparable. But neither seem to be the prevailing winds that are sought on the side of pan-Africanism [...] Be that as it may, pan-Africanism, joined with this neutrality between the East and the West which we have already evoked, seems to be the real hobbyhorse of Sekou Touré. It is, therefore, according to this, in part, that we should judge our relations with Guinea.[43]

France saw Pan-Africanism as ideologically flexible, and Touré as a committed Pan-Africanist willing and capable of drawing resources from both Western and Eastern blocs in order to advance his agenda. The British Foreign Office considered 'communism' and 'the Afro-Asian movement' as 'external threats to British protected and Commonwealth territories in Africa'.[44] Their view of the Ghana–Guinea Union, and the Pan-African aspiration that it embodied, was more ambivalent. In 1958, as soon as the Union was declared, it was thought that it might exacerbate Pan-Africanism's subversive potential.[45] Specifically, if Ghana and Guinea formed 'a unitary state', this could have posed 'important strategic problems' because of its proximity to the British colonies of Sierra Leone and Nigeria.[46] Two years later, 'a positive Western approach towards Pan-Africanism' and the Union was seen as an effective tool to prevent the spread of communism in West Africa.[47] In other words, the Union's international legitimacy shifted and partly reflected how Ghana and imperial powers summoned the 'spectre of communism'. The Union's branding as a Pan-African (rather than socialist) project depended, in turn, on presenting Pan-Africanism and communism as mutually exclusive.[48]

The Union's anti-colonial potential was not limited to its member countries. In 1961, the Chief Minister of the Gambia declared that his country might join the Union after becoming independent, while the British Foreign Office thought that the leaders of the GGMU would encourage Upper Volta

43 'Après neuf mois de l'indépendance guinéenne'.

44 Secret Ghana/Guinea, memo from W.P. Oliver to Mr Allen, 28 November 1958, TNA, DC35/9353.

45 *Ibid.*

46 *Ibid.*

47 Secret Inward Saving Telegram from Conakry to Foreign Office, 21 March 1960, p.2, TNA, DO35/93983.

48 On this, the classic text (and crucial for the context described) is George Padmore, *Pan-Africanism or Communism? The Coming Struggle for Africa* (London, 1956).

(Burkina Faso) to join too.[49] Upper Volta and the Gambia represented intuitive candidates, and served as a reminder of the salience of the union's promises of West African economic integration for small national markets. However, not all countries that expressed an interest in joining were in West Africa. In Nyasaland (Malawi), for example, a future within the Union was inscribed into the present anti-colonial struggle:

> Mr KANYAMA Chiume, Propaganda Secretary of the Malawi Congress Party of Nyasaland, said that after the independence of his country, his Party would bring about the adherence of Nyasaland to the Ghana–Guinea–Mali Union.
>
> This really makes very little sense geographically, but I thought it just worth recording, as it indicates the appeal which the Union may be having politically.[50]

However, the Union's appeal can be overestimated. Nigeria, for example, reassured the British Secretary of State for the Colonies that the country 'had enough to do for the next two years to prepare for her own independence and to maintain economic progress without getting involved in matters like this'.[51] Similarly, from Sierra Leone, Milton Margai remarked that 'he and his party base themselves firmly in independence within the Commonwealth'.[52] As will be shown in the next section, it would be inaccurate to assume that the Union posed as a complete, and mutually exclusive, alternative to the Commonwealth. Nevertheless, the Sierra Leonean perception is significant precisely because it shows the variety of images and fears conjured by the Union in different actors. Margai, for example, added that 'people here have a high regard of Ghana, but they would not approve of forced labour, suppression of Chiefs, one party rule, or Communist influence in Guinea'.[53]

49 Inward Telegram to Commonwealth Relations Office, from Accra to Gambia, 13 June 1961, TNA, FO371/155571; Confidential Telegram from Bamako to Foreign Office, 26 June 1961, TNA, FO371/155571.

50 D.A. Logan to C.T.E. Ewart-Briggs, 8 February 1961, TNA, FO371/155571. In August 1960, shortly after the Congolese independence, Patrice Lumumba signed a secret agreement to establish the 'Ghana-Congo Union', Frank Gerits, *The Ideological Scramble for Africa: How the Pursuit of Anticolonial Modernity Shaped a Postcolonial Order, 1945–1966* (Ithaca NY and London, 2023), 107–8. The agreement, similar to 'the pattern of the Ghana-Guinea-Mali Union' is reproduced in Kwame Nkrumah, *Challenge of the Congo* (New York, 1967), 30–1.

51 Secret Inward Telegram to Secretary of State for the Colonies from Federation of Nigeria (Sir J. Robertson), 26 November 1958, TNA, PREM11/2894. However, following a trip to Ghana in 1961, Obafemi Awolowo recommended that Nigeria should join the GGM, Olubomehin, 'Ghana-Guinea-Mali Union', 107.

52 Secret Inward Telegram to the Secretary of State for the Colonies from Sierra Leone (Sir M. Dorman), 24 November 1958, TNA, PREM11/2894.

53 *Ibid.*

More importantly, a Union between Ghana, Guinea, Mali, Malawi, and the Gambia does not fit into the various ways in which African countries have typically been grouped or classified; it does not map neatly onto the Monrovia, Casablanca, and Brazzaville blocs, and even less onto the Cold War divide. This suggests that, regardless of its outcome, the Union acted as a recurring device for claim-making, through which countries that were still fighting for independence imagined alternative political and economic cartographies and tried to haunt the dreams of the colonisers and challenge their post-imperial projects.

Spectral Sovereignty

Osesirefa suro ɔsaman ɛna ɔsaman nso suro Osesirefa

'Osesirefa is afraid of the ghost and the ghost is also afraid of Osesirefa'.[54]

The vagueness surrounding the institutional forms conjured by the Union contributed to its spectral appearance (as far as its contours were difficult to distinguish) and reinforced its haunting potential. Indeed, despite thinking it unlikely that the Ghana–Guinea Union would be 'as close as that which binds Egypt to Yemen', Britain and France were left to ponder the implications of the alternative economic and political arrangements that could have resulted from it.[55] In the immediate aftermath of the November 1958 communiqué, the French deemed the Union 'likely to have far-reaching consequences for not only political, economic and cultural relations between Ghana and Guinea, but also for forthcoming events in West Africa'.[56] Despite having different political cultures, both Britain and France were most distressed about an idea that Guinea would join the Commonwealth.[57] The British Secretary of State expressed concern about the fact that 'any proposal that an independent foreign State should merge in or federate with a member of the Commonwealth would raise issues of principle, quite apart from practical difficulties, such as the effect on our relations with France'.[58] The Union certainly strained the latter, as the French suspected the Union of being part of Britain's design to undermine their

54 Augustine Kofi Tieku, *The Scrolls of Ashanti Proverbs (Asantefoɔ Nnwoma). Sɛ Wo Bu Bɛ A, Menso Me Te Bɛ (If You Know Proverbs, I also Understand Proverbs) Grouped into Chapters and Verses* (No place, 2022), 25.

55 Copie d'une communications de notre ambassadeur à Londres en date du 24 novembre 1958, Centre des Archives Diplomatiques de Nantes (CADN hereafter), 183PO/1/121.

56 Télégramme de Accra à Dakar, 28 November 1958, CADN, 183PO/1/121.

57 Nouvelles de la république de Guinée, 11 December 1958, CADN, 183PO/1/121.

58 Draft memorandum, Mr Allen 12/58, The Ghana-Guinea Union, December 1958, TNA, DO35/9353.

presence in Africa. Not only was Britain 'the first Western country to recognise Guinea' as an independent country, but what did the High Commissioner in London mean with the 'cryptic declaration' that 'Ghana has never sought to bring Guinea into the Commonwealth through the back door.[59] The Executive Director of the Bank of England reassured the French that the Union between Ghana and Guinea was a cause of embarrassment in London, and 'there was no premeditation on the British side'. This was particularly pertinent 'at a time when a lively controversy opposes the British and the French about the subject of the common market and the free trade zone'.[60] Interestingly, the British Foreign Office felt compelled to declare even to the North Atlantic Treaty Organisation (NATO) that it did not orchestrate nor assist the Union between Ghana and Guinea in any way.[61]

Fearing the Ghana–Guinea union might set a precedent for 'any union between a Commonwealth country and a sovereign foreign State with no historical, linguistic or cultural connections with the Commonwealth', Britain amplified these concerns to 'all UK High Commissioners in member countries'.[62] Regardless of a monetary union, a federation between Ghana and Guinea, with the latter joining the Commonwealth, would raise problems across multiple policy areas. These included, among others, issues of representation in Commonwealth organisations (such as the Imperial Forestry Institute and the Commonwealth Agricultural Bureaux), recognition of approved medical practitioners, new procedures to authenticate legal documents for court use, an 'extensive overhaul' of legislation on extradition, the extension to Guinea of schemes to repatriate British citizens and 'former enemy persons for the restoration of, or compensation for, property taken over by France during the war'.[63] If Ghana and Guinea intended to form an actual union, rather than just a federation, there were decisions to be made about the adoption of the British or French legal model and, most likely, would have implied Ghana's severance of subjecthood to the Crown.[64] The different models discussed also had implications for the projection of African nations' sovereignty onto the international sphere: a merger between Guinea and Ghana would leave the Commonwealth's

59 'Après neuf mois de l'indépendance guinéenne'.

60 Prêt de £10 million consenti par le Ghana à la Guinée, adhésion de la Guinée au Commonwealth, 5 December 1958, BFA, 1466200601 AR 430. See also Nouvelles de la république de Guinée, 27 November 1958, CADN, 183PO/1/121.

61 Telegram from Foreign Office to United Kingdom Delegation to NATO Paris, 25 November 1958, TNA, PREM 11/2894.

62 Draft memorandum, Mr Allen 12/58, The Ghana-Guinea Union, December 1958, TNA, DO35/9353.

63 Untitled document, 28 November 1958, TNA, DO 35/9353.

64 Ghana/Guinea, 27 November 1958, TNA, DO 35/9353.

and Africa's representation at the United Nations (UN) the same, while Guinea joining the UN as its own country would create additional pressure.[65]

The announcement of the Union raised critical issues regarding the adaptability of the Commonwealth's legal and institutional infrastructure.[66] This is clearest in a report by the Constitutional Department, which postulated the possible implications of Ghana and Guinea either becoming a 'new' country or a federation.[67] Another significant distinction would be if the new political formation would be republican or monarchical (or at any rate dependent on the British crown). In the latter case, the Queen's approval was necessary for a new flag. More importantly, the union between the two states would mean that 'Guineans will have to be recognised in United Kingdom law as Commonwealth Citizens and British Subjects'.[68] Interestingly, the Constitution Department pointed out a third scenario beyond a federation and a new unitary state: something like the Franco-British Union envisaged in June 1940. This was the closest instance of a foreign sovereign state becoming part of the Commonwealth, but since the plan for how it would operate was never actualised due to France's occupation by Nazi Germany, the Franco-British Union did not 'offer a precedent for permanent arrangements in peace time'.[69] This suggests that not only did the Union threaten the Commonwealth's future (or, rather Britain's view of the Commonwealth at the time), but it also evoked stylised interpretations of specific episodes and formations in European and American history.

While the term 'sovereignty' does not recur too often in the GGMU's archival trails, it represented a key issue. By generating narratives that conflated multiple futures and pasts, and reconfigured their relationship, the GGMU embodied a 'spectral sovereignty', defined by post-colonial theorist Homi K. Bhabha as 'a semblance of the past as it passes into the history of the present'.[70] Yet, the GGMU's incarnation of 'spectral sovereignty' acquires a wider meaning: besides re-enacting a semblance of the past into the present, it derived its spectrality from its capacity to conflate imagined pasts and futures, and in the process raise profound questions about alternative political forms. The proverb 'Osesirefa is afraid of the ghost and the

65 Ghana/Guinea Union, memo from H.G.M. Bass to Mr Allen, 25 November 1958, TNA, DO35/9353.

66 Ghana/Guinea, Note by Constitutional Department, TNA, DO35/9353. There were also exceptions: one of the few observers minimising the potential impact of the Union on the Commonwealth was A.E. Parsons, 26 November 1958, TNA, DO35/9353.

67 Ghana/Guinea, Note by Constitutional Department, TNA, DO35/9353. The French seemed more convinced that Guinea would have been 'absorbed' by Ghana, Nouvelles de la république de Guinée – L'union du Ghana et de la Guinée, 12/58, CADN, 183PO/1/121.

68 Ghana/Guinea, Note by Constitutional Department, TNA, DO35/9353.

69 *Ibid.*

70 Bhabha, 'Spectral sovereignty', 143.

ghost is also afraid of Osesirefa' is typically deployed to describe a situation in which the exercise of sovereign power is constrained by a system of checks and balances.[71]

When applied to the GGMU, this proverb reiterates the vital role of fear as a catalyst of political imagination. However, if the Union is 'the ghost', who is Osesirefa? While it might be tempting to equate it with Britain and France, this section has emphasised the multi-layered questioning of sovereignty posed by the 'spectral' Union: this included issues of agency (and of the continued role played by Britain and France in the post-colonial lives of their former colonies, but also the evolving relation between Ghana and Guinea), dynamics of inclusion and exclusion (such as in the Commonwealth context), and of political forms (the kind of federation that would result from the Union, the projection of sovereignty at the United Nations, etc). However, underneath all of this, the GGMU's sovereignty was contested and redefined through money. Money simultaneously unleashed the Union's full hauntological potential, and constituted the privileged field of neo-colonial intervention.

Spectral Money

Ɔsaman a onni din no, yɛnto no nkra
'A ghost that has no name has no address'.[72]

For Marx, money was the spectral substance *par excellence*. Derrida read Marx's *A Contribution to the Critique of Political Economy* as a 'spectralising disincarnation' marking the 'apparition of the bodiless body of money'.[73] Derrida also noted that 'Marx always described money, and more precisely the monetary sign, in the figure of the appearance or simulacrum, more exactly of the ghost' – the 'movement of idealisation that Marx describes [...] is a production of ghosts, illusions, simulacra, appearances or apparitions'.[74] Although Marx understood money's spectral nature primarily in relation to the creation of exchange value and its complementarity with the mystification of commodity fetishism, he did not ignore completely money's 'other' side – its

71 Tieku, *The Scrolls of Ashanti Proverbs*, 25.
72 *Ibid.*, 29.
73 Derrida, *Specters of Marx*, 41; Karl Marx, *A Contribution to the Critique of Political Economy* (orig. 1859) https://www.marxists.org/archive/marx/works/download/Marx_Contribution_to_the_Critique_of_Political_Economy.pdf (accessed 1 June 2023).
74 Derrida, *Specters of Marx*, 45.

nature as 'an emblem instituted for a community in the name of an instance of sovereignty'.[75]

Yet, despite its centrality in both Nkrumah's vision for the Union and his overall Pan-African agenda, a new supra-national currency did not exhaust money's hauntological role.[76] In the Union, this was activated primarily by loans from Ghana to Guinea and Mali. In response to Guinea's choice to become independent outside De Gaulle's Franco-African Community, France was determined to make an example of them. As noted by Ladipo Adamolekun, the 'French government took the Guinean decision as an act of "secession", stopped all technical, economic, and financial aid with immediate effect'.[77] This made necessary a massive capital injection: Touré specified that a loan was required for 'development expenditure' and that 'it would be difficult to set an upper limit to the amount of money they would need to finance their development'.[78] Ghana agreed to lend Guinea £10 million. Signed by Ghanaian Finance Minister K.A. Gbedemah and Sékou Touré, the loan was spread over four years, with an interest rate of 2% per annum.[79] The first interest payment, paid by Guinea in December 1960, amounted to around £110,000, and was refunded to them upon Nkrumah's request.[80] As Nkrumah declared that 'an entirely new conception of the Commonwealth is evolving', the uncertainties surrounding the loan rearticulated the boundaries between the financial and political aspects of the new community.[81] This is evident in the response of

75 'The independent existence of the exchange-value of a commodity is here a transient apparition, by means of which the commodity is immediately replaced by another commodity', Karl Marx, *Capital: A Critique of Political Economy, Volume 1* (orig. 1867), 84. https://www.marxists.org/archive/marx/works/download/pdf/Capital-Volume-I.pdf (accessed 24 March 2025); Keith Hart, 'Heads or tails? Two sides of the coin', *Man* 21:4 (1986), 637–56. On Marx's monetary thought, see Suzanne de Brunhoff, *Marx on Money* (London, 2015; orig. 1973); on Marx and monetary sovereignty see Stefan Eich, *The Currency of Politics: The Political Theory of Money from Aristotle to Keynes* (Princeton, 2022), 105–38. The last quotation is from Massimo Amato, *L'enigma della moneta e l'inizio dell'economia* (Napoli-Salerno, 2016, orig. 2010), 95, trans. by Gerardo Serra.

76 Nkrumah, *Africa Must Unite*, 163.

77 Ladipo Adamolekun, *Sékou Touré's Guinea: An Experiment in Nation-Building* (London, 1976), 1.

78 Note on the meeting held on the 2nd December, 1958, at the President's Residence, PRAAD, RG6/3/31/18.

79 Conditions of the loan of £G10,000,000, 5 December 1958, PRAAD RG6/3/31/15.

80 Copy of letter from H.A. Flack to J.O. Moreton, 30 January 1961, TNA, FO371/155571.

81 Draft memorandum, Mr. Allen 12/58, The Ghana-Guinea Union, December 1958, TNA, DO35/9353.

the Bank of England, which was suspected by the French of being complicit in facilitating the loan:[82]

> the Bank of England has not yet, at this time, been consulted about the subject of this loan. The Bank of England cannot oppose a transfer from a Ghanaian account to a Guinean account: such a transfer is lawful under the terms of British exchange regulation. But [...] a transaction of this kind is certainly not in accordance with the spirit of the regulations, the authors of which may well have envisaged transfers of capital for investments, for example, but had not thought of transfers of capital for political reasons. As well, it is only on the political level, and by the British government approaching the Ghanaian government, that one could try to oppose the transfer. But the Bank of England absolutely cannot intervene with the Bank of Ghana, although its Governor is an Englishman.[83]

When Mali joined, the centrality of a new common currency was revitalised: the *Financial Times* reported that during their meeting in Accra, Ghana, Guinea, and Mali 'were to consider a political union of the three countries, a common currency, and a common bank'.[84] Ghana also gave a loan to Mali, 'delivered in Bamako by air in the form of bundles of CFA franc notes'.[85] A telegram to the British Foreign Office discussed it in considerable detail:

> Representatives of the Export Credits Guarantee Department, who have just visited here [Conakry], tell me that there is evidence in London that Ghana has recently realised sterling securities to the sum of about £4 ½ million, which I believe is the amount of the proposed Ghana loan to Mali.
>
> The US Embassy has also told me in strict confidence that Guinea now has about £4 million sterling in an account at the Bank of America in London.
>
> This leads one to speculate whether Guinea has not participated in the arrangement. Where else would Ghana get bundles of CFA notes from? Ghana would get the credit, Mali the cash, and Guinea convertible currency for her blocked francs. I cannot obtain any direct confirmation here but the

82 Ghana-Guinea, memo from H.L. Jenkyns to Sir Denis Rickett, 9 May 1960, TNA, DO35/9383.

83 'Prêt de £10 million consenti par le Ghana à la Guinée, adhésion de la Guinée au Commonwealth', 5 December 1958, BFA, 1466200601 AR 430.

84 '3-Nations Talk in Accra To-Day', *Financial Times*, 9 January 1961. However, the possibility of a common currency was not mentioned in the Joint Communiqué that formalised Mali's entrance into the Union.

85 Confidential – Mr. D.A. Logan, African Department, JU1023/8, 3 February 1961, TNA, FO371/155571.

> US Embassy, to whom I put this possibility, now tell me that they have received some sort of confirmation of it from Paris.
>
> I shall be glad to know whether there is any evidence elsewhere that some such triangular deal has been arranged.[86]

This telegram reveals the willingness of Britain, France, and the United States of America to go to considerable lengths to gather financial information about the Union. Their commitment to knowing the financial transactions between Ghana, Guinea, and Mali was dictated by their potential political and economic ramifications. More importantly, the degree of uncertainty pervading the telegram gestures at the intersections between the 'continuous' space of global capital and the 'discrete' ones of nation-states using monetary transfers as tools to define the contours of their newly acquired sovereignty. The former colonisers were even more worried that behind the simple topography of Ghana's transfers to Guinea and Mali (and Nkrumah's request that British aid to Ghana could be partly used for this cause) lurked more ambitious plans, as discussed by the Commonwealth Relations Office:

> I suspect that Dr. Nkrumah's idea of our giving aid to Ghana so that she can help Guinea and other independent territories has been superseded by Dr. Nkrumah's proposal for a Colombo Plan for Africa, which reinforces my fear that any such plan could not be confined to the Commonwealth.[87]

Once again, the Union raised the possibility of establishing frameworks alternative to those which Britain and France imagined in the post-colonial world. However, the idea of creating a new currency for the Union, heartily supported by Nkrumah, and the meaning of higher economic integration between Ghana and Guinea remained contested. It was unclear what Ghana would gain from a closer integration with Guinea, a country roughly the same size as Ghana, but with a much smaller population (2.5 million vs. almost 7 million), very high infant mortality (284/1000), and much lower levels of formal education (37,000 children in primary school vs. about 500,000 in Ghana; 1,200 in secondary school vs. 7,000 in Ghana).[88] One of the key institutions envisaged was the Joint Economic Commission, whose task was to 'study the economic and financial consequences of Guinea adopting a joint currency with Ghana, or a currency backed by Ghana, and to make joint plans for dealing with balance of payment

86 Mr. D.A. Logan, Inward Saving Telegram from Conakry to Foreign Office, 6 February 1961, TNA, FO371/155571.

87 Memo from H.A.F. Rumbold to Mr Cole, 6 May 1960, TNA, DO35/9383.

88 Guinea: some figures, PRAAD, RG6/3/31/9.

problems'.[89] In the absence of a central bank in Guinea, the Bank of Ghana would be the pillar of the new monetary architecture, tasked with discussing the technical details of the union with the Bank of England and the French Institut d'Emission.[90] The Joint Economic Commission – initially labelled Joint Economic Planning Commission – was also expected to harmonise Ghana's and Guinea's development planning, and thus provide a framework for a common economic policy.

Gbedemah pushed back, saying that the transformation from Joint Economic Planning Committee into Joint Economic Committee was necessary because it 'would not deal with economic planning of both countries'. Further, since 'Ghana's Second Development Plan was nearly ready for submission to Parliament', 'it would not be appropriate to arrest progress towards implementing the plan at this stage'.[91] While Guinea conceded this point, they also enquired when the Joint Committee would become operative. Specifically, as the country was engaged in 'very complex and delicate financial talks with the French Government', 'with a view to settlement agreement' over the financial aspects such as African military and civil service pensions, and foreign interests in bauxite, the Joint Economic Committee should be established after the end of these negotiations.[92]

When it was finally established, the Joint Economic Committee did not foster resolutions to adopt a common currency. Indeed, by 1960 (and until Mali joined, when some of these discussions were resumed) it was clear that the Guinean government did 'not contemplate anything in the nature of a common currency with Ghana at the present'.[93] Guinea left the franc zone and, on 1 March 1960, issued its own currency, the Guinean franc. Much to Britain's relief, when Gbedemah visited Guinea in 1960 to discuss the Union's priorities of currency and defence, the Guineans insisted that these two subjects should be reserved for discussion at the Head of the State level.[94] The updated joint communiqué from 1 June 1960, co-signed by Gbedemah and Camara Bengaly (Guinea's Minister of Labour and Social Affairs), contained no references to the possibility of a common currency.[95] Instead, the envisaged economic integration revolved primarily around trade: Guinean products of interest to

89 Confidential – Matters to be discussed by the Finance Minister K.A. Gbedemah and the Hon. M.A. Welbeck with Monsieur Sekou Toure [sic], President of the Government of Guinea, PRAAD, RG6/3/31/2.

90 *Ibid.*

91 Note of the Meeting Held on the 2nd November, 1958 at the President's Residence, PRAAD RG6/3/31/18.

92 *Ibid.*, PRAAD, RG6/3/31/19.

93 Aide memoire for Minister of Finance, PRAAD, RG6/3/31/24.

94 Hugh Jones, Confidential Telegram from Conakry to Foreign Office, 3 June 1960, TNA, DO35/9383.

95 Joint Communiqué issued by the Ghana-Guinea Conference held in Conakry from the 30th May to the 1st June, 1960, PRAAD, RG6/3/31/89.

Ghana included N'dama cattle, alumina, and fish; while Ghana was keen to export to Guinea manufactured products such as biscuits, cigarettes, shirts, matches, and aluminium roofing sheets.[96]

Despite being 'annoyed with Guinea for departing from the spirit of the original Ghana/Guinea union by issuing new currency of her own without consultation with Ghana', Nkrumah was still considering ways to bring Guinea into the sterling zone.[97] Once again, he emphasised the danger of excessive Soviet influence if this did not occur, and capitalised on the Union's monetary aspects to suggest a longer list of requests and grievances to the British Prime Minister, including a reminder of the illegitimacy of South Africa's stronghold over Namibia and the need for the release of Jomo Kenyatta.[98] However, the British pointed out that the possibility of the joint circulation of the Ghana and Guinea currency was unlikely:

> Unless the Guinean franc were devalued, any arrangement involving joint circulation of the Ghana and Guinea currencies and automatic convertibility between the two could be exceedingly expensive for Ghana. This is because the French West African franc (and hence the Guinean franc) is grossly overvalued in relation to the £. The operation could only have a chance of making economic sense if it were preceded by a very substantial devaluation of the Guinea franc.[99]

Still, the hauntological effect of the Union's monetary discourse left the British confused and frustrated:

> We also had confusing discussion about New Guinean currency. Nkrumah wants this currency to be backed up by Ghana or perhaps even to have joint currency, but he is imprecise and muddle-headed and I fear some nonsense may result, with awkward sterling area ramifications, unless we can steer things on right lines.[100]

96 Ghana-Guinea Union, Appendix I, Points agreed by both delegations regarding trade and financial relations, PRAAD, RG6/3/31/90–91.

97 Inward Telegram from Accra to Commonwealth Relations Office, 6 May 1960, TNA, PREM11/2894. The reference to the 'worthless notes' is in Record of a Conversation between the Prime Minister and Dr Nkrumah at 10, Downing Street at 3 p.m on Monday, 2 May 1960, p. 1, TNA, PREM11/2894.

98 Confidential Outward Telegram from Commonwealth Relations Office to Accra, 6 May 1960; Record of a Conversation between the Prime Minister and Dr Nkrumah at 10, Downing Street at 3 p.m on Monday, May 2, 1960, p. 3, both documents in TNA, PREM11/2894.

99 R.B. Norman, Record Copy – Secret, Commonwealth Relations Office, 9 May 1960, TNA, DO35/9383.

100 Secret Inward Telegram from Accra to Commonwealth Relations Office, 28 April 1960, TNA, PREM11/2894.

What did it mean to 'steer things on right lines'? In the immediate aftermath of the declaration of the union between Ghana and Guinea, a meeting between representatives of the Bank of England, the Board of Trade, the Treasury, and the Foreign Office concluded that:

> It is awkward for us politically openly [sic] to seek to dissuade Ghana from going ahead with the project of a union with Guinea. It is, however, quite possible, consistently with this, to draw the attention of the Ghanaians, particularly Mr Gbedemah, to the problems which would arise from any Union in the economic field and the draft [of a telegram sent to Gdebemah ahead of a meeting with him] therefore emphasizes the difficulties and the disadvantages both to Guinea and to Ghana, while being reasonably fair and objective.[101]

With its reification of the distinction between the 'political' and the 'economic', this passage lends some support to Nkrumah's definition of 'neo-colonialism', the essence of which is that 'the State which is subject to it is, in theory, independent and has all the outward trappings of international sovereignty. Its economic system and thus its political policy is directed from outside'.[102] In May 1960, Nkrumah discussed the issue of the monetary implications of the Union with the Chancellor of the Exchequer. Nkrumah expressed concern over the fact that the new Guinean franc had no regular backing, since out of the £10 million promised, only 4 million had been drawn. Nkrumah wanted to use the remaining (and more if necessary) 'so that the Bank of Ghana could back the Guinea franc as well as the Ghana pound'.[103] The Chancellor said that

> it would be necessary for Ghana to be very careful that it did not take on an unlimited commitment, and damage its own credit in the course of doing so. Ghana would also have to be careful that it did not prejudice the success of current negotiations for finance for the Volta River project. The U. K. was itself faced with the problem of not overstraining its resources in attempts to help newly-emergent countries all over the globe, and Ghana also must be careful not to overreach itself in seeking to assist its neighbours.[104]

While promoting its image as a disinterested provider of aid to the developing world, Britain subtly used the Volta River project, which was clearly a strategic

101 Memo from H.A.F. Rumbold to Mr A.W. Snelling, Sir Henry Lintott, Sir Gilbert Laithwaite, 26 November 1958, TNA, DO35/9383.
102 Kwame Nkrumah, *Neocolonialism: The Last Stage of Imperialism* (London, 1974; orig. 1965), ix.
103 Note for the Record, Ghana/Guinea, TNA, DO35/9383.
104 *Ibid.*

priority for Ghana, to dissuade the country from getting too involved with Guinea. This is a reminder of the potential importance of financial capital and credit as tools through which the former colonisers constrain the policy horizon of independent countries and acquire a bigger share in their markets.[105] Consistent with this, Britain was hoping to play a bigger role in Guinea, and favoured an increased US presence. It was agreed that a selective combination of diplomatic action and 'discreetly chosen aid' would be cheaper and more effective than 'seeking to negotiate programmes with the Guinean authorities'.[106] While trade expectations remained low 'until the Guineans [established] their [...] London trade account and send trade delegation to the United Kingdom', cultural exchanges and management changes represented valuable opportunities. These included the expanded role of the British Council and of the British Broadcasting Corporation (BBC) in teaching English, and the expectation that the latter would start an African service in French. Since 'the Guineans are still starved of direct contact with the non-French western world', it was hoped that by establishing connections and exchange visits between 'Western youth, women's and, if possible, trade union organizations' and their Guinean counterparts, Britain could 'make an impression on these important sections of Guinean opinion'.[107] The fluid situation created by Guinea leaving the franc zone meant an opportunity for the renegotiation of business hierarchies, with the hope that 'British, Canadian (and American) industry and commerce established in Guinea under French management should now switch to more manifest British, Canadian (and American) management': the list included 'Compagnie Minière (Tuxcore); Bauxite du Midi (Alcan); [...]; British Aluminium, etc.; Compagnie Niger (Unilever); Sogui Nex Diamonds (under British management); B. P. and Shell'.[108]

However, for former colonisers, to 'steer things on right lines' could mean vastly different things in practice. To punish Guinea for having left the franc zone and launching its own currency, France orchestrated the infamous 'Operation Persil', which consisted of printing millions of fake Guinean franc notes (the original ones were printed in Czechoslovakia), to flood the economy, causing hyperinflation and economic collapse.[109] Keïta, who firmly believed that 'political power is always and necessarily accompanied by the sovereign right to mint currency, that monetary power is inseparable from national

105 Moreover, the Chancellor's statement presents some analogies with the dichotomous conception of capital that emerged from the telegram analysed above (pages 212–13).

106 Secret Inward Saving Telegram from Conakry to Foreign Office, 17 March 1960, TNA, DO35/9383.

107 *Ibid.*

108 *Ibid.*

109 Fanny Pigeaud and Ndongo Samba Sylla, *Africa's Last Colonial Currency: The CFA Franc Story*, trans. Thomas Fazi (London, 2020), 43.

sovereignty', also found his policies highly constrained.[110] Following the creation of a national bank and a new currency, Malian economic independence was immediately hampered by the other countries in the French-approved Union Monétaire Ouest Africaine. By restricting trade with Mali, they caused a depreciation in the value of the Malian franc, and eventually forced Keïta to re-enter the franc zone in 1967.[111] He was overthrown one year later. Far from being an expression of sovereignty, the CFA franc is the 'invisible weapon of French neo-colonialism' and an index of *servitude monétaire*.[112] In July 1965, Ghana abandoned the Ghanaian pound and launched the *cedi*. The new currency acted as a vessel for national sovereignty by promoting the iconography of Nkrumah as the founder of the nation, and abandoning British units of measurement in favour of decimalisation (Figure 8.2).

Another proverb goes 'A ghost that has no name has no address' or, more literally, 'if a ghost has no name, we can't invoke him'.[113] The proverb also suggests that only one's ancestors, rather than ghosts, can receive and deliver messages to, and thus effectively intercede with, the Supreme Being.[114] When applied to the monetary imaginaries and practices set in motion by the GGMU, this proverb captures money as the intersection between the reification of a delineated (and thus *named*) political community, and the fluidity of money as 'global' capital (which seems to have *no address*). On the one hand, by attempting to assert their monetary sovereignty, the Union's countries tried to sever links with their monetary past. It is possible to think of the GGMU as a 'ghost' that could have affirmed its identity by imagining (and thus naming) a new supranational currency that subverted national and imperial topographies. Ghana's simultaneous adoption of a new currency *and* decimalisation marked the rejection of the colonial 'spaces' and metrics that, by facilitating the 'delivery' of specific messages, had perpetuated dependency on the 'Supreme Being' of Capital.[115] On the other hand, the lack of address, and the ghost's impossibility of delivering a message, recast neo-colonial machinations as processes that, through 'money' (as currency, as in the case of Operation Persil, or as capital, like in the British case), disfigure the developing world's attempts to articulate a new relationship between 'name' and 'place', and thus, the institution of alternative political and economic sovereignties.

110 Quoted in Pigeaud and Sylla, *Africa's Last Colonial Currency*, 46.

111 *Ibid.*, 47.

112 *Ibid.*; Kako Nubukpo, Martial Ze Belinga, Bruno Tinel, Demba Moussa Dembele (eds) *Sortir l'Afrique de la servitude monétaire: À qui profite le franc CFA ?* (Paris, 2016).

113 Tieku, *The Scrolls of Ashanti Proverbs*, p. 29.

114 Thanks to Kofi Adjepong-Boateng for this clarification.

115 On the politics of decimalisation, cf. Aashish Velkar, 'Rethinking metrology, nationalism and development in India, 1833–1956', *Past & Present* 239:1 (2018), 143–79.

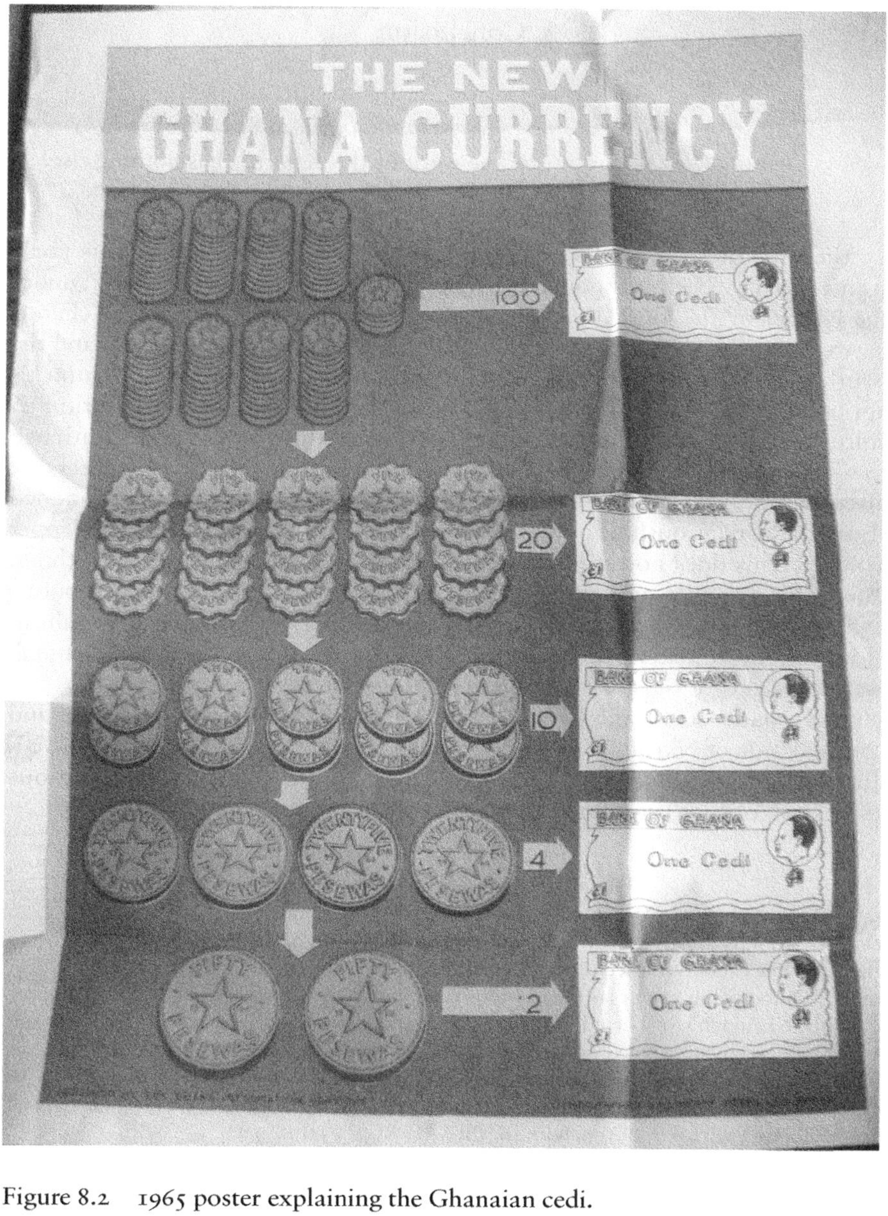

Figure 8.2 1965 poster explaining the Ghanaian cedi.
Source: PRAAD, ADM7/18/13. Reproduced with permission.

Conclusion

Ɔsaman nni biribi a, ɔwɔ abyebyɛwakyire

'If the spirit of the departed has nothing else, he has something to be inherited'.[116]

By the time of the GGMU's dissolution in 1963, its most ambitious goals seemed to have been postponed to an indeterminate future.[117] However, under the banner of the GGMU, strides were made to generate further exchange between the three countries, and between the Francophone countries and the 'world'. These included improved transport and communication, Guinea's application to join the International Postal Union, and the organisation of cultural exchanges.[118] Until Nkrumah's overthrow in 1966, Ghana continued to work closely with Guinea and Mali, and this became increasingly necessary after the 1965 Organisation of African Unity conference in Accra which added strain to the relationships between Ghana and Côte d'Ivoire, Niger and Upper Volta.[119] This does not imply that the GGMU leaders agreed on everything. Touré, for example, was concerned by Nkrumah's recognition of Mobutu's regime in Congo, which he saw as an advancement of neo-colonial imperialism. However, Touré reiterated that adopting a common position with Nkrumah was necessary for the construction of a 'progressive Africa'.[120]

In a broader sense, the GMMU laid the foundation for the expansion and consolidation of Nkrumah's Pan-African ideas. In the same year as the GGMU's dissolution, Nkrumah published *Africa Must Unite*, the most ambitious expression of his vision for continental political and economic integration.[121]

116 Appiah, Appiah, Agyeman-Duah, *Bu Me Bɛ*, proverb no. 5232.

117 Historians disagree on the reasons behind the dissolution: while Getachew emphasised 'disagreements about the precise balance between federal union and independence of member states', Olubomehin favours other economic and political factors, such as Ghana's import controls, Nkrumah's suspected implication in the assassination of Sylvanus Olympio, and the trade agreements signed between individual GGMU countries and foreign ones. See Getachew, *Worldmaking*, 110; Olubomehin, 'Ghana-Guinea-Mali Union', 109.

118 Ghana-Guinea Union, points agreed by both delegations regarding trade and financial relations, Appendix II and Appendix III, PRAAD RG6/3/31/92–93.

119 Mali hosted the meeting between Nkrumah and the leaders of Ivory Coast and Upper Volta which produced a Joint Communiqué on non-interference. This is reproduced in Letter from AFRISEC to Ghana Bureau, Conakry, 14 October 1965, PRAAD, RG17/1/429/61–62. It should also be remembered that Sékou Touré hosted Nkrumah in Conakry between the coup and his death in 1972.

120 Letter of Sékou Touré to Nkrumah, 11 December 1965, PRAAD, RG17/1/429/80.

121 Nkrumah, *Africa Must Unite*.

A note from the same year, found in an archival folder on the Bank of Ghana, reiterated that 'a common currency' was one of the four key policy areas (alongside a common defence, a common foreign policy and diplomacy, and coordinated economic planning) necessary for the unification of Africa.[122] In 1964, 'The Republic of Ghana' produced a Draft Constitution of the Union of African States, which extended to the continental level and expanded the goals of the Charter signed by Ghana, Guinea, and Mali. Besides establishing a central planning agency, creating preconditions for African industrialisation and electrification, providing universal education, and establishing a development fund to eliminate inequalities among the member states, the Union would also 'establish a Union Central Bank, a uniform fiscal and budgetary system and adopt other measures, aiming at stabilising the currency and strengthening the financial basis of the Federation'.[123]

The GGMU should not be reduced to a failed experiment crushed by the gap between its rhetoric and reality.[124] A proverb affirms 'If the spirit of the departed has nothing else, he has something to be inherited'.[125] Drawing inspiration from Derrida has allowed us to take a close look at the ways in which the Union haunted the former colonisers and constituted new imaginaries. We have found traces of this spectrality in how Nkrumah invoked 'the ghost of communism' to navigate the Cold War, in the theoretical and practical challenges raised by the Union to the Commonwealth, the sterling area and the CFA franc, and in the alternative political and economic forms that the GGMU conjured.

From this point of view, the GGMU presents some parallels with the West Indies Federation (1961–62), and with the United Arab States, the federation that, between 1958 and 1961, united Egypt (including Gaza which was ruled by Egypt at the time), Syria (the two already forming the United Arab Republic), and Yemen.[126] These parallels point to the proliferation of federal and supranational political forms as a key aspect of decolonisation. Although many were

122 Notes on Ghana's African Policy, PRAAD RG17/2/183/1–2.

123 Provisional Draft of the Principles of the Constitution (Fundamental Laws) of the Union of African States with Explanatory Note, p. 14, PRAAD, RG17/2/553.

124 The dream of a continental currency still lingers in the recent past, as indicated by artists Mansour Ciss Kanakassy and Baruch Gottlieb, who in 2002 presented at the Dakar biennale a prototype of AFRO, an imagined Pan-African currency. https://digital.lib.uiowa.edu/islandora/object/ui%3Auima_17021 There is, however, an unintended irony in the fact that one of the banknote's sides depicts Léopold Sédar Senghor, who allegedly supported Operation Persil (Pigeaud and Sylla, *Africa's Last Colonial Currency*, 43). Thanks to Karin Pallaver for making us aware of this work of art.

125 Appiah, Appiah, Agyeman-Duah, *Bu Me Bɛ*, proverb no. 5232.

126 Getachew, *Worldmaking*, 125–31; Adeed Dawisha, *Arab Nationalism in the Twentieth Century: From Triumph to Despair* (Princeton, 2003), 160–213. Thanks to Roy Bar Sadeh for this suggestion.

short-lived, dismissing them entirely or reducing them to failed experiments, roads not taken, or precursors of later arrangements misses the point. The GGMU invites us to complicate the history of how empires become nation-states, how nation-states re-arrange themselves, and how we historicise these processes. Moyn has remarked that 'for the history of federalism to be more than trivia, it has to be shown that it was actually possible'.[127] In contrast, this chapter suggests that what is 'possible' at a given time and place depends on how we choose to interrogate it. A more expansive political economy can simultaneously account for the hauntological effects that characterised these otherwise elusive political forms, and expand the canon of authors, discourses, and epistemologies upon which we draw when writing their economic history. The invitation to reconstruct spectral political economies is an important part of the GGMU's legacy, that mysterious 'something to be inherited'.

127 Samuel Moyn, 'Fantasies of federalism', *Dissent* (2015), https://www.dissentmagazine.org/article/fantasies-of-federalism/ (accessed 14 August 2025).

9

Cooperatives and Cocoa in Ghana, 1931–61

Nikolay Kamenov

Cooperatives are economic institutions that, based on contractual agreements, pool resources to create economies of scale. In contrast to joint stock companies and corporations, however, cooperatives exhibit a specific form of ownership in relation to profit and, at least in theory and related to the issue of proprietary rights, a different mechanism for making decisions. While cooperatives generate revenue, the distribution of profit is not necessarily proportionate to the capital investments. In other words, profits and in particular residual returns are not paid back to investors but to member-owners. Depending on the by-laws of the specific cooperative, this could be proportionate to the extent of cooperative services that the specific member acquired. For example, a member-owner of a consumer cooperative might receive a pay-back proportionate to the sum of purchases they have made. Similarly, members of a credit society *de facto* share in the profit proportionately to their borrowings through a lower interest rate that keeps the cooperative break-even. In the case of marketing cooperatives, i.e., societies that bring members' produce to the market, the type of cooperative most pertinent to the discussion of the history of the institution in Ghana, the profit distribution is proportionate to the amount of goods members sell through the cooperative. In addition, while in practice the management of cooperatives could take a bewildering variety of forms, in theory the decision making is based on voting rights that are non-proportional to the amount of investment, i.e., member-owners usually have equal say – one vote each – in governing the organisation.

By bypassing existing market structures, such as moneylenders, middlemen, and/or processing units, the main historical function of agricultural cooperatives was to smooth processes of commercialisation. Cooperatives thus excel in rural settings where cash crops have recently brought about dynamic market forces. In contrast, subsistence or stagnant rural economies tend to slacken the pace of cooperative development. In essence, these are market organisations that are well aligned with broader economic developments. It is thus not by chance that agricultural cooperatives, admittedly often introduced from above, started to spread rapidly among farmers in regional pockets of Asia and Africa, experiencing such commercialisation during and immediately after the so-called 'first wave of globalisation', 1870–1914.[1] From the late 1880s, Ghana fulfilled the above criteria to the letter. Using and developing the region's comparative advantage, farmers captured a rare opportunity created by an explosion in global demand for one particular cash crop – cocoa. Meanwhile, the colonial state, favouring the development of transport infrastructure and, more broadly, the creation of an open economy, attended a profound process of commercialisation in the Gold Coast and Ashanti. Following on the heels of these comprehensive market forces, cooperatives came to ameliorate some of the more turbulent effects on the economy and society.

The suggestion that this organisational form was suitable for the Ghanaian farmer and the cocoa supply chain first gained currency in the 1920s. The most important figure in the early promotion of cooperation was G.G. Auchinleck, while investigating cocoa quality for the Agricultural Department in the Gold Coast in the late 1920s. Employing his experience and knowledge from a previous post in Ceylon, he enthusiastically advocated the organisation as a panacea against various issues plaguing the marketing of cocoa.[2] Following the enactment of the Co-operative Societies Ordinance (4) by the colonial government in April 1931 and based almost exclusively on cocoa-marketing cooperatives, the movement slowly took off in the 1930s.[3] It consolidated and gained speed in the 1940s and reached its pinnacle in the 1950s.

Through intensified state support and control, the early independence period saw a further, albeit short-lived burst of cooperation. The general downturn of the economy from the mid-1960s onwards and the failed government projects, some of which engaging directly with cooperatives, and, finally, the *de facto* nationalisation of cocoa-marketing structures, left then a scarring mark on the movement.

1 For the original proposition see Jeffrey G. Williamson, 'Land, labor, and globalization in the Third World, 1870–1940', *Journal of Economic History* 62:1 (2002), 55–85 and Kevin O'Rourke and Jeffrey G. Williamson, 'When did globalisation begin?', *European Review of Economic History* 6:1 (2002), 23–50. The debate built on the Heckser-Ohlin theory, postulating that intensified global trade led to a convergence not only of commodity prices but also in factor markets. In the case of Asia and Africa, this type of globalisation should be taken with a grain of salt, but there were pockets that became more integrated into a market. For Ghana it has been argued that the most substantial change from 1874 to 1939 was the formation and expansion of markets for land-use and free labour – see Gareth Austin, 'Labour and land in Ghana, 1874–1939: a shifting ratio and an institutional revolution', *Australian Economic History Review* 47:1 (2007), 95–120.

2 Nikolay Kamenov, 'Imperial cooperative experiments and global market capitalism, c.1900–c.1960', *Journal of Global History* 14:2 (2019), 230.

3 It is important to note here that the sources refer to the first, primary farmers' cooperatives as producers' cooperatives. These were, however, *de facto* preoccupied with marketing, as the production of cooperatives remained the private business of members, i.e., most assets and labour employed remained outside the cooperative.

While going through these episodes in some detail, this chapter contends that cooperatives are very well suited to study the political economy of Ghana in the half century surrounding the Second World War, and, further, that the Ghanaian case provides a fascinating window into the study of cooperation. The first part of this bidirectional approach was already substantiated by Hill in the mid-1950s, who observed that, as an example, the study of labour in cocoa production necessitated a variety of information and that the

> only organisation keeping the necessary records was the Gold Coast co-operative movement. The co-operative societies handle a fifth of all the Gold Coast's cocoa [1954–5], are widely distributed, keep excellent records and know a lot about their members, who are expected to market all their cocoa through the society to which they belong. There is reason to think that co-operators as a group are reasonably representative of Gold Coast cocoa farmers.[4]

While the last point is certainly debatable, read critically cooperative records could be rather illuminating.[5] Although many of these excellent materials are irrecoverable as archival records were lost in the turbulence of the late 1960s, this author firmly believes that much remains to be discovered and that the literature so far has made very little use of some official, published documents, for example the annual Reports of the Registrar of Co-operatives, that are readily available in different libraries around the world. The second part of the approach, i.e., Ghana as a case study of cooperation, might provide very useful insights for the recent debate regarding the incorporation of the 'global countryside' in the world market economy.[6] In the case of the cocoa cooperatives in Ghana, we can see the sharp contours of an organisational form acting as an interface between the state, the market, and the agricultural producers.

Cooperatives tried to adapt in accordance with the relative strength of these actors and/or with the divergence or confluence of their interests. As I will show below, once the issue of financing cooperatives was incorporated within the movement through the establishment of an apex bank, the initial

4 Polly Hill, *The Gold Coast Cocoa Farmer* (London, 1956), 2.

5 Hill herself notes that the cooperators applying for certain loans through the cooperative system were not the 'typical pledgors', *ibid.*, 74–7. Another study has shown that the composition of cooperatives in the 1930s changed over time, suggesting that they were initiated by wealthier farmers investing more capital and, in later years, joined by farmers of more modest means, bringing the overall per capita capitalisation down – Chiara Cazzuffi and Alexander Moradi, 'Membership size and cooperative performance: evidence from Ghanaian cocoa producers' societies, 1930–36', *Economic History of Developing Regions* 27:1 (2012), 67–92.

6 Sven Beckert, Ulbe Bosma, Mindi Schneider and Eric Vanhaute, 'Commodity frontiers and the transformation of the global countryside: a research agenda', *Journal of Global History* 16:3 (2021), 435–50.

foundational phase in the 1930s was followed by a period of aggressive growth in the late 1940s and 50s.[7] The success of cooperatives, however, was short-lived – pressures on the movement proved too strong as market and state collapsed into one entity, global cocoa prices sank, and an overly ambitious developmental plan required generous cash infusions.

Despite this short-lived but intense institutional importance that cooperatives had, and the rare glance they offer into the economic history of Ghana, little scholarly historiography is available. A recent and excellent econometric study by Cazzuffi and Moradi is unfortunately limited to a part of the 1930s only.[8] Moreover, a handful of older studies, are either hagiographic in nature or have romanticised the precursors and potential of modern cooperation.[9] While this chapter lies a substantial distance away from a comprehensive study of cooperation, it maps the most significant developments in the early history of cooperatives in Ghana, sketches some of the movement's characteristics particular to the region and provides some suggestions for the further study of the subject. Before we turn to the cooperatives as such, however, we should first revisit some of the structural characteristics of the economy as well as some of the staples of the early cocoa boom that were to prove later of considerable influence on the fortunes of the movement.

Cocoa Boom and Cooperative Beginnings

The cocoa boom was central to the transformation of the political economy of Ghana between 1890 and the 1930s. As its various aspects are discussed at length in this edited volume, the following section will point only to some of the surrounding issues that were central for the establishment of cooperative legislation and cooperatives as well as the further development and eventual – yet temporary – demise of the movement. The cocoa boom in Ghana was part of a broader cash-crop revolution that took place in parts of West Africa in the period between c. 1890 and 1930. The revolution was best articulated in regions endowed with favourable land and was characterised by a substantial growth in the export of agricultural produce.[10]

7 As the number of cooperatives multiplied and new legislation came into existence, associations and unions were formed. In the case of Ghana, we can see that these secondary and apex institutions were Marketing Committees, a union of cooperatives, and eventually a Bank.

8 Cazzuffi and Moradi, 'Membership size'.

9 J.C. de Graft-Johnson, *African Experiment: Cooperative Agriculture and Banking in West Africa* (London, 1958); Marvin Miracle and Ann Seidman, *Agricultural Cooperatives and Quasi-Cooperatives in Ghana, 1951–1965* (Madison WI, 1968); Department of Cooperatives, *History of Ghana Cooperatives* (Accra, 1990).

10 Gareth Austin, 'Explaining and evaluating the cash crop revolution in the "peasant" colonies of Tropical Africa, c. 1890–c. 1930: beyond "vent for surplus"', in Emmanuel Akyeampong, Robert H. Bates, Nathan Nunn and James Robinson (eds), *Africa's*

Imports closely followed the exports, the latter being manufactured goods, textiles, and processed food. The Gold Coast and Ashanti and their bulging cocoa complex – including the production, marketing and transportation, and corollary capital allocation – were at the absolute forefront of the cash-crop revolution in West Africa. While the Ghanaian case partially fulfilled the so-called 'vent for surplus' theory originally postulated by Myint, particularly in the more intensive use and reclamation of land, a more remarkable aspect was the substantial increase in labour productivity.[11] In the long run, however, perhaps the most impactful developments were the institutional transformations that took place during the cocoa boom. Pledging of farms and markets in land-use rights and hired labour became widespread.[12]

The global market (read rising global demand) for cocoa was initially represented by several expatriate firms and an expanding and dynamic corpus of intermediaries. The United Africa Company, the offspring of the former Royal Niger Company, bought by W.H. Lever, and the African & Eastern Trade Corporation together with Miller Bros and F. & A. Swanzy, all merging in 1929, alone handled half of the overseas trade of West Africa in the 1930s. Tapping into the cocoa boom, there were also companies that specialised particularly in this commodity, the most prominent example of which was Cadbury. While there was also established merchant capital in the case of the Syrian-Lebanese traders as well as attempts to create export companies with indigenous or US American capital – we will return to the case of Winifred Tete-Ansa below – the fact remained that European firms dominated the export of cocoa up to the Second World War and the later creation of a state marketing board.

Here again, it should be noted that the companies' outreach was made possible by a growing number of Ghanaian traders, who bought cocoa and sold consumer goods that were the chief motivation to participate in an export economy in the first place. In the inter-war period, a complex and dynamic system of intermediaries or brokers existed and continually transformed. The relations and the relative power balance between the producers, brokers, and the expatriate firms have been the subject of a number of influential studies on the cocoa export economy and the series of hold-ups in the 1920s and 1930s. The commercial environment in the inter-war period favoured big export firms that had the capital to sustain a slump in the global prices and were able to advance money into the expanding trading networks in Ghana. The body of middlemen was highly diverse, including big cocoa farmers and salaried company brokers. The interests of the intermediaries were sometimes more aligned with those of the firms and sometimes closer to those of the producers – indeed, the

---

Development in Historical Perspective (Cambridge, 2014), 295–320; cf. A.G. Hopkins, *An Economic History of West Africa. Second Edition* (London, 2020 [1973]), 218–38.

11 Gareth Austin, 'Vent for surplus or productivity breakthrough? The Ghanaian cocoa take-off, c. 1890–1936', *Economic History Review*, 67:4 (2014), 1035–64.

12 Austin, 'Labour and land in Ghana'.

effectiveness of the ultimate hold-up of 1937–8 owed much to the participation of the brokers. While this network of intermediaries was in flux and various interests tried to subordinate it in part or as a whole, it should be reiterated that it was indispensable for both the expatriate firms and the producers.[13]

While the cocoa boom had brought affluence and dynamism to the rural economy of Ghana in an unprecedented way, it also entailed a number of risks and problems. For one, imports and exports were closely matched. This meant that negative trade terms could not only foment popular discontent when it came to a shrinking consumer basket, but also that they could hamper the diversification of the economy when it came to the import of machinery and other capital inputs. Further, in contrast to other agrarian economies where the highest portion of the revenue was made by taxes on land, the colonial state was for all intents and purposes dependent on cocoa exports for its budget. Around independence, foreign trade made around 30 per cent of the Gross Domestic Product of Ghana, and cocoa would have made around 60 per cent of the foreign trade on average in the same period.[14] The dependence on global demand and subsequently global pricing of cocoa, however, had introduced this volatility into the economy a long time ago.

Already in the 1920s, the colonial government identified two related problems regarding marketing. First, rather than a prime product on world markets, Ghanaian cocoa was more of a 'bulk' commodity. The reasons for this are beyond the scope of this chapter, but it suffices to say that the colonial government naively sought a fix that could improve the quality of cocoa and thus increase the state revenue. Second, a decisive component of the marketing of cocoa was the aforementioned system of advances that included European, Syro-Lebanese, and African cocoa-buyers and was 'locking farms to credit'.[15] Could cooperatives provide a possible solution to these issues?

Colonial officials certainly thought so. I have shown elsewhere that colonial civil servants prodded into existence a cooperative movement in South Asia around the turn of the century. The institution then gained speed and through the active propagation by cooperative experts cum imperial administrators became a role model for diverse regions of Africa and Asia.[16] Two figures illustrate this imperial connection in the formation of cooperative legislation

13 See for example Rhoda Howard, 'Differential class participation in an African protest movement: the Ghana cocoa boycott of 1937–38', *Canadian Journal of African Studies*, 10:3 (1976), 469–80.

14 Tony Killick, *Development Economics in Action: A Study of Economic Policies in Ghana* (2nd edn.: London, 2010 [1978]), 3.

15 Gareth Austin, *Labour, Land and Capital in Ghana: From Slavery to Free Labour in Asante, 1807–1956* (Rochester NY, 2005), 278–303.

16 Kamenov, 'Imperial cooperative', 219–37; see also Aaron Windel, *Cooperative Rule: Community Development in Britain's Late Empire* (Berkeley, 2021).

in Ghana. First, the aforementioned G.G. Auchinleck led the administrative attempts in Accra in seeking to emulate the South-Asian know-how. Auchinleck had previously worked in Mauritius and later in Ceylon, where, as a Divisional Agricultural Officer for North Ceylon, he published a study on West African palm oils. Auchinleck suggested that instead of improving the production in Africa, the 'foundation of a systemic plantation industry' could be pursued elsewhere, read Ceylon.[17] Ironically, his foremost task at his new post at the Agricultural Department of the Gold Coast was to find a way to improve the quality of cocoa. He advocated marketing cooperatives, started organising such and 'was mainly responsible for drawing up' the Cooperative Ordinance Bill in 1929.[18]

Around the same time the Department of Agriculture sent another official on a tour to India and Ceylon.[19] On a broader level, of particular importance was Claude Strickland, a former cooperative registrar for Punjab, who published a celebrated appeal for the formation of cooperatives throughout British Africa and, as cooperatives were seen as a perfect tool for indirect rule, the booklet was adorned with an introductory endorsement by Lord Lugard.[20] Strickland participated in the late 1920s in the editing for the Bill for the Gold Coast and Ashanti.[21]

I turn to the Ordinance below as it marked the official beginning of the movement in Ghana, but first two stories deserve some attention. The first is an African attempt formally to organise cooperative societies and a union with the hope on the one hand to consolidate a brokerage position and on the other to bypass the expatriate firms as an overseas exporter. The second story is the broader, non-contractual form of collaboration. Both had some bearing on the later development of cooperatives and deserve to be mentioned.

Winifred Tete-Ansa has been studied in the context of budding nationalism and its expression through economic activities. Hopkins identified Tete-Ansa as 'the most important figure' in translating the difficulties and frustration faced by West African farmers and entrepreneurs in their constrained pursuit of business expansion in the period between the First World War and the mid-1930s into anti-colonial sentiment and economic policies. Although his attempts were ultimately to prove unsuccessful, Tete-Ansa did not lose spirit

17 G.G. Auchinleck, *The West African Oil Palm and Its Products* (Colombo, 1923).

18 The British National Archives (henceforth TNA) CO96/688, *Co-operative Societies Ordinance*, unpaginated.

19 A.W. Paterson, *Studies in Co-operation in India and Ceylon* (London, 1929).

20 Claude Strickland, *Co-operation for Africa* (London, 1933); TNA, CO96/688, *Co-operative Societies Ordinance*, unpaginated.

21 Kamenov, 'Imperial cooperative', 29–34.

in his all-encompassing attempts at creating a vertical structure supposed to finance, market and export cocoa from the Gold Coast and Nigeria.[22]

Less attention has been paid to the fact that Tete-Ansa had chosen cooperatives as the institutional form that was supposed to supersede the European firms and retain surplus in Ghana and with the producers or, as he put it, 'the benefits [should] accrue to the Negro Race in world commerce.'[23] A central entity in Tete-Ansa's initial plan in the mid-1920s was the *West African Co-operative Producers*, an organisation registered as a company – it will be remembered no cooperative legislation existed at the time in the Gold Coast and Nigeria. The organisation, registered with limited liability, was supposed on the one hand to work as a marketing union for the producers of cocoa and on the other help in the formation of primary cooperative societies.[24] To supplement the cooperative, Tete-Ansa also registered a bank to extend loans to the cocoa producers. While these organisations were soon to go bankrupt, it seems that Tete-Ansa's efforts had a formative effect on the Department of Agriculture – '[t]he need of an organised system of Agricultural Credit on the Gold Coast was brought into prominence in 1925 by certain African gentlemen in Accra who placed a proposal before government for the establishment of Agricultural Bank.'[25] In reaction to this, the Department of Agriculture then decided to come up with its own program for the establishment of cooperatives. We will return to the question of capital allocation within this official scheme below.

Apart from Tete-Ansa's cooperative efforts that preceded the Ordinance, there was also the question of what might be called traditional forms of cooperation. As in every other society in the world, there were different forms of sharing of common resources in Ghana. Authors critical of the colonial cooperative scheme, early on criticised the alleged official disregard of such existing practices of cooperation. For example John C. de Graft-Johnson, a champion of cooperation, claimed – albeit fancifully – that the early success of the cocoa boom in Ghana was partially based on customary cooperation and particularly on 'the communal system of production and the communistic basis of native political organisation, [that] checked the spirit of selfishness which might have retarded the expansion of the industry.'[26] In contrast, scholars have duly laid emphasis on self-interest as the engine behind the cocoa boom and have shown how labour relations specific to the capitalist

22 A.G. Hopkins, 'Economic aspects of political movements in Nigeria and in the Gold Coast 1918–1939', *Journal of African History* 7:1 (1966), 133–52.

23 Winifred Tete-Ansa, *Africa at Work* (New York, 1930), 68.

24 *Ibid.*, 80–1.

25 Paterson, *Studies*, 1.

26 e Graft-Johnson, *African Experiment.*, p. 51.

mode of production emerged within the cocoa sector.[27] One particular form of 'cooperation,' that allegedly was wilfully disregarded by the colonial official in their formulation of cooperative laws, was the rotating credit and saving association known as *susu*.[28]

Both charges are not entirely unfounded but are also not completely fair. During the discussions of a cooperative legislation, it seems that traditional practices of sharing common resources were noted and the head of the Department of Agriculture G.G. Auchinleck expressed hopes that a modern cooperative movement would re-awaken a spirit of communal cultivation and sharing.[29] In the context of Nigeria, Strickland for his part commented clearly that he did not hope to reform the *Esusu* through cooperative law, but he also admitted that it was 'not without value if properly conducted.'[30]

This brings us, however, to one aspect of the initial cooperative legislation that invites more scepticism about the intentions of the colonial government – the issue of credit. The Gold Coast Ordinance, in contrast to its South Asian predecessors, provided neither for state support in terms of credit nor for a system for financing. Indeed, the issue was not simply neglected, but rather intentionally left unresolved. As I have shown elsewhere, European export firms were wary of the proposal to initiate a cooperative movement in Ghana, some even contacting the Secretary of State for the Colonies and claiming that much of the commercial and physical infrastructure in Ghana was owed to their investments. The Niger Company and the African & Eastern Trade Company thus commented that it would be wrong for the government to manage, control, and/or finance cooperatives.[31] It seems that the colonial government was receptive to this critique and

27 Gareth Austin, 'The emergence of capitalist relations in South Asante cocoa-farming c. 1916–33', *Journal of African History* 28:2 (1987), 259–79. It is interesting to note here that the Shephard report does not mention any previous form of cooperation or communal spirit that might have played a role in the cocoa boom, but rather dated the Ghanaian cooperative movement to Auchinleck's efforts starting in 1925. See C.Y. Shephard, *Report on the Economics of Peasant Agriculture in the Gold Coast* (Accra, 1936), 26.

28 This institution was borrowed from the Nigerian *esusu* (Yoruba) and *isusu* (Igbo). On the various types of rotating credit see Gareth Austin, 'Indigenous credit institutions in West Africa, c.1750–c. 1960,' in Gareth Austin and Kaoru Sugihara,(eds), *Local Suppliers of Credit in the Third World, 1750–1960* (Basingstoke, 1993), 93–159, particularly 102–3; William Bascom, 'The *esusu*: a credit institution of the Yoruba', in *Journal of the Royal Anthropological Institute of Great Britain and Ireland* 82:1 (1952), 63–9. In one of his discussions on the prospects of cooperatives in the Gold Coast in 1927, Auchinleck dismissed the *susu* as an institution unrelated to profitable and productive business: see Austin, *Labour, Land and Capital*, 537, n. 81.

29 de Graft-Johnson, *African Experiment*, 56.

30 C.F. Strickland, 'Report on the introduction of co-operative societies into Nigeria', in David Sunderland and Godfrey N. Uzoigwe, (eds), *Economic Development of Africa, 1880–1939*, vol. 5 (London, 2017 [1934]), 239.

31 Kamenov, 'Imperial cooperative', 232.

there was no provision for financial unions in the 1931 Ordinance. There were two crucial aspects in the here simplified chain between producer-broker-exporter: credit and the quality of the beans. The advancing of money to brokers was 'locking farms to credit'.[32] In the crop year 1933/4, for example, it was reported that 75 per cent of the farmers had pledged at least part of their next crop in return for advances.[33] Meanwhile, the firms and colonial government were preoccupied with the question of quality, blaming producers for the low grade of cocoa. Brokers were the fulcrum – they were the conduit of credit to producers and the controller of quality. As the new legislation was to foster new cooperative organisations, envisaged as a future replacement of the brokers, the relative emphasis on these two issues was decisive.

Indeed, cooperatives were initially seen as an institution that could teach producers to improve their cocoa and only parenthetically, if at all, as an institution that could allocate capital in efficient way. As a way of illustrating the last point, it suffices here to quote from the yearbook of the Department of Agriculture for 1930, where Capt. John Wingate provided a short guide for officers engaged in 'founding agricultural cooperative societies.' After calling the Omanhene of the division and asking him to use his influence with his chiefs in promoting cooperatives, meetings with farmers were to be meticulously planned. The first point to be raised at such a meeting concerned quality – '[t]he purity of Gold Coast cacao is lower than that of Ceylon, Java, and the West Indies. In those countries the farmers get a higher price for their cacao because they have prepared it much better than the Gold Coast farmers have done.'[34] In contrast, the issue of credit and finance was to be raised only as a fifth potential point, self-referentially noting that the government seeks to 'promote thrift amongst farmers' through the cooperatives.[35] The numbers of the pilot societies, formed before the Ordinance was passed, corroborate this bias – of the 116 societies operational in April 1931, 113 societies were cocoa producers' cooperatives, one was producing rice, and two were thrift and loan societies.[36]

The crux of the issue, however, was that there was no apex financing institution from which the cooperatives could borrow as legal entities in order to bypass the existing advances system. It was not until 1937 when the Ghanaian Ordinance was amended in accordance with the Nigerian one, itself providing for financial unions, that the issue of credit was addressed at least legally. It bears mentioning here that, while various authorities gave advice on how the

32 Austin, *Labour, Land and Capital*, 278–303.

33 Shephard, *Report*, 41.

34 John Wingate, 'Hints on forming co-operative societies', in Department of Agriculture, *Year-book 1930* (Accra, 1931), 12.

35 *Ibid.*, 13.

36 As mentioned above, producers' cooperatives were in fact marketing the produce of their members, see fn. 3.

Department should regulate and supervise credit *within* the societies, there were indications that cooperative members themselves insisted throughout the 1930s and early 40s that an apex bank should be created. The Shephard report, for example, remarked curtly that many:

> societies and individuals expressed a keen desire for the formation of an agricultural bank. There is a consensus of opinion that government should provide the entire capital, but no unanimity as to the amount required. The more modest advocates suggest an initial capital of £1,000,000. Bolder individuals consider that 'several millions' would be necessary [...][37]

Over ten years later, in 1948, the report of the Watson commission enquiring into the 'disturbances' of the same year, still similarly recommended the 'establishment by the Cocoa Marketing Board of a Cocoa Farmers Bank or Discount House' that was to perform credit services to farmers and cooperatives.[38]

So how did the initial 113 producer societies operate? First, it should be noted that they were concentrated in clusters, the more prominent of which were around Kumasi (the districts of Ashanti-Akim, Mampong, and Bekwai having altogether 42 societies) and Kofridua. An explicit goal of the Agricultural Department were villages around 'motorable roads'.[39] In practical terms, the societies collected the already fermented and dried beans of the members in a storage facility and, upon acquiring a sufficient amount, the beans would be certified by an officer of the Agricultural Department for quality and would be sold to the closest buying centre.[40] It bears mentioning here, however, that the Nowell report commented some eight year later that most 'societies have no store of their own and members keep their own stores or those of richer members of the Society pending its sale.'[41] A major goal of the early societies was to establish an economy of scale that in turn could improve the quality of the beans. In pursuing this objective, investments could include the creation of a larger drying facility – conventionally farmers would use a raised mat, but bigger operations could afford also sliding roofs of galvanised iron – and more conventionally scales, bags, and transport.[42]

According to various reports, the quality of the cocoa produced by the cooperatives for the year of 1930–31 was indeed substantially higher than the

37 Shepard, *Report*, 58.

38 Colonial Office, *Report of the Commission of Enquiry into Disturbances in the Gold Coast, 1948* (London: His Majesty's Stationary Office, 1948), 53.

39 J.C. Muir, 'Work of Co-operative Societies During 1930–31', in Department of Agriculture, *Year-Book 1930* (Accra, 1931), 16–25.

40 See for example Cazzuffi and Moradi, 'Membership size', 70.

41 William Nowell et al., *Report of the Commission on the Marketing of West African Cocoa* (London, 1938), 41.

42 Shephard, *Report*, 9–15, 26–31; cf. Cazzuffi and Moradi, 'Membership size', 74.

average obtained in the Gold Coast.[43] As a consequence, societies received a higher price from the buyers, the society keeping usually half of this difference – six pence from a shilling per load – leaving a modest mark up on the producer's profits.[44] There are conflicting numbers on the membership and the tonnage sold for the year, but it is safe to say that the were no fewer than 743 members who sold at least 516 tonnes through their respective cooperatives.[45] There were societies that reported profits, stemming from these service fees and from interest on credit disbursed to members, and distributed them as dividends.[46] This brings us to the issue of credit – the producers'/marketing cooperatives serviced their members with credit but only to the extent of the capital invested by members, as the cooperative itself was initially unable to borrow from elsewhere.

Even without a clear stipulation on how the question of credit and advances should – or even could – be bypassed, the cooperative movement took off slowly in the early 1930s, largely thanks to the continuous efforts of the Agricultural Department. Reports showed that most new societies were created as a result of active persuasion during agricultural instructors' field work in villages. As has been made clear by the quote from Wingate's 'hints' above, the nature of voluntary membership, one of the classical principles of cooperation, was severely challenged by the language and actions of the Agricultural Department.

Further evidence, for example from Birim North, corroborates the fact that the nascent cooperative movement in Ghana was not just top heavy but originally rather a colonial project. One document suggested that cocoa producers were cajoled into forming cooperatives – 'nine villages [in] some farmers, 49 in all, agreed to form societies, and at four other villages societies will probably be formed soon'.[47] The arrogance and frustration of one Captain V.W. Bratton, the main figure responsible for initiating these nine societies, is perceptible in his discussion of the difficulties in convincing farmers of the advantages of cooperation – the 'attitude of the people [towards the new organisation] was found to be one made up of the following elements: laziness, doubt and fear.'[48] Other reports related active propaganda work to a growing

43 According to the Shephard report it was 96.8 per cent as opposed to 89.1 per cent, a number that remained around the same mark in the following years: Shephard, *Report*, 15.

44 By 1938, there were commentators who argued that this small margin was not worth the extra costs and efforts that cooperative members had to put in, explaining why the growth rate of the cooperative movement did not meet previous expectations – Nowell, *Report*, 43.

45 Muir, 'Work', 16; cf. Shephard, *Report*, 26.

46 Muir, 'Work', 17–18.

47 Department of Agriculture Gold Coast, *Monthly News-Letter* (henceforth DAGC, *MNL*), 35, 1 April 1931, 6.

48 V.W. Bratton, 'The Co-operative Movement in North Birim', Department of Agriculture, *Year-Book 1930* (Accra, 1931), 28.

interest in cooperatives.[49] In contrast, slow progress was often associated with the hesitation of paramount chiefs to cooperate. Thus, in the state of Ajumaku, Saltpond District, the 'progress is hindered by the failure [sic] of the Omanhene to give his approval of the cooperative movement'.[50] There were also reports of 'anti-propaganda' carried out by brokers and intermediaries.[51]

Nonetheless, by the beginning of September 1931 the Agricultural Department could boast 205 societies, with a projection of 500 in 1932 and up to 1,000 in 1933. Simultaneously, a process of consolidation began. Dysfunctional societies were closed and inactive members expelled from the societies.[52] 'Disloyalty' remained a problem throughout the 1930s, partially due to the fact that members joining – or even founding – a society had typically already pledged a part of their produce.[53] It was estimated that even in 1936–37 more than a fifth of the cooperative members did not sell any cocoa through them.[54]

The most important development in the mid-1930s, however, was the formation of a secondary tier of cooperatives – District Unions and Joint Marketing Committees.[55] If the primary cooperatives were meant to replace brokers collecting cocoa directly from the villages, these new associations were meant to bypass brokers and intermediaries further down the commodity chain and sell directly to firms. By 1934 there were at least 127 of those, responsible for the sale of cocoa – an official from the department invited tenders from European firms. 'The tenders are then passed on to the committee of the Society or of the Union which is offering the cocoa, for its decision. When sold, the cocoa may be delivered by the Societies to the buyer's grading station by means of hired lorries, or it may be fetched by the buyer.'[56]

Despite all progress, the expectations for a meteoric growth proved unfounded. The number of cooperative cocoa societies in the Gold Coast and Ashanti in March 1938 stood at 385, with a membership of 9,711 and a 'paid-up' share capital of £26,422.[57] In the financial year 1936–7, leading up to the key political and economic event of the decade, the 'hold-up' of 1937–8, provoked by a price-fixing agreement among cocoa-buying firms, cooperatives marketed some 7,807 tonnes of cocoa for £318,371: a meagre 2.6 per cent of the overall supply.[58]

49 DAGC, *MNL*, 37, 15 June 1931, 4.
50 DAGC, *MNL*, 39, 15 August 1931, 8.
51 DAGC, *MNL*, 35, 1 April 1931, 5.
52 Department of Cooperatives, *History*, 31–2.
53 Cazzuffi and Moradi, 'Membership size', 81.
54 Nowell, *Report*, 41.
55 Department of Cooperatives, *History*, 32.
56 Nowell, *Report*, 41.
57 Nowell, *Report*, 40.
58 *Ibid*.

Growth and Consolidation: From War to the Golden 1950s?

To paraphrase an early analyst of cooperatives in the Gold Coast, both the 'hold-up' and the Second World War bore mixed blessings for the movement. Late 1939 saw the development of a controlled marketing scheme, under which the colonial government purchased the entire cocoa crop at a set price. While the scheme was initially planned as a temporary, wartime measure, it proved to be the origin of the Ghana Cocoa Marketing Board. Further, although the new system could be clearly traced back to the 'hold-up', it was in stark contrast to the recommendations of the Nowell commission that had suggested a drastic reorganisation of the cocoa marketing system, including the formation of a Farmers' Association with mandatory membership. This organisation was to take over the function of brokers and has been deemed a 'statutorily monopsonistic farmers' cooperative'.[59] In contrast, the marketing board allocated quotas to firms in accordance with their pre-war performance, securing *de facto* and *de jure* the market share of the European companies, which were now designated as 'A' shippers.

Cooperatives were classed as 'B' shippers, with a correspondingly small quota. However, the cooperatives' quota was raised by the government during the war, a move that with time encouraged loyalty in members, i.e., encouraged them to ship more of their produce through their societies.[60] While the number of members initially dropped, it rebounded by the end of the war. In the six-year span between 1938/39 and 1943/44, the proportion of cooperatively shipped cocoa to the gross tonnage of the Gold Coast rose four times, reaching in absolute terms 12,419 tonnes and rising from 1.6 per cent to 6.4 per cent of the overall Gold Coast production. The sales per member also rose substantially – from 0.498 to 1.928 tonnes per member, an almost four-fold increase. The wartime ban on advances theoretically also worked in favour of cooperatives, as brokers could not use their previous advantage, while members of cooperatives could borrow within the existing organisational structure. The growth of volume shipped by the cooperatives was reflected in the establishment of a new Department of Co-operation in 1944.

It should be noted that around the same time, the colonial policy hitherto regarding cooperation came under harsh criticism. In its report of 1945 on cooperatives in the colonies, the Fabian Colonial Bureau – an offshoot of the socialist Fabian Society, established during the war to investigate and incite public debate on colonial policies – pronounced that the administration in the

59 Rod Alence, 'The 1937–1938 Gold Coast cocoa crisis: the political economy of commercial stalemate', *African Economic History* (1990–1991) 19, 77–104.

60 Public Records and Archives Administration Department (PRAAD hereafter), RG4/2/4, Gold Coast Cooperative Societies, Annual Audit Report 1941–42, 2; cf. Department of Cooperatives, *History*, 47–9.

Gold Coast has 'repeated the mistakes of other Colonies'. Work was left to the Department of Agriculture instead of a dedicated Department of Co-operation with 'staff specially trained in the science of cooperation', resulting in 'wrong methods adopted in many instances.'[61] Moreover, the report claimed that the whole movement was an example of myopia and 'over-emphasis on immediate gains' rather than long-term planning and investment in education.[62]

Around the same time, Sir Alan Burns, the governor of the Gold Coast, published a plan for the development of the colony, contending that the building of the cooperative movement was his 'considered policy' and that the establishment of a dedicated department should ensure the conversion of marketing societies into credit and production societies.[63] The creation of the Department of Cooperation, which was inaugurated in April 1944, was thus meant to give the movement further impetus. The renewed institutional zeal was personified by recruits and consultants such as Brewster Surridge, formerly a registrar in Cyprus, and Captain Walter Cheesman, who was transferred from Nigeria. Apart from the now full-time positions of the Registrar, the Deputy Registrars and the Financial Officer, there were some 38 junior staff members, mostly seconded from the Department of Agriculture and other departments, but also around 10 fresh recruits. Junior staff members received a three-month in class course in the fundamentals of cooperation before being sent to the field.[64]

The first task of the newly established department was the further consolidation of the existing societies. From 1945 to 1946 the number of primaries fell further from 150 to 97, while the membership numbers rose another 10 per cent to reach 6,712. In its novel attempt to introduce smoother credit and clearing operations, the department insisted on the build-up of reserve funds. The reserves of the primary societies almost doubled between 1945 and 1946 from £4,531 to £8,326.[65] The most important development, however, came in October 1946. The Gold Coast Co-operative Bank was registered following the Co-operative Societies Ordinance of 1937 and allowed all registered societies – both primaries and unions – to be members of the bank. The decade following the creation of the Department of Co-operation and the apex bank was marked by a substantial growth – both nominally and proportionately – in the volume of cocoa shipped through cooperatives as well as a substantial growth in the cooperatives' assets and reserves.

Cooperative credit was at the absolute core of these developments; indeed, it could be argued that capital allocation was the stepping stone for the growth in

61 Fabian Colonial Society, *Co-operation in the Colonies: A Report from a Special Committee to the Fabian Colonial Bureau* (London, 1945), 70.

62 *Ibid.*, 72.

63 Alan Burns, *General Plan for Development in the Gold Coast* (Accra, 1944), 2.

64 Department of Cooperatives, *History*, 53.

65 *Ibid.*, 62.

the period. Between 1944 and 1952, credit disbursed on the primary level grew more than 25-fold from £8,339 to £214,944![66] More than doubling again in the span of three years, by 1955 loans to primaries reached their highest point at £526,036.[67] For the year 1951–52, for example, the Bank issued loans to the tune of £107,973, of which £90,673 was seasonal credit. The bank borrowed at 3 to 3½ per cent and lent at 3¾ to 6 per cent. Unions could loan further to primaries at a higher rate.[68] For the year 1955/6, the Bank had issued £241,000 in short-term loans and another £78,000 in long-term loans. In addition, it functioned as a midway house, between the Marketing Association and commercial banks, the latter extending credit to cooperative Marketing Unions through the bank – £425,000 in the mid-crop season and another £6,290,000 during the main season.

The accumulation of assets and the build-up of liquid reserves in the cooperatives were not exceptional but rather aligned with a broader colonial policy. In anticipation of a precipitous fall in world cocoa prices during the war, the core function of the Board, at least in theory, was to stabilise prices – build reserves while high prices and fat years lasted, cushion the blow when prices dropped. In addition, reserves from the board could also hypothetically be used for investments and a much-needed diversification of the economy. In practice, the board was used as a control mechanism against inflation.[69] As already noted imports were tightly bound to cocoa exports. This meant that once the world prices for cocoa started to improve in 1942/3, the restriction on prices paid to farmers by the board translated directly into a control of prices or, in other words, a regulation of inflation. In this sense, the build-up of reserves within the cooperatives was part of a general pattern of state-enforced prudence. Bypassing the question whether diligence and planning was in itself inefficient and whether market forces could have allocated resources more efficiently in the short run, it should be noted that in the long run neither the board nor the cooperative movement succeeded in diversifying or modernising the cocoa economy.

The cocoa cooperatives continued to grow at a spectacular rate in the late 1940s and the early 1950s. In the year 1953/4, the cooperatives marketed around 20 per cent of the produce purchased by the Cocoa Marketing Board, totalling £5,428,088. For the region of Ashanti, the figure marked by cooperatives was

66 Gold Coast Government, *Annual Report of the Department of Co-operation for the Year 1951–52* (Accra, 1953), 3.

67 Department of Co-operation, *Annual Report of the Department of Co-operation* (Accra, 1957), 1.

68 Gold Coast Government, *Annual Report*, 1953, 4.

69 Rod Alence, 'Colonial government, social conflict and state involvement in Africa's open economies: the origins of the Ghana Cocoa Marketing Board, 1939–46', *Journal of African History* 42:3 (2001), 397–416.

even higher, probably reaching 25 per cent.[70] These developments were also reflected in the fortunes of the apex bank in the mid-1950s, by now operating on a government guarantee of £1,500,000 and reaching a turn-over with its commercial bank clients of around £7,500,000 in the year 1956.[71] The leader of the Convention People's Party (CPP) and prime minister, Dr Kwame Nkrumah, laid the foundation stone of a new six-storey bank building in 1955. Cooperatives now owned a small fleet of trucks for the transport of produce.[72] Perhaps the most important development, however, was the continuous swelling of the number of members of primary societies, prompting one report to note that this was an 'indication that gradually the movement [was] getting down to the real farmer level and breaking through the screen of brokers at varying levels.'[73]

Downturn and Legacy

On the one hand, the ascendancy of the cooperatives as marketing and credit agent for the cocoa farmers played a crucial role in their own undoing. Cooperatives proved a huge temptation for the state, and in a way were victims of their own success story. On the other hand, while the growth could be easily mistaken for success, some of the structural problems leading to the demise of the movement were, if not apparent, already existent in the early 1950s. We look at those in turn.

The Gold Coast became independent from the United Kingdom in March 1957. The CPP had embraced cooperatives as a central organisation model in its programme and vested substantial hopes for the role of the institution in Ghana's prospective socialist development. The newly independent state, however, sought not just a continuation of standing practices but rather a leading role in the transformation of existing, and the creation of new, cooperative structures.[74] Cooperatives were to be subsumed under the heading of aggressive state developmentalist projects – the prime example being the Volta River Project. As the annual report on the development of cooperatives noted in 1953:

70 Department of Co-operation, *Report on the Department of Co-operation for the Year 1953–54* (Accra 1955), 1–3.

71 Department of Co-operation, *Annual Report*, 1957, 2.

72 Miracle and Seidman, *Agricultural Cooperatives*, 10.

73 Department of Co-operation, *Annual Report*, 1955, 3.

74 Keri Lambert, '"It's all work and happiness on the farms": agricultural development between the blocs in Nkrumah's Ghana', *Journal of African History* 60:1 (2019), 25–44; Ama Biney, *The Political and Social Thought of Kwame Nkrumah* (Basingstoke, 2011), 99–118; Gillian Brophy, 'African Socialism: The Theory and Practice of Kwame Nkrumah' (MA dissertation, Australian National University, 1972).

> [Ghana] is a country emergent, full of ambitious schemes and in a great hurry to execute them. The greatest is the [...] exploitation of bauxite deposits but carries with it potentials for irrigation, and for electrification on which the prospects of future secondary industries must so largely depend. [...] In such developments there will no doubt be opportunities for co-operative associations.[75]

Theoretically, the Marketing Board promised a floor price for producers when global demand was down.[76] In practice, however, during the Second World War the real producer prices were the lowest on record, while the board incurred a deficit only in the year 1941–2 and substantial surpluses in all other years between 1940 and 1945.[77] It could be argued that the price disincentive was exacerbated by the board.[78] As prices rebounded in the years following the war and culminating in 1955, the value of exported cocoa grew between 1945 and 1955. The volume of exports, or in other words of output, however, did not respond correspondingly, stagnating between 1940 and 1960 and, in fact, reaching and surpassing the record volume of 1936/7 only in the 1960s. Apart from the issue of nominal prices, perhaps the most important factor was the commodity terms of trade. While these fluctuated in the 1950s, it is important to note that in the years 1956 and 1957, Ghana's trade balance was in deficit for the first time in more than thirty years with the sole exception of 1937.[79] The introduction of a potentially non-convertible currency in 1961 exacerbated the inflation further. If 'extra-economic' factors, such as earlier attempts to control the expansionist planting of cocoa – for example the 1938 Ashanti Confederacy Council's prohibition of the formation of new cocoa farms – and swollen shoot disease, might have also contributed to the stagnation of exports, it seems evident by way of comparison that farmers in the 1940s and beginning of the 1950s were lacking the incentives that fuelled the previous

75 Gold Coast Government, *Annual Report*, 1953, 1.

76 See for example the *Report on Cocoa Control in West Africa and Statements on Future Policy*, Cmd 6554, (London 1944), in Geoffrey Kay (ed.) *The Political Economy of Colonialism in Ghana: A Collection of Documents and Statistics, 1900–1960* (London, 1972), 267–72.

77 Austin, *Labour, Land and Capital*, 331; Jonathan H. Frimpong-Ansah, *The Vampire State in Africa: The Political Economy of Decline in Ghana* (New Jersey, 1991), 57, 89; cf. Alence, 'Colonial government', 406.

78 P.T. Bauer, *West African Trade: A Study of Competition, Oligopoly and Monopoly in a Changing Economy*, (Cambridge, 1954); Douglas Rimmer, *Staying Poor: Ghana's Political Economy 1950–1990* (Oxford, 1992).

79 While the terms of trade cannot be extrapolated purely from trade balance numbers and *vice versa*, it could be noted that balance of payments crisis does point to imbalances in the domestic economy: J. Clark Leith, *Foreign Trade Regimes and Economic Development: Ghana* (New York, 1974). See, further, Alence's chapter in this volume.

expansion of the cocoa frontier.[80] After reaching a peak in 1964/5, production started to decline steadily for the next two decades. The decline of the Ghanaian industry was paralleled by the rise of cocoa production in the Côte d'Ivoire, Ghana progressively losing its share in the world market, from roughly 35 per cent in 1965 to just over 10 per cent by 1983.[81] Cooperatives were caught up in this broader picture.

When we combine the macroeconomic frame with the CPP's plans for a 'big push' towards the end of the 1950s, it becomes clear that the statutory monopoly could not suffice for the ambitions of the newly independent state – new sources for fiscal income were necessary. The focus of the state fell upon the cooperative movement which, as noted above, by this time was gradually replacing the old system of brokerage, not least by means of expanding credit services. By 1960, cooperatives had taken over some 40 per cent of the marketing of cocoa.[82] Shortly after 1957, it became evident that the CPP had planned a complete overhaul of the existing cooperative structures. The United Ghana Farmers' Council (UGFC) had been founded in 1953 as part of CPP's attempt to organise cocoa farmers and bring them into the fold of its political and economic goals.[83] At independence, the government instructed the state Cocoa Marketing Board to subsidise the UGFC annually and make it one of its licensed buying agents, recognised the latter as an official representative of Ghana's farmers, and undertook to build a not inexpensive headquarters for the Council.[84] A branch of the UGFC called the Ghana Farmers Marketing Co-operatives Limited started operations in the same year. Two more events in the following years had a crucial bearing on the faith in the cooperative movement.

Fractures and imbalances along territorial lines were coming to the surface throughout the decade. In 1954, the National Liberation Movement (NLM) was inaugurated in Kumasi, an Ashanti-based political party with the avowed goal of creating a federal state in opposition to what its leaders believe were centralist tendencies emanating from the CPP. The foremost goal of the NLM in economic terms was to devise policies to retain more of the surplus generated

80 On the new cocoa farms see Austin, *Labour, Land and Capital*, 325–32. See, further, Austin's chapter in this volume.

81 Francis Teal, 'The foreign exchange regime and growth: a comparison of Ghana and the Ivory Coast', *African Affairs* 85:339 (1986), 267–82; Jeffrey Herbst, *The Politics of Reform in Ghana, 1982–1991* (Berkeley, 1993), 17–37.

82 Miracle and Seidman, *Agricultural Cooperatives*, 14.

83 For the most detailed study of the UGFC see Björn Beckman, *Organising the Farmers: Cocoa Politics and National Development in Ghana* (Uppsala, 1976).

84 Department of Cooperatives, *History*, 70.

by cocoa for the farmers – read more money for the region.[85] These developments had an effect on the cooperative movement.

A year later, in 1955, an Ashanti regional organisation broke off from the major umbrella organisation, the Ghana Co-operative Marketing Associations Limited (GCMA), causing issues in accounting as well as concern and exasperation within the existing cooperative structures. The annual report of the department claimed that there were indications that 'the formation of the Region was not based on the clear understanding of the implications by the common body of members, but was rather an institution forced from above, by a small number of the 'leaders' of Ashanti Co-operative thought.'[86] In the following year, four of the seven local unions of the new 'region' decided to rejoin the original cooperative association. This 'served only to harden the resolve of the supporters of the "Ashanti Region" plan. These consisted of the Kumasi, Sunyani and Sechere-Mponua Unions'.[87] To resolve the issue, the cooperative association held a number of meetings with the cooperative 'separatists', offering Kumasi a more substantial representation on the board. The proposition was accepted and a 'dangerous split' seemed temporarily averted. In 1960, however, the cooperatives in Ashanti, Brong Ahafo and Sefwi formed a new Cooperative Association, ABASCO.

Even more destabilising for the existing cooperative edifice was the government assault on the Bank. In 1960, the department report described the bank as 'the financial nerve-centre of the Movement'.[88] The Bank was in process of reform, for example now directly seeking to recover arrears and collateral from defaulting primaries rather than from their unions. The repayment of loans seemed to be improving owing to a new 'policy of discriminating between good and bad borrowers more rigorously.' This involved the holding of 'itinerant meetings at the headquarters of various unions, where the officers of the societies and unions met the Bank Committee, listened to some home truths, and received assistance in devising methods of recovering amounts long outstanding,' as well as an extension of the medium-term loans 'to accord more with realities.' In addition, the finances of the Bank were further strengthened by growing public trust in its savings department.[89] Such developments notwithstanding, a campaign criticising the workings of the bank, carried out by the press associated with the CPP, instigated a number of

85 See for example Jean Marie Allman, *The Quills of the Porcupine* (Madison WI, 1993), 16–50.

86 Department of Co-operation, *Annual Report*, 1955, p. 3.

87 Registrar of Co-operative Societies, *Annual Report of the Registrar of Co-operative Societies, 1954–55*, (Accra, 1956), 2.

88 Department of Co-operation, *Annual Report of the Department of Co-operation for the year 1958–59* (Accra 1960), 1.

89 *Ibid.*, 9.

enquiries. While some of these, for example the Gotts Enquiry, which reported in July 1960, did not consider that the bank should be closed,[90] its registration was revoked in November 1960 and liquidators were appointed. At the time of liquidation all cooperative financing for production and marketing as well as short-term and long-term loans were managed by the bank. It was also the repository of various thrift and saving societies.[91] While this restructuring certainly threw the existing cooperative system in disarray, it could be argued that it further had a destabilising effect on the whole economy.

The 'Dawn Broadcast' is often quoted as a turning point in Ghanaian history. Four years after independence, in April 1961, Kwame Nkrumah's broadcast criticised party members for amassing personal wealth and charted a new course towards a 'socialist pattern of society'. In matters of cocoa, Nkrumah informed his listeners that he had 'instructed that the United Ghana Farmers' Council, which embraces all the farmers of Ghana, should be given the sole responsibility for organising the purchase of all cocoa produced in Ghana on behalf of the Cocoa Marketing Board.'[92] What deserves attention in this chapter is that the broadcast spelled the end of the cooperative movement as it had existed so far. Existing cooperative licensed marketing agents like the GCMA and ABASCO lost their legal status. In June they were nationalised – the Ministry of Agriculture directed the UGFC immediately to take over all assets and liabilities of the existing cooperatives. While the UGFC bought much of the fixed capital of the foreign buying agents, now forced to leave, it did not give compensation for any cooperative assets, which at the time were valued at around £4.5 million. Indeed, the long-term credibility of the cooperative institution was further damaged by the disregard of much of the liabilities that cooperatives had incurred to date.[93]

Cooperatives were now practically a state instrument for taxation. Moreover, they were now caught up in a macroeconomic framework in which the state and the market for the still most important cash crop had coalesced into one entity. While the predicament of the cooperatives could be seen as part of the problem facing the economy as a whole, the movement had failed to diversify. It is beyond the scope of this chapter to go into the details of that story. It suffices to note that the two most promising attempts in this regard were the formation of a consumer cooperatives association that proved to be

90 Government of Ghana, *Report of the Commission of Enquiry into the Circumstances leading to the take-over by the erstwhile United Ghana Farmers Council Co-operatives of the Business and Assets of the Former Co-operative Societies* Part I (Accra, 1960), 23.

91 Department of Cooperatives, *History*, p. 73.

92 Kwame Nkrumah, 'Dawn Broadcast', https://www.eaumf.org/ejm-blog/2018/4/8/april-8–1961-nkrumahs-dawn-broadcast-condemns-corruption-in-the-cpp-and-government (accessed 8 April, 2024).

93 Department of Cooperatives, *History*, 85.

uncompetitive vis-à-vis the trade networks distributing consumables in the early 1950s, and a diamond cooperative. State-led attempts to diversify the agricultural sector through cooperatives and state farms could not turn the tide in the 1960s.[94]

While mild attempts between 1966 and 1972 to undo some of the harmful effects of state control failed genuinely to liberalise the economy, it could be argued that they succeeded in erasing the ideological underpinnings of the CPP's 'socialist pattern'.[95] The cooperatives, now turned into more conventional businesses and devoid of additional services and benefits, could not achieve the prominence and effectiveness they had enjoyed in the 1950s.[96] New grass-roots organisations have appeared since the 1990s and in some cases, such as the Kuapa cooperative (examined in Amoah-Boampong's chapter, next), have shown considerable resilience.

Conclusion

The economic fortunes of Ghana in the twentieth century were tightly connected to the trade associated with one dominant cash crop – cocoa. The history of cooperatives can be plotted in parallel with this story of boom and bust. They came into prominence with a promise for the creation of economies of scale and the introduction of stability in a system of marketing otherwise marked by enormous flux and dynamics. However, while these remained only promises, the original impetus given by the colonial state – itself aspiring to higher revenues – focused on the question of the quality of produce and neglected the more pressing issue of financing and, more broadly, capital allocation. This was only addressed towards the end of the 1930s, but any growth of the movement was now predicated on wartime realities and a new statutory monopoly by the state over the purchase and export of cocoa. While taxing continued through a marketing board after 1945, real prices improved and a cooperative movement centred around a new apex bank grew rapidly in the late 1940s and 1950s. Indeed, the cooperatives were so successful in replacing the existing system of brokerage that they soon proved too influential for their own good. As independence dawned, cooperatives came to signify a supplementary opportunity for the extraction of surplus. As state and market became one, the future of the institution became even more bound to the

94 Miracle and Seidman, *Agricultural Cooperatives*. For a recent appraisal of the social function of state farms under the CPP see Sarah Kunkel, 'Modernising the village: state farms, agricultural development, and nation-building in 1960s Ghana', *Zeitschrift für Unternehmensgeschichte* 67:2 (2022), 219–44.

95 Killick, *Development Economics in Action*, 32, 60–72.

96 E.g. Crawford Young, Neal P. Sherman and Tim H. Rose, *Cooperatives and Development: Agricultural Politics in Ghana and Uganda* (Madison WI, 1981), 203–14.

macroeconomic path of the country. While the story of Ghana's cooperatives is not one of linear progress, it does tell us much about the institution as such. To put this in the context of previous scholarship that has blamed a 'vampire state' for the adverse economic tides[97] – cooperatives were no silver bullet. They did not diversify the agrarian economy of Ghana and were neither resilient nor agile enough to weather the severe economic downturn from the 1960s onwards.

97 To quote the title of Frimpong-Ansah's book cited above.

10

Gender, Cocoa and the Political Economy of Ghana, 1891–2011

CYRELENE AMOAH-BOAMPONG

Cocoa is one of the bedrocks of the economy of the Republic of Ghana. Women in cocoa production were an important economic force during the long twentieth century. However, women's significant roles in agriculture have not translated into equality of opportunities concerning access to productive resources, markets, and services. Globally, the confectionery companies acknowledge the importance of women at the consumer end of the cocoa-chocolate value chain; but with less recognition at the production end.

Reflecting on gender–power relations and driven by a desire to engage with women's accounts of their experiences, this chapter draws on archival documents, forty oral history interviews and ten focus groups conducted from March 2009 to July 2015. Ten men and thirty women in cocoa farming in Ashanti, Central and Western regions were interviewed to examine gender relations in cocoa production during the long twentieth century with a focus between 1993 and 2013.[1] Interviews and focus group discussion notes were transcribed and coded using a thematic approach to identify, analyse and report patterns (themes) within the data. Most of the men and women were in their sixties and seventies (62 to 78 years), which places their initial experiences of cocoa farming from the 1940s into the 1950s with the youngest respondent at 62 years being a teenager in the early 1960s. All the interviewees grew up at a time when Ghana's cocoa economy was firmly established and women's ownership of cocoa farms became far more common, although women's plots

1 Archival documents were from the Public Records and Archives Administration Department (PRAAD) Kumasi, Manhyia Archives, Cocobod and Kuapa Kokoo Farmers' Union's constitution, membership lists, minutes from Annual General Meetings (AGM), fair trade audit reports. Oral interviews were in the Juaso district in Ashanti, Twifo Praso district in the Central Region and the Asankragwa district of the Western Region. These districts were chosen as the old cocoa frontier was in the Ashanti region before it moved to the Central Region and is currently in the Western Region. Communities were also selected due to their willingness to participate and because Kuapa Kokoo Farmers' Union operated within these regions.

were generally smaller and limited, as Grier states, 'by the labor she could spare, by the willingness of her kin members and spouse to help her out, and by her ability to acquire a pawn or hire a laborer'.[2] This initial visibility of women in cocoa production documented by Okali, Grier, Allman, and Austin waned by the height of neo-liberalism in 1992 where issues of gender equality within the cocoa sphere were a matter of rhetoric with the reality being greater opportunity for men to succeed in cocoa farming.[3]

A glimmer of hope came from an unlikely quarter, namely the resurgence of cocoa cooperatives after their decline in the 1950s.[4] Cocoa farmers such as Nana Frimpong Abrebrese re-asserted the need to take collective action in defence of cocoa farmers' interests in the market as demonstrated by the Ghanaian cocoa hold-ups of 1937–38. He established a new cooperative, Kuapa Kokoo Farmers' Union (KKFU) in the cocoa boom landscape of 1993.[5] KKFU provided a much-needed avenue for some disadvantaged women in cocoa production to have a voice and agency and start to change the terms of women's engagement in the cocoa chain. This took place amidst a global cocoa boom of the 1990s that boosted the prosperity of women and men in cocoa farming as poverty rates among cocoa farmers generally more than halved.[6] Yet, beyond this macro,

2 Beverly Grier, 'Pawns, porters, and petty traders: women in the transition to cash crop agriculture in colonial Ghana', *Signs* 17:2 (1992), 304–28, at 322.

3 On initial gender relations within cocoa farming see Christine Okali, 'Kinship and Cocoa Farming in Ghana', in Christine Oppong (ed.), *Female and Male in West Africa* (London, 1983), 169–78; Jean Allman, 'Rounding up spinsters: gender chaos and unmarried women in colonial Asante', *Journal of African History*, 37 (1996), 195–214; Gareth Austin, *Labour, Land and Capital in Ghana: From Slavery to Free Labour in Asante, 1807–1956* (Rochester NY, 2005), chs 16, 18, 19.

4 For the demise see Kamenov in this volume. For the earlier history of the cooperative movement in Ghana see also John Coleman de Graft-Johnson, *African Experiment: Cooperative Agriculture and Banking in British West Africa* (London, 1958), esp. 56; Chiara Cazzuffi and Alexander Moradi, 'Why Do Cooperatives Fail? Big Versus Small in Ghanaian Cocoa Producers' Societies, 1930–36', *Working Paper Series,* 0110 (Centre for the Study of African Economies, Oxford, 2010); Cyrelene Amoah-Boampong, 'Contesting the state in Ghana's cocoa trade: the case of the Kuapa Kokoo Farmers' Union, 1957–2004' (Ph.D. dissertation, Southern Illinois University, Carbondale, 2011); Nikolay Kamenov, 'Imperial cooperative experiments and global market capitalism, c.1900–c.1960', *Journal of Global History* 14:2 (2019), 219–37.

5 Kuapa Kokoo Farmers' Union is currently known as Kuapa Kokoo Cooperative Cocoa Farmers and Marketing Union Limited-KKFU. For perspective on the history of collective action by small exporters, see Gareth Austin, 'No elders were present': commoners and private ownership in Asante, 1807–1896', *Journal of African History*, 37:1 (1996), 1–30, at 22–30.

6 The highest poverty reduction was recorded between 1991 and 1998 when national poverty reduced by 13 percentage points, compared to 11 points during 1998–2005. See World Bank, *Republic of Ghana: Ghana Work Program (FY15): Poverty and Inequality Profile,*

structural view Aryeetey and Kanbur noted that poverty has 'important gender dimensions, with most indicators showing that women face higher levels of deprivation compared with men'.[7] The micro-evidence at the farm level of high growth rates, increased producer price for cocoa, lower income poverty and wealth creation of the 1990s was not felt equally by all cocoa producers. Women in cocoa, especially female cocoa farmers, experienced limited benefits as the share of hired labour in the cocoa-farm workforce nearly halved because of rising wages charged for cocoa tasks. Male cocoa farmers, on the other hand, resorted to more affordable family labour–notably matrikin.[8] This analysis was buttressed by Berry as she noted that farmers with limited resources and negotiation powers, such as migrant labourers and women on family land, were 'systematically excluded' from the distribution of profits resulting from cocoa commercialisation.[9]

Additionally, Aryeetey and Kanbur show that there was a traumatic history to the growth story as 'the most unstable macroeconomic environment was in the 1990s with the monetary, exchange-rate and fiscal policies inconsistent with one another…the government continuously ran large deficits that had to be financed by printing money and borrowing both domestically and externally'.[10] This led to bouts of inflation, exchange-rate depreciation and high nominal and real interest rates such that by 2002, the New Patriotic Party (NPP) sought relief under the Highly Indebted Poor Countries (HIPC) Initiative. The positive macro-level data on growth and poverty was not felt equally by all cocoa farmers. Indeed, cocoa farmers are not a homogenous group but are differentiated by access to resources and profits from cocoa production based on their status, gender, land-ownership and labour arrangements. For women in cocoa, inequality increased in various dimensions after cocoa production collapsed in the 1970s to 1983 and the promise of improved living standards from then on into the 1990s became a mirage. In neighbouring Côte d'Ivoire, Chauveau and

---

Report ACS13977 (Washington DC, 2015), 8.; Ghana Statistical Service, *Poverty Trends in Ghana in the 1990s* (Accra, 2000), 3.

7 Ernest Aryeetey and Ravi Kanbur, 'Ghana's economy at half-century: an overview of stability, growth and poverty', in their (eds), *The Economy of Ghana: Analytical Perspectives on Stability, Growth and Poverty* (London, 2008), 13.

8 Marcella Vigneri and Shashi Kolavall, *Growth through Pricing Policy: The Case of Cocoa in Ghana* (Rome, 2018), 15.

9 Sara Berry, *No Condition is Permanent: The Social Dynamics of Agrarian Change in Sub-Saharan Africa* (Madison WI, 1993), 157–8.

10 Ernest Aryeetey and Ravi Kanbur, *The Economy of Ghana*, 7–8. For a review of the macroeconomic situation in the 1990s see Curtis Youngblood and David Franklin, 'Persistent public sector deficits and macroeconomic instability in Ghana', in Ernest Aryeetey and Ravi Kanbur (eds), *The Economy of Ghana: Analytical Perspectives on Stability, Growth and Poverty* (London, 2008), 78–94; Harold Coulombe and Andrew McKay, *Selective Poverty Reduction in a Slow Growth Environment: Ghana in the 1990s* (Washington DC, 2003).

Léonard assert that 'between 1988 and 1992, the effective farm gate price of cocoa fell to nearly a third of former levels. In 1988, and again in 1993, cocoa growers were not even able to sell their crop. All in all, farmers faced a reduction of 60 to 80 per cent in their monetary income'.[11]

An analytical lens of women's empowerment developed by the Bill and Melinda Gates Foundation and the Royal Tropical Institute in Amsterdam was adopted. In this study, empowerment was defined as 'the expansion of choice and the strengthening of voice' through the transformation of power relations so that women and men in cocoa-growing regions have greater control over their lives and futures.[12] In this conceptualisation, agency is at the heart of empowerment, and it is centred around the capacity to take purposeful action and the ability to express views and make decisions free from the threat of violence or retribution and the 'capacity to make decisions and act on opportunities that lead to economic advancement'.[13] However, agency needs to work in tandem with resources and institutional structures to be gender transformative and create entry points for gender-intentional interventions in the cocoa sector. This definition of empowerment does not negate male involvement, as women's engagement is relational and cannot be examined in isolation from men. The analysis in this chapter also recognises the intersectionality of women in cocoa cultivation in terms of their land ownership, labour status, and socio-economic position which impacts their empowerment.

The chapter is structured as follows. First, it sets the historical context of cocoa production focusing on gender relations and the role of women in cocoa cultivation from the Gold Coast into Ghana. The gradual move to unequal opportunities for women in cocoa production is highlighted. Finally, the role of cocoa cooperatives as an avenue for the redress of gender inequality for improving gender relations in the cocoa sector is discussed and assessed.

Gendering Cocoa Production

The conditions and experiences of women in cocoa production may be appreciated from a historical perspective. Social relations of production in agriculture in the Gold Coast transitioned from the early nineteenth century

11 Jean-Pierre Chauveau and Eric Léonard, 'Côte d'Ivoire's pioneer fronts: historical and political determinants of the spread of cocoa cultivation' in William Clarence-Smith (ed.), *Cocoa Pioneer Fronts Since 1800: The Role of Smallholders, Planters and Merchants* (London, 1996), 176–94, at 187.

12 Anouka van Eerdewijk, Franz Wong, Chloe Vaast, Julie Newton, Marcelo Tyszler and Amy Pennington, *White Paper: A Conceptual Model of Women and Girls' Empowerment* (Amsterdam, 2017), 17.

13 Erin Markel and Lindsey Jones, 'Women's economic empowerment: pushing the frontiers of inclusive market development' (USAID and LEO Brief, 2014), 3.

when export-crop cultivation commenced with oil palm plantations sustained by slave labour.[14] During this era, both men and women had access to land in principle. Land was viewed as a communal possession vested in the custodianship of traditional rulers on behalf of the living, the dead and the unborn in Ghanaian society. In practice, however, this traditional right did not operate on equal terms for both sexes. Women, who were expected to marry, married early. Indeed, all the thirty female interviewees of this study were or had been married. Women bore the burden of what Grier calls pre-capitalistic, exploitative gender relations as they engaged in domestic chores and were under the yoke of customary law obligations, which required them to assist their husbands with the cultivation of their farms.[15] Thus, to fulfil these marital duties, the few women fortunate enough to own farmland before the 1920s gave it up when they married or maintained smaller portions which they could handle alongside their husband's farm, given their inability to hire labour. Ama Akyea, a seventy-eight-year-old woman noted 'for my mother, farming for her husband came before any other activity, me and my brother and two sisters managed her food crop farm. It was hard work'.[16]

By the late nineteenth century, Amanor states that the palm oil market collapsed, and rubber production became the next big economic venture.[17] Unfortunately, the ascendancy of rubber was short-lived with shifts in global production markets as oil palm was transferred from West Africa to production on large estates in Southeast Asia against which West African producers could no longer compete. Ghanaian agricultural producers located another viable alternative for the export market. They found this in cocoa and ploughed all the profits made from oil palm and rubber plantations into the purchase of virgin forest land.[18]

As in parts of south-east Ghana, Côte d'Ivoire also turned to cocoa to cope with falling commodity prices from palm oil and rubber. However, the establishment of French rule in south-west Côte d'Ivoire, 'nipped in the bud the promising development of cash crops' as the French delayed the adoption of cocoa cultivation and relegated the people of the south-west into forced-labour reserves rather than supporting their initial foray into cash-crop agriculture.[19]

14 Austin, *Labour, Land and Capital*, 47.

15 Grier, 'Pawns, porters and petty traders', 304.

16 Personal interview with Ama Akyea, June 2009 at Juaso, Ashanti.

17 Kojo Amanor, 'Family values, land sales and agricultural commodification in south-eastern Ghana', *Africa* 80, 104–25, at 107. Also see Kwame Arhin, 'The economic and social significance of rubber production and exchange on the Gold and Ivory Coasts, 1880–1900', *Cahiers d'etudes Africaines* 20, 49–62.

18 The political economy dynamics of the cocoa value chain in Ghana dated back to 1879. See James E.K. Amoah, *Development of Consumption, Commercial Production and Marketing*, Cocoa Outline Series 1 (Accra, 1995).

19 Chauveau and Léonard, 'Côte d'Ivoire's pioneer fronts', 178.

In the case of Ghana, the cocoa industry developed independently of official policy interventions and largely on the initiatives of Ghanaian farmers.[20] Cocoa expansion was possible through the investment of family and hired migrant labourers from the northern part of Ghana and the Sahelian region who cleared the forest land and led to the institutionalisation of the cocoa industry in Ghana. Ghana became the leading cocoa producer from 1910/11 and held this position until the late 1970s.[21]

Allman contends that in these early years of the cocoa revolution, 'wives' labour increasingly became, for most men, absolutely essential for the establishment of a farm. Few had the means to pay for hired labour',[22] especially in Ashanti where Arhin noted 'in spite of their matrilineal inheritance system, the Ashanti basic unit of labour in mining, trading and farming has always been the conjugal family'.[23] Thus, the expropriation of women's labour in cocoa production had a central role in the process of capital accumulation and socio-political relations in the cocoa-growing regions of Ghana. This was because, in pre-colonial and early colonial Ghana, land was plentiful and labour scarce.[24]

Migrant labourers began to move into cocoa-producing regions by the 1920s. There were diverse labour arrangements, such as shared labour groups, payment of a fixed annual sum, payment of one-third or half of the harvested crop, and payment through sharecropping contracts. However, the struggle to gain and maintain access to, and control over, the labour-power of women (be they wives, daughters, sisters, nieces, pawns or slaves) continued as it lowered the cost of cocoa production and maximised profits. Moreover, the double reproductive power of women as producers who performed a sizeable part of the agricultural tasks and as reproducers of the labour force made women's labour prized objects of control in the cocoa economy.[25] Nevertheless, no matter how long women were tied to their husbands as sources of labour in cocoa production they benefited little from their labour, since the early cocoa farms especially in Asante were owned by men and, as Austin notes, 'the matrilineal

20 Polly Hill, *The Migrant Cocoa-Farmers of Southern Ghana: A Study in Rural Capitalism* (Cambridge, 1963), 11. Hill argues that migrant cocoa farmer constituted a class of agrarian capitalists investing in the purchase of land, and hiring of labour, and reinvesting their profits in expanding investments of land in new areas. Hill challenged the dominant assumptions of the period: 'the myth of the sedentary peasant farmers who, though unfamiliar with the cash economy, nonetheless succeeded in the space of twenty years in transforming the economy of Ghana'.

21 Austin, *Labour, Land and Capital*, 2.

22 Allman, 'Rounding up spinsters', 208.

23 Kwame Arhin, 'Succession and gold-mining at Manso Nkwanta', *Research Review* (Institute of African Studies, University of Ghana) 6:3 (1970), 101–9, at 107.

24 Austin, *Labour, Land and Capital*.

25 Grier, 'Pawns, porters and petty traders', 307.

system actually entailed the separation of husbands' and wives' possessions'.[26] The situation of women in cocoa farming was exacerbated by the land tenure system as British colonial rule placed land under the authority of chiefs. The cultural gendering of agricultural work saw men as the legitimate owners of farmland under diverse land arrangements, whereas women were 'helpers' who worked on family farms. In a focus group discussion at Juaso in the Ashanti region, Ama, a female cocoa farmer narrated 'as a woman, getting a piece of land to farm, I need the help of my husband. Here to get land is a man's work. Women who have land inherit it or have money to buy it. This is not common here.' Afia, wife of a cocoa farmer, agreed with Ama and opined that 'if a woman wants to start a cocoa farm, she needs her husband to agree and get the land for her. If you are not on good terms with the man, he will refuse to lead you.' Abena interjected that 'for the women who think they are lucky, and their husband give them land as a gift, the man can take it back whenever he feels like it. This land is not yours and you must always be quiet and do as you are told.' The lack of formal ownership of cocoa farms was problematic for women's empowerment, as women in cocoa farming had to be submissive to men to access the land 'gifted' to them.

During this initial phase of cocoa expansion in the early twentieth century, political and economic circumstances in Ghana led to the further entrenchment of colonial rule with its tax obligations. Furthermore, there was the availability of alternative sources of wage labour beyond agricultural production to meet these tax obligations. Thus, the labour of young male farm workers was diverted into mining, as they served as carriers and construction workers. This further impacted the availability of male agricultural labourers and increased the reliance on family labour, notably women. Ghana was not unique in this situation, as its neighbour Côte d'Ivoire also experienced an influx of migrants from Burkina Faso forced to migrate to meet tax obligations and also motivated by a depreciated franc that raised the local cocoa prices.[27]

The effects of British colonial rule on women in the agricultural sector were felt with the continuation of the commercialisation of land. This led to individualisation of tenure in cocoa-growing areas in favour of men and supported the accumulation interests of some men by providing an avenue of escape out of the labour force, as they dealt in land transactions as buyers and sellers instead of cultivators. Yaw Attah of Asankragwa noted, 'My father used to farm on Opanyin Kojo's farm but soon he made a lot of money selling land and we stopped going with him to that farm'.

Women, under colonial rule, experienced a new gendered pattern of production as men, who had always been culturally perceived as providing

26 Austin, *Labour, Land and Capital*, 172.

27 Chauveau and Léonard, 'Côte d'Ivoire's pioneer fronts', 179.

income, were encouraged to assume the sole privilege of cultivating cash and export crops, as well as controlling the proceeds from this venture. Women, on the other hand, continued to be marginalised in producing food crops. This dichotomy of gender roles stemmed from the degeneration of the legal status of women with the imposition of the British judicial system under the enactment of the Gold Coast Supreme Court Ordinance of 1876. This provided for the enforcement within the jurisdiction of the court of the common law, the doctrines of equity and '"the statutes of general application which were in force in England at the date when the colony obtained a local legislature, that is to say on the 24th day of July, 1874".'[28]

British jurisprudence did not recognise the rights that Ghanaian customary law afforded married women, where each party maintained a separate and distinct identity and women had a right to own property. Customarily, women during the pre-colonial era had an independent legal personality. Indeed, in the traditional political arena, women took part in the governance of their respective communities through the institution of the office of the Queen Mother who served as an adviser to the chief and played a vital role in the election and removal of future chiefs.[29] Under British law, upon marriage, there was a merger of the identity of husband and wife. The common assertion is that 'by marriage the husband and wife are one person in law and that the very being or legal existence of the woman is suspended during the marriage or at least is incorporated and consolidated into that of the husband: under whose wing, protection, and cover, she performs everything' was the norm in Britain and imposed on the people of the Gold Coast Colony.[30] This change in the legal position of women forced women in the Gold Coast to grapple with an alien system of Victorian morality and values and worsened the already comparatively inferior position vis-à-vis men. It also led to the inability of Gold Coast women to own their property and thus the loss of their farms to their husband or male kin in some cases.

A gendered division of labour between women and men characterised on-farm activities. Women's tasks of intercropping food crops, weeding the farm, harvesting the cocoa pods, breaking them open, scoping out the cocoa beans, transporting the beans to be dried, and fermenting the beans were described in terms of 'light work' and peripheral to cocoa production

28 Quoted in Gordon Woodman, 'British legislation as a source of Ghanaian law: from colonialism to technical aid', *Law and Politics in Africa, Asia and Latin America* 7:1 (1974), 19–32, at 20–1.

29 Cyrelene Amoah-Boampong, 'Women during the Nkrumah era', in Bea Lundt and Christoph Marx (eds), *Kwame Nkrumah 1909–1972: A Controversial African Visionary* (Stuttgart, 2026), 49–63, at 51.

30 William Blackstone, *Commentaries on the Laws of England* (Philadelphia: J.B. Lippincott Company, 1893), 430. Available at http://oll.libertyfund.org (accessed 20 June 2019).

as opposed to the 'heavy job' of clearing virgin land, planting and spraying. Guyer and Galletti et al. confirm this view, citing farming in Yoruba societies as largely men's work with women making some input but only at certain points. Guyer noted, 'women's indigenous obligation to supply harvest, processing and transport labour was extended to include cocoa without change in definitions of the division of labour'[31] while Galletti et al. stated, 'women's share in the farm labour is more in the harvesting of food crops, the breaking of cocoa and the carrying of produce home from the farm'.[32]

However, the experiences of the women interviewed revealed the limitations of such gendered arguments. As Aba Nyarko stated, 'It was only the spraying that is difficult for me because of the weight of the machine but, for cocoa farming we women in Juaso help at all stages of production'. The other women in her focus group jumped in with Mary Aba, sitting beside her cocoa farmer husband Tawiah, confidently saying, 'Ask him, when we started the farm, I helped him in planting the cocoa and go to the farm every day except when I am going to give birth'. Araba cut in, 'So what about all the pre-farm activities we do, fetching water, firewood, cooking, looking after children, selling some of the farm goods on our way home – do these not count? No, we do far more than the men. This farming is a hard life for me'. Oral evidence suggests that women's experiences in cocoa farming have been many and varied, but that women played a vital role in cocoa production. Indeed, the value of women's labour stands out in the drying and fermentation process to prepare the cocoa for sale. Cocoa that was not properly prepared would not earn a good price on the world market.

Oral evidence from ten women of the focus group in Juaso also indicated that beyond providing labour as a result of familial obligations, women in Ghana were cocoa farmers in their own right. They acquired farms through inheritance, purchase or gift. Amanor quoting Field asserted that:

> A husband may give his wife a farm for herself and then the profits are hers entirely, but when he gives her the farm she must give him rum before witnesses as a sign that the farm is now hers. Then, even if there is a divorce, the farm remains hers.[33]

This mode of traditionally acknowledging the contribution of women to the success of cocoa farming was not consistent and rather short-lived. Hill stated

31 Jane Guyer, 'Food, cocoa and the division of labour by sex in two West African societies', *Comparative Studies in Society and History* 22 (1980), 355–73, at 364.

32 Robert Galletti, K.D.S. Baldwin and I.O. Dina (eds.), *Nigerian Cocoa Farmers: An Economic Survey of Yoruba Cocoa-Farming Families* (London, 1956), 202.

33 Amanor, 'Family values, land sales and agricultural commodification', 115, quoting Margaret Field, *Akim Kotoku: An Oman of the Gold Coast* (London, 1948), 69.

that the perceived reciprocity implicit in women farming their husbands' farms in the hope of being gifted a portion of the land soon became complex and often filled with litigation after the death of the husband. Indeed, by the 1950s, the gift of land for the labour investment of women in their spouse's cocoa farms was no longer guaranteed. Cocoa farms were soon steeped in acrimonious litigation between women and the matrilineal relations of their spouses. For instance, the Manhyia archives recorded a case in October 1936 between Akua Komfuor (plaintiff) and Kwabena Attakora (defendant) at the Mampong Native Court.[34] Akua brought a case against Kobina, her brother-in-law, for taking over the cocoa farm that her deceased husband (Yaw Dofoo) had gifted her and her children. After inspecting the farm in question, the court ruled in December 1936 in favour of Akua Komfuor as the small farm size demonstrated that it was cultivated by a woman. Kwabena Attakora was fined £4.90.

A decade later women continued to challenge customary laws of inheritance concerning cocoa farms. In the instance of Afua Koejyah (plaintiff) and Kwasi Addai (defendant), a case was brought to the Kumasi Native Divisional Court on 14 February 1948. Afua sued Kwasi (the brother of her stepfather) for taking possession of the cocoa farm she inherited from her late mother, Abena Nyame. He also seized another farm she made herself on the same land.[35] Afua's stepfather had gifted the cocoa farm to his wife, Abena Nyame. On Abena's death, Afua inherited the cocoa farm from her mother while her stepfather was still alive. On the death of her stepfather, his brother disputed the original gift of the cocoa farm to Abena Nyame. The court pursued the case and ordered an inspection of the land in question. Hired labourers on the cocoa farm attested that Kwabena Adjei (stepfather) made a gift of land to his wife Abena Nyame. She paid for the traditional Thanksgiving items custom demanded for a gift. They also attested to Afua's inheritance and active cultivation of the land. The court found in favour of Afua Koejyah and ordered Kwasi Addai to return the plaintiff's land.

Change and continuity characterised post-colonial gender relations in the cocoa sector. Men still dominated the cocoa-production industry yet women in cocoa farming asserted themselves and a greater number of them owned farms in their own right or demanded compensation from cocoa proceeds in divorce settlements. Cocoa therefore helped to transform and redefine gender relations to the advantage of women in cocoa. Women demonstrated greater agency, especially in initiating legal action to safeguard their labour on cocoa farms. These changes occurred amidst an evolving political and economic situation in Ghana.

34 Manhyia Archives, Kumasi, MAG 9/2/73, Akua Komfour versus Kwabena Atakora.

35 Manhyia Archives, Kumasi, MAG 9/A2/2/65, Afua Koejyah versus Kwasi Addai.

The late 1950s to mid-1960s ushered in the Nkrumah regime, with colonial continuity in terms of an agricultural policy heavily reliant on the exploitation of forest rent and export crops such as cocoa. The post-colonial state instituted policies that emphasised the development and exploitation of the cash-crop sector to improve foreign exchange reserves – their main source of wealth. Cocoa producers were paid the lowest producer prices possible, so the country could funnel the appropriated incomes to bolster other economic sectors (education, health, sanitation, infrastructure) and appease the urban population who were increasingly critical of the government. In this game of political survival, female cocoa farmers and women in cocoa farming became peripheral to the state. Women did not fare any better in the political and economic mayhem of the 1970s and early 1980s with frequent military regime changes and a steady decline and near collapse of the economy due to multiple overvaluations and inconvertible currency. Austin notes that from 1975 to 1983 real Gross Domestic Product (GDP) per capita fell more than a third, inflation was over 50 per cent a year and a regime of price controls proffered fixed prices for currency, food items, textiles, cocoa and just about everything else.[36] However, women, especially those engaging in trading, were labelled as economic saboteurs. The military regime of Flight Lieutenant Jerry John Rawlings took the scapegoating of women to another level by harassing and beating female traders in the largest open-air market in West Africa, Makola Number 1 market. These women were accused of hoarding and selling above the control prices.

Despite these draconian measures, all the enforcement tactics of the Rawlings regime did not work. There was a fall in government revenue as a share of a shrinking GDP from 17.3 per cent in 1974 to 6.1 per cent in 1982.[37] Coupled with an absence of support from the Communist states of China and Russia, Rawlings' regime, the Provisional National Defence Council did a U-turn to the World Bank and International Monetary Fund (IMF) to restore market forces and revive the Ghanaian economy. This U-turn was not due to pressure from cocoa farmers but to fiscal collapse brought about by partial boycotts of official markets. The decisive role of an increasingly over-valued, decreasingly inconvertible currency sealed the deal.

Ghana suddenly underwent an economic miracle under the Structural Adjustment Programme (SAP). A higher producer share of world cocoa prices immediately made cocoa worth harvesting and the political skill of the Rawlings regime reflecting the intellectual conversion at the top helped the

36 Gareth Austin, 'Ghana and Kenya facing the 1970s commodity price shocks: the national and the global', in Shigeru Akita (ed.), *Oil Crises of the 1970s and the Transformation of International Order: Economy, Development and Aid in Asia and Africa* (London, 2023), 223–56.

37 Douglas Rimmer, *Staying Poor: Ghana's Political Economy, 1950–1990* (Oxford, 1992), 207.

economic liberalisation to work. There was a massive devaluation and floating of the currency. A realistic exchange-rate policy was adopted and the cedi was devalued in stages from 2.75 cedis per U.S. dollar in April 1983 to 90 cedis per U.S. dollar by January 1986. This was followed by a reduction in the Ghana Cocoa Board's share of the world market price for cocoa and the recovery of cocoa output.[38] Cocoa farmers halted the extensive smuggling of their crops and began to pursue sales through official channels. Investments in new cocoa farms rose from net negative to the biggest in Ghanaian history, ultimately leading to the third cocoa boom with increased output reaching over 1 million tonnes in the 2010/11 crop season.

On the macro level, SAP reversed economic decline and launched decades of growth in real per capita income and higher total factor productivity putting the Ghanaian economy on a path of long-term growth. With its gender-neutral language and focus on economic variables, the impact of SAP's resource reallocation was assumed to be equitably distributed among the population. Elson notes that this gender neutrality hid bias against women inherent in the conceptual framework of SAP. These gender biases concerned the sexual division of labour and the view that women's unpaid labour was assumed to be 'unproblematically available and infinitely elastic, able to stretch to make up the shortfalls in other resources needed for survival during adjustment'.[39] To compound the situation, there was the view that the Ghanaian household was a unified, welfare-maximising unit that pooled and shared resources so it could safely absorb the costs of adjustment. In reality, however, any reduction in government expenditure in the social sector as part of the Structural Adjustment Programme resulted in a shift in the burden of social care to women, as the income generated by men from export production was not equitably shared with their spouses. Thus, when SAP recorded 'higher productivity' it was a shift of costs from the paid to the unpaid economy, often at a cost to the health and nutrition of women.

Analysing SAP at the micro level with a gendered focus illustrated that for women, economic liberalisation through the Economic Recovery Programme (ERP) and the Structural Adjustment Programme did not alter gender relations

38 The Ghana Cocoa Board was established by ordinance in 1947 as a monopsony over local buying of cocoa beans as well as its overseas shipping and sale. For the politics of the establishment of marketing boards, see Jan-Georg Deutsch, *Educating the Middlemen: a Political and Economic History of Statutory Cocoa Marketing in Nigeria, 1936–1947* (Berlin, 1995) and Rod Alence, 'Colonial government, social conflict and state intervention in Africa's open economies: the origins of the Ghana Cocoa Marketing Board, 1939–46', *Journal of African History* 43:3 (2002), 397–416.

39 Diane Elson, 'Male bias in macroeconomics: the case of Structural Adjustment' in Elson (ed.), *Male Biases in the Development Process* (Manchester, 1991), 49. Also see Haleh Afshar and Carolyne Dennis (eds), *Women and Adjustment Policies in the Third World* (London, 1992), 46–68.

nor advance gender equality. Women still experienced a double burden. By being macroeconomic in scope, SAP ignored the reality of life at the microeconomic level and the human cost of adjustment on vulnerable groups such as women. A United Nations Children's Fund (UNICEF) study pleaded for an 'adjustment with a human face' that would reduce the costs to poor households, especially vulnerable groups such as women and children.[40] In recognition of the negative effects of the SAP and in an attempt to ease the worst effects, the government of Ghana in conjunction with the World Bank and IMF drew up a Programme of Action to Mitigate the Social Costs of Adjustment (PAMSCAD) with funds from donor countries in 1988. However, PAMSCAD's focus was on employment generation, community development, basic needs provision and addressing the educational needs of vulnerable groups. With a programme funding of $84 million for two years to target the disadvantaged in society, PAMSCAD faced challenges in implementation capacity and failed to target the rural poor especially women in cocoa farming. In the end, it became an example of the failure of large-scale social initiatives.

Amid this economic liberalisation, cocoa boom and steady growth, there was a partial, internal liberalisation of the cocoa industry. The Rawlings regime steadfastly declined to abolish the cocoa marketing board and its export monopoly – in contrast to Nigeria, for example, which abolished its marketing boards in 1986. Instead, there was continuity with the system used in 1939 in which private entities known as Licensed Buying Companies were allowed to buy cocoa at the farm gate and sell to the re-named Ghana Cocoa Board. Cocoa farmers regained their economic voice, lost after the National Liberation Movement (NLM) – Convention People's Party(CPP) inter-party struggle of 1954–56 over Ghana's independence constitution that had seen the division of cocoa farmers' unions (the Ashanti union supporting the NLM, the Gold Coast Colony union following the CPP) permanently on party lines.[41]

A group of cocoa farmers led by a visionary farmer Nana Frimpong Abrebrese motivated to do something positive about the conditions of cocoa farmers visited villages near Kumasi and started local campaigns to create awareness among farmers about the partial liberalisation of the cocoa industry. Abrebrese's group educated farmers on the need to establish a new farmer-owned organisation. Many cocoa farmers were initially sceptical and unsure about the idea of farmers having their own company. This was because of

40 UNICEF, 'Adjustment policies and programmes to protect children and vulnerable groups in Ghana', in Giovanni Andrea Cornia, Richard Jolly and Frances Stewart (eds) *Adjustment with a Human Face*, vol. 1. *Protecting the Vulnerable and Promoting Growth* (Oxford, 1987), 93–125.

41 Gareth Austin, 'National poverty and the 'vampire state' in Ghana: A review article', *Journal of International Development* 8 (1996), 553–73, at 562–4. See, further, Jean Allman, *The Quills of the Porcupine: Asante Nationalism in an Emergent Ghana* (Madison WI, 1993); Björn Beckman, *Organising the Farmers: Cocoa Politics and National Development in Ghana* (Uppsala, 1976), 65–9.

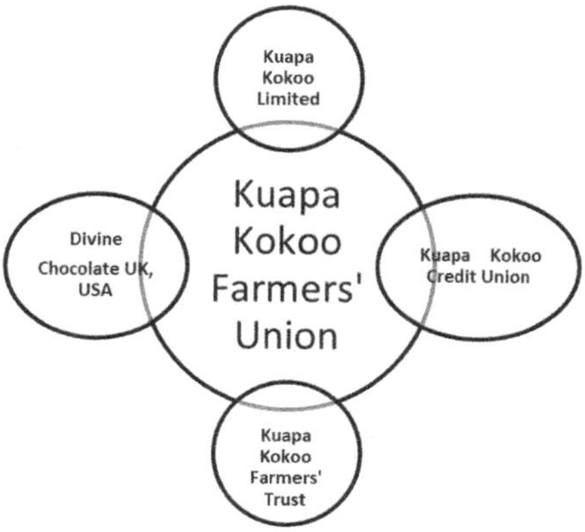

Figure 10.1
The Structure of the Kuapa Kokoo Group.

their prior experience with the United Ghana Farmers' Cooperative Council (UGFCC) in the 1960s.[42] UGFCC was initially supposed to be a farmers' organisation but had morphed into a political wing of the then ruling CPP government.

Despite these initial fears, after listening to Nana Abrebrese, a number of the older cocoa farmers saw the wisdom in his suggestion for a farmer-owned organisation that would increase the farmers' share of the profits, derived from their cocoa and their knowledge of the chocolate market. Nana Frimpong Abrebrese also won the confidence of younger farmers with the appealing name of Kuapa Kokoo Farmers' Union (KKFU-Kuapa Kokoo) and its motto. Kuapa Kokoo means 'good cocoa farmer' and the motto of 'Pa Pa Paa' means the best of the best in the Twi language.

Kuapa Kokoo embraced the cooperative principles of open and voluntary membership, democratic member control, autonomy, members' economic participation, education, training and information and concern for the community. This cocoa cooperative was formed in 1993 and registered under the Cooperative Societies decree of 1968 (NLCD 252) and Co-operative Societies regulations, 1968 (L.I. 604). It enabled its initial 2,000 cocoa farmers from 49 village societies to collect and sell their cocoa through Kuapa Kokoo Limited.[43] Figure 10.1 shows the structure of the Kuapa Kokoo group, which included a savings facility (Kuapa Kokoo Credit Union), a trust (Kuapa Kokoo Trust) and a chocolate manufacturing company (Divine Chocolate Company).

42 The UGFCC were previously the United Ghana Farmers' Council

43 Cocoa cooperatives were an initiative of the colonial Department of Agriculture to reduce farmer indebtness and maximise quality. However, an overwhelming majority of cocoa farmers did not join until the late 1950s (see Kamenov's chapter in this volume). Kuapa Kokoo has operational districts in the Ashanti, Brong Ahafo, Western North, Western South, Central and Eastern regions.

Kuapa Kokoo was able to weather its initial working capital challenges with the help of loans from TWIN and SNV.[44] It gradually increased its cocoa purchases through Kupa Kokoo Limited (KKL). The first two decades of KKL's operations demonstrated a very competitive cocoa market with the introduction of other cocoa farmer associations and cooperatives during the long twentieth century as shown in Kuapa Kokoo's varying market share in Table 1.

Table 10.1 Cocoa Purchases by Kuapa Kokoo Limited 1993/94–2013/14

Crop Season	Ghana's Total Purchases in Tonnes	KKL Tonnage Purchased	% of National Production Purchased by KKL
1993/94	254,659	1,835	0.72
1994/95	309,452	2,667	0.86
1995/96	403,843	5,192	1.30
1996/97	323,133	7,373	2.28
1997/98	409,360	13,628	3.33
1998/99	397,367	21,004	5.29
1999/00	436,906	31,852	7.29
2000/01	389,771	35,649	9.15
2001/02	340,562	35,568	10.44
2002/03	496,846	41,204	8.29
2003/04	736,975	62,443	8.47
2004/05	599,318	40,734	6.80
2005/06	740,458	48,956	6.61
2006/07	614,532	34,264	5.58
2007/08	680,781	36,025	5.29
2008/09	710,642	35,558	5.00
2009/10	632,037	30,487	4.82
2010/11	1,024,553	47,536	4.59
2011/12	879,348	43,536	4.95
2012/13	835,466	48,258	5.77
2013/14	896,220	62,232	6.94

Source: Kuapa Kokoo Farmers' Union, *Annual Reports* 1993/94–2013/14 and Cocobod, *Annual Reports* 1993–2010.

44 SNV is the Dutch development agency, and TWIN is an ethical trading body that received a grant the UK Department for International Development (DfID) to spend on Commonwealth countries to make a difference to small-scale farmers.

Changing the Terms of Women's Engagement in the Cocoa Sector

The founders of Kuapa Kokoo Farmers' Union had an enlightened attitude to gender relations culminating in an increase of women members from 26 per cent in 1996 to 40 per cent in 2019. They believed that cooperatives must ensure that they are democratic bodies which genuinely represent both male and female members. Gender issues were taken into consideration in the cooperative design: one of the three top-level objectives of its constitution required female representation at every level of the governance structure. Kuapa Kokoo operated a three-tier governance structure of elected officers at village, area and national levels. Seven elected members from the village level elected three amongst themselves to the area council. Then one member from each of the 28 area councils was in turn elected to the national executive council. From there, four members were voted to the board of Kuapa Kokoo Limited and another four to Kuapa Kokoo Farmers Trust. Farmers in every village had a direct impact on board membership.

Quotas to ensure women's representation in all village executive committees were established as part of the structure of Kuapa Kokoo by the equitable attitude of male union members. Initially, the quotas specified that at least two of the seven committee members must be women. This quota was increased in 2010: since then, three out of the seven committee members must be female. Similar quotas also exist for the 52 area-level committees: three out of the seven representatives in each area committee must be women. In addition, quotas were enforced for participation at the Annual General Meeting (AGM), which constitutes the main decision-making forum of KKFU. All primary societies sent two AGM delegates, one of which must be a woman.

The impact of gendered governance measures was evident as the quotas for women's representation on committees at the village and area levels were largely met, with 91 women out of a total of 182 representatives. Interestingly, despite the absence of gender quotas at the National Executive Committee (NEC) level, 60 per cent (12 out of 20) of the NEC Board members were female by 2010. A number of these NEC women took up key roles on the boards of Kuapa Kokoo's various subsidiaries. For example, Comfort Kumeah, a female farmer member from Antoakrom District, Ashanti Region, was elected the chairperson of KKFT from 2005 to 2012, managing an annual budget of over $1 million and ensured that the Kuapa Kokoo Farmers Trust successfully passed a FLO- CERT full systems inspection in 2009. Mavis Adu Gyamfi from the Sefwi-Akotombra Society noted,

> As soon as I joined, I was trained to improve my farming skills – how to produce pa pa paa cocoa and to improve my yields. As a result, I have doubled my yield and can now produce 40 sacks of cocoa from my 6-acre farm,

> whereas before it was only 20. Then I put myself up for election. The other farmers could see I was well educated and was good with figures, and they trusted me, a young woman, to be a recorder.[45]

In addition, during the long twentieth century, KKFU elected a woman, Christiana Ohene Agyare, as President in 2010.[46] Her election was a testament to KKFU's long-term commitment to gender equality and women's empowerment. Ms Ohene Agyare was one of five women among the eleven elected members of KKFU's National Executive Committee. The others were Fatima Ali, Juliana Fema, Esther Kuffour and Anna Were.

Kuapa Kokoo also encouraged the inclusion of women in delegations that were sent overseas to represent the organisation internationally. Most of these Kuapa Kokoo women attended the Fairtrade Fortnight as ambassadors of Kuapa and Divine Chocolate. The list includes Comfort Kumeah, Mary Nyamekye, Rijiyatu Razak, Comfort Kwasibea, Comfort Asare-Kwabi, Georgina Kwaw, Anna Awere, Veronica Mintah, Eric Kyere, Christina Ohene-Agyare, Fatima Ali, Harriet Boatemaa, Agnes Armah, Esther Mintah Ephraim, and Mary Appiah. The inclusion of these women in overseas delegations had a huge impact, not only on the self-confidence of the individual women involved but also on other female members of the cooperative, who saw these women as role models.

Beyond measures to ensure women's representation in governance, ensuring access to general membership services was vital to the attainment of gender justice and women's empowerment. Conventional cocoa farmer membership was linked to ownership of land which created a bias in favour of men, as more men than women owned land for cocoa farming. In addition, a lack of gender awareness in cooperatives meant women's needs and interests were not sufficiently taken into consideration in planning and policy-making.

To redress the gender access to resources Kuapa Kokoo's membership dues were set at 0.20 Ghana cedis (approximately $0.14) per member in the 1990s, a fee that even the poorest farmers could afford.[47] Moreover, although one must be a cocoa farmer to become a member, it was not necessary to have formal or even traditional land ownership rights over the farm. Anyone who had control of the produce from a cocoa farm could join (including sharecroppers who had control over only a portion of it). Secondly, any village society could submit a funding application to the Farmers Trust for social projects that benefit the

45 Divine Chocolate, *Empowering the Woman Cocoa Farmer of Kuapa Kokoo* (London, 2017). This report was a review of 20 years of learning and pioneering progress in addressing gender equality in the cocoa supply chain.

46 Fatima Ali, a female cocoa farmer was elected President of Kuapa Kokoo Farmers' Union in 2014.

47 Kuapa Kokoo membership dues rose to 2.00 Ghana cedis in 2025.

community, such as the construction of sanitary facilities, schools, or boreholes. To be submitted, the application must be approved by all members of the primary society executive committee, at least three of whom must be women. Moreover, the community-level committee that is appointed to oversee the implementation of an approved project must also have a female as well as a male representative. Finally, the provision of micro-credit between $20 and $600 to individual women to develop their micro-enterprises was possible as Kuapa made it easier for woment to access the credit they needed. No collateral was required to secure loans which was often a barrier for women and approval from a person's village society executive committee was all that was required to be deemed credit-worthy.

The impact of measures to ensure women's access to the full range of Kuapa Kokoo's membership services and facilities was evident through interviews conducted in three village societies in which women confirmed equal access to all Kuapa's membership services. Women in Asankragwa and Twifo Praso communities confirmed that they have received credit from Kuapa Kokoo Credit Union and used it to meet medical costs and help fund their children's education.

As part of its long-standing strategy of addressing women's empowerment, a gender assessment was carried out in 1996, soon after the formation of KKFU, leading to the establishment of a Gender Programme in 1998. This targeted support to women members was in the form of training and capacity building, skills training and the provision of credit and it promoted women's representation across the organisation. Training and capacity building targeted the development of personal leadership and management skills. Skills training focused on teaching 400 women the practical skills they need to develop collective income-generating activities during the cocoa off-season, such as farming other (non-cocoa) crops, soap-making, palm and palm kernel oil production, and bread making. Similarly, in collaboration with Divine Chocolate, which invests part of its profits directly in farmer projects addressing gender equality, the high level of illiteracy among women farmers has been drastically reduced. Intensive literacy and numeracy lessons for nine months a year, four times a week have given women the skills and confidence to participate and put themselves forward for leadership positions. As an example Fatima Ali from the Akontombra district of the Western Region decided to run for Secretary of the National Executive Council of Kuapa Kokoo and won this position in 2003.

In terms of training and capacity building, women in cocoa farming were given training in leadership skills as well as business and financial literacy which involved basic arithmetic, modules on good agronomic practices, loan management and record keeping. Record keeping enabled women to track their expenses and improve their habits of saving. Kuapa Kokoo partnered with WIEGO (Women in Informal Employment: Globalizing and Organizing) in the Business and Leadership project to deliver training to 2,800 women farmers across 670 of its primary societies. As a result of this empowerment training, women became more confident in stepping forward as leaders and in claiming their rights as evidenced by the increase in land ownership. The baseline survey at the start of the project showed that 60 per cent of women involved in the cooperative owned land separately from land owned by their husbands. This figure had surged to 89 per cent by the end of the project, primarily because of women claiming their inheritance rights and securing land from their parents, while a smaller percentage of women had been able to secure their piece of land from their husbands. There was also a noticeable increase in the percentage of women who purchased land by themselves, rising from a mere 3 per cent at the start of the project to 17 per cent at the end. The Kuapa Kokoo women interviewed claimed that the most important factor in their decision to secure land was the empowerment training which they received through the project.

The impact of training is phenomenal. Some women, such as Akua Bemo, stated that after undergoing training for a year she learnt to improve the management of her farm which has increased yields. The project also resulted in a noticeable increase in the number of women in leadership positions within the cooperative: 83 per cent of the women interviewed for the project evaluation study had become cooperative leaders. They stated that although they had previously been afraid to take on leadership roles as they had not been to school, they gained confidence through the training which equipped them with the knowledge that they needed to fulfil the responsibilities under these roles. A further 99 per cent of the women interviewed said that they would also like to take up positions of responsibility within their communities. Overall, empowering women cocoa farmers enhanced their decision-making power and control over assets within the household. It also strengthened democratic systems, encouraged a more equitable allocation of resources within Kuapa Kokoo and helped to raise productivity and improve quality.

Together with Divine Chocolate, Kuapa Kokoo became a power in establishing land rights for tenant farmers, a significant number being women. Many farmers in Ghana own dispersed plots of land and take on tenant farmers to work the plots they cannot manage themselves. In many cases, arrangements between farmers and tenants are informal and non-standardised which can lead to disputes. Kuapa Kokoo established Labour Rights Committees to raise awareness about tenant rights and progressed from verbal agreements between farmer-owners and tenant farmers to written tenancy contracts. Thirty per cent of the signatories were women and enjoyed stability of tenure.

Kuapa Kokoo's success in mainstreaming gender through various gender initiatives discussed above has not been without challenges. Some male members were initially resistant to supporting the quota system for women's representation on the village society and area committees. They felt the system was unfair because there were more male than female cocoa farmers, men tended to have larger farms and also be better educated so marginal female representation was appropriate. However, because all members must sign up to Kuapa Kokoo's gender equality principles as a condition of membership, these initially resistant men soon understood the basis of the quota system. A secondary challenge for some men comes from their perception of the Gender Programme as biased. Although most men do accept the principle of equal opportunities in governance, many continue to feel aggrieved about the Gender Programme because it offers credit and support for women only. They feel this is unfair, and that there should be a parallel programme of support for men.

Conclusion

Kuapa Kokoo's focus on gender equality has advanced women's empowerment as it targets and benefits the wives and other female relatives of male Kuapa members, as well as women who are cocoa farmers and members of Kuapa in their own right. It has been especially rewarding to see the positive impact achieved for women as they can step up and take their rightful place in the cocoa narrative.

Actors at every stage of the cocoa supply chain need to understand that gender relations are structurally and systematically entangled. Thus, there is a need to evaluate the assumptions, social norms and biases that underlie daily practices and habits toward women in cocoa farming. Currently, gender intersects with other forms of oppression to push women cocoa farmers to the margins of the supply chain. To centre women in the cocoa supply chain, an intersectional approach to understanding women's productive and reproductive contributions is needed. This intersectionality has the potential to highlight women cocoa farmers' disproportionate vulnerability to exploitative cultural norms within the cocoa sector. These prohibitive cultural norms and stereotypes inhibit women's access to critical inputs such as land, labour and capital.

However, changing the terms of engagement is a slow process and more needs to be done to address the broader structures and gender norms that constrain women's ability to take advantage of opportunities. One of the lessons that KKFU learnt is that leadership training is not sufficient. Once women have received training and built their agency, they need access to resources to reduce gender disparity and achieve empowerment. KKFU has demonstrated that cooperatives can survive and thrive in the free-market economy. Applying a gender lens to their organisational structure can empower women in the cocoa sector to break the vicious cycle of poverty and reach the global goal of gender equality, a vital component for the attainment of the 2030 agenda for sustainable development.

11

The Predicament of Youth and Ghana's Political Economy in the Long Twentieth Century

NANA YAW BOAMPONG SAPONG

The average student of Economics in Ghana throughout the second half of the twentieth century was made to learn by rote the factors of production; natural resources (land), labour (manpower), capital, and a later addition – entrepreneurship. Economists referred to the vast potential of Africa, even though colonial economic development was primarily export-oriented and raw-material based.[1] A cursory look at trade and revenue generation from the 1890s to the 1950s in Ghana (then Gold Coast) often showed a favourable balance of trade, but also revealed a heavy reliance on cash crops and extracted minerals.[2] In a pathfinding work on the political economy of pre-colonial and colonial Ghana, Austin painstakingly explored how and why an agricultural export economy developed and evolved in Asante. More importantly, this study examined the contentions surrounding the deployment of the factors of production, sometimes between individuals, families, or individuals and institutions (the state) in cocoa production.[3] In the 1930s, cocoa production was once again at the centre of rural discontent, as African producers tangled with the colonial state and private enterprise over price fixing. In 1937/38, a significant cocoa 'hold-up' occurred when expatriate firms fixed the price of cocoa without consulting African producers. Led by John Ayew and centered around the town of Suhum, as well as Kojo Broni and the Ashanti cocoa farmers' union, this discontent compelled the colonial state to denounce price-fixing

1 Ann Seidman, *An Economics Textbook for Africa* (London, 1972), 37–51. I chose this textbook because it was one of my earliest encounters with Economics as a secondary school student in the 1980s.

2 See 'Appendix D: Trade and Revenue Returns, 1853–1956' in G.E. Metcalfe (ed.), *Great Britain and Ghana: Documents of Ghana History, 1807–1957* (London, 1964), 750–52. There were, however, years such as 1920 and 1936, when imports exceeded exports by 3 million British pounds, but this did not drastically affect revenue returns.

3 Gareth Austin, *Labour, Land and Capital in Ghana: From Slavery to Free Labour in Asante, 1807–1956* (Rochester NY, 2005).

and recommend the sale of cocoa through farmers' cooperatives.[4] Generally, the late-nineteenth-century African cash-crop revolution, which spilled over into the twentieth century, and resulted in the significant expansion of export agriculture, reiterated the usefulness of African agency, as production was mainly initiated and carried out by Africans.[5]

The colonial period covered by Austin's study was also auspicious for growth, or in fashionable parlance, 'development.' Indeed, the late colonial period saw a push in what Decker and McMahon referred to as the development episteme, 'the creation of knowledge about Africa's social, economic, political, environmental, intellectual, and physical conditions and how to improve them'.[6] From the onset, British colonial officials ensconced the idea of development in 'something to be done *to* and *for* Africa, not with it'.[7] In Ghana (the Gold Coast), this culminated in the introduction of policies such as the 1940 Colonial Development and Welfare Act, a program that set aside £120 million to develop the economies and social services of colonies.[8] It should, however, be pointed out that colonial political economy did not unequivocally and solely transform post-colonial political economies in Africa. Post-colonial economies were not necessarily held hostage on predetermined paths charted by colonial economies. Commenting on the issue of 'path determination,' Austin suggests a nuanced approach by arguing that 'the "path(s)" on which African economies were ... set by the time of independence are most usefully seen not as necessarily initiated in the colonial period, but often rather as continuations and adjustments from paths of change established before the European partition of the continent'.[9] Thus, the creativity and agency of pre-colonial transactional interactions within and between polities, as well as individual, whether African or European, should not be divorced from

4 See A. Adu Boahen, *Ghana: Evolution and Change in the Nineteenth and Twentieth Centuries* (Accra, 2000), 146–8, and D.E.K. Amenumey, *Ghana* (Accra, 2008), 197–8.

5 Gareth Austin, 'Explaining and evaluating the cash crop revolution in the "peasant" colonies of Tropical Africa, c. 1890–c. 1930: beyond "vent for surplus"' in Emmanuel Akyeampong, Robert H. Bates, Nathan Nunn and James A. Robinson (eds), *Africa's Development in Historical Perspective* (Cambridge, 2014), 295–320. Also see John Tosh, 'The cash crop revolution in Tropical Africa: an agricultural reappraisal', *African Affairs* 79:314 (1980), 79–94.

6 Corrie Decker and Elisabeth McMahon, *The Idea of Development in Africa: A History* (Cambridge, 2021), 15.

7 Frederick Cooper, 'Modernizing bureaucrats, backward Africans, and the development concept' in Frederick Cooper and Randall Packard (eds), *International Development and the Social Sciences* (Berkeley, 1997), 65.

8 See Jon Olav Hove, 'Development and Decolonisation: The Gold Coast (Ghana), 1940–1957' (Ph.D. dissertation, NTNU, Trondheim, 2013).

9 Gareth Austin, 'African economic development and colonial legacies', *International Development Policy*, 1 (2010) , http://poldev.revues.org/78 (accessed 1 March, 2013).

the making of post-colonial political economies. More importantly, it would be useful to perceive linkages between the state-organised youth schemes of the post-independence era (especially the late 1960s to early 1980s) and the pre-colonial mobilisation of youth in the *asafo*.[10] Indeed, in 1969, Prime Minister Busia appealed to history by invoking the pre-colonial image of the *asafo* to legitimise the need for a National Service Corps to serve the nation.

In the post-colonial period, Ghana's political economy witnessed a greater push towards state-led economic development. After a generation of political instability, state mismanagement of the economy and an unpredictable world marketplace, Ghana was left in tatters. This period was marked by a slow and unstable growth, punctuated by collapse in the late 1970s and early 1980s. This state of helplessness, and a general feeling of an impending doom solidified in the Ghanaian imaginary. Additionally, individual stories emerged to fuel this imaginary. In a popular and sordid tell-all narrative of this period titled *99 Days in Agege*, Yaw Brenya wrote a letter to Joe, apologising for his sudden departure from Ghana to oil-rich Nigeria in search of 'the good things in life'. The trendy catchphrase was 'Age-eege!' to which the response was, 'You go sleep Ghana rot'. The most disconcerting fact about the trip was that Mr Brenya was in his prime and gainfully employed. He would have been described as part of Ghana's youth population. After 99 difficult days in Nigeria, Yaw decided to come back home to Ghana. His experiences subsequently became the subject matter and often-cited example of hardship in the 1980s. Indeed, throughout the 1970s and 1980s, professionals in their prime left Ghana for countries such as Nigeria, the United Kingdom, Canada, and the United States when the economy took a sharp dip.[11] Things took a worse turn when in January 1983, President Shagari announced that illegal migrants were going to be arrested, tried, and sent back home if they do not leave voluntarily. Subsequently, Nigeria deported some two million illegal migrants from the subregion, about 50 per cent of whom were from Ghana.[12] Others took the path of con-artistry and deception, as exemplified in the story of John Ackah Blay-Miezah, the man who misled two military governments in Ghana and defrauded western investors through the Oman Ghana Trust Fund.[13]

10 Historically, *asafo* is the name for a group of active, strong and healthy young men who were usually assigned protective duties, communal work or conscripted for warfare.

11 Yaw Brenya, *99 Days in Agege: Yaw Brenya's Experience* (Accra, 1981).

12 See Samuel Fury Childs Daly, 'Ghana must go: nativism and the politics of expulsion in West Africa, 1969–1985', *Past & Present* 259:1 (2023), 229–61; and Shola Lawal 'Ghana must go: the ugly history of Africa's most famous bag', https://atavist.mg.co.za/ghana-must-go-the-ugly-history-of-africas-most-famous-bag/ (accessed 22 July 2023).

13 'Oman Ghana Trust Fund: $10m in Soon', *Daily Graphic*, 7 January 1975. Also Yepoka Yeebo, *Anansi's Gold: The Man Who Looted the West, Outfoxed Washington, and Swindled the World* (London, 2023).

By the 1980s, some macro-historical analyses of Ghana's political economy often lamented the missed chances and wasted opportunities. In his 1988 J.B. Danquah Memorial Lectures at the Ghana Academy of Arts and Sciences, Adu Boahen analysed Ghana's political economy and pointed out that Ghana posed a riddle. He wondered why Ghana wallowed in poverty despite the presence of some classical factors of production such as natural resources and manpower (including youth labour). The key to unraveling the riddle, Boahen posited, was a question of leadership, and governance in general.[14] On the other hand, alternative views pointed to recovery and a steady growth from the mid-1980s, due to political stability, structural changes, contingencies and the imperceptible moments of history.[15] Ultimately, despite the different perspectives, all point to the inseparable bond between politics and the economy.

Propositions, Definitions and Historiographic Issues

In 1848, John Stuart Mill's *Principles of Political Economy* provided an early classic indication of the inextricable relationship between politics and the economy. Indeed, the pantheon of classical economists – Adam Smith, David Ricardo and Mill – referred to themselves as political economists. By the 1970s, political economy increasingly came to represent 'the integration of political and economic factors in our analysis of modern society'.[16] The state of the political economy of a country is mainly determined by an interplay and synergetic relationship between political forces and economic forces. Generally, the narrative on the political economy of post-colonial Africa is beset with instances of weak governance and political instability, which greatly affected its youth populations. According to Olivier de Sardan, this situation is due to the presence of four main gate keepers. In a reflective piece on the political economy of Niger, he surmised that these 'four prisons of power' (*les quatre prisons du pouvoir*) include big business, bureaucrats, international

14 A. Adu Boahen, *The Ghanaian Sphinx: Reflections on the Contemporary History of Ghana, 1972–1987* (Accra, 1992). Also see Zaya Yeebo, *Ghana: The Struggle for Popular Power* (London, 1991); Kevin Shillington, *Ghana and the Rawlings Factor* (New York, 1992); Paul Nugent, *Big Men, Small Boys and Politics in Ghana* (London, 1995).

15 See Gareth Austin, 'Ghana's Economic Development Since Independence, 1957–2017,' public lecture at the Institute of Economic Affairs Ghana, 26 September 2017. The literature on Ghana's economic recovery and the structural adjustment programmes is copious. For instance, see Ebo Hutchful, 'IMF Adjustment Policies in Ghana Since 1966', *Africa Development* 10:1–2 (1985), 122–36.

16 Jeffrey Frieden, 'The political economy of economic policy', *Finance & Development* 57:2 (2020), 4–9, at 9.

experts, and political party courtiers and 'foot soldiers'.[17] Similarly, in Nigeria's post-colonial development crisis, its youth have been neglected and repressed, creating a restive youth population, especially in the Niger Delta region.[18]

In the case of Ghana, the history of its political economy in the twentieth century has been a story of how the creation of the colonial and post-colonial states have been influenced by interest groups, the market, and a development episteme.[19] We may infer an inseparable bond between Ghana's political and economic fortunes; a situation in which the youth will have access to quality education and professional development. In a classical liberal moment, both labour and entrepreneurship, crucial constituents of production, derive fulfilment from an educated, healthy, enthusiastic, and patriotic youthful population. Likewise, political elite blocs pursuing political power rely on the support of the youth, a critical mass in winning power, either through the ballot box or by coercion. Unfortunately, there is a persistent construction of African youth as a threat,[20] a perception which does not augur well for Africa's political economy.

Using youth as a trope, this work makes four interdependent propositions. The first proposition is that throughout Ghana's history, both the state and society have created or invented organisations and associations to channel youth energy, creativity and potential towards politics and the economy. This has been the case in both pre-colonial and post-colonial periods. However, this process seldom reached the intended outcome as the state (and traditional authority) inevitably subverted the role of youth as a constituent of state-making, governance, and wealth creation. Thus, the concept of youth in Ghana, that uncertain and restive stage, mirrored the ups and downs of Ghana's political economy and its misdirected, exploited, and truncated potential. Secondly and paradoxically, the long twentieth century, especially the long 1970s,[21] a

17 Jean-Pierre Olivier de Sardan, 'Niger: les quatre prisons du pouvoir.' Published 4 January 2016. https://www.marianne.net/agora/tribunes (accessed 16 April 2025). Also see Gilles O. Yabi, 'The Sahel's intertwined challenges', *Finance & Development* 61:3 (2024), 55–7.

18 Arowosegbe Jeremiah, 'Violence and national development in Nigeria: the political economy of youth restiveness in the Niger Delta', *Review of African Political Economy* 36:122 (2009), 575–94.

19 The development episteme, based on the Enlightenment project's mission to civilise, and hegemonic western perceptions of African people and societies' path to 'development', has been the driving force behind World Bank and International Monetary Fund (IMF) initiatives in postcolonial Africa.

20 Mamadou Diouf, 'Engaging postcolonial cultures: African youth and public spaces', *African Studies Review* 46:2 (2003), 1–12.

21 I use the phrase 'long 1970s' to represent the years 1966 to 1979. For a conceptual explanation, see Elisa Prosperetti and Claire Nicolas, 'Ghana's long 1970s: historical contingency and the dark side of nation building', *Ghana Studies* 27 (2024), 1–23, and Nana Yaw

period of cataclysmic economic slump, also witnessed substantive efforts to integrate the youth into Ghana's response to economic crisis. Through the National Service Corps and the National Service Scheme, the state (especially the National Redemption Council – NRC) attempted to seize the rhetoric of power by revisiting Ghana's self-help and Africa-centered posture. Decker and McMahon would argue that this approach by the state demonstrates that Africans have always 'co-opted,' contested, and 'reformed' the idea of development.[22] Thirdly, and unfortunately, policy documents from these initiatives in the long 1970s imposed gender-biased assumptions and revealed a lopsided attempt at dealing with the youth question. Finally, these propositions are a methodological push to encourage a deeper reflection on historical change, and the *longue durée*, which takes cognizance of those quotidian, contingent and imperceptible moments of history, in the study of the history of Ghana's political economy.[23] It is important to state that this chapter is not a study of the psychology of 'youth', but rather a reading of the historical relations between the state and a socio-economic and political segment of the population whose place is fluid and paradoxical.

The operational definition of youth remains a shifting category. However, according to a 2013 United Nations Development Programme estimate, nearly half of the world's population is under 30 years old. In the same year, 25 per cent of this number is of working age, according to an estimate by the International Labour Organisation and the Food and Agriculture Organisation. Yet, most of them are not part of decision-making at the higher levels of government.[24] The United Nations (UN), as well as the World Health Organisation (WHO), describe the youth as people between the ages of 15 to 24. These world bodies, however, added that the range is not prejudicial to any national or regional interpretation.[25] Thus, in Africa, the age range for youth can sometimes be between 15 to 35, or in a certain context evasive, since this could include students, teachers, farmers, doctors, nurses, soldiers, lawyers, fishermen, and mineworkers.

Most political parties in Ghana have had an independent operational definition for 'youth.' Kwame Nkrumah's Convention People's Party of Ghana (CPP) was very clear on the place of Ghana's young people. According to the

Boampong Sapong, '1966 and the foreshortening of Ghana's history', *Ghana Studies* 27 (2024), 24–31.

22 Decker and McMahon, *The Idea of Development in Africa*, 3.

23 See Emmanuel Akyeampong, Robert H. Bates, Nathan Nunn and James A. Robinson (eds), *Africa's Development in Historical Perspective* (Cambridge, 2014) for a *longue durée* analysis of Africa's development challenges.

24 See https://www.un.org/youthenvoy/political-participation/ and https://www.un.org/youthenvoy/employment/ respectively.

25 See https://www.un.org/en/global-issues/youth.

constitution and rules of the CPP, youth and sports organisations could apply to be affiliated to the party. Additionally, youth presence at the national annual conference of the CPP was guaranteed through both affiliated youth organisations and the Ghana Youth League. Furthermore, the National Executive Council of the party included two youth representatives from youth organisations. Finally, the 'inner party organisation' is powered by four interworking components. These are a National Secretariat, a Women's Section, the Party Youth League, and a Publications wing. The Party Youth League, among its duties, was responsible for organising young Ghanaians, who are under the age of eighteen, into Party Youth Clubs.[26] In contemporary Ghana, political parties still recognise the value of their 'youth' constituents. Intriguingly, the National Democratic Congress (NDC) has no age limit for 'youth' in the party ranks, while the New Patriotic Party (NPP) has an age range from 18 to 39 years. On the other hand, the Convention People's Party (not to be confused with the one chaired by Nkrumah) dropped the minimum age lower by defining 'youth' as anyone between 14 and 38 years.[27]

The concept of 'youth' or 'young men' has been historically evolving. In pre-colonial Ghana, the idea of youth was often mediated through initiation rites into societies and guilds, through organs of state formation, or through social class formation. On a simplistic level, the term 'youth' or *mmerante* among the Akan represented a social class of both young and old commoners 'who do not belong to the 'aristocratic' classes'.[28] However, the most ubiquitous symbol of youth in several pre-colonial polities was the *Asafo*. The *Asafo* was a group of able-bodied male adults in the community who were rallied together for any purpose, especially warfare. Indeed, the *Asafo* units or companies were often referred to as 'organised military bands.' According to J.C. de Graft Johnson, *Asafo* in a specific sense implied 'the third estate or common people' who were 'referred to, politically, as *mbrantsie* or "young men" to distinguish them from the *mpanyinfu*, chiefs and elders'.[29] It is generally agreed that the concept and practice of *Asafo* was already visible in pre-colonial Akan polities, especially among the Fante. Each Fante state, such as Oguaa (Cape Coast), Abura, Ekumfi, Elmina, Anomabo and Mankesim had several *Asafo* companies. It was from these small coastal states that the *Asafo* institution spread to the larger and more centralised Akan states in the forest regions. The membership

26 John Arthur, *Freedom for Africa* (Accra, 1961), 45–55.

27 See Ransford E.V. Gyampo, 'The youth and political ideology in Ghanaian politics: the case of the Fourth Republic' *Africa Development* 37:2 (2012), 139–40. Also see the constitutions of the various political parties.

28 F.K. Buah, *A History of Ghana* (London, 1998), 49.

29 J.C. de Graft Johnson, 'The Fanti Asafu' *Africa* 5:3 (1932), 307–22, at 308. Also see Ansu K. Datta and R. Porter, 'The Asafo system in historical perspective,' *Journal of African History* 12:2 (1971), 279–97, at 279.

base of the *Asafo* companies was often patrilineal and from social groups mainly identified as 'commoners'. Thus, the *Asafo* were frequently presumed to be speaking for the common people and their interests. Indeed, during the colonial period, the *Asafo* arrogated the role 'as a medium of popular protest against escalating exploitation by chiefs and, indirectly, against the colonial administration'.[30] Although most *Asafo* companies did not explicitly exclude women and old men, membership and activities of the companies remained predominantly a world of young men or *mbrantsie*.

In eighteenth-century Akyem Abuakwa, the *Amantoomiensa*[31] or national *Asafo* was formed to mobilise warriors expeditiously to protect the *Okyenhene* against foreign invasions, especially surprise attacks from Asante. However, by the mid-nineteenth century, the *Amantoomiensa* had evolved 'into a pressure group of sorts and asserted a claim to recognition as the "mouthpiece" of the ordinary citizens'.[32] Indeed, a later generation of mission-school educated youth in the *Asafo* began demanding more decision-making roles from traditional authority. By the turn of the twentieth century, the perception by some chiefs of Akyem Abuakwa youth as rabble-rousers and usurpers was solidified when the *Amantoomiensa* presented 28 demands to *Okyenhene* Nana Ofori Atta in May 1916. These demands included absolution from punishment for swearing the *Okyenhene*'s oath, and unrestricted access to the king's palace. Additionally, in May 1918, the *Asafo* of Apiramang attempted to destool Nana Kofi Boateng II by entering his palace and initiating the process without recourse to Abuakwa custom and constitution.[33] However, the most poignant example of the *asafo*–chief strife came in November 1918 when the *Amantoomiensa* attempted to destool Nana Ofori Atta for allegedly using the paramount stool as collateral for a loan from the Colonial Bank.[34]

Similarly, in nineteenth-century Asante, the *nkwankwaa* or 'young men' were youth who were excluded from political office by traditional requirements, and

30 Per Hernaes, 'Asafo history: an introduction', *Transactions of the Historical Society of Ghana* New Series, 2 (1998), 2. This article was part of a special issue of the journal *Transactions of the Historical Society of Ghana* on the *Asafo* in Ghana. This was a result of the research collaboration between the University of Ghana, Legon and the Norwegian University of Science and Technology, Trondheim.

31 The *Amantoomiensa*, also known as *Ofori Nkonnwa ho asraafoo* (soldiers of the Ofori stool), served as a standing army for Akyem Abuakwa whenever the need arose. Also, *Okyenhene* is the official title of the king of Akyem Abuakwa. See Robert Addo-Fening, *Akyem Abuakwa 1700–1943, from Ofori Panin to Sir Ofori Atta* (Trondheim, 2001), 10.

32 Addo-Fening, *Akyem Abuakwa*, 14.

33 The word 'destool' involves an act of severing the link between a chief and his stool, a socio-religious and political symbol of office. A similar word in this context would be to 'dethrone'.

34 Robert Addo-Fening, 'The Akyem Abuakwa Asafo, 1700–1918', *Transactions of the Historical Society of Ghana* New Series 2 (1998), 16–18.

financially limited by state monopoly on economic activities, especially trade.[35] However, far from being a helpless and hapless social group, Jean Allman observed that the *nkwankwaa* were 'artful initiators' of alliances and 'displayed an historical ability to take advantage of the fluid nature of Asante politics' by 'playing power against power.'[36] They are remembered for being at the centre of Asantehene Mensa Bonsu's destoolment in 1883, as well as the unsuccessful cocoa hold-up in Asante in 1934. In the case of the Volta River basin, especially among the inland *Ewedometowo* of Vakpo and Anfoega, members of the *Asafo* companies were able-bodied men who were neither teenagers nor members of the council of elders. Apart from martial duties, they also provided communal labour to the communities. The most striking feature of the *Asafo* in these areas was a heavy Akan influence in organisation and performance.[37]

By the latter part of the nineteenth century, apart from the *Asafo*, new social groups such as an educated Ghanaian elite had emerged. This western or mission-educated group included lawyers, doctors, engineers, and intellectuals in the upper echelons. However, in the mid and lower rungs were teachers, the clergy (mainly catechists), junior civil servants, small traders, clerks, and messengers. It was this lower group of 'young men' or youth who played a crucial role in the nationalist politics of the late colonial period.[38] These 'young men' of the late colonial period were neither members of the chiefly families nor the intelligentsia, nor commoners. They were unable to stay in the countryside or villages, and 'unable to find satisfactory alternative opportunities in the towns'. It was from this same population set that the CPP youth involved in the independence movement, commonly referred to as the 'verandah boys', were drawn.[39] However, from a more nuanced explanation, youth had several inferences. While it was a term used for the physically active segment of Ghana's population, and a particular component of the populace who were excluded from exercising power because they did not possess the material and (or) lineage requirements, there was also a gendered angle. In the case of women, marriage

35 See Ivor Wilks, *Asante in the Nineteenth Century: The Structure and Evolution of a Political Order* (Cambridge, 1975) and Jean Allman, 'The Youngman and the porcupine: class, nationalism and Asante's struggle for self-determination, 1954–57', *Journal of African History* 31:2 (1990), 263–79.

36 Jean Allman, 'The Youngman and the porcupine,' 269–70.

37 Kofi Baku, 'The Asafo in two Ewe states', *Transactions of the Historical Society of Ghana* New Series 2 (1998), 2–28.

38 Adu Boahen, *Ghana*, 102–3.

39 Roger Genoud, *Nationalism and Economic Development in Ghana* (New York, 1969), 51. Also see George M. Bob-Milliar, 'Verandah boys versus reactionary lawyers: nationalist activism in Ghana, 1946–1956' *International Journal of African Historical Studies* 47:2 (2014), 287–318 and Nana Yaw Boampong Sapong, 'Framing contentious politics in the Gold Coast: The Nkrumah contingency, 1948–1951' in Bea Lundt and Christoph Marx (eds), *Kwame Nkrumah, 1909–1972: A Controversial African Visionary* (Stuttgart, 2016).

and childbirth was a foremost determinant of whether one stayed in or left the youth bracket, while age lost its power as a significant factor.[40]

Under the colonial state's watch, the paradox of youth became evident. On one hand, the state had harnessed the energies of the youth 'as uniformed *askaris* and petty functionaries in the colonial bureaucracy, as catechists and teachers and as labourers building a modern economic infrastructure'.[41] On the other hand, these 'westernised' youth 'threatened to antagonise powerful constituencies ... on which colonial states depended'.[42] The process of 'westernisation,' including education and employment, 'gave the young confidence and the resources to challenge their elders' authority'.[43] Elsewhere on the Gold Coast in the nineteenth century, aspiring young men were often caught in the throes of a troubled global economy and traditional power politics. Emmanuel Akyeampong's work on Christian Jacobson is illustrative, as it shows economic decline in West Africa, the unsavory business practices of established traders in the metropole and on the Gold Coast, and the limitations these placed on young traders in late-nineteenth-century Gold Coast. European business partners who had filed for bankruptcy in Britain kept that information from their associates in the Gold Coast. Thus, young enterprising traders such as Christian Jacobson fell victim to this omission and later incurred losses. Additionally, although Jacobson regarded himself as a business associate of Chief Akolatse of Anlo, he was saddled with the repayment of monies he had taken from Chief Akolatse to go into doomed business partnerships. Indeed, an 1892 lawsuit in the Supreme Court of the Gold Coast revealed that Chief Akolatse allegedly retained the services of Jacobson as a clerk from 1880 to 1886, but later declined to settle his wages.[44]

The script of potential contestation between the state and youth over the future of the continent and its individual countries remained in the post-colonial period. Interestingly, the post-colonial state did not stray too far from the colonial state's paradoxical attitude towards and approach to the youth question. Ultimately, looking at the concept of youth through specific

40 Kojo S. Amanor, "Rural Youth and the Right to a Livelihood in Ghana," a paper delivered at 'Conference on Youth and the Global South: Religion, Politics and the Making of Youth in Africa, Asia and the Middle East,' CODESRIA, Dakar, Senegal, 13–15 October, 2006, 2. Also see Kojo S. Amanor, *Global Restructuring and Land Rights in Ghana: Forest Food Chains, Timber and Rural Livelihoods* (Uppsala, 1999).

41 Richard Waller, 'Rebellious youth in colonial Africa', *Journal of African History* 47:1 (2006), 78.

42 *Ibid.*, 78.

43 *Ibid.*, 79.

44 Emmanuel Akyeampong, 'Commerce, credit, and mobility in late nineteenth-century Gold Coast: changing dynamics in Euro-African trade' in Emmanuel Akyeampong, Robert H. Bates, Nathan Nunn and James A. Robinson (eds), *Africa's Development in Historical Perspective* (Cambridge, 2014), 255–8.

time periods present scholars and students with an opportunity to explore the contextual circumstances and anxieties, and measure the opportunities and risks associated with the youth and Ghana's political economy.

Youth, Anxieties and Silences: The Long 1970s

Power and historical agency play a crucial role in why and how youth narratives are generated.[45] On the African continent, youth are 'particularly sensitive to transformations in the economy as their activities, prospects, and ambitions are dislocated and redirected'.[46] Additionally, they tend to be caught in an unending cycle of being used and discarded in emergent forms of political participation and influence. Furthermore, youth is a period when young people live in what Honwana described as 'waithood,' a protracted, uncertain, problematic, and dynamic transition into adulthood. In the quotidian details of everyday life, young adults learn to 'wait for their turn'.[47] In the long 1970s (mid-1960s and 1970s), the state attempted to seize the rhetoric of power by appropriating youth energies through Ghana's self-help desire for the nation and the continent.

In the post-colonial moment, the state endeavored to be creative as it tried to harness the potential of its teeming youth. In the 1960s, the songwriter Jonathan Michael Teye Dosoo (J.M.T. Dosoo), seized by nationalist *zeitgeist*, composed the song 'Arise Ghana Youth.'

Arise Ghana youth for your country
The nation demands your devotion
Let us all unite to uphold her
And make her great and strong

Refrain:

We are all involved
We are all involved
We are all involved
In building our motherland

This song was augmented by other patriotic songs aimed at workers (of which a majority were 'young men') such as the Ramblers Dance Band rendition of

45 See Deborah Durham, 'Youth and the social imagination in Africa: introduction to Parts 1 and 2.' *Anthropological Quarterly* 73:3 (2000), 113–20. On the topic of hegemonic narratives, see Michel-Rolph Trouillot, *Silencing the Past: Power and the Production of History* (Boston, 1995).

46 Durham, 'Youth and the Social Imagination', 114.

47 Alcinda Manuel Honwana, 'Youth struggles: from the Arab Spring to Black Lives Matter and beyond', *African Studies Review* 62:1 (2019), 8–21.

'Work and Happiness.' Paradoxically, these songs present a habitual conundrum in Ghana's political economy, which generated anxieties for the country's youth population. In colonial Africa, the youth were active agents in liberation movements and the process of decolonisation. Yet, in the post-colonial period, demographic changes and an increase in youth population led to anxieties about young people in Africa.[48] Indeed, a consistent rise in Ghana's population signalled a burden on the country's existing resources. The 1960 population census of Ghana recorded a 63.3 per cent increase in Ghana's population over the 1948 census.[49] By 1960, an estimated 2.5 million people, most of who were in the 'young men' category, were working as railway workers, miners, carpenters, construction site labourers, prostitutes, among other vocations. Frequently, these workers formed associations and unions which engaged the state in contentions.[50]

After the 1966 coup d'état, a concatenation of happenstances made it cumbersome to separate events of the mid-1960s from those of the 1970s. The National Liberation Council (NLC) gradually came to terms with its fragility and impermanence, especially after the death of Kotoka,[51] and mounting economic problems. Additionally, events such as the cocoa slump beginning in 1969 ensured a toning down of the euphoria that greeted the 'liberation' from Nkrumah's government. Thus, the 'long 1970s' (1966–79) came to represent a puzzling admixture of economic decay and survival, an inexplicable period sullied by state incompetence but considered redeemable by the 'self-help' spirit of the people. The crisis of the 'long 1970s' generated anxieties for Ghana's post-colonial population, especially the youth. Population growth and unemployment, as well as the rising cost of living, triggered a sense of desperation. Nonetheless, the Ghanaian state created associations to direct the energy and potential of its youthful population towards political and economic ends. The long 1970s, a period of uncertainty in Ghana's political economy, also

48 See Diouf, 'Engaging postcolonial cultures', 1–12; and Michelle Gavin, 'Africa's restless youth', *Current History* 106:700 (2007), 220–6.

49 From 4,118,450 in 1948 to 6,726,815 in 1960. See B. Gil and K.T. de Graft-Johnson, *1960 Population Census of Ghana*, Volume V, *General Report* (Accra 1964), xxii. Note that figures for the 1948 census missed a significant number of people. See Austin's revised estimate in the introduction to this volume.

50 For more on railway workers during the Nkrumah era, see Richard Jeffries, *Class, Power and Ideology in Ghana: the Railwaymen of Sekondi* (Cambridge, 1978). Also, on workers' discontent, see Nana Osei-Opare, '"If you trouble a hungry snake, you will force it to bite you": rethinking postcolonial African archival pessimism, worker discontent, and petition writing in Ghana, 1957–66', *Journal of African History* 62:1 (2021), 59–78.

51 On Monday, 17 April 1967, Lt. Gen. E.K. Kotoka, a member of the NLC, was assassinated by rogue members of the Ghana Armed Forces. See 'Kotoka Killed' *Daily Graphic*, 18 April 1967. Also see 'Attempted Coup is Crushed', *Daily Graphic*, 18 April 1967; and 'Arthur Planned Abortive Coup', *Daily Graphic*, 29 April 1967.

witnessed substantive efforts to integrate the youth into Ghana's response to economic crisis. Through youth-centered initiatives such as the National Service Corps and the National Service Scheme, Ghana reconsidered its self-help and Africa-centered posture.

Youth as a Third Force: The National Service Corps (NSC), 1969–1972

In late August 1969, a general election was held in Ghana, which was won by K. A. Busia's Progress Party. Thus began Ghana's second post-colonial attempt at representative government on 1 October 1969.[52] Faced with the enormity of a crippling external debt, high unemployment, and a general lack of provision for basic and essential needs especially in the rural areas, the Busia government tried different remedies, including stirring the youth into action. At a seminar titled 'The Youth and the Second Republic', Mr. A.A. Munufie, the Minister of Social and Rural Development, admonished the youth to form a 'third force' in Ghana's reconstruction.[53] In a 15 December 1969 radio and television broadcast, Prime Minister Busia announced the founding of the National Service Corps (NSC) under the Office of the Prime Minister. The Gliding School at Afienya[54] was to become the headquarters for training supervisors and executives of the NSC. The NSC was founded to revive the spirit of accomplishing things together as a community. It was intended to serve as an organising and rallying point for voluntary service to the nation. Citing *Asafo* companies as a traditional form of voluntary service, Prime Minister Busia appealed to Ghanaians to join his quest to solve 'our problems of hunger, illiteracy, disease and unemployment'.[55] The NSC was to be engaged in farming, road construction, community healthcare, sanitation projects, building affordable housing, constructing boreholes and wells, and generally expanding amenities to towns and villages. In terms of organisation, the NSC was headed by a director, who was aided by a National Committee. This committee included ministers of state, representatives from the Ministries of Agriculture, Finance and Economic Planning, Lands and Mineral Resources, Works and Interior, and representatives from the National Youth Council, Trades Union Congress, and the defence services.

52 'Ghana Returns to Civil Rule' *Daily Graphic*, 2 October 1969.

53 'Towards National Reconstruction: The Youth as a Third Force', *Daily Graphic*, 4 November 1969.

54 For more discussion on the gliding school, see Jean Allman, 'Phantoms of the archive: Kwame Nkrumah, a Nazi pilot named Hanna, and the contingencies of postcolonial history-writing', *American Historical Review* 118:1 (2013), 104–29.

55 Republic of Ghana, *A Call to Service: Radio and Television Broadcast by Dr. the Rt. Hon. K.A. Busia Prime Minister*, 15 December 1969. Also see 'National Service Corps Formed', *Daily Graphic*, 16 December 1969.

At inception, the NSC was envisioned to be the organising body for an obligatory training in responsible citizenship and service for university and secondary school students. Consistent with intrigues surrounding initiatives involving the youth, Busia had to fend off accusations of creating a paramilitary organisation. Indeed, one of Busia's central preoccupations was to rechannel youth energies into the national development discourse, as he was concerned with the anxieties associated with a youthful, unemployed population. He emphasised that when 'youth talk of war, and seek to tread the paths of war, they are doing nothing new; they are merely seeking to tread again the paths which have always led to disaster'.[56] Thus, the NSC through selfless service and camaraderie, will pursue 'nation-building, national unity, and peace'.[57] Furthermore, the NSC programme was to provide training to the youth but in the long term, it was to provide opportunities for employment. Additionally, the NSC was meant to complement and not to replace existing youth-oriented associations such as the Workers Brigade, the National Youth Council, Voluntary Workcamps Association of Ghana, and the National Union of Ghana Students (NUGS).

Ultimately, the success of this initiative was dependent, not only on the Office of the Prime Minister but also on stakeholders such as the universities, polytechnics, teacher training colleges, secondary schools, and vocational schools. An initial concern was how to align the timetable of the NSC to the academic schedule of public universities. An instance of this situation was the decision by the Academic Board of University of Science and Technology, Kumasi, to ask for exemption from voluntary service during the long vacation. This decision was based on the premise that students undertook their practical training during this period.[58] Certain departments at the University of Ghana and the University College of Cape Coast expressed similar concerns. Despite these apparent issues, the NSC had established several training centres across the country by early 1971. These included the Avenorpeme Centre in the Volta Region, the Wa Farming Project in the Upper Region, and the University of Science and Technology NSC Training Centre in Kumasi. The courses ranged from Home Science, pottery, crop farming, livestock farming to building

56 'Address by the Rt. Hon. The Prime Minister at the Inaugural Meeting of the National Committee of the National Service Corps at the Castle Conference Room on Friday, the 8th of January, 1971, at 10.00 A.M.' Press Release, Ministry of Information, Accra, 8 January 1971. Public Records and Archives Administration Department (PRAAD hereafter) GH/PRAAD/RG3/5/2525.

57 *Ibid.*

58 Letter from the Registrar's office, University of Science and Technology, Kumasi, to the Principal Secretary, National Council for Higher Education, 9 October 1970.

construction. There were also plans to start programmes at Afienya in masonry, roofing, painting, carpentry, plumbing and electricals.[59]

By June 1971, the NSC had ongoing projects in Greater Accra, Volta, Western, Central, Ashanti, Eastern, Brong Ahafo, Northern and Upper regions. These projects were mainly in construction, and included pit latrines, health posts, schools, community centres, markets and postal agencies. In a total of 96 projects across the 9 regions, 41 (42.7 per cent) were pit latrines, 30 (31.3 per cent) were health posts and 12 (12.5 per cent) were schools. The rest included three postal agencies, three community centres, two markets and five miscellaneous projects. In the Ashanti Region, one interesting addition was the construction of a 2.5-mile wall around Wesley College, Kumasi.[60] Busia, coincidentally, was an alumnus of Wesley College.

Table 11.1 National Service Corps Projects by Region

Region	**Number of NSC Projects**	**Description**
Central	23	Pit latrines, health posts, schools, postal agency
Eastern	18	Health posts, pit latrines, schools, market, drainage
Ashanti	13	Pit latrines, health posts, community centre, school, house, 2.5-mile wall
Brong Ahafo	10	Schools, pit latrines, postal agency, house craft centre, village improvement
Western	10	Health posts, pit latrines, schools
Greater Accra	8	Pit latrines, health posts, school
Northern	6	Pit latrines
Upper	5	Community centres, pit latrines, market
Volta	3	Pit latrine, school, feeder road
Total	96	

Unfortunately, these programmes were disrupted when the Second Republic was truncated by the National Redemption Council (NRC).

On January 13, 1972, Col. I. K. Acheampong announced the overthrow of the Busia-led Progress Party. The reasons for the coup d'état included

59 'Report of the Sub-Committee on Training (NSC) to the National Committee', GH/PRAAD/RG3/5/2525.

60 These statistics were generated by author using data from 9 regions. See 'Progress Report on National Service Corps Projects as on 30th June, 1971', NSC Sub-Committee on Training, GH/PRAAD/RG3/5/2403.

corruption, arbitrary dismissal of civil servants, devaluation of the cedi, and economic mismanagement.[61] Indeed, the National Redemption Council (NRC) formed under Acheampong referred to the takeover as a revolution. The NRC referred to a revolution that must lead to the discovery of a capacity for self-reliance, cooperation and self-development. Considering this, the NRC drew up a charter that had seven goals:

1. One Nation, One People, One Destiny
2. Total Manpower Development and Deployment
3. Revolutionary Discipline
4. Self-Reliance
5. Service to the People
6. Patriotism and International Brotherhood
7. Mobilisation of Spiritual, Intellectual and Willpower[62]

Initially, the NRC had a lot of goodwill from professionals, students, traditional rulers, civil servants and farmers. The state initiated several agricultural policies including 'Operation Feed Yourself' and 'Operation Feed Your Industries.' These policies were aimed at ending Ghana's dependence on food imports and increasing the production of cash crops such as rice, sugarcane, rubber, and cotton. There is the often-told story of over 700 students from University of Cape Coast and Komenda Teachers Training College who harvested about 80 tonnes of sugarcane to feed the sugar factory at Komenda. To its credit, the NRC initially united the country to solve the food problem. This chapter maintains that those early years of the NRC also witnessed an attempt to address the youth question. This culminated in the founding of the National Service Scheme (NSS).

The National Service Scheme [63]

In a broadcast statement on the revised budget for the 1971–72 fiscal year, Col. Acheampong hinted that his government intended to abolish the National Service Corps and merge it with the Department of Social Welfare and

61 'Coup! Army Takes Over', *Daily Graphic*, January 14, 1972.

62 Republic of Ghana, *Two Years in Office of Colonel Ignatius Kutu Acheampong, 13th January 1972–12th January 1974* (Tema, 1974), 15–22.

63 For a detailed discussion of the NSS, see Sylvester Akyea, 'A History of the National Service Scheme in Ghana, 1973–2000' (BA Long Essay, University of Ghana, 2018). His study of the NSS was conducted under my supervision in the 2017–18 academic year.

Community Development.[64] The National Service Corps (NSC) was subsequently dissolved by the NRC Decree 47 (23-3-72). The decree also disposed of the assets and liabilities of the NSC. In the following year, the National Service Scheme (NSS) was established by National Redemption Council Decree (NRCD) 208. The provisions of the decree stipulated that any Ghanaian who completed any course of study at any of Ghana's public universities (UG, KNUST, UCC), and any other educational institution prescribed by the Commissioner of Education, shall serve the country for a year in certain key areas. These included education, health, rural development, agriculture, local government, youth programmes, cooperatives, or any other area deemed critical by the NRC. The NSS was compulsory and abstention punishable by law (section 3 of the NRCD 208). According to Akyea, the NSS has undergone three phases of transformation since its founding in 1973. These are evolution (1973–1983), progression (1983–2000) and innovation (2000–present). However, this chapter's focus is on the long 1970s, a period in which the state found an avenue to keep its youth and unemployed 'productive'. The long 1970s overlaps with the period of evolution in the history of the NSS, an era that laid a solid foundation for subsequent periods.

In May 1978, the Supreme Military Council[65] approved the setting up of a committee to review the NSS. It was chaired by F.K. Buah, a historian and chair of the Council of the University of Cape Coast. The report generated by this committee was released in June 1979, and it proved to be a constructive assessment of the first 5 years of the NSS.[66] Known as the F.K. Buah Report, it laid out some of the problems encountered by the NSS, including interference from government officials and parents, lack of decent accommodation and reliable transportation, and lack of enthusiasm from service persons. The report then recommended several action points, including sustaining the NSS, decentralising the administration of the NSS, assigning more service persons to rural schools, increasing the duration of service to 2 years and integrating military training into the NSS. The report also contained statistics on annual NSS assignments across the country from 1973 to 1978.

64 Col. I.K. Acheampong, *Speeches and Interviews by Col. I.K. Acheampong* (Tema, 1973), 47. GPC/A18/10,000/1/73.

65 In 1975, the Head of State Col. I.K. Acheampong replaced three top members of the NRC (Maj. K. Baah, Maj. K.B. Agbo and Maj. Anthony Selormey) with heads of units in the Ghana Armed Forces, to form the Supreme Military Council I (SMC I). Ironically, in July 1978, Acheampong was forced to step down by commanders from units in the armed forces. Lt. Gen. F.W. K. Akuffo became the new leader of the reconstituted SMC II.

66 'Report of the Committee on the National Service Scheme' June 1979, GH/PRAAD/RG8/2/492.

Table 11.2 National Service Scheme Assignments 1973–78[67]

NSS Year	Number of NSS Persons
1973–1974	1,330
1974–1975	1,350
1975–1976	1,450
1976–1977	1,500
1977–1978	1,550
Total	7,180

The above figures seem negligible when compared to Ghana's population size, which was estimated to be 9.44 million in 1972, 10.3 million in 1975, and 11.25 million in 1978.[68] However, it is important to point out that, unlike the NSC which opened its doors to all volunteers, the NSS was mainly serviced by educational institutions whose students were already a privileged minority. The F.K. Buah Report was a driving force behind subsequent changes which took place in the NSS, starting with the 1980 Ghana National Service Scheme Act 426.

By 1978, the synergy between the NRC/Supreme Military Council (SMC) and Ghanaians, especially the youth, had been whittled away by acts of corruption, nepotism, hoarding, profiteering, political intimidation and arbitrary arrests. The last straw was when the SMC under Acheampong attempted to prolong his hold on power by forcing a referendum to be held on the 'union government' idea. The youth on university campuses joined other groups and associations to criticise the government. In a remedial attempt, the SMC removed Acheampong and initiated a schedule to return Ghana to civil rule. However, on June 4, 1979, junior officers in the Ghana Armed Forces orchestrated a coup d'état which brought in the Armed Forces Revolutionary Council.

Gender in National Service Narratives[69]

States throughout Ghana's pre-colonial, colonial and post-colonial eras have sought to capture agency when it came to determining what to do with its youthful populations. Nonetheless, what was more striking was a conscious

67 *Ibid.*

68 See https://data.worldbank.org/indicator/SP.POP.TOTL?locations=GH (accessed 4 June 2025).

69 This topic is the subject of ongoing research by the author.

attempt to delineate and reinforce gender roles in official approach to the youth question. In the long 1970s, policy documents and government pronouncements reinforced prevailing perceptions of gender roles in training, capacity building and work. NSC programmes were particularly cast in this mould. In 1971, a report from the Sub-committee on Training of the NSC indicated that a majority of Middle School Form 4 girls did not have employable skills.[70] To mitigate this situation, however, policy documents and actions from state initiatives in the long 1970s imposed gender assumptions and revealed an uneven attempt at dealing with the youth question. In a call to action towards nation-building, national unity, and peace, the state appealed to a 'brotherhood in action,' setting the tone for a gender-biased approach.

In Brakwa (Central Region), one of the early laboratories of testing NSC initiatives, the Ministries of Health, Education, Youth and Rural Development, Information, and the Ghana Red Cross, took 35 women and girls through a training course in health at home, village sanitation, home improvement, simple nutrition, mother and childcare and serving. Additionally, selected women were taken through short courses to prepare them for feeding and house-keeping duties at project sites throughout the country. On 22 February 1971, the Avenorpeme Centre, which was founded solely for women, held its first 4-week course for 35 women volunteers from the Volta Region. The coterie of courses included Home Science and pottery, mainstays in all approved NSC programmes designed for women.[71] The programmes designed for men, however, included a wider variety of courses, making them more employable than the women. These included livestock farming, building construction, masonry, roofing, painting, carpentry, plumbing and electricals.

Conclusion: Youth Within and Beyond the Long Twentieth Century

Ghana's long twentieth century offers a unique opportunity to interrogate the concept of youth through time. Although more emphasis was placed on the long 1970s in this chapter, it is important to reiterate that the history of Ghana's political economy in the long twentieth century has been a story of how an unholy alliance of the state (and traditional authority), interest groups and the market colluded to take advantage of a vulnerable but volatile youth population through invented traditions and associations. Additionally, despite periodic cycles of economic slump, the state sought to integrate the youth into

70 Minutes of the Meeting of the National Service Corps Sub-Committee on Training Held in the Office of the Chief Education Officer, Ministry of Education, on Saturday, 23 January 1971, GH/PRAAD/RG3/5/2403.

71 'Address by the Rt. Hon. The Prime Minister', GH/PRAAD/RG3/5/2525'.

economic and political solutions. Furthermore, as a part of this chapter has shown, the long 1970s abounded in programmes to harness youth potential, which frequently employed language that differentiated between gender roles, and assigned specific tasks, training and career trajectory to women.

The years 1979 (June 4) and 1981 (December 31) saw the occurrence of two military coup d'état, which some regarded as comeuppance for the political elites' inability to reverse Ghana's economic miasma and ill fortune. In the eye of the political storm were actors who fell within the 'youth' category. These included servicemen and women, students and workers who provided a support base for the coup d'état. Consequently, the political and economic contexts of the early 1980s subsumed youth under populist rhetoric, movements, and 'organs' of revolution. The Provisional National Defence Council (PNDC) set up public committees such as the People's Defence Committee (PDC), which later morphed into the Committee for the Defence of the Revolution (CDR). The CDRs were in both the rural and urban areas and extended their activities to the workplaces and the communities. In 1982, the 31 December Women's Movement was also created to promote the interest of women. During this period, the youth question was rephrased and subsumed under revolutionary rhetoric, as the existence and survival of the nation was declared paramount.

However, by the late 1980s, contingencies of history, political stability, and structural changes in the economy initiated a neo-liberal phase in Ghana's political economy. The story of Ghana as a 'star pupil' in IMF and World Bank-inspired initiatives is a well-known trope, but how did this create a safety net for the country's vulnerable, teeming youth? Amanor is of the view that neo-liberal reforms in Ghana, starting with those of the late-twentieth century, gradually created a hostile environment for the youth in rural areas. The creeping power of chiefs over land and natural resources, and an openness to large-scale foreign capital investment in rural areas has gradually closed the door on alternative livelihoods for rural youth.[72] Perhaps the life story of Francis is illustrative. In 1990 in the Ashanti region of Ghana, Francis, also known as Rootman, was born to a tailor and a petty trader. He was the fourth of eleven children, and a gifted soccer player who had ambitions of playing in a major league. However, he had to give up his dream because he could not rely on his parents' meagre income. At age 17, Rootman moved to Ashiaman, a shanty peri-urban sprawl in Greater Accra. There, he became an apprentice to a master tiler. Interestingly, throughout these years Rootman never gave up on soccer. He used to make his way to Madina to play colt soccer. After four years of apprenticeship, Rootman graduated and set up his own tiling business. His children want to

72 Kojo Amanor, 'Rural Youth and the Right to a Livelihood in Ghana', 19.

become medical doctors and military officers. Ironically, Rootman still dreams of soccer, and is open to travel opportunities.[73]

The twenty-first century presented its unique set of problems for governments in Africa, but the youth question remained. In Ghana's urban, peri-urban and rural areas, the opportunities and challenges of having a 'youth bulge' was ever-present. The youth served as an untapped reservoir of human capital but were also a wellspring of 'foot soldiers' for the main political parties during election cycles. On the negative side, a host of unemployed youth could spell trouble for any government. The state's attempt to solve this conundrum included state-sponsored youth programmes.[74] In 2006, the National Youth Employment Programme (NYEP) was inaugurated under the Office of the President, similar to Busia's attempt to by-pass bureaucratic limitations to establish the NSC. Couched in the shadow of the Millenium Development Goals, the NYEP was, among other things, intended to reduce poverty, increase access to education, and improve healthcare. More importantly, the NYEP was envisioned to tackle youth unemployment and pre-empt its undesirable consequences. Six years later, the state reconstituted the NYEP into the Ghana Youth Employment and Entrepreneurial Agency. Furthermore, the state initiated the process to imbue this initiative with legal backing by passing the Youth Employment Agency Bill (Youth Employment Agency Act 2015, Act 887) through Parliament. A subsequent law, the Youth Employment Agency Regulations 2016, L.I. 2231, was passed to enforce Act 887. Thus, the Youth Employment Agency was born 'to oversee the development, coordination, supervision and facilitation of employment for the youth and related matters in Ghana'.[75] Oddly, the National Service Scheme is still running concurrently with the YEA.

Although the usefulness of youth-focused initiatives such as the National Service Corps, the National Service Scheme, the National Youth Employment Programme, the Ghana Youth Employment and Entrepreneurial Agency, and the Youth Employment Agency in Ghana cannot be denied, the potential for state capture is ever-present. Throughout its short existence in the Second Republic, Busia had continuously to reassure Ghanaians that the NSC was not a paramilitary organisation. The PNDC on the other hand did not hide its intentions on the function of the CDRs in the early 1980s. Elsewhere in Africa, in Zimbabwe, the National Youth Service (NYS) was founded in 2001. This organisation became an instrument of the Zimbabwe African National Union - Patriotic Front party. Through the NYS, the state coerced young adults into engaging in acts that consolidated the party's hold on power. Generally,

73 Personal interview with Francis, a.k.a Rootman, July 2023, in Kwashieman, Accra.

74 See Emmanuel A. Codjoe, 'The prospects and challenges of a youthful population in achieving economic and social transformation in Ghana', in Ernest Aryeetey and Ravi Kanbur (eds), *The Economy of Ghana Sixty Years after Independence* (Oxford, 2017).

75 https://yea.gov.gh/index.php/about-us (accessed 30 September 2024).

these young people were unduly influenced and exploited because of their economic vulnerability.[76] Such examples do not give a bright prognosis for youth and historical agency in the twenty-first century. Perhaps lessons can be learned from pre-colonial groupings such as the *asafo*, who often seized historical agency, unlike the top-down, post-independence organisations set up as conduits for youthful energies. Nonetheless, the presence of an educated, healthy and hopeful youth augurs well for future of this continent, and Ghana in particular. In this future, youth in sub-Saharan Africa will be a significant catalyst for change.[77] It is undeniable that they have consistently been a catalyst for change in Ghana's political economy throughout the long twentieth century, and indeed in Ghana's long 1970s.

76 Ivo Mhike, 'Political violence in Zimbabwe's National Youth Service, 2001–2007', in Elina Oinas, Henri Onodera, and Leena Suurpaa (eds), *What Politics? Youth and Political Engagement in Africa* (Leiden, 2018), 246–64.

77 Gavin, 'Africa's Restless Youth', 220.

12

From Geological Pathfinder, through Illicit Undertaking to Indispensable Income-Earning Activity: Reflecting on the Multiple Roles of Small-Scale Gold Mining in Ghana, 1957–2024

Gavin Hilson

Over the past two decades, few subjects have attracted more media attention in Ghana than artisanal and small-scale mining (ASM).[1] Despite making formalisation of ASM a centrepiece of his campaign for the December 2016 election, in office President Nana Akufo-Addo chose to do the exact opposite following his inauguration: to eradicate, with force, all unlicensed ASM activities in the country. But a campaign that began with the launch of *Operation Vanguard*, a military-led 'crusade' aimed at bringing *illegal* mining to a grinding halt – which, in its inaugural months, was buoyed by a fervent media that had galvanised around imagery of defaced landscapes and polluted waterbodies – rapidly became a debacle.

The original plan was to recruit 500 men and women from the army, navy and police to execute *Operation Vanguard*; they would subsequently make their way across Ghana, shutting down all unlicensed ASM operations in their paths. Three months after the operation was launched in April 2017, the government published its *Multi-Sectoral Mining Integrated Project* (MMIP), a project conceived by the Ministry of Lands and Natural Resources 'to ensure the systematic and sustainable development of Artisanal and Small-Scale Mining in Ghana'.[2] A 'strategy' which officials believed legitimised *Operation Vanguard*, *Operation Halt II* (its successor) and more broadly,

1 Whilst the precise definitions vary from location-to-location, ASM is widely regarded as low-tech, labour-intensive mineral extraction and processing. Experts recognise it as the category of activities comprising the most rudimentary branch of the mining sector. Ghana, like most countries in sub-Saharan Africa, has a diversified ASM economy but this chapter focuses exclusively on gold, its largest segment.

2 Ministry of Lands and Natural Resources (MLNR), 'Project Appraisal and Implementation Document' (PAID), Multi-Sectoral Mining Integrated Project (MMIP) (Accra, 2017), 18.

military intervention in Ghana's ASM communities, the MMIP was conceived by the government, 'upon assumption of office', believing it was 'further demonstration of its commitment to addressing the menace of illegal and unsustainable mining practices'. What remains unclear, however, is how the government believed 'Measures Taken to Address the Illegal Mining Menace' were in any way an appropriate course of action 'to ensure the systematic and sustainable development of Artisanal and Small-Scale Mining in Ghana', the stated goal of the MMIP.[3]

Operation Vanguard could not be sustained because the government was unable to mobilise the finance needed to carry out regular monitoring of communities. Arrests were made and excavators seized but this did little to reduce ASM activity; it did little more than appease a hungry media and stoke further public resentment of *galamsey* activity.[4] Once knowledge of the timings of *Vanguard* visits was gained, miners were able to elude soldiers and police, and proceeded to warn colleagues in neighbouring villages in advance of their arrival; some savvy individuals began working after dark in order to avoid being caught.

The government, it seems, assumed incorrectly that donors – in particular, the World Bank – would finance *Operation Vanguard*, either directly or indirectly. Believing this was the case, officials at the Ministry of Lands and Natural Resources would identify, in the MMIP Project Appraisal Document, 'five interrelated components' (of the MMIP), with dollar figures attached. They were as follows: (1) Review and Enforce the Legal and Regulatory Regime (US$10 million); (2) Reclamation of Degraded Lands, Dredge silted Estuaries and Waterways and Free Lands for Agribusiness (US$100 million); (3) Implementation of Social Interventions to facilitate sustainable livelihood creation in mining communities (US$50 million); (4) Adoption of Technology to ensure efficient mining, processing, environmental and monitoring activities (US$20 million); and (5) Capacity Building of ASM, and Regulatory Institutions and Project Management including Communication (US$20 million).

The Akufo-Addo Government expected external partners to fund 80 per cent of these activities. The likely reasons why the World Bank shied away from supporting this particular version of the MMIP, however, were the controversial measures[5] being proposed by the government to 'sanitise' ASM, and

3 *Ibid.*, 13, 18.

4 *Galamsey* is a label used in Ghana for illegal mining, the meaning of which is 'gather them and sell'.

5 This largely has to do with the context in which the MMIP was due to be implemented: specifically, at a time when *Operation Vanguard* was in full force. For example, establishing Mining Intelligence Committees (MICs) under 'Review and Enforce the Legal and Regulatory Regime', and installing systems to track heavy equipment used in mining/construction and use drones to track ASM activities under 'Adoption of Technology to ensure efficient mining,

it having already provided tens of millions of dollars in technical assistance for ASM in Ghana under previous projects (with disappointing results).[6] It is probably no coincidence that in light of these developments, the World Bank elected to revise in advance its plans to provide additional technical support for ASM in Ghana, the details of which it circulated in early 2021. The COVID-19 pandemic provided Bank officials with an excuse to delay the launch of a revised project; they proceeded to revisit elements of the proposed US$47.8 million *Ghana: Artisanal and Small-Scale Mining Formalization Project* (P168002)[7] and US$62.76 million *Landscape Restoration and Ecosystem Management for Sustainable Food Systems Project* (P171933).[8] Yet, before the former had even been finalised, the government had declared – rather disconcertingly – that the 'The World Bank has approved 50 million dollars to support the government's efforts at addressing illegal small-scale mining under activities outlined in the Multi-Sectoral Mining Integrated Project (MMIP)'. Specifically, 'The draft manual of activities would be sponsored by the Bank and presented to its top management'.[9] Tense discussions between government officials and World Bank technical staff followed, culminating in one amalgamated *Ghana Landscape Restoration and Small-Scale Mining Project*. This project was officially launched in 2022 but with a significantly reduced budget of US$70 million.

Professor Frimpong Boateng, the Minister for Environment, Science, Technology and Innovation, was commissioned by the president to coordinate *Operation Vanguard*.[10] His rhetoric and energy proved instrumental in sustaining the exercise: despite only receiving sporadic injections of finance, he managed to keep it going for 20 months, until December 2018. When it emerged that the government could or would no longer pay *Vanguard* staff, many of the police officers and soldiers recruited for patrols began seizing heavy machinery (including those belonging to licensed small-scale miners),

---

processing, environmental and monitoring activities' were condemned by Bank officials, who viewed this as legitimising *Operation Vanguard*.

6 See World Bank *Project Performance Assessment Report Ghana, Natural Resources and Environmental Governance: First Development Policy Operation* (IDA-44260), *Second Natural Resources and Environmental Governance Development Policy Operation* (IDA-46270), *Third Natural Resources and Environmental Governance Development Policy Operation* (IDA-47460). All World Bank (Washington DC, 2014).

7 World Bank, *Project Information Document: Ghana: Artisanal and Small-Scale Mining Formalisation* (P168002) (Washington DC, 2019).

8 World Bank, *Project Information Document: Landscape Restoration and Ecosystem Management for Sustainable Food Systems Project* (P171933) (Washington DC, 2019).

9 'World Bank approves $50m for fight against galamsey', www.graphic.com.gh/news/general-news/world-bank-approves-50m-for-fight-against-galamsey.html (Accessed 4 July 2025).

10 The president was acting in his capacity as chair of the government's Inter-Ministerial Committee on Illegal Mining. The committee would be dissolved in 2021.

setting excavators ablaze and even mining themselves. It was the missing machinery seized during raids of sites, however, that caught the media's attention, sparking rumours that politicians had taken possession of them to lease them to *galamsey* operators themselves. Professor Frimpong-Boateng himself was accused of orchestrating this and was removed from his post in 2021.[11] He was found to be in possession of ASM concessions but it was ruled later that he had acquired them legally.[12]

Others were not so lucky, including influential figures such as the MP for Manso Nkwanta, Joseph Albert Quarm; the late Mr Owusu Afriyie, the former CEO of the Forestry Commission; the Minister for Information, Mr Kojo Oppong Nkrumah; and Lord Commey, Charles Nii Teiko and Frank Asiedu Bekoe, three appointees at Jubilee House, the seat of the presidency.[13]

But rather than taking stock of the limitations of *Operation Vanguard*, the Akufo-Addo Government maintained a militarised approach to manage ASM. It launched *Operation Halt II* in April 2021, an exercise 'made up of personnel from the Ghana Armed Forces' which seeks 'to remove all persons and mining equipment from water bodies and forest reserves in the country, including decommissioning and demobilising equipment where necessary'.[14] Much like its predecessor, however, *Operation Halt II* has failed to reduce unlicensed ASM activity across the country; it yielded the occasional flurry of arrests but little more.[15] The current National Democratic Congress (NDC)

11 Soldiers allegedly immobilised 700 excavators but only 150–200 remained at the end of the operation. See 'Frimpong-Boateng indicts NPP officials, others in "bombshell" galamsey report', https://citinewsroom.com/2023/04/frimpong-boateng-indicts-npp-officials-others-in-bombshell-galamsey-report/ (accessed 21 April 2025).

12 'Prof. Frimpong-Boateng was not involved in any illegal mining – CHRAJ boss', www.modernghana.com/news/1226719/prof-frimpong-boateng-was-not-involved-in-any.html (accessed 3 December 2025).

13 See 'Frimpong-Boateng lied, I don't own any mining concession – Former MP Joseph Albert Quarm denies illegal mining allegations', https://ghstandard.com/frimpong-boateng-lied-i-dont-own-any-mining-concession-former-mp-joseph-albert-quarm-denies-illegal-mining-allegations/79101/ (accessed 22 April 2025); 'Sir John had Chinese "gangs" mining on his behalf – Frimpong-Boateng's report reveals', https://www.modernghana.com/news/1225908/sir-john-had-chinese-gangsmining-on-his-behalf.html (accessed 23 April 2025); 'Professor Frimpong-Boateng Names 3 Jubilee House Appointees Supporting Illegal Mining', https://yen.com.gh/ghana/232132-professor-frimpong-boateng-names-3-jubilee-house-appointees-supporting-illegal-mining/ (accessed 1 May 2025).

14 'Operation Halt II relaunched: As chiefs, MMDCEs empowered', https://www.graphic.com.gh/news/general-news/operation-halt-ii-relaunched-as-chiefs-mmdces-empowered.html (accessed 3 April 2025).

15 The author has requested, from the Ministry of Defence and Ministry of the Interior, data on the number of arrests but each inquiry elicited a response explaining that this information is unavailable. Throughout Nana Akufo-Addo's presidential term (2017–2025), Ghanaian media outlets were littered with headlines that documented individual arrests

Government, in place since January 2025, has continued, in various guises, the work initiated by its predecessor to eradicate unlicensed ASM activity. It recently announced – possibly in a bid to appease the general public – that it had arrested at least 1,345 people engaged in 'illegal mining' in its first seven months in office.[16]

Significantly, the fanfare surrounding *Operation Vanguard*, *Operation Halt II* and the MMIP, and the – more often than not, exaggerated – media coverage they have attracted has overshadowed the many roles and functions, actual and perceived, ASM has played in Ghana over the past 100 years. The purpose of this chapter is to revisit these ideas, with the goal of reviving debates on the importance of ASM – referred to here as its *livelihoods dimension* – in rural Ghana. Pre-MMIP, there was vibrant discussion on this very subject that informed and shaped broader debates on the economic and social impacts of ASM in sub-Saharan Africa. Scholars are now in broad agreement that ASM is the most important rural non-farm activity in the region, generating disposable incomes that millions of people rely upon to support their family farms, and to cover other household expenses such as school fees, rent and transport (for example, payment for buses to and from markets, schools and villages). Many people who engage in ASM have reinvested their earnings in other business ventures, including restaurants, equipment (for leasing), transport and food provision services. These dynamics apply to Ghana, where today, over one million people rely on ASM directly for a large proportion of their incomes, and millions more livelihoods are linked (downstream and upstream) to the sector.

The chapter picks out certain points over the past 100 years to underscore how ASM's role and functions have changed in Ghana, despite the physical state of the sector itself evolving minimally during this time. An alluvial gold site in Tarkwa in the late 1800s mirrors the sprawling *galamsey* operations that now dot the landscape of the likes of Oda, Kade and Birim North in

and/or seizures of equipment from unlicensed ASM sites. Examples include "Over 800 illegal miners arrested since 2023, Foresters urge dialogue to end galamsey' see https://www.myjoyonline.com/over-800-illegal-miners-arrested-since-2023-foresters-urge-dialogue-to-end-galamsey/ (accessed 3 June 2025), and 'Galamsey: 5 arrested, 40 changfans burnt on Birim River' (see https://citinewsroom.com/2024/10/galamsey-5-arrested-40-changfans-burnt-on-birim-river/ (accessed 3 June 2025). There was an announcement made by the-then Attorney General and Minister of Justice toward the end of the Akufo-Addo presidency (October 2024) that between August 2021 and October 2024, at least 76 people, including 18 foreigners, were convicted on charges of illegal mining. See '76 people have been convicted for illegal mining since 2021 – Godfred Dame', https://www.myjoyonline.com/76-people-have-been-convicted-for-illegal-mining-since-2021-godfred-dame/ (accessed 4 July 2025).

16 'Ghana illegal mining: At least 1,345 people arrested in seven months. The government says the arrests were part of government's broader commitment to combating illegal mining', https://trt.global/afrika-english/article/2c2fe14c5fb7 (accessed 20 August 2025).

Ghana's Eastern Region. The only significant differences – which are discussed below – are that today, ASM is firmly entrenched in the informal economy, and is relied upon, as a *primary* source of income, by many more people. In Ghana, the economic impacts of ASM could be fully realised, and more impactful monitoring of the sector's activities would take place, if more effective formalisation strategies were in place. The country's ASM formalisation 'project', which is now in its fourth decade, has fallen short of its objectives. Rather than bringing operators into the legal domain, it has *created* and *perpetuated* the sector's informality. The widespread environmental degradation and numerous social 'ills' associated with the informal ASM economy that has burgeoned as a result have been easy targets for successive governments to create a narrative which, despite being simplistic and failing to explain most elements of the *galamsey* story, has proved effective in engaging the local media and general public.[17] It has obfuscated the economic, social and cultural importance of ASM in Ghana, and the impact it has had, historically, within its territories.

More People, More Activities but Little Change in the Past Century

Since independence, Ghana has experienced pronounced economic and political change. Against the background of these changes, the roles and functions played by (and perceptions of) ASM in wider Ghanaian society have also shifted markedly. This is despite the physical state of ASM itself evolving minimally during this time.

Much has been written about ASM sites in Ghana in recent years, from operations in Tarkwa in the Western Region; through Noyem and Dunkwa in the Eastern Region and Central Region, respectively; to former Talensi-Nabdam District in the Upper East Region.[18] Analysis of the findings reported reveals that each ASM site in Ghana exhibits unique attributes, organisationally, in its

17 Gavin Hilson,'"Creating" rural informality: the case of artisanal gold mining in Sub-Saharan Africa.', *SAIS Review of International Affairs* 33:1 (2013), 51–64; Gavin Hilson, Ekow Bartels, Yanfei Hu, 'Brick by brick, block by block: building and sustainable formalisation strategy for small-scale gold mining in Ghana', *Environmental Science and Policy* 35: (2022), 207–25.

18 T.R. Zolnikov, 'Effects of the government's ban in Ghana on women in artisanal and small-scale gold mining', *Resources Policy* 65 (2020), Art. 101561; H. Orleans-Boham, G.B. Sakyi-Addo, A. Tahiru and R. Amankwah, 'Women in artisanal mining: Reflections on the impacts of a ban on operations in Ghana', *The Extractive Industries and Society* 7:2 (2020), 583–6; Francis Arthur-Holmes and Kwaku Abrefa Busia, 'Women, North-South migration and artisanal and small-scale mining in Ghana: motivations, drivers and socio-economic implications', *The Extractive Industries and Society* 10 (2022), Art. 101076; Elizabeth Koomson-Yalley and Justice Richard Kwabena Owusu Kyei, '"We are mine workers": Feminists' political economy in artisanal and Small Scale gold mining in the Talensi District, Ghana', *Journal of Rural Studies* 95 (2022), 140–7.

own right; the design of every operation is influenced heavily by the types of gold deposits (alluvial or hardrock) being worked. Similar equipment, however, is generally found from site to site. Moreover, and as indicated, processing and extraction techniques employed have changed very little, which a rapid survey of the literature confirms.[19]

It starts with the basic structure and foundation of ASM operations. As several studies have shown, there is a broad and largely gender-based division of labour discernible at most ASM sites in the country. This is particularly evident with licensed operations; most titleholders are male (only 4 per cent of Ghana's small-scale mine license holders are women).[20] It is also men who generally amalgamate gold, operate heavy machinery and work as financiers. Women tend to be most concentrated at the lower tiers of the sector's labour pyramid, carrying out general labour such as ore hauling and washing. Over 100 years ago, Macdonald observed similar dynamics at ASM sites in Akan-speaking regions:

> Each woman is furnished with a number of large and small wooden bowls or calabashes, which are filled with the earth and sand obtained by the men from the manholes. This earth is repeatedly washed with fresh water in a most adept manner, the stones and earth being thrown out by a rapid rotary motion of the bowl till it is cleaned from all the earthy matters. The gold on account of its weight sinks to the bottom of the tray.[21]

In addition to the general division of labour, many of the practices employed at sites 100 years ago continue to feature today. For example, accounts of 'fire setting', of the process of heating rocks (achieved via similar means, including rudimentary furnaces), which breaks down sulphides,[22] can be found as far back as the 1880s, when it was observed to be widely practised in Prestea's hardrock environments.[23] Today, this (ore roasting) is common in all Ghana's hardrock settings, as is the 'timbering of shafts', which Dumett reported was taking place in the Gold Coast Colony by 'gold mining companies for pit

19 See, for example, Emmanuel Terray, 'Long-distance exchange and the formation of the state: the case of the Abron Kingdom of Gyaman', *Economy and Society* 3:3 (1974), 315–45; Emmanuel Ababio Ofosu-Mensah (2011), 'Historical overview of traditional and modern gold mining in Ghana', *International Research Journal of Library, Information and Archival Studies* 1:1 (2011), 6–22.

20 World Bank, *Ghana Landscape Restoration and Small Scale Mining Project*, Project Appraisal Document (Washington DC, 2021).

21 George Macdonald, 'Gold in West Africa', *Journal of the Royal African Society* 1:4 (1902), 416–30.

22 David Amaldi, 'A study of pre-colonial and contemporary methods of gold mining in Ghana', *Frontiers of Library, Information and Computer Sciences* 1:1 (2015), 27–42.

23 Winfried Peters, *History of Gold Mining in Ghana* (Geo-Leo e-docs, Lizenz, 2013).

props (underground timbering) and as fuel'.[24] Today, timber harvested from local forests and shrubbery is used to support mine shafts in locations where ore is being extracted underground, including in the likes of the aforementioned Prestea (Western Region), Talensi (Upper East Region) and Konongo (Ashanti Region).[25] During the colonial period, it was quite common that the 'roof of each pit was supported with timber to prevent the shaft from caving in or collapsing, just as galamsey operators do today'.[26]

Two other implements that continue to feature prominently in Ghana's ASM are bowls and weights. The former are used for sampling and washing gold. As indicated, in the Gold Coast, gold-aggregated ore was washed in calabashes and carved wooden bowls. Macdonald's descriptions from the early 1900s could apply to a typical ASM site today: how ore is repeatedly washed with fresh water 'in a most adept manner', and 'The gold on account of its weight sinks to the bottom of the tray' and residue is 'then passed to a smaller tray and the process repeated until nothing is left but the grains of gold and a little sand, which are again washed and the gold finally extracted'.[27] The only difference is that today, the principal sampling instrument used by artisanal and small-scale miners is the inner tube of an automobile tyre.[28] The same applies to the way in which gold is weighed. In his seminal work on Akan weights, Garrard[29] spoke about the castings (with symbolic meanings) used to weigh gold dust and determine the prices it fetched during the seventeenth to nineteenth centuries. Today, these weights have been replaced with items that are widely available in rural markets, such as razor blades and match sticks. Purchase of gold amalgam by local buyers is therefore typically quoted in 'sticks' and 'blades'.

The dependency of Ghana's ASM operators on mercury also remains unchanged. For centuries, mercury has been relied upon by miners operating in all corners of the globe to extract gold from ore as a stable amalgam,

24 Raymond E. Dumett, 'Tropical Forests and West African Enterprise: The Early History of the Ghana Timber Trade', *African Economic History* 29 (2001), 79–116, at 106.

25 Amegbey, N.A., Dankwa, J.B.K., Al-Hassan, 'Small scale mining in Ghana – techniques and environmental considerations', *International Journal of Surface Mining, Reclamation and Environment* 11:3 (1997), 135–8; Frank.K. Nyame and J. Andrew Grant, 'The political economy of transitory mining in Ghana: understanding the trajectories, triumphs, and tribulations of artisanal and small-scale operators', *The Extractive Industries and Society* 1:1 (2014), 75–85; K.J. Bansah, A.B. Yalley and N. Dumankor-Dupey, 'The hazardous nature of small scale underground mining in Ghana', *Journal of Sustainable Mining* 15:1 (2016), 8–25.

26 Emmanuel Ababio Ofosu-Mensah, 'Historical and modern artisanal small-scale mining in Akyem Abuakwa, Ghana', *Africa Today* 64:2 (2017), 69–81, at 72.

27 Macdonald, 'Gold', 422.

28 Gavin Hilson and Sandra Pardie, 'Mercury: an agent of poverty in Ghana's small-scale gold-mining sector?', *Resources Policy* 31:2 (2006), 106–16.

29 Timothy F. Garrard, *Akan Weights and the Gold Trade* (London, 1980).

coveted for its efficiency, ease of use and cost-effectiveness.[30] When released into the natural environment, however, mercury methylates can bioaccumulate to toxic levels, posing a series of threats to human health and wildlife. It is now widely known that in methylated form, mercury can disperse throughout the bloodstream, targeting the central nervous system and – in elevated concentrations – can cause coordination problems, hearing and vision impairment, convulsions and even death.[31] Regulation of the use of mercury in the country's gold mining commenced in 1933, following the passage of the Mercury Ordinance. The move, however, was not motivated by a desire to protect the environment but was rather a deliberate attempt by the colonial administration to weaken local chiefs' influence over the gold trade and facilitate a transfer of control of the mineral-rich territories to Europeans. The Mercury Ordinance prohibited the sale of mercury to locals, in the process effectively criminalising indigenous gold mining,[32] developments which Armah et al. reflect on in depth:

> The pre-colonial period was characterized by private and collective interest; no written policy; no nation-state (even though states existed); and social, cultural, and economic values guided mining.... Private Ghanaian gold miners were banned in 1932 from operating mines due to the promulgation of the Mercury Ordinance. This ban compelled indigenous miners to go into hiding so that their unregulated activities were carried out in secrecy. It marked the beginning of the criminalization of indigenous, small-scale gold mining until 1989 when the small-scale mining law was enacted by the Provisional National Defence Council (PNDC) to give legal status to the sector again.[33]

With the use of mercury by the colony's miners banned, traditional gold extraction setups rapidly eroded because 'Without mining, the chiefs did not have the same influence and control over their subjects, because they did not have leverage in terms of labour demands anymore'.[34] It was not until 1989, following passage of the Mercury Law (PNDCL 217) that Ghanaians were once

30 Lindsey Konkel, 'Safer gold rush? Curbing mercury pollution in artisanal and small-scale gold mining', *Environmental Health Perspectives* 127:1 (2019), 112001–1 – 112001–6.
31 Marti F. Wolfe, Steven Schwarzbach and Rini A. Sulaiman. 'Effects of mercury on wildlife: a comprehensive review', *Environmental Toxicology and Chemistry* 17:2 (1998), 146–160; Young-Seoub Hong, Yu-Mi Kim, and Kyung-Eun Lee, 'Methylmercury exposure and health effects', *Journal of Preventive Medicine and Public Health* 45:6 (2012), 353–63.
32 T. Aubynn, 'Regulatory Structures and challenges to Developmental Extractives: Some practical Observations from Ghana', WIDER Working Paper 2017/179, United Nations University (Helsinki, 2017), p. 5.
33 Frederick A. Armah, Isaac Luginaah and Justice Odoi, 'Artisanal small-scale mining and mercury pollution in Ghana: a critical examination of a messy minerals and gold mining policy', *Journal of Environmental Studies and Science* 3:4 (2013), 381–90, at 383–4.
34 Ofosu-Mensah, 'Historical overview', 18.

again authorised to sell mercury. It was passed alongside the Small-Scale Gold Mining Law (PNDCL 218) and Precious Minerals Marketing Corporation Law (PNDCL 219) as part of a three-pronged regulatory apparatus that officially legalised small-scale mining in the country.[35]

The environmental and health-related impacts of mercury use in ASM did not start attracting the attention of scholars until the late 1990s and early 2000s. They were first brought to the attention of the global public in the 1980s during the heyday of the Brazilian *garimpeiro* gold rushes. In Ghana itself, a steady stream of donor-funded work has been commissioned in recent years to explore the (methyl) mercury pollution problem in the country's ASM communities.[36] It has confirmed, *inter alia*, that mercury has long been released indiscriminately by ASM operators in all corners of the country. The mercury baseline study conducted in 2019 as part of Ghana's ratification of the Minamata Convention on Mercury[37] reaffirmed this: that annually, ASM accounts for the release of between 42.5 and 62 tonnes of mercury in the country, close to 13 per cent of national (mercury) emissions.[38] But it was not until the media began to showcase the work being carried out under *Operation Vanguard* and scholars and news outlets began to profile – in many instances, selectively – the damage ASM activities were causing to the country's waterbodies that the sector's mercury pollution problem began to be scrutinised, publicly, by Ghana's policymakers, Non-Governmental Organisation (NGO) officials and citizens.[39]

35 Fui S. Tsikata, 'The vicissitudes of mineral policy in Ghana', *Resources Policy* 23:1–2 (1997), 9–14.

36 Jeffrey Davidson, 'The transformation and successful development of small-scale mining enterprises in developing countries', *Natural Resources Forum* 17:4 (1993), 315–25; M. Babut, R. Sekyi, A. Rambaud, M. Potin-Gautier, S. Tellier, W. Bannerman, C. Beinhoff, 'Improving the environmental management of small-scale gold mining in Ghana: a case study of Dumasi', *Journal of Cleaner Production* 11:2 (2003), 215–21; Hilson and Pardie, 'Mercury'.

37 '*Garimpeiro*' is a local term used in Brazil for 'mineral prospector'. A significant amount of research was conducted during the 1980s which provided a glimpse of the environmental damage – principally, deforestation and methylmercury contamination – that gold rush activities were causing in sections of the Brazilian Amazon. See e.g., Luiz Drude de Lacerda, Wolfgang Christian Pfeiffer, Ari Teixeria Ott and Ene Gloria da Silveira, 'Mercury contamination in the Madeira river, Amazon-Hg Inputs to the Environment', *Biotropica* 21 (1989), 91–3; Wolfgang Christian Pfeiffer, O. Malm, C.M.M. Souza, Luiz Drude de Lacerda, Ene Gloria da Silveira, W.R. Bastos, 'Mercury in the Madeira river ecosystem, Rondônia, Brazil', *Forest Ecology and Management* 38:3–4 (1991), 239–45.

38 Global Environmental Facility and Ghana Environmental Protection Agency, *National Action Plan to Reduce and Where Feasible Eliminate Mercury Use in Artisanal and Small-Scale Gold Mining in Ghana* (Accra, 2020).

39 See e.g., '"We are poisoning ourselves": Ghana gold rush sparks environmental disaster', https://www.bbc.co.uk/news/articles/cn9dn8xq92jo (accessed 4 May 2025); 'A

In summary, ASM in Ghana has barely evolved over the past 100 years. It remains largely low-tech and labour-intensive, featuring similar techniques and similar divisions of labour. The growing presence of excavators in the sector is often mistakenly portrayed as 'mechanisation' when, in fact, these machines are relied upon to remove overburden and near-surface gravels. In the early 1900s, the 'native miner' was observed as 'having but few implements: a long-bladed spud or digger, a wooden bucket for baling out the water or hoisting up the stuff, and a bowl for washing or "panning" make up the list'.[40] Today, most ASM operators have a similar inventory, apart from the occasional pump and crushing machine (and possibly, an excavator). But whilst the organisational and technological dynamics of Ghana's ASM sector have changed minimally over time, its role and functions have changed a lot. Greater appreciation of ASM's importance in Ghanaian society would yield more dynamic solutions to reduce informal ASM activity than shortsighted interventions such as *Operation Vanguard*, as well as go a long way toward rewriting the narrative on *galamsey*.

The next section highlights the key junctures in the sector's journey over the past 100 years.

From Geological Pathfinder, through Illicit Undertaking to Indispensable Income-Earning Activity: The Multiple Roles of Small-Scale Gold Mining in Ghana

Ironically, *Operation Vanguard*, *Operation Halt II* and the MMIP emerged at a time when the 'livelihoods dimension' of ASM had started to catch the attention of donors. This has been particularly reflected in recent World Bank initiatives aimed at supporting ASM, including work carried out in Mali, Tanzania, Mozambique and Ghana. In these, and other, cases, technical assistance financed by Bank officials has been multifaceted; it has explored a range of issues, including gender equality, formalisation of ASM activities and links between agriculture and the sector's operations. Whilst only those in possession of a licence or the requisite permits (more on the Ghana case shortly) – i.e., only a small fraction of the ASM population – are able to access this support, significantly, it is a radical departure from the mostly technical-oriented assistance administered by donors to the sector in the 1990s and early 2000s. Galvanising debates on ASM's economic importance worldwide culminated in the launch,

---

price too high to pay? Pollution from Ghana's gold rush sparks maternal health fears', https://edition.cnn.com/interactive/asequals/ghana-illegal-gold-mining-galamsey-birth-defects-as-equals-intl-cmd/ (accessed 3 June 2025); A.K. Saim, 'Mercury (Hg) use and pollution assessment of ASGM in Ghana: challenges and strategies towards Hg reduction', *Environmental Science and Pollution Research* 28 (2021), 61919–28.

40 Macdonald, 'Gold', 424.

in 2018, of DELVE,[41] a platform established to share fresh information about the sector, with the goal of facilitating the design of more appropriate laws and policies for its operators.

In Ghana specifically, pre-pandemic, scholars, donors and NGOs were all doing their part to showcase ASM's livelihoods dimension. But very little work has since been conducted that challenges the government's militarised stance toward *galamsey*. A rapid examination of the multiple economic functions ASM has had in Ghana during and since the colonial period could go a long way toward reviving fruitful discussion on the sector's livelihoods dimension.

The Pathfinder, 1880s–Present

It is widely known that in Ghana multinationals have, for decades, relied on artisanal miners as pathfinders,[42] tapping into their knowledge of the local terrain to locate gold deposits. From the point at which the Europeans first arrived in Gold Coast by 1471 to the time the colony was officially established, there was a vibrant indigenous alluvial gold mining sector that was very much part of the local and regional cultural fabric. The first Europeans in the Gold Coast, however, had come into contact with a sector that was already many centuries old and populated by individuals armed with significant experience and geological knowledge. It was therefore deeply rooted and probably provided Europeans with many important clues on what the foundation of a commercial gold mining hub needed to look like.

Up until the late 1870s, attempts were made by the British – albeit, with limited success – to 'scale up' *hitherto* low-tech alluvial gold-mining. But interests soon shifted to lode mining; the completion of the railway from Sekondi to Tarkwa in 1901, Obuasi in 1903 and Prestea in 1910 opened up previously-impassable terrain. South African engineers who had visited Tarkwa in the late 1800s claimed that the reefs here were of higher grade than deposits in Johannesburg. By this time, some significant groundwork had already been laid: foreign prospecting commenced in the 1870s, the first concessions of the Bibiani mine were granted in 1891, there was one company operating in Prestea in 1885, and the Ashanti Goldfields Corporation began working the rich reefs at Obuasi in 1897.[43] Moreover, by 1883, four companies were already producing gold –

41 DELVE, https://delvedatabase.org (accessed 30 June 2023).

42 Gavin Hilson, Natalia Yakovleva and Sadia Mohammed Banchirigah, '"To move or not to move": Reflections on the resettlement of artisanal miners in the Western Region of Ghana', *African Affairs* 106:424 (2007), 413–36; Nyame and Grant, 'The political economy of transitory mining'; Sabine Luning and Robert J. Pijpers, 'Governing access to gold in Ghana: in-depth geopolitics on mining concessions', *Africa* 87:4 (2017), 758–79.

43 G.B. Cartland, 'The Gold Coast – an historical approach', *African Affairs* 46:183 (1947), 89–97; G.K. Allen, 'Gold mining in Ghana', *African Affairs* 57:228 (1958), 221–40.

albeit, intermittently – in Tarkwa, made possible by the ore-crushing machinery and extraction technology installed at their sites. These were the African Gold Coast Company (a French corporation), the Wassaw Gold Mining Company, the Gold Coast Mining Company and the Effuenta Mining Company.[44]

The Gold Coast Colony's 'jungle boom' of 1901–2 followed, a period in which 400 mining companies were established. Whilst most failed to produce, significant gold prospecting of unexplored terrain took place during this time.[45] Many of the colony's first gold-mining companies, including Taquah and Abosso Mines Ltd., Amalgamated Banket Areas Ltd. and the aforementioned Ashanti Goldfields Corporation, were very much the products of knowledge acquired from analysis of the alluvial gold mining sector. Its participants offered important clues on the orientation of rocks and the location of economic mineral deposits. An intimate knowledge of alluvial gold prospecting was gained through observing and interacting with indigenous miners (information that would, in turn, fuel European efforts to establish alluvial gold mining operations themselves). This included insight on how to sample soils, search for the 'flower line', and trace the courses of rivers and streams where (gold) deposits were located.[46]

Dumett's authoritative text offers important clues on developments that unfolded in the late 1800s that would ultimately catalyse, in a short time, the transformation of the Gold Coast's *hitherto* artisanal gold-panning sector into a dynamic large-scale commercial mining hub.[47] One of the key objectives of his landmark work was to demonstrate how adoption of some of the techniques used by indigenous alluvial gold miners ('fire setting', for example) facilitated the expansion of European-backed gold exploitation in the Gold Coast in the late 1800s.[48] Knowledge of indigenous gold workings jumpstarted and ultimately helped to sustain European-backed mining activity in the Gold Coast Colony. The reality for Europeans was that 'despite claims of European technological superiority, it was some thirty years after the gold rush had begun before European prospectors were able to find a gold deposit not already known to, and worked by, African diggers'.[49]

44 H.T. Bevin, 'The Gold Coast economy about 1880', *Transactions of the Gold Coast & Togoland Historical Society* 2:2 (1956), 73–86.

45 Allen, 'Gold mining in Ghana'.

46 Francis N.N. Botchway, 'Pre-colonial methods of gold mining and environmental protection in Ghana', *Journal of Energy and Natural Resources Law* 13:4 (1995), 299–311.

47 Raymond E. Dumett, *El Dorado in West Africa The Gold Mining Frontier, African Labor, and Colonial Capitalism in the Gold Coast, 1875–1900* (Athens OH, 1998).

48 Lorenzo D'Angelo, 'Technology', in Lorenzo D'Angelo and Robert Jan Pijpers (eds), *The Anthropology of Resource Extraction* (London, 2022), 167–83.

49 Jim Silver, 'The failure of European mining companies in the nineteenth-century Gold Coast', *Journal of African History* 22:4 (1981), 520–1.

It is now widely recognised by mining company officials and donors that artisanal operators are among the best 'pathfinders'. No hired foreign geologist could possibly acquire a comparable level of knowledge of a mineralised terrain in a short time. Thus, in spite of the tenuous relationship the management of most mining companies has with artisanal miners, any reference to their presence does, in some way, provide assurance to their investors that – in this instance – gold is present within demarcated concessions. This could explain why, in the case of Ghana, most Gold Coast Chamber of Mines Annual Reports (through to 1957) and the earliest Ghana Chamber of Mines Annual Reports (from 1960 onward) make reference throughout to local (small-scale) mining activities and alluvial settings. It also explains why most contemporary feasibility studies of gold-rich territories in sub-Saharan Africa often – and very casually – make reference to local artisanal mining activities. Examples from Ghana include:

- The Feasibility Report Prepared for Gold Fields Limited and IAMGold Corporation (Damang), 25 October 2004, by SRK Consulting. It states that 'Small scale gold mining activities in the area date back to the late 19th Century, but the most significant operation on the Damang lease area comprised the now abandoned Abosso Mine which exploited Banket conglomerates to a depth of approximately 850 m', and 'here artisanal miners were exploiting alluvium shedding from two low ridges. Gold appeared to be associated with both Banket conglomerates and a flat lying quartz vein system'.[50]
- The NI 43–101 Technical Report and Feasibility Study produced for Asanko Gold Mine, Ghana, also by SRK Consulting. It states, *inter alia*, that 'The main land uses include secondary forest, subsistence and cash crop farming, and artisanal gold mining', and 'Artisanal mining has occurred at a number of the AGM target areas, focusing mainly on placer gold production'.[51]

Of course, the international consultants commissioned by multinational gold mining companies to conduct ore feasibility analysis cannot rely exclusively on conclusions drawn from examinations of existing and previous artisanal workings. But there is broad recognition across the industry that the long-term presence of artisanal mining activities is an encouraging sign of there being potential mineable deposits within the immediate vicinity and/

50 SRK Consulting, 'An Independent Technical Report on the Damang Gold Mine, Ghana' (Cardiff, 2004).

51 SRK Consulting. 2023. 'The NI 43–101 Technical Report and Feasibility Study for Asanko Gold Mine, Ghana', prepared for Galiano Gold Inc. (Cardiff, 2023).

or in adjacent territories. Making reference to these activities in a feasibility report, therefore, is essential, as it is an important confidence-builder in a such a high-risk industry.

In summary, small-scale operators are valued pathfinders and relied upon by international mining companies to locate and ultimately develop orebodies on a commercial scale. In Ghana, the historical workings of artisanal miners and more recently, the movements of *galamsey* groups, are routinely studied by gold mining companies; the knowledge acquired has played an important role in facilitating the development and design of their operations.

An Indispensable Economic Activity, 1990s–Present

In the 1990s, perceptions of ASM started to change. Experts began to make the case that it is more than just an industry providing opportunities to rogue entrepreneurs; the growing consensus at the time was that the sector provided a livelihood to tens of millions of people across sub-Saharan Africa. Works which identified different groups of people who pursue employment in ASM, along with analysis that broadened understanding of what was triggering movement into the sector and the impact this was having economically, began to surface.[52] The idea that ASM sites may be populated by people other than professional miners, in particular, individuals driven to the sector because of personal hardship, began to gain traction following the World Bank-hosted International Roundtable on Artisanal Mining, in May 1995.[53] Here, ASM was referred to as a 'poverty-driven activity' for the first time, introducing an entirely different lens through which the dynamics of the sector's workforce have henceforth been analysed, particularly in sub-Saharan Africa.

In Ghana today, most people engaged in ASM fall squarely into the category of 'poverty-driven' operator, akin to what is commonly referred to in the business and management literature as 'necessity-based entrepreneur'. Broadly, these are people who move into the sector out of desperation. Unprecedentedly high gold prices (over US$4,000/oz), which people have associated with 'rush-type' activity spearheaded by rogue entrepreneurs, have obfuscated why today, so many Ghanaians continue to move into ASM: because there are few alternative sources of employment. Whilst many individuals who fall into the 'poverty-driven' category have agriculture or (large-scale) mining backgrounds, it is not uncommon to encounter former public-sector workers

52 See e.g., Davidson, 'Transformation', Béatrice Labonne, 'Artisanal mining: an economic stepping stone for women', *Natural Resources Forum* 20:2 (1996), 117–22; International Labour Organization, *Social and Labour Issues in Small-Scale Mining* (Geneva, 1999).

53 M. Barry (ed.), *Regularizing Informal Mining: A Summary of the Proceedings of the International Roundtable on Artisanal Mining* (W Washington DC, 1996).

or individuals with university degrees at sites.[54] The composition of Ghana's ASM workforce has become highly eclectic in only a few decades, populated by hundreds of thousands of individuals, each of whom is associated with their own livelihood trajectory. Structural adjustment,[55] which caused mass unemployment in industries such as manufacturing and forestry, and the public sector, has been heavily responsible for the dynamic makeup of the ASM workforce. A typical ASM site is one of few places in Ghana where today, a subsistence farmer can be seen working shoulder-to-shoulder with a trained accountant or school teacher.

The 'poverty-driven' narrative is one of two categories of drivers used by ASM scholars to contextualise movements into the sector; the other is 'get rich quick'. The efforts made following the conclusion of the International Roundtable on Artisanal Mining (1995) to place individuals engaged in ASM into different categories were commendable, although most of the ideas presented were imagined or based largely on casual observations, as opposed to grounded analysis of the organisational structures of sites. The typology conceived by World Bank officials shortly after the roundtable and later endorsed by the United Nations Economic Commission for Africa was no exception.[56] World Bank experts identified, and provided accompanying explanations for, the following four categories of ASM: (1) permanent artisanal and small-scale miners; (2) seasonal artisanal and small-scale miners; (3) poverty-driven artisanal and small-scale miners; and (4) gold-rush artisanal and small-scale miners. The Bank's push to categorise ASM motivated others to do the same. Examples include the NGO PACT's assessment (1. Full-time, 2. Seasonal, 3. Occasional);[57] the Alliance for Responsible Mining's four-part

54 Sadia Mohammed Banchirigah, 'How have reforms fuelled the expansion of artisanal mining? Evidence from Sub-Saharan Africa', *Resources Policy* 31:3 (2006), 165–71; Isaah Baddianaah, Ibrahim Abu Abdulai and Felix Dordaa, 'Sorting the facts from the lots: contribution of artisanal and small-scale mining (galamsey) to rural livelihood configurations in sub-Saharan Africa', *Journal of Degraded and Mining Lands Management* 11:1 (2023), 5025–36.

55 Structural adjustment loans were made by the International Monetary Fund and the World Bank, predominantly in the 1980s and 1990s. In exchange for funds, both organisations demanded that borrowing countries implement sweeping changes, including devaluing their currencies, privatising state assets, liberalising agriculture, reducing their public and manufacturing sectors, and deregulating industries.

56 M.J. Weber-Fahr, R. Strongman, G. Kunanayagam, G. McMahon, C. Sheldon, *Mining and Poverty Reduction* (Washington DC, 2001); United Nations Economic Commission for Africa, *Report on Selected Themes in Natural Resources Development in Africa: Artisanal and Small-Scale Mining and Technology Challenges in Africa* (Addis Ababa, 2003).

57 PACT Institute, *2008 Regional Workshop: Small-scale Mining in Africa – A Case for Sustainable Livelihood* (Washington DC, 2008).

framework (permanent, seasonal, rush-type and shock-push);[58] and the World Gold Council's more recent and elaborate five-segment typology of traditional (mining), seasonal, permanent, migrant influx, and 'shock' or 'disaster'.[59]

For simplicity, the analysis here sticks with the two broad categories of 'poverty-driven' (necessity-based entrepreneurship) and 'get rich quick' (opportunity-based entrepreneurship), a distinction which has gained considerable traction in the literature over the years.[60]

'Poverty-Driven'

The unemployment issue in Ghana today is multifaceted; there is no one single cause of the country's widespread joblessness. Some of the more recent claims that have been made include that the jobs available for the country's youth are not particularly appealing, that they are unsuitable for university graduates, and that young women in particular face significant cultural barriers when attempting to enter the labour market.[61] What *has* been established, however, is – as already hinted – that structural adjustment has had a devastating impact on Ghana's industrial development and labour market.[62] The resulting

58 Alliance for Responsible Mining, *Addressing Forced Labor in Artisanal and Small-scale Mining* (Bogota, 2014).

59 See World Gold Council, *Lessons Learned on Managing the Interface Between Large-scale and Artisanal and Small-Scale Gold Mining* (London, 2022). By 'traditional mining' (admittedly, a rather ambiguous term), World Gold council officials mean work undertaken 'where gold mining has occurred in a region for many years and plays a central role in local incomes' and where 'Mining skills may be passed down through families and be an important element in the cultural identity of some communities' (p. 11).

60 Thomas Hentschel, Felix Hruschka and Michael Priester, *Global Report on Artisanal & Small-Scale Mining* (London, 2002); J.S. Andrew, 'Potential application of mediation to land use conflicts in small-scale mining', *Journal of Cleaner Production* 11:2 (2003), 117–30; Gavin Hilson, '"Once a miner, always a miner": poverty and livelihood diversification in Akwatia, Ghana', *Journal of Rural Studies* 263 (2010), 296–307.

61 Michael Poku-Boansi and Sam Afrane, 'Magnitude and impact of youth unemployment in Ghana', *West Africa Review* 18 (2011), 73–89; William Baah-Boateng, 'Determinants of unemployment in Ghana', *African Development Review* 25:4 (2013), 385–99; Charity Sylvia Akotia and Adote Anum, 'Gender, culture, and inequality in Ghana: an examination of sociocultural determinants of gender disparity', in Saba Safdar and Natasza Kosakowska-Berezecha (eds), *Psychology of Gender Through the Lens of Culture: Theories and Applications* (New York, 2015), 375–94; Emmanuel Affum-Osei, Eric Asante, Solomon Kwaretng Korkouh, Osei Michael Aboagye and Collins Opoku Antwi, 'Unemployment trends and labour market entry in Ghana: job search methods perspective', *Labor History* 60:2 (2019), 716–33.

62 See e.g., Kwame Boafo-Arthur, 'Ghana: Structural Adjustment, democratization, and the politics of continuity', *African Studies Review* 42:2 (1999), 41–72; Timon Forster, Alexander E. Kentikelenis, Bernhard Reinsberg, Thomas H. Stubbs and Lawrence P. King, 'How structural adjustment programs affect inequality: A disaggregated analysis of IMF conditionality, 1980–2014', *Social Science Research* 80 (2019), 83–113.

joblessness is likely to have played a role in fuelling the growth of the country's ASM sector over the years.

On the rationale for pursuing adjustment lending, there was, on the one hand, certainly a precedent for pursuing a fresh development strategy in Ghana in the early 1980s because by this time, economic conditions in the country had deteriorated markedly. Annual growth of real Gross Domestic Product (GDP) had fallen from 6.4 per cent between 1965 and 1973 to 3.2 per cent in the period from 1973 to 1980, and further declined to 0.7 per cent in 1982. It reached a record low of 0.2 per cent in 1983, accompanied by marked declines in average income per capita, formal sector employment and per-capita food consumption.[63] The finance the Government of Ghana would receive from the World Bank and IMF to address these economic woes were contingent upon it making a series of sweeping policy changes. These included devaluing the *cedi*; liberalising agriculture; privatising further the enterprises in which the state had a majority or minority stake in at the time (determined to be 235 in 1984); and implementing the financial incentives needed to stimulate increased foreign investment.

On the other hand, these changes, which were pronounced and sudden, had an immediate impact on the country's workforce Total employment in the large- and medium-scale formal sector (enterprises with 30 or more employees) fell from 464,000 in 1985 to 394,000 in 1987 and to 186,000 in 1991, representing 'a decline of almost 60% in five or six years'.[64] Policy reforms implemented in the agricultural sector, which 'focused preponderantly on rehabilitation of the cocoa industry and reform of its marketing system',[65] resulted in the elimination of 80,000 job positions on the Cocoa Board; upward of 45,000 additional civil servants were immediately 'redeployed' (29,000 were dismissed in 1988, and the remainder in 1989); and hundreds of private sector employees lost textile and manufacturing jobs as a result of import liberalisation.[66] Recently, there has been some speculation that in Ghana, a link exists between structural adjustment and unemployment on the one hand, and the growth of ASM on the other hand.[67] If this is, indeed, the case, which of the country's poverty-driven groups, impacted by adjustment, have turned to ASM for work?

63 Akilagpa Sawyerr, *The Political Dimension of Structural Adjustment Programmes in Sub-Saharan Africa* (Accra, 1990); John Toye, 'Structural Adjustment: context, assumptions, origin and diversity', in Rolf Van der Hoeven and Fred Van der Kraaij (eds), *Structural Adjustment and Beyond in Sub-Saharan Africa* (The Hague, 1994), 18–35.

64 Eboe Hutchful, *Ghana's Adjustment Experience: The Paradox of Reform* (Geneva, 2002), 90.

65 *Ibid.*, p. 67.

66 Stephen R. Wiessman, 'Structural Adjustment in Africa: insights from the experiences of Ghana and Senegal', *World Development* 18:12 (1990), 1621–34, at 1629.

67 Gavin Hilson and Clive Potter, 'Structural Adjustment and subsistence industry: artisanal gold mining in Ghana', *Development and Change* 36:1 (2005), 103–31.

One group of individuals who have made the move are vulnerable youth and women; today, they can be seen working in all areas of the ASM 'ecosystem'. Yakovleva[68] produced the first comprehensive study on women in Ghanaian ASM communities, research for which was conducted in the Ntronang and Noyem communities in the country's Eastern Region. Here, it was observed that women's work in ASM was linked to their household responsibilities – that movement into the sector was governed by their need to cover child care costs, and secure monies to support family farms. At the time, they were employed at sites as diggers, haulers and service providers (supplying equipment, food and clothing), work which generated the ready cash needed to cover these household expenses. Studies have since been undertaken which further nuance women's participation in ASM and the impact this work has had on their livelihoods. Arthur-Holmes and Busia,[69] for example, observed that in Prestea, most women miners did not pool mine earnings with those of their husbands, electing rather to contribute to the household in ways mirroring what was reported in Noyem and Ntronang. Examples include food preparation and financing children's education. Similar observations were made by Mengba et al.[70] in north-eastern Ghana, where more pronouncedly, 'Gender-based roles and responsibilities at the mining sites are deeply entrenched and actually reflect the cultural expectations of women and men within the "private" sphere of the home in the mining communities'.[71] According to the authors, this explains why, at most sites here, which now dot the landscapes in which the 'male-dominant patriarchal systems [that have] pervaded the social fabric of the Talensi people' are found, most women working in ASM engage in the loading and transportation of ore.[72]

Youth involvement at ASM sites in Ghana and elsewhere in sub-Saharan Africa should be viewed as an 'expression' of a much bigger development problem. Half of the region's population is under the age of 25 and cannot afford *not* to work. In Ghana itself, within localities such as Bekwai Municipality in the Ashanti Region, it has been observed that ASM 'enables some students to save money to pay their school fees, and it further provides employment to

68 Natalia Yakovleva, 'Perspectives on female participation in artisanal and small-scale mining: a case study of Birim North District of Ghana', *Resources Policy* 32:1–2 (2007), 29–41.

69 Francis Arthur-Holmes and Kwaku Abrefa Busia, 'Household dynamics and the bargaining power of women in artisanal and small-scale mining in sub-Saharan Africa: a Ghanaian case study', *Resources Policy* 69 (2020), Art. 101884.

70 Jennifer Dokbila Mengba, Raymond Aitibasa Atanga and Constance Awinpoka Akurugu, 'Small-scale gold mining and gender roles: critical reflections on socio-cultural dynamics in north-eastern Ghana', SN Social Sciences 3:4 (2023), https://doi.org/10.1007/s43545-022-00591-6 (accessed 25 May 2026).

71 *Ibid.*, p. 3.

72 *Ibid.*, p. 15.

the majority of youth with low skills'.[73] In response to public criticism of the impact of their ASM operations on the environment, the youth often claim that whilst they are aware of the consequences of their actions, their financial situations and need to survive take priority over any such cost.[74] Ghana's youth blame their growing reliance on *galamsey* activities for their livelihoods on successive governments' failure to invest in future generations and create the skilled jobs which the country's secondary institutions prepare them for. In established mining communities such as Prestea, the youth have reached the point where they now view *galamsey* as an acceptable career path, despite public condemnation of its existence.[75] In towns such as these, local university graduates are increasingly viewing ASM as an arena in which they can apply their skills, in response to the acute shortage of alternative income-earning opportunities locally and in the cities.[76] Another more recent trend observed is young people migrating to ASM settlements from other areas of the country for months – and sometimes, for years – out of desperation. They do so with hopes of accumulating enough money, before returning, to purchase a motorbike, build a better-quality house or pay for their university expenses.[77]

A second group of individuals are those with farming backgrounds who carry out ASM seasonally or alongside agriculture. In Ghana, the two activities have long been inseparable: capital and labour flow between the two and often engage entire families. A large number of individuals found working at ASM sites in Ghana have agricultural backgrounds. This is consistent with observations made elsewhere in sub-Saharan Africa. Specifically, in countries such as Sierra Leone, Liberia and Malawi, scholars have carried out research and produced evidence that points to ASM and subsistence farming being inseparable, observed to dovetail one another seasonally, or the former generating

73 Kwame Asamoah and Alex Osei-Kojo, 'A contextual analysis of implementation challenges of small-scale mining laws in Ghana: a case study of Bekwai municipality', *Sage Open* 6:3 (2016), 1–11, p. 9.

74 Lydia Osei, Godwin Arku and Isaac Luginaah, '"We have done nothing wrong": youth miners' perceptions of the environmental consequences of artisanal and small-scale mining (ASM) in Ghana', *The Extractive Industries and Society* 12 (2022), Art. 101179.

75 Paul W.K. Yankson and Katherine V. Gough, 'Gold in Ghana: the effects of changes in large-scale mining on artisanal and small-scale mining (ASM)', *The Extractive Industries and Society* 6:1 (2018), 120–8.

76 Francis Arthur-Holmes, Kwaku Abrefa Busia, Diego Alfonso Vazquez-Brust and Natalia Yakovleva, 'Graduate unemployment, artisanal and small-scale mining, and rural transformation in Ghana: what does the "educated" youth involvement offer?', *Journal of Rural Studies* 95 (2022), 125–39.

77 Katherine V. Gough and Torben Birch-Thomsen, 'Mobile rural youth in northern Ghana: combining near and distant opportunity spaces', in Katherine V. Gough and Thilde Langevang (eds), *Young Entrepreneurs in Sub-Saharan Africa* (London, 2017), 117–31.

revenue that is used to finance the purchase of inputs that feature in the latter, including fertilisers and pesticides.[78]

More on the Impact of the Farming-ASM Nexus

By supporting agriculture economically, ASM has undoubtedly helped to stabilise the food security situation facing thousands of Ghanaian households. Such a claim may seem highly controversial in light of recent assertions that *galamsey* activities are destroying arable lands used to support agriculture.[79] But there are several points that should be considered before reaching this conclusion, the first being that there is a long history in Ghana of families engaging in both mining and agriculture simultaneously. The accounts found in the literature share details about members of farming families pursuing mine work and the impact this has had on others in their households. These range from reports of women using calabashes to wash gold to the well-documented movement of male farmers from the Northern Territories of the Gold Coast to the south to take up work as labourers at mines opened by Europeans.[80] The point that needs to be emphasised here is that in Ghana, the movement of farm hands into low- and semi-skilled positions at gold mines – typically, seasonally – can be traced back to the colonial period. There is evidence, too, of the earnings generated from mine work being used to support family-oriented farming activities in migrant workers' hometowns. In other words, in Ghana, there is a *history*, reinforced by scattered accounts in the literature, of mine earnings stabilising the food security situation at the household level.[81]

The second point that needs to be made here is that there are clues that, historically, Ghanaian families have engaged in both ASM and farming

78 Roy Maconachie and J.A. Binns, '"Farming miners" or "mining farmers"?: diamond mining and rural development in post-conflict Sierra Leone', *Journal of Rural Studies* 23:3 (2007), 367–80; Roy Maconachie, 'Re-agrarianising livelihoods in post-conflict Sierra Leone? Mineral wealth and rural change in artisanal and small-scale mining communities', *Journal of International Development* 23:8 (2011), 1054–67; Gavin Hilson and Steven Van Bockstael, 'Diamond mining, rice farming and a "maggi cube": a viable survival strategy in rural Liberia?', *Journal of International Development* 23:8 (2011), 1042–53; Paul Justice Kamlongera, 'Making the poor "poorer" or alleviating poverty? Artisanal mining livelihoods in rural Malawi', *Journal of International Development* 23:8 (2011), 1128–39.

79 Daniel Siaw, George Ofosu and David Sarpong, 'Cocoa production, farmlands, and the galamsey: examining current and emerging trends in the ASM-agriculture nexus', *Journal of Rural Studies* 101 (2023), Art. 103044.

80 A.E. Kitson, 'The Gold Coast: some considerations of its structure, people, and natural history', *Geographical Journal* 48:5 (1916), 369–91; Dumett, *El Dorado in West Africa*.

81 Emmanuel Ababio Ofosu-Mensah, 'Labour migration during the colonial period to the Obuasi mines in Ghana', *International Research Journal of Library, Information and Archival Studies* 1:3 (2011), 68–80; Ofosu-Mensah, 'Transformation of artisanal small-scale mining (ASM) in Ghana: from pre-colonial to the modern era', *Journal of African Policy Studies* 27:1 (2021), 57–94.

simultaneously for the purposes of diversifying and supplementing their income sources. During the colonial period, for many households in the Northern Territories, this diversification was undoubtedly set in motion – or at least accelerated – by the migration of men to mining towns located in the south of the country for extended periods of time. Curless explains how:[82]

> Many northern migrants to the mining towns viewed wage labor as a temporary stage in their lives which would enable them to acquire the capital to fulfill customary roles expected of them with regard to gender, generation, and the demands of agricultural living back in the north…Significantly, the economic changes that compelled men to seek out work in the south also contributed to the increased commodification of women's domestic labor. The absence of male agricultural labor for months at a time meant that women were required to cultivate cash-crops which could be sold at market to generate the income required to purchase food staples.

Recent accounts of small-scale miners degrading farmlands, whilst potentially accurate, fail to capture the complete story. Specifically, and inferring from what has taken place since Ghana's colonial period, individual family members are migrating to ASM sites to earn money, portions of which are remitted to their home towns, where they are invested in agriculture. This does not mean that the irreversible land degradation that may be occurring in and around ASM sites should be condoned but it is imperative that the complete picture be captured as it is ensures that the general public is not misled.

In Akan-speaking areas of Ghana, the influence of agriculture on the local governance structures now in place for ASM is additional evidence of the two activities long being interconnected at the household level. Men digging and crushing ore, and women subsequently washing it brokered, with local and paramount chiefs, agreements that mirrored the *abusa* system (see p. 32) which they were no doubt exposed to, and familiar with, through their farming. Under this setup, the gold miner was 'obliged to present gifts of a prescribed value to the local stool in return for the right to commence mining operations, and then to pay one-third of his production to the local stool for as long as he continued to mine on the stool land'. Moreover, 'The paramount chief was also entitled to a share, which usually consisted of either all nuggets found on the land, or, as was the case in the Tarkwa area, the proceeds of Saturday's work'.[83]

Third and interrelatedly, the historical dimensions of the linkages between agriculture and ASM in Ghana have been obfuscated by coverage of the different roles each has played at the household level in recent years. Specifically, among

82 Gareth Curless, 'The worlds of labor in Ghana's gold mining industry, c.1895–1957', *International Labor and Working-Class History* 107 (2025), 30–47, at 41, 34.

83 Silver, 'The failure of European mining companies', 512.

households engaged in both activities, findings consistently show that ASM generates more disposable income than farming.[84] Whilst a surging gold price is one obvious reason why this may now be the case, what also cannot be ignored are the many factors that limit productivity (and ultimately, profit-making ability) in the country's smallholder farming sector. The list includes intermittent rainfall, and limited access to markets, finance and technology.[85] These livelihood dynamics are perhaps most visible at the household level in Ghana within the Eastern Region, where livelihoods have long been observed to revolve around farming and a range of different ASM activities.[86] This may be a more recent development, as the government claims, but there is little disputing that both activities are interconnected and integral components of income portfolios in this area of the country. In communities such as Noyem, Kibi, Ntronang, Kobriso and Oda, all of which have lengthy farming traditions, ASM has rapidly become indispensable, economically, for tens of thousands of people.[87] The evidence points to most of the farmers engaged in ASM in the Eastern Region doing so because of hardship or being 'poverty-driven' but at the same time, not abandoning their agricultural activities.

Lastly, claims that ASM is destroying lands on which cocoa, long the country's chief cash crop, is being harvested are not entirely accurate. There is now a sizeable body of work that aims to make this case, drawing on satellite

84 I.K. Osumanu, 'Small-scale mining and livelihood dynamics in north-eastern Ghana: sustaining rural livelihoods in a changing environment', *Progress in Development Studies* 20:3 (2010), 208–22; Issah Baddianaah, Gordon N-yelkabu Tuu, Bernard Nuoleyeng Baatuuwiw, 'Livelihood implications of artisanal gold mining in farming communities: insight from the Wa East District, Ghana', *Ghana Journal of Geography* 13:3 (2021), 85–119; Franklin N. Mabe, Ebenezer Owusu-Sekyere and Olluyemi Theoophilus Adeosun, 'Livelihood coping strategies among displaced small scale miners in Ghana', *Resources Policy* 74 (2021), Art. 102291.

85 T.S. Jayne, David Mather and Elliot Mghenyi, 'Principal challenges confronting smallholder agriculture in Sub-Saharan Africa', *World Development* 38:1 (2010), 1394–98; P.W.K. Yankson, A.B. Owusu and S. Frimpong, 'Challenges and strategies for improving the agricultural marketing environment in developing countries: evidence from Ghana', *Journal of Agricultural & Food Information* 17:1 (2016), 49–61; Seth Opoku Mensah, Bismark Sei-Acheampong, Brent Jacobs, Rebecca Cunningham, Akwasi Bamfo Akoto, 'Smallholder farmers' climate change adaptation in Ghana: a systematic literature review and future directions', *Journal of Environmental Management* 384 (2025), Art. 125598.

86 See e.g., Sadia Mohammed Banchirigah, 'Challenges with eradicating illegal mining in Ghana: a perspective from the grassroots', *Resources Policy* 33:1 (2008), 29–38; Gavin Hilson and Chris Garforth, '"Everyone now is concentrating on the mining": drivers and implications of rural economic transition in the Eastern Region of Ghana', *Journal of Development Studies* 49:3 (2013), 348–64.

87 See Yakovleva, 'Perspectives on female participation'; Banchirigah, 'Challenges with eradicating illegal mining'; Hilson, '"Once a miner, always a Miner"'; Hilson and Garforth, '"Everyone now is concentrating on the mining"'.

imagery, interview data and photography to illustrate how *galamsey* activities are adversely impacting cocoa production in districts such as Atiwa, Amenfi West and Amansie West. It argues that the growing presence of ASM activities in these, and other, areas of Ghana has put the smallholder cocoa farmer under considerable strain by absorbing workers and therefore causing labour shortages; polluting waterbodies relied upon for irrigation; and contaminating soils.[88] Reports that ASM may be impacting cocoa-growing sections of Ghana has even piqued the interests of the editors of *National Geographic*, who published the article, 'Illegal Gold Mining Boom Threatens Cocoa Farmers (And Your Chocolate)', in 2018.[89]

But before accepting that *galamsey* activities are a 'menace' to cocoa-producing areas of Ghana, as many commentators have declared,[90] it is important that the economics of this alleged interface and the circumstances facing the individuals involved are studied more closely. There is the likelihood of there being individuals who engage in both activities simultaneously. For these people, carrying out environmentally-destructive ASM activity would be illogical because it would cannibalise opportunities to engage in lucrative cocoa farming. What *is* happening, however, is that cocoa farmers are selling their plots to *galamsey* groups. Some scholars[91] suggest that some cocoa farmers have been coerced into selling lands but there are others who have clearly willingly done so, principally because of the sums of money involved.[92] There are others still who keep their cocoa plots and jump into the ASM sector itself, citing low harvest prices, rising costs of farm inputs and intermittent production as the

88 Denis Owusu Boateng, Francis Nana Yaw Codjoe and Johnnson Ofori, 'Impact of illegal small scale mining (Galamsey) on cocoa production in Atiwa district of Ghana', *International Journal of Advance Agricultural Research* 2, 89–99; B. Snapir, D.M. Simms and T.W. Waine, 'Mapping the expansion of galamsey gold mines in the cocoa growing area of Ghana using optical remote sensing', *International Journal of Applied Earth Observation and Geoinformation* 58: (2017), 225–33.

89 "Illegal Gold Mining Boom Threatens Cocoa Farmers (And Your Chocolate)", https://www.nationalgeographic.com/science/article/ghana-gold-mining-cocoa-environment (accessed 4 October 2025).

90 See e.g., "Fresh Galamsey Invasion Ravages Cocoa Farms at Asante Akyem Bompata Baadu", https://www.myjoyonline.com/fresh-galamsey-invasion-ravages-cocoa-farms-at-asante-akyem-bompata-baadu/ (accessed 9 November 2025); '"Cocoa Production Under "Galamsey" Threat', https://thechronicle.com.gh/cocoa-production-under-galamsey-threat/#google_vignette",thechronicle.com.gh/cocoa-production-under-galamsey-threat/ (accessed 3 November 2025).

91 Siaw, Ofosu and Sarpong. 'Cocoa production, farmlands, and the galamsey'.

92 "Why cocoa farmers are 'ditching' business, selling their lands to illegal miners", https://www.ghanaweb.com/GhanaHomePage/business/Why-cocoa-farmers-are-ditching-business-selling-their-lands-to-illegal-miners-1979295 (accessed 2 December 2025).

main reasons behind the move.[93] This is precisely the opposite of what was on display in the 1920s and 1930s, when migrants chose to pursue employment in the country's booming cocoa farming sector as opposed to the mines, where work was more arduous, wages were lower and sanitary conditions of the towns in which they lived were poor.[94] The contribution that cocoa farming and engagement in the cash-crop economy makes to household income and food security in Ghana today has been well documented in the literature.[95] Could it, therefore, simply be that for cocoa farmers who have jumped into the *galamsey* sector for work, ASM now plays the major part in ensuring food security?

A final point worth noting is the potential selectivity of sites visited by researchers and journalists intent on proving that mushrooming *galamsey* activity is impairing cocoa production. As part of the World Bank's US$70 million *Ghana Landscape Restoration and Small-Scale Mining Project*, preliminary work carried out in the two exclusive project districts revealed that there was minimal overlap between ASM and cocoa farming, and that 'The suggestion that they [i.e., *galamsey* operations] are destroying active cocoa lands is sensational'. It furthermore revealed that where *galamsey* is degrading lands supporting cocoa farming, that these are likely 'splinter illegal ASM activities' and little more.[96] In summary, it is not being suggested here that *galamsey* activities *are not* destroying arable lands that support cocoa farming. Rather, the point being made is that the cocoa farming–ASM story in Ghana is far more complex than what has been reported, as is the role played by the latter in generating income and improving food security for many households in the country. Rarely are these details shared in sweeping condemnations of *galamsey* activities.

93 "Cocoa farmer realities: Frederick speaks about the difficulties for young farmers", https://equaltradeglobal.org/cocoa-farmer-realities-frederick-speaks-about-the-difficulties-for-young-farmers/ (accessed 4 December 2025); Sylvia Kyerewaa Appiah, Collins Osei, Kwadwo Amankwah, Enoch Kwame Tham-Agyekum, John-Eudes Andivi Bakang and Fred Ankuyi, 'Galamsey's grip: unravelling the impact of illegal small-scale mining on cocoa farming and livelihoods', *Agricultural Socio-Economics Journal* 24:1 (2024), 49–58.

94 Curless, 'The worlds of labor in Ghana's gold mining'; Ellie Gore, 'Colonial afterlives in the global cocoa supply chain: sharecropping, labour exploitation, and gendered (re) production', *Review of International Political Economy* 33:1 (2025), https://doi.org/10.1080/09692290.2025.2567360 (accessed 25 May 2026).

95 See e.g., Sophie Graefe, Lennart Flavio Meyer-Sand, Katja Chauvette, Issaka Abdulai, Laurence Jassogne, Philippe Vaast and Richard Asare, 'Evaluating farmers' knowledge of shade trees in different cocoa agro-ecological zones in Ghana', *Human Ecology* 45 (2017), 321–32; Ishmael Hashmiu, Olivia Agbenyega and Evans Dawoe, 'Cash crops and food security: evidence from smallholder cocoa and cashew farmers in Ghana', *Agriculture & Food Security* 11:12 (2022), Art. 12.

96 Personal Communication, World Bank Consultant, 28 October 2025.

'Get Rich Quick'

As indicated, it is not uncommon to encounter university graduates and/or professionals working in ASM communities in Ghana. Hilson and Potter reflected, nearly two decades ago, on the direct impact that structural adjustment had on the country's ASM sector, creating a burgeoning pool of unemployed people, many of whom migrated to sites for the first time.[97] As the sector has grown, this pattern has become more pronounced: seeing someone with a higher university degree in a non-mining subject (i.e., *not* mining engineering or geology) no longer surprises.

Reiterating points already raised, many people now found at ASM sites were laid off by large-scale mines; they often arrive with skills and experience (blasting, processing, machine operation, etc.). In other instances, sites are populated by 'generational miners' who have acquired skills in the sector, over time, and have moved elsewhere to apply them. It is the arrival time of most of these individuals, along with many educated people (accountants, financiers, etc.), to sites that differentiates them from the other groups mentioned. Specifically, whereas the women, youth and farming groups who gravitate to manual work arrive when sites are *established* and when there is demand for their labour, generational miners and experienced/educated individuals tend to be responsible for *establishing* operations and spearheading mineral rushes. They are the closest examples of the 'get rich quick' type of operator, who will continue mining no matter what other 'alternative livelihoods' or income-earning opportunities are made available.

These dynamics are perhaps most visible in the Western Region, one of Ghana's most established gold mining hubs. In localities such as Tarkwa and Prestea, gold mining has taken place for hundreds of years. Individuals who were once employed by the State Gold Mining Corporation are now found in both localities; many have taken up work in ASM. They have struggled for decades to secure small-scale mining licences to work in landscapes that have come increasingly under the control of large-scale mining and mineral exploration companies. In both Tarkwa and Prestea, there is a mining company that is in possession of a vast concession, which has prevented locals from securing licences to work (mostly vacant) areas. In the former, the entire town has been engulfed by a concession awarded to the South Africa-headquartered multinational, Gold Fields; here, the company operates its Tarkwa mine. In the latter, the situation is slightly more complex, as the Prestea Underground, the property of the State Gold Mining Corporation up until the 1990s and which was subsequently acquired by the junior mining company, Bogoso Gold Limited in the 1990s, and then Golden Star Resources (it acquired Bogoso Gold Limited in

97 Hilson and Potter, 'Structural Adjustment and subsistence industry'.

1999), has never been freed up by the government for ASM, despite proving unviable to mine on a large scale. Ex-State Gold Mining Corporation workers, with their wealth of experience and skills, now control the town (and to some extent, Tarkwa), having built careers in the local *galamsey* economy.[98]

An Illicit Undertaking and 'Menace', 2000-Present

Resuscitating discussion on the 'poverty-driven' – 'get rich quick' typology would go a long way towards neutralising claims made by the Government of Ghana, local media channels and even academics that ASM is a 'menace'. The origins of this narrative, and ultimately the alleged rationale for launching *Operation Vanguard* and *Operation Halt II*, are environmental concerns. The Government of Ghana has used images of river pollution caused by *galamsey* activities to mobilise public support for military action. It seems unjustifiable, however, to take such action when the 'illegality and informality of [this] ASM is caused by the state itself in large measure, but worse, the decision to act to stop it is so often politicised'.[99] The evidence points to the state making it exceptionally difficult for small-scale miners to operate legally, and then proceeding to condemn the informal activities – which it does not monitor nor support – that emerge as a result. All signs point to this behaviour being attributable to the rent-seeking culture that has emerged around large-scale mining.

At the time of writing, there were 130 active (large-scale) prospecting licences (each granted for three years with possibility of renewal for up to three more years) and 165 mining leases linked to gold extraction.[100] The country is effectively a series of sizeable and contiguous plots now in the hands of a range of companies headquartered in different corners of the globe: over 30 per cent of Ghana's land is in the hands of the large-scale mineral exploration and mining sector at any given time.[101] For each Prospecting Licence awarded, the Government of Ghana earns tens of thousands of dollars in permit fees (formal and informal).

98 See Gavin Hilson and Natalia Yakovleva, 'Trained relations: A critical analysis of the mining conflict in Prestea, Ghana', *Political Geography* 26:1 (2007), 98–119; Arthur-Holmes and Busia, 'Women, North-South migration and artisanal and small-scale mining'.

99 Jasper Abembia Atyelazuno and Lord Mawuko-Yevugah, 'Large-scale mining and ecological imperialism in Africa: the politics of mining and conservation of the ecology in Ghana', *Journal of Political Ecology* 26:1 (2019), 243–62, at 244.

100 Data extracted from 'Ghana Mining Repository', https://ghana.revenuedev.org/dashboard (accessed 29 May 2024).

101 Gavin Hilson and Roy Maconachie, 'For the environment: an assessment of recent military intervention in informal gold mining communities in Ghana', *Land Use Policy* 96 (2020), Art. 104706.

To facilitate large-scale mineral exploration companies gaining access to lands, successive government have, as indicated, made it difficult for prospective small-scale licencees to register and operate legally. The issue is cost: applicants must make a series of payments, which have made securing a Small-Scale Mining Licence in Ghana challenging and at times, impossible.[102] There is the fee administered by the Environmental Protection Agency (EPA) for the 'Application for Environmental Permit to Undertake Small/Medium Scale Mining'. Between 2001 and 2011, a nominal GHS100 permit fee was charged by the EPA. But in 2012, it increased to GHS750, and in March 2016, rose to GHS5,000 with an added GHS1,000 processing fee, despite mounting complaints from ASM groups. A *Water Use Permit* which also costs in the range of GHS5,000 must also be obtained; this is supplied by the Water Resources Commission. Then applicants must turn to the Small-Scale Mining Licence itself, which requires engaging with officers at the Minerals Commission,[103] to which they must pay US$70 for the application form, US$150 for processing, GHS3,400 for the licence itself, US$120 for annual mineral rights per concession, and a GHS600 fee for the gazetting of land documents. Individuals could find themselves paying in excess of US$20,000 for a Small-Scale Mining Licence. An additional challenge is that decisions on licence applications take many months and in many cases, years.

The 'menace' narrative that has emerged in the past decade used to justify the launch of *Operation Vanguard* and *Operation Halt* has been a convenient distraction for a government which appears committed to developing large-scale gold mining at all costs.

The 'Ecosystem', 2021-Present

An emerging narrative that could help to generate fresh policy dialogue on the livelihoods dimension of ASM in Ghana, post-pandemic, is the idea that each (ASM) site is the nucleus of a broader rural economic 'ecosystem'.[104] What is

102 See e.g., Hilson and Potter, 'Structural Adjustment and subsistence industry'; Francis Arthur-Holmes, Kwaku Abrefa Busia, Diego Alfonso Vazquez-Brust and Natalia Yakovleva, 'Artisanal and small-scale mining methods and the Sustainable Development Goal 6: Perceived implications for clean water supply', *Environmental Science & Policy* 137 (2022), 205–15; and Ferdinand Adu-Baffour, Thomas Daum and Regina Birner, 'Governance challenges of small-scale gold mining in Ghana: Insights from a process net-map study', *Land Use Policy* 102 (2021), Art. 105271.

103 The Minerals Commission is the government body in Ghana tasked with developing mining policies and monitoring their implementation. See 'Minerals Commission', https://www.mincom.gov.gh (accessed 29 May 2024).

104 Massaran Traoré, Gavin Hilson and Abigail Hilson, 'Reimagining entrepreneurship in the artisanal and small-scale mining sector: fresh insights from Sub-Saharan Africa', *Arica*

routinely overlooked in critiques of ASM communities in Ghana and wider sub-Saharan Africa is the series of support industries that the sector spawns. There are more people employed or directly dependent upon the incomes generated from ancillary income-earning activities linked to the sector than those who pursue work directly as miners. A typical cross section of an ASM site would reveal as much: that people working at sites need transportation 'in and out', clothing to wear, food to eat, equipment to use, finance to pay workers and to acquire machines, and security for protection.

Research carried out in recent years has captured the breadth of these ancillary industries, which, at an established site, can range from carpentry and machine repair, through to ore sack sales. The livelihood trajectories of those engaged, however, are not always the same. Some initially take up work as miners, driven to the sector because of poverty (as indicated above), and then, after some time, pursue and achieve some level of success in an ancillary trade. Others aim to establish themselves at sites because they are pursuing an opportunity they have identified. Significantly, rarely have assessments of entrepreneurship at sites extended to the ancillary industries now inseparable from the sector. This is why, when analysing the economic impacts of ASM with the goal of building a case for formalising its activities, the sector must be viewed as an 'ecosystem'.[105]

Again, it is difficult to generalise about the different types of actors found at ASM sites in Ghana and sub-Saharan Africa more broadly. Each individual found working at a site chooses to mine for different reasons and, therefore, it is impossible to devise concrete categories of operator/worker. Whilst simplistic, the typology of 'poverty-driven' – 'get rich quick' does provide a useful starting point for identifying groups of people at sites because it maintains focus on their motivations for pursuing work in ASM in the first place.

The ecosystem narrative is, in essence, a reimagination of ASM that takes into account work and linkages beyond (mine) operations. Holistic pictures of sites could go a long way toward neutralising government rhetoric about ASM and build the momentum needed to revitalise interest in the sector's livelihoods 'dimension' and, broadly, formalisation of its activities.

Journal of Management (2024), https://doi.org/10.1080/23322373.2024.2349481 (accessed 25 May 2026).

105 Gavin Hilson and Yanfei Hu, 'Changing priorities, shifting narratives: remapping rural livelihoods in Africa's artisanal and small-scale mining sector', *Journal of Rural Studies* 92:3 (2022), 93–108.

Concluding Remarks

The Government of Ghana's decision to take military action against *galamsey* operators has overshadowed ASM's economic importance in the country. There is a need to resuscitate discussion on this strategy, which was gaining traction in policymaking debates long before the launch of *Operation Vanguard* in April 2017. The objective of this chapter was to help jumpstart this discussion by showcasing the roles – many of them indispensable – ASM has played in Ghana over the past 100 years. A comprehensive unpacking of these points, alongside a more logical interrogation of the 'menace' that the label *galamsey* now carries, should form the basis of a more productive discussion moving forward.

The current media campaign and protests waged against *galamsey* are unhelpful because they fail to pinpoint, and more importantly, unpack, the reasons why people turn to ASM for their livelihoods. It is a sector that is not going to go away, despite the best efforts of the government and the general public: it has existed for centuries, is firmly embedded in Ghana's rural economy, and will continue to flourish for many more decades. The key, therefore, is ensuring that ASM operations are regulated effectively, monitored regularly and properly supported. This cannot be achieved unless miners are in a position to formalise their operations, which, as indicated in this chapter, is far from being the case.

Importantly, Ghana has the capacity to do this. It has in place a comprehensive regulatory apparatus for small-scale mining, supported by a number of regulatory bodies, including the Minerals Commission, Ghana Geological Survey Authority, EPA and the Water Resources Commission. Ghana has also received millions of dollars in technical assistance over the years to support efforts to formalise ASM. This has been supplied by the likes of the World Bank, bilateral agencies and various divisions of the United Nations. For the media and general public, rather than focusing exclusively on the *galamsey* sector and condemning its environmental impacts, which are ultimately the products of unchecked ASM activity, more attention should be paid to understanding what can be achieved if the sector is formalised and ultimately, regulated and supported more effectively.

13

Post-Independence Structural Transformation in Ghana: The Drivers, Constraints and (Missed) Opportunities for Manufacturing

Emmanuel Abbey and Emmanuel Adu-Danso

When Ghana gained independence in 1957, it stood at a crossroads, facing both significant opportunities and substantial challenges in pursuing economic development. Although Ghana possessed the potential to pioneer its course towards an economic transformation and development that could inspire other African countries, the economic situation at independence was far from being inspirational. Nevertheless, this historic milestone represented a turning point, offering hope for shaping Ghana's future and influencing development approaches throughout the continent.

Despite the prevalence of several competing models of economic development in the 1950s and 1960s, such as the linear stages-of-growth model associated with Walt W. Rostow,[1] the structural change theory exemplified by Arthur Lewis's dual-sector model[2] and the international dependency theory advanced by Andre Gunder Frank,[3] Ghana's first president, Dr Kwame Nkrumah, gravitated more towards the socialist approach that emphasised state-led economic planning and industrialisation. He conceptualised a transformation agenda that sought political and economic independence from the West, even though the centrepiece of this agenda was a hydroelectric and aluminium project financed by the World Bank and built by an American company. He, therefore, envisioned a centrally planned economy driven by state-led enterprises with complementary import-substitution strategies aimed at reducing the country's overdependence on former colonial powers and foreign products. His ambitions also centred on modernising agriculture and pursuing an industrialisation agenda while delivering key social services,

1 W.W. Rostow, *The Stages of Economic Growth: A Non-Communist Manifesto* (Cambridge, 1960).

2 W. Arthur Lewis, 'Economic development with unlimited supplies of labour', *Manchester School*, 22:2 (1954), 139–91.

3 Andre Gunder Frank, *Capitalism and Underdevelopment in Latin America: Historical Studies of Chile and Brazil* (New York, 1967).

including universal education and healthcare. Decades after his overthrow, key economic decisions and policymaking continued to be influenced by elements of his views on transformation.

This chapter contributes to the literature on Ghana's post-independence structural transformation by providing a review of the country's industrial development trajectory from independence to 2010, as we explore drivers, constraints and missed opportunities that have shaped Ghana's industrialisation agenda through manufacturing. Building on seminal works such as Killick's *Development Economics in Action*, which analysed Ghana's economic policies from independence to the 1980s, with an update in 2010,[4] this chapter extends the historical perspective to examine more recent industrial policies and outcomes. It addresses the challenges of premature deindustrialisation highlighted by Nxumalo and Raju,[5] while also incorporating insights from recent studies on Ghana's economic complexity and export diversification potential, including studies by the Brookings Institution.[6] By synthesising these various strands of literature and relating them to the present, this chapter provides a holistic view of the key drivers (enablers) of the transformation process, the constraints (or challenges) and (missed) opportunities for shaping Ghana's manufacturing sector.

Indeed, Nkrumah's idea of structural transformation was based on a capital-intensive Import-Substitution Industrialisation (ISI) strategy driven by the central government.[7] The rationale was to free the country from the colonial situation of depending on advanced economies for manufactured goods and industrialise to meet domestic consumption needs. Ghana had a vibrant agricultural sector at independence, and the intention was that surpluses from agriculture should be used to support the nascent manufacturing sector.[8] These ideas aligned quite well with the emerging view by some prominent African leaders (notably Julius Nyerere of Tanzania, Kenneth Kaunda of Zambia and Leopold Senghor of Senegal) of communalism and humanism, and they were

4 Tony Killick, *Development Economics in Action: A Study of Economic Policies in Ghana* (London, 1978; 2nd edn, 2010). The references below are to the second edition.

5 Mpumelelo Nxumalo and Dhushyanth Raju, 'Structural Transformation and Labor Market Performance in Ghana', *World Bank Jobs Working Paper* 55 (2020).

6 See William Baah-Boateng and Eric Kofi Twum, 'Pathways to structural transformation of the Ghanaian economy – and some roadblocks', *Africa in Focus* (2020) https://www.brookings.edu/articles/pathways-to-structural-transformation-of-the-ghanaian-economy-and-some-roadblocks/ (accessed 25 May 2026).

7 Robert Darko Osei and Remi Jedwab, 'Structural change in a poor African country: new historical evidence from Ghana', in Margaret McMillan, Dani Rodrik and Claudia Sepúlveda (eds), *Structural Change, Fundamentals and Growth: A Framework and Case Studies* (Washington DC, 2016), 161–96; Killick, *Development Economics in Action*; Douglas Rimmer, *Staying Poor: Ghana's Political Economy, 1950–1990* (Oxford, 1992).

8 Killick, *Development Economics in Action*.

seen as a good way of addressing the disruption caused by colonial structures.[9] However, Nkrumah's agenda contrasted with the more general model of structural transformation as postulated by Arthur Lewis, which assumed labour surplus in agriculture.

When Lewis was invited as an economic adviser to Nkrumah, he took a different view of the path that the new nation had to take for transformation.[10] Having observed that Ghana, like much of Sub-Saharan Africa at the time, did not possess a surplus of agricultural labour for structural transformation, Lewis tailored his recommendations to the region's widespread labour scarcity, advocating capital-intensive agriculture to raise productivity and gradually release labour for industrial development. He did not believe that the country was ready to undertake the kind of industrialisation drive it was embarking on. As a result of this, he frequently clashed with Nkrumah over what he saw as wasteful 'white elephant' projects that were undertaken in the name of industrialisation. His disappointment at the repeated missed opportunities for genuine structural transformation, among other fundamental disagreements with Nkrumah's goals, ultimately led to his resignation in December 1958.[11]

The early promise of a buoyant Ghanaian economy succumbed to various underlying economic and political tensions.[12] But it is important to note that the situation at independence in March 1957 was not as robust as the prevailing optimism suggested. The economy's heavy dependence on cocoa exports made it vulnerable to global price fluctuations, and the country faced significant challenges in economic diversification and industrial development. The euphoria of independence, reflected in the mood of the time, obscured these realities. The subsequent economic difficulties were thus not solely due to post-independence

9 Although communism and humanism are not directly linked, the challenges of early European industrialisation spurred socialist, communist, and humanist philosophies, which emphasised social equality and collective welfare. African leaders such as Nyerere, Kaunda, and Senghor adapted these ideas, combining them with indigenous communal traditions, to forge national ideologies aimed at countering the disruptions of colonialism in ways suited to their own societies.

10 Arthur Lewis published his influential *Report on Industrialisation and the Gold Coast* in 1953, before his appointment as Chief Economic Adviser to Kwame Nkrumah. The report was formally received and debated by the Legislative Assembly and is widely cited as an early analytical input into Ghanaian industrial policy, although later work suggests that Nkrumah's own industrialisation drive only partly reflected Lewis's more cautious recommendations. See the discussion by Ravi Kanbur, 'W. Arthur Lewis and the roots of Ghanaian economic policy', in Ernest Aryeetey and Ravi Kanbur (eds), *The Economy of Ghana Sixty Years After Independence* (Oxford, 2017), 16–27; and Kanbur's chapter in this volume.

11 Robert L. Tignor, *W. Arthur Lewis and the Birth of Development Economics* (Princeton, 2006).

12 Killick, *Development Economics in Action*; Rimmer, *Staying Poor*, ch. 2.

policies but also stemmed from pre-existing structural issues that were not immediately apparent amid the celebrations of newfound sovereignty.

Less than a decade after independence, Nkrumah's approach to development became unpopular, and economic hardship began to mount.[13] The country subsequently witnessed a series of military coups and fragile political regimes over the next fifteen years (or more, if one includes the fragility of the Provisional National Defence Council (PNDC) in 1981–83).[14] But, until 1983, Ghana did not significantly deviate from Nkrumah's idea of using ISI to structurally transform the economy. From April 1983, under a new era of international economic liberalisation, a strategy based on free trade and the free market, designed to break the legacy of state-led industrialisation, was pursued. Industrialisation followed a more market-oriented strategy. From 2001, economic liberalisation was complemented by a private-sector-led accelerated industrial strategy through the reform of the investment climate and adaptation to an emerging natural resource boom. Recently, attempts have been made to incorporate science, technology, and innovation in industrial policy.[15]

The continuous renewal of the country's industrialisation policies, with a view to developing a buoyant manufacturing sector, was generally aimed at transforming the economy to meet the aspirations of Ghanaians, including the provision of higher-quality jobs and incomes. Ghana's post-independence structural transformation has been a journey of contrasts. The initial period of state-led import-substitution industrialisation policies from 1957 to 1983 ultimately led to economic decline, with Gross Domestic Product (GDP) per capita falling below independence levels. From 1983, a market-oriented, private-sector-driven strategy, initially as part of a broader Economic Recovery Programme that sparked sustained economic growth (averaging 3.6 per cent during 1983–86 and 4.8 per cent in 1987–91) by reducing fiscal deficits, improving infrastructure, and promoting exports (averaging 8.2 per cent of GDP during 1983–86, and 15.5 per cent in 1987–91).[16] Despite this decisive shift, significant industrialisation has not materialised. Instead, the economy transitioned from being agriculture-led to being service-led, with manufacturing remaining stagnant (see Figure 13.1). This trajectory stands in contrast to Ghana's early

13 *Ibid.*

14 Baffour Agyeman-Duah, 'Ghana, 1982–6: the politics of the P.N.D.C.', *Journal of Modern African Studies* 25:4 (1987), 613–42.

15 Nkechi Owoo and John Page, 'Industrial policy in Ghana: from dominant state to resource abundance', in Ernest Aryeetey and Ravi Kanbur (eds), *The Economy of Ghana Sixty Years after Independence* (Oxford, 2017), 176–91; Peter Quartey, F.E. Turkson, E. Abbey and M.M. Butu, *Impact and Lessons from COVID-19 and the Pathways for Industrialization and Trade in Ghana (Industrial and Manufacturing Sector)*. Project report prepared for the African Development Bank (Accra, 2020).

16 Rimmer, *Staying Poor*; Jonathan H. Frimpong-Ansah, *The Vampire State in Africa: The Political Economy of Decline in Ghana* (London, 1991).

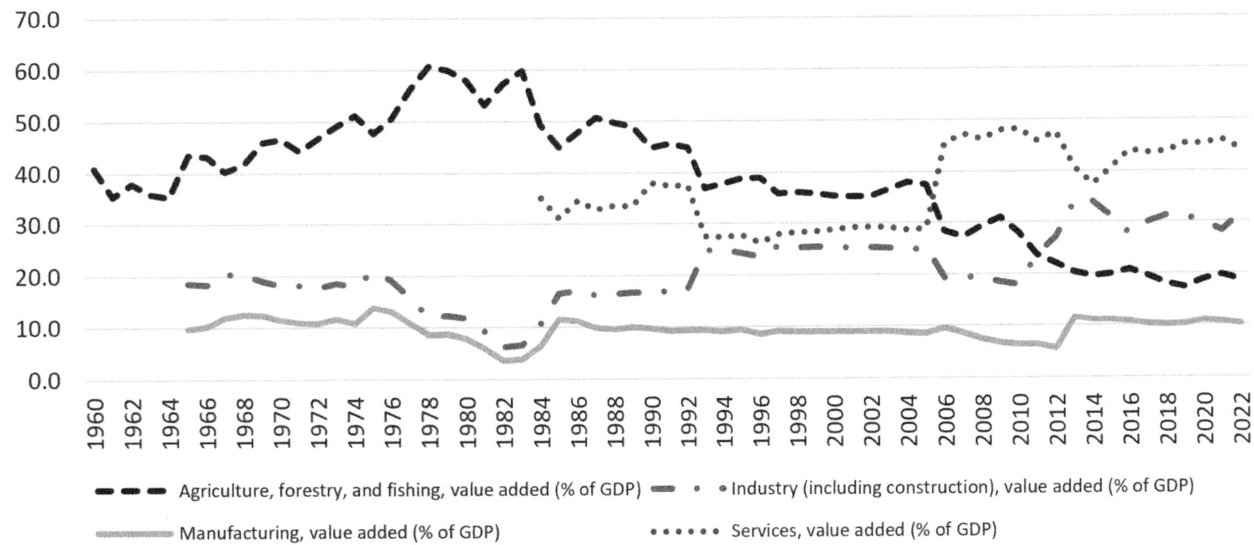

Figure 13.1 Sectoral Contribution to GDP (%).

Source: World Development Indicators, 2024.

post-independence performance, which closely matched that of South Korea around 1957; both countries then exhibited similar levels of GDP per capita, before Korea's rapid ascent, as against the slower progress in Ghana. After nearly seven decades of effort, Ghana's structural transformation remains incomplete, facing ongoing challenges in achieving comprehensive economic diversification and industrial development.

Lewis's Model of Structural Transformation Revisited

Arthur Lewis's 1954 dual-sector or structural transformation model remains one of the most influential frameworks in development economics.[17] It presents the economy as comprising two sectors: a subsistence agricultural sector with surplus, low-productivity labour, and a capitalist industrial sector characterised by higher productivity, capital accumulation, and profit-oriented expansion. Economic development, in Lewis's view, hinges on the transfer of surplus labour from agriculture to industry, where workers earn a higher, institutionally fixed wage, typically about 30 per cent above subsistence levels. This wage differential drives rural–urban migration, enabling the industrial sector to expand and accelerate growth.

A key dynamic of the model is the reinvestment of industrial profits. As workers move from agriculture to industry, industrial output and profits rise, encouraging further reinvestment and continued capital accumulation. During this phase, the supply of labour to industry remains elastic, keeping real wages stable and sustaining profitability. The process continues until the so-called 'Lewis Turning Point', when surplus labour is fully absorbed. Beyond this point, any labour withdrawal from agriculture reduces food output, and wages in both sectors begin to rise, signalling the onset of labour scarcity, slower growth, and higher production costs. Lewis emphasised that sustained growth required rising agricultural productivity, as each advance would release more labour and resources for industry. Although the Lewis model remains a cornerstone of development economics, it has attracted substantial criticism for its simplifying assumptions and limited realism. Accordingly, later theories have refined its framework by integrating labour market dualism, informality, and sectoral diversity.[18] Nonetheless, Lewis's core

17 Lewis, 'Economic development with unlimited supplies of labour'.

18 John R. Harris and Michael P. Todaro, 'Migration, unemployment and development: a two-sector analysis', *American Economic Review* 60:1 (1970), 126–42.

proposition remains influential and has been revisited and partly qualified by modern studies, including those of McMillan and Rodrik.[19]

Lewis's experience in Ghana underscores the practical complexities of applying his own framework. He quickly observed that Ghana lacked the large pool of surplus agricultural labour his model assumed and did not yet possess the skilled workforce necessary for rapid industrialisation. In his advisory report to Dr Kwame Nkrumah's government, Lewis proposed a gradual, sequenced approach: improving agricultural productivity, building human capital, and enhancing public services before attempting large-scale industrialisation.[20] He warned that using agriculture to finance capital-intensive, state-led industrial ventures would prove unsustainable without first strengthening the rural economy. Ghana's decision to pursue import-substitution industrialisation, contrary to these recommendations, underscored the tension between political ambition and economic realism, a dynamic that contributed to both policy failure and Lewis's early resignation.[21] Lewis's framework, though originally designed for mid-twentieth-century economies, continues to inform policy debates. Its core message, that productive transformation must be anchored in agriculture and supported by reinvestment and skill development, however, remains relevant today.

A Historical Account of Ghana's Structural Transformation Path

This section traces the key developments that shaped the kind of transformation that took place within the periods discussed. It highlights these key drivers of change in the economy, tracing developments from the colonial period through the post-independence era. In doing so, we show some of the constraints that emerged and the opportunities (including those missed) that emerged.

The Colonial Era, to 1957

Before independence, Ghana's economy was predominantly rural and heavily dependent on agriculture, with smallholder farmers playing a central role. Cocoa cultivation began in the late nineteenth century and quickly spread

19 Margaret McMillan and Dani Rodrik, 'Globalization, structural change, and economic growth', National Bureau of Economic Research *(NBER) Working Paper Series*, Working Paper 17143 (Cambridge MA, 2011).

20 W. Arthur Lewis, *Report on Industrialisation and the Gold Coast* (Accra, 1953). For a much more detailed discussion of the report, see Kanbur's chapter in this volume.

21 See, for example, Kanbur, 'W. Arthur Lewis', which documents Lewis's advisory role to Nkrumah, his proposals for more gradual, productivity-oriented development, the government's decision to pursue ambitious import-substituting, capital-intensive industrialisation instead, and his resignation as chief economic adviser in 1958.

across southern Ghana.[22] In 1910/11, Ghana became the world's leading producer of cocoa, marking some transformation within agriculture and the economy. Cocoa farming involved significant entrepreneurial activity, particularly by migrant farmers who moved to fertile areas, acquired land, and invested profits to expand production.[23] This export-crop sector was crucial to Ghana's colonial and post-colonial economy, underpinning export revenues and shaping economic structures. The colonial administration supported cocoa expansion through infrastructure development and incentives, while migrant labour from neighbouring regions contributed to sector growth.

Structural transformation in Ghana's colonial era was characterised by what A.G. Hopkins termed an 'open economy' policy.[24] During this time, the colonial government prioritised export-oriented agriculture, particularly cocoa, alongside the extraction of minerals and timber. This approach facilitated the Gold Coast's integration into global trade networks but left the economy vulnerable to external shocks and price fluctuations.[25] A notable change occurred in 1939 with the establishment of a parastatal export monopsony for cocoa, which was institutionalised after the Second World War through the retention of the Cocoa Marketing Board (CMB). This marked a shift toward a more state-controlled or 'closed' economic model. State-led promotion of economic development by colonial administrations, which began as early as the 1890s (though not very effectively) and was notably advanced by Governor Guggisberg, laid important foundations for later industrialisation. Rather than a post-war emergence, these initiatives reflected a gradual shift towards greater state involvement in economic planning well before independence.

The Nkrumah Era, 1957–66

Moved by a desire to dismantle the colonial legacy and to transform the Ghanaian economy, Ghana's first president adopted a state-led industrialisation programme that sought to reduce or eliminate the country's dependence on imports of finished goods. The ISI strategy of the central government was at complete variance with the prescription of the country's economic adviser at the time, Lewis, who believed that the conditions in the 1950s were not right. Lewis adduced two main reasons for this: first, that land was still relatively abundant to accommodate agricultural expansion, while the price of labour was too high; second, the supply of skilled labour was inadequate to support capital-intensive manufacturing. Lewis's recommendation to the Nkrumah government was for a 'vigorous agricultural programme' underpinned by the

22 See Austin's chapter.
23 Polly Hill, *The Migrant Cocoa-Farmers of Southern Ghana* (Cambridge, 1963).
24 A.G. Hopkins, *An Economic History of West Africa*, 2nd edn (London, 2019).
25 See Alence's chapter.

provision of infrastructure and investment in human capital, which would lay the required foundation for the country's future industrialisation: a labour-push approach. He believed in dealing first with what Rodrik later characterised as the 'fundamental' challenges to transforming Ghana, including better institutions, health and education, technologies, and policies.[26]

Nkrumah disagreed with this view and went ahead to pursue massive state-led ISI. The focus of policy was on nurturing the development of the state enterprises through trade protectionism and preferential access to finance and foreign exchange. Effective protection was over 100 per cent by the end of the 1960s for the majority of manufacturing firms, prompting a shift in import structure from consumer goods to capital inputs.[27]

There was a substantial increase in public investments, mostly in infrastructure. A centrepiece of this effort was the integrated hydroelectric dam, the aluminium industry project, and the associated Volta Aluminium Company (VALCO). The Akosombo Dam, completed in 1965 at a cost of US$130 million, provided hydroelectric power to support industrial activities, particularly aluminium production.[28] Osei and Jedwab note that only Nkrumah, given the kind of political support that he received, could implement this 'big push', which resulted in some structural changes in the Ghanaian economy.[29] But by 1966, Ghana faced significant external and internal debts totalling nearly US$1 billion due to heavy borrowing to finance these projects.

Agriculture remained dominant in its contribution to the growth of the Ghanaian economy. It also remained the leading source of employment. The share of manufacturing in Ghana's GDP did rise over time, but it remained relatively small. Ghana's manufacturing sector experienced modest growth in its share of GDP, rising from 10 per cent in 1960 to 14 per cent by 1970. Most of the large-scale industries established during Nkrumah's leadership remained in their infancy and failed to mature into competitive

26 Dani Rodrik, 'An African growth miracle?', *Journal of African Economies* 27:1 (2018), 10–27.

27 Charles Ackah, Charles Adjasi and Festus Turkson, 'Scoping study on the evolution of industry in Ghana', *WIDER Working Paper*, 2014/075 (Helsinki, 2014).

28 This project was salvaged by a World Bank loan, secured with the backing of the US government following prolonged negotiations by Dr Nkrumah. This became necessary after Britain abandoned the original colonial scheme. The Akosombo Dam formed part of the Volta River Project and was central to Ghana's industrialisation strategy. It supported aluminium smelting through VALCO, which consumed 60 per cent of the dam's hydroelectric power and produced up to 200,000 tonnes of aluminium annually during the 1970s. However, challenges such as global oversupply of bauxite and economic recession later undermined this initiative: Library of Congress (LaVerle Berry, ed.), *Ghana: A Country Study* (Washington DC, 2nd edn, 1980), 322–7.

29 Osei and Jedwab, 'Structural change'.

or self-sustaining enterprises. Manufacturing had little impact on per capita income and employment (and may even have reduced overall welfare once the fiscal and efficiency costs of subsidies and protection are taken into account), with many manufacturing firms remaining small and informal.[30]

Nkrumah's pursuit of development through rapid state-led industrialisation faced serious implementation challenges. For instance, there was a dearth of feasibility studies on potential markets and raw material needs preceding the massive investments.[31] There were also issues with the siting of manufacturing plants, which appeared largely politically motivated.[32] Subsequent mismanagement and the inflationary effect of import restrictions exacerbated the challenges of the endeavour.[33] Nkrumah's political vision of transforming the Ghanaian economy through the driving force of state-led manufacturing took off but proved unsustainable and was cut short by his overthrow in 1966.[34] A key observation from the era is that structural constraints and policy missteps can significantly hinder structural transformation.

Manufacturing, during that era, was uncompetitive mainly because firm-level productivity (technical efficiency) was far too low to offset production costs, especially wages, so that Ghanaian firms could not profitably export manufactures even at relatively low wage levels.[35] Comparing Ghana to Mauritius, Teal argued that the latter's manufacturing firms were several times more efficient than Ghanaian firms, which meant that, despite paying higher wages, Mauritian producers had much lower unit labour costs and could compete successfully in export markets while Ghanaian firms, facing low efficiency and weak productivity growth, remained largely inward-looking and uncompetitive internationally.[36] Frankema and Van Waijenburg argued that relatively high wages in Ghana were linked to the relative scarcity of labour compared to land and natural resources, contrasting with the labour-surplus economies

30 Friedrich Ebert Foundation, *Privatization of State-Owned Enterprises in Ghana: Proceedings of a Workshop Organized for Members of the Finance Committee of Parliament, 18–20 November* (Accra, 1994); Rajiv Ball, 'The "long depression" and the growth of small-scale industries in Ghana, 1970–mid-1980s', in Gareth Austin (ed.), 'Industrial Growth in the Third World, 1870–1990', LSE Working Papers in Economic History, 44/98 (London, 1998), 73–87.

31 Kodwo Ewusi, *The Process of Industrialization in Ghana: 1950–75* (Legon, 1981).

32 Leslie E. Grayson, 'A conglomerate in Africa: public-sector manufacturing enterprises in Ghana, 1962–71', *African Studies Review* 16:3 (1973), 315–45.

33 Osei and Jedwab, 'Structural change'.

34 Rimmer, *Staying Poor.*

35 See Francis Teal, 'Why can Mauritius export manufactures and Ghana not?', *The World Economy* 22:7 (1999), 981–93.

36 *Ibid.*

of Asia, where real wages were relatively lower.[37] This made Ghana's manufacturing uncompetitive and rendered the pursuit of industrialisation costly for the state.[38]

The Post-Nkrumah Era to Structural Adjustment, 1966–82

Between 1966 and 1979, Ghana vacillated between periods of autocratic military rule and fragile democratic governance. Although economic policies varied with political dispensations, Nkrumah's legacy of state-led ISI persisted in this period. Various constraints compelled succeeding governments to pursue a variant of Nkrumah's ISI rather than promoting manufacturing for exports. Structural challenges, including wage disparities and limited technological capacity, remained key constraints. The National Liberation Council (NLC), which overthrew Kwame Nkrumah in 1966, started the exercise of privatising uncompetitive state-owned enterprises. The NLC inherited an economy characterised by macroeconomic instability, unsustainable fiscal and external balances, inefficient and politicised state enterprises, and declining competitiveness in key sectors. This meant limited financial resources along with overbearing government consumption expenditure, fleeting foreign reserves and ballooning external debt. Existing manufacturing firms were already overstaffed, uncompetitive and politicised. Government divestment (divestiture) became one of the manufacturing renaissance solutions, although there were reservations about mass privatisation.[39]

A brief return to democracy from 1969 to 1972 under the Kofi Busia government saw the continuation and extension of liberal economic measures first initiated under the NLC, including new incentives and institutional support for domestic and foreign private investors, together with a large IMF-backed devaluation of the cedi in 1971 that the government reluctantly accepted amid mounting balance-of-payments pressures, as part of broader efforts to open the economy.[40] These were, however, not enough to stem the decline in total factor productivity and physical capital's contribution to GDP.[41]

37 Ewout Frankema and Marlous van Waijenburg, 'Structural impediments to African growth? New evidence from real wages in British Africa, 1880–1965', *Journal of Economic History* 72:4 (2012), 895–926.

38 See Teal, 'Why can Mauritius export manufactures and Ghana not?'; Gareth Austin, Ewout Frankema and Morten Jerven, 'Patterns of manufacturing growth in Sub-Saharan Africa', in Kevin O'Rourke and Jeffrey G. Williamson (eds), *The Spread of Modern Industry to the Periphery since 1871* (Oxford, 2017), 345–74.

39 Friedrich Ebert Foundation, *Privatization of State-Owned Enterprises in Ghana.*

40 Augustin Fosu and Ernest Aryeetey, 'Economic Growth in Ghana, 1960–2000', in B. Ndulu, S. O'Connell, J. Azam, R. Bates, A. Fosu, J. Gunning, and D. Njinkeu (eds), *The Political Economy of Economic Growth in Africa, 1960–2000*, vol. 2: *Country Case Studies* (New York, 2008).

41 Fosu and Aryeetey, 'Economic Growth in Ghana, 1960–2000'.

The National Redemption Council (NRC), led by Colonel (later General) Ignatius Acheampong, which took power in 1972 and was reconstituted as the Supreme Military Council in 1975, launched the flagship agricultural development programme Operation Feed Yourself, an initiative that initially expanded domestic food production but began to falter by the mid-1970s amid shortages and high food prices. Under the programme, the state committed resources to increase the output of staples such as rice and maize to meet domestic food needs. Agriculture continued to grow in importance, with its contribution to GDP rising to one of the highest levels in Ghana's post-independence history, contributing about 60 per cent of the country's GDP (see Figure 13.1). Ordinarily, this should have provided the momentum for a labour-push industrial transformation. However, Ghana's agricultural sector continued to be dominated by smallholder farming, and the rising agricultural output was pursued largely through increasing the area under cultivation, given that land remained relatively abundant. The structure of the economy remained largely unchanged, and what structural change did occur tended to be growth-reducing, as labour moved out of agriculture into low-productivity informal services rather than into higher-productivity manufacturing or modern services, so that the reallocation contributed little to, and sometimes detracted from, overall productivity growth.[42]

Domestic and international shocks, together with mounting balance-of-payments pressures and widening fiscal deficits, had pushed the economy into a severe crisis by 1979, with negative per-capita growth, chronic shortages of foreign exchange and imported goods, very high inflation and large external payment arrears. A junior officers' coup in June 1979 brought Flight Lieutenant Jerry John Rawlings and the Armed Forces Revolutionary Council briefly to power, in a 'house-cleaning' operation forcibly acting against inflation and corruption. The 'June Fourth Revolution' government ceded power to the democratically elected People's National Party (PNP), led by Hilla Limann. The PNP attempted to address economic imbalances through policy reforms, but these measures were insufficient to reverse the economic decline. Within two years, perceived incompetence and worsening economic conditions led to another military intervention. On 31 December, 1981, Rawlings staged a coup and established the PNDC, initially pursuing a radical populist agenda that tightened state control over prices, imports, and marketing while promoting new organs of grassroots political participation such as workers' and people's defence committees. Only later, after the failure of this strategy and the drying-up of support from socialist allies, did the regime turn to IMF- and

42 Osei and Jedwab, 'Structural Change'.

World Bank-backed economic liberalisation as a pragmatic response to the deepening crisis.[43]

By 1982, the private sector remained largely underdeveloped, given the dominance of the state in economic and social life. Supporting infrastructure, key to sustaining a burgeoning private sector, was virtually nonexistent following years of policies that essentially crowded out entrepreneurship. Significant deindustrialisation took place during this period as manufacturing's share of GDP declined to its lowest level since independence (see Figure 13.1). Nonetheless, the share of agriculture in GDP was rising, a legacy of Operation Feed Yourself and related policies that channelled resources and incentives toward food production. One distinctive feature of this era was the adoption of exceptionally stringent foreign-exchange and trade-control measures in the name of import-substituting industrialisation, going far beyond earlier control regimes. These policies combined very tight quantitative restrictions on imports, sweeping foreign-exchange licensing and rationing, and an exchange-rate policy that held the cedi at a steeply overvalued level for prolonged periods, even by comparison with the severe controls of the 1940s.[44]

The Era of Liberalisation and Economic Recovery, 1983–2000

By 1983, Ghana had been through five military coups and two fragile democratic dispensations. The economy reeled under international shocks, the worst drought in the last fifty years, and stagflation. Real GDP fell more than 30 per cent between 1975 and 1982, and foreign reserves were completely depleted.[45] Like many other economies that adopted state-led industrialisation, in Ghana, ISI failed to transform the economy.

Restoring a market-oriented economy, on a scale not seen since before the creation of the cocoa export marketing board in 1939, came to be viewed as the only credible programme, with the Bretton Woods institutions seen as the indispensable source of external finance to support such far-reaching reforms. The PNDC signed onto the International Monetary Fund (IMF) and World Bank-sponsored programmes, although it was not the first time Ghana had sought external fiscal relief. From 1983 to 1992, Ghana went through six programmes, which included three standby agreements in 1984, 1985 and 1986,

43 Paul Nugent, *Big Men, Small Boys and Politics in Ghana: Power, Ideology and the Burden of History*, 1982–1994 (London, 1995); Emmanuel Hansen, *Ghana under Rawlings: Early Years* (Lagos, 1991).

44 Gareth Austin, 'Ghana and Kenya facing the 1970s commodity price shocks: the national and the global', in Shigeru Akita (ed.), *Oil Crises of the 1970s and the Transformation of International Order: Economy, Development and Aid in Asia and Africa* (London, 2023), 223–56.

45 International Monetary Fund, *Annual Report of the Executive Board for the Financial Year Ended April 30, 1991* (Washington DC, 1991).

the Extended Fund Facility with a Structural Adjustment Facility (SAF) in 1987, the enhanced SAF between 1988 and 1991, and the Fund Monitored Programme from 1992.[46]

Along with the Economic Recovery Programme, the Structural Adjustment Programme (SAP) aimed to rehabilitate the economy through liberalisation itself, that is, by restoring the price mechanism and opening up the economy, and the April 1983 budget inaugurated these liberalising measures before the subsequent upturn in output and growth. Under the programmes, the currency was devalued and later floated, and trade was liberalised. There were substantial shifts in public expenditure aimed at restoring fiscal and monetary discipline and enhancing efficiency: overall public investment was sharply reduced in the early 1980s, wage bills were compressed and about 200,000 public-sector workers were retrenched, even as selected items such as the real minimum wage and salaries for key professional groups were raised and spending on basic education and primary health care began to recover later in the decade.[47] Structural and institutional reforms included the privatisation of state-owned enterprises. The reforms sought to restore the fundamentals of the economy, fix some of the major distortions (including the Acheampong regime's control-price system, especially the rationing and extreme overvaluation), and expand private sector participation in the economy. The official rate had been kept so high relative to market conditions that it severely penalised exporters, fuelled shortages and a flourishing black market, and contributed directly to the collapse in recorded output before April 1983, as Austin and others emphasise.[48]

The programmes produced a paradigm shift in the industrial policy from the traditional import substitution and overprotected industrial strategy to an outward liberalised private sector-led industrial strategy.[49] A key element of the industrial strategy under the Economic Recovery Programme (ERP) was the shift from the government being the main driver of industrial development to placing greater emphasis on private sector participation, with a focus on small- and medium-sized business, which it was hoped would create jobs. This was anticipated to help absorb retrenched public sector workers and new entrants into the labour market. Industrial policy focused on abolishing the import licensing regime, introducing market exchange rates, removing price controls and liberalising interest rates. To increase efficiency and reduce anti-export bias, quantitative import controls were also eliminated. State-owned

46 Matthew Martin, 'Neither phoenix nor Icarus: negotiating economic reform in Ghana and Zambia, 1983–92', in Thomas M. Callaghy and John Ravenhill (eds), *Hemmed In: Responses to Africa's Economic Decline* (New York, 1993), 130–79.

47 International Monetary Fund, *Ghana: Adjustment and Growth, 1983–91* (Washington DC, 1992), which documents the evolution of public expenditure, public employment and wages during the ERP/SAP period.

48 Austin, 'Ghana and Kenya facing the 1970s commodity price shocks'.

49 Ackah, Adjasi and Turkson, 'Scoping study'.

enterprises were targeted for privatisation, and the Ghana Investment Centre was established.

Despite the sweeping reforms, manufacturing never fully took off, as its share of GDP remained at about 10 per cent over the following two decades (Figure 13.1). Agriculture's contribution to both output and employment continued to decline, with its share of GDP falling to a record low, compared with the early post-independence period, when agriculture dominated output and employment. Industry, however, did witness some recovery, with its share of GDP rising for most of the recovery period.

In 1992, elections were held, and the Fourth Republic was inaugurated in January 1993. Since then, Ghana has experienced political stability, with regular alternation of power between the major parties, while successive governments have broadly sustained a liberal, market-oriented policy framework initiated under the PNDC. However, structural transformation remains incomplete due to persistent challenges such as a weak industrial base, inefficiencies in agriculture, and reliance on low-productivity services. The creation of the Export Processing Zones at Tema and Sekondi (in 1996) was among the significant industrial advances during the earlier phases of this period, as these zones provided purpose-built enclaves with fiscal and regulatory incentives to attract export-oriented manufacturing and foreign investment.

The Era of Democratic Consolidation, 2000 and Beyond

This period began with a peaceful transfer of power between democratically elected governments. Since then, Ghana has experienced sustained competitive multiparty democracy. Additionally, the era has been distinguished by an accelerated industrial development strategy driven primarily by the private sector. An industrial architecture based on value-added processing of Ghana's natural resource endowments was created.[50] Industrial policy emphasised the growth of rural enterprises, micro, small, and medium enterprises, as well as strengthening links between agriculture and industry (manufacturing).

An industrial policy was launched by the John Evans Atta Mills government in 2011 to encourage agro-based industrial growth, enhance technological capabilities in manufacturing, and establish a modern, productive economy characterised by high value addition. It also aimed to offer consumers better-quality goods and services at reasonable prices. This policy framework comprised a range of targeted tools and measures designed to improve the economy's access to competitive production factors and to strengthen Ghana's industrial sector (manufacturing) in terms of productivity, efficiency, and expansion. The policy identified four main components covering a comprehensive range of initiatives

50 *Ibid.*

across twenty-one subject areas: production and distribution, technology and innovation, incentives and regulatory frameworks, and cross-cutting issues.

The rise of the industrial sector was largely unsupported by adequate public investments in skills and economic infrastructure, and private investment in these areas also remained limited. Evaluations based on Doing Business metrics[51] (a set of indicators used to evaluate how conducive a country's regulatory environment is to starting and operating a business) seemed to be unproductive since they diverted attention away from other important aspects of the investment climate and the task of working with the private sector to create legally binding restrictions for increased business productivity. The rate of industrial growth increased slightly between 2000 and 2020, although the mix shifted away from manufacturing towards mining, quarrying, and construction. Nkechi Owoo and John Page indicated that the mining and quarrying sector grew by roughly 206.5 per cent in 2011 alone, and this was largely due to the onset of commercial offshore oil production.[52] This remarkable expansion contributed to Ghana's overall economic performance that year, with growth in extractive activities, especially gold mining and offshore petroleum production, playing a key role in driving GDP growth. Specific one-off developments, including the start-up and rapid scaling-up of offshore oil production and related services, led to the services sector surpassing agriculture in its contribution to GDP, while industry remained below.

Since the late 2000s, two major programmes have been introduced by the government of Ghana, specifically led by the Ministry of Trade and Industry, to support industrialisation. The first was the Ghana Industrial Sector Support Programme (ISSP), introduced in the late 2000s, and the second was the Ghana Ten-Point Agenda (announced in 2017). The ISSP was a 'special purpose vehicle' designed to implement Ghana's industrial policy within the context of the broader vision of transforming the Ghanaian economy into one driven by an industrial development model, capable of delivering widespread, equitable, and sustainable impacts, particularly in terms of inclusive growth, decent jobs, and poverty reduction to achieve balanced social and economic development. By facilitating targeted interventions, the ISSP helped increase Ghana's industrial competitiveness, supported value addition to natural resources, and fostered private-sector growth, thereby advancing the country's industrial transformation goals. When ISSP was pursued, the industrial sector underperformed with an aggregate growth rate that was relatively low. According to Pokua

51 World Bank, *The Development Effectiveness of the Use of Doing Business Indicators, Fiscal Years 2010–20* (Washington DC, 2022).

52 Owoo and Page, 'Industrial policy in Ghana'.

Fenny,[53] the underperformance of the industrial sector between 2006 and 2014 was largely due to the reduction in electricity supply and rising fuel prices, which compelled many firms, especially those operating in import-dependent manufacturing activities, to cut production.

For the first time, the share of industry in GDP surpassed that of agriculture. While the economic downturn that began in 2011 and lasted until 2014 may have contributed to ISSP's inability to achieve improved industrial performance, other parts of the industrial sector – construction, mining, and quarrying – performed quite well. In 2012, oil production contributed considerably to the growth of the economy, which reached 14.9 per cent. The implementation of the ISSP has been successful in specific industrial sector activities, including providing food-processing skills training to low-income and otherwise disadvantaged men and women, improving the manufacture of processing equipment and spare parts, assisting manufacturing companies to obtain export approval within the West African sub-region, and supporting system reforms at the ports, including customs and logistics procedures.

According to Esther Ofei-Aboagye, the underperformance of the industrial sector in 2016 was also attributable to the introduction of new taxes and increases in withholding taxes on rental income, which sought to reduce Ghana's fiscal deficit.[54] These policies had adverse effects on manufacturing sector activities. The energy crisis during that period, combined with infrastructure shortcomings, high interest rates, inadequate investment promotion, the ISSP's failure to leverage R&D along with science and technology to boost productivity, and the government's inability to strengthen and support institutions aiding industrial sector activities, collectively led to the industry's underperformance. Between 2017 and 2019, the industrial sector experienced growth, peaking at 15.7 per cent in 2017 and reaching its lowest point at 10.0 per cent in 2018. This growth was supported by key industrial sector initiatives carried out under the commerce development programme and the business development and promotion programme.

The second industrialisation-support programme, known as the Ten-Point Agenda, was introduced by the government of Ghana under President Nana Addo Dankwa Akufo-Addo in 2017. It was designed to build upon the industrial policy initiatives established in 2010, under President Atta Mills, highlighting how successive administrations have contributed to the evolution of Ghana's industrial policy. It aimed to align closely with Ghana's medium- to long-term development goals as outlined in the Ghana Beyond Aid Charter and Strategy, adopted in April 2019 as a framework for pursuing industrialisation,

53 Ama Pokua Fenny, 'Ghana's path to an industrial-led growth: the role of decentralisation policies', *International Journal of Economics and Finance* 9:11 (2017), 22–34.

54 Esther Ofei-Aboagye, *An Analysis of Existing Industrial Policies and State Implementation in Six (6) African Countries: A Synthesis Report* (Accra, 2018).

export diversification, and job creation with reduced reliance on external aid. This positioning underscored the Ten-Point Agenda's role in supporting a self-reliant, value-adding economy rather than one dependent on primary commodity exports and concessional finance.

A distinguishing feature of the democratic consolidation era is the structural change in sectoral contribution to GDP. As a result of the 2010 rebasing exercise, which adopted 2006 as its base year and incorporated previously under-recorded activities, the services sector was recognised as the largest contributor to the country's GDP, although a significant part of the activities carried out are within the informal economy (Figure 13.1).[55] The start of oil exports in 2010 opened new potential avenues for industrialising the economy, but also raised concerns about 'Dutch Disease' effects that could hinder manufacturing. In 2012, industry overtook agriculture to become the second-largest contributor to GDP. The manufacturing sub-sector's share of GDP has remained the smallest of the three main sectors throughout the period.

Drivers of Structural Transformation in Ghana

A significant share of the extant analyses of the theoretical frameworks for structural transformation has focused on the growth of sectoral labour productivity and employment to identify their underlying drivers. We rely on these same indicators to demonstrate that structural transformation has not been fully achieved in Ghana, despite noticeable changes in sectoral contributions to GDP in recent years. We limit the analysis to Ghana's Fourth Republic, a period when the country witnessed marked changes in sectoral contributions to both GDP and employment, with the share of services in GDP outpacing agriculture. It is worth noting that although sectoral shares in the period 1951 to 1989 showed agriculture's share of both employment and GDP decline significantly, it nonetheless remained the largest sector throughout the period (Figure 13.1).

Our analysis is based on data from the Groningen Growth and Development Centre (GGDC).[56] Its limitations are largely inherent to cross-country

55 GDP rebasing involves updating the base year used to calculate a country's GDP. This process provides a more accurate picture of the current economic structure by incorporating new industries, updated production methods, and changes in relative prices.

56 Gaaitzen de Vries, Linda Arfelt, Dorothea Drees, Mareike Godemann, Calumn Hamilton, Bente Jessen-Thiesen, Ahmet Ihsan Kaya, Hagen Kruse, Emmanuel Mensah and Pieter Woltjer, 'The Economic Transformation Database: Content, Sources, and Methods', WIDER Technical Note (2021). The GGDC datasets are a prominent resource in empirical economics, widely acknowledged for the rigour of the editors' efforts at standardisation and cross-national comparability. Gaaitzen de Vries, Klaas de Vries, Reitze Gouma, Stefan Pahl and Marcel P. Timmer, 'GGDC 10-Sector Database: Contents, Sources and Methods', *Groningen Growth and Development Centre* (2014). Confidence in the dataset is generally

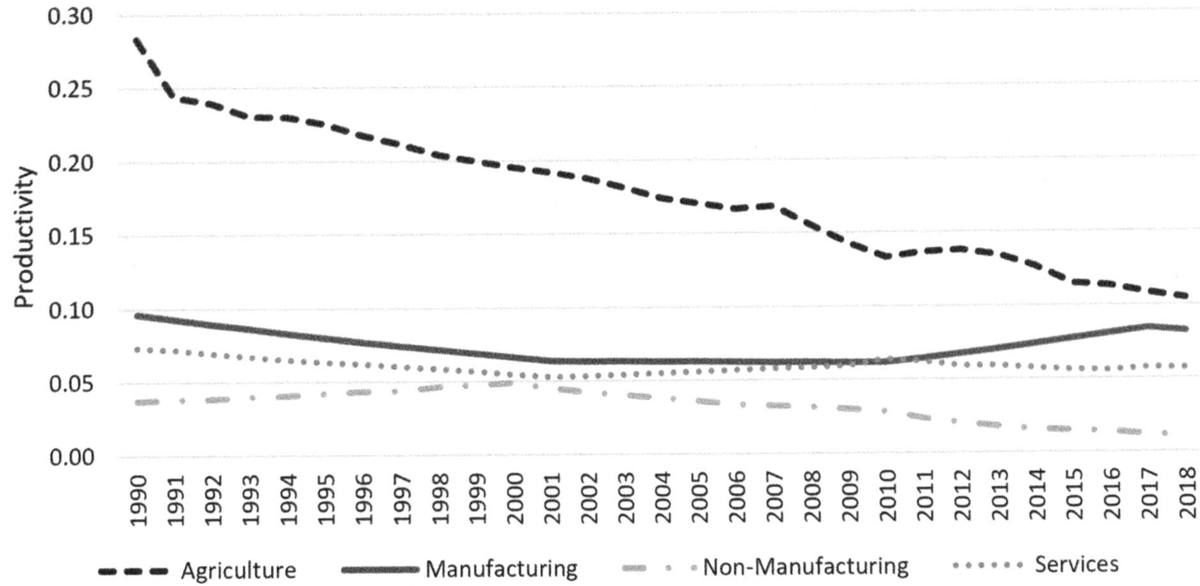

Figure 13.2 Aggregate Labour Productivity by Major Sectors, 1990–2018 (annual real gross value added per worker).

Source: Calculated from GGDC data.

datasets, particularly the uneven quality of data across countries and over different periods. We present line plots of two indicators for four major sectors of the economy: agriculture (including forestry and fishing), manufacturing, non-manufacturing industry (i.e. mining, utilities and construction) and services (i.e. trade, transport, business, and financial services). Figure 13.2 plots the shares of aggregate labour productivity for the sectors between 1990 and 2018, and Figure 13.3 plots the sectoral shares of total employment over the same period.

It is apparent from both figures that the gap between agriculture's and manufacturing's shares of aggregate labour productivity, as well as of employment, has been narrowing. One way of looking at the near convergence is that the economy was on a path of change, but transformation did not take place. Aggregate labour productivity in agriculture generally followed a significant downward trend, while that of manufacturing declined only marginally and recovered, thereby narrowing the gap between the two sectors. The share of agricultural employment also significantly declined, while that of the manufacturing sector increased, albeit marginally. The analysis is no different if aggregate manufacturing is added to the non-manufacturing industry, with almost the same trend emerging.

Several factors have influenced the changes in the distribution of employment. While technological change, in terms of product innovation, has been positively linked to job creation, particularly in manufacturing and service sectors, the introduction of more capital-intensive technology has also led to significant short-term job destruction due to labour-saving mechanisms.[57] Over time, however, the new technology has compensated for job losses by creating new opportunities, especially in higher-skill occupations.[58] The penetration of telecommunications has boosted productivity, with Information and Communications Technology (ICT) adoption driving efficiency gains and enabling sectoral transformation. Manufacturing has seen a slight shift towards higher-value activities, but the overall mix remains

---

robust, reflecting the GGDC's commitment to employing sound methodologies in data compilation and harmonisation, often drawing upon primary data from national statistical agencies and international organisations. Robert Inklaar and Marcel P. Timmer, 'GGDC productivity level database: International comparisons of output, inputs and productivity at the industry level' (Growth and Development Centre, University of Groningen, 2008).

57 See for instance, Agyapomaa Gyeke-Dako, Abena D. Oduro, F. Ebo Turkson, Priscilla Twumasi Baffour, and Emmanuel Abbey, *The Effect of Technological Innovation on the Quantity and Quality of Employment in Ghana*, R4D Working Paper 9 (Swiss Programme for Research on Global Issues for Development, 2016).

58 World Bank, 'Ghana Can Create Better Jobs through Accelerated Economic Transformation' (2021) https://www.worldbank.org/en/news/press-release/2021/11/24/ghana-can-create-better-jobs-through-accelerated-economic-transformation (accessed 3 December 2024).

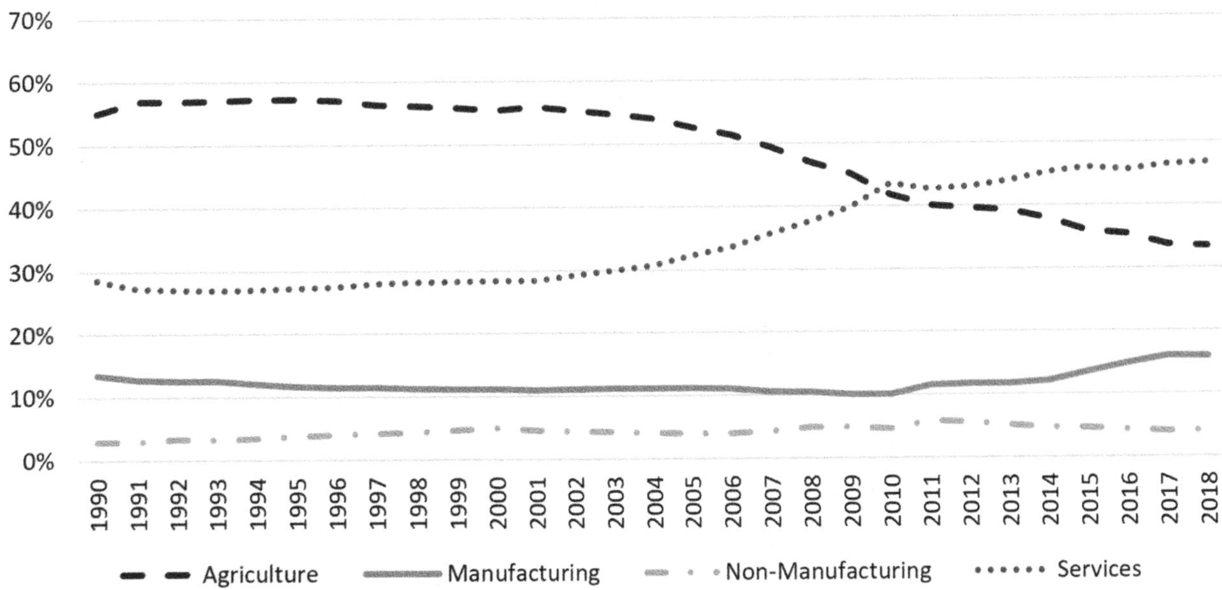

Figure 13.3 Share of Employment by Major Sectors, 1990–2018.

Source: Calculated from GGDC data.

constrained by limited structural transformation. Improvements in transport infrastructure have supported connectivity and trade, contributing to spatial transformation and facilitating movement into higher-productivity sectors. However, Ghana's economic transformation remains incomplete, as evidenced by the persistent though narrowing gap between labour productivity in agriculture and manufacturing.

Ghana's path towards structural transformation has therefore been shaped by a significant decline in aggregate labour productivity in agriculture and sluggish growth in labour productivity in manufacturing. It is important to distinguish export crops, especially cocoa, from domestic food crops, because the aggregate decline in agricultural labour productivity hides contrasting trends between them. Cocoa, grown mainly for export, saw a marked rise in labour productivity during the 2000s boom, while productivity in staple food crops such as maize, cassava and yam remained low and largely stagnant. Manufacturing has simply not been able to compensate for the decline in productivity in agriculture. Although labour productivity growth appears marginal in the services sector, it has attracted a fairly large share of total employment. The modest economic growth achieved over the years, the thriving informal economy and the discovery of new mineral resources may have provided good support for business services. (The effective stock of some older resources has in fact declined, as pressures on cultivable land have intensified, not least through the spread of small-scale and often illegal gold mining, with associated land degradation and loss of agricultural potential.) Additionally, the country has, in recent times, witnessed robust growth in education, health and ICT services. In education, initiatives like the Free Compulsory Universal Basic Education programme, launched in 1995 and implemented from 1996, boosted primary enrolment. In health, the national e-health strategy launched in 2010 has introduced telemedicine and web-based health consultancy services to improve access, especially in remote areas. Ghana's ICT sector has also shown robust growth, contributing significantly to economic development. Government initiatives such as digitising fiscal systems, expanding fibre-optic networks, and promoting digital literacy have positioned Ghana as a leader in mobile payments and ICT-enabled services in Africa. These advances collectively reflect the country's commitment to leveraging technology and policy reforms.

In sum, structural transformation is yet to take place in Ghana, despite the noticeable changes in sectoral contribution to GDP. It is important to stress that the more recent changes in sectoral contribution to GDP may also be an outcome of the rebasing exercise and not entirely from the process of structural transformation, as suggested by the sectoral shift in labour productivity and employment. Agriculture remains the second-largest sector, employing a significant proportion of the labour force, but with persistently low productivity and precarious employment. The manufacturing sector, which is typically central to structural transformation due to its potential for high productivity and job creation, has either stagnated or declined. The industrial policies that have been pursued, although largely useful, have not entirely led to the type of transformation conceptualised for the country. The services sector dominates GDP and employment but is characterised by low-value, informal activities such as petty trading, which do not significantly enhance incomes or productivity. Accordingly, Kunal Sen has classified Ghana among the 'structurally developing' economies of the world – alongside Brazil, China, Indonesia, Morocco, and South Africa[59] – defined by having a services sector which employs the largest share of the labour force, followed by agriculture, with industry accounting for the smallest share. Challenges such as macroeconomic instability, weak infrastructure, limited access to credit, inefficiencies in trade facilitation, and a mismatch between labour skills and market demands exacerbate the difficulty of achieving structural transformation. Addressing these issues through targeted reforms in education, industrial development, and infrastructure remains essential for Ghana's transition towards a more inclusive and resilient economic structure.

The Constraints on Structural Transformation: Why has Manufacturing not responded?

It is clear from the foregoing discussion that manufacturing in Ghana has been and continues to be severely constrained despite attempts to promote structural transformation through industrialisation. Relying on manufacturing to transform the Ghanaian economy has failed to produce the desired results. What accounted for this? What could explain the sluggish growth in aggregate labour productivity in manufacturing? Why has the manufacturing sector not attracted surpluses from agriculture as envisioned by the country's industrial policy?

A careful examination of the literature shows that one of the binding constraints to structural transformation has been weak managerial capacity and a limited skilled workforce.[60] Right from independence, it was clear that there were challenges with the type of skilled workforce that the country had, as it was unable to support the type of capital-intensive ISI strategy that the country intended to pursue. This point was made by Arthur Lewis[61] over seventy years ago and formed the basis of his conclusion that Ghana should proceed cautiously with the implementation of an ISI strategy and rather seek to enhance productivity in agriculture, whilst investing in human

59 Kunal Sen, 'Structural transformation around the world: patterns and drivers', *Asian Development Review* 36:2 (2019), 1–31.

60 Ackah, Adjasi and Turkson, 'Scoping study'.

61 Lewis, *Report on Industrialisation*.

capital. Not surprisingly, weak managerial capacity and a shortage of skilled labour continued to plague manufacturing well beyond the Nkrumah era.[62] In the post-Nkrumah era, mismanagement became more prominent, and it underpinned the drive for the privatisation of state-owned enterprises. The culmination of these challenges more recently features in the form of jobless growth, and unstable and vulnerable work.[63] Twumasi Baffour and Ackah[64] highlighted the persistence of vulnerable employment, noting that it accounted for about 66 per cent of total employment in Ghana around 2017. A significant proportion of jobs in which the youth are engaged are vulnerable and typically on a part-time/temporary basis. The unemployment rate among the youth in 2019 remained higher than for the general population, with an average national unemployment rate of around 6 per cent; youth unemployment was estimated as substantially higher. About 59.6 per cent of young people (aged 15 to 35) were employed, 12.1 per cent were unemployed, while the remaining 28.3 per cent were out of the labour force. Also, nearly one in three young people (31.8 per cent) was employed as an own-account[65] worker outside agriculture.

Another binding constraint relates to the difficult macroeconomic environment, mostly precipitated by the persistent and large fiscal deficits (Table 13.1). Fiscal deficits have dominated the larger part of the post-independence era, resulting in the country's debt levels remaining unsustainably high. Interest rates have also remained high, raising the cost of doing business. Intense competition for funds in the financial market (exacerbated by government borrowing that crowds out the private sector) has reduced private investment, undermining the growth of a private-sector-led manufacturing base. Persistent fiscal deficits have driven reliance on external debt financing, expressed in a growing appetite for concessionary support from the IMF and the World Bank, and, more recently, for resources mobilised from international capital markets. Combined with an unfettered national dependence on imported goods, these factors have consistently exerted intense downward pressure on the exchange rate, thereby raising the cost of doing business in the country and, given the economy's heavy reliance on imported inputs, often undermining competitiveness and impeding the growth of a private-sector-led manufacturing base.

62 Osei and Jedwab, 'Structural change'.

63 Mostly affecting self-employed people and contributing family workers.

64 Priscilla Twumasi Baffour and Charles G. Ackah, 'Employment vulnerabilities and the COVID-19 pandemic in Ghana', in *The Socio-Economic Impact of the COVID-19 Pandemic on Ghana 2020–2021*, edited by ISSER (University of Ghana), and United Nations Development Programme (Accra, 2021), 74–94.

65 Youth employed in self-employment, typically informal or non-agricultural.

Table 13.1 Fiscal Deficits: Key Events and Economic Impact

Year	Fiscal Deficit as % of GDP	Key Events and Policies	Economic Impact
1959	First budget deficit	Post-independence expansionary policies, including import substitution and infrastructure projects.	Fiscal deficits became a recurring issue.
1980s	Fiscal deficits increased significantly.	Economic reforms under the IMF and World Bank, including structural adjustment programmes.	High inflation and economic instability.
1990s	Fiscal indiscipline led to HIPC status in 2001	Ghana was declared a Heavily Indebted Poor Country (HIPC) due to high debt levels.	Debt relief programmes were implemented.
2000	6.1% of GDP	Fiscal deficits contributed to high inflation (25.1%).	Economic growth challenged due to fiscal instability.
2006	Low of 2.96% of GDP	Significant debt reduction following HIPC relief.	Improved fiscal sustainability temporarily.
2007–2008	Increased to 7.2% and 8.0% of GDP	Election-related expenditures and spending increases.	High inflation rates (18.1% in 2008).
2010–2018	Persistent fiscal deficits	Government spending outpaced revenue, leading to high debt levels.	Continued economic challenges and inflationary pressures.
2013	Public debt to GDP ratio rose to 57.7%	Fiscal slippages were exacerbated by wage bill increases and weak revenue mobilisation.	Debt sustainability concerns.
2018	Fiscal deficit management improved under the IMF programme.	Strict adherence to zero central bank financing of deficits helped reduce inflation to 9.4%.	Improved monetary policy credibility.
2025	Projected fiscal deficit of 3.1% of GDP	Primary surplus target of 1.5% contingent on reversing fiscal slippages.	Ongoing efforts to stabilise fiscal policy.

Again, structural transformation in Ghana has been impeded by a combination of exogenous shocks and institutional constraints, notably weak policy frameworks and deficiencies in policy coordination. The World Bank noted in 1985 that a combination of unfavourable international economic factors (for instance, a shortage of foreign exchange due to a recession that affected export demand) and a distorted domestic incentive and policy framework had adversely affected manufacturing.[66] The Bank also showed how an overvalued exchange rate and import restrictions, which provided massive protection to ISI strategies in the 1970s, severely constrained manufacturing exports. The high costs of doing business, unreliable energy, constrained access to finance, poor state–business relations and insecure land rights – none of them adequately addressed by policy – were the main challenges constraining industrialisation through manufacturing.[67] Despite some significant improvements in these institutional factors following the liberalisation of the economy, the generally weak economic export potential made the country largely vulnerable.

Furthermore, some supply-side constraints, including challenges associated with the availability of inputs to support manufacturing, remain key in explaining why manufacturing has struggled. In the era of ISI, the limited availability of raw materials domestically compelled some state-owned factories to rely on imported inputs – a situation that seemed intractable. With declining agricultural productivity as well as output, most agro-processing firms had difficulties obtaining inputs for production. Even when they existed, binding constraints, including ineffective input delivery, limited capacity to produce on a large scale, and poor marketing strategies, hampered growth and development. Moreover, physical bottlenecks, including the absence of a functioning rail network and unreliable energy supply, remain important obstacles. And so, despite being endowed with considerable natural resources as a nation, it has been difficult to harness these resources in an effective way for the benefit of manufacturing.

Another significant impediment to structural transformation is the inadequacy of both hard infrastructure (such as transport, telecommunications) and soft infrastructure base (including institutional capacity, regulatory systems) to support industrial production. Domestic production of manufactures has remained low because of over-reliance on inefficient technologies. Also, spatial disparities in infrastructure reflect the dynamics of what Lipton termed urban bias, whereby state policies and investments disproportionately

66 World Bank, Ghana: Industrial Policy, Performance and Recovery, World Bank Report 5716GH (Washington DC, 1985).

67 Owoo and Page, 'Industrial policy in Ghana'.

favour economically and politically dominant urban centres.[68] The historical concentration of economic activity in the south has attracted greater public and private infrastructural investment, thereby reinforcing regional inequalities between the less developed north and the more urbanised south, and contributing to the patterns of north–south migration analysed by Bob-Milliar and Mano-Osafo in Chapter 3. That notwithstanding, there have been some significant successes or improvements. Institutional reforms that have been adopted in ICT, at the ports and harbours, roads, and reforms of the water utility have substantially contributed to this success. Ghana has succeeded in increasing household access to telephone, power, and water services by developing its national infrastructure backbone. These successes are not entirely confined to urban areas, as rural water-supply initiatives such as the Community Water and Sanitation Programme[69] and the National Electrification Scheme[70] have extended access to previously underserved districts, while rapid expansion of telephony (driven by both private and public investments) has resulted in higher coverage rates even in remote rural areas.[71]

Lastly, a significant political economy concern stems from a crisis of credibility in the country's governance and policy framework, which has, over time, inadvertently undermined policy consistency and investor confidence. As Resnick has demonstrated, policy backtracking has increasingly permeated policymaking decisions around macroeconomic fundamentals, with serious adverse implications for the manufacturing sector.[72] An example of this backtracking is Ghana's repeated reversal of fuel and electricity subsidy removal; governments announce subsidy cuts to restore macroeconomic stability but later reinstate them, especially around elections, undermining fiscal consolidation and harming the manufacturing sector through renewed inflationary and cost pressures.[73] Ghana's policy choices in recent decades have been shaped by the dual imperative of stabilising macroeconomic fundamentals

68 Michael Lipton, *Why Poor People Stay Poor: A Study of Urban Bias in World Development* (London, 1977); Robert H. Bates, *Markets and States in Tropical Africa: The Political Basis of Agricultural Policies* (Berkeley, 1981).

69 Republic of Ghana, *Community Water and Sanitation Programme: National Strategy* (Accra, 1994).

70 Republic of Ghana, *National Electrification Scheme Master Plan* (Accra, 1989).

71 International Telecommunication Union, *Measuring the Information Society Report 2018* (Geneva, 2018).

72 Danielle Resnick, 'Strong Economy, Weak State: The Political Economy of Ghana's Stalled Structural Transformation', in Xinshen Diao, Peter Hazell, Shashidhara Kolavalli, and Danielle Resnick (eds), *Ghana's Economic and Agricultural Transformation: Past Performance and Future Prospects* (Washington DC, 2019), 49–95.

73 Danielle Resnick, 'Strong Democracy, Weak State: The Political Economy of Ghana's Stalled Structural Transformation', IFPRI Discussion Paper 01586, International Food Policy Research Institute (Washington DC, 2016).

while addressing poverty and inequality.[74] The 'Ghana Beyond Aid' agenda, announced in 2017 and codified in the 2019 Charter, for instance, exemplifies policy efforts to accelerate growth through agricultural modernisation and export-led industrialisation, based on mobilising domestic resources, with the stated goal of transitioning Ghana to an upper-middle-income country.[75] However, challenges persist due to policy inconsistencies and backtracking, which undermine manufacturing growth and broader economic development.[76] Political economy concerns, including credibility crises stemming from frequent shifts in policy direction, exacerbate these issues. The reliance on evidence-based policymaking remains limited, with political motives often overshadowing long-term developmental goals. To achieve sustainable growth, Ghana must prioritise consistent policies that foster private sector competitiveness, improve human capital, and leverage regional markets while addressing governance and institutional weaknesses. Successive governments have failed actively to consolidate the gains from industrialisation and build a strong, productive and competitive private sector. The distrust and alienation of the private sector that characterised previous government administrations remain a historical legacy.

Missed Opportunities in Structural Transformation: What are the opportunities for enhancing Manufacturing in Ghana?

Ghana's structural transformation has unfolded along a markedly different path from that of late industrialisers, particularly the East Asian 'miracle' economies between the 1960s and mid-1980s. While these economies successfully leveraged coordinated industrial policies, export-oriented manufacturing and strategic state intervention, Ghana's trajectory has been more chequered, punctuated by periods of policy reversal, macroeconomic and political instability. Comparisons with both these high-growth economies and selected African peers reveal key moments at which Ghana missed opportunities to embed manufacturing at the centre of its growth strategy. Recognising these gaps provides a basis for a paradigm shift in the country's industrialisation agenda to identify concrete avenues for rethinking manufacturing.

Several missed opportunities arose in the early post-independence era, during which the global economy was less integrated compared with the post-1980s

74 Ernest Aryeetey and William Baah-Boateng, *Understanding Ghana's Growth Success Story and Job Creation Challenges*, WIDER Working Paper No. 2015/140 (Helsinki: UNU-WIDER, 2015).

75 Government of Ghana, *Ghana Beyond Aid Charter and Strategy Document* (Accra, April 2019).

76 *Ibid.*

wave of globalisation, which was driven by liberalisation and financial deregulation. Ghana's efforts at transformation at the time centred largely on breaking free from colonial dependency for development. But this was pursued without an adequate appreciation of the country's specific constraints, its comparative advantages, and a determination of the conditions necessary to sustain the initial protectionist and interventionist policies. The experiences of late industrialisers demonstrated that protectionist and interventionist policies can be highly effective when implemented alongside favourable but context-specific conditions. Ghana's industrialisation efforts can be contrasted with those of South Korea, a latecomer industrialiser that successfully transformed its economy through targeted strategies. While both countries initially employed protectionist and interventionist measures, South Korea distinguished itself by thoroughly assessing its constraints, leveraging its comparative advantages such as skilled and relatively cheap labour in the early years of its industrialisation and export-oriented sectors, and instituting durable support mechanisms. For example, from the early 1960s, South Korea shifted from its earlier import-substitution approach to an export-oriented industrialisation strategy, prioritising export promotion, technological upgrading, and state-led investment in strategic sectors such as electronics, shipbuilding, steel, and chemicals, a shift facilitated by its front-line position in the Cold War, which brought substantial access to US markets and balance-of-payments support tied to military spending.[77] This contrast underscores how successful protectionist and interventionist policies ought to be aligned with national institutional capacity, comparative advantage and a long-term development vision.

Another missed opportunity lay in Ghana's prolonged emphasis on ISI industrialisation at the expense of sectors where the country held a real comparative advantage. Historically, Ghana's comparative advantage resided in agriculture – a legacy reinforced by colonial economic policy. Yet, post-independence industrial strategies relied heavily on developing manufacturing in areas where Ghana lacked both comparative advantage and the requisite structural and institutional capacity for success, including technology, skilled labour and enabling infrastructure. This mismatch between policy direction and the underlying economic realities significantly hampered the long-term sustainability of ISI-led growth. Moreover, opportunities to explore relevant value chains in various agricultural products such as cocoa, oil palm and rice, using rising agricultural productivity and surplus rural labour to feed into processing

77 See Akio Hosono, 'Industrial policies for learning, innovation, and transformation: insights from Japan and selected countries', in Izumi Ohno, Kuniaki Amatsu, and Akio Hosono (eds), *Policy Learning for Industrial Development and the Role of Development Cooperation* (Tokyo, 2022); Keun Lee, *Innovation–Development Detours for Latecomers* (Cambridge, 2024); Alice Amsden, *Asia's Next Giant: South Korea and Late Industrialisation* (New York, 1989).

and light manufacturing in the Lewis-type 'labour-push' sense, were not fully utilised, even though such an approach has become more feasible with today's market access, technology, and regional demand conditions. While the intention of using surpluses in agriculture to industrialise was ideal, the incentives that would ensure that the transition took place were absent. The country also missed the opportunity to develop relevant linkages in the agricultural value chain that could facilitate development. For example, maize, rice, and soybean, which are vital to Ghana's food security and economy, faced challenges such as limited access to high-quality inputs (fertilisers and seeds), inadequate mechanisation, and poor market connectivity. Additionally, the mango value chain in regions such as the Volta Region struggled from the 2000s onwards due to a lack of credit, inadequate infrastructure, and ineffective pest control measures. Without sustainable linkages between production, processing, and marketing, Ghana's agricultural sector has been unable to maximise its potential for job creation, export growth, and poverty reduction. Strengthening these linkages remains essential for transforming agriculture into a driver of economic growth.

Additionally, during the liberalisation, Ghana missed a crucial opportunity to strengthen private sector engagement in the economic life of Ghana, amid the relative political and policy stability of the Fourth Republic. The distrust of private enterprise, manifested in government dealings during the years leading up to the beginning of the Fourth Republic (for example, the use of the divestiture process primarily as an instrument of political patronage rather than as a vehicle for efficiency and growth), undermined efforts to divest state-owned enterprises and nurture a truly vibrant and dynamic private sector.[78] More so, the current 'winner-takes-all' system that has dominated the political landscape continues to hamper the proper development of the private sector. An example of this can be seen in the award of government contracts, which are often granted to individuals or companies perceived as loyal to the ruling political party, sidelining competent private sector actors who lack political affiliations. This practice not only undermines fair competition but also discourages private sector investment and innovation, as businesses are unable to rely on merit-based opportunities. Additionally, when governments change, contracts awarded by previous administrations are frequently cancelled or renegotiated, leading to financial losses and instability for private enterprises.[79] Opportunities to enshrine national development plans in the constitution remain largely unexploited, perpetuating the instability that undermines the sustainable growth of the private sector.

78 See Kojo Appiah, 'State-owned enterprises and privatisation in Ghana', *Journal of Modern African Studies* 39:2 (2001), 197–229.

79 Ransford Gyampo, 'Dealing with winner takes all politics in Ghana: the case of national development planning', *Governance: A Publication of the Institute of Economic Affairs* 20:1 (2016), 1–12.

The discovery of oil offered Ghana another chance to drive structural transformation through the development of upstream and downstream industries. However, this potential has remained elusive, constrained by the strategic positioning of political leaders and the utilisation of oil revenues. As Owoo and Page point out,[80] meaningful diversification will remain elusive unless critical preconditions are met. These include the formulation of a coherent long-term industrialisation policy, strategic public investment and effective management of the resource-curse risks that the discovery presents. While the discovery of oil offers some significant opportunities for economic transformation, there are risks of the resource curse (Dutch disease), whereby oil revenue inflows lead to currency appreciation that weakens the competitiveness of non-oil sectors like agriculture and manufacturing, effectively reducing their contribution to GDP. Between 2013 and 2018, Ghana's real effective exchange rate appreciation primarily undermined the competitiveness of non-traditional exports such as pineapples. Its effect on cocoa operated less through world-price competition and more through the mechanism by which a stronger cedi translated a given dollar-denominated world price into fewer cedis at the farm gate, weakening producers' incentives unless domestic pricing rules offset the appreciation. Furthermore, the concentration of investments in oil-related activities crowded out labour and resources from other sectors, exacerbating structural imbalances. To address these risks, civil society and policymakers proposed strategies such as establishing a sovereign wealth fund to manage oil revenues sustainably, formulating coherent industrialisation policies, investing strategically in infrastructure, and ensuring transparent governance to prevent corruption and rent-seeking behaviour. Without these measures, Ghana risks missing the transformative potential of its oil wealth.

Are there credible prospects for advancing structural transformation in Ghana through industrial development, particularly in manufacturing? We contend that achieving this will necessitate strategic interventions. Chief among these is a substantial investment in infrastructure, such as road networks that connect vital agricultural production zones to industrial centres. While infrastructure investment is not a panacea, foundational spending that facilitates manufacturing has underpinned successful industrial diversification globally. China exemplifies this pattern with its extraordinary industrialisation driven by massive infrastructure investment in communications technology, energy, and transportation, which has enabled rapid scaling up of manufacturing activity and economic expansion.

There is also the need to address various supply-side constraints to industrialisation in the form of reliable energy supply, access to low-cost credit, practices of informal competitors, and customs and trade regulations. Manufacturing

80 Owoo and Page, 'Industrial policy in Ghana'.

must be pursued by leveraging the opportunities that exist in innovation, digitisation and regional integration. In countries where manufacturing has been an important contributor to growth, digital technologies and innovation have been important in enhancing operations, particularly in the trade-related areas. Regional integration can act as a catalyst for structural transformation through expanded access to resources, fostering competitive markets and enhancing trade and investment flows, as evidenced in regions where economic blocs have reduced barriers and coordinated industrial policies.

A stable macroeconomic environment must be pursued to create conditions conducive to private sector growth and business expansion. The large fiscal deficits, as well as interest rates, require urgent corrective measures, while a predictable political climate that safeguards private sector participation is essential for the transformation process. Equally, enhancing the skills of the labour force should be prioritised. While the different policies targeted at general education are commendable, a more targeted approach to developing skills essential for agricultural development, mining, and industrialisation will be indispensable in laying the solid foundations for sustainable economic transformation.

Ghana's progress towards structural transformation has been heavily conditioned by the quality, scale and coherence of infrastructure investment.[81] While successive governments have expanded road networks, invested in energy generation and pursued improvements in ports and trade corridors, these efforts have not consistently kept pace with the needs of a diversifying economy or been tightly aligned with an explicit industrial strategy.[82] Persistent bottlenecks in reliable and affordable power, transport logistics and trade facilitation have raised production costs for firms, limited agglomeration effects, and weakened the competitiveness of manufacturing relative to both imports and resource-based activities.[83]

81 Remi Jedwab, 'Structural Change in Ghana, 1960–2010', Institute for International Economic Policy Working Paper, George Washington University (2013); World Bank, *Economic Diversification through Productivity Enhancement: Ghana Country Economic Memorandum* (Washington DC, 2020).

82 World Bank, *Ghana's Infrastructure: A Continental Perspective* (Washington DC, 2016); Charles Ackah, Charles Adjasi and Festus Turkson, 'Industrial policy in Ghana: its evolution and impact', in Carol Newman, John Page, John Rand, Abebe Shimeles, Måns Söderbom and Finn Tarp (eds), *Manufacturing Transformations: Comparative Studies of Industrial Development in Africa and Emerging Asia* (Oxford, 2016), 50–71; Ernest Aryeetey and Nkechi S. Owoo, 'Ghana's experiments with business-government coordination', in John Page and Finn Tarp (eds), *The Practice of Industrial Policy: Government-Business Coordination in Africa and East Asia* (Oxford, 2017), 255–74.

83 Asuamah Yeboah, 'Unleashing Ghana's Manufacturing Might: Performance, Constraints and Policy Priorities', *MPRA Working Paper* (2023).

These infrastructure gaps interact with deeper supply-side constraints to slow the reallocation of labour into higher-productivity sectors. Small and medium manufacturing firms continue to face high input and financing costs, limited access to serviced industrial land, and weak links to technology, skills and export markets. In agriculture, similar constraints in irrigation, storage, rural roads and extension services dampen productivity growth and reduce the scope for agro-processing linkages. Together, these factors have contributed to a pattern of growth that is driven more by resource booms and consumption than by sustained productivity gains in tradable manufacturing and modern services.[84]

At the same time, Ghana has begun to develop capabilities in innovation and digital technologies that could support a more dynamic pattern of structural change.[85] The rapid diffusion of mobile connectivity, digital financial services and emerging e-commerce platforms is creating new opportunities for firms to access markets, manage supply chains and adopt more efficient business practices, even though their use in manufacturing remains limited.[86] Digitisation's contribution to structural transformation will depend critically on targeted measures to diffuse digital tools, skills and standards into production networks and value chains.[87]

Regional integration provides an additional avenue for hastening structural transformation. Ghana's participation in the Economic Community of West African States and the African Continental Free Trade Area, combined with investments in transport and trade infrastructure, has the potential to underpin regional production networks in agro-processing, light manufacturing and business services.[88] Realising these gains will require aligning infrastructure spending and industrial policy with the explicit objective of integrating Ghanaian firms into regional markets, including through trade facilitation reforms, standards harmonisation and targeted support for export-oriented clusters. In this sense, strengthening infrastructure networks, easing supply-side constraints and harnessing innovation, digitisation and regional integration emerge as complementary pillars of a more coherent transformation strategy, rather than disconnected policy aspirations.[89]

84 Nxumalo and Raju, 'Structural Transformation and Labor Market Performance'.

85 World Bank, *Ghana Digital Acceleration Project: Project Appraisal Document* (Washington DC, 2022).

86 African Center for Economic Transformation, *Ghana: Country Economic Transformation Outlook* (Accra, 2023).

87 African Center for Economic Transformation, *Innovation Meets Growth? Navigating the Digital Landscape in Ghana* (Accra, 2024).

88 UNCTAD, *Structural Transformation and Industrial Policy: Trade and Development Report 2016* (Geneva, 2016).

89 Nxumalo and Raju, 'Structural Transformation and Labor Market Performance'; Ackah, Adjasi and Turkson, 'Industrial policy in Ghana'.

With global demand for green minerals expected to rise sharply in the coming decade, Ghana stands at a potentially transformative juncture. Decades of often painful experience with gold, cocoa and oil have generated a deep repository of lessons on how not to manage resource booms, but also on what is needed to capture more value domestically, from stronger local content rules to more capable state institutions.[90] A new generation of policies, including Ghana's emerging green minerals framework and continental strategies on critical minerals, reflects an explicit shift from raw commodity export towards value addition at or near the mine head.[91] Lithium, manganese and other transition minerals offer not just another enclave export story, but a platform around which to organise a more ambitious industrial strategy.

If these resources are leveraged effectively and placed in the service of an inclusive transformation rather than a residual sector,[92] the prize is not simply higher GDP, but a structural shift in which a larger share of workers move into more productive, better-paid, and more formal employment, with stronger linkages to the rest of the economy.[93] This requires deliberate investment in midstream and downstream capabilities (from chemical processing and battery precursor production to components for electric vehicles and grid-scale storage) rather than treating mining as a fiscal cash cow.

Artificial intelligence and related digital technologies now provide a critical additional lever in this project.[94] In mining itself, AI is already being used globally to optimise exploration, reduce waste, monitor environmental impacts and improve safety, lowering costs while raising standards.[95] More importantly for Ghana's long-term development, AI-enabled design, process control and logistics can help compensate for gaps in experience and infrastructure in adjacent manufacturing activities, allowing late industrialisers to

90 Paul Collier and Anthony J. Venables (eds), *Plundered Nations? Successes and Failures in Natural Resource Extraction* (London, 2011); World Bank, *The Case of the Manufacturing Sector in Africa* (Washington DC, 2020).

91 Government of Ghana, Ministry of Lands and Natural Resources, *Green Minerals Policy and Investment Guide* (Accra, 2023).

92 Dani Rodrik, 'Premature deindustrialization', *Journal of Economic Growth* 21:1 (2016), 1–33; Carol Newman, John Page, John Rand, Abebe Shimeles, Måns Söderbom and Finn Tarp (eds), *Made in Africa: Learning to Compete in Industry* (Washington DC, 2016).

93 Margaret McMillan and Kenneth Harttgen, 'What is driving the "African Growth Miracle"?', *NBER Working Paper* No. 20077 (2014).

94 UNCTAD, *Technology and Innovation Report 2021: Catching Technological Waves – Innovation with Equity* (Geneva, 2021).

95 'AI innovations in mining: beyond compliance', *Ghana Mining Review*, special issue (January–February 2025).

leapfrog some stages of learning while still building domestic capabilities.[96] When combined with Ghana's increasingly educated, relatively low-cost labour force, this creates a distinctive opportunity to integrate labour-intensive production with more knowledge- and technology-intensive niches.[97] Yet the experience documented by Teal and others, of African manufacturing firms struggling with high costs, unreliable power and intense international competition, remains a powerful warning against technological determinism.[98] AI will not, by itself, reverse decades of underinvestment in infrastructure, skills systems and firm capabilities, nor will green minerals automatically deliver broad-based prosperity.[99] The central question is whether Ghana can use this conjuncture (abundant critical minerals, a more educated labour force, and rapidly advancing digital technologies) to forge a state coordinated but private-sector-driven industrial strategy that avoids the enclave trap and embeds learning, upgrading and diversification over time.[100]

Conclusions

In this chapter, we have traced Ghana's post-independence structural transformation path, highlighting the key drivers, constraints and (missed) opportunities with a particular focus on manufacturing. We have shown that Ghana has yet to achieve the kind of structural transformation in which labour shifts from low-productivity sectors like agriculture to high-labour-productivity sectors such as manufacturing and modern services. A significant decline in agricultural labour productivity, coupled with only marginal gains in manufacturing labour productivity, has shaped this trajectory. These patterns largely reflect persistent constraints in smallholder agriculture (including low technology adoption, climate vulnerability and weak extension and input systems) alongside a manufacturing sector dominated by small, low-capital firms that struggle to upgrade and expand. Constraints such as weak managerial capacity and low

96 UNIDO, *Industrialization in the Digital Age: Transforming Manufacturing in Developing Countries* (Vienna, 2020).

97 Gareth Austin, 'Is Africa too late for "late development"? Gerschenkron south of the Sahara', in Martin Andersson and Tobias Axelsson (eds), *Diverse Development Paths and Structural Transformation in the Escape from Poverty* (Oxford, 2016), 206–35; Christopher Cramer, John Sender and Arkebe Oqubay, *African Economic Development: Evidence, Theory, Policy* (Oxford, 2020).

98 Teal, 'Why can Mauritius export manufactures and Ghana not?'; Collier and Venables, *Plundered Nations?*

99 World Bank, *Case of the Manufacturing Sector in Africa.*

100 Austin, 'Is Africa too late for "late development"?'; Rodrik, 'Premature deindustrialization'.

skill of the workforce, persistent fiscal deficits, exogenous shocks, and institutional obstacles, including poor policy coherence, supply-side bottlenecks, and a polarised political environment, continue to hamper progress.

We have argued that the country can hasten the pace of structural transformation by strengthening infrastructure networks, addressing supply-side challenges, as well as harnessing the potential of innovation, digitisation and regional integration. Strategic and transparent use of the rents from natural resources such as oil and, more recently, lithium, offers a viable path to financing these essentials. With global demand for green minerals expected to rise sharply in the coming decade, and with decades of lessons from gold, cocoa and oil exports, Ghana is well positioned to chart a new course. If these resources are leveraged effectively and placed in the service of a coherent industrial strategy, manufacturing could become the engine of sustained and inclusive transformation.

14

The Politics of Managing the Economy of Ghana: Different Political Regimes, Same Economic Decisions

Ernest Aryeetey

The public perception that Ghanaian political parties have differed in their understanding of the role of the state in long-term development and transformation is not necessarily supported by the evidence. It is our view that the role of the state in national development, largely reflected by how public spending is done, has not varied much and has not been subject to any significant debates over the years. Macroeconomic instability, caused mainly by large fiscal deficits and how they are financed, is a consequence of an environment where there is no contest of ideas and no accountability. Policy choices do not result from ideological or similar contests but reflect mainly external influences and narrow short-term political objectives.

This chapter shows that this difficult political governance practice has severely constrained economic development in the country, through macroeconomic instability.

Introduction

There was much optimism at independence that it would pave the way for rapid growth and development. Kwame Nkrumah emphasised the need for transformation by pursuing a development approach based on import-substitution industrialisation that placed indigenous people at the centre. The state wanted to provide all that was needed for the rapid transformation of the country, including major investments in infrastructure and state-owned industries. The adoption of this system of economic governance was partly a pushback to colonial policies and reflected some of the new thinking of development economics at the time.[1]

Indeed, the country witnessed reasonable growth and development immediately after independence. The expansionary fiscal policy regime pursued by the Nkrumah regime boosted economic growth and set the pace for the significant expansion of the economy. However, the early promise of a buoyant Ghanaian economy was not fulfilled. Financing the massive investments proved difficult. With time, the country's economic indicators started deteriorating and the fiscal position became vulnerable to various economic shocks. Within a few years, the fiscal balance deteriorated significantly, per-capita Gross Domestic Product (GDP) became lower than its value at the time of independence, the external reserves began running down and the balance of payments and credit ratings of the country became generally poor.

Nkrumah's pride of place as the champion of socialism was short-lived. His political vision came under intense questioning. His overthrow and the subsequent experiments with liberalisation appeared to have changed the narrative, but not for long. After the major economic challenges and political instability of the 1970s, the economic liberalisation of the 1980s followed by the political liberalisation of the 1990s significantly reversed the negative economic trends. After that, the politics of managing the Ghanaian economy became almost predictable under the different political regimes as there have been many instances where governments have pursued policy choices that did not reflect their true or self-professed 'traditions' or 'ideologies'. What is interesting is the fact that there have been no major debates about this development.

The role of the state in economic development has not been subjected to any significant debates in recent times. Public expenditure management has simply become an instrument for short- to medium-term objectives. It is unclear whether current practices create the right conditions for the country's longer-term development. Macroeconomic instability, caused mainly by large fiscal deficits and how they are financed, is a consequence of an environment where there is no contest of ideas and no accountability. Policy choices about public spending are not the result of any significant debates but rather reflect external influences and narrow political objectives. Indeed, for most of the post-independence years, the country has recorded large fiscal deficits, and financing these deficits has also followed a common and anticipated pattern where the government has repeatedly sought budgetary support from the Bretton Woods institutions and/or the banking system. Reforms with taxation to support the country's budgetary process appear not to have been successful.

1 Augustin K. Fosu and Ernest Aryeetey, 'Ghana's post-independence economic growth', in Ernest Aryeetey and Ravi Kanbur (eds), *The Economy of Ghana: Analytical Perspectives on Stability, Growth and Poverty* (Woodbridge, 2008), 36–77.

This chapter presents an account of the politics of managing the economy of Ghana since independence. The main point made here is that although there are differences in the self-professed ideologies of the different political regimes, the main economic decisions appear to be the same. This chapter will focus on the approach to government spending and financing to make the point, citing the relatively large fiscal deficits associated with different governments and the difficulties encountered in financing these. It will argue that because of the new political culture that has emerged, ideologies or any sets of ideas to guide development paths no longer matter. Only the political objectives matter.

Trends in Economic Indicators

GDP Growth Record

Ghana's growth performance has no doubt been uneven. It has largely been episodic and can easily be associated with specific historical episodes including trade shocks. The growth performance mimics developments in political governance: (i) Nkrumah's years of strong state involvement in all sectors, (ii) the first military regime, (iii) the brief Busia regime, (iv) the second military intervention, (v) more stable reform years, (vi) the return of growth episodes (see Figure 14.1).

With reasonably high GDP growth in the early 1960s, the period between 1966 and 1984 corresponded with some major turbulence, with negative growth rates recorded in 1966, 1972, 1975, 1979 and 1981–83. These periods of turbulent growth corresponded with five different political regimes, with most years of negative GDP growth reflecting a change in political governance. The periods after 1984 saw relative stability in GDP growth, averaging 4.8 per cent until the early 2000s. This corresponded with Ghana's Fourth Republic with no military coup. Stability in GDP growth was sustained for some years, until 2007 when the global financial crisis hit. GDP growth, after 2006, once again became turbulent, although well above the rates in the early post-independence period. There were, however, some significant declines in 2014/15, during the commodity super-cycle burst, and in 2020 during the Covid-19 pandemic. In the most recent years, per-capita GDP has risen above US$2,000. The growth in the latter years of post-independence Ghana has been impressive. Not surprisingly, the country's GDP per capita (Figure 14.2) has been increasing steadily. While driven mainly by an increase in the extraction of natural resources, it aligns with stability in political governance.

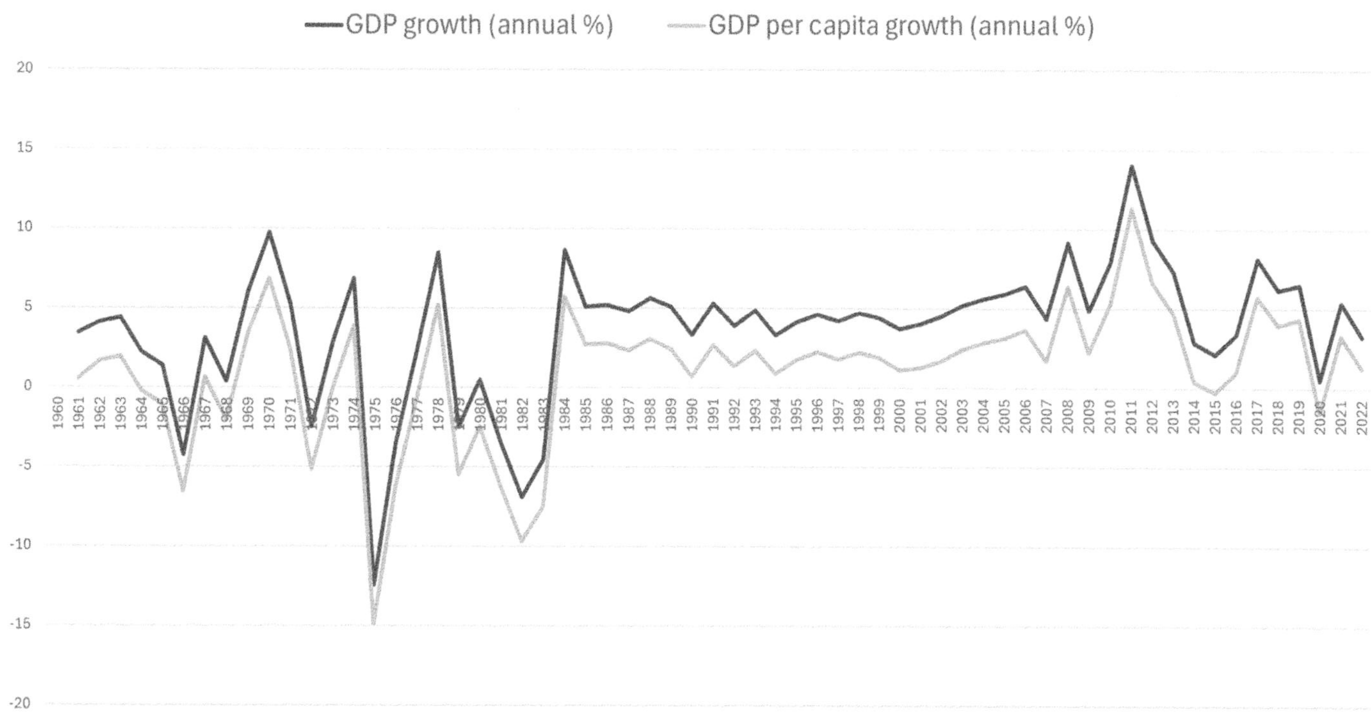

Figure 14.1 Real GDP Growth and Per Capita Growth.
Source: World Bank, *World Development Indicators.*

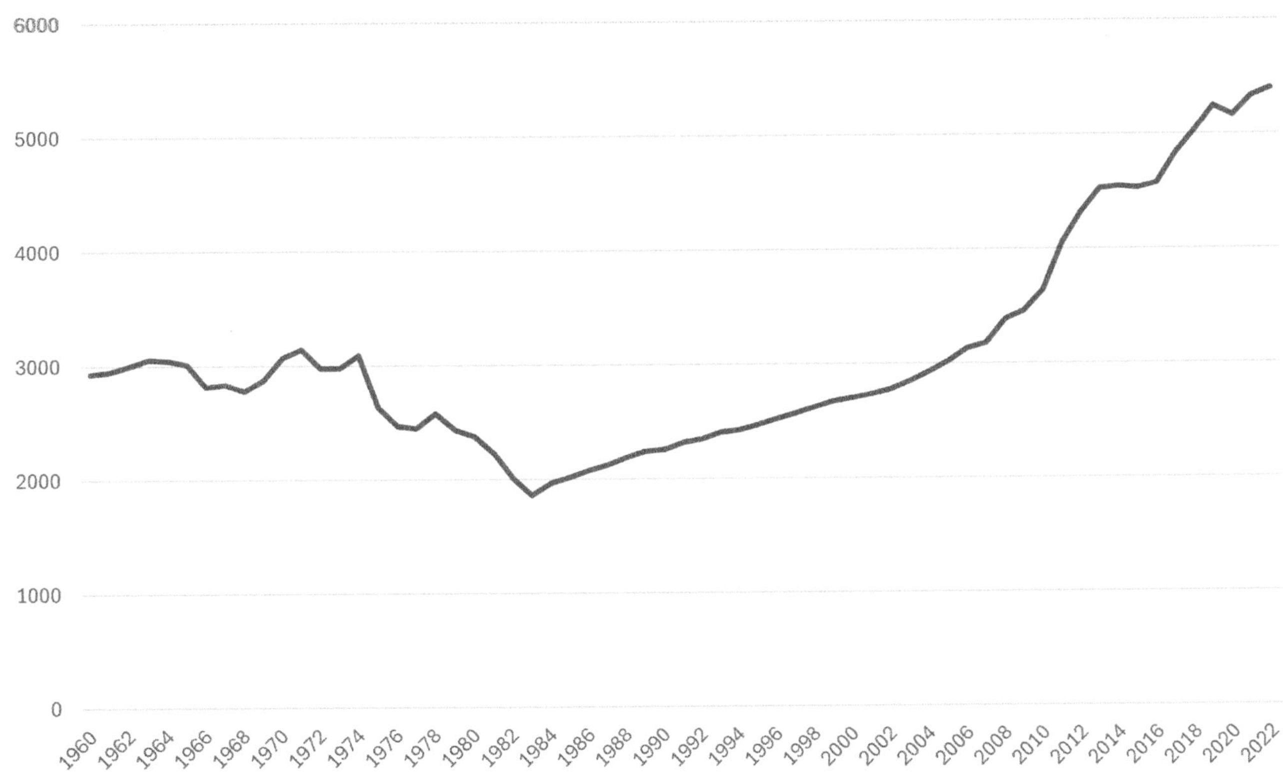

Figure 14.2 GDP Per Capita (Local Currency Unit).
Source: World Bank, *World Development Indicators*.

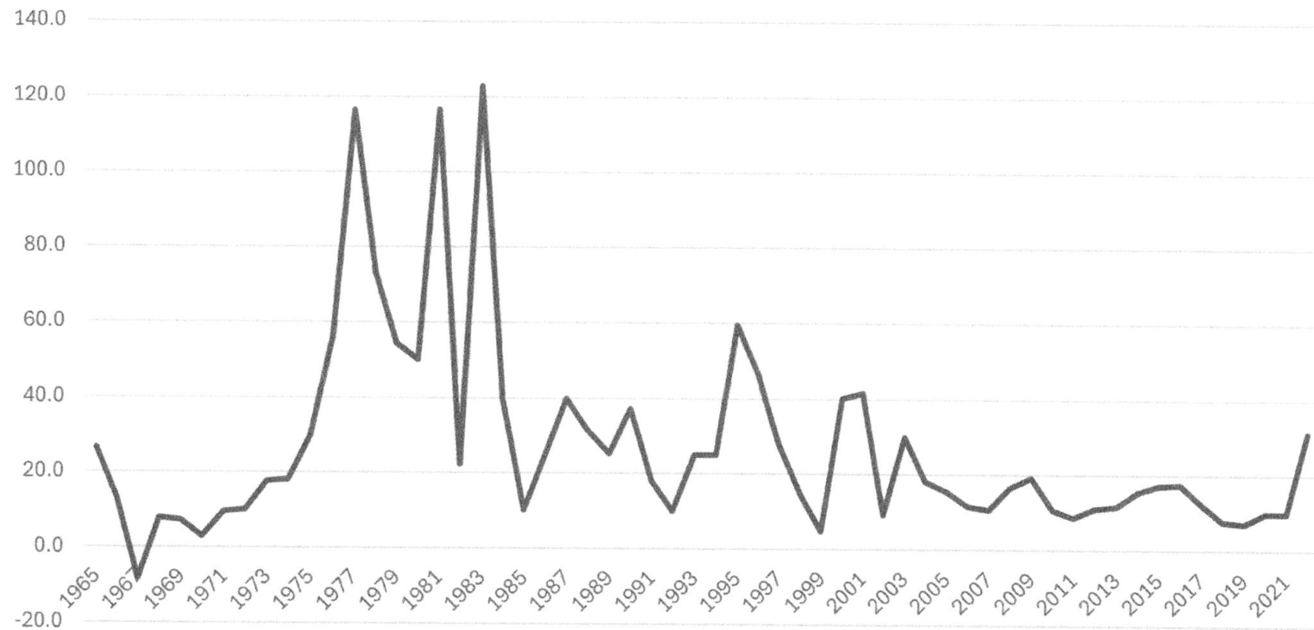

Figure 14.3 Inflation, Consumer Prices (Annual %).
Source: World Bank, *World Development Indicators*.

Inflationary Trends

The trends in inflation also follow developments in political governance and macroeconomic performance. Largely because of the expansionary fiscal regime that was pursued immediately after independence, inflation trended upwards. The exchange-rate controls introduced in the 1970s, and the subsequent economic challenges, including the large fiscal deficits and large debts, accounted for the high inflation episodes between 1975 and 1985. Indeed, in the Ghanaian literature, Chhibber and Shafik concluded that the high inflation episodes observed during this period were largely a result of monetary expansion and large inflows of external resources that also increased the country's money stock.[2] Sowa also attributed it to inconsistencies in the pursuit of fiscal policy.[3]

Inflationary trends in the periods after 1985, although remaining relatively low, were again episodic. Largely because of the reforms, inflation remained stable for several years until the early 1990s. For instance, the spike witnessed in 1995 was a result of the surge in spending. This was followed by another spike in 2000. Between 2000 and 2005, improvements in the budget balance were reflected in a reduction in inflation. Some lagged effects were also observed as a worsening budget balance in 2006 and 2021 resulted in rising inflation rates the following year. Lately, inflation has been on the rise, and this has been accompanied by large fiscal and external imbalances which have tended to rise after every election, declining reserves, depreciation of the cedi, high interest rates and a growing wage bill.

Government Expenditures

The trends in government expenditures have been closely associated with developments in political governance in the country. Immediately after independence, there was a gradual increase in government expenditures to enable the massive investments in infrastructure and the pursuit of import-substitution industrialisation. Between, 1960 and 1968, the country's expenditures were well above those of the years soon after independence (Figure 14.4). Government expenditure peaked at 16.8 per cent of GDP in 1968. A year later, following an IMF-sponsored monetary reform, devaluation of the

2 Ajay Chhibber and Nemat Shafik, 'Exchange Reform, Parallel Markets, and Inflation in Africa: the Case of Ghana', World Bank Policy Research Working Paper 427 (Washington DC, 1990).

3 N.K. Sowa, 'Fiscal deficits, output growth and inflation targets in Ghana', *World Development* 22:8 (1994), 1105–17.

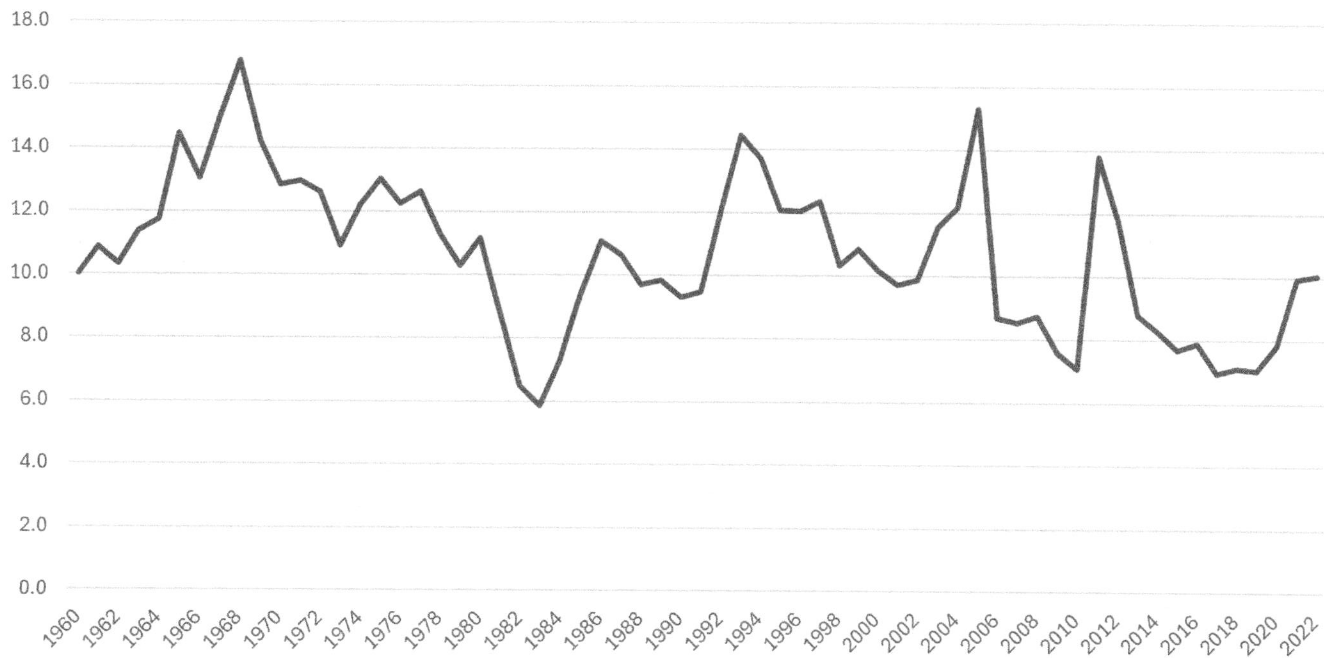

Figure 14.4 Government Expenditure (% of GDP).
Source: World Bank, *World Development Indicators*.

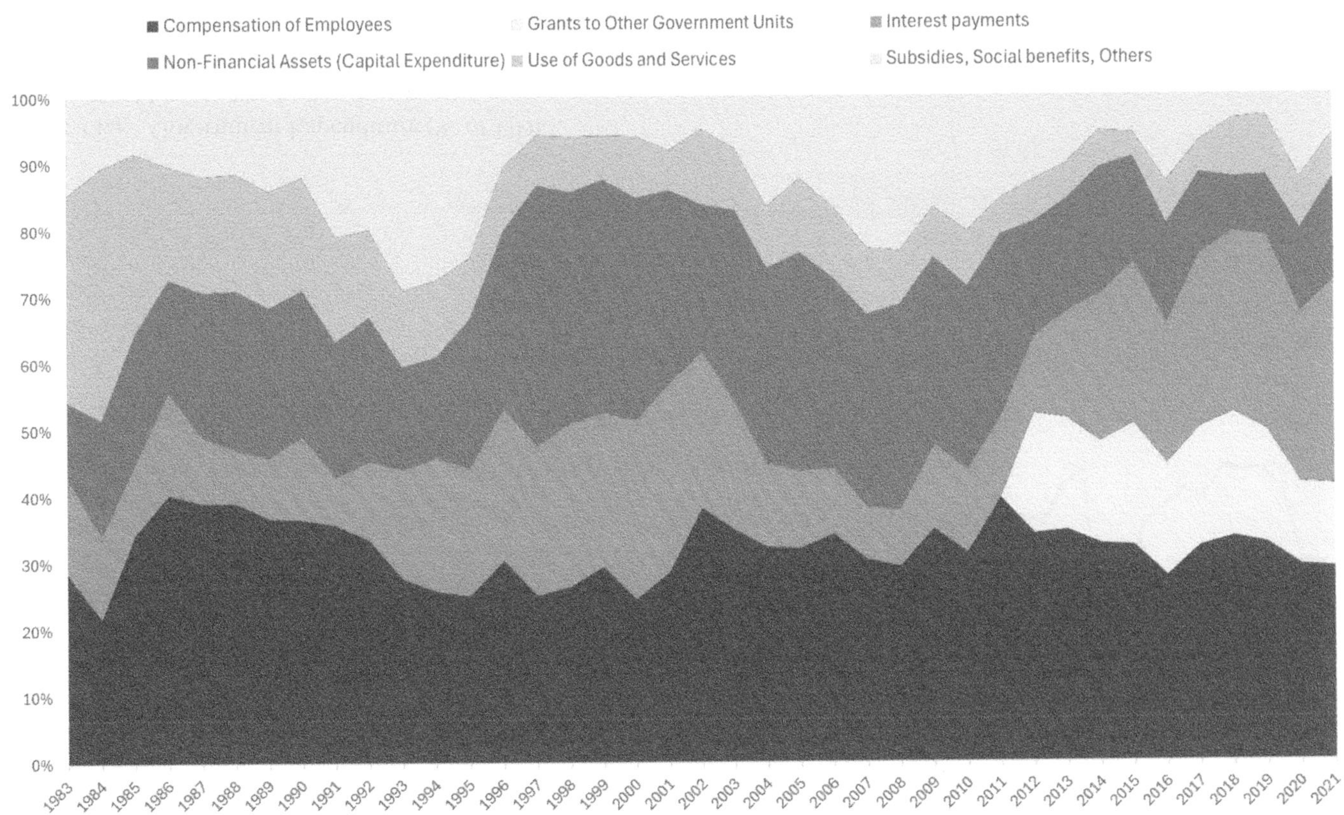

Figure 14.5 Breakdown of Public Expenditure (% of Total Expenditure and Net Lending).

Source: World Bank, *World Development Indicators*.

currency in 1967, liberalisation of the external sector and an effort to address excessive fiscal deficits, there was a drastic reduction in government spending. It is important to understand that in 1972, following general hardship with high prices, there was a second military takeover. The new regime declined to continue with the IMF programme. This led to a whole decade of limited opportunity for increases in government spending.

This declining trend was halted in 1983, when it reached a trough of about 6 per cent of GDP. Subsequently, government expenditures began to rise again with the economic reforms that began in that year and saw a significant injection of capital into the economy, largely through aid. In the early reform years, public expenditures averaged 9 per cent of GDP. Starting from 1992/93, a new trend in public expenditures began, reflecting the massive new increases in spending to coincide with national elections. This was observed again around the elections of 2004 and 2012. The situation was not bad in 2016, but it occurred again in 2020/21. Most of the increases in government expenditures were recurrent.[4]

A breakdown of the country's public expenditures shows that almost a third have been in the form of compensation to government employees. Beginning in 2012, the country introduced grants to other government units as a major component of public expenditure. Together with interest payments, compensation of employees and grants to other government units have constituted more than seventy per cent of public expenditures in recent years. The overall effect of this is that capital expenditure has consistently been declining.

Government Revenues

Although the country has undertaken several tax and non-tax policy reforms, especially during the 1980s and under the auspices of the IMF and the World Bank, Ghana has not performed particularly well with revenue mobilisation. Figure 14.6 shows the growth of real total revenue and grants between 1993 and 2020. Although no predictable pattern can be observed when relating to political governance, the declining trend has been of concern. This has led to the growth of the country's debt stock and debt service payments. The peak in the growth of revenues in 2011 was mainly due to new oil revenues.

4 Robert Darko Osei and Henry Telli, 'Sixty years of fiscal policy in Ghana: outcomes and lessons', in Ernest Aryeetey and Ravi Kanbur (eds), *The Economy of Ghana Sixty Years after Independence* (Oxford, 2017), 66–87.

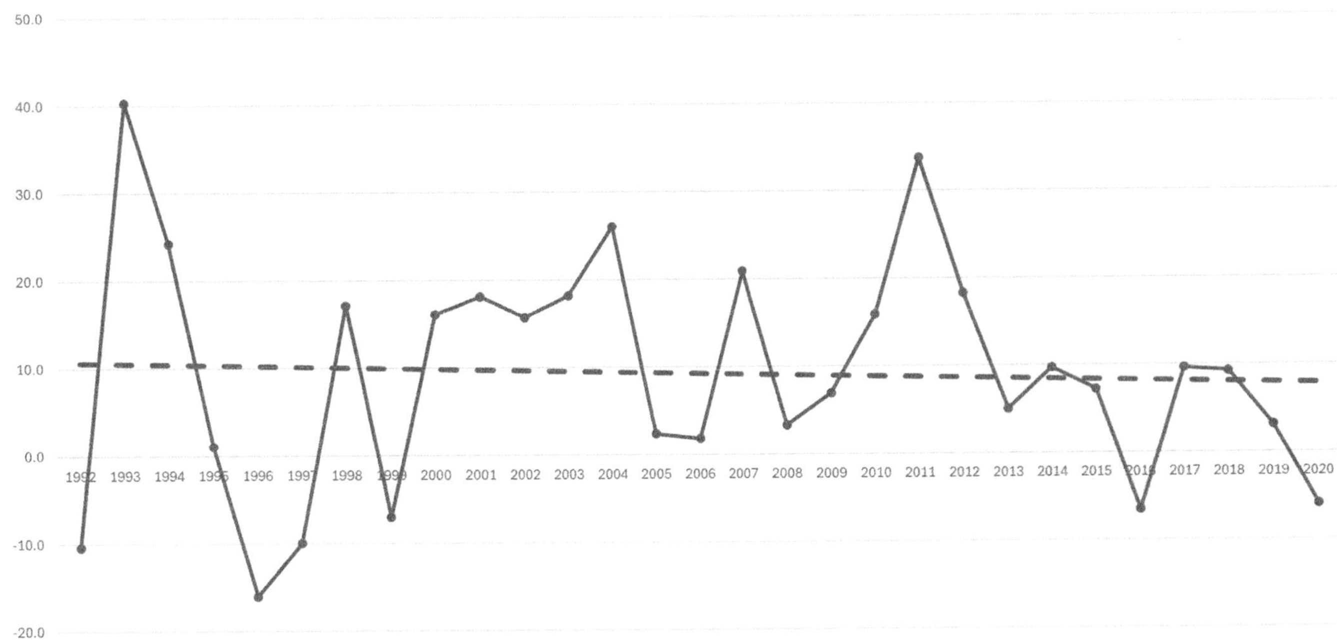

Figure 14.6 Growth Rate of Real Total Revenue and Grants, 1993–2020.
Source: World Bank, *World Development Indicators*.

Politics and Public Spending in Ghana

Politics around the world is generally organised around political parties with different sets of ideas or ideologies on how to relate to the market and its principles. In relation to the market, several considerations are made by the parties with respect to individual rights and how these are affected by such concepts as the separation of powers under a constitution, the organisation of elections, civil society, the rule of law, etc.

Ghana prides itself on being a democracy, especially since 1992. This means that political parties are expected to contest political power supposedly riding on the back of ideas for the people's welfare against which their performance can be measured and possibly translated into votes. But the contest of ideas has simply become mainly a contest over how much the government is willing to spend on people to win their votes.

This section argues that macroeconomic instability, caused mainly by large fiscal deficits and how they are financed, is a consequence of an environment where there is no contest of ideas for long-term development and no accountability. The section again shows that most of the policy decisions about public spending are not the result of any significant debates, but rather reflect external influences and narrow short-term political objectives.

Politics and Public Spending Before 1983 Reforms

Ghana's post-independence macroeconomic outcomes have largely reflected the efforts of the different political ideologies and their practices. Amidst all the developments, which include the early involvement of the military governments and the subsequent institution of democratic governance, Ghana's economy remained robust against many different economic shocks. This notwithstanding, the country has struggled with maintaining fiscal discipline as its fiscal balance has consistently been negative. In the post-independence era, the country has enjoyed only about ten years of a surplus in its fiscal balance. Government spending has increased, without any serious effort to enhance tax revenues.

1957–66 (Kwame Nkrumah)

Kwame Nkrumah was very anxious to modernise the economy of Ghana as quickly as possible. He saw the state's role in directly investing in infrastructure and in the production of goods and services as inevitable in the absence of large private capital to do this. Thus, from the dawn of independence, the rapid and significant increases in government spending, without much effort to consolidate the budget, led to a worsening fiscal balance. This in turn led to the country recording its first deficit in 1959, with a deficit-to-GDP ratio of

1.8 per cent.[5] The worsening fiscal situation was associated with declining total factor productivity (TFP) and deteriorating external reserves such that by 1966, the country's external reserves became negative: -US$391 million.[6] The balance of payments and credit ratings of the country became poor. Nkrumah's pride of place as the champion in the fight against neo-colonialism prevented his government from seeking budgetary support from the Bretton Woods institutions, whose activities he viewed as imperialistic.[7]

1967–72 (The National Liberation Council and Progress Party Years)

The later 1960s saw the country move from being a one-party dictatorship, first to a military regime and then to the elected government of the Progress Party. It was supposed to be a more neo-liberal system that emphasised market-led economic decision-making. Indeed, following the overthrow of the Nkrumah government, the National Liberation Council (1966–69) and the Progress Party (1969–72), attempted to stabilise the economy by relying on a couple of macroeconomic measures, including an IMF-sponsored monetary reform, devaluation of the currency and liberalisation of the external sector. Among many other things, the intention was to address the worsening fiscal situation. Fosu and Aryeetey indicated that the stabilisation effort was largely successful, as the deficit situation improved (1 per cent in 1970) following positive economic growth rates and an improvement in the balance of trade.[8] They argued, however, that growth fell significantly, as TFP continued to decline between 1965 and 1969 at roughly the 1960–64 rate of about two percentage points a year, and the accumulation of physical capital also slowed.[9] It is important to observe that there was very little difference in the spending patterns compared to the Nkrumah era. For example, spending on the public sector, including on state-owned enterprises, did not diminish. The country's deficit in this period was almost fully financed from external borrowing.[10]

1972–83

The Progress Party government led by Prime Minister K.A. Busia was overthrown in January 1972. One of the first things that the new military regime did was partially to reverse the devaluation of the currency, leading to a very short-term reprieve in the cost of living. Between 1972 and 1983, it was very difficult to describe economic policymaking and the ideas that influenced the

5 Osei and Telli, 'Sixty years of fiscal policy'.
6 Fosu and Aryeetey, 'Ghana's post-independence economic growth'.
7 Sowa, 'Fiscal deficits'.
8 Fosu and Aryeetey, 'Ghana's post-independence economic growth'.
9 *Ibid.*
10 Sowa, 'Fiscal deficits'.

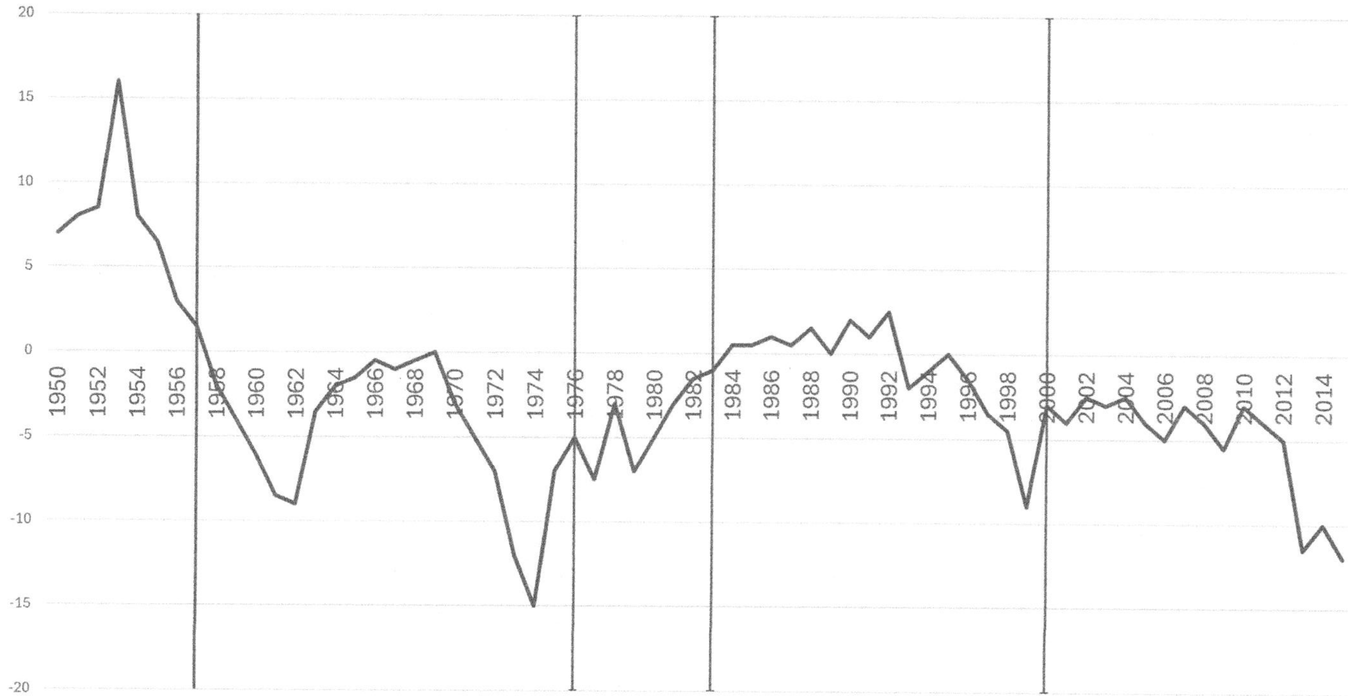

Figure 14.7 Fiscal Balances, 1950–2015.

Source: Robert Darko Osei and Henry Telli, 'Sixty years of fiscal policy in Ghana: outcomes and lessons', in Ernest Aryeetey and Ravi Kanbur (eds), *The Economy of Ghana Sixty Years after Independence* (Oxford, 2017), 66–87, at 69.

choices made. The management of the economy was not driven by any clear set of ideas as it appeared to respond mainly to various exigencies of the time, including terms-of-trade shocks and the non-availability of foreign exchange as a result. The first two years of the regime saw a clear effort 'to live within its means' as international capital markets were not available to the military regime. Things changed in 1973 with the first oil price shock and the declining cocoa prices. The country subsequently had one of its worst economic outcomes. The deficit grew rapidly, going beyond 10 per cent of GDP in 1974 for the first time. Although the military regime was not identifying or associating itself with any ideology, it had some interest in state controls and import-substitution industrialisation, just as Kwame Nkrumah did. It embarked on several large-scale state-sponsored infrastructure projects, including irrigation schemes and other large agricultural projects without much long-term finance. The challenges of the time forced it to operate a restrictive foreign exchange regime and apply quantitative restrictions on imports and general price controls. Not surprisingly, there was a significant reduction in agricultural output with food crop production reducing significantly and cocoa exports falling remarkably. There was a sustained deterioration in the economy and the cost of living which was far worse than under previous political regimes. Fiscal deficits remained very high for most parts of this period, averaging 7 per cent of GDP. The policy of overvaluation of the currency and the imposition of import controls remained the identifying modus operandi of the National Redemption Council/Supreme Military Council government.

It is important to note that in 1978, changes in the military regime led to a short-lived liberalisation of markets. This was followed by the first appearance of Jerry Rawlings on the scene, motivated mainly by the need for 'house-cleaning'. He was followed by the Hilla Limann government, which came to power promising to complete the work that had been started by Kwame Nkrumah. It is our assessment that these changes had no perceptible impact on policymaking. The Limann government was in office for too short a time to have been able to resurrect the Nkrumah legacy of state interventions in several different sectors.

Politics and Public Spending After 1983 Reforms

Following the very challenging economic situation of the early 1980s, exacerbated by drought, widespread bush fires and the expulsion of some one million Ghanaians from Nigeria in early 1983, it was hardly surprising that the return of Jerry Rawlings saw his government looking outside for help. Thus, the period after 1983 corresponded with economic reforms that had significant support from the World Bank and the IMF. The intention was, among other things, to reverse the growth of the fiscal deficit, address the country's debt problems that made access to capital markets impossible, and improve the macroeconomic situation in preparation for the rehabilitation of the real economy.

1984–2000

The 1984–2000 period was associated with reforms that began following the adoption of a stabilisation programme - the Economic Recovery Programme (ERP) in 1983 and later the Structural Adjustment Programme in 1986 with support from the IMF and the World Bank. Both programmes sought to correct structural imbalances including improving the country's deficit situation. The ERP led to the liberalisation of various sectors of the economy and significant changes were made in the management of the exchange rate, fiscal and monetary policies and trade policy. Privatisation of state-owned enterprises was deemed to be a major instrument for cutting back significantly on public spending. The economy witnessed significant growth and most macroeconomic indicators improved considerably as the fiscal situation changed. Between 1986 and 1991, the economy experienced brief periods of budget surpluses. One important factor that led to the rapid correction of this imbalance was the significant growth in external grants. Between 1992 and 1993, however, the country returned to a significant deficit situation in the build-up towards the first elections after the return to democratic rule in 1992. Things improved in 1994, 1995 and 1997, when the economy once again recorded budget surpluses, but this was short-lived as it returned to unsustainable large fiscal deficits after 1997.

It is our assessment that the decision to accept a very neo-liberal approach to economic policymaking was not the consequence of any significant policy debate, except within the core of the ruling government. In the end, the neo-liberal approach won because its proponents argued strongly that there was no alternative as the inflow of resources, especially foreign capital, depended on the adoption of such policies. They were not necessarily thinking about long-term development and structural transformation.

2000–08

The early part of this period is generally associated with the persistence of large fiscal deficits associated with election cycles. The spikes in government spending were always noticeable during election years. Interestingly, after each election-related over-spending, serious effort went into reducing spending significantly. For most of those periods, the containment of the deficit was associated with debt relief arrangements, including from bilateral and multilateral creditors, such as the Heavily Indebted Poor Country (HIPC) and

Multilateral Debt Relief (MDR) initiatives of the early 2000s. These have been followed by Extended Credit/Fund Facilities in more recent years. Managing the deficit has also involved a combination of debt-service savings (which affected government expenditure positively) and increased external grant revenue (which shored up total government revenue).

2009–16

Since 2009, the main motivations behind rapidly increasing public spending have changed and the way of financing them has also changed. Ghana began to get deeply involved with expanded infrastructure development and pursued this programme with a combination of Chinese government initiatives and financing from European capital markets. The excessive spending and borrowing of the period were on the back of growing expectations from new oil revenues, having discovered sizeable oil reserves in 2007. However, the oil revenues did not have much impact on the deficits as Ghana's fiscal deficits started worsening again during the period 2009–16. During this period, the country relied on extended credit facilities from the IMF on two occasions: 2009 and 2015. The 2014/15 commodity super-cycle burst appeared to have significantly affected the country.

2017–Present

Although the period beginning in 2017 was associated with declining fiscal deficits as the growth in public spending slowed down, the situation became worse subsequently, reaching a nadir of −15.2 per cent in 2020. The country witnessed an alarming increase in public spending in the period. Worsened by the debilitating effects of the Covid-19 pandemic, which narrowed the country's fiscal space and expanded debt levels (due to the heightened recourse to borrowing to finance the widening fiscal deficit), the country's fiscal position once again became extremely vulnerable. Fiscal deficits were financed through both domestic sources and international capital markets. The 2023 budget, for instance, indicated that about 85 per cent of the deficit in 2022 was financed mainly through domestic sources. This situation was warranted by the limited availability of finance from the capital markets. This had a significant effect on other macroeconomic variables, including the excessive depreciation of the local currency and rising interest rates.

In sum, Ghana's fiscal situation has been challenging for most of the post-independence period. Steadily rising public spending without steady improvements in revenue generation has led to the situation. The promise of significant revenue from oil did not materialise as expected. The resort to non-concessional borrowing in recent times to finance rapidly growing public expenditures has made debt servicing an increasingly significant item in the payments to be made

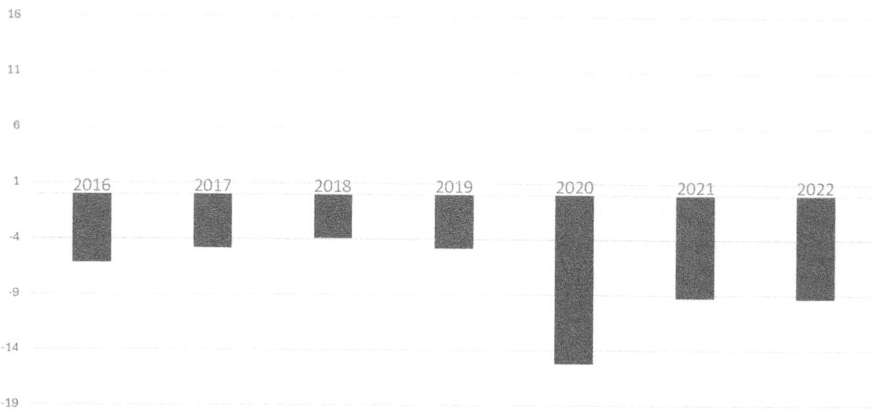

Figure 14.8 The Trend in Overall Fiscal Deficit, 2016–22.
Source: World Development Indicators.

from year to year. This has been so under both dominant political parties that have governed Ghana since the return to constitutional rule. Their approaches to public spending have been comparable and their methods for financing deficits have been similar, as we will see in the next section. Their spending is largely motivated by a strong desire to win elections. While the international capital markets offered some reprieve in more recent times, the situation got worse after the Covid-19 pandemic and the Russia–Ukraine war, which affected the prices of some imports.

Financing Growing Deficits

In the early days of independence, the quest to develop the economy rapidly led to large increases in public investment. The first government basically financed the massive investment needs by drawing down reserves as well as relying on suppliers' credit. Nkrumah's government did not request budgetary support from the Bretton Woods institutions. Rather, there was the reliance on treasury bills as well as heavy borrowing from the domestic monetary system as additional funding sources for government expenditure. The international capital markets were not necessarily available to the Nkrumah government.

Following the overthrow of the Nkrumah government in 1966, the military government of the National Liberation Council initially pursued a stabilisation programme, slashing the capital budget and rescheduling most short-term debt. This gave the government some initial relief as the pressure was reduced significantly. Unfortunately, there was a continuing decline in tax revenue and this worsened the deficit situation subsequently. The country had to rely on IMF-sponsored monetary reform to stabilise the economy.

In 1969, when the country returned to democratic rule, the new Busia government was not only critical of economic management under the Nkrumah regime but sought to reverse some of its tenets. A major policy change was the gradual elimination of all import licensing. In the absence of the necessary resources to back this policy shift, however, the budget deficit worsened with the growing demand for imports. It is important to mention that the Busia government did not completely abandon the Nkrumah ideal of reaching the 'commanding heights' of the economy, but attempted minor tweaks. The focus on rural development added a new twist to state-owned enterprises.

The military regime that overthrew the Busia government in 1972 did not inherit an improved economy, as the underlying fundamentals had not improved. It initially promised fiscal prudence, but the budgetary limits were often ignored, and the revenue measures were not getting any better. By 1976, the deficit of 11 per cent of GDP was financed mainly by the domestic monetary system and not international borrowing. The Acheampong government's commitment to operating a self-reliant government ensured that it did not add to the country's foreign debt. It could not have sustained any external debt servicing as it had become apparent that the country could not settle the pre-1966 supplier credits. This was in addition to all the other debts that were on its books. Following debt negotiations, the Paris Club in 1974 took the initiative to spread the country's debt over 28 years including an 11-year grant period at a 2.5 per cent moratorium interest rate (almost halving the debt in nominal terms). The military regime struggled with revenue generation throughout its time in office, even through the different incarnations of the National Redemption Council (NRC) and Supreme Military Council (SMC) governments. This forced it to ration every available public resource, which it did opaquely and corruptly. Real import duty collection dropped following the lack of foreign exchange at the fixed nominal exchange rate. By 1978 government revenue amounted to a mere 7 per cent of GDP.

The period from 1979 until the end of 1981, when the Limann government was overthrown, did not change the pattern of development financing. The government began negotiations with the Bretton Woods institutions for support for a new economic programme, but this was not concluded before the overthrow of the regime.

From 1983, Ghana's reforms were focused on reducing the persistent fiscal deficits. This was to be achieved through the rationalisation of government activity and tax reforms, focus on the creation of an efficient tax system, expanding the revenue base and strengthening tax administration. Major fiscal measures under the ERP between 1983 and 1986 included cost-recovery measures, reductions in subsidies and the divestiture of state-owned enterprises. Civil servants were retrenched, while the salaries of those who remained were raised to narrow the gap with private-sector pay, particularly for highly skilled workers. On the revenue side, the tax reforms prioritised raising revenue while decreasing dependency on cocoa and creating a tax structure that encourages growth through lower tax rates and the widening of the tax base. This political regime was largely successful in managing fiscal deficits in the country until the late 1990s.

What is evident is that various tweaks to the tax system have not led to a significant expansion of the base and sustainable improvements in revenue generation. As expenditures have not been held in check, that has always meant looking outwards for support in managing the gaps in the budget. This has been so for all governments since 1983, regardless of ideology or public posture (see Figures 14.9 and 14.10 below).

Indeed, the story of how Ghana has managed its large public spending over the years is dominated by how governments have related to or been seen by potential financiers as they have relied heavily on both domestic and external borrowing. The consequence is the large build-up of both domestic and external debt. The significant drop in external debt between 2000 and 2006 is largely a result of the massive debt cancellation obtained through the HIPC initiative and, from 2006, the MDR initiative. Largely because domestic debt competes with lending to the private sector, this has led to rising interest rates. Not surprisingly, total debt servicing has also increased astronomically. HIPC again reduced interest payments on debt from 42.3 per cent in 2000 to 15.3 per cent in 2006 as a share of total revenue. More recent schemes to finance Ghana's rising fiscal deficit have seen the reliance on external borrowing that came from commercial and other non-concessional sources, including China.

Many African countries face public debt challenges similar to Ghana's, and this is typically marked by heavy dependence on both domestic and external borrowing and participation in schemes such as the HIPC and MDR debt relief initiatives. African nations, including Zambia, Cameroon and Ethiopia, continue to grapple with high debt burdens driven by persistent fiscal deficits, currency depreciation, and a complex creditor landscape that now includes traditional lenders alongside emerging ones like China. The difficulties encountered in coordinating debt restructuring under frameworks such as the G20 Common Framework highlight systemic issues on the continent. Also, weak legal frameworks for debt management and limited transparency exacerbate debt sustainability problems, indicating that debt relief programmes alone are insufficient without broader reforms in public financial management and economic policy.

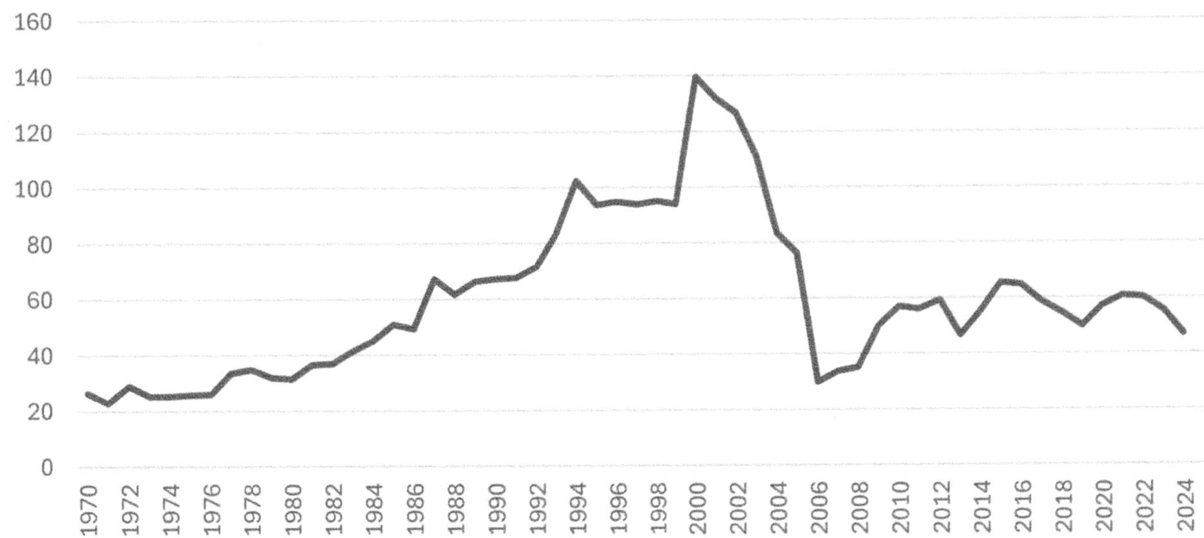

Figure 14.9 External Debt as % of Gross National Income.
Source: World Bank, *World Development Indicators*.

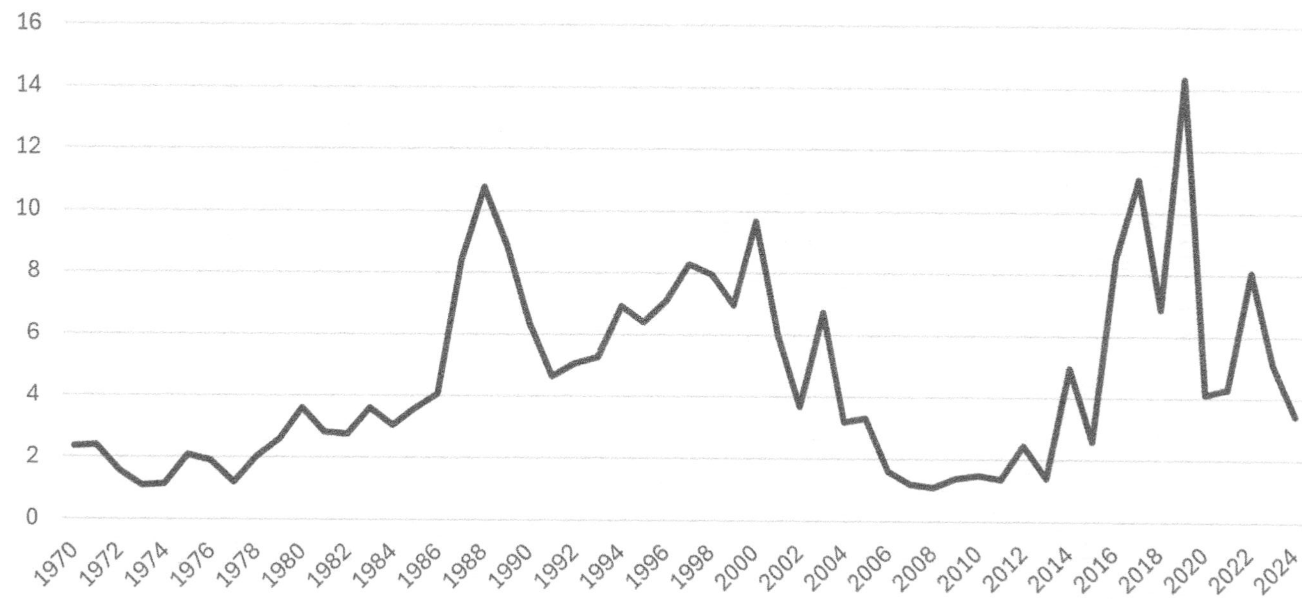

Figure 14.10 Total Debt Service as % of Gross National Income.
Source: World Bank, *World Development Indicators*.

The Politics of Managing Fiscal Behaviour in Ghana

We have described elsewhere the new political culture that has emerged in Ghana following the 1992 constitution, which simply suggests to many that the President of Ghana has unlimited power to do anything that he/she chooses to do.[11] In this new culture, the system of checks and balances that limits the authority of the different arms of government, namely the Executive, the Legislature and the Judiciary, is ineffective as they all look up to the Head of State for resources and other support, especially as individuals. In that new culture, the independence of different actors, including the Central Bank, is significantly compromised and they are not able to participate in or conduct policy decision-making in an effective way. It is for this and many other reasons that several actors have called for a revision of the 1992 Constitution.[12] It is our view that the lack of policy debates that can orient or shape public spending and revenue generation are direct outcomes of this new culture.

In explaining the drivers of change, Killick relied on the political science term *neo-patrimonial* to describe African states.[13] The term simply describes a state in which there is little sense of the public good or public service, and where the resources of the state are part of the estate of the ruler and his court. Killick discussed the dangers of neo-patrimonialism for development and how it has exhibited itself in almost all the different political regimes in Ghana.[14] There are clear signs of neo-patrimonial behaviour in managing public spending in modern Ghana, and this has not deviated much from the thinking associated with most of the post-independence era.

While Ghana has been able to document clearly that the desire was to ensure fiscal stability and the need to pursue that institutionally, this has been very difficult to achieve to achieve. Essentially, the ruling party/central government has dominated in every fiscal consideration. The politics of clientelism appears to have taken over economic management. The examples below are intended to highlight situations where rules were simply set aside in undertaking budgetary decision-making.

In the first example, we note that the 1992 Constitution, which is the primary legislative instrument that supports the legal framework for public debt

11 Ernest Aryeetey, 'Threats and Challenges to Constitutional Governance: Political Culture, Corruption and Missing Civil Societies' (2021). Speech at the Ghana Academy of Arts and Sciences Founders Week. https://gaas-gh.org/wp-content/uploads/2021/11/GAAS-Founders-Week-2021-Address-by-Ernest-Aryeetey.pdf (accessed 25 May 2026).

12 Gideon Afful Amoako, '"Review portions of the constitution for a transformed Ghana" – Dr. Kingsley Y. Amoako', *Modern Ghana* (2023) https://www.modernghana.com/news/1241698/review-portions-of-the-constitution-for-a-transfo.html (accessed 25 May 2026).

13 Tony Killick, 'What drives change in Ghana?', in Ernest Aryeetey and Ravi Kanbur (eds), *The Economy of Ghana: Analytical Perspectives on Stability, Growth and Poverty* (Woodbridge, 2008), 20–35.

14 *Ibid.*

management, provides very clear indications of the need for fiscal prudence. This followed many economic forums where the desire and need for fiscal prudence were expressed by a cross-section of participants. As a result, in 2018, Ghana instituted a Fiscal Responsibility Act, which is supposed to be one of the main secondary instruments that provide support for the management of public debt in Ghana. The Act is intended to correct distorted incentives, ensure fiscal discipline, prevent fiscal slippages, and improve fiscal and debt sustainability. The law places a statutory 5 per cent cap on fiscal deficits. A Fiscal Council (independent) and a Financial Stability Council (institutional representation) were also set up by Executive Instrument in late 2018 to promote fiscal responsibility and to support the objectives of the Act. Throughout 2023 the Fiscal Council never met.

It has generally been difficult to implement the law because of the procyclical nature of the country's public expenditures. In 2020, the law was eventually set aside by the Minister of Finance with approval from parliament, with dire implications for the economy. There are again several challenges with the establishment of the Fiscal Council. Its independence is questionable because of its limited legal authority. It is not devoid of political interference and strong pressure in times of large fiscal overruns.

Another example relates to the independence of the Central Bank. The Bank of Ghana Act, 2002 (Act 612), as amended by the Bank of Ghana (Amendment) Act, 2016 (Act 918), assures the Bank of its independence as stated here: 'Except as provided in the Constitution, the Bank of Ghana, in the performance of its functions under this Act, shall not be subject to the direction of any person or authority'. It is generally difficult to accept that the Central Bank is independent simply because of how it has been used in the past years. The Bank has, on some occasions, lacked the legal authority to enforce its recommendations which are critical to ensuring fiscal prudence. The government has relied heavily on the Central Bank to finance its deficits, in breach of the statutory limits on central-bank financing of government, with dire macroeconomic consequences.

Clearly, Ghana has not been able to legislate good behaviour in fiscal management under the new political culture. The politics of clientelism has led to a situation where institutions tasked with managing the governance processes lack the capacity to exercise free will and independence, and this has hindered the effective development and implementation of policies. Although there are rules that could be followed to ensure prudent fiscal management, the political culture that drives the need to win elections at all costs, together with weaknesses in public administration, has often meant that these rules are ignored. Most fiscal decisions are managed by small, politically linked groups. There is no significant contest of ideas and no accountability. Fiscal rules are simply set aside with no consequences.

A fallout from the current situation is that most public spending is associated with expected political dividends accruing to the party in power and its individual members. The public does not have a long-term expectation of such spending and its possible development impact. The perception that politically connected individuals benefit from all spending fuels expectations of corruption around many public projects.

It is important to indicate that Ghana's economic and political experiences are paralleled by several African nations, notable examples being Zambia and Nigeria, each marked by unique complexities. Like Ghana, Zambia initially adopted import-substitution industrialisation after independence, accumulating debt to support state-led development, but later encountered economic crises that prompted the implementation of structural adjustment programmes by the IMF and World Bank, which emphasised liberalisation and privatisation.[15] Despite shifts in political leadership and ideologies, Zambia faced challenges in maintaining fiscal discipline and frequently resorted to external borrowing. This reflects a broader issue in Africa, where there is a general difficulty in translating political transitions into sustainable economic governance.

Since its independence in 1960, Nigeria, much like Ghana, has alternated between periods of state-led economic intervention and neo-liberal reforms.[16] The oil boom of the 1970s spurred rapid growth in government spending and state control over the economy. However, in the 1980s, economic decline and falling oil prices led Nigeria to adopt structural adjustment programmes under the guidance of the IMF and World Bank, embracing neo-liberal policies such as privatisation and fiscal austerity. Just as in Ghana, Nigeria has struggled with governance deficits and limited public debate on economic management. However, Nigeria's greater ethnic complexity, larger economy, and cultural influence add further layers to its political economy. Nigeria's history of military coups, civil war, and governance challenges parallels Ghana's struggles with economic management and limited public discourse. However, Nigeria's greater ethnic complexity, larger economy, and cultural influence add further layers to its political economy.

Zimbabwe, Uganda, Kenya and others have also experienced shifts in economic policies, often driven by external pressures and political expediency rather than

15 Wilfred C. Lombe, 'Local content in Zambia – a faltering experience?' in John Page and Finn Tarp (eds), *Mining for Change: Natural Resources and Industry in Africa* (Oxford, 2020), 422–46.

16 International Monetary Fund, 'Economic and political setting', in International Monetary Fund, *Nigeria: Experience with Structural Adjustment* (Washington DC, 1997). https://www.elibrary.imf.org/display/book/9781557756305/ch002.xml (accessed 25 May 2026).

ideological clarity or inclusive debate.[17] Across these nations, the dominance of narrow political interests and the absence of robust public engagement have perpetuated macroeconomic instability and hindered development, underscoring the urgent need for a new political culture that promotes transparency, accountability, and coherent economic strategies.

Concluding Remarks

This chapter has argued that since independence, Ghanaian governments have generally presented themselves as different from others in terms of their approach to long-term development and economic transformation, but in practice, their methods and approaches have been the same. The main reason for this is that, after the initial interest in rapid industrialisation and the challenges that came with it, they have all devoted most of their energies to short-term survival and convenience, and in that space, there is very little room for any contest over ideas and debates about the most appropriate development paths.

In the early years, the limited space was exhibited by how quickly the import-substitution industrialisation dream fizzled out, never to be replaced. When governments professed to be more market-oriented, attempts to free the markets proved very expensive, especially with no external support. As domestic prices rose sharply, they reduced the use of markets in allocating resources, and the role of the state became as prominent as before.

Since 1983, the basic tools for managing the economy have been drawn from the economic reforms of that year. However, the tenets of those reforms have been muted by the new political culture that encourages governments to ignore other voices in policymaking. There is no contest of ideas in the pursuit of development and transformation. There is instead a contest for political power fuelled mainly by how much public spending is done, regardless of the long-term consequences. In the end, the governments are all the same.

The key lesson for African countries drawn from Ghana's development experience is that without a true dedication to long-term economic transformation and a political culture that embraces diverse perspectives and open debate, governments often focus on short-term survival and political convenience at the expense of sustainable progress. Although there were early ambitions for industrialisation and market reforms, the ongoing emphasis on immediate challenges and political power struggles has resulted in repetitive policy cycles and limited economic advancement. For genuine development to take hold, there needs to be a shift towards a more inclusive and participatory political environment where civil society and citizens play an active role in

17 Graham Harrison, 'Authoritarian neoliberalism and capitalist transformation in Africa: all pain, no gain', *Globalizations*, 16:3 (2019), 274–88.

shaping policies. Only through such engagement can economic transformation become a lasting priority, moving beyond temporary fixes to achieve sustained growth and development.

It is our hope that a more accommodating and progressive political culture will emerge from the interventions of civil society and other like-minded individuals and groups. There appears to be a growing view that 'things cannot continue like this forever', and this is often expressed on radio programmes by ordinary citizens. When that culture emerges, the need for economic transformation will drive the economic policy agenda.

Table 14.1 Ghana's History of Lending Commitments

Facility	Date of Arrangement	Expiration Date	Amount Agreed ('000 SDR)	Amount Drawn ('000 SDR)	Amount Outstanding ('000 SDR)
Extended Credit Facility	17 May 2023	15 May 2026	2,242,000	451,400	1,790,600
Extended Credit Facility	3 April 2015	2 April 2019	664,200	531,360	531,360
Extended Credit Facility	15 July 2009	23 July 2012	387,450	387,450	257,641
Poverty Reduction and Growth Facility	9 May 2003	31 October 2006	184,500	184,500	0
Poverty Reduction and Growth Facility	3 May 1999	30 November 2002	228,800	176,218	0
Enhanced Structural Adjustment Facility	30 June 1995	2 May 1999	164,400	137,000	0
Enhanced Structural Adjustment Facility	9 November 1988	5 March 1992	388,550	388,550	0
Structural Adjustment Facility Commitment	6 November 1987	9 November 1988	129,858	40,900	0
Extended Fund Facility	6 November 1987	9 November 1988	245,400	97,550	0
Stand-by Arrangement	15 October 1986	14 October 1987	81,800	81,800	0
Stand-by Arrangement	27 August 1984	31 December 1985	180,000	180,000	0
Stand-by Arrangement	3 August 1983	2 August 1984	238,500	238,500	0
Stand-by Arrangement	10 January 1979	9 January 1980	53,000	32,000	0
Stand-by Arrangement	29 May 1969	28 May 1970	5,000	5,000	0
Stand-by Arrangement	28 May 1968	27 May 1969	12,000	12,000	0
Stand-by Arrangement	25 May 1967	24 May 1968	25,000	25,000	0
Stand-by Arrangement	17 May 1966	16 May 1967	36,400	31,400	0
Total			5,266,858	3,000,628	2,579,601

Source: IMF, 'Ghana: History of Lending Commitments', https://www.imf.org/external/np/fin/tad/extarr2.aspx?memberKey1= (accessed 25 May 2026).

Index

People, Markets, Goods: Economies and Societies in History

Previously published

1. *Landlords and Tenants in Britain, 1440–1660: Tawney's* Agrarian Problem *Revisited*, edited by Jane Whittle, 2013

2. *Child Workers and Industrial Health in Britain, 1780–1850*, Peter Kirby, 2013

3. *Publishing Business in Eighteenth-Century England*, James Raven, 2014

4. *The First Century of Welfare: Poverty and Poor Relief in Lancashire, 1620–1730*, Jonathan Healey, 2014

5. *Population, Welfare and Economic Change in Britain 1290–1834*, edited by Chris Briggs, P. M. Kitson and S. J. Thompson, 2014

6. *Crises in Economic and Social History: A Comparative Perspective*, edited by A. T. Brown, Andy Burn and Rob Doherty, 2015

7. *Slavery Hinterland: Transatlantic Slavery and Continental Europe, 1680–1850*, edited by Felix Brahm and Eve Rosenhaft, 2016

8. *Almshouses in Early Modern England: Charitable Housing in the Mixed Economy of Welfare, 1550–1725*, Angela Nicholls, 2017

9. *People, Places and Business Cultures: Essays in Honour of Francesca Carnevali*, edited by Paolo Di Martino, Andrew Popp and Peter Scott, 2017

10. *Cameralism in Practice: State Administration and Economy in Early Modern Europe*, edited by Marten Seppel and Keith Tribe, 2017

11. *Servants in Rural Europe, 1400–1900*, edited by Jane Whittle, 2017

12. *The Age of Machinery: Engineering the Industrial Revolution, 1770–1850*, Gillian Cookson, 2018

13. *Shoplifting in Eighteenth-Century England*, Shelley Tickell, 2018

14. *Money and Markets: Essays in Honour of Martin Daunton*, edited by Julian Hoppit, Duncan Needham and Adrian Leonard, 2019

15. *Women and the Land, 1500–1900*, edited by Amanda L. Capern, Briony McDonagh and Jennifer Aston, 2019

16. *Globalized Peripheries: Central Europe and the Atlantic World, 1680–1860*, edited by Jutta Wimmler and Klaus Weber, 2020

17. *Financing Cotton: British Industrial Growth and Decline, 1780–2000*, Steven Toms, 2020

18. *Quakers in the British Atlantic World, c.1660–1800*, Esther Sahle, 2021

19. *The Great Famine in Ireland and Britain's Financial Crisis*, Charles Read, 2022

20. *Family Firms in Postwar Britain and Germany: Competing Approaches to Business*, David Paulson, 2023

21. *Labour Laws in Preindustrial Europe: The Coercion and Regulation of Wage Labour, c.1350–1850*, edited by Jane Whittle and Thijs Lambrecht, 2023

22. *Financial Failure in Early Modern England*, Aidan Collins, 2024

23. *Capitalism: Histories*, edited by Robert G. Ingram and James M. Vaughn, 2025

24. *Mobility, Belonging and Identity in Freetown during the Era of Abolition*, Mégane L. Coulon, 2026

Printed and bound by CPI Group (UK) Ltd, Croydon, CR0 4YY

05/10/2026

14975256-0003